Applied Mathematics–I

Applied Mathematics–I

Abhimanyu Singh

Lecturer, Applied Mathematics
Baghway Pavshoraw Institute of Technology
Appiliated to GGSIPU, Delhi

Ane Books Pvt. Ltd.

New Delhi ♦ Chennai

Applied Mathematics–I

Abhimanyu Singh

First Edition : 2010
Reprint : 2015, 2020

Published by

Ane Books Pvt. Ltd.
4821, Parwana Bhawan, 1st Floor, 24 Ansari Road,
Darya Ganj, **New Delhi** - 110 002, India
Tel.: +91(011) 23276843-44, Fax: +91(011) 23276863
e-mail: kapoor@anebooks.com, Website: www.anebooks.com

Branch Office:

- Avantika Niwas, 1st Floor, 19 Doraiswamy Road, T. Nagar, **Chennai** - 600 017, Tel.: +91(044) 28141554, 28141209
e-mail: anebooks_tn@airtelmail.in

ISBN : 978-93-8015-632-3

Preface

It is a great pleasure to bring out the first edition of the book *Applied Mathematics-I*, which is written to completely fulfil the requirement of first semester students of B. Tech., GGSIPU, Delhi. The book also takes care of most of the requirements of first semester students of Delhi Technological University and Jamia Miliya Islamiya University (Delhi), and other Indian and International Engineering and Technological Institutions.

The subject matter is divided into 13 chapters and has been presented in a simple and lucid manner. The book features a large number of solved and unsolved problems. I hope the book will turn out to be a great source of information.

My sincere thanks to Prof. V.P. Mishra (Former HOD, Applied Mathematics DCE); Prof. H.C. Taneja (HOD, Applied Mathematics, DTU); Prof. V.P. Jaggi; Prof. B.S. Gupta; Prof. Sushma Jain; Prof. R.C. Sharma (Dean International Collaboration, DTU); Prof. V.K. Sharma (DU); Dr. R. Srivastava (Senior faculty, Applied Maths, DTU), whose love and guidance have always encouraged me.

I am thankful to management and staff of BPIT, Dr. Siddharth Sirohi (Assistant Prof., DU); Dr. Abhijit Nayak (Assistant Prof., BPIT), and my colleagues and friends.

I am grateful to the authors and the publishers of books, which were freely referred to for my work.

I am grateful to Mr. Sunil Saxena, Mr. Jai Raj Kapoor and Mr. Nishant Saini for making great efforts to bring the first edition in the best possible form.

I thank my wife Poonam Singh for her cooperation and encouragement and my son Aditya Pratap Singh for restricting his naughty activities during the preparation of the manuscript.

I am highly obliged to Prof. P.B. Sharma, Vice-chancellor, Delhi Technological University and Shri Atam Prakash Kaushik (Hon'ble Chairman, BPIT) who have always been the source of inspiration.

Last but not the least, I thank my parents for their blessings and my well-wishers for their constant support.

Suggestion from the readers will always be welcomed to improve the next edition.

Author

Syllabus for

Guru Gobind Singh Indraprastha University

B. Tech. (Bachelor of Technology)

Semester–I

Paper Code : ETMA-101 : Applied Mathematics–I

Unit–I : Complex Numbers and Infinite Series

De Moivre's theorem and roots of complex numbers, Euler's theorem, Logarithmic Functions, Circular, Hyperbolic Functions and their Inverses.

Convergence and Divergence of Infinite series, Comparison test D'Alembert's ratio test. Higher ratio test, Cauchy's root test. Alternating series, Leionitz test, Absolute and conditional convergence.

Unit–II : Calculus of one Variable

Successive differentiation. Leibnitz theorem (without proof) Maclaurin's and Taylor's series expansion of functions, errors and approximation. Asymptotes of Cartesian curves.

Curvature of curves in Cartesian, parametric and polar coordinates. Tracing of curves in Cartesian, parametric and polar (like conies, astroid, hypocycloid, Folium of forms Descartes, Cycloid, Circle, Cardide. Lemniscate of Bernoulli, equiangular spiral).

Reduction Formulae for evaluating.

Finding area under the curves, length of the curves, volume and surface of solids of revolution.

Unit–III : Linear Algebra-Matrices

Rank of matrix, Linear transformations, Hermitian and skew-Hermitian forms. Inverse of matrix by elementary operations. Consistency of linear simultaneous equations, Diagonalisation of a matrix, Eigen values and eigen vectors. Caley-Hamilton theorem (without proof).

Unit–IV : Ordinary Differential Equations

First order differential equations-exact and reducible to exact form. Linear differential equations of higher order with constant coefficients. Solution of simultaneous differential equations. Variation of parameters. Solution of homogeneous differential equations-Cauchy and Legendre forms.

Contents

1

Complex Numbers

INTRODUCTION

To get the solution of the equations of the form $x^2 + 1 = 0$, the concept of imaginary numbers was developed by Euler, because there are no real numbers which satisfy this type of equations. An imaginary number is a number whose square is –*ve* real number or in other words square roots of –*ve* real numbers are the imaginary numbers, *i.e.*

$$\sqrt{(-4)} = \sqrt{(-1)} \cdot \sqrt{4} = \pm 2i$$

where $\quad i = \sqrt{(-1)}$, is termed as 'iota'.

COMPLEX NUMBERS

A number z defined by $z = x + iy$, $x, y \in R$, is called a complex number, where x is called real part of the complex number z and is denoted by $Re\,(z)$, y is called imaginary part of the complex number z and is denoted by $I_m\,(z)$.

If $y = 0$, then z is said to be purely real and if $x = 0$, then z is said to be purely imaginary. Thus, every real number is a complex number and every imaginary number is a complex number.

Introduction of complex numbers equipped the mathematicians with the solution of the quadratic equations whose discriminant are negative real numbers.

Algebra of Complex Numbers

If $z_1 = x_1 + iy_1$, $z_2 = x_2 + iy_2$, then

(*i*) **Equality of two complex numbers:**

$$z_1 = x_1 + iy_1,\ z_2 = x_2 + iy_2$$

are said to be equal if $x_1 = x_2$ and $y_1 = y_2$.

(*ii*) **Addition of two complex numbers:**

$$z_1 + z_2 = (x_1 + x_2) + i(y_1 + y_2).$$

Since x_1, x_2, y_1, y_2 are all real numbers,

so are $x_1 + x_2$ and $y_1 + y_2$.

Therefore, the sum of two complex numbers is also a complex number.

Thus, the set of complex numbers is closed with respect to the operation of addition.

- Since $z_1 + z_2 = z_2 + z_1$

  Therefore, addition of complex numbers is commutative.

- Since $(z_1 + z_2) + (z_3) = z_1 + (z_2 + z_3)$

  Therefore, addition of complex numbers is associative.

(*iii*) **Subtraction of two complex numbers:**

$$z_1 - z_2 = (x_1 - x_2) + i(y_1 - y_2)$$

Since x_1, x_2, y_1, y_2 are real, so are $x_1 - x_2, y_1 - y_2$.

Therefore, the difference of two complex numbers is also a complex number.

Thus, the set of complex numbers is closed with respect to the operation of subtraction.

- Since$z_1 - z_2 \neq z_2 - z_1$.

Therefore, subtraction of complex numbers is not commutative.

(*iv*) **Multiplication of two complex numbers:**

$$z_1 \cdot z_2 = (x_1 + iy_1)(x_2 + iy_2) = x_1x_2 + iy_1x_2 + i\,y_2x_1 + i^2y_1y_2$$

$$= (x_1x_2 - y_1y_2) + i\,(x_1y_2 + x_2y_1) \qquad [\because\ i^2 = -1]$$

Since x_1, y_1, x_2, y_2 are real, so are $x_1x_2 - y_1y_2$ and $x_1y_2 + y_1x_2$.

Therefore, the product of two complex numbers is also a complex number.

- Since $z_1z_2 = z_2z_1$

Therefore, multiplication of complex numbers is commutative.

(*v*) **Division of two complex numbers:**

$$\frac{z_1}{z_2} = \frac{(x_1 + iy_1)}{x_2 + iy_2} = \frac{x_1x_2 + y_1y_2}{x_2^2 + y_2^2} + i\frac{(y_1x_2 - y_2x_1)}{x_2^2 + y_2^2}$$

Thus $\frac{z_1}{z_2}$ is also a complex number, $(z_2 \neq 0)$

Thus, the quotient of two complex numbers is also a complex number.

Further more :

(*a*) **There are two complex numbers zero (0), and unity (1) such that**

$$z + 0 = 0 + z = z,\ 1.z = z.1 = z$$

0 is called additive identity and 1 is called multiplicative identity.

(*b*) **Additive inverse**

If z_1 and z_2 are two complex numbers such that $z_1 + z_2 = 0$, then z_1 and z_2 are said to be the additive inverse of each other.

(*c*) **Multiplicative inverse**

If z_1 and z_2 are two non-zero complex numbers such that $z_1 \cdot z_2 = z_2 \cdot z_1 = 1$, then z_1 and z_2 are said to be the inverse of each other and are denoted by $z_1^{-1} = z_2$ and $z_2^{-1} = z_1$.

Geometrical Representation of Complex Numbers

Let $z = x + iy$ be represented by an ordered pair $P\ (x, y)$, which represents the position of the point P in rectangular coordinate system $X'OX$ and $Y'OY$ in a plane. Thus there exists a one–one correspondence between the set of complex numbers $z = x + iy$ and position of a point in the coordinate system $X'OX$ and $Y'OY$.

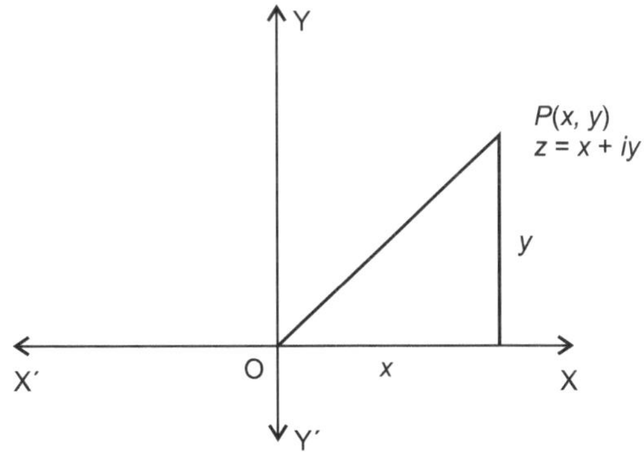

This representation of z is called Argand diagram and the plane is called a complex plane.

Polar form of a Complex Number

If P(x, y) represents a complex numberz, then

$z = x + iy$, which is represented in the Argand diagram as in Fig. 1.2.

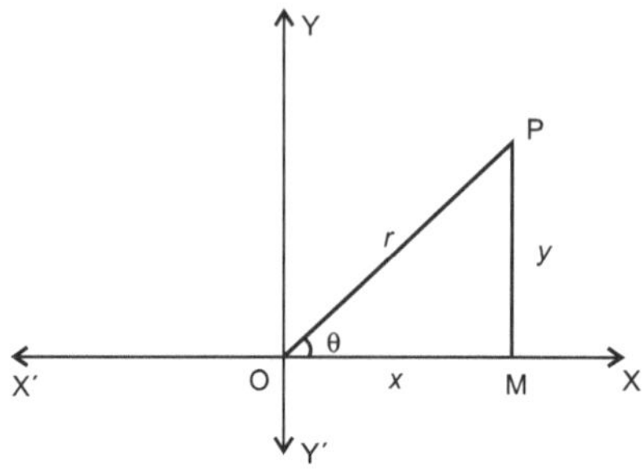

If (r, θ) are the polar coordinates of the same point P, then x, y, r,θ are as given in the Fig. 1.2.

Thus $x = r\cos\theta$

$y = r\sin\theta$

∴ $z = r[\cos\theta + i\sin\theta]$

and $r^2 = x^2 + y^2$

∴ $r = \sqrt{x^2 + y^2}$, is called modulus of the complex number z and is denoted by $|z|$.

And $\theta = \tan^{-1}\left(\frac{y}{x}\right)$ such that $0 \le \theta \le 2\pi$, is called amplitude or argument of the complex number z. The value of θ lying in $[0, 2\pi]$ is called principal value. Sometimes $-\pi \le \theta \le \pi$.

Geometrical Representation of $z_1 + z_2$

Let $z_1 = x_1 + iy_1$, $z_2 = x_2 + iy_2$ be two complex numbers, then

$$z_1 + z_2 = (x_1 + x_2) + i(y_1 + y_2).$$

Thus $z_1 + z_2$ is a complex number whose real part is $x_1 + x_2$ and imaginary part is $y_1 + y_2$, which is represented by the point R.

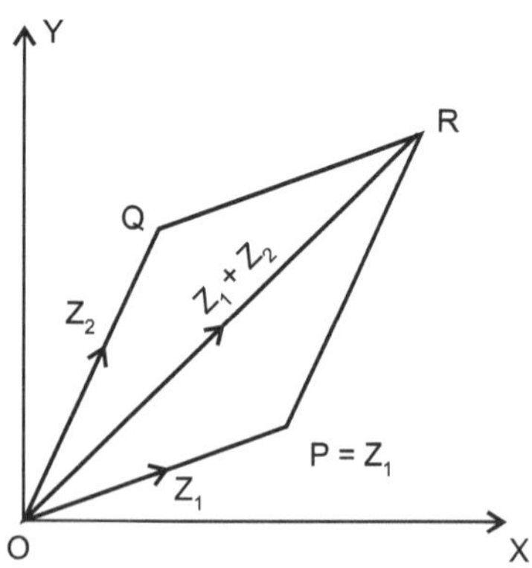

Geometrical Representation of $z_1 - z_2$

Let $$z_1 = x_1 + iy_1,\ z_2 = x_2 + i\,y_2.$$

$$\therefore \quad z_1 - z_2 = (x_1 - x_2) + i(y_1 - y_2).$$

$z_1 - z_2$ is also a complex number.

Then R is the point which represents $z_1 - z_2$, whose real part is $x_1 - x_2$ and imaginary part is $y_1 - y_2$.

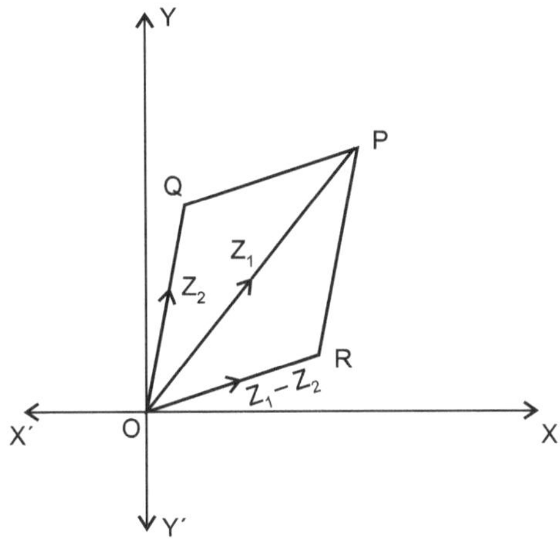

Geometrical Representation of $z_1 \cdot z_2$

Let $$z_1 = r_1\,(\cos\theta_1 + i\sin\theta_1)$$

$$z_2 = r_2\,(\cos\theta_2 + i\sin\theta_2)$$

$$\therefore \quad z_1 \cdot z_2 = r_1 \cdot r_2\,[\cos(\theta_1 + \theta_2) + i\sin(\theta_1 + \theta_2)]$$

$$\therefore \quad |z_1 \cdot z_2| = |z_1| \,.\, |z_2|$$

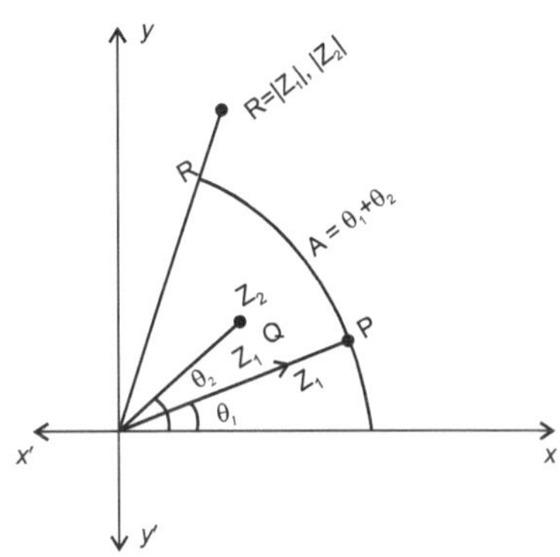

Thus the Modulus of the product of two complex numbers is equal to the product of their moduli, and

$$\arg(z_1 \cdot z_2) = \theta_1 + \theta_2$$

$$= \arg(z_1) + \arg(z_2).$$

Geometrical Representation of $\frac{z_1}{z_2}$

$$\frac{z_1}{z_2} = \frac{r_1\,(\cos\theta_1 + i\sin\theta_1)}{r_2\,(\cos\theta_2 + i\sin\theta_2)}$$

$$= \left(\frac{r_1}{r_2}\right) \cdot [\cos(\theta_1 - \theta_2) + i \sin(\theta_1 - \theta_2)]$$

$$\therefore \qquad \left|\frac{z_1}{z_2}\right| = \frac{r_1}{r_2} = \frac{|z_1|}{|z_2|}$$

$$\& \qquad \arg\left(\frac{z_1}{z_2}\right) = \theta_1 - \theta_2$$

$$= \arg(z_1) - \arg(z_2)$$

Thus, the modulus of the quotient is equal to the quotient of their moduli and the argument of the quotient is equal to the difference of their arguments (arg. N^r – arg. D^r).

Complex Conjugate of z = x + iy

Corresponding to each complex number $z = x + iy$, there is defined a complex number denoted by $\bar{z}$ and defined by $\bar{z} = x - iy$, called conjugate of z.

If $\quad z = x + iy \quad$ then $\quad \bar{z} = x - iy.$

therefore $\quad z\bar{z} = (x + iy)(x-iy) = x^2 + y^2 = |z|^2$

$$\therefore \qquad |z| = \sqrt{z\bar{z}}$$

$$\text{and} \qquad z + \bar{z} = 2x$$

$$\therefore \qquad x = \frac{1}{2}[z + \bar{z}]$$

$$y = \frac{1}{2i}[z - \bar{z}]$$

$$\therefore \qquad \frac{1}{2}[z + \bar{z}] = \text{Re}(z),$$

$$\frac{1}{2i}[z - \bar{z}] = \text{Im}(z).$$

$$\text{and} \qquad |z| = \sqrt{x^2 + y^2}$$

$$|\bar{z}| = \sqrt{x^2 + (-y)^2}$$

$$= \sqrt{x^2 + y^2} = |z|$$

Thus $|z| = |\overline{z}|$.

If in polar form z is represented by (r, θ) then, $\overline{z}$ is represented by $(r, -\theta)$.

Important Results about Complex Conjugates

(*i*) If $z_1 = z_2$ then $\overline{z}_1 = \overline{z}_2$.

(*ii*) $\overline{\overline{(z)}} = z$.

(*iii*) $(\overline{z_1 + z_2}) = \overline{z}_1 + \overline{z}_2$.

(*iv*) $(\overline{z_1 \cdot z_2}) = \overline{z}_1 . \overline{z}_2$.

BINOMIAL THEOREM

If z_1 and z_2 are two complex numbers and n is a positive integer, then

$$(z_1 + z_2)^n = z_1^n + {}^nc_1\, z_1^{n-1} \cdot z_2 + {}^nc_2 \,.\, z_1^{n-2} \cdot z_2^2 + \ldots$$
$$+ {}^nc_2 \,.\, z_1^{n-2}\, z_2^2 + \ldots + {}^nc_n \cdot z_2^n$$

Distance between two complex numbers z_1 and z_2

It is defined as $d = |z_1 - z_2|$

If $z_1 = x_1 + iy_1\,, \quad z_2 = x_2 + iy_2$

then $d = |z_1 - z_2| = \sqrt{(x_2 - x_1)^2 + (y_2 - y_1)^2}$.

SOLVED EXAMPLES

Example 1. If z_1 and z_2 are two complex numbers, prove that

$$|z_1 + z_2|^2 = |z_1|^2 + |z_2|^2$$

if and only if, $z_1\, \overline{z}_2$ is purely imaginary.

Solution: We know that $|z|^2 = z.\overline{z}$

$$\therefore \quad |z_1 + z_2|^2 = (z_1 + z_2)\ (\overline{z_1 + z_2})$$
$$= (z_1 + z_2)\ (\overline{z}_1 + \overline{z}_2)$$
$$= z_1\,\overline{z}_1 + z_2\,\overline{z}_1 + z_1\,\overline{z}_2 + z_2\,\overline{z}_2$$
$$= |z_1|^2 + z_2\,\overline{z}_1 + z_1\,\overline{z}_2 + |z_2|^2$$
$$= |z_1|^2 + |z_2|^2 + (z_1\,\overline{z}_2 + z_2\,\overline{z}_1)$$

If $|z_1 + z_2|^2 = |z_1|^2 + |z_2|^2$

then $z_1 \overline{z}_2 + \overline{z}_1 z_2 = 0$

$\Rightarrow \quad z_1 \overline{z}_2 + (\overline{z_1 \overline{z}_2}) = 0$

$\Rightarrow \quad \text{Re}\,(z_1 \overline{z}_2) = 0$

$\Rightarrow z_1 \overline{z}_2$ is purely imaginary.

Example 2. Express $(1 + \cos\alpha + i \sin\alpha)$ in the form $r(\cos\theta + i \sin\theta)$.

Solution: Let $1 + \cos\alpha + i \sin\alpha = r(\cos\theta + i \sin\theta)$

$\therefore 1 + \cos\alpha + i \sin\alpha = r \cos\theta + i\, r \sin\theta$

Equating real and imaginary parts, we have

$$1 + \cos\alpha = r\cos\theta \qquad ...(1)$$

$$\sin\alpha = r\sin\theta \qquad ...(2)$$

Squaring (1) and (2) and adding, we have

$$r^2 = 1 + \cos^2\alpha + 2\cos\alpha + \sin^2\alpha$$

$$= 2 + 2\cos\alpha$$

$$= 2(1 + \cos\alpha)$$

$$= 2.2\cos^2\alpha/2$$

$$\therefore \quad r = 2\cos\alpha/2$$

Also by dividing (2) by (1), we have

$$\cot\theta = \left(\frac{1+\cos\alpha}{\sin\alpha}\right) = \left(\frac{2\cos^2(\alpha/2)}{2\sin(\alpha/2)\cos(\alpha/2)}\right)$$

$$= \cot(\alpha/2)$$

$$\therefore \quad \theta = \tan\frac{\alpha}{2}$$

$$\therefore\ 1 + \cos\alpha + i\sin\alpha = 2\cos\frac{\alpha}{2} \cdot \left[\cos\frac{\alpha}{2} + i\sin\frac{\alpha}{2}\right]$$

De Moivre's Theorem

Whether n is +ve or –ve, integral or fractional, the value or one of the values of $(\cos\theta + i\sin\theta)^n$ is $\cos n\theta + i\sin n\theta$.

Proof: **Case I.** When n is +ve integer

$$(\cos\theta_1 + i\sin\theta_1)(\cos\theta_2 + i\sin\theta_2)$$

$$= \cos\theta_1\cos\theta_2 - \sin\theta_1\sin\theta_2 + i(\sin\theta_1\cos\theta_2 + \sin\theta_2\cos\theta_1)$$

$$= \cos(\theta_1 + \theta_2) + i\sin(\theta_1 + \theta_2) \qquad \text{...(1)}$$

Again

$$(\cos\theta_1 + \sin\theta_1)(\cos\theta_2 + i\sin\theta_2)(\cos\theta_3 + i\sin\theta_3)$$

$$= \{\cos(\theta_1 + \theta_2) + i\sin(\theta_1 + \theta_2)\}(\cos\theta_3 + i\sin\theta_3).$$

$$= \cos(\theta_1 + \theta_2 + \theta_3) + i\sin(\theta_1 + \theta_2 + \theta_3) \qquad \text{...(2)}$$

Proceeding in the same way, we have

$$(\cos\theta_1 + i\sin\theta_1)(\cos\theta_2 + i\sin\theta_2)\ldots(\cos\theta_n + i\sin\theta_n) \qquad \text{...(3)}$$

$$= \cos(\theta_1 + \theta_2 + \theta_3 + \ldots\theta_n) + \text{i}\sin(\theta_1 + \theta_2 + \ldots\theta_n)$$

Taking $\theta_1 = \theta_2 = \theta_3 \ldots = \theta_n = \theta$. in (3), we have

$$(\cos\theta + i\sin\theta)^n = \cos n\theta + i\sin n\theta.$$

Thus, the theorem is proved for positive integral value of n.

Case II. When n is *–ve* integer

Let $n = -m$ (m being +*ve* integer)

$$(\cos\theta + i\sin\theta)^n = (\cos\theta + i\sin\theta)^{-m}$$

$$= \frac{1}{(\cos\theta + i\sin\theta)^m}$$

$$= \frac{1}{(\cos m\theta + i\sin m\theta)}$$

$$= \frac{\cos m\theta - i\sin m\theta}{(\cos m\theta + i\sin m\theta)(\cos m\theta - i\sin m\theta)}$$

$$= \frac{\cos m\theta - i\sin m\theta}{\cos^2 m\theta + \sin^2 m\theta}$$

$$= \cos m\theta - i\sin m\theta$$

$$= \cos(-m)\theta + i\sin(-m\theta)$$

$$= \cos n\theta + i\sin n\theta$$

Thus, the theorem is proved for negative integral value of n.

Case III. When n is fractional

Suppose $n = p/q$ where p, q are integers $(q \neq 0)$.

$$\left(\cos\frac{\theta}{q} + i\sin\frac{\theta}{q}\right)^q = (\cos q\frac{\theta}{q} + i\sin q\frac{\theta}{q})$$

$$= \cos\theta + i\sin\theta.$$

$\therefore$ $\cos\theta + i\sin\theta$ is one of the values of $\left(\cos\frac{\theta}{q} + i\frac{\sin\theta}{q}\right)^q$

$$(\cos\theta + i\sin\theta)^{1/q} = (\cos\frac{\theta}{q} + i\sin\frac{\theta}{q})$$

Raising both sides to power p, we have

$$(\cos\theta + i\sin\theta)^{p/q} = (\cos\frac{\theta}{q} + i\sin\frac{\theta}{q})^p$$

$$= (\cos p\frac{\theta}{q} + i\sin p\frac{\theta}{q})$$

$$\therefore \quad (\cos\theta + i\sin\theta)^n = \cos n\theta + i\sin n\theta.$$

Thus, the theorem is proved for fractional value of n.

SOLVED EXAMPLES

Example 1. If $x = \cos\theta + i\sin\theta$, prove that

(i) $x^n + x^{-n} = 2\cos n\theta$

(ii) $x^n - x^{-n} = 2i\sin n\theta$

Solution: Since $x = \cos\theta + i\sin\theta$

$$\therefore \quad x^n = (\cos\theta + i\sin\theta)^n$$

$$= \cos n\theta + i\sin n\theta \quad \text{(By De-Moivre's theorem)}$$

and

$$x^{-n} = (\cos\theta + i\sin\theta)^{-n}$$

$$= \cos(-n\theta) + i\sin(-n\theta)$$

$$= \cos n\theta - i \sin n\theta$$

$\therefore$ $$x^n + x^{-n} = 2\cos n\theta$$

and $$x^n - x^{-n} = 2i \sin n\theta.$$

Example 2. If α and β are real, prove that

$$(\alpha + i\beta)^{m/n} + (\alpha - i\beta)^{m/n} = 2.(\alpha^2 + \beta^2)^{m/2n} . \cos\left(\frac{m}{n}\tan^{-1}\frac{\beta}{\alpha}\right).$$

Solution: Let $\alpha + i\beta = r(\cos\theta + i\sin\theta)$

$$\alpha = r\cos\theta$$

$$\beta = r\sin\theta$$

$\therefore$ $$\alpha^2 + \beta^2 = r^2$$

$\Rightarrow$ $$r = (\alpha^2 + \beta^2)^{1/2}$$

and $$\tan\theta = \left(\frac{\beta}{\alpha}\right)$$

$\therefore$ $$\theta = \tan^{-1}\left(\frac{\beta}{\alpha}\right)$$

$\therefore$ $$(\alpha + i\beta)^{m/n} = r^{m/n}\left(\cos\frac{m}{n}\theta + i\sin\frac{m}{n}\theta\right)$$

and $$(\alpha - i\beta)^{m/n} = r^{m/n}\left(\cos\frac{m}{n}\theta - i\sin\frac{m}{n}\theta\right)$$

$\therefore$ $$(\alpha+i\beta)^{m/n} + (\alpha-i\beta)^{m/n} = 2r^{m/n} . \cos\left(\frac{m}{n}\theta\right)$$

$$= 2 . (\alpha^2 + \beta^2)^{m/2n} . \cos\left(m.\tan^{-1}\frac{\beta}{\alpha}\right)$$

$$= 2 . (\alpha^2 + \beta^2)^{m/2n} . \cos\left(m\tan^{-1}\frac{\beta}{\alpha}\right)$$

and $$(\alpha+i\beta)^{m/n} - (\alpha-i\beta)^{m/n} = 2i(\alpha^2 + \beta^2)^{m/2n} . \sin\left(m\tan^{-1}\frac{\beta}{\alpha}\right)$$

Example 3. If $a = \cos 2\alpha + i\sin 2\alpha$, $b = \cos 2\beta + i\sin 2\beta$,
$c = \cos 2\gamma + i\sin 2\gamma$, $d = \cos 2\delta + i\sin 2\delta$.

Show that

$$\sqrt{\frac{ab}{cd}}+\sqrt{\frac{cd}{ab}} = 2\cos(\alpha+\beta-\gamma-\delta).$$

Solution: We have

$$\frac{ab}{cd} = \frac{(\cos 2\alpha + i\sin 2\alpha)(\cos 2\beta + i\sin 2\beta)}{(\cos 2\gamma + i\sin 2\gamma)(\cos 2\delta + i\sin 2\delta)}$$

$$= \frac{\cos(2\alpha+2\beta)+i\sin(2\alpha+2\beta)}{\cos(2\gamma+2\delta)+i\sin(2\gamma+2\delta)}$$

$$= [\cos(2\alpha + 2\beta) + i\sin(2\alpha + 2\beta)]$$
$$[\cos(2\gamma + 2\delta) + i\sin(2\gamma + 2\delta)]^{-1}$$

$$= [\cos(2\delta + 2\beta) + i\sin(2\alpha + 2\beta)]$$
$$[\cos(2\gamma + 2\delta) - i\sin(2\gamma + 2\delta)]$$

$$= [\cos(2\alpha + 2\beta - 2\gamma - 2\delta)$$
$$+ i\sin(2\alpha + 2\beta - 2\gamma - 2\delta)$$

$$\therefore \quad \sqrt{\frac{ab}{cd}} = [\cos(2\alpha + 2\beta - 2\gamma - 2\delta)$$
$$+ i\sin(2\alpha + 2\beta - 2\gamma - 2\delta)]^{1/2}$$
$$= \cos(\alpha + \beta - \gamma - \delta) + i\sin(\alpha + \beta - \gamma - \delta)$$

Similarly,
$$\sqrt{\frac{cd}{ad}} = \left(\sqrt{\frac{ab}{cd}}\right)^{-1}$$

$$= [\cos(\alpha + \beta - \gamma - \delta) + i\sin(\alpha + \beta - \gamma - \delta)]^{-1}$$
$$= [\cos(\alpha + \beta - \gamma - \delta) - i\sin(\alpha + \beta - \gamma - \delta)]$$

$$\therefore \quad \sqrt{\frac{ab}{cd}}+\sqrt{\frac{cd}{ab}} = 2\cos(\alpha+\beta-\gamma-\delta).$$

Example 4. Find the equation whose roots are the mth powers of the roots of $x^2 - 2x\cos\theta + 1 = 0$.

Solution: Let α, β be the roots of $x^2 - 2x\cos\theta + 1 = 0$.

$$\therefore \quad \alpha, \beta = \frac{2\cos\theta \pm \sqrt{4\cos^2\theta - 4}}{2}$$

$$= \frac{2\cos\theta \pm 2\sqrt{-\sin^2\theta}}{2}$$

$$\alpha, \beta = \cos\theta \pm i\sin\theta.$$

Let $\alpha = \cos\theta + i\sin\theta.$

$\therefore$ $\beta = \cos\theta - i\sin\theta.$

$\therefore$ $\alpha^m = \cos m\theta + i\sin m\theta.$

$\beta^m = \cos m\theta - i\sin m\theta.$

$\therefore$ $\alpha^m + \beta^m = 2\cos m\theta.$

and $\alpha^m \cdot \beta^m = 1$

$\therefore$ The required equation is

$$= x^2 - x\,(\text{sum of roots}) + \text{product of roots} = 0$$

$$= x^2 - 2x\cos m\theta + 1 = 0$$

Example 5. If $x_r = \cos\left(\frac{\pi}{2^r}\right) + i\sin\left(\frac{\pi}{2^r}\right)$, prove that

$$x_1\,x_2\,x_3 \ldots x_r \ldots \text{to } \infty = -1.$$

Solution: We are given that

$$x_r = \cos\frac{\pi}{2^r} + i\sin\frac{\pi}{2^r}$$

$\therefore$ $$x_1 = \cos\frac{\pi}{2} + i\sin\frac{\pi}{2},$$

$$x_2 = \cos\frac{\pi}{2^2} + i\sin\frac{\pi}{2^2},$$

$$x_3 = \cos\frac{\pi}{2^3} + i\sin\frac{\pi}{2^3}$$

$\therefore$ $x_1 . x_2 . x_2 \ldots x_r \ldots$ to ∞

$$= (\cos\frac{\pi}{2} + i\sin\frac{\pi}{2}) . (\cos\frac{\pi}{2^2} + i\sin\frac{\pi}{2^2}) .$$

$$(\cos\frac{\pi}{2^3} + i\sin\frac{\pi}{2^3}) \ldots (\cos\frac{\pi}{2^r} + i\sin\frac{\pi}{2^r}) \ldots \text{upto } \infty.$$

$$= \cos\frac{\pi}{2}\left[1 + \frac{1}{2} + \frac{1}{2^2} + \frac{1}{2^3} + \ldots\text{to } \infty\right]$$

$$+ i \sin \frac{\pi}{2}\left[1+\frac{1}{2}+\frac{1}{2^2}+\frac{1}{2^3}+\ldots\text{to } \infty\right]$$

$$= \cos\frac{\pi}{2}\left[\frac{1}{1-\frac{1}{2}}\right]+ i \sin \frac{\pi}{2}\left[\frac{1}{1-\frac{1}{2}}\right]$$

$$= \cos\pi + i \sin\pi = -1.$$

Example 6. Find $x \in$ R, such that

$$\frac{(x+\alpha)^n-(x+\beta)^n}{\alpha-\beta}=\frac{\sin n\theta}{\sin^n \theta}$$

Where α, β are the roots of $t^2 - 2t + 2 = 0$.

Solution: Since α, β are the roots of $t^2 - 2t + 2 = 0$.

$$\therefore \quad \alpha, \beta = \frac{2 \pm \sqrt{4-8}}{2} \qquad \ldots (1)$$

$$\alpha, \beta = \frac{2 \pm 2i}{2}$$

$$\alpha, \beta = 1 \pm i.$$

Let $\alpha = 1 + i.$

$\therefore$ $\beta = 1 - i.$

$\therefore$ $\alpha - \beta = 2i.$

Now, let $x + \alpha = (x + 1 + i) = r(\cos\phi + i \sin\phi)$

$\therefore$ $x + \beta = (x + 1 - i) = r(\cos\phi - i \sin\phi)$

$\therefore$ $x + 1 = r\cos\phi,$ ...(2)

$1 = r\sin\phi$ ...(3)

Substituting these in the given equation, we get

$$\frac{r^n[\cos\phi + i\sin\phi]^n - r^n[\cos\phi - i\sin\phi]^n}{2i} = \frac{\sin n\theta}{\sin^n\theta}$$

or

$$\frac{r^n.2i\sin n\phi}{2i} = \frac{\sin n\theta}{\sin^n\theta}$$

$$r^n.\sin n\phi = \frac{\sin n\theta}{\sin^n\theta}$$

$$\frac{\sin n\phi}{\sin^n \phi} = \frac{\sin n\theta}{\sin^n \theta} \quad \left(\because r = \frac{1}{\sin \phi}\right)$$

$\Rightarrow$ $\phi = \theta.$

Putting this in equations (2) and (3), we get

$$x + 1 = r \cos\phi = r \cos\theta.$$

$$1 = r \sin\phi = r \sin\theta.$$

$\therefore$ $x + 1 = \cot\theta$

or $x = \cot \theta - 1.$

Example 7. If $\sin\alpha + \sin\beta + \sin\gamma = 0 = \cos\alpha + \cos\beta + \cos\gamma$, prove that

(i) $\cos3\alpha + \cos3\beta + \cos3\gamma = 3 \cos (\alpha + \beta + \gamma)$

(ii) $\sin3\alpha + \sin3\beta + \sin3\gamma = 3 \sin (\alpha + \beta + \gamma)$

(iii) $\cos (\beta + \gamma) + \cos (\gamma + \alpha) + \cos (\alpha + \beta) = 0 = \sin (\alpha + \beta) + \sin(\beta + \gamma) + \sin (\gamma + \alpha)$.

Solution: Let $x = \cos\alpha + i \sin\alpha,$ ...(1)

$y = \cos\beta + i \sin \beta$ ...(2)

and $z = \cos\gamma + i \sin\gamma$ ...(3)

$\therefore$ $x + y + z = \cos\alpha + \cos\beta + \cos\gamma + i (\sin\alpha + \sin\beta + \sin\gamma)$

$= 0 + i.0$

$x + y + z = 0$ ...(4)

$\therefore$ $x + y = -z$

Cubing both sides, we get

$$x^3 + y^3 + 3xy (x + y) = -z^3$$

or $x^3 + y^3 + 3xy (-z) = -z^3$

$$x^3 + y^3 - 3xyz = -z^3$$

$\therefore$ $x^3 + y^3 + z^3 = 3xyz$ ....(5)

Substituting x, y, z in equation (5), we get

$(\cos\alpha + i \sin\alpha)^3 + (\cos\beta + i \sin\beta)^3 + (\cos\gamma + i \sin\gamma)^3$

$= 3 (\cos\alpha + i \sin\alpha) (\cos\beta + i \sin\beta) (\cos\gamma + i \sin\gamma)$

$\cos3\alpha + i \sin3\alpha + \cos3\beta + i \sin3\beta + \cos3\gamma + i \sin3\gamma$

$= 3[\cos (\alpha + \beta + \gamma) + i \sin (\alpha + \beta + \gamma)]$

$\therefore$ $\cos3\alpha + \cos3\beta + \cos3\gamma + i (\sin3\alpha + \sin3\beta + \sin3\gamma)$

$= 3[\cos (\alpha + \beta + \gamma) + i \sin (\alpha + \beta + \gamma)]$

Equating real and imaginary parts, we get

$\cos3\alpha + \cos3\beta + \cos3\gamma = 3 \cos (\alpha + \beta + \gamma)$

and

$\sin3\alpha + \sin3\beta + \sin3\gamma = 3\sin (\alpha + \beta + \gamma).$

Now $$\frac{1}{x}+\frac{1}{y}+\frac{1}{z} = \frac{1}{\cos\alpha+i\sin\alpha}+\frac{1}{\cos\beta+i\sin\beta}+\frac{1}{\cos\gamma+i\sin\gamma}$$

$$= (\cos\alpha - i\sin\alpha) + (\cos\beta - i\sin\beta) + (\cos\gamma - i\sin\gamma)$$

$$= \cos\alpha + \cos\beta + \cos\gamma - i(\sin\alpha + \sin\beta + \sin\gamma)$$
$$= 0 - i \,.\, 0$$
$$= 0.$$

$\therefore$ $$\frac{1}{x}+\frac{1}{y}+\frac{1}{z} = 0$$

$\Rightarrow$ $xy + yz + zx = 0$

$\Rightarrow$ $(\cos\alpha + i\sin\alpha)(\cos\beta + i\sin\beta) + (\cos\beta + i\sin\beta)(\cos\gamma + i\sin\gamma)$
$+ (\cos\gamma + i\sin\gamma)(\cos\alpha + i\sin\alpha) = 0$

$\Rightarrow \cos(\alpha + \beta) + i\sin(\alpha + \beta) + \cos(\beta + \gamma) + i\sin(\beta + \gamma) + \cos(\gamma + \alpha)$
$+ i\sin(\gamma + \alpha) = 0$

Equating real and imaginary parts, we get

$$\cos(\alpha + \beta) + \cos(\beta + \gamma) + \cos(\gamma + \alpha) = 0$$

and $$\sin(\alpha + \beta) + \sin(\beta + \gamma) + \sin(\gamma + \alpha) = 0.$$

Roots of a Complex Number

We know that $\cos\theta$ and $\sin\theta$ are periodic functions of period $2m\pi$, where m is an integer.

Then $\cos\theta + i\sin\theta = \cos(2m\pi + \theta) + i\sin(2m\pi + \theta)$

$\therefore$ $$(\cos\theta + i\sin\theta)^{1/n} = \cos\frac{2m\pi+\theta}{n} + i\sin\frac{2m\pi+\theta}{n}$$

for $m = 0, 1, 2, 3 \ldots n-1$ all the values obtained, when raised to power n give $\cos\theta + i\sin\theta$.

Thus, all the values, so obtained are the nth roots of $\cos\theta + i\sin\theta$.

SOLVED EXAMPLES

Example 1. Show that the nth roots of $(\cos\theta + i\sin\theta)$ form a G.P. and further show that there are n and only n distinct roots.

Solution: The nth roots of $\cos\theta + i\sin\theta$ are given by

$$= \cos\frac{2m\pi+\theta}{n} + i\sin\frac{2m\pi+\theta}{n}, \quad m = 0, 1, 2, \ldots n-1$$

$$= \left(\cos\frac{2\pi}{n}+i\sin\frac{2\pi}{n}\right)^m\left(\cos\frac{\theta}{n}+i\sin\frac{\theta}{n}\right)$$

where $m = 0, 1, 2, 3, ...n-1$

Let $\cos\dfrac{2\pi}{n} + i\sin\dfrac{2\pi}{n} = a$

and $\cos\dfrac{\theta}{n} + i\sin\dfrac{\theta}{n} = b$

Then the roots are $b, ab, a^2b, a^3b \ .... \ a^{n-1}b.$

Obviously, they form a G.P.,

when $m = n$, then the root z_{n+1} is

$$z_{n+1} = a^n.b$$

$$= \left(\cos\frac{2\pi}{n} + i\sin\frac{2\pi}{n}\right)^n . b$$

$$= (\cos 2\pi + i\sin 2\pi) . b$$

$$= b$$

Which is the root, which is obtained for $m = 0$.

Thus, after $m = n - 1$, roots begin to repeat.

Hence, we get n and only n distinct roots.

Note: Angular difference between any two successive roots, *i.e.*, z_i, z_{i-1} is the same. Thus all the roots are uniformly distributed in the Z-plane.

Example 2. Find five 5th roots of unity and further show that the sum of their n^{th} powers vanishes, if n is not a multiple of 5 and is 5, if n is a multiple of 5.

Solution: We know that

$$1 = \cos 0 + i\sin 0$$

$$= \cos 2n\pi + i\sin 2n\pi$$

$$\therefore \quad (1)^{\frac{1}{5}} = \cos\frac{2n\pi}{5} + i\sin\frac{2n\pi}{5}$$

$$n = 0, 1, 2, 3, 4$$

$\therefore$ The 5th roots of unity are

$$z_1 \text{ (for } n = 0) = \cos 0 + i\sin 0 = 1$$

$$z_2 \text{ (for } n = 1) = \cos\frac{2\pi}{5} + i\sin\frac{2\pi}{5}$$

$$z_3 \text{ (for } n = 2) = \cos\frac{4\pi}{5} + i\sin\frac{4\pi}{5}$$

$$z_4 \text{ (for } n = 3) = \cos\frac{6\pi}{5} + i\sin\frac{6\pi}{5}$$

$$z_5 \text{ (for } n = 4) = \cos\frac{8\pi}{5} + i\sin\frac{8\pi}{5}$$

Further, let $\left[\cos\frac{2\pi}{5} + i\sin\frac{2\pi}{5}\right] = \alpha$

Thus, the roots are 1, α, α^2, α^3, α^4.

$\therefore$ sum of the roots $= 1 + \alpha + \alpha^2 + \alpha^3 + \alpha^4$

$$= \frac{1-\alpha^5}{1-\alpha}$$

$$= \frac{1-1}{1-\alpha} \quad (\alpha^5 = 1, \alpha \neq 1)$$

$$= 0$$

Now S_n = sum of nth powers of the roots

$$= 1^n + \alpha^n + \alpha^{2n} + \alpha^{3n} + \alpha^{4n}$$

$$= \frac{1-\alpha^{5n}}{1-\alpha^n}$$

If n is not a multiple of 5

then $\alpha^n \neq 1$, $\alpha^{5n} = (\alpha^5)^n = 1^n = 1$

$$\therefore \quad S_n = \frac{1-1}{1-\alpha^n} = 0$$

$\therefore$ $S_n = 0$, if n is not a multiple of 5.

Now, if n is a multiple of 5, then $n = 5k$ (k is an integer).

$$\therefore \quad \alpha^n = \alpha^{5k} = (\alpha^5)^k$$

$$= (1)^k$$

$$= 1$$

$$\therefore \quad \alpha^n = 1$$

$$\alpha^{2n} = \alpha^{3n} = \alpha^{4n} = 1.$$

$$1 + \alpha^n + \alpha^{2n} + \alpha^{3n} + \alpha^{4n} = 1 + 1 + 1 + 1 + 1$$

$$= 5.$$

Example 3. Find all the values of $(i)^{1/6}$.

Solution: We have

$$i = \cos\frac{\pi}{2} + i\sin\frac{\pi}{2}$$

$$i = \cos\left(2n\pi + \frac{\pi}{2}\right) + i\sin\left(2n\pi + \frac{\pi}{2}\right)$$

$\therefore$
$$(i)^{1/6} = \left[\cos(4n+1)\frac{\pi}{2} + i\sin(4n+1)\frac{\pi}{2}\right]^{1/6}$$

$$= \cos(4n+1)\frac{\pi}{12} + i\sin(4n+1)\frac{\pi}{12}$$

where $n = 0, 1, 2, 3, 5$

putting $n = 0, 1, 2, 3, 4, 5$, we get the required six roots as

$$z_1 = \cos\frac{\pi}{12} + i\sin\frac{\pi}{12}.$$

$$z_2 = \cos\frac{5\pi}{12} + i\sin\frac{5\pi}{12}.$$

$$z_3 = \cos\frac{9\pi}{12} + i\sin\frac{9\pi}{12}.$$

$$z_4 = \cos\frac{13\pi}{12} + i\sin\frac{13\pi}{12} = -\left(\cos\frac{\pi}{12} + i\sin\frac{\pi}{12}\right)$$

$$z_5 = \cos\frac{17\pi}{12} + i\sin\frac{17\pi}{12} = -\left(\cos\frac{5\pi}{12} + i\sin\frac{5\pi}{12}\right)$$

$$z_6 = \cos\frac{21\pi}{12} + i\sin\frac{21\pi}{12} = -\left(\cos\frac{9\pi}{12} + i\sin\frac{9\pi}{12}\right)$$

$\therefore$ The required roots are $\pm\left(\cos\frac{\pi}{12} + i\sin\frac{\pi}{12}\right)$, $\pm\left(\cos\frac{5\pi}{12} + i\sin\frac{5\pi}{12}\right)$

$\pm\left(\cos\frac{9\pi}{12} + i\sin\frac{9\pi}{12}\right)$.

Example 4. Solve the equation $x^6 + x^5 + x^4 + x^3 + x^2 + x + 1 = 0$.

Solution: Multiplying the given equation by $(x - 1)$, we have

$$(x - 1)(x^6 + x^5 + x^4 + x^3 + x^2 + x + 1) = 0$$

or
$$x^7 - 1 = 0$$

or $\qquad x^7 = 1$

$$x = (1)^{1/7}$$

Now $\qquad 1 = \cos 0 + i \sin 0$

$$= \cos 2n\pi + i \sin 2n\pi$$

$\therefore \qquad (1)^{1/7} = \cos\frac{2n\pi}{7} + \text{i} \sin\frac{2n\pi}{7}$, where $n = 0, 1, 2, \ldots 6.$

Putting $n = 0, 1, 2, 3, 4, 5, 6$ we get the roots as $1, \cos\frac{2\pi}{7} \pm i \sin\frac{2\pi}{7}$,

$\cos\frac{4\pi}{7} \pm i \sin\frac{4\pi}{7}, \cos\frac{6\pi}{7} \pm i \sin\frac{6\pi}{7}$.

Out of these roots $x = 1$ is corresponding to the factor $(x - 1)$, with which we multiplied the given equation.

So, leaving this root, rest of the roots are the roots of the given equation.

Thus, the roots of the given equation are $\cos\frac{2\pi}{7} \pm i \sin\frac{2\pi}{7}$, $\cos\frac{4\pi}{7} \pm i \sin\frac{4\pi}{7}$, and $\cos\frac{6\pi}{7} \pm i \sin\frac{6\pi}{7}$.

Example 5. Solve the equation $x^4 - x^3 + x^2 - x + 1 = 0$.

Solution: The given equation is

$$x^4 - x^3 + x^2 - x + 1 = 0 \qquad \ldots(1)$$

Multiplying the given equation by $(x + 1)$,

we have $(x + 1), (x^4 - x^3 + x^2 - x + 1) = 0$

$$x^5 + 1 = 0$$

$$x^5 = -1.$$

$\therefore \qquad x = (-1)^{1/5}$.

We know that $\qquad -1 = \cos\pi + i \sin\pi$

$$= \cos (2n + 1) \pi + i \sin (2n + 1) \pi$$

$$(-1)^{1/5} = \cos (2n + 1) \frac{\pi}{5} + i \sin (2n + 1) \frac{\pi}{5}$$

$$n = 0, 1, 2, 3, 4.$$

for $n = 0, 1, 2, 3, 4$ the roots are $\cos\frac{\pi}{5} + i \sin\frac{\pi}{5}, \cos\frac{3\pi}{5} + i \sin\frac{3\pi}{5}$,

$\cos\pi + i \sin\pi, \cos\frac{7\pi}{5} + i \sin\frac{7\pi}{5}, \cos\frac{9\pi}{5} + i \sin\frac{9\pi}{5}$

or

$$\cos\frac{\pi}{5} \pm i\sin\frac{\pi}{5},\ \cos\frac{3\pi}{5} \pm i\sin\frac{3\pi}{5},\ -1.$$

leaving –1, which is corresponding to the factor $(x + 1) = 0$, rest of the roots are the roots of the given equation.

Example 6. Solve $x^9 - x^5 + x^4 - 1 = 0$.

Solution: The given equation is

$$x^9 - x^5 + x^4 - 1 = 0$$

$$x^5 (x^4 - 1) + 1 (x^4 - 1) = 0$$

or $$(1 + x^5)(x^4 - 1) = 0$$

$\therefore$ $$x^5 + 1 = 0.$$

$\Rightarrow$ $$x = (-1)^{1/5}$$

and $$x^4 - 1 = 0$$

$$x = (1)^{1/4}.$$

Thus, roots of $x^5 + 1 = 0$ and $x^4 - 1 = 0$ are the roots of the given equation. Which is left as an exercise for the students.

Example 7. Find all the values of $\left(1 - i\sqrt{3}\right)^{1/3}$.

Solution: Let $\left(1 - i\sqrt{3}\right) = r(\cos\theta + i\sin\theta)$ ...(1)

Equating real and imaginary parts on both sides,

We have

$$1 = r\cos\theta \quad ....(2)$$

$$-\sqrt{3} = r\sin\theta \quad ....(3)$$

Squaring and adding (2) and (3), we get

$$4 = r^2$$

$\therefore$ $r = 2$ (+ve roots are to be considered)

Dividing (3) by (2), we have

$$\tan\theta = -\sqrt{3}$$

$$\theta = -\frac{\pi}{3}$$

$\therefore$ $$1 - i\sqrt{3} = 2\left[\cos\frac{\pi}{3} - i\sin\frac{\pi}{3}\right].$$

$$= 2\left[\cos\left(2n\pi + \frac{\pi}{3}\right) - i\sin\left(2n\pi + \frac{\pi}{3}\right)\right]$$

$$\therefore \quad (1 - i\sqrt{3})^{1/3} = 2^{1/3}\left[\cos(6n+1)\frac{\pi}{9} - i\sin(6n+1)\frac{\pi}{9}\right]$$

$$n = 0, 1, 2.$$

Putting $n = 0, 1, 2$ we get the three values of $(1 - i\sqrt{3})^{1/3}$.

Example 8. Show that the roots of the equation $(x - 1)^n = x^n$, are given by $\frac{1}{2}\left[1 + i\cot\frac{r\pi}{n}\right]$, $r = 0, 1, 2, ... (n - 1)$.

Solution: The given equation is

$$(x - 1)^n = x^n$$

$$\therefore \quad \left(\frac{x-1}{x}\right)^n = 1$$

$$\text{or} \quad \left(1 - \frac{1}{x}\right)^n = 1$$

$$= \cos 2r\pi + \text{i} \sin 2r\pi$$

$$\therefore \quad \left(1 - \frac{1}{x}\right) = [\cos 2r\pi + i \sin 2r\pi]^{1/n}$$

$$= \cos\frac{2r\pi}{n} + i \sin\frac{2r\pi}{n}.$$

where $\quad r = 0, 1, 2, ... (n - 1)$

$$\therefore 1 - \cos\frac{2r\pi}{n} - i \sin\frac{2r\pi}{n} = \frac{1}{x}$$

$$\text{or} \quad x = \frac{1}{1 - \cos\frac{2r\pi}{n} - i\sin\frac{2r\pi}{n}}$$

$$= \frac{1}{2\sin^2\frac{r\pi}{n} - 2i\sin\frac{r\pi}{n}.\cos\frac{r\pi}{n}}$$

$$= \frac{1}{2\sin\frac{r\pi}{n}\left[\sin\frac{r\pi}{n} - i\cos\frac{r\pi}{n}\right]}$$

$$= \frac{1}{2\sin\frac{r\pi}{n}}\left[\frac{\sin\frac{r\pi}{n} + i\cos\frac{r\pi}{n}}{\sin^2\frac{r\pi}{n} + \cos^2\frac{r\pi}{n}}\right]$$

$$= \frac{1}{2}.\frac{1}{\sin\left(\frac{r\pi}{n}\right)}\left[\sin\frac{r\pi}{n} + i\cos\frac{r\pi}{n}\right]$$

$$= \frac{1}{2}\left[1 + i\cot\frac{r\pi}{n}\right]. \text{ where} r = 0, 1, 2, \ldots n - 1.$$

EXERCISE

1. Show that:

$$\frac{(\cos 2\theta + i\sin 2\theta)^3 (\cos 3\theta - i\sin 3\theta)^4}{(\cos 3\theta + i\sin 3\theta)^2 (\cos 3\theta + i\sin 3\theta)^{-4}} = 1.$$

2. If $x + \frac{1}{x} = 2\cos\theta$ and $y + \frac{1}{y} = 2\cos\phi$,

Prove that:

(i) $x^m y^n + \left(\frac{1}{x^m y^n}\right) = 2\cos(m\theta + n\phi)$

(ii) $\frac{x^m}{y^n} + \frac{y^n}{x^m} = 2\cos(m\theta - n\phi)$

3. Show that:

$[\cos\theta + i\sin\theta) + (\cos\phi + i\sin\phi)]^n + [(\cos\theta - i\sin\theta) +$

$(\cos\phi - i\sin\phi)]^n = 2^{n+1} . \cos^n\left(\frac{\theta - \phi}{2}\right). \cos^n\left(\frac{\theta + \phi}{2}\right).$

4. Prove that:

$(1 + i)^n + (1 - i)^n = 2^{n/2+1} . \cos\frac{n\pi}{4}.$

5. If $\sin\alpha + \sin\beta + \sin\gamma = \cos\alpha + \cos\beta + \cos\gamma = 0$, then show that : $\Sigma \sin^2\alpha = \Sigma \cos^2\alpha$.
6. Find the general value of θ which satisfies the equation
$(\cos\theta + i\sin\theta)(\cos 2\theta + i\sin 2\theta) \ldots (\cos n\theta + i\sin n\theta) = 1.$
7. If α, β are the roots of the equation $y^2 - 2y + 4 = 0$, then show that
$$\alpha^n + \beta^n = 2^{n+1} \cdot \cos\left(\frac{n\pi}{3}\right).$$
8. If $x = \cos\theta + i\sin\theta$ and $nc - 1 = \sqrt{1-c^2}$, then show that
$$1 + c \cdot \cos\theta = \frac{c}{2n}(1 + nx)\left(1 + \frac{n}{x}\right).$$
9. Find all the values of $(-i)^{1/6}$.
10. Find all the values of $\left[\frac{1}{2} + \frac{i}{2}\sqrt{3}\right]^{\frac{3}{4}}$ and hence, show that their continued product is unity.
11. Prove that the n, n^{th} roots of unity form a G.P., and their product is $(-1)^{n-1}$.
12. Solve the following equations
(i) $x^4 + x^3 + x^2 + x + 1 = 0$
(ii) $x^5 - x^4 + x^3 - x^2 + x - 1 = 0$
(iii) $x^7 + x^4 + x^3 + 1 = 0$.
13. Show that the roots of the equation $(1 + x)^{2n} + (1 - x)^{2n} = 0$, are given by
$$x = \pm i \tan\frac{(2k-1)\pi}{4n}, \text{ where } k = 0, 1, 2, 3, \ldots n.$$

Answers:

Ans. 6. $\theta = \dfrac{4m\pi}{n(n+1)}$, $m \in I$.

Ans. 9. $\pm\left(\cos\dfrac{n\pi}{12} - i\sin\dfrac{n\pi}{12}\right)$, $n = 1, 5, 9$.

Ans. 10. $\cos\dfrac{(2n+1)\pi}{4} + i\sin(2n+1)\dfrac{\pi}{4}$, $n = 0, 1, 2, 3$.

Ans. 12. (i) $\cos\dfrac{2\pi}{5} \pm i\sin\dfrac{2\pi}{5}$, $\cos\dfrac{4\pi}{5} \pm i\sin\dfrac{4\pi}{5}$.

(ii) $\frac{1}{2} \pm i\frac{\sqrt{3}}{2}, -\frac{1}{2} \pm i\frac{\sqrt{3}}{2}, 1.$

(iii) $-1, \frac{1}{2}(1 \pm i\sqrt{3}), \frac{(\pm 1 \pm i)}{\sqrt{2}}.$

Expansions of sin *n*q, cos *n*θ in powers of sinq and cosθ (when *n* is a + ve integer)

By De-Moivre's Theorem, we have

$$(\cos\theta + i \sin\theta)^n = \cos n\theta + i \sin n\theta \qquad ...(1)$$

since n is a +ve integer, then expanding $(\cos\theta + i \sin\theta)^n$ by binomial theorem, we have

$$(\cos\theta + i \sin\theta)^n = \cos^n\theta + nc_1 . \cos^{n-1}\theta\,(i \sin\theta) + nc_2 . \cos^{n-2}\theta\,(i \sin\theta)^2 + nc_3 . \cos^{n-3}\theta\,(i \sin\theta)^3 + ...$$

$$= \cos^n\theta + i\, nc_1 . \cos^{n-1}\theta . \sin\theta - nc_2 \cos^{n-2}\theta . \sin^2\theta - i . nc_3 \cos^{n-3}\theta \sin^3\theta + ...$$

$$= \cos^n\theta - nc_2 . \cos^{n-2}\theta . \sin^2\theta + nc_4 . \cos^{n-4}\theta . \sin^4\theta ... + i\,[nc_1 . \cos^{n-1}\theta \sin\theta - nc_3 \cos^{n-3}\theta \sin^3\theta + ...$$

Equating the R.H.S. of the equation (1) and (2), we have

$$\cos n\theta + i \sin n\theta = \cos^n\theta - nc_2 . \cos^{n-2}\theta \sin^2\theta + nc_4 \cos^{n-4}\theta \sin^4 + ... + i\,[nc_1 . \cos^{n-1}\theta \sin\theta - nc_3 \cos^{n-3}\theta \sin^3\theta + nc_5 \cos^{n-5}\theta . \sin^5\theta ...]$$

Equating real and imaginary parts, we have

$$\cos n\theta = \cos^n\theta - nc_2 . \cos^{n-2}\theta . \sin^2\theta + nc_4 \cos^{n-4}\theta \sin^4\theta + ...$$

$$\sin n\theta = nc_1 . \cos^{n-1}\theta . \sin\theta - nc_3 . \cos^{n-3}\theta \sin^3\theta +$$

$$+ nc_5 \cos^{n-5}\theta \sin^5\theta + ...$$

Expansion of tan *n*θ in Powers of tanθ

From the previous results, we know that

$$\cos n\theta = \cos^n\theta - nc_2 . \cos^{n-2}\theta . \sin^2\theta$$

$$+ nc_4.\cos^{n-4}\theta.\sin^4\theta + \ldots \qquad \ldots(1)$$

and
$$\sin n\theta = nc_1.\cos^{n-1}\theta.\sin\theta - nc_3 \cos^{n-3}\theta.\ \sin^3\theta + \ldots$$

$$+ nc_5 \cos^{n-5}\theta.\ \sin^5\theta + \ldots \qquad \ldots(2)$$

Dividing equation (2) by (1), we have

$$\tan n\theta = \frac{nc_1.\cos^{n-1}\theta.\sin\theta - nc_3.\cos^{n-3}\theta.\sin^3\theta + \ldots}{\cos^n\theta - nc_2 \cos^{n-2}\theta.\sin^2\theta + nc_4.\cos^{n-4}.\sin^4\theta + \ldots}$$

Dividing N^r. & D^r. by $\cos^n\theta$, we get

$$\tan n\theta = \frac{nc_1\ .\tan\theta - nc_3 \tan^3\theta + nc_5 \tan^5\theta \ldots.}{1 - nc_2.\tan^2\theta + nc_4.\tan^4\theta \ldots}$$

Expansion of $\cos^n\theta$, in Series of cosines of Multiples of θ. (n being a +ve integer)

Let
$$x = \cos\theta + i\sin\theta$$

$$\therefore \quad \frac{1}{x} = \cos\theta - i\sin\theta$$

$$x^n = \cos n\theta + i\sin n\theta$$

$$\therefore \quad \frac{1}{x^n} = \cos n\theta - i\sin n\theta$$

$$x + \frac{1}{x} = 2\cos\theta$$

$$\therefore \quad (2\cos\theta)^n = \left(x + \frac{1}{x}\right)^n$$

$$= x^n + nc_1.\ x^{n-2} + nc_2\ .\ x^{n-4} \ldots$$

$$+ nc_{n-1}\ .\ \frac{1}{x^{n-2}} + \frac{1}{x^n}$$

$$= \left(x^n + \frac{1}{x^n}\right) + nc_1.\left[x^{n-2} + \frac{1}{x^{n-2}}\right]$$

$$+ nc_2.\left[x^{n-4} + \frac{1}{x^{n-4}}\right] + \dots\dots\dots\dots$$

$$= 2\cos n\theta + nc_1.2\cos(n-2)\theta + nc_2\, 2\cos\ (n-4)\theta + \dots$$

$$\therefore \qquad \cos^n\theta = \frac{1}{2^{n-1}}[\cos n\theta + nc_1.\cos(n-2)\theta + nc_2.\cos(n-4)\theta + \dots.$$

Expansion of $\sin^n\theta$ in Series of Sines of Multiples of θ (n being a +ve integer)

Let $\qquad x = \cos\theta + i\sin\theta$

$\therefore \qquad \dfrac{1}{x} = \cos\theta + i\sin\theta$

$\therefore \qquad x^n = \cos n\theta + i\sin n\theta$ and $x^{-n} = \cos n\theta - i\sin n\theta$.

$$x^n + \frac{1}{x^n} = 2\cos n\theta \text{ and } x^n - \frac{1}{x^n} = 2\, i\sin n\theta.$$

Now $\qquad 2i\sin\theta = \left(x - \dfrac{1}{x}\right)$

$$(2i\sin\theta)^n = \left(x - \frac{1}{x}\right)^n$$

$$= x^n - nc_1.x^{n-2} + nc_2\, .\, x^{n-4} - nc_{3.}\, x^{n-6} \dots$$

$$+ nc_{n-1}.\,(-1)^{n-1}\,\frac{1}{x^{n-2}} + \left(-\frac{1}{x}\right)^n.$$

Case I. When n is even:

$$= \left(x^n + \frac{1}{x^n}\right) - nc_1.\left(x^{n-2} + \frac{1}{x^{n-2}}\right)$$

$$+ nc_2\left(x^{n-4} + \frac{1}{x^{n-4}}\right) \dots$$

$$= 2\cos n\theta - nc_1.2\cos(n-2)\theta + nc_4.2\cos(n-4)\theta \dots$$

$$\therefore \qquad 2^{n-1}.i^n\sin^n\theta = \cos n\theta - nc_1\cdot\cos(n-2)\theta + nc_2.\cos(n-4)\theta\dots$$

Case II. When n is odd:

$$2^n.i^n \sin^n\theta = \left(x - \frac{1}{x}\right)^n$$

$$= x^n - nc_1.x^{n-2} + nc_2 \,.\, x^{n-4} - nc_3\, x^{n-6} \ldots$$

$$+ nc_{n-1}.\frac{1}{x^{n-2}} + \left(-\frac{1}{x}\right)^n$$

$$= \left(x^n - \frac{1}{x^n}\right) - nc_1.\left(x^{n-2} - \frac{1}{x^{n-2}}\right)$$

$$+ nc_2.\left(x^{n-4} - \frac{1}{x^{n-4}}\right)$$

$$= 2\,i \sin n\theta - nc_1.i\; 2\sin(n-2)\theta +$$
$$nc_2 \,.\, 2\,i \sin(n-4)\theta + \ldots$$

$$\therefore\; 2^{n-1}.i^{n-1} \sin^n\theta = \sin n\theta - nc_1\, .\sin(n-2)\theta + nc_2\, .\sin(n-4)\theta + \ldots.$$

SOLVED EXAMPLES

Example 1. Expand cos7θ and sin7θ in powers of sinθ and cosθ.

Solution: We have

$$(\cos\theta + i\sin\theta)^7 = \cos 7\theta + i\sin 7\theta \text{ (using De-Moivre's theorem)}$$

$$\text{Also, } (\cos\theta + i\sin\theta)^7 = \cos^7\theta + 7c_1.\cos^6\theta\,(i\sin\theta)$$
$$+ 7c_2.\cos^5\theta\,(i\sin\theta)^2 + 7c_3.\cos^4\theta(\,i\sin\theta)^3$$
$$+ 7c_4.\cos^3\theta\,(i\sin\theta)^4 + 7c_5\cdot \cos^2\theta.(i\sin\theta)^5$$
$$+ 7c_6.\,\cos\theta(i\sin\theta)^6 + 7c_7\,(i\sin\theta)^7$$
$$= \cos^7\theta + i.\,7c_1\,\cos^6\theta.\,\sin\theta - 7c_2\cdot\cos^5\theta.\,\sin^2\theta$$
$$- i.\,7c_3\,\cos^4\theta.\,\sin^3\theta + {}^7c_4.\cos^3\theta\,\sin^4\theta$$
$$+ i.\,7c_5\cdot\cos^2\theta\,\sin^5\theta - 7c_6\cdot\cos\theta.\sin^6\theta - i7c_7\,\sin^7\theta \quad \ldots.(2)$$

Equating real and imaginary parts on R.H.S. of equation (1) & (2), we get

$$\cos 7\theta = \cos^7\theta - 7c_2\,\cos^5\theta\,\sin^2\theta + 7c_4\,\cos^3\theta.\sin^4\theta$$
$$- 7c_6\,\cos\theta.\sin^6\theta. \quad \ldots(3)$$

and

$$\sin 7\theta = 7c_1\cdot\cos^6\theta.\,\sin\theta - 7c_3\cdot\cos^4\theta\,\sin^3\theta +$$
$${}^7c_5\,\cos^2\theta.\,\sin^7\theta - {}^7c_7\,\sin^7\theta. \quad \ldots.(4)$$

Expansions given by equation (3) and (4) are the required expansions.

Example 2. Show that:

$$\tan 5\theta = \frac{5\tan\theta - 10\tan^3\theta + \tan^5\theta}{1 - 10\tan^2\theta + 5\tan^4\theta}$$

Solution: We know that

$$\tan n\theta = \frac{nc_1.\tan\theta - nc_3\tan^3\theta + nc_5\tan^5\theta + ...}{1 - nc_2\tan^2\theta + nc_4.\tan^4\theta - ...}$$

Putting $n = 5$, we have

$$\tan 5\theta = \frac{5c_1.\tan\theta - 5c_3.\tan^3\theta + 5c_5.\tan^5\theta}{1 - 5c_2\tan^2\theta + 5c_4.\tan^4\theta \; ...}$$

or $$\tan 5\theta = \frac{5.\tan\theta - 10\tan^3\theta + \tan^5\theta}{1 - 10\tan^2\theta + 5\tan^4\theta}.$$

Example 3. Form the equation whose roots are:

$$\pm\tan\left(\frac{\pi}{7}\right), \pm\tan\left(\frac{2\pi}{7}\right), \pm\tan\left(\frac{3\pi}{7}\right).$$

Solution: Let θ be any of the angles

$$\frac{\pi}{7}, \frac{2\pi}{7}, \frac{3\pi}{7}, \frac{4\pi}{7}, \frac{5\pi}{7}, \frac{6\pi}{7}, \frac{7\pi}{7}.$$

then $$7\theta = \pi, 2\pi, 3\pi, 4\pi, 5\pi, 6\pi, 7\pi.$$

or $$7\theta = n\pi, \qquad n = 0, 1, 2, ...7$$

$\therefore$ $$\tan 7\theta = \tan n\pi \qquad ...(1)$$

or $$\tan 7\theta = 0 \qquad ...(2)$$

$$\Rightarrow 7c_1 . \tan\theta - 7c_3 . \tan^3\theta + 7c_5 . \tan^5\theta - 7c_7 . \tan^7\theta = 0$$

$$\Rightarrow \tan\theta\,[7 - 35\tan^2\theta + 21\tan^4\theta - \tan^6\theta] = 0 \qquad ...(3)$$

If $$\tan\theta \neq 0$$

i.e. $$\theta \neq \frac{7\pi}{7}$$

then, substituting $\tan\theta = x$,

we have $\tan\frac{\pi}{7}, \tan\frac{2\pi}{7}, \tan\frac{3\pi}{7} \ldots \tan\frac{6\pi}{7}$ are the roots of

$$7 - 35x^2 + 21x^4 - x^6 = 0$$

i.e. $x^6 - 21x^4 + 35x^2 - 7 = 0$ ...(4)

$\therefore$ The roots of the above equation (4) are $\tan\frac{\pi}{7}, \tan\frac{2\pi}{7}, \tan\frac{3\pi}{7}, \tan\frac{4\pi}{7}$, $\tan\frac{5\pi}{7}$ and $\tan\frac{6\pi}{7}$

since $\tan\frac{4\pi}{7} = \tan\left(\pi - \frac{3\pi}{7}\right) = -\tan\frac{3\pi}{7}$.

$$\tan\left(\frac{5\pi}{7}\right) = \tan\left(\pi - \frac{2\pi}{7}\right) = -\tan\left(\frac{2\pi}{7}\right)$$

and $\tan\left(\frac{6\pi}{7}\right) = \tan\left(\pi - \frac{\pi}{7}\right)$

$$= -\tan\frac{\pi}{7}$$

$\therefore$ The equation (4) is the equation whose roots are $\pm\tan\frac{\pi}{7}, \pm\tan\frac{2\pi}{7}$, $\pm\tan\frac{3\pi}{7}$, *i.e.,* the equation is $x^6–21x^4+35x^2–7=0$.

EXERCISE

1. Prove that:
   $\cos 7\theta = 64\cos^7\theta - 112\cos^5\theta + 56\cos^3\theta - 7\cos\theta$.
2. Form the equation whose roots are $\cos\frac{2\pi}{7}, \cos\frac{4\pi}{7}, \cos\frac{6\pi}{7}$.

Ans. $8x^3 + 4x^2 - 4x - 1 = 0$.

Exponential Function of a Complex Variable

If $x \in$ R, then $e^x = 1 + x + \frac{x^2}{2!} + \frac{x^3}{3!} + \frac{x^4}{4!} \ldots$

Similarly, we define an exponential function of a complex variable $z\ (= x + i\ y)$ as

$$e^z = 1 + z + \frac{z^2}{2!} + \frac{z^3}{3!} + \frac{z^4}{4!} \ldots$$

Taking $x = 0$, *i.e.*, $z = i\ y$, we have

$$e^{iy} = 1 + (iy) + \frac{(iy)^2}{2!} + \frac{(iy)^3}{3!} + \frac{(iy)^4}{4!} + \frac{(iy)^5}{5!} + \frac{(iy)^6}{6!} \ldots$$

$$= 1 + iy - \frac{y^2}{2!} + \frac{iy^3}{3!} + \frac{y^4}{4!} + \frac{iy^5}{5!} - \frac{y^6}{6!} - \frac{iy^7}{7!} + \frac{y^8}{8!} + \ldots$$

$$= \left(1 - \frac{y^2}{2!} + \frac{y^4}{4!} - \frac{y^6}{6!} + \frac{y^8}{8!} \ldots.\right)$$

$$+ i\left(y - \frac{y^3}{3!} + \frac{y^5}{5!} - \frac{y^7}{7!} + \frac{y^9}{9!} \ldots\right)$$

$\therefore$ $$e^{iy} = \cos y + i \sin y \quad \ldots(1)$$

Changing i by $-i$, we have

$$e^{-iy} = \cos y - i \sin y \quad \ldots(2)$$

Adding (1) and (2), we get

$$e^{iy} + e^{-iy} = 2 \cos y$$

$\therefore$ $$\cos y = \frac{e^{iy} + e^{-iy}}{2} \quad \ldots(3)$$

Similarly

$$\sin y = \frac{e^{iy} - e^{-iy}}{2i} \quad \ldots(4)$$

Formulae (3) and (4) are known as **Euler's formulae.**

Periodicity of e^z, sin z, cos z and tan z.

(i) e^z is a periodic function of period $2\pi i$.

We have $e^{z+2n\pi i}$

$$= e^z \,.\, e^{2n\pi i}$$

$$= e^z . (\cos 2n\pi + i \sin 2n\pi)$$
$$= e^z . 1 = e^z.$$

Thus, e^z is a periodic function of period $2\pi i$.

(ii) $\sin z$ is a periodic function of periodics 2π.

$$\sin (z + 2n\pi) = \sin z \cos 2n\pi + \cos z . \sin 2n\pi,\ n \in I.$$
$$= \sin z \cdot 1 + 0. = \sin z$$

Thus, $\sin z$ is periodic of period 2π

Similarly $\cos z$ and $\tan z$ are periodic functions of period 2π and π respectively.

De-Moivre's Theorem for Complex Arguments

De-Moivre's theorem can be extended for complex values of θ.

We have

$$(e^{i\theta})^n = e^{in\theta} : \qquad \text{(where } \theta \text{ is real or complex)}$$

or $\quad (\cos\theta + i \sin\theta)^n = \cos n\theta + i \sin n\theta$. (By Euler's formula)

This shows that the theorem is true for θ being real or complex.

All the trigonometric results can be verified by Euler's formulae, *i.e.,*

(i) $\sin^2 x + \cos^2 x = 1$

(ii) $\sin 2x = 2\sin x . \cos x$

(iii) $\cos 2x = \cos^2 x - \sin^2 x$.

Proof:

(i) We know that

$$\sin x = \left(\frac{e^{ix} - e^{-ix}}{2i}\right)$$

$$\cos x = \left(\frac{e^{ix} + e^{-ix}}{2}\right)$$

$$\therefore \qquad \sin^2 x + \cos^2 x = -\frac{1}{4}[e^{2ix} + e^{-2ix} - 2.e^{ix}.e^{-ix}]$$

$$+ \frac{1}{4}[e^{2ix} + e^{-2ix} + 2.e^{ix}.e^{-ix}]$$

$$= \frac{1}{4}[-e^{2ix} - e^{-2ix} + 2 + e^{2ix} + e^{-2ix} + 2]$$

$$= \frac{1}{4}[4] = 1$$

(ii) $$\sin 2x = \left(\frac{e^{2ix} - e^{-2ix}}{2i}\right)$$

$$= 2.\left(\frac{e^{ix} - e^{-ix}}{2i}\right).\left(\frac{e^{ix} + e^{-ix}}{2i}\right)$$

$$= 2.\sin x \ . \cos x.$$

$$\therefore \quad \sin 2x = 2 \sin x. \cos x$$

(iii) $$\cos^2 x - \sin^2 x = \frac{1}{4}[(e^{ix} + e^{-ix})^2 + (e^{ix} - e^{-ix})^2]$$

$$= \frac{1}{4}\left[e^{2ix} + e^{-2ix} + 2 + e^{2ix} + e^{-2ix} - 2\right]$$

$$= \frac{1}{4}[2(e^{2ix} + e^{-2ix})]$$

$$= \frac{1}{4}.2.2 \cos 2x.$$

$$= \cos 2x.$$

HYPERBOLIC FUNCTIONS

For all values of x whether real or complex, the expressions $\frac{e^x + e^{-x}}{2}$ and $\frac{e^x - e^{-x}}{2}$ are defined as hyperbolic cosine of x and hyperbolic sine of x and are denoted by cos hx and sin hx respectively

$$\therefore \quad \cos hx = \frac{e^x + e^{-x}}{2}$$

$$\sin hx = \frac{e^x - e^{-x}}{2}$$

Similarly $$\tan hx = \frac{\sin hx}{\cos hx} = \frac{e^x - e^{-x}}{e^x + e^{-x}}.$$

$$\sec hx = \frac{2}{e^x + e^{-x}}.$$

$$\cot hx = \frac{e^x + e^{-x}}{e^x - e^{-x}}.$$

And $$\operatorname{cosec} hx = \frac{2}{e^x - e^{-x}}.$$

As the circular functions sin x, cos x, tan x ... etc. are connected with a circle, similarly hyperbolic functions are connected with a hyperbola.

Relation between Hyperbolic and Circular Functions

We know that

$$\sin (x) = \frac{e^{ix} - e^{-ix}}{2i}$$

Replacing x by ix, we have

$$\sin (ix) = \frac{e^{i(ix)} - e^{-i(ix)}}{2i}$$

$$= \frac{e^{-x} - e^{x}}{2i}$$

$$= \frac{(-1)}{i}\left[\frac{e^x - e^{-x}}{2}\right].$$

$$= \frac{\left(i^2\right)}{i}\left[\frac{e^x - e^{-x}}{2}\right].$$

$\therefore$ $$\boxed{\sin(ix) = i \sin hx}$$

$$\cos ix = \frac{e^{i(ix)} + e^{-i(ix)}}{2}$$

$$= \frac{e^{-x} + e^{x}}{2}$$

$$= \cos hx$$

$\therefore$ $$\boxed{\cos(ix) = \cos hx}$$

$$\tan (ix) = \frac{\sin(ix)}{\cos(ix)}$$

$$= \frac{i \sin hx}{\cos hx}$$

$$= i \tan hx.$$

$\therefore$ $\boxed{\tan(ix) = i \tan hx}$

Similarly we can see that,

$$\cot(ix) = -i \cot hx$$

$$\sec(ix) = \sec hx$$

and $\quad \operatorname{cosec}(ix) = -i \operatorname{cosec} hx.$

Properties of Hyperbolic Functions

Relations between hyperbolic functions can be derived from the relations between circular functions.

(i) We know that $\cos^2 x + \sin^2 x = 1.$

Replacing x by (ix) we get

$$\cos^2(ix) + \sin^2(ix) = 1$$

or $\quad (\cos h\ x)^2 + (i \sin h\ x)^2 = 1$

or $\quad \cdot\left(i\ \frac{\pi}{2} - \log\ e \right)$

(ii) $\quad \sin 2ix = 2 \sin ix.\ \cos ix$

$$\sin(2ix) = 2 \sin ix \cos ix$$

or $\quad i \sin h2x = 2\, i \sin hx\ .\ \cos hx$

$\therefore$ $\boxed{\sin h2x = 2 \sin hx.\cos hx}$

(iii) $\quad \cos 2x = \cos^2 x - \sin^2 x$

Replacing x by ix, we get

$$\cos 2ix = \cos^2(ix) - \sin^2(ix)$$

$$\cos h\ 2x = \cos h^2 x + \sin h^2 x.$$

$\therefore$ $\boxed{\cos h2x = \cos h^2 x + \sin h^2 x}$

(iv) $$\sin(x+y) = \sin x.\cos y + \cos x.\sin y$$

Replacing x and y by ix and iy respectively, we get

$$\sin i(x+y) = \sin(ix).\cos(iy) + \cos(ix).\sin(iy)$$

$$i \sin h(x+y) = i \sin hx.\cos hy + i \cos hx.\sin hy$$

$$\therefore \quad \boxed{\sin h(x+y) = \sin hx.\cos hy + \cos hx.\sin hy}$$

Similarly taking into account the relation between circular and hyperbolic functions, all relations corresponding to each circular relation can be obtained. Some of them are mentioned below:

(v) $1 - \tan h^2 x = \operatorname{sech}^2 x$

(vi) $\tan h\, 2x = \dfrac{2\tan hx}{1+\tan h^2 x}$

(vii) $\sin h\, 2x = \dfrac{2\tan hx}{1-\tan h^2 x}$

(viii) $\cos h\, 2x = \dfrac{1+\tan h^2 x}{1-\tan h^2 x}$

(ix) $\cos h(x+y) = \cos hx.\cos hy + \sin hx.\sin hy$

(x) $\sin h\, 3x = 3\sin hx + 4\sin h^3 x.$

(xi) $\cos h\, 3x = 4\cos h^3 x - 3\cos hx.$

(xii) $\tan h3x = \dfrac{3\tan hx + \tan h^3 x}{1+3\tan h^2 x}$

Series Expansion for sin *hx* and cos *hx*

We have

$$\sin hx = \left[\frac{e^x - e^{-x}}{2}\right]$$

$$= \frac{1}{2}\left[(1+x+\frac{x^2}{2!}+\frac{x^3}{3!}...) - (1-x+\frac{x^2}{2!}-\frac{x^3}{3!}....)\right]$$

$$\sin hx = x + \frac{x^3}{3!} + \frac{x^5}{5!} + \frac{x^7}{7!} \text{...to } \infty.$$

Similarly

$$\cos hx = 1 + \frac{x^2}{2!} + \frac{x^4}{4!} + \frac{x^6}{6!} \text{...to } \infty.$$

Periodicty of Hyperbolic Functions

We know that

$$e^{2n\pi i} = \cos 2n\pi + i \sin 2n\pi \qquad \text{[by Euler's theorem]}$$

$$= 1 + i.0 = 1.$$

And

$$e^{-2n\pi i} = \cos(2n\pi) - i \sin(2n\pi)$$

$$= 1 + i.0 = 1.$$

If n is an integer, then

$$\sin h\,(x + 2n\pi i) = \frac{e^{x+2n\pi i} - e^{-(x+2n\pi i)}}{2}$$

$$= \frac{e^x . e^{2n\pi i} - e^{-x} . e^{-2n\pi i}}{2}$$

$$= \frac{e^x .1 - e^{-x} .1}{2}$$

$$= \sin hx.$$

$$\sin h\,(x + 2n\pi i) = \sin hx$$

$\therefore$ $\sin h\,(x)$ is a periodic function of period $2\pi i$.

Similarly, we can see that $\cos hx$ is periodic function of period $2\pi i$ and $\tan hx$ is periodic of period πi.

Separation into Real and Imaginary parts

Separation into real and imaginary parts means to express a complex number in the form $x + iy$, where x and y are real.

I. Using expansions of circular or hyperbolic function.

II. When a complex number is given in fractional form in which N^r. and D^r. both are complex numbers, to convert it in $x + iy$ form we multiply D^r. and N^r. by the conjuate of D^r. to make D^r. a real.

SOLVED EXAMPLES

Example 1. Resolve sin $(\theta + i\phi)$ into real and imaginary parts.

Solution: $\sin(\theta + i\phi) = \sin\theta.\ \cos(i\phi) + \cos\theta.\ \sin(i\phi)$

$$= \sin\theta.\ \cos h\phi + i\cos\theta.\ \sin h\phi.$$

$\therefore$ Real part $= \sin\theta.\ \cos h\phi.$

Imaginary part $= \cos\theta\ \sin h\phi.$

Similarly, we can resolve $\sin(\theta - i\phi)$, $\cos(\theta \pm i\phi)$ into real and imaginary parts.

Example 2. Resolve tan $(\alpha + i\beta)$ into real and imaginary parts.

Solution:
$$\tan(\alpha + i\beta) = \frac{\sin(\alpha + i\beta)}{\cos(\alpha + i\beta)}$$

$$= \frac{2\sin(\alpha + i\beta)\cos(\alpha - i\beta)}{2\cos(\alpha + i\beta)\cos(\alpha - i\beta)}$$

$$= \frac{\sin(2\alpha) + \sin(2i\beta)}{\cos(2\alpha) + \cos(2i\beta)}$$

$$= \frac{\sin 2\alpha + i\sin h2\beta}{\cos 2\alpha + \cos h2\beta}$$

$$\therefore \quad \text{Real part} = \frac{\sin 2\alpha}{\cos 2\alpha + \cos h2\beta}$$

$$\text{Imaginary part} = \frac{\sin h2\beta}{\cos 2\alpha + \cos h2\beta}$$

Similarly multiplying by the conjugate of the D^r., we can resolve into real and imaginary parts of the expressions $\tan(\alpha - i\beta)$, $\sec(\alpha \pm i\beta)$, $\cot(\alpha \pm i\beta)$, $\operatorname{cosec}(\alpha \pm i\beta)$.

Example 3. Resolve sin $h(\alpha + i\beta)$ into real and imaginary parts.

Solution:

$$\sin h(\alpha + i\beta) = \frac{1}{i}\sin(i\alpha + i^2\beta)$$

$$= \frac{1}{i}\sin(i\alpha - \beta)$$

$$= \frac{1}{i}[\sin(i\alpha).\ \cos\beta - \cos(i\alpha)\ .\ \sin\beta]$$

$$= \frac{1}{i}[i \sin h\alpha . \cos\beta - \sin\beta . \cos h\alpha]$$

$$= \sin h\alpha . \cos\beta - \frac{1}{i}\sin\beta . \cos h\alpha$$

$$= \sin h\alpha \cos\beta + \frac{i^2}{i}\sin \beta \cos h\alpha$$

$$= \sin h\alpha . \cos\beta + i \sin \beta . \cos h\alpha$$

$\therefore$ Real part $= \sin h\alpha . \cos\beta$

Imaginary part $= \cos h\alpha . \sin\beta$.

Example 4. Resolve $\tan h\,(\alpha - i\beta)$ into real and imaginary parts.

Solution:

$$\tan h\,(\alpha - i\beta) = \frac{i}{i}\tan h\,(\alpha - i\beta)$$

$$= \frac{1}{i}\tan h\,(i\alpha + i\beta) \qquad (i^2 = -1)$$

$$= \frac{1}{i}\tan(\beta + i\alpha)$$

$$= \frac{1}{i}\frac{\sin(\beta + i\alpha)}{\cos(\beta + i\alpha)}$$

$$= \frac{1}{i}.\frac{2\sin(\beta + i\alpha)\cos(\beta - i\alpha)}{2\cos(\beta + i\alpha)\cos(\beta - i\alpha)}$$

$$= \frac{1}{i}\left[\frac{\sin 2\beta + \sin 2i\alpha}{\cos 2\beta + \cos 2i\alpha}\right]$$

$$= \frac{1}{i}\left[\frac{\sin 2\beta + i\sin h2\alpha}{\cos 2\beta + \cos h2\alpha}\right]$$

$$= \frac{\sin h2\alpha}{\cos 2\beta + \cos h2\alpha} + \frac{1}{i}.\frac{\sin h2\beta}{\cos 2\beta + \cos h2\alpha}$$

$$= \frac{\sin h2\alpha}{\cos 2\beta + \cos h2\alpha} - \frac{i\sin h2\beta}{\cos 2\beta + \cos h2\alpha}$$

$$\therefore \qquad \text{Real part} = \frac{\sin h2\alpha}{\cos 2\beta + \cos h2\alpha}$$

$$\text{Imaginary part} = \frac{-\sin h2\beta}{\cos 2\beta + \cos h2\alpha}.$$

Similarly multiplying N^r. and D^r. by the conjugate of D^r, we can resolve tan h ($\alpha + i\ \beta$), cot h ($\alpha \pm i\ \beta$), sec h ($\alpha + i\ \beta$), cosec h ($\alpha \pm i\ \beta$) into real and imaginary parts.

Example 5. $e^{\cos(x+iy)}$ into real and imaginary parts.

Solution: We have

$$= e^{\cos(x+iy)}.$$

$$= e^{\cos x\,.\,\cos iy - \sin x\,.\,\sin iy}$$

$$= e^{\cos x\,.\,\cos hy - i \sin x \sin hy}$$

$$= e^{\cos x \cos hy}\,.\,e^{-i \sin x \sin hy}$$

$$= e^{\cos x \cos hy}\,[\cos(\sin x\,.\,\sin hy) - i \sin(\sin x \sin hy)]$$

$$\therefore \qquad \text{Real part} = e^{\cos x \cos hy}\,.\,\cos(\sin x \sin hy)$$

$$\text{Imaginary part} = -e^{\cos x\,.\,\cos hy}\,.\,\sin(\sin x \sin hy)$$

Example 6. Resolve $e^{\cos h(x-iy)}$ into real and imaginary parts.

Solution: We have

$$= e^{\cos h(x-iy)}.$$

$$= e^{\cos(ix - i^2 y)}$$

$$= e^{\cos(ix + y)}$$

$$= e^{\cos(ix) \cos y - \sin(ix) \sin y}$$

$$= e^{\cos hx\,.\,\cos y - i \sin hx \sin y}$$

$$= e^{\cos hx \cos y}.\,e^{-i \sin hx \sin y}$$

$$= e^{\cos hx \cos y}\,[\cos(\sin hx \sin y) - i \sin(\sin hx \sin y)]$$

$$\therefore \qquad \text{Real part} = e^{\cos hx\,.\,\cos y}\,.\,\cos(\sin hx \sin y).$$

$$\text{Imaginary part} = -e^{\cos hx \cos y} \sin(\sin hx \sin y).$$

Example 7. If tan ($\theta + i\phi$) = sin ($x + iy$), then prove that

$$\cot hy\,.\,\sin h2\phi = \cot x\,.\,\sin 2\theta.$$

Solution: We have

$$\tan(\theta + i\phi) = \sin(x + iy)$$

$$\frac{2\sin(\theta+i\phi).\cos(\theta-i\phi)}{2\cos(\theta+i\phi)\cos(\theta-i\phi)} = \sin x \cos iy + \cos x \sin iy$$

or $$\frac{\sin 2\theta + \sin 2i\phi}{\cos 2\theta + \cos 2i\phi} = \sin x \cos iy + \cos x \sin iy$$

or $$\frac{\sin 2\theta + i\sin h2\phi}{\cos 2\theta + \cos h2\phi} = \sin x \cos hy + i \cos x \sin hy$$

Equating real and imaginary parts, we have

$$\sin x.\ \cos hy = \frac{\sin 2\theta}{\cos 2\theta + \cos h2\phi} \qquad ...(1)$$

$$\cos x\ .\ \sin hy = \frac{\sin h2\phi}{\cos 2\theta + \cos h2\phi} \qquad ...(2)$$

Dividing (1) by (2), we get

$$\frac{\sin x \cos hy}{\cos x \sin hy} = \frac{\sin 2\theta}{\sin h2\phi}$$

$$\frac{\cot hy}{\cot x} = \frac{\sin 2\theta}{\sin h2\phi}$$

$\therefore$ $\cot hy.\ \sin h\ 2\phi = \cot x\ .\ \sin 2\theta.$

Example 8. If $\tan(\alpha + i\beta) = x + iy$, prove that

(i) $x^2 + y^2 + 2x \cot 2\alpha = 1$

(ii) $x^2 + y^2 - 2y \cot h\ 2\beta = -1$

(iii) $x \cot h\ 2\alpha + y \cot h\ 2\beta = 1.$

Solution: We have

$$\tan(\alpha + i\beta) = x + iy \qquad ...(1)$$

$$\therefore \quad \tan(\alpha - i\beta) = x - iy \qquad ...(2)$$

(i) Now $2\alpha = (\alpha + i\beta) + (\alpha - i\beta)$

$\therefore$ $\tan(2\alpha) = \tan[(\alpha + i\beta) + (\alpha - i\beta)]$

$$= \frac{\tan(\alpha+i\beta) + \tan(\alpha-i\beta)}{1-\tan(\alpha+i\beta).\tan(\alpha-i\beta)}$$

$$= \frac{x+iy+x-iy}{1-(x+iy)(x-iy)}$$

$$\tan 2\alpha = \frac{2x}{1-\left(x^2+y^2\right)}$$

$$\therefore \qquad \cot 2\alpha = \frac{1-x^2-y^2}{2x}$$

$$\Rightarrow \qquad 2x \cot 2\alpha = 1 - x^2 - y^2$$

$$\therefore\ x^2 + y^2 + 2x \cot 2\alpha = 1 \qquad \text{...(3)}$$

(ii) $$2i\beta = (\alpha + i\beta) - (\alpha - i\beta)$$

$$\therefore \qquad \tan(2i\beta) = \tan[(\alpha + i\beta) - (\alpha - i\beta)]$$

$$= \frac{\tan(\alpha+i\beta)-\tan(\alpha-i\beta)}{1+\tan(\alpha+i\beta).\tan(\alpha-i\beta)}$$

$$= \frac{(x+iy)-(x-iy)}{1+(x+iy)(x-iy)}$$

$$i \tan h\, 2\beta = \frac{2iy}{1+\left(x^2+y^2\right)}$$

$$\therefore \qquad \cot h\, 2\beta = \frac{1+x^2+y^2}{2y}$$

$$\Rightarrow \qquad x^2 + y^2 + 1 = 2y \cot h\, 2\beta$$

$$\therefore\ x^2+y^2-2y \cot h\, 2\beta = -1. \qquad \text{...(4)}$$

(iii) Subtracting (4) from (3), we have

$$2x \cot 2\alpha + 2y \cot h\, 2\beta = 2$$

$$x \cot 2\alpha + y \cot h2\beta = 1 \qquad (5)$$

Example 9. If $\tan(\theta + i\phi) = \cos\alpha + i \sin\alpha$, prove that

(i) $\theta = \dfrac{n\pi}{2} + \dfrac{\pi}{4}$

(ii) $\phi = \dfrac{1}{2}\log \tan\left(\dfrac{\pi}{4}+\dfrac{\alpha}{2}\right)$.

Solution: We have

$$\therefore \quad \tan(\theta + i\phi) = \cos\alpha + i\sin\alpha \qquad ...(1)$$

$$\tan(\theta - i\phi) = \cos\alpha - i\sin\alpha \qquad ...(2)$$

$$2\theta = (\theta + i\phi) + (\theta - i\phi)$$

$$\therefore \quad \tan 2\theta = \tan[(\theta + i\phi) + (\theta - i\phi)]$$

$$= \frac{\tan(\theta + i\phi) + \tan(\theta - i\phi)}{1 - \tan(\theta + i\phi)\tan(\theta - i\phi)}$$

$$= \frac{\cos\alpha + i\sin\alpha + \cos\alpha - i\sin\alpha}{1 - (\cos\alpha + i\sin\alpha)(\cos\alpha - i\sin\alpha)}$$

$$= \frac{2\cos\alpha}{1-1}$$

$$= \frac{2\cos\alpha}{0} = \infty \text{ if } \alpha \neq \frac{\pi}{2}$$

$$\therefore \quad \tan 2\theta = \tan\frac{\pi}{2}$$

$$\Rightarrow \quad 2\theta = \frac{\pi}{2}$$

$$\Rightarrow \quad 2\theta = \frac{\pi}{2} + n\pi$$

$$\therefore \quad \theta = \frac{n\pi}{2} + \frac{\pi}{4} \qquad ...(3)$$

Now

$$2i\phi = (\theta + i\phi) - (\theta - i\phi)$$

$$\therefore \quad \tan(2i\phi) = \tan[(\theta + i\phi) - (\theta - i\phi)]$$

$$= \frac{\tan(\theta + i\phi) - \tan(\theta - i\phi)}{1 + \tan(\theta + i\phi).\tan(\theta - i\phi)}$$

$$= \frac{2i\sin\alpha}{1+1}$$

$$i\tan h\, 2\phi = \frac{2i\sin\alpha}{2}$$

$$\Rightarrow \quad \tan h\, 2\phi = 1\ \sin\alpha$$

$$\therefore \qquad \frac{e^{2\phi} - e^{-2\phi}}{e^{2\phi} + e^{-2\phi}} = \frac{\sin\alpha}{1}$$

Applying componendo and dividendo, we have

$$\frac{2e^{2\phi}}{2e^{-2\phi}} = \frac{1+\sin\alpha}{1-\sin\alpha}$$

$$e^{4\phi} = \frac{\sin^2\alpha/2 + \cos^2\alpha/2 + 2\sin\alpha/2\ \cos\alpha/2}{\sin^2\alpha/2 + \cos^2\alpha/2 - 2\sin\alpha/2\ \cos\alpha/2}$$

$$= \frac{[\cos\alpha/2 + \sin\alpha/2]^2}{[\cos\alpha/2 - \sin\alpha/2]^2}$$

$$\therefore \qquad e^{2\phi} = \frac{\cos\alpha/2 + \sin\alpha/2}{\cos\alpha/2 - \sin\alpha/2} = \frac{1+\tan(\alpha/2)}{1-\tan(\alpha/2)}$$

$$\Rightarrow \qquad e^{2\phi} = \tan\left(\frac{\pi}{4} + \frac{\alpha}{2}\right)$$

$$\Rightarrow \qquad 2\phi = \log\tan\left(\frac{\pi}{4} + \frac{\alpha}{2}\right)$$

$$\therefore \qquad \phi = \frac{1}{2}.\log\tan\left(\frac{\pi}{4} + \frac{\alpha}{2}\right)$$

Example 10. If $\sin(\theta + i\phi) = e^{i\alpha}$, prove that

$$\cos^2\theta = \sin h^2\phi = \pm\ \sin\alpha.$$

Solution: Given that

$$\sin(\theta + i\phi) = e^{i\alpha}$$

$\therefore$ $\sin\theta \cos i\phi + \cos\theta \sin i\phi = \cos\alpha + i \sin\alpha$

or $\sin\theta \cos h\phi + i \cos\theta \sin h\phi = \cos\alpha + i \sin\alpha$

Equating real and imaginary parts, we have

$$\sin\theta \cos h\phi = \cos\alpha \qquad \text{...(1)}$$

$$\cos\theta \sin h\phi = \sin\alpha \qquad \text{...(2)}$$

Eliminating ϕ between (1) and (2), we have

$$\frac{\cos^2\alpha}{\sin^2\theta} - \frac{\sin^2\alpha}{\cos^2\theta} = 1.$$

$\Rightarrow$ $\cos^2\alpha \cos^2\theta - \sin^2\alpha \sin^2\theta = \sin^2\theta \cos^2\theta$

$\Rightarrow$ $(1 - \sin^2\alpha) \cos^2\theta - \sin^2\alpha (1 - \cos^2\theta) = (1 - \cos^2\theta) \cos^2\theta$

$\Rightarrow$ $\cos^2\theta - \sin^2\alpha \cos^2\theta - \sin^2\alpha + \sin^2\alpha \cos^2\theta = \cos^2\theta - \cos^4\theta$

$$\cos^4\theta = \sin^2\alpha$$

$\therefore$ $\cos^2\theta = \pm \sin\alpha.$

Substituting $\cos^2\theta$ in equation 2 we have $\sin h^2\phi = \pm \sin\alpha$.

EXERCISE

1. Using Euler's formula, prove that

   (i) $\cos 2z = 2\cos^2 z - 1$

   (ii) $\sin 3z = 3 \sin z - 4 \sin^3 z$.

   (iii) $\sin (x \pm y) = \sin x \cos y \pm \cos x \sin y$.

2. Show that:

   $[\sin (\theta + \alpha) - e^{i\alpha} \sin\theta]^n = \sin^n\alpha \, e^{-n\theta i}$.

3. Separate following into real and imaginary parts:

   (i) $\cot (\alpha + i\beta)$

   (ii) $\tan h (\alpha + i\beta)$

   (iii) $e^{\sin (\alpha + i\beta)}$

   (iv) $\sec (\alpha + i\beta)$.

4. If $u = \log \tan\left(\frac{\pi}{4} + \frac{\theta}{2}\right)$, show that.

   (i) $\tan h \left(\frac{u}{2}\right) = \tan \left(\frac{\theta}{2}\right)$

   (ii) $\theta = -i \log \tan \left(\frac{\pi}{4} + \frac{iu}{2}\right)$.

5. If $\sin (x + iy) \sin (\theta + i\phi) = 1$, show that.

   (i) $\tan h^2 y \cos h^2\phi = \cos^2\theta$

   (ii) $\tan h^2\phi \cos h^2 y = \cos^2 x$.

6. If $\cos(\theta + i\phi) = \rho(\cos\alpha + i\sin\alpha)$, show that

$$\phi = \frac{1}{2}.\log\frac{\sin(\theta-\alpha)}{\sin(\theta+\alpha)}.$$

7. If $\tan(\alpha + i\beta) = i$, where $\alpha, \beta \in R$, show that α is indeterminate and β is infinite.

8. If $\tan(\theta + i\phi) = \tan\alpha + i\sec\alpha$, prove that:

(i) $\theta = \frac{n\pi}{2} + \frac{\pi}{4} + \frac{\alpha}{2}$

(ii) $e^{2\phi} = \pm\cot\left(\frac{\alpha}{2}\right)$.

9. If $\sin(\alpha + i\beta) = x + iy$, show that:

(i) $\frac{x^2}{\cos h^2\beta} + \frac{y^2}{\sin h^2\beta} = 1$

(ii) $\frac{x^2}{\sin^2\alpha} - \frac{y^2}{\cos^2\alpha} = 1.$

10. If $\sin(\theta + i\phi) = \tan\alpha + i\sec\alpha$, then prove that:

$\cos 2\theta \cos h\, 2\phi = 3.$

11. If $x = 2\cos\alpha \cos h\beta$ and $y = 2\sin\alpha \sin h\beta$, show that.

(i) $\sec(\alpha + i\beta) + \sec(\alpha - i\beta) = \frac{4x}{x^2 + y^2}$

(ii) $\sec(\alpha + i\beta) - \sec(\alpha - i\beta) = \frac{4iy}{x^2 + y^2}$.

Answers :

3. (i) Re. part $= \frac{\sin 2\alpha}{\cos h\, 2\beta - \cos 2\alpha}$

Im. part $= \frac{-\sin h\, 2\beta}{\cos h\, 2\beta - \cos 2\alpha}$

(ii) Re. part $= \frac{\sin h\, 2\alpha}{\cos 2\beta + \cos h\, 2\alpha}$

$$\text{Im. part} = \frac{\sin 2\beta}{\cos 2\beta + \cos h2\alpha}$$

(iii) Re. part = $e^{\sin\alpha \cos h\beta}$. cos (cosα sin $h\beta$).

Im. part = $e^{\sin\alpha \cosh\beta}$ sin (cosα sin$h\beta$)

(iv) $$\text{Re. part} = \frac{2\cos\alpha\cos h\beta}{\cos 2\alpha + \cos h2\beta}$$

$$\text{Im. part} = \frac{2\sin\alpha\sin h\beta}{\cos 2\alpha + \cos h2\beta}$$

LOGARITHM OF COMPLEX QUANTITIES

If w and z be two complex numbers such that $w = e^z$, then z is called the logarithm of w to the base e and is written as

$$z = \log e^w$$

or $$z = \log e^w$$

the base e is understood.

Logarithm of a Complex Number is a Multi valued Function

If $\log w = z$

$\therefore$ $w = e^z$

$$e^{z + 2n\pi i} = e^z \,.\, e^{2n\pi i}$$

$$= e^z \,.\, (\cos 2n\pi + i \sin 2n\pi)$$

$$= e^z \,.\, 1$$

$$= e^z = w$$

$$\log w = z + 2n\pi i$$

Thus, the logarithm of a complex number is a multi valued function.

Principal and General values of Logarithm of a Non-zero Complex Number

Let $z = x + iy$, be a non-zero complex number.

Suppose $\log_e z = \alpha + i\beta \quad (\alpha, \beta \in R)$. ...(1)

Then $z = e^{\alpha + i\beta} = e^{\alpha} \,.\, e^{i\beta}$

$$z = e^{\alpha}\,[\cos\beta \; i \sin\beta]$$

$\therefore$ $x + iy = e^{\alpha}\,[\cos\beta + i \sin\beta]$

Equating real and imaginary parts, we have

$$x = e^{\alpha} \cos\beta \quad ...(2)$$

$$y = e^{\alpha} \sin\beta \quad ...(3)$$

$\because$ $$x^2 + y^2 = e^{2\alpha}$$

$\therefore$ $$2\alpha = \log (x^2 + y^2)$$

$\therefore$ $$\alpha = \frac{1}{2} . \log (x^2 + y^2) \quad ...(4)$$

Dividing (3) by (2), we get

$$\tan\beta = \frac{y}{x}$$

$\therefore$ $$\beta = \tan^{-1}\left(\frac{y}{x}\right)$$

$\therefore$ $$\log (x + iy) = \frac{1}{2} .\log (x^2 + y^2) + i \tan^{-1}\left(\frac{y}{x}\right)$$

is called the principal value and $\frac{1}{2} .\log (x^2 + y^2) + i \tan^{-1}\left(\frac{y}{x}\right) + 2n\pi i$ is called the general value and is denoted by log $(x + iy)$.

$\therefore$ $$\log (x + iy) = \frac{1}{2} .\log (x^2 + y^2) + i \tan^{-1}\left(\frac{y}{x}\right) + 2n\pi i.$$

Logarithm of a +ve Real Number in the Set of Complex Numbers

Let x be a +ve real number

Then $$x = x + i. 0$$

$$= r (\cos\theta + i \sin\theta)$$

Equating real and imaginary parts, we have

$$x = r \cos\theta$$

$$0 = r \sin\theta$$

$\therefore$ $$r = x \text{ and } \theta = 0$$

$$\therefore \qquad \log(x) = \frac{1}{2}\log(x^2+0) + i\tan^{-1}\left(\frac{0}{x}\right).$$

$$\therefore \qquad \log(x) = \log x + i.0$$

$$\log(x) = \log x$$

$$\therefore \qquad \log(x) = \log x + 2n\pi i.$$

Thus, in the set of complex numbers the logarithm of a +ve real number has infinitely many values, out of which only one is real which is obtained for $n = 0$.

Logarithm of a –ve Real Number

Let x be a –ve real number then $-x$ is a +ve real number.

$$\therefore \qquad x = -y, \text{ where } y > 0.$$

$$\therefore \qquad \log(x) = \log(-y)$$

$$\log x = \log(y) + \log(-1)$$

$$= \log(y) + \log[e^{(2n+1)\pi i}]$$

$$= \log(y) + (2n+1)\pi i$$

$$\therefore \qquad \log(x) = \log(-x) + (2n+1)\pi i \qquad \ldots(1)$$

for $\qquad n = 0$

$$\log(x) = \log(-x) + \pi i$$

is the principal value of the logarithm of a –ve real number.

SOLVED EXAMPLES

Example1. Find the principal and general values of $\log(1+i)$.

Solution: We know that

$$\log(x+iy) = \frac{1}{2}.\log(x^2+y^2) + i\tan^{-1}\left(\frac{y}{x}\right) + 2n\pi i$$

$$\log(1+i) = \left(\frac{y}{x}\right).\log(1+1) + i\tan^{-1}\left(\frac{1}{1}\right) + 2n\pi i$$

$$= \frac{1}{2}.\log(2) + i\frac{\pi}{4} + 2n\pi i$$

$$= \frac{1}{2}.\log (2) + \left(2n\pi + \frac{\pi}{4}\right) i \qquad ...(1)$$

Putting $n = 0$, we get

$$\log (1 + i) = \frac{1}{2}.\log 2 + \frac{i\pi}{4} \qquad ...(2)$$

The value given by (1) is called the general value and that given by (2) is called the principal value.

Example 2. Find the principal and general values of log (–7).

Solution: We know that

$$\log (-x) = \log (-x) + (2n + 1)\, \pi i$$

$$\log (-7) = \log (7) + (2n + 1)\, \pi i \qquad ...(1)$$

is the general value of log (–7).

putting $n = 0$, we get principal value as

$$\log (-7) = \pi i + \log (7). \qquad ...(2)$$

Example 3. Prove that $\log \left(\frac{a+ib}{a-ib}\right) = 2i \tan^{-1}\left(\frac{b}{a}\right)$.

Solution: $\log \left(\frac{a+ib}{a-ib}\right) = \log (a + ib) - \log (a - ib)$

$$= \frac{1}{2}.\log (a^2 + b^2) + i \tan^{-1}\left(\frac{b}{a}\right)$$

$$- \frac{1}{2}.\log (a^2+(-b)^2) - i \tan^{-1}\left(\frac{-b}{a}\right)$$

$$= \frac{1}{2}.\log (a^2 + b^2) + i \tan^{-1}\left(\frac{b}{a}\right)$$

$$- \frac{1}{2}.\log (a^2+b^2) + i \tan^{-1}\left(\frac{b}{a}\right)$$

$$= 2i \tan^{-1}\left(\frac{b}{a}\right).$$

GENERAL EXPONENTIAL FUNCTION

Let a and z be any two complex numbers then the general exponential function a^z is defined as

$$a^z = e^{z \log a}$$

we know that log (a) is a multi valued function.

Thus

$$a^z = e^{z \log a}$$

$$= e^{z\,(\log a\, +\, 2n\pi i)}$$

and the principal value is obtained for $n = 0$, given by $e^{z \log a}$.

With the help of this general exponential function we can resolve $(a+ib)^{\,p+iq}$ in A+iB form.

Example 4. Prove that the principal value of log (i^i) is $-\dfrac{\pi}{2}$.

Solution: We know that

$$a^z = e^{z \log a}$$

$$\therefore \qquad (i)^i = e^{i \log i}$$

$$= e^{i \log\left(e^{\frac{i\pi}{2}}\right)}$$

$$= e^{i\left[i\frac{\pi}{2}\log e\right]}$$

$$= e^{i\left(i\frac{\pi}{2}\right)}$$

$$= e^{-\frac{\pi}{2}}.$$

$$\therefore \qquad \log(i^i) = \log\left(e^{-\frac{\pi}{2}}\right)$$

$$= -\frac{\pi}{2}.\log e$$

$$= -\frac{\pi}{2}$$

$$\therefore \qquad \log(i^i) = -\frac{\pi}{2}.$$

Example 5. Prove that the real part of the principal value of $(i)^{\log(1+i)}$ is $e^{\frac{-\pi^2}{8}} . \cos\left(\frac{\pi}{4}.\log 2\right)$.

Solution: We know that $a^z = e^{z \log a}$.

$$(i)^{\log(1+i)} = e^{\log(1+i)\ \log(i)}$$

$$= e^{\left[\frac{1}{2}\log 2 + i\tan^{-1}(1)\right]\log\left(e^{\frac{i\pi}{2}}\right)}$$

$$= e^{\left[\frac{1}{2}\log 2 + i\frac{\pi}{4}\right]\cdot\left(i\frac{\pi}{2}\log e\right)}$$

$$= e^{\left[\frac{1}{2}\log 2 + i\frac{\pi}{4}\right]\cdot\frac{i\pi}{2}}$$

$$= e^{\frac{-\pi^2}{8} + i\frac{\pi}{4}\log 2}$$

$$= e^{\frac{-\pi^2}{8}} . e^{i\frac{\pi}{4}\log 2}$$

$$= e^{\frac{-\pi^2}{8}}\left[\cos\left(\frac{\pi}{4}\log 2\right) + i\sin\left(\frac{\pi}{4}\log 2\right)\right]$$

$\therefore$ Real part of the principal value of $(i)^{\log(1+i)} = e^{\frac{-\pi^2}{8}} . \cos\left(\frac{\pi}{4} . \log 2\right)$.

INVERSE HYPERBOLIC FUNCTION

If w and z are two complex quantities such that $w = \sin hz$, then z is defined as the inverse hyperbolic sine of z and is written as $z = \sin h^{-1}w$. Other inverse hyperbolic functions $\cos h^{-1}w$, $\tan h^{-1}w$, $\text{cosec}\ h^{-1}w$ are defined in the same way.

Logarithmic Representation of Inverse Hyperbolic Functions of Sine, Cosine and Tangent.

(i) **To prove that** $\sin h^{-1} w = \log\left[w + \sqrt{w^2 + 1}\right]$.

Proof:

Let $\sinh^{-1} w = z$

$\therefore$ $\sin hz = w$

$\therefore$ $\cos hz = \sqrt{1+\sin h^2 z} = \sqrt{w^2+1}.$

Now $\sin hz + \cos hz = w + \sqrt{w^2+1}.$

or $\dfrac{e^z - e^z}{2} + \dfrac{e^z + e^{-z}}{2} = w + \sqrt{w^2+1}.$

or $e^z = \sqrt{w^2+1.} + w$

or $z = \log\left[w + \sqrt{w^2+1}\right]$

or $\boxed{\sin h^{-1} w = \log\left[w + \sqrt{w^2+1}\right]}$

(ii) $\mathbf{\cos h^{-1} w = \left[w + \sqrt{w^2 - 1}\right]}$

Proof: Let $\cos h^{-1} w = z$

$\therefore$ $\cos hz = w$ ...(1)

$\sin hz = \sqrt{\cos h^2 z - 1}$

$\therefore$ $\sin hz = \sqrt{(w^2-1)}$ ...(2)

Adding (1) and (2), we get

$$\cos hz + \sin hz = w + \sqrt{w^2-1}$$

$\therefore$ $\dfrac{e^z + e^{-z}}{2} + \dfrac{e^z - e^{-z}}{2} = w + \sqrt{(w^2-1)}$

$\therefore$ $e^z = w + \sqrt{(w^2-1)}$

$$z = \log\left[w + \sqrt{w^2-1}\right]$$

or $$\boxed{\cos h^{-1} w = \log\left[w + \sqrt{w^2 + 1}\right]}$$

(iii) $\mathbf{\tan h^{-1} w = \frac{1}{2} \cdot \log\left(\frac{1+w`}{1-w}\right).}$

Proof: Let $\tan h^{-1} w = z$ ...(1)

$\therefore$ $\tan hz = w$ ...(2)

$$\therefore \quad \frac{e^z - e^{-z}}{e^z + e^{-z}} = \frac{w}{1}$$

Applying componendo and dividendo, we have

$$\frac{2e^z}{2e^{-z}} = \frac{1+w}{1-w}$$

$$e^{2z} = \frac{1+w}{1-w}$$

$$\therefore \quad 2z = \log\left(\frac{1+w}{1-w}\right)$$

$$\therefore \quad z = \frac{1}{2}\log\left(\frac{1+w}{1-w}\right)$$

or $$\boxed{\tan h^{-1} w = \frac{1}{2}\log\left(\frac{1+w}{1-w}\right)}$$

Similarly, we can show that

$$\boxed{\cot h^{-1} w = \frac{1}{2}\log\left(\frac{w+1}{w-1}\right)}$$

General Values of Sin h^{-1} (w), Cos h^{-1} (w) and Tan h^{-1} (w), Denoted by Sin h^{-1} w, Cos h^{-1} w and Tan h^{-1} w are given by

$$\text{Sin } h^{-1}(w) = 2n\pi i + (-1)^n \log\left[w + \sqrt{(w^2+1)}\right]$$

$$\text{Cos } h^{-1}(w) = 2n\pi i \pm \log\left[w + \sqrt{(w^2-1)}\right]$$

and $$\text{Tan}\, h^{-1}(w) = n\pi i + \frac{1}{2}\log\left(\frac{1+w}{1-w}\right).$$

Relation Between Inverse Hyperbolic Function and Inverse Circular Functions.

(i) $$\sin h^{-1}(w) = -i \sin^{-1}(iw)$$

Proof: Let $\sin h^{-1}(w) = u$

$\therefore$ $$w = \sin hu$$

or $$iw = i \sin hu$$

or $$iw = \sin(iu)$$

or $$iu = \sin^{-1}(iw)$$

or $$u = \frac{1}{i}\sin^{-1}(iw)$$

or $$u = -i \sin^{-1}(iw)$$

$\therefore$ $$\boxed{\sin h^{-1}(w) = -i \sin^{-1}(iw)}$$

Similarly, we can show that

$$\boxed{\cos h^{-1} w = -i \cos^{-1}(w)}$$

$$\boxed{\tan h^{-1}(iw) = -i \tan^{-1}(iw)}$$

SOLVED EXAMPLES

Example 1. Separate $\sin^{-1}(\cos\theta + i\sin\theta)$ into real and imaginary parts, where θ is a +ve acute angle.

Solution: Let $\sin^{-1}(\cos\theta + i\sin\theta) = A + i\,B$, $(A, B \in R)$ ...(1)

$\therefore$ $$\sin(A + i\beta) = \cos\theta + i\sin\theta$$

$$\sin A\cos(i\beta) + \cos A\sin(i\beta) = \cos\theta + i\sin\theta$$

$$\sin A\cos h\beta + i\cos A\sin h\beta = \cos\theta + i\sin\theta \quad ...(2)$$

Equating real and imaginary parts on both sides of (2), we have

$$\sin A\cos h\beta = \cos\theta \quad ...(3)$$

$$\cos A\sin h\beta = \sin\theta \quad ...(4)$$

Eliminating β between (3) and (4), we get

$$\frac{\cos^2\theta}{\sin^2 A} - \frac{\sin^2\theta}{\cos^2 A} = 1$$

$$\cos^2 A\,(1 - \sin^2\theta) - (1 - \cos^2 A)\sin^2\theta = \cos^2 A\,(1 - \cos^2 A)$$

or $$\cos^2 A - \cos^2 A\sin^2\theta - \sin^2\theta + \cos^2 A\sin^2\theta = \cos^2 A - \cos^4 A$$

$$\therefore \quad \cos^4 A = \sin^2\theta$$

$$\Rightarrow \quad \cos^2 A = \sin\theta$$

$$\therefore \quad \cos A = \pm\sqrt{\sin\theta}$$

Since A is the real part of $\sin^{-1}(\cos\theta + i\sin\theta)$

Therefore $\frac{-\pi}{2} \le A \le \frac{\pi}{2}$.

so, $$\cos A = \sqrt{\sin\theta}$$

$$\therefore \quad A = \cos^{-1}\left(\sqrt{\sin\theta}\right) \qquad (5)$$

Substituting this in equation (4), we have

$$\sin h\,\beta = \sqrt{\sin\theta}$$

$$\therefore \quad \beta = \sin h^{-1}\left(\sqrt{\sin\theta}\right)$$

or $$\beta = \log\left[\sqrt{\sin\theta} + \sqrt{1 + \sin\theta}\right]$$

$$\therefore \quad A + i\beta = \cos^{-1}\left(\sqrt{\sin\theta}\right) + i\log\left[\sqrt{\sin\theta} + \sqrt{1 + \sin\theta}\right]$$

$$\therefore \sin^{-1}(\cos\theta + i\sin\theta) = \cos^{-1}\left(\sqrt{\sin\theta}\right) + i\log\left[\sqrt{\sin\theta} + \sqrt{1 + \sin\theta}\right].$$

Example 2. Show that $\sin^{-1}(ix) = n\pi + i(-1)^n \log\left[x+\sqrt{(1+x^2)}\right]$.

Solution: Let $\sin^{-1}(ix) = z$ ...(1)

$$\therefore \quad \sin z = ix$$

$$\therefore \quad \cos^2 z = 1 + x^2$$

$$\text{or} \quad \cos z = \sqrt{(1+x^2)}$$

$$\therefore \quad \cos z + i \sin z = \sqrt{1+x^2} - x$$

$$\text{or} \quad e^{iz} = \sqrt{1+x^2} - x$$

$$\therefore \quad z = \frac{1}{i}\log\left[\sqrt{1+x^2} - x\right]$$

$$= -i\log\left[\sqrt{1+x^2} - x\right]$$

$$= -i\log\left[\frac{(1+x^2) - x^2}{\sqrt{1+x^2} + x}\right]$$

$$= i\log\left[x + \sqrt{1+x^2}\right] \quad ...(2)$$

$$\therefore \quad \sin^{-1}(ix) = i\log\left[x + \sqrt{1+x^2}\right]$$

$\therefore$ The general value is

$$\sin^{-1}(ix) = n\pi + (-1)^n . i\log\left[\sqrt{(1+x^2)} + x\right] \quad ...(3)$$

on putting $x = 1$ in (3), we get the principal value as

$$\sin^{-1}(i) = i\log\left(1+\sqrt{2}\right).$$

Example 3. Prove that the principal value of $(a + ib)^{(c + id)}$ is wholly real or wholly imaginary accordingly as $\tan^{-1}(b/a) + \frac{1}{2} d \log (a^2 + b^2)$ is an even or an odd multiple of $\frac{\pi}{2}$.

In case it is wholly real, prove that

$$(a + ib)^{(c + id)} = (a^2 + b^2)^{(c^2 + d^2)/2c}$$

Solution: We know that

$$a^z = e^{z \log a}$$

$$\therefore \qquad (a + ib)^{(c + id)} = e^{(c + id).\log (a + ib)}$$

$$= e^{(c+id).\left[\frac{1}{2}\log\left(a^2+b^2\right)+i\tan^{-1}\left(\frac{b}{a}\right)\right]}$$

$$= e^{\frac{1}{2}.c.\log\left(a^2+b^2\right)-d\tan^{-1}\left(\frac{b}{a}\right)+i\left[\frac{d}{2}\log\left(a^2+b^2\right)+c\tan^{-1}\left(\frac{b}{a}\right)\right]}$$

$$= e^{\frac{1}{2}.c.\log\left(a^2+b^2\right)-d\tan^{-1}\left(\frac{b}{a}\right)}.e^{i\left[\frac{d}{2}\log\left(a^2+b^2\right)+c.\tan^{-1}\left(\frac{b}{a}\right)\right]}$$

$$= e^{\frac{c}{2}.\log\left(a^2+b^2\right)-d\tan^{-1}\left(\frac{b}{a}\right)}.\left[\cos\left\{\frac{d}{2}\log\left(a^2+b^2\right)+c\tan^{1}\left(\frac{b}{a}\right)\right\}\right.$$

$$\left.+i\sin\left\{\frac{d}{2}.\log\left(a^2+b^2\right)+c.\tan^{-1}\left(\frac{b}{a}\right)\right\}\right]$$

If this is wholly real,

$$\sin\left[\frac{d}{2}.\log\left(a^2+b^2\right)+c.\tan^{-1}\left(\frac{b}{a}\right)\right]=0$$

if $$\frac{d}{2}\log\left(a^2+b^2\right)+c.\tan^{-1}\left(\frac{b}{a}\right) = n\pi = 2n.\frac{\pi}{2}$$

$$= \text{an even multiple of } \frac{\pi}{2}.$$

If it is wholly imaginary, then

$$\cos\left[\frac{d}{2}.\log\left(a^2+b^2\right)+c.\tan^{-1}\left(\frac{b}{a}\right)\right]=0$$

i.e. $\frac{d}{2}\log\left(a^2+b^2\right)+c.\tan^{-1}\left(\frac{b}{a}\right)$ is an odd multiple of $\frac{\pi}{2}$.

If this is wholly real, then

$$\frac{d}{2}\log\left(a^2+b^2\right)+c.\tan^{-1}\left(\frac{b}{a}\right)=0$$

or $$c.\tan^{-1}\left(\frac{b}{a}\right) = -\frac{d}{2}.\log\left(a^2+b^2\right)$$

Then, the value of the expression becomes

$$(a+ib)^{(c+id)} = e^{\frac{c}{2}\log\left(a^2+b^2\right)+\frac{d^2}{2c}.\log\left(a^2+b^2\right)}$$

$$= e^{\frac{\left(c^2+d^2\right)}{2c}.\log\left(a^2+b^2\right)}$$

$$= e^{\log\left[\left(a^2+b^2\right)^{\left(\frac{c^2+d^2}{2c}\right)}\right]}.$$

$$= \left(a^2+b^2\right)^{\left(\frac{c^2+d^2}{2c}\right)}$$

Example 4. Prove that the general value of $(1 + i\tan\alpha)^{-i}$ is $e^{\alpha+2n\pi}$. $[\cos(\log\cos\alpha) + i\sin(\log\cos\alpha)]$

Solution: We know

$$(1+i\tan\alpha)^{-i} = e^{-i\log(1+i\tan\alpha)}$$

$$= e^{-i\left[\frac{1}{2}\log\left(1+\tan^2\alpha\right)+i\tan^{-1}(\tan\alpha)+2n\pi i\right]}$$

$$= e^{-i\left[\frac{1}{2}\log\sec^2\alpha+i\alpha+2n\pi i\right]}$$

$$= e^{-i\log\sec\alpha+\alpha+2n\pi}$$

$$= e^{\alpha+2n\pi}.e^{i\log\cos\alpha}$$

$$= e^{\alpha+2n\pi}.[\cos(\log\cos\alpha)+i\sin(\log\cos\alpha)].$$

Example 5. If $\cos hx = \sec\alpha$, then show that $x = \log(\sec\theta \pm \tan\theta)$

Solution: Given that

$$\cos hx = \sec\theta$$

$$\therefore \qquad \frac{e^x + e^{-x}}{2} = \sec\theta$$

or $e^{2x} - 2e^x \sec\theta + 1 = 0$, which is quadratic in e^x

$$\therefore \qquad e^x = \frac{2\sec\theta \pm \sqrt{4\sec^2\theta - 4}}{2}$$

$$= \sec\theta \pm \tan\theta$$

$$\therefore \qquad x = \log(\sec\theta \pm \tan\theta).$$

Example 6. If $\sin^{-1}(\theta + i\phi) = \alpha + i\beta$, then prove that $\sin^2\alpha$ and $\cos h^2\beta$ are the roots of the equation $x^2 - x(1 + \theta^2 + \phi^2) + \theta^2 = 0$

Solution: We have

$$\sin^{-1}(\theta + i\phi) = \alpha + i\beta \qquad ...(1)$$

$$\therefore \qquad \sin(\alpha + i\beta) = \theta + i\phi$$

$$\sin\alpha \cos h\beta + i \cos\alpha \sin h\beta = \theta + i\phi$$

Equating real and imaginary parts, we have

$$\sin\alpha \cos h\beta = \theta \qquad ...(2)$$

$$\cos\alpha \sin h\beta = \phi \qquad ...(3)$$

$$1+\theta^2 + \phi^2 = 1 + \sin^2\alpha \cos h^2\beta + \cos^2\alpha \sin h^2\beta.$$

$$= 1 + \sin^2\alpha \cos h^2\beta + (1 - \sin^2\alpha)(\cos h^2\beta - 1)$$

$$= 1 + \sin^2\alpha.\cos h^2\beta + \cos h^2\beta - \sin^2\alpha \cos h^2\beta - 1 + \sin^2\alpha.$$

$$\therefore \qquad 1 + \theta^2 + \phi^2 = \sin^2\alpha + \cos h^2\beta.$$

And from (2)

$$\sin^2\alpha.\cos h^2\beta = \theta^2$$

$\therefore$ The equation whose roots are $\sin^2\alpha$ and $\cos h^2\beta$ is

$$x^2 - (\sin^2\alpha + \cos h^2\beta)x + \sin^2\alpha \cos h^2\beta = 0$$

or $x^2 - (1 + \theta^2 + \phi^2)x + \theta^2 = 0.$

Example 7. Prove that $\tan h^{-1}(x) = \sin h^{-1}\left(\dfrac{x}{\sqrt{1-x^2}}\right)$.

Solution: Let $\tan h^{-1}(x)=y$ ...(1)

$$\Rightarrow \quad \tan hy = x.$$

$$\therefore \quad x^2 = \tan h^2 y$$

and $$1 - x^2 = 1 - \tan h^2 y$$

$$1 - x^2 = \sec h^2 y$$

$$\therefore \quad \frac{x}{\sqrt{1-x^2}} = \frac{\tan hy}{\sec hy}$$

$$\therefore \quad \frac{x}{\sqrt{1-x^2}} = \sin hy$$

so $$y = \sin h^{-1}\frac{x}{\sqrt{1-x^2}} \quad ...(2)$$

$\therefore$ From (1) and (2)

$$\tan h^{-1}(x) = \sin h^{-1}\frac{x}{\sqrt{1-x^2}}.$$

Example 8. Prove that.

$$\sin^{-1}(\text{cosec}\theta) = [2n + (-1)^n \frac{\pi}{2} + i\,[(-1)^n \log\cot\frac{\theta}{2}\,],\ (\theta \in R)$$

Solution: If θ is real, then $\text{cosec}\,\theta \geq 1$.

Therefore, $\sin^{-1}(\text{cosec}\theta)$ is a complex number

Let $\sin^{-1}(\text{cosec}\theta) = \alpha + i\beta$

$$\therefore \quad \sin(\alpha + i\beta) = \text{cosec}\theta$$

or $\sin\alpha \cos h\beta + i \cos\alpha \sin h\beta = \text{cosec}\theta$

Equating real and imaginary parts, we have

$$\sin\alpha \cos h\beta = \text{cosec}\theta \quad ...(1)$$

and $$\cos\alpha \sin h\beta = 0 \quad ...(2)$$

From (2), $\cos\alpha = 0$

$\because$ $\sin h\beta \neq 0$

(If $\sin h\beta = 0 \Rightarrow \beta = 0$ which makes $\sin^{-1}(\text{cosec}\theta)$ (a purely real, which is not)

$\therefore$ $\alpha = \dfrac{\pi}{2}$

Putting $\alpha = \dfrac{\pi}{2}$ in equation (1), we have

$$\sin\frac{\pi}{2} . \cos h\beta = \text{cosec}\theta$$

$\therefore$ $\cos h\beta = \text{cosec}\theta$

or $\beta = \cos h^{-1}(\text{cosec}\theta)$

$$\therefore \quad \beta = \log\left[\text{cosec}\theta + \sqrt{\text{cosec}^2\theta - 1}\right]$$

$$= \log(\text{cosec}\theta + \cot\theta)$$

$$= \log\left(\frac{1+\cos\theta}{\sin\theta}\right)$$

$$= \log\left(\cot\frac{\theta}{2}\right)$$

$$\sin^{-1}(\text{cosec}\theta) = \alpha + i\beta = \frac{\pi}{2} + i\log\left(\cot\frac{\theta}{2}\right)$$

Hence, $\sin^{-1}(\text{cosec}\theta) = n\pi + (-1)^n(\alpha + i\beta)$

$$= n\pi + (-1)^n\left[\frac{\pi}{2} + i\log\cot\frac{\theta}{2}\right]$$

$$= [2n + (-1)^n]\frac{\pi}{2} + i(-1)^n\log\cot\frac{\theta}{2}.$$

EXERCISE

1. Separate into real and imaginary parts.

$$\cos^{-1}(\cos\theta + i\sin\theta).$$

2. Prove that $\cot h^{-1}\left(\dfrac{2}{x}\right) = \sin h^{-1}\left(\dfrac{x}{\sqrt{4-x^2}}\right)$.

3. Prove that $\tan^{-1} i = \left(\frac{x-a}{x+a}\right) = \frac{-i}{2}\log\left(\frac{a}{x}\right)$.

4. Prove that $\log\tan\left(\frac{\pi}{4}+\frac{ix}{2}\right) = i\tan^{-1}(\sin hx)$.

5. If $\cos h^{-1}(x+iy) + \cos h^{-1}(x-iy) = \cos h^{-1}(a)$, show that

$$2(a-1)x^2 + 2(a+1)y^2 = a^2 - 1.$$

6. If $\cos^{-1}(\alpha + i\beta) = \theta + i\phi$, then prove that

   (i) $\alpha^2 \sec h^2\phi + \beta^2 \operatorname{cosec} h^2\phi = 1$ and

   (ii) $\alpha^2\sec^2\theta - \beta^2 \operatorname{cosec}^2\theta = 1$.

7. Prove that

$$\tan^{-1}(\cos\theta + i\sin\theta) = n\pi + \frac{\pi}{4} - \frac{i}{2}\log\tan\left(\frac{\pi}{4}-\frac{\theta}{2}\right).$$

8. Separate $\tan h^{-1}(x+iy)$ into A + iB form and hence deduce the value of $\tan h^{-1}(iy)$.

9. If $i^{i^{i\ldots\infty}} = A + i\beta$, prove that

   (i) $\tan\left(\frac{\pi A}{2}\right) = \frac{\beta}{A}$

and (ii) $A^2 + \beta^2 = e^{-\pi\beta}$.

10. Prove that $\tan\left[i\log\left(\frac{a-ib}{a+ib}\right)\right] = \frac{2ab}{a^2-b^2}$.

11. If $\cos^{-1}(u+iv) = \alpha + i\beta$, prove that $\cos^2\alpha$ and $\cos h^2\beta$ are the roots of equation $x^2 - (1+u^2+v^2)x + u^2 = 0$.

Answers

1. $\sin^{-1}\left(\sqrt{\sin\theta}\right) + i\log\left[\sqrt{1+\sin\theta} - \sqrt{\sin\theta}\right]$

8. $\frac{1}{2}\tan h^{-1}\left(\frac{2x}{1+x^2+y^2}\right) + i\frac{1}{2}\tan^{-1}\left(\frac{2y}{1-x^2-y^2}\right)$.

2

Infinite Series

An expression $u_1 + u_2 + u_3 + u_4 + \dots u_n + \dots$ is called a series if each term is followed by another according to some definite rule.

If the number of terms in the series is finite, say n, it is called a finite series and is denoted by $\sum_{r=1}^{n} u_r$.

If the number of terms in the series is infinite, it is called an infinite series and is denoted by $\sum_{n=1}^{\infty} u_n$ or $\sum u_n$.

As, it is obvious by the name infinite series, our discussion will be regarding the infinite series. Further we shall use the term 'series' for infinite series.

Convergence and divergence of series:

Let $S_n = u_1 + u_2 + u_3 + u_4 + \dots u_n + \dots$

then a series $\sum u_n$ is said to be a convergent series if

$$\underset{n\to\infty}{\text{Lt}}\ S_n = \text{a finite quantity}$$

Divergent series if

$$\underset{n\to\infty}{\text{Lt}}\ S_n = \infty \text{ or } -\infty$$

and is said to be an oscillatory series if $\underset{x\to\infty}{\text{Lt}}\ S_n$ neither tends to a definite value nor to $+\infty$ or $-\infty$.

The series is said to oscillate finitely, if $\underset{n\to\infty}{\text{Lt}}\ S_n$ fluctuates within a finite range.

SOLVED EXAMPLES

Example 1. $\sum u_n = 1+\frac{1}{2}+\frac{1}{2^2}+\frac{1}{3^2}+\frac{1}{4^2}+...$

Solution: Here

$$S_n = 1+\frac{1}{2}+\frac{1}{2^2}+\frac{1}{2^3}+...+\frac{1}{2^n}$$

$$= \frac{1\left(1-\left(\frac{1}{2}\right)^n\right)}{\left(1-\frac{1}{2}\right)}$$

$$S_n = 2\left[1-\left(\frac{1}{2}\right)^n\right]$$

$$\therefore \quad \underset{n\to\infty}{\text{Lt}}\ S_n = \underset{n\to\infty}{\text{Lt}}\ 2\left[1-\left(\frac{1}{2}\right)^n\right]$$

$$= 2\,[1-0] = 2 \text{ (a finite quantity)}$$

$$\therefore \quad \sum u_n = \sum_{n=1}^{\infty}\frac{1}{2^{n-1.}} \text{ is a convergent series.}$$

Example 2. $\sum u_n = 1 + 4 + 9 + 16 + ...$

Solution: $\because\ S_n = 1^2 + 2^2 + 3^2 + 4^2 + ... + n^2$

$$= \frac{n(n+1).(2n+1)}{6}$$

$$\therefore \quad \underset{n\to\infty}{\text{Lt}}\ S_n = \infty$$

$$\Rightarrow \quad \sum u_n = 1 + 4 + 9 + 16 + ... \text{ is a divergent series.}$$

Example 3. $\sum u_n = 3 - 3 + 3 - 3 + 3 - 3 ...$

Solution: Here

$S_n = 3$, if n is odd.

$= 0$, if n is even.

$\underset{n\to\infty}{\text{Lt}}\ S_n$ is neither finite nor ∞, it fluctuates between 0 and 3. So $\sum u_n$ is oscillatory series with finite oscillation.

Some Properties of Infinite Series

1. Nature of a series does not change if :
   (i) The signs of all the terms of a series are changed.
   (ii) Each term is multiplied or divided by a non-zero number k.
   (iii) Finite number of terms are added into or omitted from the series.
2. If $\sum u_n$, $\sum v_n$ be two convergent series, converging to P and Q respectively, then $\sum (u_n + v_n)$ is also a convergent series, converging to $P + Q$.
3. If $\sum u_n$ converges to P, then $\sum ku_n$ converges to kP.
4. If $\sum u_n$ & $\sum v_n$ be two convergent series converging to P & Q respectively, then $\sum (au_n + bv_n)$ converges to aP + bQ.
5. If $\sum u_n$, $\sum v_n$ be two +ve terms divergent series, then $\sum (au_n + bv_n)$ is also divergent.

Necessary Condition for Convergence

If $\sum u_n$ is a convergent series then $\underset{n\to\infty}{\text{Lt}}\ u_n = 0$.

or

For every convergent series $\sum u_n$, $\underset{n\to\infty}{\text{Lt}}\ u_n = 0$.

Let $\sum u_n$ be a +ve terms convergent series

Then $$S_n = u_1 + u_2 + u_3 + u_4 + \ldots\ u_{n-1} + \ldots + u_n$$

$$S_{n-1} = u_1 + u_2 + u_3 + \ldots\ u_{n-1}$$

$\therefore$ $$S_n - S_{n-1} = u_n.$$

$$\underset{n\to\infty}{\text{Lt}}\ (S_n - S_{n-1}) = \underset{n\to\infty}{\text{Lt}}\ u_n$$

If $\sum u_n$ is a convergent series, then

$$\underset{n\to\infty}{\text{Lt}}\ S_n = \underset{n\to\infty}{\text{Lt}}\ S_{n-1}$$

$\therefore$ $$\underset{n\to\infty}{\text{Lt}}\ u_n = 0.$$ (Hence the condition)

Convergence of a Geometric Series

Solution. Let us consider the geometric series

$$a + ar + ar^2 + ar^3 + \ldots + ar^{n-1} + \ldots$$

Let S_n be the sum of first n terms of the series

$$\therefore \qquad S_n = \frac{a\left(1-r^n\right)}{1-r}, \text{ if } r < 1.$$

$$= \frac{a\left(r^n - 1\right)}{\left(r-1\right)}, \text{ if } r > 1.$$

Case I. When $|r| < 1$, *i.e.* $-1 < r < 1$.

If $|r| < 1$

$$\therefore \qquad \underset{n\to\infty}{\text{Lt}}\ r^n \to 0.$$

$$\underset{n\to\infty}{\text{Lt}}\ S_n = \underset{n\to\infty}{\text{Lt}}\ \frac{a\left(1-r^n\right)}{\left(1-r\right)}$$

$$= \frac{a\left(1-0\right)}{1-r}$$

$$= \frac{a}{1-r}, \text{ which is a finite quantity.}$$

$\therefore \sum u_n$ converges, if $|r| < 1$.

Case II. When $r = 1$.

for $\qquad r = 1,$

$$S_n = a + a + a + \ldots n \text{ times}$$

$$= na$$

$$\therefore \qquad \underset{n\to\infty}{\text{Lt}}\ S_n = \infty \text{ or } -\infty \text{ as } a \text{ is +ve or –ve.}$$

Hence, the series $\sum u_n$ is divergent.

Case III. When $r > 1$.

If $r > 1$, $\underset{n\to\infty}{\text{Lt}}\ r^n \to \infty$

$$\therefore \qquad \underset{n\to\infty}{\text{Lt}}\ S_n = \infty \text{ or } -\infty \text{ as } a > 0 \text{ or } a < 0.$$

Hence, the series is divergent.

Case IV. When $r = -1$.

$$S_n = a - a + a - a + a \ldots n \text{ times}$$

$$= a, \text{ if } n \text{ is odd.}$$

$$= 0, \text{ if } n \text{ is even.}$$

Hence, the series $\sum u_n$ is oscillatory for $r = -1$.

Case V. When $r < -1$.

Let $\qquad r = -r_1$

If $\qquad r < -1, r_1 > 1$

$$\therefore \qquad S_n = \frac{a(1 - r^n)}{1 - r}$$

$$= \frac{a\left[1 - (-r_1)^n\right]}{1 + r_1}$$

$$= \frac{a\left[1 + r_1^n\right]}{1 + r} \text{ or } \frac{a\left[1 - r_1^n\right]}{1 + r}$$

accordingly as n is odd or even.

$\underset{n\to\infty}{\text{Lt}}\ S_n \to \infty$ or $-\infty$ accordingly as $a > 0$ or $a < 0$.

Therefore, in this case the series is oscillatory with infinite oscillation.

Hence, the geometric series $a + ar + ar^2 + ar^3 + \ldots + ar^n + \ldots \infty$

(i) Converges, if $|r| < 1$.
(ii) Diverges, if $r \geq 1$.
(iii) Oscillatory, if $r \leq -1$.

Series of Positive terms: If $\sum u_n$ is a series such that $u_n > 0 \; \forall \; n$. Then $\sum u_n$ is said to be a series of positive terms.

Some results regarding the convergence or divergence of positive terms series.

1. A series $\sum u_n$ converges if and only if there exists a number k such that $u_1 + u_2 + u_3 + \ldots + u_n < k \; \forall \; n$.
2. A series of +ve terms diverges if each term after a fixed term is greater than some fixed positive number.
3. If $\sum u_n$, $\sum v_n$ be two +ve terms series such that:

   (i) $u_n \le v_n \; \forall_n$, then $\sum u_n$ converges if $\sum v_n$ is convergent.

   (ii) $u_n \ge v_n \; \forall_n$, then $\sum u_n$ diverges if $\sum v_n$ is divergent.

Convergence or Divergence of the Auxiliary Series

$$\sum n^{-p} = \sum \frac{1}{n^p}.$$

The infinite series

$$\sum \frac{1}{n^p} = \frac{1}{1^p} + \frac{1}{2^p} + \frac{1}{3^p} + \ldots + \frac{1}{n^p} + \ldots$$

(i) Converges if $p > 1$.

(ii) Diverges if $p \le 1$.

Proof: Case I. $p > 1$.

$$\therefore \quad \frac{1}{1^p} + \frac{1}{2^p} + \frac{1}{3^p} + \frac{1}{4^p} + \frac{1}{5^p} + \frac{1}{6^p} + \ldots$$

$$= \frac{1}{1^p} + \left(\frac{1}{2^p} + \frac{1}{3^p}\right) + \left(\frac{1}{4^p} + \frac{1}{5^p} + \frac{1}{6^p} + \frac{1}{7^p}\right)$$

$$+ \left(\frac{1}{8^p} + \frac{1}{9^p} + \ldots + \frac{1}{15^p}\right) + \ldots$$

when $p > 1$, $\qquad 2^p < 3^p$

$$\therefore \qquad \frac{1}{2^p} > \frac{1}{3^p}$$

$$\therefore \qquad \frac{1}{2^p}+\frac{1}{3^p} < \frac{1}{2^p}+\frac{1}{2^p}$$

$$\frac{2}{2^p}=\frac{1}{2^{p-1}}$$

$$\frac{1}{4^p}+\frac{1}{5^p}+\frac{1}{6^p}+\frac{1}{7^p} < \frac{1}{4^p}+\frac{1}{4^p}+\frac{1}{4^p}+\frac{1}{4^p}$$

$$< \frac{4}{4^p}$$

$$< \frac{1}{4^{p-1}}$$

$$< \frac{1}{2^{2(p-1)}}$$

$$\frac{1}{8^p}+\frac{1}{9^p}+\frac{1}{10^p}+\ldots+\frac{1}{15^p} < \frac{1}{8^p}+\frac{1}{8^p}+\ldots 8 \text{ times}$$

$$< \frac{8}{8^p}$$

$$= \frac{1}{8^{p-1}}$$

$$= \frac{1}{2^{3(p-1)}}.$$

and so on.

$$\frac{1}{1^p}+\frac{1}{2^p}+\frac{1}{3^p}+\ldots+\frac{1}{n^p}+\ldots$$

$$< 1+\frac{1}{2^{p-1}}+\frac{1}{2^{2(p-1)}}+\frac{1}{2^{3(p-1)}}+\ldots$$

But the series on R.H.S. is an infinite geometric series with common ratio $\frac{1}{2^{p-1}} < 1$ since $(p > 1)$

Thus, the series on R.H.S. is a convergent series. Thus the series on L.H.S. is an infinite series which is term by term less than a convergent series.

So, L.H.S. is also a convergent series.

Case II. When $p = 1$.

$$1+\frac{1}{2}+\frac{1}{3}+\frac{1}{4}+\frac{1}{5}+\frac{1}{6}+\frac{1}{7}+\frac{1}{8}+\frac{1}{9}+\dots$$

$$= 1+\frac{1}{2}+\left(\frac{1}{3}+\frac{1}{4}\right)+\left(\frac{1}{5}+\frac{1}{6}+\frac{1}{7}+\frac{1}{8}\right)$$

$$+\left(\frac{1}{9}+\frac{1}{10}+\dots\frac{1}{16}\right)+\dots$$

Now, $$\frac{1}{3}+\frac{1}{4} > \frac{1}{4}+\frac{1}{4}$$

$$> \frac{2}{4}$$

$$> \frac{1}{2}$$

$$\frac{1}{5}+\frac{1}{6}+\frac{1}{7}+\frac{1}{8} > \frac{1}{8}+\frac{1}{8}+\frac{1}{8}+\frac{1}{8}$$

$$> \frac{1}{2}$$

$$\frac{1}{9}+\frac{1}{10}+\frac{1}{11}+\dots\frac{1}{16} > \frac{1}{16}+\frac{1}{16}\dots \text{ 8 times}$$

$$> \frac{8}{16}$$

$$> \frac{1}{2}.$$

Thus,

$$1+\frac{1}{2}+\frac{1}{3}+\frac{1}{4}+\frac{1}{5}+\frac{1}{6}+\dots > 1+\frac{1}{2}+\frac{1}{2}+\frac{1}{2}+\frac{1}{2}+\dots$$

S_n = sum of n terms of the series on R.H.S.

$$= 1 + (n-1)\frac{1}{2}$$

$$= \frac{(n+1)}{2}$$

$$\therefore \qquad \operatorname*{Lt}_{n\to\infty} S_n = \infty$$

$\Rightarrow \quad \sum u_n$ diverges, if $p = 1$.

Case III. When $p < 1$.

then $$n^p < n$$

$$\therefore \qquad \frac{1}{n^p} > \frac{1}{n}$$

$$\Rightarrow \qquad \sum \frac{1}{n^p} > \sum \frac{1}{n}$$

We know that, $\sum \frac{1}{n}$ is divergent (being p-series for $p = 1$)

The series on L.H.S. also diverges.

Thus, the series $\sum \frac{1}{n^p}$.

(i) Converges, if $p > 1$.

(ii) Diverges, if $p \le 1$.

COMPARISON TEST

If $\sum u_n$ and $\sum v_n$ be two +ve terms series, such that $\operatorname*{Lt}_{n\to\infty} \frac{u_n}{v_n} = e$ (finite and non-zero), then $\sum u_n$ and $\sum v_n$ both are of the same nature, *i.e.,* either both converge or both diverge.

Proof: Let $\operatorname*{Lt}_{n\to\infty} \frac{u_n}{v_n} = e$, then by definition of limit, there exists a +ve number $\in > 0$, such that $\left|\frac{u_n}{v_n} - e\right| < \in \forall\, n$.

or $$-\in < \frac{u_n}{v_n} - e < \in$$

or $$e - \in < \frac{u_n}{v_n} < e + \in \qquad ...(1)$$

Case I. When $\sum v_n$ is convergent then $\sum (e+\in) v_n$ is also convergent,

then from equation (1),

$u_n < (e+\in) v_n$.

since $\sum (e+\in) v_n$ is convergent, so is $\sum u_n$

[since $\sum u_n$ is term by term less than $\sum (e+\in) v_n$]

Case II. When $\sum v_n$ is divergent,

and $$u_n > (e-\in) v_n \;\forall n,$$

or $$\sum u_n > \sum (e-\in) v_n$$

Since $\sum v_n$ is divergent

$\therefore$ $\sum (e-\in) v_n$ is also divergent.

Since $\sum u_n$ is term by term greater than $\sum (e-\in) v_n$.

$\therefore$ $\sum u_n$ is also divergent.

Procedure for Applying Comparison Test

This test is applied when the *n*th term u_n, of $\sum u_n$ contains the powers of n only, which may be positive, negative or fractional or u_n contains some trigonometric terms like sin, tan of n or functions of n, of which limit can be evaluated by some suitable choice of $\sum v_n \left(\sum \frac{1}{n^p} \right)$.

In case u_n contains powers of n, then v_n is chosen by $v_n = \dfrac{1}{n^{p-q}}$.

where p = deg. of n in the D^r. of u_n.

q = deg. of n in the N^r. of u_n.

Some Important Limits

1. $\underset{n \to \infty}{\text{Lt}} \left(1 + \frac{x}{n} \right)^n = e^x$

2. $\underset{n\to\infty}{\text{Lt}}\left(1+\frac{x}{n}\right)^{p} = 1$, if p is finite.

3. $\underset{n\to\infty}{\text{Lt}}\ n^{\frac{1}{n}} = 1$

4. $\underset{n\to\infty}{\text{Lt}}\ \frac{\log n}{n} = 0$

5. $\underset{n\to\infty}{\text{Lt}}\left(\frac{n^n}{n!}\right)^{1/n} = e.$

SOLVED EXAMPLES

Example 1. Test the convergence of the series

$$\sum u_n = \frac{1}{2}+\frac{2}{5}+\frac{3}{10}+\ldots+\frac{n}{n^2+1}.$$

Solution: For the given series

$$u_n = \frac{n}{n^2+1}\ldots$$

$$\underset{n\to\infty}{\text{Lt}}\ u_n = 0$$

Now, let $$v_n = \frac{1}{n}$$

$$\therefore \quad \frac{u_n}{v_n} = \frac{n^2}{n^2+1}$$

$$\underset{n\to\infty}{\text{Lt}}\ \frac{u_n}{v_n} = \underset{n\to\infty}{\text{Lt}}\ \frac{n^2}{n^2+1}$$

$$= \underset{n\to\infty}{\text{Lt}}\ \frac{1}{1+\frac{1}{x^2}}$$

$$= \frac{1}{1+0} = 1 \text{ (non-zero finite).}$$

$\therefore$ By comparison test, both the series $\sum u_n$ and $\sum v_n$ are of the same nature.

But $\sum v_n = \sum \frac{1}{n}$ is divergent, so $\sum u_n$ is also divergent.

Example 2. Discuss the convergence of the series

$$\frac{1}{2}+\frac{4}{5}+\frac{9}{10}+\frac{16}{17}+\ldots\frac{n^2}{n^2+1}.$$

Solution: Here,

$$u_n = \frac{n^2}{n^2+1}$$

$$\underset{n\to\infty}{\text{Lt}}\ u_n = \underset{n\to\infty}{\text{Lt}}\ \frac{n^2}{n^2+1}$$

$$= \underset{n\to\infty}{\text{Lt}}\ \frac{1}{1+\frac{1}{n^2}}$$

$$= 1.$$

$\therefore$ $\underset{n\to\infty}{\text{Lt}}\ u_n \neq 0 \Rightarrow \sum u_n$ is divergent.

Example 3. Test the following series for convergence, whose n^{th} terms are given by:

(i) $\frac{\sqrt{n}}{n^3+1}$ (ii) $\sin\left(\frac{1}{n}\right)$

(iii) $\tan^{-1}\left(\frac{1}{n}\right)$ (iv) $\frac{1}{3^n+5^n}$

(v) $\frac{1}{n^3}\left(\frac{n+2}{n+3}\right)^n$ (vi) $\sqrt{n^4+1}-\sqrt{n^4-1}.$

Solution: (i)

$$u_n = \frac{\sqrt{n}}{n^3+1}$$

Here,

$$u_n = \frac{\sqrt{n}}{n^3+1}$$

$\therefore$ Let

$$v_n = \frac{1}{n^{5/2}}$$

$$\therefore \qquad \frac{u_n}{v_n} = \frac{n^{1/2}.n^{5/2}}{n^3+1}$$

$$= \frac{n^3}{n^3+1} = \frac{1}{1+\frac{1}{n^3}}$$

$$\therefore \qquad \underset{n\to\infty}{\text{Lt}} \frac{u_n}{v_n} = \underset{n\to\infty}{\text{Lt}} \frac{1}{1+\frac{1}{n^3}}$$

$$= \frac{1}{1+0}$$

$$= 1 \text{ (Non-zero finite).}$$

$\therefore$ By comparison test $\sum u_n$ and $\sum v_n$ both are of the same nature.

But $\sum v_n = \sum \frac{1}{n^{5/2}}$ is convergent ($p > 1$).

$\therefore \sum u_n$ is also convergent

Thus $\sum u_n = \sum \frac{\sqrt{n}}{n^3+1}$ is convergent.

(ii) $u_n = \sin\frac{1}{n}$

We know that

$$\sin x = x - \frac{x^3}{3!} + \frac{x^5}{5!} - \frac{x^7}{7!}\cdots$$

$$\therefore \qquad \sin\left(\frac{1}{n}\right) = \frac{1}{n} - \frac{1}{3!n^3} + \frac{1}{5!}\frac{1}{n^5}\cdots$$

$$\therefore \qquad \sin\left(\frac{1}{n}\right) = \frac{1}{n}\left[1 - \frac{1}{3!n^2} + \frac{1}{5!}\frac{1}{n^4}\right]$$

Let $v_n = \frac{1}{n}$

$$\therefore \qquad \frac{u_n}{v_n} = \frac{\sin\left(\frac{1}{n}\right)}{\left(\frac{1}{n}\right)} = 1 - \frac{1}{3!n^2} + \frac{1}{5!n^4} \cdots$$

$$\therefore \qquad \underset{n\to\infty}{\text{Lt}} \frac{u_n}{v_n} = \underset{n\to\infty}{\text{Lt}} \left[1 - \frac{1}{3!n^2} + \frac{1}{5!n^4} \cdots\right]$$

$$= 1 \text{ (Non-zero finite).}$$

$\therefore$ By comparison test, both the series are of the same nature.

But $\qquad \sum v_n = \sum \frac{1}{n}$ is divergent

So $\sum u_n$ is also divergent.

Thus $\sum u_n = \sin\frac{1}{n}$ is divergent.

(iii) $u_n = \tan^{-1}\left(\frac{1}{n}\right)$

We know that

$$\tan^{-1}(x) = x - \frac{x^3}{3} + \frac{x^5}{5} \cdots$$

$$\therefore \qquad \tan^{-1}\left(\frac{1}{n}\right) = \frac{1}{n} - \frac{1}{3n^3} + \frac{1}{5n^5} \cdots$$

$$u_n = \frac{1}{n}\left[1 - \frac{1}{3n^2} + \frac{1}{5n^4} \cdots\right]$$

Now, let $\qquad V_n = \frac{1}{n}$

$$\therefore \qquad \frac{u_n}{v_n} = \frac{n}{n}\left[1 - \frac{1}{3n^2} + \frac{1}{5n^4} \cdots\right]$$

$$= 1 - \frac{1}{3n^2} + \frac{1}{5n^4} \cdots$$

$$\therefore \qquad \underset{n\to\infty}{\text{Lt}} \frac{u_n}{v_n} = \underset{n\to\infty}{\text{Lt}} \left[1 - \frac{1}{3n^2} + \frac{1}{5n^4} \cdots\right]$$

$$\underset{n\to\infty}{\text{Lt}} \frac{u_n}{v_n} = [1 - 0]$$

$$= 1 \text{ (Non-zero finite)}$$

$\therefore$ $\sum u_n$ and $\sum v_n$ both the series are of the same nature.

But $\sum v_n = \sum \frac{1}{n}$ is divergent. So $\sum u_n = \tan^{-1}\frac{1}{n}$ is also divergent.

(iv) $$u_n = \frac{1}{3^n + 5^n}$$

$$= \frac{1}{5^n\left[1+\left(\frac{3}{5}\right)^n\right]}$$

$$= \frac{1}{5^n}\left[\frac{1}{1+\left(\frac{3}{5}\right)^n}\right]$$

Let $$v_n = \frac{1}{5^n}$$

$\therefore$ $$\frac{u_n}{v_n} = \frac{5^n}{5^n}\left[\frac{1}{1+\left(\frac{3}{5}\right)^n}\right]$$

$$= \frac{1}{1+\left(\frac{3}{5}\right)^n}$$

$\therefore$ $$\underset{n\to\infty}{\text{Lt}} \frac{u_n}{v_n} = \underset{n\to\infty}{\text{Lt}} \frac{1}{1+\left(\frac{3}{5}\right)^n}$$

$$= \frac{1}{1+0} = 1 \text{ (non-zero finite).}$$

$\therefore \quad \sum u_n \;\&\; \sum v_n$ both are of the same nature,

but $\sum v_n = \sum \frac{1}{5^n}$ is convergent [being infinite G.P. with common ratio $\frac{1}{5} < 1$].

$\therefore \; \sum u_n = \frac{1}{3^n + 5^n}$ is also convergent.

(v) $u_n = \frac{1}{n^3}\left(\frac{n+2}{n+3}\right)^n$.

Let $v_n = \frac{1}{n^3}$

$$\therefore \qquad \frac{u_n}{v_n} = \frac{n^3}{n^3}\left[\left(\frac{n+2}{n+3}\right)^n\right]$$

$$= \frac{(n+2)^n}{(n+3)^n}$$

$$\frac{u_n}{v_n} = \frac{\left(1+\frac{2}{n}\right)^n}{\left(1+\frac{3}{n}\right)^n}$$

$$\therefore \qquad \operatorname*{Lt}_{n\to\infty} \frac{u_n}{v_n} = \frac{\operatorname*{Lt}_{n\to\infty}\left(1+\frac{2}{n}\right)^n}{\operatorname*{Lt}_{n\to\infty}\left(1+\frac{3}{n}\right)^n}$$

$$= \frac{e^2}{e^3} = \frac{1}{e} \text{ (Non-zero finite).}$$

$\therefore \quad \sum u_n \;\&\; \sum v_n$ both are of the same nature, but $\sum v_n = \sum \frac{1}{n^3}$ is convergent.

$\therefore \ \sum u_n = \sum \frac{1}{n^3}\left(\frac{n+2}{n+3}\right)^n$ is also convergent.

(vi) Here $u_n = \sqrt{n^4+1} - \sqrt{n^4-1}$.

$$= \left[\sqrt{n^4+1} - \sqrt{n^4-1}\right] \frac{\left[\sqrt{n^4+1} + \sqrt{n^4-1}\right]}{\left[\sqrt{n^4+1} + \sqrt{n^4+1}\right]}$$

$$= \frac{n^4+1-\left(n^4-1\right)}{\sqrt{n^4+1} + \sqrt{n^4-1}} = \frac{2}{\sqrt{n^4+1+\sqrt{n^4-1}}}$$

$$= \frac{2}{n^2}\left[\frac{1}{\sqrt{1+\frac{1}{n^4}} + \sqrt{1-\frac{1}{n^4}}}\right]$$

Now let $\qquad V_n = \frac{1}{n^2}$

$$\therefore \qquad \frac{u_n}{v_n} = \frac{2n^2}{n^2} \frac{1}{\sqrt{1+\frac{1}{n^4}} + \sqrt{1-\frac{1}{n^4}}}$$

$$= \frac{2}{\sqrt{1+\frac{1}{n^4}} + \sqrt{1-\frac{1}{n^4}}}$$

$$\therefore \qquad \underset{n\to\infty}{\text{Lt}} \frac{u_n}{v_n} = \underset{n\to\infty}{\text{Lt}} \frac{2}{\sqrt{1+\frac{1}{n^4}} + \sqrt{1-\frac{1}{n^4}}}$$

$$= \frac{2}{\sqrt{1+0}+\sqrt{1-0}} = \frac{2}{2} = 1 \text{ (Non-zero finite)}$$

$\therefore$ $\sum u_n$ & $\sum v_n$ both are of the same nature, but $\sum v_n = \sum \frac{1}{n^2}$ is convergent.

$\therefore$ the given series $\sum\left(\sqrt{n^4+1}-\sqrt{n^4-1}\right)$ is also convergent.

Example 4. Test the convergence of the series:

$$\frac{1}{1.3}+\frac{1}{3.5}+\frac{1}{5.7}+\ldots$$

Solution: Here $u_n = \dfrac{1}{(2n-1)(2n+1)}$

Let $v_n = \dfrac{1}{n^2}$

$$\therefore \quad \frac{u_n}{v_n} = \frac{n^2}{(2n-1)(2n+1)}$$

$$= \frac{n^2}{n^2\left[2+\frac{1}{n}\right]\left[2-\frac{1}{n}\right]}$$

$$\frac{u_n}{v_n} = \frac{1}{\left(2+\frac{1}{n}\right)\left(2-\frac{1}{n}\right)}$$

$$\therefore \quad \operatorname*{Lt}_{n\to\infty}\frac{u_n}{v_n} = \operatorname*{Lt}_{n\to\infty}\frac{1}{\left(2+\frac{1}{n}\right)\left(2-\frac{1}{n}\right)}$$

$$= \frac{1}{(2+0)(2-0)} = \frac{1}{4} \text{ (Non-zero finite)}$$

$\therefore$ $\sum u_n$ & $\sum v_n$ both are of the same nature. But $\sum v_n = \sum \frac{1}{n^2}$ is convergent. So $\sum u_n = \frac{1}{(2n-1)(2n+1)}$ is also convergent.

Example 5. Discuss the convergence of the series:

$$\frac{1}{1.2.3} + \frac{3}{2.3.4} + \frac{5}{3.4.5} + \ldots$$

Solution: Here $$u_n = \frac{(2n-1)}{n(n+1)(n+2)}$$

Let $$v_n = \frac{1}{n^2}$$

$$\therefore \quad \frac{u_n}{v_n} = \frac{n^2[2n-1]}{n(n+1)(n+2)}$$

$$= \frac{n^2 . n\left[2 - \frac{1}{n}\right]}{n^3 .\left(1+\frac{1}{n}\right)\left[1+\frac{2}{n}\right]}$$

$$= \frac{\left(2-\frac{1}{n}\right)}{\left(1+\frac{1}{n}\right)\left[1+\frac{2}{n}\right]}$$

$$\therefore \quad \underset{n\to\infty}{\text{Lt}} \frac{u_n}{v_n} = \underset{n\to\infty}{\text{Lt}} \frac{\left(2-\frac{1}{n}\right)}{\left(1+\frac{1}{n}\right)\left[1+\frac{2}{n}\right]}$$

$$= \frac{(2-0)}{(1+0)(1+0)} = 2 \text{ (Non-zero finite)}$$

$\therefore$ $\sum u_n$ & $\sum v_n$ both are of the same nature. But $\sum v_n = \sum \frac{1}{n^2}$ is convergent. So $\sum u_n = \sum \frac{(2n-1)}{n(n+1)(n+2)}$ is also convergent.

EXERCISE

Test the following series for convergence or divergence:

1. $\frac{1}{2}+\frac{2}{3}+\frac{3}{4}+\frac{4}{5}+\ldots$

2. $\frac{1}{\log 2}+\frac{1}{\log 3}+\frac{1}{\log 4}+\ldots+\frac{1}{\log n}+\ldots$

3. $\sum_{n=1}^{\infty} \frac{1}{n^{\left(a+\frac{b}{n}\right)}}$

4. $\sum_{n=1}^{\infty} \frac{1}{2^n+3^n}$

5. $\sum\left[\sqrt[3]{(n+1)}-\sqrt[3]{n}\right]$

6. $\sum \sin\left(\frac{1}{n^2}\right)$

7. $\frac{1}{1.2.3.}+\frac{3}{2.3.4}+\frac{5}{3.4.5}+\ldots$

8. $\sum \frac{1}{\sqrt{n}} \tan\left(\frac{1}{n}\right)$

9. $\sum \frac{1}{n^{1+1/n}}$

Answers:

1. Divergent.
2. Divergent.
3. Convergent if $a > 1$.
   Divergent if $a \leq 1$.
4. Convergent.

5. Divergent.
6. Convergent.
7. Convergent.
8. Convergent.
9. Divergent.

CAUCHY'S ROOT TEST

If $\sum u_n$ be a series of +ve terms such that from and after some particular term

$$\underset{n\to\infty}{\text{Lt}} (u_n)^{1/n} = e, \text{ then}$$

(i) Σu_n converges if $e < 1$

(ii) Σu_n diverges if $e > 1$

(iii) The test fails if $e = 1$.

Proof: Let $\Sigma u_n = u_1 + u_2 + u_3 + \ldots u_n + \ldots$

since $u_n > 0$ for all n and $(u_n)^{1/n}$ stands for the positive nth root of u_n.

$$\therefore \quad \underset{n\to\infty}{\text{Lt}} (u_n)^{1/n} = e \geq 0.$$

$\therefore$ By definition

$$|u_n^{1/n} - e| < \in$$

i.e. $$-\in < (u_n)^{1/n} - e < \in .$$

or $$e - \in < (u_n)^{1/n} < e + \in$$

or $$(e - \in)^n < u_n < (e + \in)^n \qquad \ldots(1)$$

Case I. When $e < 1$. We can find a number $r = e + \in < 1, \in > 0$

$\therefore \quad 0 \leq e < r < 1.$

From equation (1), $u_n < r^n \ \forall n.$

Since Σr^n is a geometric series with common ratios $r < 1$.

$\therefore$ Σr^n is convergent.

$\therefore$ By comparison test, Σu_n is convergent.

(ii) When $r > 1$, we can find $r = e - \in > 1$.

$\therefore$ From equation (1), $u_n > r^n \quad \forall\, n$.

But Σr^n is a geometric series with common ratio $r > 1$ for which it is divergent. Therefore, by comparison test Σu_n is divergent.

(iii) When $e = 1$.

$$\text{Let} \qquad \Sigma u_n = \Sigma \frac{1}{n}$$

$$\therefore \qquad u_n = \frac{1}{n}$$

$$\underset{n\to\infty}{\text{Lt}} (u_n)^{1/n} = \underset{n\to\infty}{\text{Lt}} \left(\frac{1}{n}\right)^{1/n}$$

$$= \underset{n\to\infty}{\text{Lt}} \frac{1}{(n)^{1/n}}$$

$$= 1.$$

Since $\Sigma \frac{1}{n}$ is divergent.

$\therefore$ If $\underset{n\to\infty}{\text{Lt}} (u_n)^{1/n} = 1$, then Σu_n may be divergent.

$$\text{Secondly let} \qquad \Sigma u_n = \Sigma \frac{1}{n^2}$$

$$\therefore \qquad u_n = \frac{1}{n^2}.$$

$$\therefore \qquad \underset{n\to\infty}{\text{Lt}} (u_n)^{1/n} = \underset{n\to\infty}{\text{Lt}} \frac{1}{\left(n^{1/n}\right)^2} = 1.$$

Since $\Sigma \frac{1}{n^2}$ is convergent and we observe that $\underset{n\to\infty}{\text{Lt}} (u_n)^{1/n} = 1$.

The series Σu_n may be convergent. Thus we have observed that the Cauchy's root test fails if $e = 1$.

SOLVED EXAMPLES

Example 1. Test the following series for convergence.

(i) $\Sigma\left(1+\frac{1}{n}\right)^{-n^2}$

(ii) $\Sigma\left(\frac{n+1}{n+2}\right)^{n}.x^n$

(iii) $\Sigma\left(\frac{n}{n+1}\right)^{n^2}$.

Solution: (i) Here $u_n = \left(1+\frac{1}{n}\right)^{-n^2}$

$$\therefore \quad (u_n)^{1/n} = \left(1+\frac{1}{n}\right)^{-n}$$

$$= \frac{1}{\left(1+\frac{1}{n}\right)^{n}}$$

$$\therefore \quad \underset{n\to\infty}{\text{Lt}} (u_n)^{1/n} = \underset{n\to\infty}{\text{Lt}} \frac{1}{\left(1+\frac{1}{n}\right)^{n}} = \frac{1}{e} < 1.$$

By Cauchy's root test, Σu_n is convergent.

(ii) Here $u_n = \left(\frac{n+1}{n+2}\right)^{n}.x^n$

$$\therefore \quad (u_n)^{1/n} = \left(\frac{n+1}{n+2}\right).x$$

$$= \left(\frac{1+\frac{1}{n}}{1+\frac{2}{n}}\right).\,x$$

$$\therefore \quad \underset{n\to\infty}{\text{Lt}} (u_n)^{1/n} = \underset{n\to\infty}{\text{Lt}} \left(\frac{1+\frac{1}{n}}{1+\frac{2}{n}}\right) . x = x$$

$\therefore$ By Cauchy's root rest, Σu_n converges if $x < 1$ and diverges if $x > 1$.
For $x = 1$, the test fails.
Now, for $x = 1$

$$u_n = \left(\frac{n+1}{n+2}\right)^n$$

$$u_n = \frac{\left(1+\frac{1}{n}\right)^n}{\left(1+\frac{2}{n}\right)^n}$$

$$\therefore \quad \underset{n\to\infty}{\text{Lt}} u_n = \underset{n\to\infty}{\text{Lt}} \frac{\left(1+\frac{1}{n}\right)^n}{\left(1+\frac{2}{n}\right)^n}$$

$$= \frac{e}{e^2} = \frac{1}{e} > 0.$$

$\therefore \underset{n\to\infty}{\text{Lt}} u_n \neq 0 \Rightarrow \Sigma u_n$ is divergent.

Thus, Σu_n converges if $x < 1$ and diverges if $x \geq 1$.

(ii) Here $$(u_n)^{1/n} = \left(\frac{n+1}{n+2}\right)^{n^2}$$

$$\therefore \quad (u_n)^{1/n} = \left(\frac{n+1}{n+2}\right)^n$$

$$\underset{n\to\infty}{\text{Lt}} (u_n)^{1/n} = \underset{n\to\infty}{\text{Lt}} \left(\frac{n+1}{n+2}\right)^n$$

$$= \underset{n\to\infty}{\text{Lt}} \left(\frac{1+\frac{1}{n}}{1+\frac{2}{n}}\right)^n$$

$$= \underset{n\to\infty}{\text{Lt}} \frac{\left(1+\frac{1}{n}\right)^n}{\left(1+\frac{2}{n}\right)^n}$$

$$= \frac{1}{e} < 1.$$

$$\therefore \qquad \underset{n\to\infty}{\text{Lt}} (u_n)^{1/n} < 1.$$

Thus Σu_n is convergent.

EXERCISE

Test the convergence and divergence of the following series:

1. $\frac{1}{2} x + \left(\frac{2}{3}\right)^4 . x^2 + \left(\frac{3}{4}\right)^9 . x^3 + ... \left(\frac{n}{n+1}\right)^{n^2} x^n + ...$

2 $1+\frac{x}{2}+\frac{x^2}{3^2}+\frac{x^3}{4^3}+..., \; x>0.$

3. $\frac{2}{1^2} .x+\frac{3^2}{2^3} .x^2+\frac{4^3}{3^4} .x^3+...\frac{(n+1)^n}{n^{n+1}} .x^n+...$

4. $(x + 3) + 2^2 . (x + 3)^2 + 3^3 (x + 3)^3 + ...$

Answer:

1. Convergent for $x < e$ and divergent for $x \geq e$.
2. Convergent.
3. Convergent for $x \leq 1$ and divergent for $x > 1$.
4. Divergent.

D-ALENBERT'S RATIO TEST

If $\sum u_n$ be a positive terms series such that

$$\underset{n\to\infty}{\text{Lt}} \frac{u_{n+1}}{u_n} = e, \text{ then } \sum u_n$$

(i) Converges if $e < 1$.
(ii) Diverges if $e > 1$.
(iii) The test fails if $e = 1$.

Proof:

Case I. When $e < 1$.

By definition of limit, there exists a positive number $\lambda (e < \lambda < 1)$,

such that $$\frac{u_{n+1}}{u_n} < \lambda \ \forall n. \qquad ...(1)$$

Then $$\frac{u_2}{u_1} < \lambda, \ \frac{u_3}{u_2} < \lambda \ \text{........... and so on} \qquad ...(2)$$

Now, $u_1 + u_2 + u_3 + u_4 + ... \text{ to } \infty$.

$$= u_1\left[1 + \frac{u_2}{u_1} + \frac{u_3}{u_1} + \frac{u_3}{u_1} + ...\right].$$

$$= u_1\left[1 + \frac{u_2}{u_1} + \frac{u_3}{u_2}.\frac{u_2}{u_4} + \frac{u_4}{u_3}.\frac{u_3}{u_2}.\frac{u_2}{u_1}...\right]$$

$$< u_1 \ [1 + \lambda + \lambda^2 + \lambda^3 + ...]$$

$$< u_1 \ . \ \frac{1}{1-\lambda}$$

$$< \frac{u_1}{1-\lambda}, \text{ a finite quantity.}$$

$\therefore$ The series $\sum u_n$ converges when $e < 1$.

Case II. When $e > 1$, then we have

$$\frac{u_{n+1}}{u_n} > 1$$

$$\frac{u_2}{u_1} > 1, \frac{u_3}{u_2} > 1, \ \frac{u_4}{u_3} > 1 \ ...$$

$$\therefore \qquad S_n = u_1 + u_2 + u_3 + u_4 + ... + u_n$$

$$= u_1\left[1 + \frac{u_2}{u_1} + \frac{u_3}{u_1} + \frac{u_4}{u_1} + ...\right]$$

$$= u_1\left[1+\frac{u_2}{u_1}+\frac{u_3}{u_2}.\frac{u_2}{u_1}+\frac{u_4}{u_3}.\frac{u_3}{u_2}.\frac{u_2}{u_1}+...\right]$$

$$> u_1 \; [1 + 1 + 1 + 1 + ... \; n \text{ terms}]$$

$$S_n > u_{n1}$$

$$\therefore \; \underset{n\to\infty}{\text{Lt}} \; S_n \to \infty .$$

Case III. When $e = 1$, the test fails, since when $e = 1$, sometimes the series are convergent and sometimes are divergent.

For example,

Let $$\sum u_n = \sum \frac{1}{n}$$

$$\therefore \quad u_n = \frac{1}{n}$$

$$u_{n+1} = \frac{1}{n+1}$$

$$\therefore \quad \frac{u_{n+1}}{u_n} = \frac{n}{n+1} = \frac{1}{1+\frac{1}{n}}$$

$$\underset{n\to\infty}{\text{Lt}} \frac{u_{n+1}}{u_n} = \underset{n\to\infty}{\text{Lt}} \frac{1}{1+\frac{1}{n}}$$

$$= \frac{1}{1+0} = 1$$

and we know that $\sum \frac{1}{n}$ is divergent.

Secondly let

$$\sum u_n = \sum \frac{1}{n^2} \text{ which is convergent.}$$

$$\therefore \quad u_n = \frac{1}{n^2}$$

$$u_{n+1} = \frac{1}{(n+1)^2}$$

$$\therefore \quad \frac{u_{n+1}}{u_n} = \frac{n^2}{(n+1)^2} = \frac{1}{\left(1+\frac{1}{n}\right)^2}$$

$$\therefore \quad \underset{n\to\infty}{\text{Lt}} \frac{u_{n+1}}{u_n} = \underset{n\to\infty}{\text{Lt}} \frac{1}{\left(1+\frac{1}{n}\right)^2}$$

$$= \frac{1}{(1+0)^2} = 1.$$

Thus the test does not give right information when $e = 1$.

SOLVED EXAMPLES

Example 1. Discuss the convergence and divergence of the series:

$$1+\frac{x}{2^2}+\frac{x^2}{3^2}+\frac{x^3}{4^2}+\ldots$$

Solution: Here $\quad u_n = \dfrac{x^{n-1}}{n^2}$

$$\therefore \quad u_{n+1} = \frac{x^n}{(n+1)^2}$$

$$\therefore \quad \frac{u_{n+1}}{u_n} = \frac{x^n}{(n+1)^2} \cdot \frac{n^2}{x^{n-1}}$$

$$= x \cdot \frac{n^2}{(n+1)^2} = x \cdot \frac{1}{\left(1+\frac{1}{n}\right)^2}$$

$$\underset{n\to\infty}{\text{Lt}} \frac{u_{n+1}}{u_n} = x \cdot \underset{n\to\infty}{Lt} \frac{1}{\left(1+\frac{1}{n}\right)^2}$$

$$= x \cdot 1 = x$$

By D-Alembert's Ratio test, the series Σu_n converges if $x < 1$ and diverges if $x > 1$ and for $x = 1$, the test fails.

Now, for $x = 1$

$$\Sigma u_n = \Sigma \frac{1}{n^2}$$

∴ Which is p-series (Auxiliary series for $p = 2 > 1$, for which it converges.)

Thus Σu_n converges if $x \leq 1$ and diverges if $x > 1$.

Example 2. Test the convergence of the series

$$\frac{2}{1} + \frac{2.5.8}{1.5.9} + \frac{2.5.8.11}{1.5.9.13} + \ldots$$

Solution: Here,

$$u_n = \frac{2.5.8.11....(3n+2)}{1.5.9.13...(4n+1)}$$

$$u_{n+1} = \frac{2.5.8.11....(3n+2)(3n+5)}{1.5.9.13....(4n+1)(4n+5)}$$

$$\therefore \quad \frac{u_{n+1}}{u_n} = \frac{2.5.8.11....(3n+2)(3n+5)}{1.5.9....(4n+1)(4n+5)} \cdot \frac{1.5.9...(4n+1)}{2.5.8...(3n+2)}$$

$$\therefore \quad = \frac{3n+5}{4n+5}$$

$$= \frac{3+\frac{5}{n}}{4+\frac{5}{n}}$$

$$\therefore \quad \underset{n\to\infty}{\text{Lt}} \frac{u_{n+1}}{u_n} = \underset{n\to\infty}{Lt} \left(\frac{3+\frac{5}{n}}{4+\frac{5}{n}} \right)$$

$$= \frac{3}{4} < 1.$$

∴ By De-Alembert's ratio test, the series Σu_n converges.

Example 3. Discuss the convergence of the series

$$\frac{x}{a.1^2+b}+\frac{2x^2}{a.2^2+b}+\frac{3x^3}{a.3^2+b}+\ldots$$

Solution: Here,

$$u_n = \frac{nx^n}{a.n^2+b}$$

$$\therefore \qquad u_{n+1} = \frac{(n+1)x^{n+1}}{a.(n+1)^2+b}$$

$$\frac{u_{n+1}}{u_n} = \frac{(n+1)x^{n+1}}{n.x^n}\cdot\frac{(a.n^2+b)}{\left[a.(n+1)^2+b\right]}$$

$$= \left(1+\frac{1}{n}\right)\cdot\frac{x.\left[a+\frac{b}{n^2}\right]}{\left[a\left(1+\frac{1}{n}\right)^2+\frac{b}{n^2}\right]}$$

$$\therefore \qquad \underset{n\to\infty}{\text{Lt}}\frac{u_{n+1}}{u_n} = \underset{n\to\infty}{Lt}\left(1+\frac{1}{n}\right)\frac{x.\underset{n\to\infty}{Lt}\left[a+\frac{b}{n^2}\right]}{\underset{n\to\infty}{Lt}\left[a\left(1+\frac{1}{n}\right)^2+\frac{b}{n^2}\right]}$$

$$= \frac{1.x.a}{a} = x$$

$\therefore$ By D-Alembert's ratio test, the series Σu_n converges if $x < 1$ and diverges if $x > 1$.

for $\quad x = 1$, the test fails

Now, for $\quad x = 1$

$$u_n = \frac{n}{an^2+b}$$

$$\therefore \qquad \underset{n\to\infty}{\text{Lt}}\, u_n = \underset{n\to\infty}{Lt}\frac{1}{an+\frac{b}{n}} = 0$$

$\therefore$ Σu_n may be convergent or divergent.

Let $$v_n = \frac{1}{n}$$

$$\therefore \quad \frac{u_n}{v_n} = \frac{n^2}{a.n^2 + b}$$

$$= \frac{1}{a + \frac{b}{n^2}}$$

$$\therefore \quad \underset{n\to\infty}{\text{Lt}} \frac{u_n}{v_n} = \frac{1}{a} \text{ (non-zero finite)}$$

$\therefore$ Σu_n and Σv_n both are of the same nature, but $\Sigma v_n = \Sigma \frac{1}{n}$ is divergent.

$\therefore$ Σu_n is also divergent.

Thus, Σu_n converges if $x < 1$ and diverges if $x \geq 1$.

Example 4. Test the following series for convergence:

(i) $\Sigma \frac{n!3^n}{n^n}$ (ii) $\frac{n^n}{n!}$

(iii) $\Sigma \frac{2^n - 1}{3^{n-1}}$ (iv) $\frac{x^n}{x^n + a^n}$ $(x > 0, a > 0)$

Solution: (*i*) Here $$u_n = \frac{n!.3^n}{n^n}$$

$$\therefore \quad u_{n+1} = \frac{(n+1)!\ 3^{n+1}}{(n+1)^{n+1}}$$

$$\therefore \quad \frac{u_{n+1}}{u_n} = \frac{(n+1)!}{n!} \frac{3^{n+1}}{3^n} . \frac{n^n}{(n+1)^{n+1}}$$

$$= (n + 1) . 3 . \frac{n^n}{(n+1)^{n+1}}$$

$$= \frac{3 \cdot n^n}{(n+1)^n}$$

$$\frac{u_{n+1}}{u_n} = \frac{3}{\left(1+\frac{1}{n}\right)^n}$$

$$\therefore \quad \underset{n\to\infty}{\text{Lt}} \frac{u_{n+1}}{u_n} = \underset{n\to\infty}{Lt} \frac{3}{\left(1+\frac{1}{n}\right)^n}$$

$$= \frac{3}{e} = \frac{3}{e} > 1.$$

By D-Alembert's ratio test, the series Σu_n diverges.

(ii) Here $u_n = \dfrac{n^n}{n!}$

$$\therefore \quad u_{n+1} = \frac{(n+1)^{n+1}}{(n+1)!}$$

$$\frac{u_{n+1}}{u_n} = \frac{(n+1)^{n+1}}{n^n} \cdot \frac{n!}{(n+1)!}$$

$$= \frac{(n+1)^n}{n^n}$$

$$\frac{u_{n+1}}{u_n} = \left(1+\frac{1}{n}\right)^n$$

$$\therefore \quad \underset{n\to\infty}{\text{Lt}} \frac{u_{n+1}}{u_n} = \underset{n\to\infty}{Lt} \left(1+\frac{1}{n}\right)^n$$

$$= e > 1$$

By D-Alembert's ratio test, the series Σu_n is divergent.

(iii) $u_n = \dfrac{2^n - 1}{3^n - 1}$.

$$\therefore \qquad u_{n+1} = \frac{2^{n+1}-1}{3^{n+1}-1}.$$

$$\therefore \qquad \frac{u_{n+1}}{u_n} = \frac{2^{n+1}-1}{(2^n-1)} \cdot \frac{3^n-1}{3^{n+1}-1}$$

$$= \frac{2}{3} \cdot \frac{\left(1-\frac{1}{2^{n+1}}\right)}{\left(1-\frac{1}{2^n}\right)} \cdot \frac{\left(1-\frac{1}{3^n}\right)}{\left(1-\frac{1}{3^{n+1}}\right)}$$

$$\therefore \qquad \underset{n\to\infty}{\text{Lt}} \frac{u_{n+1}}{u_n} = \underset{n\to\infty}{Lt} \frac{2}{3} \cdot \frac{\left(1-\frac{1}{2^{n+1}}\right)}{\left(1-\frac{1}{2^n}\right)} \cdot \frac{\left(1-\frac{1}{3^n}\right)}{\left(1-\frac{1}{3^{n+1}}\right)} = \frac{2}{3}(<1)$$

$\therefore$ By D-Alembert's ratio test, the series Σu_n is convergent.

(iv) Here $$u_n = \frac{x^n}{x^n + a^n}$$

$$\therefore \qquad u_{n+1} = \frac{x^{n+1}}{x^{n+1} + a^{n+1}}.$$

Case I. When $x < a$.

$$\therefore \qquad \frac{u_{n+1}}{u_n} = \frac{x^{n+1}}{x^n} \cdot \frac{x^n + a^n}{x^{n+1} + a^{n+1}}$$

$$= \frac{x}{a} \cdot \frac{\left[1+\left(\frac{x}{a}\right)^n\right]}{\left[1+\left(\frac{x}{a}\right)^{n+1}\right]}$$

$$\therefore \qquad \underset{n\to\infty}{\text{Lt}} \frac{u_{n+1}}{u_n} = \frac{x}{a} < 1.$$

$\therefore$ By D-Alembert's ratio test, Σu_n is convergent.

Case II. When $x = a$.

then $$u_n = \frac{a^n}{a^n + a^n} = \frac{1}{2} \ \forall n.$$

$\therefore$ $$\underset{n\to\infty}{\text{Lt}}\ u_n = \frac{1}{2}(\neq 0).$$

$\therefore$ Σu_n is divergent for $x = a$.

Case III. When $x > a$.

then $$u_n = \frac{x^n}{x^n + a^n}.$$

$$= \frac{1}{1+\left(\frac{a}{x}\right)^n}$$

$\therefore$ $$\underset{n\to\infty}{\text{Lt}}\ u_n = \frac{1}{1+0} = 1 \ (\neq 0)$$

$\therefore$ Σu_n is diverent. Thus Σu_n

(i) Converges if $x < a$

(ii) Diverges if $x \geq a$.

Example 5. Discuss the convergence of the series

$$\Sigma u_n = \frac{n^2 - 1}{n^2 + 1} . x^n.$$

Solution: Here $$u_n = \frac{n^2 - 1}{n^2 + 1} . x^n$$

$\therefore$ $$u_{n+1} = \frac{(n+1)^2 - 1}{(n+1)^2 + 1} . x^{n+1}$$

$\therefore$ $$\frac{u_{n+1}}{u_n} = \frac{(n+1)^2 - 1}{(n+1)^2 + 1} . \frac{n^2 + 1}{n^2 - 1} . x$$

$$= \frac{\left[\left(1+\frac{1}{n}\right)^2 - \frac{1}{n^2}\right] \cdot \left(1+\frac{1}{n^2}\right)}{\left[\left(1+\frac{1}{n}\right)^2 + \frac{1}{n^2}\right] \cdot \left[1-\frac{1}{n^2}\right]} \cdot x$$

$$\therefore \qquad \underset{n\to\infty}{\text{Lt}} \frac{u_{n+1}}{u_n} = \frac{1.1}{1.1} \cdot x = x$$

$\therefore$ By D-Alembert's ratio test, the series Σu_n converges, if $x < 1$ and diverges if $x > 1$.

For $x = 1$, test fails.

Now, for $\qquad x = 1$

$$u_n = \frac{n^2 - 1}{n^2 + 1}.$$

$$= \left[\frac{1-\frac{1}{n^2}}{1+\frac{1}{n^2}}\right]$$

$$\therefore \qquad \underset{n\to\infty}{\text{Lt}} (u_n) = \underset{n\to\infty}{Lt} \left[\frac{1-\frac{1}{n^2}}{1+\frac{1}{n^2}}\right]$$

$$= 1 \neq 0.$$

$\therefore$ Σu_n is divergent.

Thus, Σu_n, converges, if $x < 1$ and diverges, if $x \geq 1$.

EXERCISE

Test the convergence of the following series:

1. $1 + 3x + 5x^2 + 7x^3 + \ldots$

2. $\frac{1}{1^p} + \frac{x}{3^p} + \frac{x^3}{7^p} + \ldots$

3. $1 + \frac{1^2.2^2}{1.3.5} + \frac{1^2.2^2.3^2}{1.3.5.7.9} + \ldots$

4. $1+\frac{2^p}{2!}+\frac{3^p}{3!}+\frac{4^p}{4!}+...$

5. Show that the series

$$1+\frac{\alpha+1}{\beta+1}+\frac{(\alpha+1)(2\alpha+1)}{(\beta+1)(2\beta+1)}+\frac{(\alpha+1)(2\alpha+1)(3\alpha+1)}{(\beta+1)(2\beta+1)(3\beta+1)}+...$$

6. Discuss the convergence of the series

$$\Sigma\frac{a^n}{x^n+a^n}$$

7. Test for convergence the series given below:

$$\frac{1}{2\sqrt{1}}+\frac{x^2}{3\sqrt{2}}+\frac{x^4}{4\sqrt{3}}+\frac{x^6}{5\sqrt{4}}+...$$

8. Test the convergence of the series given below:

$$1+\frac{2}{5}x+\frac{6}{9}x^2+\frac{14}{17}x^3+...+\frac{2^n-2}{2^n+1}x^{n-1}+...$$

Answers:

1. Convergence $x<1$ and divergence for $x \geq 1$.
2. Convergence for $x<1$ and divergence for $x>1$.
   for $x = 1$, convergent, if $P>1$ and divergence, if $P \leq 1$.
3. Convergent.
4. Convergent.
5. Converges, if $\beta>\alpha>0$ and diverges if $\alpha \geq \beta > 0$ [$\alpha > 0, \beta . 0$]
6. Convergent, if $x>a$ and divergent for $x \leq a$.
7. Convergent, if $x^2 \leq 1$ and divergent for $x^2>1$.
8. Convergent, if $x<1$ and divergent if $x^2 \geq 1$.

COMPARISON OF RATIOS

If Σu_n, Σv_n are two positive terms series, such that:

(i) $\frac{u_n}{u_{n+1}}<\frac{v_n}{v_{n+1}}$

(ii) Σv_n is divergent, then Σu_n is also divergent.

Proof: Given that $\frac{u_{n+1}}{u_n}>\frac{v_{n+1}}{v_n}$

i.e. $$\frac{u_2}{u_1} > \frac{v_2}{v_1}, \frac{u_3}{u_2} > \frac{v_3}{v_2}, \frac{u_4}{u_3} > \frac{v_4}{v_3} \dots$$

Now

$$u_1 + u_2 + u_3 + u_4 + u_5 + \dots = u_1\left[1 + \frac{u_2}{u_1} + \frac{u_3}{u_1} + \frac{u_4}{u_1} + \frac{u_5}{u_1} + \dots\right]$$

$$= u_1\left[1 + \frac{u_2}{u_1} + \frac{u_3}{u_2} \cdot \frac{u_2}{u_1} + \frac{u_4}{u_3} \cdot \frac{u_3}{u_2} \cdot \frac{u_2}{u_1} + \dots\right]$$

$$> u_1\left[1 + \frac{v_2}{v_1} + \frac{v_3}{v_2} \cdot \frac{v_2}{v_1} + \frac{v_4}{v_3} \cdot \frac{v_3}{v_2} \cdot \frac{v_2}{v_1} + \dots\right]$$

$$> \frac{u_1}{v_1}[v_1 + v_2 + v_3 + v_4 + \dots]$$

Series on R.H.S. is divergent, so that the series on L.H.S. is also divergent.

Thus Σu_n is divergent.

Similarly, we can show that:

If (i) $\frac{u_n}{u_{n+1}} > \frac{v_n}{v_{n+1}}$ and

(ii) Σv_n is convergent, then Σu_n is also convergent.

RAABE'S TEST

If Σu_n be a series of positive terms such that

$$\underset{n\to\infty}{\text{Lt}}\ n\left(\frac{u_n}{u_{n+1}} - 1\right) = e, \text{ then } \Sigma u_n$$

(i) Converges, if $e > 1$.

(ii) Diverges, if $e < 1$ and the test fails if, $e = 1$.

Proof: Let $u_1 + u_2 + u_3 + u_4 + \dots$ be the series of positive terms.

Case I: When $e > 1$.

We can find a positive number p such that $e > p > 1$.

Then $\Sigma v_n = \Sigma \frac{1}{n^p}$, is convergent. Then by comparison of ratios, Σu_n is convergent, if after some particular term.

If $$\frac{u_n}{u_{n+1}} > \frac{v_n}{v_{n+1}}$$

If $$\frac{u_n}{u_{n+1}} > \frac{\frac{1}{n^p}}{\frac{1}{(n+1)^p}}$$

If $$\frac{u_n}{u_{n+1}} > \frac{(n+1)^p}{n^p}$$

If $$\frac{u_n}{u_{n+1}} > \left(1+\frac{1}{n}\right)^p$$

If $$> 1 + p.\frac{1}{n} + \frac{p(p-1)}{2!}\frac{1}{n^2} + \frac{p(p-1)(p-2)}{3!}\frac{1}{n^3} + \ldots$$

If $$\frac{u_n}{u_{n+1}} - 1 > \frac{p}{n} + \frac{p(p-1)}{2!}\frac{1}{n^2} + \frac{p(p-1)(p-2)}{3!}\frac{1}{n^3}\ldots$$

If $$n\left(\frac{u_n}{u_{n+1}} - 1\right) > p + \frac{p(p-1)}{2!}\frac{1}{n} + \frac{p(p-1)(p-2)}{3!\,n^2}\ldots$$

If $$\underset{n\to\infty}{\text{Lt}}\; n\left(\frac{u_n}{u_{n+1}} - 1\right) > p$$

If $$e > p$$

Which is true.

$\therefore$ Σu_n converges, if $e > 1$.

Case II: When $e < 1$.

We can find a positive number p, such that $e < p < 1$.

Let $$\Sigma v_n = \Sigma \frac{1}{n^p}, \text{ which is divergent } (\because p < 1)$$

$\therefore$ Σu_n will be divergent, if

$$\frac{u_n}{u_{n+1}} < \frac{v_n}{v_{n+1}}$$

If $$\frac{u_n}{u_{n+1}} < \frac{(n+1)^p}{n^p}$$

$$< \left(1+\frac{1}{n}\right)^p$$

If $$\frac{u_n}{u_{n+1}} < 1+\frac{p}{n}+\frac{p(p-1)}{2!}.\frac{1}{n^2}+\frac{p(p-1)(p-2)}{3!}\frac{1}{n^3}+\ldots$$

If $$\frac{u_n}{u_{n+1}} - 1 < \frac{p}{n}+\frac{p(p-1)}{2!}.\frac{1}{n^2}+\ldots$$

If $$n\left(\frac{u_n}{u_{n+1}}-1\right) < p+\frac{p(p-1)}{2!}.\frac{1}{n}+\ldots$$

If $\underset{n\to\infty}{\text{Lt}}\ n\left(\dfrac{u_n}{u_{n+1}}-1\right) < p.$

If $e < p,$ which is true.

Thus, the series Σu_n is divergent.

SOLVED EXAMPLES

Example 1. Test the convergence of the series

$$\Sigma\frac{n!\ x^n}{3.5.7\ldots(2n+1).}$$

Solution: Here $$u_n = \frac{n!\ x^n}{3.5.7\ldots(2n+1).}$$

$\therefore$ $$u_{n+1} = \frac{(n+1)!\ x^{n+1}}{3.5.7\ \ldots(2n+1)(2n+3)}.$$

$$\therefore \quad \frac{u_{n+1}}{u_n} = \frac{(n+1)!}{n!} \frac{x^{n+1}}{x^n} \cdot \frac{3.5.7 \ldots (2n+1)}{3.5.7 \ldots (2n+1)(2n+3)}$$

$$= (n+1) \cdot x \cdot \frac{1}{(2n+3)}$$

$$= \left(\frac{n+1}{2n+3}\right) \cdot x$$

$$\frac{u_{n+1}}{u_n} = \frac{\left(1+\frac{1}{n}\right)}{\left(2+\frac{3}{n}\right)} \cdot x$$

$$\therefore \quad \underset{n\to\infty}{\text{Lt}} \frac{u_{n+1}}{u_n} = \underset{n\to\infty}{Lt} \frac{\left(1+\frac{1}{n}\right)}{\left(2+\frac{3}{n}\right)} \cdot x$$

$$= \frac{x}{2}$$

Therefore, by D-Alembert's ratio test, the series Σu_n converges, if $\frac{x}{2} < 1$.

i.e. $x < 2$ and diverges, if $\frac{x}{2} > 1$, *i.e.*, $x > 2$.

For $x = 2$, the test fails.

Now, For $x = 2$.

$$\frac{u_{n+1}}{u_n} = \frac{2n+2}{2n+3}$$

$$\therefore \quad \frac{u_n}{u_{n+1}} = \frac{2n+3}{2n+2}$$

$$\therefore \quad \frac{u_n}{u_{n+1}} - 1 = \frac{1}{2n+2}$$

$$\therefore \quad n\left(\frac{u_n}{u_{n+2}}-1\right) = \frac{n}{2n+2}$$

$$n\left(\frac{u_n}{u_{n+2}}-1\right) = \frac{1}{2+\frac{2}{n}}$$

$$\therefore \quad \underset{n\to\infty}{\text{Lt}}\, n\left(\frac{u_n}{u_{n+2}}-1\right) = \underset{n\to\infty}{Lt}\left(\frac{1}{2+\frac{2}{n}}\right)$$

$$= \frac{1}{2} < 1.$$

$\therefore$ By Raabe's test, Σu_n diverges for $x = 2$

Thus, Σu_n converges, if $x < 2$ and diverges, if $x \geq 2$.

Example 2: Discuss the convergence of the series

$$\frac{2}{5}\,.\,x+\frac{2.4}{5.8}x^2+\frac{2.4.6}{5.8.11}x^3+\ldots$$

Solution: Here
$$u_n = \frac{2.4.6\ldots(2n)}{5.8.11\ldots(3n+2)}\,.\,x^n$$

$$\therefore \quad u_{n+1} = \frac{2.4.6\ldots(2n)(2n+2)}{5.8.11\ldots(3n+2)(3n+5)}\,.\,x^{n+1}$$

$$\therefore \quad \frac{u_{n+1}}{u_n} = \frac{(2n+2)}{(3n+5)}\,.\,x$$

$$= \frac{2\left[1+\frac{1}{n}\right].x}{\left(3+\frac{5}{n}\right)}$$

$$\therefore \quad \underset{n\to\infty}{\text{Lt}}\frac{u_{n+1}}{u_n} = \frac{2.x}{3} = \frac{2x}{3}.$$

By D-Alembert's ratio test, Σu_n converges, if $\frac{2x}{3} < 1$, *i.e.*, $x < \frac{3}{2}$ and divergent, if $\frac{2x}{3} > 1$, *i.e.*, $x > \frac{3}{2}$.

For $x = \frac{3}{2}$, the test fails.

Now, for $$x = \frac{3}{2}$$

$$\frac{u_{n+1}}{u_n} = \frac{3n+3}{3n+5}$$

$$\therefore \quad \frac{u_n}{u_{n+1}} = \frac{3n+5}{3n+3}$$

$$\therefore \quad \frac{u_n}{u_{n+1}} - 1 = \frac{2}{2n+3}$$

or $$n\left(\frac{u_n}{u_{n+1}} - 1\right) = \frac{2n}{3n+3}$$

$$\therefore \quad \underset{n\to\infty}{\text{Lt}}\ n\left(\frac{u_n}{u_{n+1}} - 1\right) = \underset{n\to\infty}{Lt}\ \frac{2n}{3n+3} = \frac{2}{3} < 1.$$

By Raabe's test, Σu_n is divergent.

Thus, Σu_n converges, if $x < \frac{3}{2}$ and diverges, if $x \geq \frac{3}{2}$.

EXERCISE

Discuss the convergence of the following series:

1. $\frac{1^2}{4^2} + \frac{1^2.5^2}{4^2.8^2} + \frac{1^2.5^2.9^2}{4^2.8^2.12^2} + \frac{1^2.5^2.9^2.13^2}{4^2.8^2.12^2.16^2} + \ldots$

2. $\frac{3}{7}.x + \frac{3.6}{7.10}x^2 + \frac{3.6.9}{7.10.13}x^3 + \ldots$

3. $\frac{1}{3}x + \frac{1.2}{3.5}x^2 + \frac{1.2.3}{3.5.7}x^3 + \ldots$

4. $1+a+\frac{a(a+1)}{1.2}+\frac{a(a+1)(a+2)}{1.2.3}$

5. $\Sigma\frac{4.7\ldots(3n+1)}{1.2.3\ldots n}x^n$.

6. $\frac{a}{a+3}+\frac{a(a+2)}{(a+3)(a+5)}x+\frac{a(a+2)(a+3)}{(a+3)(a+5)(a+7)}x^2+\ldots$

Answers:

1. Convergent
2. Convergent if $x \leq 1$ and divergent if $x > 1$.
3. Convergent if $x < 2$ and divergent if $x \geq 2$.
4. Convergent if $a \leq 0$ and divergent if $a > 0$.
5. Convergent if $x < \frac{1}{3}$ and divergent if $x \geq \frac{1}{3}$.
6. Convergent if $x \leq 1$ and divergent if $x > 1$.

LOGARITHMIC TEST

If Σu_n is a +ve terms series, such that

$$\underset{n\to\infty}{\text{Lt}}\ n\log\left(\frac{u_n}{u_{n+1}}\right) = e, \text{ then } \Sigma u_n$$

Converges, if $e > 1$ and diverges, if $e < 1$.
For $e = 1$, the test fails.

Proof: Let $u_1 + u_2 + u_3 + u_4 + \ldots u_n + \ldots$ be the series of positive terms.

Case I: When $e > 1$

We can choose a positive number p such that $e > p > 1$.

Now, for this value of p (>1) the series $\Sigma v_n = \frac{1}{n^p}$ is convergent.

Now Σu_n is convergent, if

$$\frac{u_n}{u_{n+1}} > \frac{v_n}{v_{n+1}}$$

If $$\frac{u_n}{u_{n+1}} > \frac{(n+1)^p}{n^p}$$

$$> \left(1+\frac{1}{n}\right)^p$$

If $$\log\left(\frac{u_n}{u_{n+1}}\right) > p\log\left(1+\frac{1}{n}\right)$$

$$> p\left[\frac{1}{n}-\frac{1}{2n^2}+\frac{1}{3n^3}...\right]$$

If $$n\log\left(\frac{u_n}{u_{n+1}}\right) > p\left[\frac{1}{1}-\frac{1}{2n}+\frac{1}{3n^2}...\right]$$

If $$\underset{n\to\infty}{\text{Lt}}\ n\log\left(\frac{u_n}{u_{n+1}}\right) > p$$

If $e > p$, which is true.

$\therefore\ \Sigma u_n$ is convergent, if $e > 1$.

Case II: When $e < 1$

This result is left as an exercise for the students which can be proved in the same way.

SOLVED EXAMPLES

Example 1: Test the convergence of the series

$$1+\frac{2x}{2!}+\frac{3^2.x^2}{3!}+\frac{4^3.x^3}{4!}+\frac{5^4.x^4}{5!}+...$$

Solution: Here $$u_n = \frac{n^{n-1}.x^{n-1}}{n!}$$

$\therefore$ $$u_{n+1} = \frac{(n+1)^n.x^n}{(n+1)!}$$

$$\therefore \qquad \frac{u_{n+1}}{u_n} = \frac{(n+1)^n}{n^{n-1}} \cdot \frac{n!}{(n+1)!} x.$$

$$= \frac{(n+1)^{n-1}}{n^{n-1}} . x$$

$$\in = \left(1+\frac{1}{n}\right)^{n-1} . x$$

$$\therefore \qquad \underset{n\to\infty}{\text{Lt}} \frac{u_{n+1}}{u_n} = ex.$$

$\therefore$ By D-Alembert's ratio test, Σu_n converges, if $ex < 1$ or $x < \frac{1}{e}$ and Σu_n diverges, if $x > \frac{1}{e}$.

For $\qquad x = \frac{1}{e}$, the test fails.

Now, for $\qquad x = \frac{1}{e}$

$$\frac{u_{n+1}}{u_n} = \left(1+\frac{1}{n}\right)^{n-1} . \frac{1}{e}$$

$$\therefore \qquad \frac{u_n}{u_{n+1}} = \frac{e}{\left(1+\frac{1}{n}\right)^{n-1}}$$

$$\therefore \qquad \log\left(\frac{u_n}{u_{n+1}}\right) = \log e - (n-1)\log\left(1+\frac{1}{n}\right)$$

$$= 1 - (n-1)\left[\frac{1}{n} - \frac{1}{2n^2} + \frac{1}{3n^2} \cdots\right]$$

$$= 1 - \left[1 - \frac{1}{2n} + \frac{1}{3n^2} \cdots - \frac{1}{n} + \frac{1}{2n^2} - \frac{1}{3n^3} \cdots\right]$$

$$= \frac{1}{2n} - \frac{1}{3n^2} \cdots + \frac{1}{n} - \frac{1}{2n^2} + \frac{1}{3n^3}$$

$$= \frac{3}{2n} - \frac{5}{6n^2} - \ldots$$

$$\therefore \quad n \log\left(\frac{u_n}{u_{n+1}}\right) = \frac{3}{2} - \frac{5}{6n} \ldots$$

$$\operatorname*{Lt}_{n\to\infty} n \log\left(\frac{u_n}{u_{n+1}}\right) = \frac{3}{2} > 1.$$

$\therefore$ By logarithmic test, Σu_n converges for $x = \frac{1}{e}$.

Thus Σu_n is

(i) Convergent for $x \le \frac{1}{e}$.

(ii) Divergent for $x > \frac{1}{e}$.

Example 2: Test the convergence of the series

$$\frac{(a+x)}{1!} + \frac{(a+2x)^2}{2!} + \frac{(a+3x)^3}{3!} + \ldots$$

Solution: Here $$u_n = \frac{(a+nx)^n}{n!}$$

$$\therefore \quad u_{n+1} = \frac{[a+(n+1)x]^{n+1}}{(n+1)!}$$

$$\therefore \quad \frac{u_{n+1}}{u_n} = \frac{[a+(n+1)x]^{n+1}}{(a+nx)^n} \cdot \frac{n!}{(n+1)!}$$

$$= \frac{[a+(n+1)x]^{n+1}}{(a+nx)^n} \cdot \frac{1}{(n+1)}$$

$$= \frac{(n+1)^{n+1} . x^{n+1}\left[1 + \frac{a}{(n+1)x}\right]^{n+1}}{n^n . x^n \left[1 + \frac{a}{nx}\right]^n . (n+1)}$$

$$= \frac{(n+1)^n . x . \left[1+\frac{(a/x)}{n+1}\right]^{n+1}}{\left[1+\frac{(a/x)}{n}\right]^n}$$

$$\therefore \qquad \underset{n\to\infty}{\text{Lt}} \frac{u_{n+1}}{u_n} = \underset{n\to\infty}{\text{Lt}} \frac{\left(1+\frac{1}{n}\right)^n . x . \left[1+\frac{(a/x)}{n+1}\right]^{n+1}}{\left[1+\frac{(a/x)}{n}\right]^n}$$

$$= e. \, x \, . \, \frac{e^{a/x}}{e^{a/x}}$$

$$\therefore \qquad \underset{n\to\infty}{\text{Lt}} \frac{u_{n+1}}{u_n} = ex.$$

$\therefore$ Σu_n coverges, if $ex < 1$ or $x < \frac{1}{e}$ and Σu_n diverges, if $x > \frac{1}{e}$.

For $x = \frac{1}{e}$, the test fails.

Now, for $\qquad x = \frac{1}{e}$

$$\frac{u_n}{u_{n+1}} = \frac{e.\left[1+\frac{ae}{n}\right]^n}{\left(1+\frac{1}{n}\right)^n . \left[1+\frac{ae}{n+1}\right]^{n+1}}.$$

$$\therefore \qquad \log\left(\frac{u_n}{u_{n+1}}\right) = \log e + n \log\left(1+\frac{ea}{n}\right) - n \log\left(1+\frac{1}{n}\right)$$

$$- (n+1) \log\left(1+\frac{ea}{n+1}\right)$$

$$= 1 + n\left[\frac{ea}{n} - \frac{e^2a^2}{2n^2} + \frac{e^3a^3}{3n^3} \ldots\right]$$

$$-n\left[\frac{1}{n}-\frac{1}{2n^2}+\frac{1}{3n^3}-\frac{1}{4n^4}\cdots\right]-$$

$$(n+1)\,.\left[\frac{ae}{n+1}-\frac{1a^2e^2}{2(n+1)^2}+\frac{1a^3e^3}{3(n+1)^3}\cdots\right]$$

$$n\log\frac{u_n}{u_{n+1}}=n\left[\left(\frac{-e^2a^2}{n}+\frac{1}{2n}\right)+\frac{e^2a^2}{2(n+1)}+\left(\frac{e^3a^3}{3}-\frac{1}{3}\right)\frac{1}{x^2}\cdots\right]$$

$$\underset{n\to\infty}{\text{Lt}}\ n\log\frac{u_n}{u_{n+1}}=\frac{-e^2a^2}{2}+\frac{1}{2}+\frac{e^2a^2}{2}$$

$$=\frac{1}{2}<1.$$

$\therefore\ \Sigma u_n$ diverges, if $x=\frac{1}{e}$

Thus the series Σu_n

(i) Converges, if $x>\frac{1}{e}$.

(ii) Diverges, if $x\geq\frac{1}{e}$.

EXERCISE

Test the convergence of the series

1. $\Sigma\frac{(n-1)^{n-1}}{n^n}$

2. $1^p+\left(\frac{1}{2}\right)^p+\left(\frac{1.3}{2.4}\right)^p+\left(\frac{1.3.5}{2.4.6}\right)^p+\ldots$

3. $\frac{1}{(\log 2)^p}+\frac{1}{(\log 3)^p}+\frac{1}{(\log 4)^p}+\ldots$

Answers:

1. Convergent.
2. Convergent, if $p>2$ and divergent, if $p<2$.
3. Divergent.

INTEGRAL TEST

Let $f(x)$ be a non-negative, monotonically decreasing, integrable function on $[1, \infty]$. Then the series $\sum_{n=1}^{\infty} f(n)$ and the improper integral $\int_1^{\infty} f(x)\,dx$ converge or diverge together, *i.e.,* the series $\Sigma f(n)$ converges or diverges accordingly as $\int_1^{\infty} f(x)\,dx$ tends to a definite limit or ∞.

SOLVED EXAMPLES

Example 1. Apply integral test to prove the convergence of $\sum \frac{1}{n\sqrt{n^2-1}}$.

Solution: Here $\quad f(n) = \frac{1}{n\sqrt{n^2-1}} \quad$ for $n \in [2, \infty]$

$\because$ $f(n) > 0$ and monotonically decreasing when $n \geq 2$.

$$\therefore \quad \int_2^n \frac{1}{x\sqrt{x^2-1}}\,dx = \left[\sec^{-1} x\right]_2^n = \sec^{-1}(n) - \sec^{-1}(2)$$

$$\therefore \quad \underset{n\to\infty}{\text{Lt}} \int_2^n \frac{1}{x\sqrt{x^2-1}}\,dx = \underset{n\to\infty}{\text{Lt}} [\sec^{-1}(n) - \sec^{-1}(2)]$$

$$= \frac{\pi}{2} - \sec^{-1} 2$$ which is finite, therefore by Cauchy's integral test, the series

$$\Sigma f(n) = \sum_{n=2}^{\infty} \frac{1}{n\sqrt{n^2-1}}$$ is convergent.

Example 2. Using integral test, check the convergence of the series $\sum \frac{1}{n^2+1}$.

Solution: Here $\quad f(x) = \frac{1}{x^2+1}$

$\therefore$ $f(x) > 0$ and it is monotonically decreasing in $(1, \infty)$.

$$\therefore \quad \int_1^{\infty} \frac{1}{x^2+1}\,dx = \left(\tan^{-1} x\right)_1^{\infty} = \tan^{-1}(\infty) - \tan^{-1}(1)$$

$$= \frac{\pi}{2} - \frac{\pi}{4} = \frac{\pi}{4} \text{ (finite)}$$

$\therefore$ By integral test, the series $\sum \frac{1}{n^2+1}$ is convergent.

Example 3. Show by integral test that the series $\Sigma \frac{1}{n^p}$ $(p > 0)$ converges, if $p > 1$ and diverges, if $p \leq 1$.

Solution: Let $f(n) = \frac{1}{n^p}$, $p > 0$ and $n \in [1, \infty]$, thus $f(n) > 0$ and is monotonically decreasing on $[1, \infty]$.

$$\therefore \quad I = \int_1^n \frac{1}{x^p}\,dx = \int_1^n x^{-p}\,dx$$

$$= \begin{cases} \dfrac{n^{1-p}}{1-p} - \dfrac{1}{1-p} & \text{if } p \neq 1. \\ \log n & \text{if } p = 1. \end{cases}$$

If $\quad p > 1 \; \underset{n\to\infty}{\text{Lt}} \; I = 0 - \frac{1}{1-p} = \frac{1}{1-p}$

If $p < 1$ then $\underset{n\to\infty}{\text{Lt}} \; I_n = \infty$

$\therefore \sum_{n=1}^{\infty} \frac{1}{n^p}$ $(p > 0)$

(i) Converges, if $p > 1$.

(ii) Diverges, if $p \leq 1$.

ALTERNATING SERIES

Definition :

An infinite series in which the terms are alternatively positive and negative is called an Alternating Series.

Leibnitz's test for convergence of an alternating series S$(-1)^{n-1}$. u_n.

The alternating series

$$u_1 - u_2 + u_3 - u_4 + u_5 + \ldots (-1)^{n-1}\, u_n + \ldots (u_n > 0).$$

converges, if

(i) $u_{n+1} < u_n \quad \forall\, n.$

and (ii) $\underset{n\to\infty}{\text{Lt}}\; u_n = 0$

Proof: The given series is:

$$u_1 - u_2 + u_3 - u_4 + u_5 - u_6 + \ldots$$

Since

(i) $u_1 > u_2,\, u_3 > u_4,\, u_5 > u_6$

$\therefore \quad u_1 - u_2 > 0, \;\; u_3 - u_4 > 0, \;\; u_5 - u_6 > 0.$

(ii) $\underset{n\to\infty}{\text{Lt}}\; u_n = 0$

Then
$$S_{2n} = u_1 - u_2 + u_3 - u_4 + u_5 - u_6 + \ldots$$
$$= (u_1 - u_2) + (u_3 - u_4) + (u_5 - u_6) + \ldots$$

Since each term within the bracket is +ve

$$\therefore \quad S_{2n} > 0$$
$$S_{2n+1} = u_1 - u_2 + u_3 - u_4 + \ldots - u_{2n} + u_{2n+1}$$
$$S_{2n+1} = u_1 - [(u_2 - u_3) + (u_4 - u_5) + \ldots + (u_{2n} - u_{2n+1})]$$

The quantity within each bracket is +ve.

$$\therefore \quad S_{2n+1} \leq u_1$$

Thus S_{2n} is +ve and increases with n and always remains less than u_1.

$$\therefore \quad S_{2n+1} = S_{2n} + u_{2n+1}$$

$$\therefore \quad \underset{n\to\infty}{\text{Lt}}\; S_{2n+1} = \underset{n\to\infty}{\text{Lt}}\; S_{2n} + \underset{n\to\infty}{Lt}\; u_{2n+1}$$

$$\underset{n\to\infty}{\text{Lt}}\; S_{2n+1} = \underset{n\to\infty}{\text{Lt}}\; S_{2n} + 0$$

Thus $\underset{n\to\infty}{\text{Lt}} S_n$ tends to the same limit.

Hence, the given series is convergent.

SOLVED EXAMPLES

Example 1. $\frac{1}{1.2}-\frac{1}{3.4}+\frac{1}{5.6}-\frac{1}{7.8}+\ldots$

Solution:
$$u_n = \frac{(-1)^{n-1}.1}{(2n-1)(2n)}$$

$$\therefore \quad |u_n| = \frac{1}{(2n-1)(2n)}$$

$$\therefore \quad |u_{n+1}| = \frac{1}{(2n+1)(2n+2)}$$

$$\therefore \quad |u_{n+1}| - |u_n| = \frac{1}{(2n+1)(2n+2)} - \frac{1}{(2n-1)(2n)}$$

$$= \frac{(2n-1)\,2n-(2n+1)(2n+2)}{(2n-1)(2n)(2n+1)(2n+2)}$$

$$= \frac{-8n-2}{(2n-1)(2n)(2n+1)(2n+2)}$$

$$= \frac{-2(4+1)}{(2n-1)(2n)(2n+1)(2n+2)} < 0$$

$$\therefore \quad u_{n+1} - u_n < 0$$

$$\therefore \quad (u_{n+1}) < u_n$$

and
$$u_n = \frac{(-1)^{n-1}.1}{(2n-1)(2n)}$$

$$\therefore \quad \underset{n\to\infty}{\text{Lt}}\ u_n = 0$$

Thus by Leibnitz's test, the given series is convergent.

Example 2. Test the convergence of the series.

$$\frac{1}{\log 2}-\frac{1}{\log 3}+\frac{1}{\log 4}-\frac{1}{\log 5}+\ldots$$

Solution: Here $u_n = \dfrac{1}{\log n}$

$$\therefore \quad u_{n+1} = \frac{1}{\log(n+1)}$$

$$\therefore \quad u_{n+1} - u_n = \frac{1}{\log(n+1)} - \frac{1}{\log n}$$

$$= \frac{\log(n)-\log(n+1)}{\log(n+1)\log(n)}$$

$$\therefore \quad \log(n+1) > \log(n)$$

$$\therefore \quad u_{n+1} - u_n < 0$$

or $$u_{n+1} < u_n \qquad \ldots(1)$$

and $$u_n = \frac{1}{\log(n)}$$

$$\therefore \quad \underset{n\to\infty}{\text{Lt}}\, u_n = \underset{n\to\infty}{Lt}\, \frac{1}{\log(n)} = 0$$

Thus, by Leibnitz's test the alternating series is convergent.

Example 3. Discuss the convergence of the series

$$x-\frac{x^2}{2}+\frac{x^3}{3}-\frac{x^4}{4}+\frac{x^5}{5}\ldots$$

Solution: Here $u_n = (-1)^{n-1} \cdot \dfrac{x^n}{n}$

$$\therefore \quad u_{n+1} = (-1)^n \frac{x^{n+1}}{(n+1)}$$

$$\left|\frac{u_{n+1}}{u_n}\right| = \left|\frac{x^{n+1}}{n+1}\cdot\frac{n}{x^n}\right|$$

$$= |x| \cdot \frac{n}{n+1}$$

$$\therefore \qquad \underset{n\to\infty}{\text{Lt}} \left|\frac{u_{n+1}}{u_n}\right| = |x| \cdot \underset{n\to\infty}{\text{Lt}} \left(\frac{1}{1+\frac{1}{n}}\right)$$

$$= |x| .1 = |x|$$

$\therefore$ By Leibnitz's test the given series converges, if $|x| < 1$ and diverges, if $|x| > 1$.

for $\qquad |x| = 1$ the test fails

for $\qquad x = 1$, we get

$$u_n = (-1)^n \cdot \frac{1}{n}$$

$$\therefore \qquad |u_n| = \frac{1}{n}$$

$$|u_{n+1}| = \frac{1}{n+1}$$

It is obvious that $u_{n+1} < u_n$

$$\underset{n\to\infty}{\text{Lt}}\ u_n = \underset{n\to\infty}{\text{Lt}}\ \frac{1}{n}$$

$$= 0$$

$\therefore$ By Leibnitz's test the given series is convergent.

Thus, the given series is:

(i) converges, if $|x| \leq 1$ (ii) diverges, if $|x| > 1$.

ABSOLUTE CONVERGENCE

An infinite altenating series Σu_n is said to be absolutely convergent, if Σu_n and $\Sigma |u_n|$ both are convergent.

CONDITIONAL CONVERGENCE

An alternating series Σu_n is said to be conditionally convergent, if Σu_n converges but $\Sigma |u_n|$ does not converge.

Example 4. Discuss the absolute or conditional convergence of the series

$$x - \frac{x^2}{2} + \frac{x^3}{3} - \frac{x^4}{4} + \frac{x^5}{5} \ldots$$

Solution: Here the given series is

$$x - \frac{x^2}{2} + \frac{x^3}{3} - \frac{x^4}{4} + \frac{x^5}{5} \ldots$$

$$\therefore \qquad \Sigma |u_n| = x + \frac{x^2}{2} + \frac{x^3}{3} + \frac{x^4}{4} + \frac{x^5}{5} \ldots$$

$$u_n = \frac{x^n}{n}$$

$$\therefore \qquad u_{n+1} = \frac{x^{n+1}}{(n+1)}$$

$$\therefore \qquad \left|\frac{u_{n+1}}{u_n}\right| = |x| \frac{n}{n+1}$$

$$\therefore \qquad \underset{n\to\infty}{\text{Lt}} \left|\frac{u_{n+1}}{u_n}\right| = |x| \,.\, \underset{n\to\infty}{\text{Lt}} \left(\frac{1}{1+\frac{1}{n}}\right)$$

$$= |x| \,.\, 1 = |x|$$

$\Sigma |u_n|$ converges, if $|x| < 1$ and diverges, if $|x| > 1$.

For $|x| = 1$, the test fails

for $x = 1$

$$u_n = \frac{1}{n} \,.\, (-1)^{n-1}$$

$$\therefore \qquad |u_{n+1}| < |u_n|$$

and

$$\underset{n\to\infty}{\text{Lt}} u_n = \underset{n\to\infty}{\text{Lt}} \left(\frac{1}{n}\right)$$

$$= 0$$

$\therefore$ By Leibnitz's test, the series converges.

Now, for $x = 1 \ \Sigma|u_n| = \Sigma\frac{1}{n}$

$\therefore$ For $x = 1, \Sigma\frac{1}{n}$ is divergent.

$\therefore$ $\Sigma|u_n|$ is divergent.

Hence, Σu_n is conditionally convergent.

Example 5. Show that the series

$\frac{2}{1^2}-\frac{3}{2^2}+\frac{4}{3^2}-\frac{5}{4^2}+\ldots$ converges conditionally.

Solution: The given series is an alternating series $\sum_{n=1}^{\infty}(-1)^{n-1} u_n$, where

$$u_n = \frac{n+1}{n^2} > 0.$$

Now,
$$u_n - u_{n+1} = \frac{n+1}{n^2} - \frac{n+2}{(n+1)^2}$$

$$= \frac{n^3+1+3n^2+3n-2n^2}{n^2(n+1)^2}$$

$$= \frac{n^2+3n+1}{n^2(n+1)^2} > 0 \quad \forall n.$$

$\therefore$
$$u_n - u_{n+1} > 0 \ \forall n$$

$\Rightarrow$
$$u_n > u_{n+1}$$

$$\underset{n\to\infty}{\text{Lt}} u_n = \underset{n\to\infty}{\text{Lt}} \left(\frac{n+1}{n^2}\right)$$

$$= \underset{n\to\infty}{\text{Lt}} \left(\frac{1}{n}+\frac{1}{n^2}\right) = 0$$

By Leibnitz's test, the given series is convergent.

Now,
$$|(-1)^{n-1} u_n| = \frac{n+1}{n^2}$$

Let $$v_n = \frac{1}{n}.$$

$$\underset{n\to\infty}{\text{Lt}} \frac{u_n}{v_n} = \underset{n\to\infty}{\text{Lt}} \frac{n+1}{n}$$

$$= \underset{n\to\infty}{\text{Lt}} \frac{\left(1+\frac{1}{n}\right)}{1} = 1 \times (\neq 0) \text{ finite.}$$

$\therefore$ By comparison test, both the series are either convergent or divergent.

But $$\Sigma v_n = \Sigma \frac{1}{n} \text{ is divergent}$$

$\therefore$ $\Sigma|u_n|$ is also divergent.

Thus, the given alternating series is conditionally convergent.

EXERCISE

1. Test the convergence of the series

$$1 - \frac{1}{1!} + \frac{1}{2!} - \frac{1}{3!} + \frac{1}{4!} \ldots$$

2. $\log\left(\frac{2}{1}\right) - \log\left(\frac{3}{2}\right) + \log\left(\frac{4}{3}\right) - \log + \left(\frac{5}{4}\right) + \ldots$

3. Test the series given below for convergence:

$$\frac{1}{x} - \frac{1}{x+a} + \frac{1}{x+2a} - \frac{1}{x+3a} + \ldots \qquad x > 0, a > 0$$

4. Test the absolute or conditional convergence af the series given below:

(i) $\sum$

(ii) $\Sigma(-1)^{n-1} \frac{n^2}{(n+1)!}$

(iii) $\sum_{n=1}^{\infty} (-1)^{n+1}.\left(\sqrt{n+1} - \sqrt{n}\right)$

(iv) $\sum_{n=1}^{\infty} \frac{(-1)^{n-1}}{\left(\sqrt{n}+\sqrt{a}\right)^{2}}$

Answers:

1. Convergent.
2. Convergent.
3. Convergent.
4. (i) Absolutely convergent.
   (ii) Absolutely convergent.
   (iii) Conditionally convergent.
   (iv) Conditionally convergent.

3

Successive Differentiation

INTRODUCTION

Let $y = f(x)$ be a function of x, then $\dfrac{dy}{dx}$ is either constant or a function of x.

If this is differentiated again, then this derivative is denoted by $\dfrac{d}{dx}\left[\dfrac{dy}{dx}\right] = \dfrac{d^2y}{dx^2}$, called the second order derivative of y. Here in this chapter we will disucss the ways of finding the nth derivatives of functions, which can be expressed in terms of some standard functions whose n^{th} derivatives are known to us.

n^{th} DERIVATIVES OF SOME STANDARD FUNCTIONS

(*i*) If $y = e^{ax}$

then

$$y_1 = ae^{ax}$$

$$y_2 = a^2e^{ax}$$

$$y_3 = a^3e^{ax}$$

$$y_n = a^ne^{ax}$$

$$\vdots$$

Thus $\boxed{y_n = a^n e^{ax}}$

(*ii*) If $$y = \log (ax + b)$$

then $$y_1 = \frac{a}{ax+b}$$

$$= a \,.\, (ax + b)^{-1}$$

$$y_2 = a(-1) \,.\, (ax + b)^{-2} \,.\, a$$

$$= a^2 (-1) \,.\, (ax + x)^{-2}$$

$$y_3 = a^2 (-1) (-2) (ax + b)^{-3} \,.\, a$$

$$= a^3(-1)^2 \,.\, 2! \,(ax + b)^{-3}$$

$$\vdots$$

$$y_n = a^n (-1)^{n-1} (n - 1)! \,(ax + b)^{-n}$$

Thus $$\boxed{\begin{aligned} &\text{if } \boldsymbol{y = \log(ax+b)} \\ &\boldsymbol{y_n = a^n (-1)^{n-1} .(n-1)!(ax+b)^{-n}} \end{aligned}}$$

(*iii*) If $$y = (ax + b)^m$$

$$y_1 = m \,.\, a\, (ax + b)^{m-1}$$

$$y_2 = m(m - 1) \,.\, a^2 (ax + b)^{m-2}$$

$$y_3 = m(m - 1) (m - 2) \,.\, a^3 (ax + b)^{m-3}$$

$$\vdots$$

$$y_n = m(m - 1) (m - 2) \ldots [m - (n - 1)].a^n(ax + b)^{m-n}$$

$$y_n = m(m - 1) (m - 2) \ldots (m - n + 1) \,.\, a^n (ax + b)^{m-n}$$

(*a*) When *m* is a +ve integer

Case I. When $m > n$

$$y_n = \frac{m(m-1)\ldots(m-n+1)(m-n)(m-n-1)\ldots 3.2.1\, a^n}{(m-n)(m-n-1)\ldots 3.2.1}$$

$$= .\, (ax + b)^{m-n}$$

$$\boxed{\boldsymbol{y_n = \frac{m!}{(m-n)!} a^n (ax+b)^{m-n}}}$$

Case II. When $m = n$

$$y_n = \frac{n!}{0!} a^n (ax + b)^0$$

$$\boxed{y_n = n! a^n}$$

Case III. When $\mathbf{m < n}$

$$y_n = 0$$

(*b*) When $m = -1$

$$y_n = (-1)(-2)(-3) \ldots (-1 - n + 1) \, . \, a^n (ax + b)^{-1-n}$$

$$\boxed{y_n = (-1)^n . n! a^n (ax + b)^{-(n+1)}}$$

Case IV. If $y = \sin (ax + b)$

then $y_1 = \cos (ax + b) \, . \, a$

$$= a \, . \, \sin \left(ax + b + \frac{\pi}{2} \right)$$

$$y_2 = a \, . \, \cos \left(ax + b + \frac{\pi}{2} \right) \, . \, a$$

$$= -a^2 \, . \, \sin \left(ax + b + \frac{\pi}{2} \right)$$

$$= a^2 \, . \, \sin \left(ax + b + 2\frac{\pi}{2} \right)$$

$$\vdots$$

$$\boxed{y_n = a^n \sin \left(ax + b + \frac{n\pi}{2} \right)}$$

Case V. If $y = \cos (ax + b)$

then $$\boxed{y_n = a^n . \cos \left(ax + b + \frac{n\pi}{2} \right)}$$

Case VI. When $y = e^{ax} . \sin(bx + c)$

$$y_1 = ae^{ax} . \sin(bx + c) + b\, e^{ax} . \cos(bx + c)$$

$$= e^{ax}[a \sin(bx + c) + b \cos(bx + c)]$$

Let $a = r\cos\theta,\ b = r\sin\theta.,$

then $y_1 = e^{ax}[r\sin(bx + c) . \cos\theta + r\cos(bx + c)\sin\theta]$

$$= r\, e^{ax} . \sin(bx + c + \theta)$$

Similarly, we have

$$y_2 = r^2 e^{ax} . \sin(bx + c + 2\theta)$$

$$y_3 = r^3 e^{ax} . \sin(bx + c + 3\theta)$$

$$\vdots$$

$$y_n = r^n e^{ax} . \sin(bx + c + n\theta)$$

$$= \left(a^2 + b^2\right)^{\frac{n}{2}} . e^{ax} . \sin\left\{bx + c + n.\tan^{-1}\left(\frac{b}{a}\right)\right\}$$

$$\boxed{\boldsymbol{y_n = \left(a^2 + b^2\right)^{\frac{n}{2}} .e^{ax} .\sin\left(bx + c + n.\tan^{-1}\left(\frac{b}{a}\right)\right)}}$$

Similarly, if $y = e^{ax} . \cos(bx + c)$

Then $$\boxed{\boldsymbol{y_n = \left(a^2 + b^2\right)^{\frac{n}{2}} .e^{ax} .\cos\left(bx + c + n.\tan^{-1}\left(\frac{b}{a}\right)\right)}}$$

SOLVED EXAMPLES

Example 1. If $y = \sin kx + \cos kx$, show that

$$y_n = k^n \{1 + (-1)^n \sin 2kx\}^{1/2}$$

Solution: Given that

$$y = \sin kx + \cos kx$$

$$\therefore \quad y_n = k^n \sin\left(kx + \frac{n\pi}{2}\right) + k^n \cos\left(kx + \frac{n\pi}{2}\right)$$

$$= k^n \left\{\left[\sin\left(kx+\frac{n\pi}{2}\right)+\cos\left(kx+\frac{n\pi}{2}\right)\right]^2\right\}^{1/2}$$

$$= k^n \left\{\sin^2\left(kx+\frac{n\pi}{2}\right)+\cos^2\left(kx+\frac{n\pi}{2}\right)\right.$$

$$\left.+2\sin\left(kx+\frac{n\pi}{2}\right)\cos\left(kx+\frac{n\pi}{2}\right)\right\}^{1/2}$$

$$= k^n \left\{1+\sin 2\left(kx+\frac{n\pi}{2}\right)\right\}^{1/2}$$

$$= k^n[1 + \sin (2kx + n\pi)]^{1/2}$$

$$= k^n[1 + \sin 2kx .\cos n\pi]^{1/2}$$

$$= k^n[1 + (-1)^n \sin 2kx]^{1/2}.$$

Example 2. Find the nth derivative of

$$y = \frac{3x-1}{(x-1)(x+4)}.$$

Solution: Here

$$y = \frac{3x-1}{(x-1)(x+4)}$$

$$y = \frac{2}{5}.\frac{1}{x-1}+\frac{13}{5}.\frac{1}{(x+4)}$$

$$y = \frac{2}{5}(x-1)^{-1} + \frac{13}{5}(x+4)^{-1}$$

Now, differentiating n times, we get

$$y_n = \frac{2}{5}.(-1)^n\, n!\,(x-1)^{-(n+1)} + \frac{13}{5}(-1)^n\, n!\,(x+4)^{-(n+1)}$$

$$= (-1)^n\, n!\left[\frac{2}{5}.(x-1)^{-(n+1)}+\frac{13}{15}(x+4)^{-(n+1)}\right]$$

$$= (-1)^n\, n!\left[\frac{2}{5(x-1)^{n+1}}+\frac{13}{5}\frac{1}{(x+4)^{n+1}}\right]$$

Example 3. Find the nth derivative of sin 5x cos 2x.

Solution: Here
$$y = \sin 5x \cos 2x$$
$$= \frac{1}{2}[2\sin 5x \cos 2x]$$
$$y = \frac{1}{2}\,.\sin 7x + \frac{1}{2}\sin 3x$$

Differentiating n times, we get,
$$y_n = \frac{1}{2}7^n \sin\left(7x+\frac{n\pi}{2}\right) + \frac{1}{2}3^n\,.\sin\left(3x+\frac{n\pi}{2}\right)$$
$$= \frac{1}{2}7^n \sin\left(7x+\frac{n\pi}{2}\right) + \frac{3^n}{2}\,.\sin\left(3x+\frac{n\pi}{2}\right)$$

Example 4. If $y = \tan^{-1} x$, prove that
$$y_n = (n-1)!\cos\left\{ny+(n-1)\frac{\pi}{2}\right\}\cos^n y.$$

Solution: Here
$$y = \tan^{-1} x \qquad ...(1)$$
$$\therefore \qquad y_1 = \frac{1}{1+x^2} = \frac{1}{(x+i)(x-i)}$$
$$= \frac{1}{2i}\left[\frac{1}{(x-i)}-\frac{1}{(x+i)}\right]$$
$$= \frac{1}{2i}[(x-i)^{-1}-(x+i)^{-1}] \qquad ...(2)$$

Now, differentiating $(n-1)$ times, we get
$$y_n = \frac{1}{2i}[(-1)^{n-1}(n-1)!\,(x-i)^{-n}-(-1)^{n-1}(n-1)!\,(x+i)^{-n}]$$
$$= \frac{1}{2i}(-1)^{n-!}(n-1)!\,[(x-i)^{-n}-(x+i)^{-n}]$$

Let $\qquad x = r\cos\phi,\ 1 = r\sin\phi,$

then
$$y_n = \frac{(-1)^{n-1}}{2i}(n-1)!\,[r^{-n}(\cos\phi - i\sin\phi)^{-n} - r^{-n}.\,(\cos\phi - i\sin\phi)^{-n}]$$

$$= \frac{(-1)^{n-1}}{2i} (n-1)!\, r^{-n} [\cos n\phi + i \sin n\phi$$

$$- \cos n\phi + i \sin n\phi]$$

$$= (-1)^{n-1} (n-1)!\, r^{-n} \sin n\phi$$

$$y_n = (-1)^{n-1} (n-1)! \sin^n\phi \sin n\phi \qquad \text{...(3)}$$

Given that $y = \tan^{-1}x$

$\therefore$ $x = \tan y$

and $x = \cot \phi$ (as assumed)

$\therefore$ $\cot \phi = \tan y$

$$y = \frac{\pi}{2} - \phi$$

or $\phi = \frac{\pi}{2} - y$

$\therefore$

$$y_n = (n-1)! \sin^n \left(\frac{\pi}{2} - y\right) .\cos (n-1)\pi.\sin n \left(\frac{\pi}{2} - y\right)$$

$$= (n-1)! \cos^n y \,.\, \sin \left[\frac{n\pi}{2} - ny - (n-1)\pi\right]$$

$$= (n-1)! \cos^n y \sin \left[-ny - \frac{n\pi}{2} + \pi\right]$$

$$= (n-1)! \cos^n y \cos \left[\frac{\pi}{2} + ny + \frac{n\pi}{2} - \pi\right]$$

$$= (n-1)! \cos^n y \cos \left[ny + (n-1)\frac{\pi}{2}\right]$$

$$y_n = (n-1)! \cos (ny + (n-1)\frac{\pi}{2}) \cos^n y.$$

Example 5. If $y = x \log\left(\frac{x-1}{x+1}\right)$, prove that

$$y_n = (-1)^n (n-2)! \left[\frac{x-n}{(x-1)^n} - \frac{x+n}{(x+1)^n}\right]$$

Solution: Here $$y = x\log\left(\frac{x-1}{x+1}\right)$$

$$y = x\log(x-1) - x\log(x+1) \qquad ...(1)$$

Differentiating w.r.t. x, we get

$$y_1 = 1\,.\log(x-1) + x\,.\,\frac{1}{x-1} - 1\,.\log(x+1) - \frac{x}{x+1}$$

$$= \log(x-1) - \log(x+1) + \frac{1}{x-1} + \frac{1}{x+1}$$

$$y_1 = \log(x-1) - \log(x+1) + (x-1)^{-1} + (x+1)^{-1}$$

Now differentiating $(n-1)$ times, we have

$$y_n = (-1)^{n-2}(n-2)!\,[(x-1)^{-(n-1)} - (x+1)^{-n-1}]$$

$$+ (-1)^{n-1}(n-1)!\,[(x-1)^{-n} + (x+1)^{-n}]$$

$$= (-1)^n (n-2)!\,[(x-1)^{-n}\{(x-1)-(n-1)\}$$

$$-(x+1)^{-n}(x+1+n-1)]$$

$$y_n = (-1)^n (n-2)!\left[\frac{x-n}{(x-1)^n} - \frac{x+n}{(x+1)^n}\right].$$

Example 6. Find the nth derivative of $\tan^{-1}\left(\frac{x}{a}\right)$.

Solution: $$y = \tan^{-1}\left(\frac{x}{a}\right) \qquad ...(1)$$

Differentiating (1) w.r.t. x, we have

$$y_1 = \frac{a}{x^2+a^2} \qquad ...(2)$$

$$= \frac{a}{(x+ia)(x-ia)}$$

$$= \frac{1}{2i}\left[\frac{1}{(x-ia)} - \frac{1}{(x+ia)}\right]$$

$$y_1 = \frac{1}{2i}[(x - ia)^{-1} - (x + ia)^{-1}] \qquad (3)$$

Differentiating (3), $(n - 1)$ times w.r.t. x, we have

$$y_n = \frac{1}{2i}[(-1)^{n-1} . (n - 1)!\{(x - ia)^{-n} - (x + ia)^{-n}\}]$$

$$y_n = \frac{1}{2i}(-1)^{n-1} . (n - 1)!\{(x - ia)^{-n} - (x + ia)^{-n}\}$$

Putting $x = r\cos\phi$, $a = r\sin\phi$,

$$y_n = \frac{1}{2i}(-1)^{n-1} . (n - 1)!r^{-n}[\cos\phi - i\sin\phi)^{-n}$$

$$- (\cos\phi + i\sin\phi)^{-n}]$$

$$= \frac{(-1)^{n-1}.(n-1)!}{2i} r^{-n}. 2i\sin n\phi$$

$$= (-1)^{n-1}(n - 1)!\, r^{-n}. \sin n\phi$$

$$= \frac{(-1)^{n-1}.(n-1)!}{a^n}\sin^n\phi \sin n\phi$$

$$\therefore \qquad y_n = \frac{(-1)^{n-1}.(n-1)!}{a^n}\sin^n\phi \sin n\phi$$

where $\phi = \tan^{-1}\left(\frac{x}{a}\right)$

Example 7. Prove that the nth derivative of $\frac{x^3}{x^2-1}$ for $x = 0$, is zero, when n is even and $-(n!)$, when n is odd and greater than one.

Solution: Here $y = \frac{x^3}{x^2-1}$

$$= x + \frac{x}{x^2-1}$$

$$y = x + \frac{1}{2(x-1)} + \frac{1}{2(x+1)}$$

$$= x + \frac{1}{2}(x-1)^{-1} + \frac{1}{2}(x+1)^{-1}$$

Differentiating n times, we get

$$y_n = +\frac{1}{2} \cdot (-1)^n \cdot n! \; [(x-1)^{-(n+1)} + (x+1)^{-(n+1)}]$$

If $n > 1$

for $\qquad x = 0$

$$y_n(0) = +\frac{1}{2} \cdot (-1)^n \cdot n! \; [(-1)^{-(n+1)} + (1)^{-(n+1)}]$$

Case I. If n is even, then $(n + 1)$ is odd and consequently $(-1)^{n+1} = -1$.

$$\therefore \quad y_n(0) = +\frac{1}{2} \cdot (-1)^n \cdot n! \; [-1 + 1] = 0$$

$$\therefore \quad y_n(0) = 0$$

Case II. If n is odd, then $(n + 1)$ is even

$$\therefore \quad (-1)^{n+1} = +1.$$

and
$$y_n(0) = -\frac{1}{2}(-1)^n \cdot n! \; [1 + 1]$$

$$= -\frac{1}{2} 1 \cdot n! \; 2$$

$$y_n(0) = -(n!)$$

Thus
$$y_n(0) = 0, \text{ if } n \text{ is even}$$
$$= -(n!), \text{ if } n \text{ is odd.}$$

Example 8. Find the nth derivative of $e^{2x}. \sin 3x \cdot \cos 2x$.

Solution: Here
$$y = e^{2x}. \sin^3 x \cdot \cos^2 x$$

$$y = \frac{e^{2x}}{2}[2 \sin 3x \cdot \cos 2x]$$

$$= \frac{e^{2x}}{2}[\sin 5x + \sin x]$$

$$\therefore \qquad y = \frac{1}{2} e^{2x} \, . \, \sin 5x + \frac{1}{2} e^{2x} \sin x \qquad ...(1)$$

Differentiating n times, we have

$$y_n = \frac{1}{2}(2^2 + 5^2)^{n/2} \sin\left[5x + n\tan^{-1}\left(\frac{5}{2}\right)\right]$$

$$+ \frac{1}{2}(2^2 + 1^2)^{n/2} \sin\left[x + n\tan^{-1}\left(\frac{1}{2}\right)\right]$$

$$y_n = \frac{1}{2}\left[(29)^{n/2} \sin\left\{5x + n.\tan^{-1}\left(\frac{5}{2}\right)\right\}\right.$$

$$\left. + 5^{n/2} \sin\left(x + n.\tan^{-1}\frac{1}{2}\right)\right].$$

EXERCISE

1. Find the nth derivative of the following:

(i) $y = \dfrac{x^2 + 4x + 1}{x^3 + 2x^2 - x - 2}$

(ii) $y = \dfrac{1}{(1 - 5x + 6x^2)}$

(iii) $y = \tan^{-1}\left(\dfrac{2x}{1 - x^2}\right)$

(iv) $y = \dfrac{x^4}{(x-1)(x-2)}$

(v) $y = \dfrac{x^4}{(x-1)^2(x-2)}$

(vi) $y = e^{ax} \, . \, \cos^2 bx.$

2. If $y = \frac{1}{2} \log \left(\frac{2x+1}{x-2}\right)$, show that

$$y_n = \frac{1}{2} . (-1)^{n-1} . (n-1)! \left[\frac{2^n}{(2x+1)^n} - \frac{1}{(x-2)^n}\right].$$

3. If $y = e^{x\cos\beta} \cos (x \sin\beta)$, show that

$y_n = e^{x\cos\beta} . \cos (x \sin \beta + n\beta)$.

4. If $y = x \log (x + 1)$, show that

$$y_n = \frac{(-1)^{n-2} .(n-2)!(x+n)}{(x+1)^n}$$

5. If $y = \tan^{-1}x$, show that

$$y_n = (-1)^{n-1} (n-1)! \sin n \left(\frac{\pi}{2} - y\right) . \cos^n y.$$

Answers:

1. (i) $y_n = (-1)^n n! \left[\frac{1}{(x-1)^{n+1}} + \frac{1}{(x+1)^{n+1}} - \frac{1}{(x+2)^{n+1}}\right]$

(ii) $y_n = n! \left[\frac{3^{n+1}}{(1-3x)^{n+1}} - \frac{2^{n+1}}{(1-2x)^{n+1}}\right]$

(iii) $y_n = 2(-1)^{n-1} . (n-1)! \sin n\theta \sin^n\theta$

where $\theta = \tan^{-1}\left(\frac{1}{x}\right)$

(iv) $y_n = (-1)^n n! \left[\frac{16}{(x-2)^{n+1}} - \frac{1}{(x-1)^{n+1}}\right]$

(v) $y_n = (-1)^n \left[\frac{(n+1)!}{3(x-1)^{n+2}} + \frac{5n!}{9(x-1)^{n+1}} + \frac{4n!}{9(x+2)^{n+1}}\right]$

(vi). $y_n = \dfrac{e^{ax}}{2}\left[a^n + \left(a^2+4b^2\right)^{\frac{n}{2}}.\cos\left\{2bx + n\tan^{-1}\left(\dfrac{2b}{a}\right)\right\}\right]$

LEIBNITZ'S THEOREM

If u and v are functions of x, each having n^{th} derivatives *w.r.t.* x, then

$$D^n\,(u.v) = D^n(u)\,.\,v + {}^nc_1\,.\,D^{n-1}(u)\,.\,D(v) + {}^nc_2\,D^{n-2}(u)\,.\,D^2(v) + {}^nc_3\,D^{n-3}(u)\,D^3\,(v) + \ldots + \ldots\,{}^nc_{n-1}\,D(u)\,D^{n-1}(v) + {}^nc_n\,u.\,D^n(v).$$

SOLVED EXAMPLES

Example 1. Find the nth derivative of $e^x.\log x$.

Solution: Here $u = e^x,\ v = \log x$

$$D^n\,(e^x) = e^x$$

$$D^n\,(\log x) = (-1)^{n-1}\,(n-1)!\,x^{-n}$$

$$\therefore\quad D^n\,(e^x\,.\,\log x) = D^n\,(e^x)\,.\,\log x. + nc_1\,.\,D^{n-1}\,(e^x).\,D\,(\log x) + nc_2\,D^{n-2}\,(e^x).\,D^2\,(\log x) + \ldots + \ldots + nc_n\,.\,e^x.\,D^n\,(\log x)$$

$$= e^x\,.\,\log x + nc_1\,.\,e^x\,\frac{1}{x}\,.+ nc_2\,.\,e^x\,.\,\frac{-1}{x^2} + \ldots + nc_n\,.\,e^x\,.\,(-1)^{n-1}\,.\,(n-1)!\,x^{-n}.$$

$$\therefore\quad y_n = e^x\,.\,\log x + \frac{ne^x}{x} - \frac{n(n-1)}{2!}\,\frac{e^x}{x^2} + \ldots + e^x\,.\,(-1)^{n-1}.\,(n-1)!\,x^{-n}.$$

Example 2. If $y = a\cos(\log x) + b\sin(\log x)$, show that

(i) $x^2y_2 + xy_1 + y = 0$ and hence, show that

(ii) $x^2\,y_{n+2} + (2n+1)\,xy_{n+1} + (n^2+1)\,y_n = 0$

Solution: Here $y = a\cos(\log x) + b\sin(\log x)$ ...(1)

Differentiating equation (i) w.r.t. x, we have

$$y_1 = -a \sin(\log x) \cdot \frac{1}{x} + b \cos(\log x) \cdot \frac{1}{x}$$

$\therefore$ $$xy_1 = -a \sin(\log x) + b \cos(\log x)$$

Again differentiating, we have

$$xy_2 + y_1 = -a \cos(\log x)\, \frac{1}{x} \cdot - b \sin(\log x) \cdot \frac{1}{x}$$

or $$x^2y_2 + xy_1 = -[a \cos(\log x) + b \sin(\log x)]$$

or $$x^2y_2 + xy_1 + y = 0 \qquad \text{...(2)}$$

Now differentiating equation (2), n times by Leibnitz's theorem, we have

$$D^n(x^2y_2) + D^n(xy_1) + D^n(y) = 0$$

or $$x^2y_{n+2} + nc_1 \cdot (2x) \cdot y_{n+1} + nc_2 \cdot 2. y_n + y_{n+1} \cdot x + nc_1\, y_n \cdot 1 + y_n = 0$$

or $$x^2y_{n+2} + 2n\, xy_{n+1} + n(n-1)\, y_n + xy_{n+1} + ny_n + y_n = 0$$

or $$x^2y_{n+2} + (2n + 1)\, xy_{n+1} + (n^2 + 1)\, y_n = 0$$

Example 3. If $y = e^{m\cos^{-1}(x)}$, show that

$y_{n+2}(1 - x^2) - (2n + 1)\, xy_{n+1} - (n^2 + m^2)\, y_n = 0$ and hence find $y_n(0)$.

Solution: $$y = e^{m\cos^{-1}}(x) \qquad \text{...(1)}$$

$\therefore$ $$y_1 = e^{m\cos^{-1}}x \cdot \frac{-m}{\sqrt{1-x^2}}$$

or $$y_1 = y \cdot \frac{-m}{\sqrt{1-x^2}}$$

$$y_1^2(1 - x^2) = m^2y^2 \qquad \text{...(2)}$$

Differentiating (2) *w.r.t.* x, we have

$$2y_1y_2(1 - x^2) - 2xy_1^2 - m^2 \cdot 2yy_1 = 0$$

or $$y_2(1 - x^2) - xy_1 - m^2y = 0 \qquad (\because 2y_1 \neq 0)$$

$$y_2(1 - x^2) - xy_1 - m^2y = 0 \qquad \text{...(3)}$$

Now differentiating (3), n times w.r.t. x, we have

$$y_{n+2}(1 - x^2) + nc_1 \cdot y_{n+1} \cdot (-2x) + nc_2 \cdot y_n(-2)$$
$$- [xy_{n+1} + nc_1.1.y_n] - m^2y_n = 0$$

or $\quad y_{n+2}(1-x^2) - 2n\,xy_{n+1} - n(n-1)\,y_n - xy_{n+1} - ny_n - m^2y_n = 0$

or
$$y_{n+2}(1-x^2) - (2n+1)\,xy_{n+1} - n^2y_n - m^2\,y_n = 0$$

$$y_{n+2}(1-x^2) - (2n+1)\,xy_{n+1} - (n^2+m^2)\,y_n = 0 \qquad \text{...(4)}$$

Putting $x = 0$ in (4), we have

$$y_{n+2}(0) = (n^2 + m^2)\,y_n(0)$$

writing n–2 in place of n, we have

$$y_n(0) = [(n-2)^2 + m^2]\,y_{n-2}(0)$$

$$y_{n-2}(0) = [(n-4)^2 + m^2]\,y_{n-4}(0)$$

$$\ldots\ldots\ldots$$

If n is even $\quad y_n(0) = [(n-2)^2 + m^2]\,y_{n-2}(0)$

$$= [(n-2)^2 + m^2]\,[(n-4)^2 + m^2]\,y_{n-4}(0)$$

$$= [(n-2)^2 + m^2].[n-4)^2 + m^2].[n-6)^2 + m^2]\,y_{n-6}(0)$$

$$= [(n-2)^2 + m^2]\,[n-4)^2 + m^2]\,[n-6)^2 + m^2] \ldots$$

$$[0^2 + m^2]\,y(0)$$

$$= [(n-2)^2 + m^2]\,[(n-4)^2 + m^2]\,[(n-6)^2 + m^2] \ldots$$

$$m^2\,.\,e\frac{m\pi}{2}.$$

If n is odd

$$y_n(0) = [(n-2)^2 + m^2]\,[n-4)^2 + m^2]\,[n-6)^2 + m^2] \ldots$$

$$[1^2 + m^2]\,y_1(0)$$

$$= [(n-2)^2 + m^2]\,.\,[n-4)^2 + m^2]\,[n-6)^2 + m^2] \ldots$$

$$[1^2 + m^2]\,(-m)\,e\frac{m\pi}{2}.$$

Thus, if n is even

$$y_n(0) = m^2\,(2^2 + m^2)\,(4^2 + m^2) \ldots [(n-4)^2 + m^2] \ldots$$

$$[(n-2)^2 + m^2]\,e\frac{m\pi}{2}.$$

If n is odd

$$= -m(1^2 + m^2)(3^2 + m^2)(5^2 + m^2) \ldots$$

$$[(n-4)^2 + m^2] \,.\, [(n-2)^2 + m^2]\, e\frac{m\pi}{2}.$$

Example 4. If $y^{1/m} + y^{-1/m} = 2x$, prove that

$(x^2 - 1)\, y_{n+2} + (2n + 1)\, xy_{n+1} + (n^2 - m^2)\, y_n = 0$

Solution: Here $y^{1/m} + y^{-1/m} = 2x$ ...(1)

$$\therefore \quad y^{2/m} + 1 = 2xy^{1/m}$$

$$\therefore \quad y^{2/m} - 2xy^{1/m} + 1 = 0 \qquad ...(2)$$

Equation (2) is quadratic in $y^{1/m}$

$$\therefore \quad y^{1/m} = \frac{2x \pm \sqrt{4x^2 - 4}}{2}$$

$$y^{1/m} = x \pm \sqrt{x^2 - 1}$$

$$\therefore \quad y = \left[x \pm \sqrt{x^2 - 1}\right]^m \qquad ..(3)$$

Now differentiating (3) w.r.t. x we have

$$y_1 = m\left[x \pm \sqrt{x^2 - 1}\right]^{m-1} \cdot \left[1 \pm \frac{x}{\sqrt{x^2 - 1}}\right]$$

$$= m \,.\, \left[x \pm \sqrt{x^2 - 1}\right]^{m-1} \cdot \frac{\left[\sqrt{x^2 - 1} \pm x\right]}{\sqrt{x^2 - 1}} \quad .$$

$$y_1 = \frac{-my}{\sqrt{x^2 - 1}} \qquad ...(4)$$

Squaring (4), we have

$$y_1^2 = \frac{m^2 . y^2}{\left[\sqrt{(x^2 - 1)}\right]^2}$$

or $(x^2 - 1)\, y_1{}^2 = m^2y^2$

or $(x^2 - 1)\, y_1{}^2 - m^2y^2 = 0$ ...(5)

Differentiating (5) w.r.t. x, we have

$$2y_1y_2\,(x^2 - 1) + 2xy_1{}^2 - 2m^2yy_1 = 0$$

$$y_2\,(x^2 - 1) + xy_1 - m^2y = 0 \qquad ...(6)$$

Now, Differentiating (6), n times by Leibnitz's theorem, we have

$$y_{n+2} \cdot (x^2 - 1) + nc_1 \cdot y_{n+1} \cdot 2x + nc_2 \cdot y_n .2 + xy_{n+1}$$

$$+ nc_1 \,.\, 1.\, y_n - m^2\, y_n = 0$$

$$y_{n+2}\,(x^2 - 1) + 2n\, xy_{n+1} + n(n - 1)\, y_n + xy_{n+1} + ny_n - m^2y_n = 0$$

$$\text{or } y_{n+2}\,(x^2 - 1) + (2n + 1)\, xy_{n+1} + (n^2 - m^2)\, y_n = 0$$

Example 5. Show that

$$D^n\,(x^{n-1} \,.\, \log x) = \frac{(n-1)!}{x}$$

Solution: $D^n\,(x^{n-1} \,.\, \log x)$

$$= D^{n-1}\,[D\,(x^{n-1} \log x)]$$

$$= D^{n-1}\,[(n - 1) \,.\, x^{n-2} \,.\, \log x + x^{n-2}]$$

$$= (n - 1) \,.\, D^{n-1} \,.\, (x^{n-2}.\, \log x) + D^{n-1}\,(x^{n-2})$$

$$= (n - 1) \,.\, D^{n-1} \,.\, [x^{n-2}.\, \log x] + 0$$

$$= (n - 1)\, D^{n-2} \,.\, [D\,(x^{n-2}.\, \log x)]$$

$$= (n - 1)\, D^{n-2} \,.\, [(n - 2) \,.\, x^{n-3}.\, \log x + x^{n-3}]$$

$$= (n - 1)\,(n - 2)\, D^{n-2} \,.\, [x^{n-3}.\, \log x] + (n - 1)\, D^{n-2}\,[x^{n-3}]$$

$$= (n - 1)\,(n - 2)\, D^{n-2} \,.\, [x^{n-3}.\, \log x] + 0$$

$$= (n - 1)\,(n - 2)\, D^{n-2} \,.\, [x^{n-3}.\, \log x]$$

Continuing in this way, we get

$$D^n\,(x^{n-1} \,.\, \log x) = (n - 1)\,(n - 2)\,(x - 3) \ldots 3 \,.\, 2 \,.\, 1\, D\,[x^0.\, \log x]$$

$$= (n - 1)\,(n - 2)\,(n - 3) \ldots 3 \,.\, 2 \,.\, 1\, D\,[x^0.\, \log x]$$

$$= \frac{(n-1)!}{x}$$

$$\therefore \quad D^n\,(x^{n-1} \,.\, \log x) = \frac{(n-1)!}{x}.$$

EXERCISE

1. Find the nth derivative of the following :
   (i) $e^x \,.\, \log x$
   (ii) $x^2 \sin x$
   (iii) $x^2 e^x$
   (iv) $x^2 \log x.$

2. If $y = \sin^{-1}x$, show that

   $(1 - x^2)y_{n+2} - (2n + 1)xy_{n+1} - n^2y_n = 0$

3. If $y = \sin (p \sin^{-1}x)$, show that

   $(1 - x^2)\, y_2 - xy_1 + p^2y = 0$ and hence show that

   $(1 - x^2)y_{n+2} - (2n + 1)\, xy_{n+1} + (p^2 - n^2)\, y_n = 0.$

4. If $x + y = 1$, prove that

   $D^n\, [x^ny^n] = n!\, [y^n - (nc_1)^2 \,.\, y^{n-1}x + (nc_2)^2\, y^{n-2}\, x^2 - \ldots (-1)^n\, x^n].$

5. If $y = (\sin^{-1}x)^2$, show that

   $(1 - x^2)\, y_{n+2} - (2n + 1)\, xy_{n+1} - n^2y_n = 0$ and hence find $y_n(0)$.

6. If $V_n = \dfrac{dn}{dx^n}\, (x^n \log x)$, show that

   $V_n = nv_{n-1} + (n - 1)!$, hence show that

   $$V_n = n!\left[\log x + 1 + \frac{1}{2} + \frac{1}{3} + \frac{1}{4} + \ldots + \frac{1}{n}\right]$$

7. If $y = \left[x + \sqrt{x^2 + 1}\right]^m$, show that

   $(x^2 + 1)\, y_2 + xy_1 - m^2y = 0$ and hence, show that

   $y_{n+2}\, (1 + x^2) + (2n + 1)\, xy_{n+1} + (n^2 - m^2)\, y_n = 0.$

   Also find $y_n(0)$.

8. Show that

   $$D^n\left[\frac{\log x}{x}\right] = \frac{(-1)^n\, n!}{x^{n+1}}\left[\log x - 1 - \frac{1}{2} - \frac{1}{3} \ldots - \frac{1}{n}\right].$$

9. If $x = \cos h\left(\frac{1}{m}\log y\right)$, show that

$$(x^2 - 1)\, y_{n+2} + (2n + 1)\, xy_{n+1} + (n^2 - m^2)\, y_n = 0.$$

10. If $x = \sin t$, $y \cos pt$, then show that

$$(1 - x^2)\, y_2 - xy_1 + p^2y = 0, \text{ hence show that}$$

$$(1 - x^2)\, y_{n+2} - (2n + 1)\, xy_{n+1} - (n^2 - p^2)\, y_n = 0.$$

11. If $y = \log\left[x + \sqrt{1 + x^2}\right]$, prove that

$$(1 + x^2)y_{n+2} + (2n + 1)\, xy_{n+1} + n^2\, y_n = 0.$$

12. If $y = e^{m \sin^{-1} x}$, show that

$$(1 - x^2)\, y_{n+2} - (2n + 1)\, xy_{n+1} - (n^2 + m^2)\, y_n = 0.$$

Also find $y_n(0)$.

Answers:

1. (i) $e^x\left[\log x + nc_1\frac{1}{x} - nc_2\frac{1}{x^2}\cdots\right]$

(ii) $(x^2 - n^2 + n)\sin\left(x + n\frac{\pi}{2}\right) - 2nx\cos\left(x + n\frac{\pi}{2}\right)$

(iii) $e^x\,[x^2 + 2nx + n^2 - n]$

(iv) $(-1)^{n-1}\,.\,(n - 1)!\, x^{2-n} + nc_1\,(-1)^{n-2}\,(n - 2)!\, 2x^{2-n} \ldots$

5. $y_n(0) = 0$, if n is odd.

$2.2^2.4^2.6^2 \ldots (n-4)^2\,.\,(n - 2)^2$ if, n is even.

7. $y_n(0) = m^2\,(m^2 - 2^2)\,(m^2 - 4^2) \ldots [m^2 - (n - 2)^2]$, if n is even.

$= m\,.\,(m^2 - 1^2)\,(m^2 - 3^2) \ldots [m^2 - (n - 2)^2]$, if n is odd.

12. $y(0) = a\,(1^2 + a^2)\,(3^2 + a^2) \ldots [(n - 2)^2 + a^2]$, if n is odd.

or $a^2\,(2^2 + a^2)\,(4^2 + a^2) \ldots [(n - 2)^2 + a^2]$, if n is even.

4

Expansion of Functions and Approximate Calculations

INTRODUCTION

If a function $f(x)$ and all its derivatives exist finitely for $x = 0$, then it can be expanded in a convergent series of +ve integral powers of x, known as Maclaurin's series, given by

$$f(x) = f(0) + xf'(0) + x^2 \cdot \frac{f''(0)}{2!} + x^n \cdot \frac{f^n(0)}{n!} + \ \ldots.$$

MACLAURIN'S SERIES

Le $\quad f(x) = a_0 + a_1x + a_2x^2 + a_3x^3 + a_4x^4 + a_5x^5 + a_6x^6 + a_7x^7 + \ldots \quad (1)$

$$f^i(x) = a_1 + 2a_2 . x + 3a_3 . x^2 + 4a_4 . x^3 + 5a_5 . x^4 + 6a_6 . x^5 + 7a_7 . x^6 \ldots$$

$$f^{ii}(x) = 2a_2 + 3.2 . a_3x + 4.3\ a_4 . x^2 + 5.4.a_5 . x^3 + 6.5\ a_6\ x^4 + \ldots$$

$$f^{iii}(x) = 3.2.1.a_3\ x + 4.3.2.a_4x + 5.4.3.a_5\ x^2 + 6.5.4.a_6x_3 + \ldots$$

For $\quad x = 0$

$$f(0) = a_0,$$

$$f^i(0) = a_1$$

$$f^{ii}(0) = 2a_2$$

$$f^{iii}(0) = 3!a_3, \ldots f^n(0) = n!a_n \ldots$$

Substituting a_0, a_1, a_2 ... a_n in equation (1), we have

$$f(x) = f(0) + f^{i}(0) + x^2 \cdot \frac{f^{ii}(0)}{2!} + \frac{f^{iii}(0)}{3!} + \ldots$$

$$+ x^n \frac{f^{n}(0)}{n!} + \ldots$$

SOLVED EXAMPLES

Example 1. Expand tan x in powers of x.

Solution: Here $f(x) = \tan x$

$\therefore$ $f(0) = \tan 0^\circ = 0$

$f^{i}(x) = \sec^2 x$

$\therefore$ $f^{i}(0) = 1$

$f^{ii}(x) = 2\sec^2 x \cdot \tan x$

$f^{ii}(0) = 0$

$f^{ii}(x) = 2\sec^2 x \cdot \tan x$

$f^{ii}(x) = 2 \cdot f^{i}(x) \cdot f(x)$

$\therefore$ $f^{iii}(x) = 2 \cdot f^{ii}(x) \cdot f(x) + 2[f^{i}(x)]^2$

$f^{iii}(0) = 0 + 2 \cdot 1 = 2$

$f^{iv}(x) = 2f^{iii}(x) \cdot f(x) + 2 \cdot f^{ii}(x) \cdot f^{i}(x) + 2f^{i}(x) \cdot f^{ii}(x)$

$\therefore$ $f^{iv}(0) = 2f^{iii}(0) \cdot f(0) + 2 \cdot f^{ii}(0) \cdot f^{i}(0)$

$+ 2f^{i}(0) \cdot f^{ii}(0)$

$= 0$

$f^{iv}(x) = 2f^{iii}(x) \cdot f(x) + 4 \cdot f^{i}(x) f^{ii}(x)$

$f^{iv}(x) = 2f^{iii}(x) f(x) + 4 f^{i}(x) f^{ii}(x)$

$f^{v}(x) = 2f^{iv}(x) \cdot f(x) + 2 f^{iii}(x)] \cdot f^{i}(x)$

$+ 4 [f^{ii}(x)]^2 + 4 f^{i}(x) \cdot f^{iii}(x)$

$f^{v}(0) = 2 f^{iv}(0) f(0) + 6 f^{iii}(0) \cdot f^{i}(0)$

$+ 4 \cdot [f^{ii}(0)]^2$

$$= 0 + 6\,.2 + 0$$

$$= 12$$

$$f^{v}(0) = 12 \ldots$$

Thus $$f(x) = x + \frac{x^3}{3} + \frac{1.x^5}{10} + \ldots$$

$\therefore$ $$\tan x = x + \frac{x^3}{3} + \frac{1.x^5}{10} + \ldots$$

Example 2. Show that

$$e^{a\sin^{-1}x} = 1 + ax + \frac{(ax)^2}{2!} + \frac{a(1^2 + a^2)}{3!}x^3 + \frac{a^2(2^2 + a^2)}{4!}x^4 + \ldots$$

and hence show that

$$e^{\theta} = 1 + \sin\theta + \frac{\sin^2\theta}{2!} + \frac{2}{3!}\sin^3\theta + \frac{5}{4!}\sin^4\theta + \ldots$$

Solution: Here $$y = e^{a\sin^{-1}x}$$

$$y_1 = e^{a\sin^{-1}x} \cdot \frac{a}{\sqrt{1-x^2}}$$

$$= \frac{a\,y}{\sqrt{1-x^2}}$$

or $$y_1^2(1 - x^2) = a^2y^2 \qquad \ldots(1)$$

Again differentiating, we have

$$2y_1y_2(1 - x^2) - 2xy_1^2 - 2a^2yy_1 = 0$$

or $$y_2(1 - x^2) - xy_1 - a^2y = 0 \qquad \ldots(2)$$

Now diff. (2) n times by Leibnitz's theorem, we have

$$y_{n+2}(1 - x^2) + nc_1 \cdot y_{n+1} \cdot (-2x) + nc_2 \cdot y_n(-2) - xy_{n+1}$$
$$- nc_1\,y_n \cdot 1 - a^2y_n = 0$$

or $$y_{n+2}(1 - x^2) - 2n\,xy_{n+1} - n(n-1)\,y_n - xy_{n+1} - ny_n - a^2y_n = 0$$

$$y_{n+2}(1 - x^2) - (2n + 1)\,xy_{n+1} - (n^2 + a^2)\,y_n = 0 \qquad \ldots(3)$$

Putting $x = 0$, we have

$$y_{n+2}(0) = (n^2 + a^2)\, y_n(0)$$

$$y_n(0) = [(n-2)^2 + a^2]\, y_{n-2}(0)$$

$$y_{n-2}(0) = [(n-4)^2 + a^2]\, y_{n-4}(0)$$

∴ If n is even

$$y_n(0) = [(n-2)^2 + a^2]\,[(n-4)^2 + a^2] \,.\, (0^2 + a^2) \,.\, y(0)$$

$$= a^2\,(2^2 + a^2)\,(4^2 + a^2) \,\ldots\, [(n-2)^2 + a^2]$$

If n is odd

$$y_n(0) = a\,(1^2 + a^2)\,(3^2 + a^2) \,\ldots\, [(n-2)^2 + a^2]$$

Here $y(0) = e^{a\sin^{-1}(0)} = e^0 = 1$

$$y_1(0) = a$$

$$y_2(0) = a^2$$

$$y_3(0) = a(1^2 + a^2)$$

$$y_4(0) = a^2(2^2 + a^2)$$

$$y_5(0) = a(1^2 + a^2)(3^2 + a^2)$$

$$y_6(0) = a(2^2 + a^2)(4^2 + a^2)$$

∴ $$y = y(0) + y_1(0) \,.\, x + y_2(0) \,.\, \frac{x^2}{2!}$$

$$+ y_3(0) \,.\, \frac{x^3}{3!} + y_4(0) \,.\, \frac{x^4}{4!} + \ldots$$

$$= 1 + ax + \frac{a^2x^2}{2!} + \frac{a\left(1^2 + a^2\right)x^3}{3!}$$

$$+ \frac{a^2\left(2^2 + a^2\right)}{2!}\; \frac{x^4}{4!} + \ldots$$

∴ $$e^{a\sin^{-1}(x)} = 1 + ax + \frac{a^2x^2}{2!} + \frac{a\left(1^2 + a^2\right)x^3}{3!}$$

$$+ \frac{a^2(2^2+a^2)}{4!} x^4 + \dots$$

Putting $a = 1$, and $x = \sin\theta$, we have

$$e^{\theta} = 1 + \sin\theta + \frac{\sin^2\theta}{2!} + \frac{2}{3!}\sin^3\theta + \frac{5}{4!}\sin^4\theta + \dots$$

Example 3. Expand $e^{x\cos x}$ in powers of x.

Solution: We have $f(x) = e^{x\cos x}$ (1)

$\therefore$
$$f^{i}(x) = e^{x\cos x}\,.\,(\cos x - x\sin x)$$

$$f^{i}(x) = f(x)\,.\,(\cos x - x\sin x)$$

$$f^{ii}(x) = f^{i}(x)\,.\,(\cos x - x\sin x) + f(x)$$
$$(-\sin x - \sin\,.\,1 - x\cos x)$$

$$f^{ii}(x) = f^{i}(x)\,.\,(\cos x - x\sin x) - f(x)\,[2\sin x + x\cos x]$$

$$f^{iii}(x) = f^{ii}(x)\,.\,(\cos x - x\sin x) + f^{i}(x)\,[-2\sin x$$
$$- x\cos x] - f^{i}(x)\,[2\sin x + x\cos x]$$
$$- f(x)\,[2\cos x + \cos x - x\sin x]$$
$$= f^{ii}(x)\,.\,(\cos x - x\sin x) - f^{i}(x)\,.\,[2\sin x$$
$$+ x\cos x + 2\sin x + x\cos x] - f(x)$$
$$[2\cos x + - \cos x + x\sin x]$$
$$= f^{ii}(x)\,(\cos x - x\sin x) - 2f^{i}(x)\,[2\sin x + x\cos x]$$
$$- f(x)\,[3\cos x - x\sin x]$$

$\therefore$
$$f(0) = e^0 = 1.$$

$$f^{i}(0) = 1.$$

$$f^{ii}(0) = 1.$$

$$f^{iii}(0) = 1 - 3 - 0 = -2$$

$\therefore$
$$f(x) = f(0) + x f^{i}(0) + \frac{x^2}{2!} f^{ii}(0) + \frac{x^3}{3!} f^{iii}(0)$$

$$= 1 + x + \frac{x^2}{2!} - \frac{2x^3}{3!} \ldots$$

$$\therefore \qquad e^{x \cos x} = 1 + x + \frac{x^2}{2} - \frac{x^3}{3} + \ldots$$

Example 4. Expand log (1 + sin x) in ascending powers of x.

Solution:

$$f(x) = \log(1 + \sin x)$$

$$\therefore \qquad f(0) = \log(1) = 0$$

$$\therefore \qquad f^{i}(x) = \frac{\cos x}{1+\sin x}$$

$$f^{i}(0) = 1$$

$$f^{ii}(x) = \frac{-\sin x(1+\sin x) - \cos^2 x}{(1+\sin x)^2}$$

$$f^{ii}(0) = -1$$

$$f^{ii}(x) = \frac{-\sin x - \sin^2 x - \cos^2 x}{(1+\sin x)^2}$$

$$= \frac{-[1+\sin x]}{(1+\sin x)^2}$$

$$f^{ii}(x) = \frac{-1}{1+\sin x}$$

$$= -(1 + \sin x)^{-1}$$

$$f^{iii}(x) = +(1 + \sin x)^{-2} \cos x$$

$$= \frac{\cos x}{(1+\sin x)^2}$$

$$\therefore \qquad f^{iii}(0) = 1.$$

$$f^{iv}(x) = \frac{-\sin x(1+\sin x)^2 - 2\cos^2 x(1+\sin x)}{(1+\sin x)^4}$$

$$= \frac{-\sin x(1+\sin x) - 2\cos^2 x}{(1+\sin x)^3}$$

$$f^{iv}(0) = \frac{0-2}{1}$$

$$= -2$$

$$\therefore \quad f(0) = f(0) + f^{i}(0)\ x + \frac{x^2}{2!} f^{ii}(0) + \frac{x^3}{3!} f^{iii}(0)$$

$$+ \frac{x^4}{4!} f^{iv}(0) + \ldots$$

$$= x - \frac{x^2}{2!} + \frac{x^3}{3!} - 2\frac{x^4}{4!} + \ldots$$

$$\therefore \quad \log(1+\sin x) = x - \frac{x^2}{2} + \frac{x^3}{6} - \frac{x^4}{12} + \ldots$$

TAYLOR'S SERIES

If a function $f(x + h)$ can be expanded as an infinite convergent series of positive integral powers of h, then

$$f(x+h) = f(x) + h f^{i}(x) + \frac{h^2}{2!} f^{ii}(x) + \ldots + \frac{h^n}{n!} f^{n}(x) + \ldots$$

SOLVED EXAMPLES

Example 1. Expand $\tan^{-1}(x)$ in ascending powers of $\left(x - \frac{\pi}{4}\right)$.

Solution: We have to expand $\tan^{-1} x$ in powers of $x - \frac{\pi}{4}$.

$$\therefore \quad \tan^{-1}(x) = \tan^{-1}\left[\frac{\pi}{4} + \left(x - \frac{\pi}{4}\right)\right]$$

Here $\quad f(x) = \tan^{-1} x$

$$\therefore \quad f\left(\frac{\pi}{4}\right) = \tan^{-1}\left(\frac{\pi}{4}\right).$$

$$f^{i}(x) = \frac{1}{1+x^2}$$

$$\therefore \qquad f^{i}\frac{\pi}{4} = \frac{1}{1+\frac{\pi^2}{16}}$$

$$= \frac{16}{\pi^2+16}$$

$$f^{i}(x) = \frac{1}{1+x^2}$$

$$f^{ii}(x) = \frac{-2x}{\left(1+x^2\right)^2}$$

$$f^{ii}\left(\frac{\pi}{4}\right) = \frac{-2.\frac{\pi}{4}}{\left(\frac{16+\pi^2}{16}\right)^2}$$

$$= \frac{-\frac{\pi}{2}.16^2}{\left(16+\pi^2\right)^2}$$

$$= \frac{-128\pi}{\left(\pi^2+16\right)^2}$$

$$\therefore \quad \tan^{-1}(x) = \tan^{-1}\left(\frac{\pi}{4}\right) + \frac{16}{16+\pi^2}.\left(x-\frac{\pi}{4}\right) - \frac{128\pi\left(x-\frac{\pi}{4}\right)^2}{2\left(\pi^2+16\right)^2} + \ldots$$

$$= \tan^{-1}\left(\frac{\pi}{4}\right) + \frac{16}{16+\pi^2}\left(x-\frac{\pi}{4}\right) - \frac{64\pi}{\left(\pi^2+16\right)^2}\left(x-\frac{\pi}{4}\right)^2 + \ldots$$

Example 2. Expand the polynomial

$x^4 - 5x^3 + 7x^2 + 5x + 9$ in positive integral powers of $(x - 2)$.

Solution: $f(x) = f[2 + (x - 2)]$

$\therefore$ By Taylor's series, we have

$$f(x) = f[2 + (x - 2)]$$

$$= f(2) + (x - 2) f^{i}(2) + (x - 2)^2 \frac{f^{ii}(2)}{2!}$$

$$+ (x - 2)^3 . \frac{f^{iii}(2)}{3!} + (x - 2)^4 \frac{f^{iv}(2)}{4!} + \ldots$$

Here $f(x) = x^4 - 5x^3 + 7x^2 + 5x + 9$

$\therefore$ $f(2) = 16 - 40 + 28 + 10 + 9$

$= 23$

$\therefore$ $f^{i}(x) = 4x^3 - 15x^2 + 14x + 5$

$f^{i}(2) = 5$

$f^{ii}(x) = 12x^2 - 30x + 14$

$f^{ii}(2) = 2$

$f^{iii}(x) = 24x - 30$

$f^{iii}(2) = 18$

$f^{iv}(x) = 24$

$f^{iv}(2) = 24$

$f^{v}(x) = 0$

$$\therefore \quad f(x) = 23 + 5(x - 2) + \frac{2}{2!}(x - 2)^2 + \frac{18}{3!}(x - 2)^3 + \frac{24}{4!}(x - 2)^4$$

$$= 23 + 5(x - 2) + (x - 2)^2 + 3(x - 2)^3 + (x - 2)^4.$$

Example 3. If $f(x) = x^3 + 8x^2 + 15x - 24$. Find the value of $f\left(\frac{11}{10}\right)$ using Taylor's series.

Solution: By Taylor's series, we have

$$f(x + h) = f(x) + hf^{i}(x) + \frac{h^2}{2!} f^{ii}(x) + \frac{h^3}{3!} f^{iii}(x) + \ldots$$

Now $f(x) = x^3 + 8x^2 + 15x - 24$

$$\therefore \qquad f^{i}(x) = 3x^2 + 16x + 15$$

$$f^{ii}(x) = 6x + 16$$

$$f^{iii}(x) = 6$$

$$f^{iv}(x) = 0$$

To evaluate $f\left(\frac{11}{10}\right)$, we take $x = 1$ and $h = \frac{1}{10}$.

$$\therefore \qquad f(1) = 0$$

$$f^{i}(1) = 34$$

$$f^{ii}(1) = 22$$

$$f^{iii}(1) = 6$$

$$f^{iv}(1) = 0$$

$$\therefore \qquad f\left(1+\frac{1}{10}\right) = 0 + \frac{1}{10}\cdot 34 + \frac{1}{2!}\frac{1}{100}\cdot 22 + \frac{1}{3!}\frac{1.6}{100}$$

neglecting further terms.

$$= 3.4 + 0.11 + 0.001$$

$$= 3.511$$

$$\therefore \qquad f\left(\frac{11}{10}\right) = 3.511.$$

Example 4. Expand sin (x) in powers of $\left(x-\frac{\pi}{2}\right)$.

Solution: Given $\quad f(x) = \sin x$

$$\therefore \qquad f\left(\frac{\pi}{2}\right) = 1.$$

$$f^{i}(x) = \cos x$$

$$\therefore \qquad f^{i}\left(\frac{\pi}{2}\right) = 0.$$

$$f^{ii}(x) = -\sin x$$

$$\therefore \qquad f^{ii}\left(\frac{\pi}{2}\right) = -1.$$

$$f^{iii}(x) = -\cos x$$

$$\therefore \qquad f^{iii}\left(\frac{\pi}{2}\right) = 0.$$

$$f^{iv}(x) = \sin x$$

$$\therefore \qquad f^{iv}\left(\frac{\pi}{2}\right) = 1.$$

By Taylor's series

$$\sin x = \sin\left(\frac{\pi}{2}\right) + \left(x-\frac{\pi}{2}\right) . f^{i}\left(\frac{\pi}{2}\right) + \frac{1}{2!}\left(x-\frac{\pi}{2}\right)^2 .$$

$$f^{ii}\left(\frac{\pi}{2}\right) + \frac{1}{3!}\left(x-\frac{\pi}{2}\right)^3 . f^{iii}\left(\frac{\pi}{2}\right) + \frac{1}{4!}\left(x-\frac{\pi}{2}\right)^4 f^{iv}\left(\frac{\pi}{2}\right) \ldots$$

$$= 1 + 0\left(x-\frac{\pi}{2}\right) - \frac{1}{2!}\left(x-\frac{\pi}{2}\right)^2 + 0 . \frac{1}{3!}\left(x-\frac{\pi}{2}\right)^3$$

$$+ \frac{1}{4!}\left(x-\frac{\pi}{2}\right)^4 . 1 + \ldots$$

$$\sin x = 1 - \frac{1}{2!}\left(x-\frac{\pi}{2}\right)^2 + \frac{1}{4!}\left(x-\frac{\pi}{2}\right)^4 - \ldots$$

Example 4. Expand $\log x$ in powers of $(x - 2)$.

Solution: Here $f(x) = \log x$

$$\therefore \qquad \log x = \log\,[2 + (x-2)]$$

$$f(x) = f(2) + (x-2) f^{i}(2) + \frac{(x-2)^2}{2!} f^{ii}(2) + \frac{(x-2)^3}{3!}$$

$$f^{iii}(2) + \frac{(x-2)^4}{4!} f^{iv}(2) + \ldots$$

$\because \qquad f(x) = \log(x)$

$\therefore \qquad f(2) = \log 2$

$f^{i}(x) = \frac{1}{x}.$

$\therefore \qquad f^{i}(2) = \frac{1}{2}$

$f^{ii}(x) = \frac{-1}{x^2}.$

$\therefore \qquad f^{ii}(2) = -\frac{1}{4}$

$f^{iii}(x) = \frac{2}{x^3}$

$\therefore \qquad f^{iii}(2) = \frac{1}{4}.$

$f^{iv}(x) = \frac{-6}{x^4}$

$\therefore \qquad f^{iv}(2) = \frac{-3}{8}.$

....

$$\therefore \qquad \log(x) = \log(2) + \frac{1}{2}(x-2) - \frac{1}{2!}.\frac{1}{4}(x-2)^2 + \frac{1}{3!}.\frac{1}{4}(x-2)^3 - \frac{1}{4!}.\frac{3}{8}.(x-2)^4 + \ldots$$

$$\therefore \qquad \log(x) = \log 2 + \frac{(x-2)}{2} - \frac{(x-2)^2}{8} + \frac{(x-2)^3}{24} - \frac{(x-2)^4}{64} + \ldots$$

APPROXIMATE CALCULATIONS

Let y be a function of x defined by

$$y = f(x) \qquad \ldots(1)$$

then, as the value of x changes, the value of y also changes. We have to find the change Δy in y, corresponding to a small change Δx, in x.

Now, by Taylor's theorem

$$y + \Delta y = f(x + \Delta x)$$

$$\therefore \quad \Delta y = f(x + \Delta x) - y$$

$$\Delta y = f(x + \Delta x) - f(x)$$

$$\therefore \quad \Delta y = f(x) + f^{i}(x) \,.\, \Delta x + f^{ii}(x) \frac{(\Delta x)^2}{2!} + \ldots - f(x)$$

$$= f^{i}(x) \,.\, \Delta x + f^{ii}(x) \frac{(\Delta x)^2}{2!} + \ldots$$

As Δx is sufficiently small, then

$$\Delta y = f^{i}(x)\, \Delta x$$

or

$$\boxed{\Delta \boldsymbol{y} = \frac{d\boldsymbol{y}}{d\boldsymbol{x}} \,.\, \Delta \boldsymbol{x}}$$

RELATIVE ERROR

If Δx is error in x, then $\frac{\Delta x}{x}$ is called the relative error.

Percentage Error : Relative error × 100

$$= \frac{\Delta x}{x} \times 100.$$

SOLVED EXAMPLES

Example 1. ABCD is a rectangular protactor in which AB = 8 cm, BC = 2 cm and O is the mid point of the side AB. An angle BOP is set off by a mark P on the edge CD. If in setting off an angle θ degrees, a mark is made $\frac{1}{100}$ cm along the edge from the correct point, then show that the error in the angle is $\frac{9 \sin^2 \theta}{10\pi}$ degrees.

Solution:

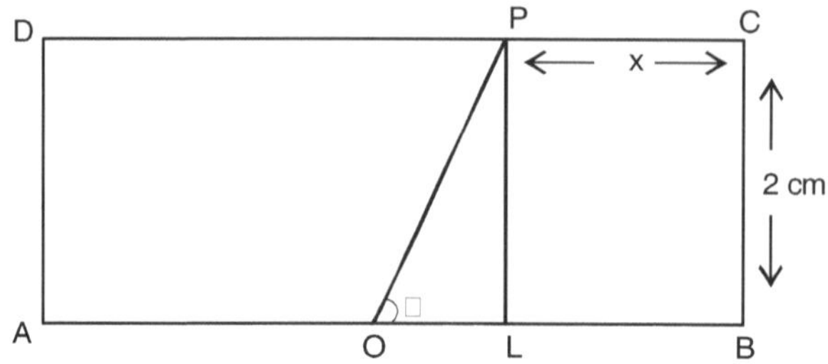

Let P be the correct position of the point P which is at a distance x from c, for which the angle BOP is θ.

Then, $$OL = 4 - x$$

In Δ LOP

$$\tan\theta = \frac{2}{4-x}$$

$$\therefore \quad 4 - x = 2\cot\theta \qquad ...(1)$$

Differentiating (1), w.r.t θ

$$\frac{-dx}{d\theta} = -2\,\text{cosec}^2\theta$$

$$\frac{d\theta}{dx} = \frac{\sin^2\theta}{2}$$

Δθ, error in θ, corresponding an error Δx in correct location of the point P is

$$\Delta\theta = \frac{d\theta}{dx}\,.\,\Delta x$$

$$= \frac{\sin^2\theta}{2}.\frac{1}{100} \text{ rad.}$$

$$= \frac{\sin^2\theta}{200}.\frac{180}{\pi} \text{ degrees.}$$

$$\Delta\theta = \frac{9\sin^2\theta}{10\pi} \text{ degrees.}$$

Example 2. Show that sin $(a + h)$ differs from $\sin a + h \cos a$ by not more than $\frac{h^2}{2}$.

Solution: By Taylor's series, we have

$$\sin (a + h) = \sin a + h \cos a + \frac{h^2}{2!} (-\sin a) - \frac{h^3}{3!}$$

$$\cos a + \frac{h^4}{4!} \sin a + ...$$

$$\therefore \quad \sin (a + h) - \sin a - h \cos a = -\frac{h^2}{2} . \sin a - \frac{h^3}{3!} \cos a ...$$

When h is sufficiently small then h^3 and higher powers are is negligible, then

$$|\sin (a + h) - \sin a - h \cos a| = \frac{h^2}{2} |\sin a|$$

$$\leq \frac{h^2}{2} \{\because |\sin a| \leq |\}.$$

Thus, $\sin (a + h)$ differs from $\sin a + h \cos a$ by not more than $\frac{h^2}{2}$.

Example 3. Expand log sin $(x + h)$ in ascending powers of h and hence find the approximate value of log sin (32°) to four places of decimal.

Solution: Here $f(x) = \log \sin x$

$\therefore \quad f^{i}(x) = \cot x$

$f^{ii}(x) = -\text{cosec}^2 x$

$f^{iii}(x) = 2 \text{cosec}^2 x \cot x$

$\therefore$ By Taylor's series, we have

$$\log \sin (x + h) = \log \sin x + h \cot x + \frac{h^2}{2!} (-\text{cosec}^2 x)$$

$$+ \frac{h^3}{3!} (2 \text{cosec}^2 x \cot x) + ...$$

$$\therefore \qquad \log \sin (x + h) = \log \sin x + h \cot x + \frac{h^2}{2} (- \text{cosec}^2 x)$$

$$+ \frac{h^3}{3} (\text{cosec}^2 x \cot x) + \ldots$$

Now to calculate approximate value of log sin (32°),

We put $$x = 30^\circ, h = 2^\circ = \frac{2.\pi}{180} = \frac{\pi}{90} \text{ rad.}$$

$$\therefore \qquad \log \sin (32^\circ) = \log (\sin 30^\circ) + \frac{\pi}{90} . \cot 30^\circ$$

$$- \left(\frac{\pi}{90}\right)^2 \text{cosec}^2 (30^\circ)$$

$$+ \left(\frac{\pi}{90}\right)^3 . \frac{1}{3} \text{cose}^2 30^\circ . \cot 30^\circ + \ldots$$

$$= \log\left(\frac{1}{2}\right) + \frac{\pi}{90}\sqrt{3} - \frac{\pi^2}{(90)^2} . 4 + \frac{\pi^3}{(90)^3} 4 . \frac{1}{3}\sqrt{3}$$

$$= -\log 2 + \frac{\pi\sqrt{3}}{90} - \frac{\pi^2}{(90)^2}.4 + \frac{\pi^3}{(90)^3} 4\sqrt{3}.\frac{1}{3}$$

$$= \bar{1}.724209$$

Example 4. Prove that

$$\tan^{-1} (x + h) = \tan^{-1} x + (h \sin \alpha) . \sin \alpha -$$

$$(h \sin \alpha)^2 . \frac{\sin 2\alpha}{2} + \frac{(h \sin \alpha)^3 . \sin 3\alpha}{3} + \ldots$$

where $$\alpha = \cot^{-1} x.$$

Solution: Here $f(x + h) = \tan^{-1} (x + h)$

$$\therefore \qquad f(x) = \tan^{-1} x$$

$$\therefore \qquad f^i (x) = \frac{1}{1 + x^2}$$

$$f^{ii}(x) = \frac{-2x}{\left(1+x^2\right)^2}$$

$$f^{iii}(x) = \frac{2\left(1-3x^2\right)}{\left(1+x^2\right)^3}$$

Substituting $x = \cot\alpha$ in the coefficients

$$f^{i}(x) = \frac{1}{1+x^2} = \frac{1}{1+\cot^2\alpha} = \sin^2\alpha$$

$$f^{ii}(x) = \frac{-2\cot\alpha}{\left(1+\cot^2\alpha\right)^2} = -2\cot\alpha \,.\, \sin^4\alpha$$

$$f^{iii}(x) = \frac{2\left(1-3x^2\right)}{\left(1+x^2\right)^3} = \frac{-2\left(1-3\cot^2\alpha\right)}{\left(1+\cot^2\alpha\right)}$$

$$= -2\left(\sin^2\alpha - 3\cos^2\alpha\right) . \sin^4\alpha$$

$$= 2 \,.\, \sin 3\alpha \,.\, \sin^3\alpha$$

By Taylor's series

$$= f(x) + hf^{i}(x) + \frac{h^2}{2!} f^{ii}(x) + \frac{h^3}{3!} f^{ii}(x) + \ldots$$

$$= \tan^{-1} x + (h \,.\, \sin\alpha) \,.\, \sin\alpha - \frac{h^2}{2!}\left(2\cot\alpha \,.\, \sin^4\alpha\right)$$

$$+ \frac{h^3}{3!}\left[2\sin 3\alpha \,.\, \sin^3\alpha\right]$$

$$\therefore \quad \tan^{-1}(x+h) = \tan^{-1}x + (h\sin\alpha) \,.\, \sin\alpha - (h\sin\alpha)^2 . \frac{\sin 2\alpha}{2}$$

$$+ \frac{(h\sin\alpha)^3 . \sin 3\alpha}{3} + \ldots$$

Example 5. A soap bubble of radius 3 cm shrinks to radius 2.9 cm. Find the approximate change in (i) volume (ii) in surface area.

Solution: If r is the radius of the spherical soap bubble

$\therefore$ Volume of the bubble

$$V = \frac{4}{3}\pi r^3 \quad ...(1)$$

and surface $S = 4\pi r^2$ ...(2)

$\therefore$ $\dfrac{dv}{dr} = 4\pi r^2$

and $\dfrac{ds}{dr} = 8\pi r$

If Δr is the change in the radius then the change ΔV and ΔS, in volume and surface area respectively, are

$$\Delta V = \frac{dV}{dr} . \Delta r$$

$$\Delta V = 4\pi r^2 . \Delta r$$

and $\Delta S = \dfrac{ds}{dr} . \Delta r$

$$\Delta S = 8\pi r \Delta r$$

for $r = 3$ cm

$\Delta r = -0.1$, we have

$$\Delta V = 4\pi\, 9\, (-0.1)$$

$$= -3.6\,\pi \text{ cc.}$$

and $\Delta s = 8\pi\, 3\, (-0.1)$

$$= -2.4\pi \text{ sq cm.}$$

Example 6. The Power p required to propel a ship of length l, moving with a velocity v is given by

$$p = kv^3 l^2$$

Prove that a 4% increase in velocity and 3% increase in length will require 18% increase in power.

Solution: Here

$$p = k.v^3 l^2$$

$$\therefore \quad \log p = \log k + 3 \log v + 2 \log l$$

$\therefore$ Differentiating

$$\frac{1}{p} dp = 0 + 3 \, . \, \frac{dv}{v} + 2\frac{dl}{l}$$

$$\therefore \quad \frac{dp}{p} \times 100 = 3\frac{dv}{v} \times 100 + 2 \, . \, \frac{dl}{l} \times 100$$

$$= 3(4) + 2(3) = 18$$

$\therefore$ The required change in power is 18%.

EXERCISE

1. Expand the following functions in Maclaurin series:

 (i) a^x

 (ii) $\log (1 + x)$

 (iii) $\tan x$

 (iv) $\tan^{-1}x$

 (v) $\sin^{-1}x$

 (vi) $\log (1 + \cos x)$

 (vii) $\log \sec x$

 (viii) $\log \cos x$

 (ix) $e^x \, . \, \sin x$

 (x) $\sin (m \sin^{-1}x)$.

2. Expand $\tan x$ in powers of $\left(x - \frac{\pi}{4}\right)$ upto third degree term.

3. Expand the polynomial $f(x) = x^3 - 2x^2 + 3x + 5$ in +ve integral powers of $(x - 2)$.

4. Apply Taylor's theorem to find the value of $f(2.001)$ when

 $f(x) = x^3 - 2x + 5$.

5. Expand e^x in powers of $(x - 1)$.

6. Expand $\tan\left(\frac{\pi}{4} + x\right)$ in +ve integral powers of x.

7. The pressure p and volume V of a gas are connected by $pV^{1.4} = \text{constant}$. Find the % change in the pressure corresponding to a decrease of 1% in the volume.

Answers

1 (i) $1 + (x \log a) + \frac{1}{2!}(x \log a)^2 + \frac{1}{3!}(x \log a)^3 + \ldots$

(ii) $x - \frac{x^2}{2} + \frac{x^3}{3} - \frac{x^4}{4} + \frac{x^5}{5}$

(iii)

(iv) $x - \frac{x^3}{3} + \frac{x^5}{5} - \frac{x^7}{7} + \ldots$

(v) $x + \frac{1}{2}.\frac{x^3}{3} - \frac{1.3}{2.4}\frac{x^5}{5} + \frac{1.3.5}{2.4.6}.\frac{x^7}{7} + \ldots$

(vi)

(vii) $\frac{x^2}{2!} + \frac{2x^4}{4!} + \frac{16.x^6}{6!} \ldots$

(viii) $-\frac{x^2}{2!} - 2.\frac{x^4}{4!} - 16.\frac{x^6}{6!} \ldots$

(ix) $x + x^2 + \frac{2x^3}{3!} - \frac{2^2.x^5}{5!} \ldots$

(x) $mx + m(1^2 - m^2)\frac{x^3}{3!} + m(1^2 - m^2)(3^2 - m^2)\frac{x^5}{5!} + \ldots$

2. $1 + 2\left(x - \frac{\pi}{4}\right) + 2\left(x - \frac{\pi}{4}\right)^2 + \frac{8}{3}\left(x - \frac{\pi}{4}\right)^3 + \ldots$

3. $11 + 7(x - 2) + 4(x - 2)^2 + (x - 2)^3$

4. 9.01 (approx.)

5. $e\left[1 + (x-1) + \frac{1}{2!}(x-1)^2 + \frac{1}{3!}(x-1)^3 + \ldots\right]$

6. $1 + 2x + 2x^2 + \frac{8}{3}x^3 + \frac{10}{3}x^4 + \ldots$

5

Asymptotes

INTRODUCTION

An asymptote to a curve is a straight line, at a finite distance from the origin, which touches the curve at infinity. Asymptotes exist for those curves only, which tend to infinity, like parabola, hyperbola, etc. and do not exist for closed curves like circles, ellipses etc.

ASYMPTOTES OF CARTESIAN CURVES

Let $\quad y = mx + c$, be an asymptote ...(1)

then

$$\frac{y}{x} = m + \frac{c}{x}$$

$$\therefore \quad \underset{x\to\infty}{\text{Lt}} \frac{y}{x} = m. \quad \text{...(2)}$$

Now let $\quad y = mx + c$ (1)

be an asymptote to the cartesian curve

$$(a_0\, x^n + a_1 x^{n-1} \,.\, y + a^2\, x^{n-2} \,.\, y^2 + \dots\, a_n y^n)$$
$$+ (b_1\, x^{n-1} + b_2\, x^{n-2} \,.\, y + b^3\, x^{n-3} \,.\, y^2 + \dots\, b_n\, y^{n-1})$$
$$+ (c_2\, x^{n-2} + c_3\, x^{n-3} \,.\, y + c_4\, x^{n-4} \,.\, y^2 + \dots\, c_n\, y^{n-2})$$
$$+ (l_{n-1}\,.\, x + l_n\,.\, y) + k_n = 0$$

Since the expressions in each of the bracket are homogeneous, then the above expression can be written as

$$x^n \phi_n\left(\frac{y}{x}\right) + x^{n-1}\phi_{n-1}\left(\frac{y}{x}\right) + \ldots + x\phi_1\left(\frac{y}{x}\right) + k_n = 0$$

$$\text{or } \phi_n\left(\frac{y}{x}\right) + \frac{1}{x}\phi_{n-1}\left(\frac{y}{x}\right) + \frac{1}{x^2}\phi_{n-2}\left(\frac{y}{x}\right) + \ldots \frac{1}{x^{n-1}}\cdot\phi_1\left(\frac{y}{x}\right) + \frac{k_n}{x^n} = 0$$

$$\underset{x\to\infty}{\text{Lt}}\left(\frac{y}{x}\right) = m \qquad \ldots(3)$$

Taking limit of equation (2), as $x \to \infty$, we have

$$\phi_n(m) = 0 \ldots \qquad \ldots(4)$$

The real roots of the equation (4) give the values of m, *i.e.*, slopes of the asymptotes.

Now $\because$
$$\frac{y}{x} = m + \frac{c}{x}$$

$$\text{Then } \phi_n\left(m+\frac{c}{x}\right) + \frac{1}{x}\phi_{n-1}\left(m+\frac{c}{x}\right) + \frac{1}{x^2}\phi_{n-2}\left(m+\frac{c}{x}\right) + \ldots = 0$$

Since x is very large so, $\frac{c}{x}$ will be very small and we can expand

$$\phi_n\left(m+\frac{c}{x}\right), \phi_{n-1}\left(m+\frac{c}{x}\right)\ldots$$

By Taylor's theorem, we have

$$\left[\phi_n(m) + \frac{c}{x}\phi_n'(m) + \frac{1}{2!}\left(\frac{c}{x}\right)^2\cdot\phi_n''(m) + \ldots\right]$$

$$+ \frac{1}{x}\left[\phi_{n-1}(m) + \frac{c}{x}\cdot\phi_{n-1}'(m) + \frac{1}{2!}\left(\frac{c}{x}\right)^2\cdot\phi_{n-1}''(m) + \ldots\right]$$

$$+ \frac{1}{x^2}\left[\phi_{n-2}(m) + \frac{c}{x}\cdot\phi_{n-2}'(m) + \frac{1}{2!}\left(\frac{c}{x}\right)^2\cdot\phi_{n-2}''(m) + \ldots\right]$$

$$= 0 \qquad \ldots(5)$$

But
$$\phi_n(m) = 0$$

Equation (5) on multiplying by x gives

$$\left[c\,.\,\phi'_n(m)+\phi_{n-1}(m)\right]+\frac{1}{x}\left[\frac{c^2}{2!}\phi''_n(m)+c\,.\,\phi'_{n-1}(m)+\phi_{n-2}(m)\right]$$

$$+\frac{1}{x^2}\left[\frac{c^3}{3!}\phi'''_n(m)+\frac{c^2}{2!}\phi''_{n-1}(m)+c\,.\,\phi'_{n-2}(m)+\phi_{n-3}(m)\right]+\ldots=0$$

Taking limit as $x \to \infty$, we have

$$c\,.\,\phi'_n(m)+\phi_{n-1}(m)=0$$

$$\therefore \qquad c=-\frac{\phi_{n-1}(m)}{\phi'n(m)} \qquad \ldots(6)$$

If all the values of m are real and distinct.

Substituting the values of m as $m_1, m_2, \ldots m_n$ we get c as $c_1, c_2, c_3 \ldots c_n$ and corresponding asymptotes as

$$y_1 = m_1x + c_1$$

$$y_2 = m_2x + c_2$$

$$y_n = m_nx + c_n$$

If two values of m are real and equal, *i.e.*, $m_1 = m_2$, then there are two parallel asymptotes and for these two values of m, c will have one value, according to equation (6).

Since $\qquad \phi_{n-1}(m) = 0$

and $\qquad \phi'_{n-1}(m) = 0$

In this case we make use of

$$\frac{c^2}{2!}\phi''_n(m) + c\,.\,\phi'_{n-1}(m) + \phi_{n-2}(m) = 0 \qquad \ldots(7)$$

and for $m_1 = m_2$, we get two values of c from the quadratic equation (7) and hence the two || asymptotes are obtained.

If $m_1 = m_2 = m_3$, then we make use of

$$\frac{c^3}{3!}\phi'''_n(m) + \frac{c^2}{2!}\phi''_{n-1}(m) + c\,\phi'_{n-2}(m) + \phi_{n-3}(m) = 0$$

and for one value of m, three values of c are obtained and hence the three parallel asymptotes are obtained.

Shorter Method

If the equation of the curve we of degree n.

In the equation of the curve we substitute $x = 1$ and $y = m$ in the nth, $(n-1)^{th}$ and $(n-2)^{th}$ degree terms and obtain $\phi_n(m)$, $\phi_{n-1}(m)$ and $\phi_{n-2}(m)$.

The values of m are obtained from

$$\phi_n(m) = 0.$$

Corresponding values of c are given by

$$c = -\frac{\phi_{n-1}(m)}{\phi'_n(m)} \text{ or otherwise.}$$

Asymptotes Parallel to Coordinate Axes

In case the asymptote is parallel to y-axis then the value of m is infinite.

In this case the asymptotes can not be determined by the method discussed earlier.

The equation of the curve (of nth degree) can be written as

$$y^n\phi(x) + y^{n-1}\phi_1(x) + y^{n-2}\phi_2(x) + \ldots = 0 \quad \ldots(1)$$

Dividing equation (1) by y^n, we have

$$\phi(x) + \frac{1}{y}\phi_1(x) + \frac{1}{y^2}\phi_2(x) + \ldots = 0 \quad \ldots(2)$$

Now as $y \to \infty$, let $x \to k$.

Under the equation (2) gives

$$\phi(k) = 0$$

Thus, k is the root of $\phi(k) = 0$

Let $\phi(k) = 0$ have roots k_1, k_2, k_3 ... etc. then the asymptotes parallel to y-axis are

$$x = k_1, k_2, k_3 \ldots \text{ etc.}$$

Thus, the asymptotes $\|$ to y-axis are obtained by equating to zero the coefficient of highest power of y (if not a constant) in the equation of the curve.

Similarly, asymptotes parallel to x-axis are obtained by equating to zero the coefficient of highest power of x (if not a constant).

If the coefficient of highest power is a constant or imaginary, then no asymptotes parallel to any of the axes oxis.

SOLVED EXAMPLES

Example 1. Find the asymptotes of the curve

$$x^2y + xy^2 + xy + y^2 + 3x = 0.$$

Solution: Putting $x = 1$, $y = m$ in third, second and linear terms in the equation (1), we have

$$x^2y + xy^2 + xy + y^2 + 3x = 0 \quad ...(1)$$

$$\phi_3(m) = m + m^2 \quad ...(2)$$

$$\phi_2(m) = m + m^2 \quad ...(3)$$

$$\phi_1(m) = 3 \quad ...(4)$$

If $\quad y = mx + c$ is an asymptote, then m are given by

$$\phi_3(m) = 0$$

i.e. $\quad m + m^2 = 0$

$$m(1 + m) = 0$$

$\therefore \quad m = 0, -1.$

$$c = \frac{-\phi_2(m)}{\phi_3'(m)}$$

$$= \frac{-(m + m^2)}{1 + 2m} \quad ...(4)$$

$$c_1 \text{ (for } m = 0_1) = 0$$

$$c_2 \text{ (for } m = -1) = 0$$

The two asymptotes are

$$y = 0.x + 0$$

$\Rightarrow \quad y = 0 \quad ...(5)$

and $\quad y = -x + 0$

$\Rightarrow \quad y + x = 0 \quad (6)$

and the asymptotes || to the coordinate axis are (1)

$$x + 1 = 0 \text{ parallel to } y\text{-axis and}$$

$$y = 0, \text{ parallel to } x\text{-axis}$$

Thus, the asymptotes of the given curve are

$$y = 0,\ y + x = 0,\ x + 1 = 0.$$

Example 2. Find all the asymptotes of the curve

$$x^3 + y^3 - 3axy = 0.$$

Solution: Here, $\phi_3(m) = 1 + m^3$

$$\phi_2(m) = -3am.$$

Let $y = mx + c$ be the asymptotes.

The values of m are given by

$$\phi_3(m) = 0$$

$$\Rightarrow \quad 1 + m^3 = 0$$

$$(m + 1)(m^2 - m + 1) = 0$$

$$\Rightarrow \quad m = -1, \text{ is the only real root.}$$

Thus, the curve has only one asymptote

Now $$c = \frac{-\phi_2(m)}{\phi_3'(m)}$$

$$= \frac{-(-3am)}{3m^2}$$

$$= \frac{a}{m}$$

$$(c)_{m=-1} = -a$$

$\therefore$ The asymptote is $y = -x - a$

or $x + y + a = 0$

Example 3. Find all the asymptotes of the curve

$$y^4 - 2xy^3 + 2x^3y - x^4 - 3x^3 + 3x^2y + 3xy^2 - 3y^3 - 2x^2 + 2y^2 - 1 = 0.$$

Solution: Here the equation of the curve is of four degree.

Putting $x = 1$, $y = m$, in the fourth, third and second degree terms in the above equation, we have

$$\phi_4\ (m) = m^4 - 2m^3 + 2m - 1$$

$$\phi_3\ (m) = -3 + 3m + 3m^2 - 3m^3$$

$$\phi_2\ (m) = -2 + 2m^2$$

$$\phi_1\ (m) = 0$$

$$\phi_0\ (m) = -1$$

Values of the slopes of the asymptotes are given by

$$\phi_4\ (m) = 0$$

i.e. $\quad m^4 - 2m^3 + 2m - 1 = 0.$

$\Rightarrow \quad (m - 1)^3 \,.\, (m + 1) = 0$

$\therefore \qquad m = 1, 1, 1, -1.$

when $\qquad m = -1$

$$c = \frac{-\phi_3(m)}{\phi_4'(m)}$$

$$= \frac{\left[-3 + 3m + 3m^2 - 3m^3\right]}{4m^3 - 6m^2 + 2}$$

$$(c_1)\ m = -1 = \frac{-[-3 - 3 + 3 + 3]}{-4.27 - 6.4 + 2} = 0$$

Since $m = 1$, is repeated three times.

Then c's are given by

$$\frac{c^3}{3!}\phi'''_4(m) + \frac{c^2}{2!}\phi''_3(m) + c\ \phi'_2(m) + \phi_1(m) = 0$$

or $\quad \dfrac{c^3}{6!}\,.\,(24\ m - 12) + \dfrac{c^2}{2}(6 - 18\ m) + c\,.\,(4\ m) + 0 = 0$

for $m = 1$, $$2c^3 - 6c^2 + 4c = 0$$

$$2c(c-1)(c-2) = 0$$

$\therefore$ $$c = 0, 1, 2.$$

Thus, the asymptotes are $y = x$, $y = x + 1$, $y = x + 2$ and $y = -x$.

Example 4. Find all the asymptotes of the curve

$$x^2y^2 = a^2(x^2 + y^2).$$

Solution: The given equation of the curve is

$$x^2y^2 - a^2x^2 - a^2y^2 = 0 \qquad ...(1)$$

This equation is of degree four and hence the curve may have four asymptotes.

Since here the coefficient of highest powers of x and y are not constant.

So, first of all we find the asymptotes || to the coordinate axes.

Asymptotes parallel to the x-axis are given by equating to zero the coeffecient of x^2, *i.e.*,

$$y^2 - a^2 = 0$$

$$(y + a)(y - a) = 0$$

The asymptotes || to x-axis are

$\therefore$ $$y = a, y = -a.$$

Similarly, asymptotes || to y-axis are

$$x = a, x = -a.$$

$\therefore$ The four asymptotes are $x = \pm a$, $y = \pm a$.

EXERCISE

1. Find all the asymptotes of the following curves:

   (i) $x^3 + x^2y - xy^2 - y^3 + 2xy + 2y^2 - 3x + y = 0$

   (ii) $x^3 + 3x^2y - 4y^3 - x + y + 3 = 0$

   (iii) $x^3 + 2x^2y - xy^2 - 2y^3 + xy - y^2 - 1 = 0$

   (iv) $x^4 - 5x^2y^2 + 4y^4 + x^2 - 2y^2 + 2x + y + 7 = 0$

   (v) $x^3 + 4x^2y + 5xy^2 + 2y^3 + 2x^2 + 4xy + 2y^2 - x - 9y + 1 = 0.$

2. Find the asymptotes || to the coordinate axes of the following curves.

(i) $(x^2 + y^2)\,x - ay^2 = 0$

(ii) $y = \dfrac{x^2 + 1}{x^2 - 1}$

(iii) $x^2y^3 + x^3y^2 = x^3 + y^3$

(iv) $y^2\,(2a - x) = x^3$.

Answers:

1. (i) $y = x + 1,\ y + x + 1 = 0,\ x + y = 2$

(ii) $x = y,\ x + 2y + 1 = 0,\ x + 2y - 1 = 0$

(iii) $x + 2y = 1,\ y = x,\ x + y + 1 = 0$.

(iv) $x \pm 2y = 0,\ x \pm y = 0$.

(v) $x + 2y + 2 = 0,\ x + y \pm \sqrt{2} = 0$

6. (i) $x = a$ (ii) $x = \pm 1,\ y = \pm 1$

(iii) $y = 1,\ x = \pm 1$ (iv) $x = 2a$.

6

Curvature

DERIVATIVES OF ARC LENGTH

Let A be a fixed point on the curve

$$y = f(x) \qquad \ldots(1)$$

and let P and Q be two adjacent points on the curve with coordinates (x, y) and $(x + \delta x, y + \delta y)$ such that the arc length

$$\overset{\frown}{AP} = s$$

$$\overset{\frown}{AQ} = s + \delta s$$

$$\therefore \quad \overset{\frown}{PQ} = \delta s$$

$$\text{Chord} \quad PQ = \delta l$$

As Q moves towards P, then the difference between arc length $\overset{\frown}{PQ}$ and chord PQ goes on decreasing.

As Q approaches P, then arc length $\overset{\frown}{PQ}$ tends to the chord length PQ.

$$\therefore \quad \underset{Q \to P}{\text{Lt}} \frac{\overset{\frown}{PQ}}{PQ} = 1.$$

We draw the perpendiculars PL and QM on x-axis from the points P and Q.

$$\text{Then} \quad PR = \delta x$$

$$RQ = \delta y$$

Now, in right-angled triangle PRQ, we have

$$PQ^2 = PR^2 + PQ^2$$

$$(\delta l)^2 = (\delta x)^2 + (\delta y)^2$$

$$\left(\frac{\delta l}{\delta x}\right)^2 = 1 + \left(\frac{\delta y}{\delta x}\right)^2$$

Now $$\frac{\delta s}{\delta x} = \frac{\delta s}{\delta l} \cdot \frac{\delta l}{\delta x}$$

$$= \frac{\delta s}{\delta l}\sqrt{1+\left(\frac{\delta y}{\delta x}\right)^2}$$

Taking limit $\delta x \to 0$, we have

As $\delta x \to 0$, *i.e.*, $Q \to P$, then $\underset{\delta x \to 0}{\text{Lt}} \dfrac{\delta s}{\delta l} \to 1.$

$\therefore$ $$\underset{\delta x \to 0}{\text{Lt}} \left(\frac{\delta s}{\delta x}\right) = 1 \,.\, \underset{\delta x \to 0}{\text{Lt}} \sqrt{1+\left(\frac{\delta y}{\delta x}\right)^2}$$

or $$\frac{ds}{dx} = \sqrt{1+\left(\frac{dy}{dx}\right)^2}$$

$\therefore$ $$\boxed{\frac{ds}{dx} = \sqrt{1+\left(\frac{dy}{dx}\right)^2}}$$

Similarly,

$$\boxed{\frac{ds}{dy} = \sqrt{1+\left(\frac{dx}{dy}\right)^2}}$$

$$\boxed{\frac{ds}{dt} = \sqrt{\left(\frac{dx}{dt}\right)^2 + \left(\frac{dy}{dt}\right)^2}}$$

$$\boxed{\frac{ds}{dr} = \sqrt{1+\left(r\frac{d\theta}{dr}\right)^2}}$$

and $$\boxed{\frac{ds}{d\theta} = \sqrt{r^2 + \left(\frac{dr}{d\theta}\right)^2}}$$

CURVATURE

Let us consider the arc of the curve $y = f(x)$. ...(1)

Let A be a fixed point on the curve such that

$$\widehat{AP} = s$$

$$\widehat{AQ} = s + \delta s$$

$$\widehat{PQ} = \delta s$$

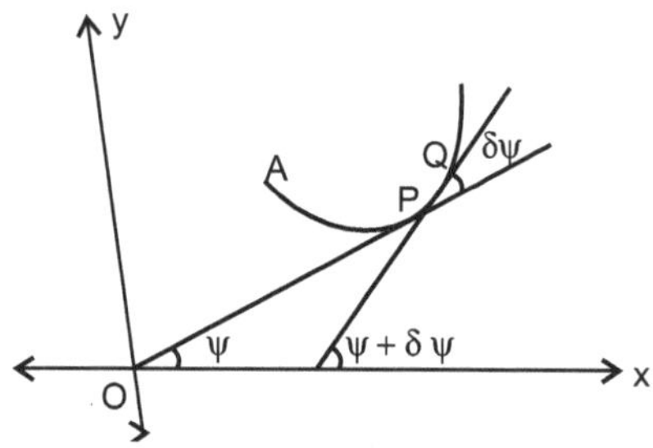

Let the tangents at the points P and Q make angles ψ and $\psi + \delta\psi$ respectively, with +ve direction of x-axis. Thus along the curve, as s changes by δs, ψ changes by $\delta\psi$.

The curvature of a curve at a point P is defined as the rate of change of the angle ψ (which the tangent to the curve at that point makes with +ve direction of x-axis) with respect to the arc length s.

i.e. $$\text{Curvature} = \underset{\delta s \to 0}{\text{Lt}} \frac{\delta\psi}{\delta s}$$

$\therefore$ $$\boxed{\text{Curvature} = \frac{d\psi}{ds}}$$

RADIUS OF CURVATURE

If the curvature of a curve at a point is not zero, then the reciprocal of curvature is defined as the radius of curvature at that point and is denoted by ρ.

Thus $$\rho = \frac{1}{\text{curvature}} = \frac{1}{\frac{d\psi}{ds}}$$

or $$\rho = \frac{ds}{d\psi}$$

ρ is always taken with +ve sign.

Radius of Curvature [Cartesian Curves].

Let the cartesian equation of a curve be

$$y = f(x) \qquad ...(1)$$

Then if ψ be the angle, which the tangent to the curve at any point, makes with +ve direction of x-axis, then

$$\tan\psi = \frac{dy}{dx} \qquad ...(2)$$

Differentiating equation (2) w.r.t. s, (the arc length), we have

$$\sec^2\psi \frac{d\psi}{ds} = \frac{d}{dx}.\left[\frac{dy}{dx}\right].\frac{dx}{ds}$$

$$= \frac{d^2y}{dx^2}.\frac{dx}{ds}$$

$$= \frac{\frac{d^2y}{dx^2}}{\frac{ds}{dx}}$$

$$\therefore \quad (1+\tan^2\psi)\frac{d\psi}{ds} = \frac{\frac{d^2y}{dx^2}}{\sqrt{1+\left(\frac{dy}{dx}\right)^2}}$$

$$\therefore \quad \frac{d\psi}{ds} = \frac{\frac{d^2y}{dx^2}}{\left[1+\left(\frac{dy}{dx}\right)^2\right]\left[1+\left(\frac{dy}{dx}\right)^2\right]^{1/2}}$$

$$\frac{d\psi}{ds} = \frac{\frac{d^2y}{dx^2}}{\left[1+\left(\frac{dy}{dx}\right)^2\right]^{3/2}}$$

$$\therefore \quad \frac{ds}{d\psi} = \frac{\left[1+\left(\frac{dy}{dx}\right)^2\right]^{3/2}}{\frac{d^2y}{dx^2}}$$

$$\therefore \quad \boxed{\rho = \frac{\left[1+\left(\frac{dy}{dx}\right)^2\right]^{3/2}}{\frac{d^2y}{dx^2}}} \quad \left[\frac{d^2y}{dx^2} \neq 0\right]$$

SOLVED EXAMPLES

Example 1. Find the radius of curvature of the curve $x^3 + y^3 = 3axy$ at $(3a/2, 3a/2)$

Solution: Equation of the curve is $x^3 + y^3 - 3axy = 0$

$$\therefore 3x^2 + 3y^2 \frac{dy}{dx} - 3ay - 3ax \frac{dy}{dx} = 0$$

$$\therefore \quad \frac{dy}{dx} = \frac{x^2 - ay}{ax - y^2}$$

and
$$\frac{d^2y}{dx^2} = \frac{\left(2x - a\frac{dy}{dx}\right)\left(ax - y^2\right) - \left(x^2 - ay\right)\left(a - 2y\frac{dy}{dx}\right)}{\left(ax - y^2\right)^2}$$

$$y_1 = \left(\frac{dy}{dx}\right)_{(3a/2, 3a/2)} = -1$$

and
$$\left(\frac{d^2y}{dx^2}\right)_{(3a/2, 3a/2)} = \frac{-32}{3a} = y_2$$

$$\text{Radius of curvature} = \left|\frac{\left(1+y_1^2\right)^{3/2}}{y_2}\right| = \left|\frac{3a\left(1+1\right)^{\frac{3}{2}}}{-32}\right|$$

$$= \frac{3a.2\sqrt{2}}{32} = \frac{3a.\sqrt{2}}{16}$$

Example 2. If ρ is the radius of curvature at any point P on the parabola $y^2 = 4ax$ and S is its focus, then show that $\rho^2 \alpha SP^3$.

Solution: Equation of the given parabola is

$$y^2 = 4ax \qquad ...(1)$$

Then its focus S is given by S(a, o)

Let P (x_1, y_1) be any point on the parabola (1), then

$$y_1{}^2 = 4ax_1 \qquad ...(2)$$

$$\therefore \quad SP = \sqrt{(x_1 - a)^2 + (y_1 - o)^2}$$

$$= \sqrt{x_1^2 + a^2 - 2ax_1 + y_1^2}$$

$$= \sqrt{x_1^2 + a^2 - 2ax_1 + 4ax_1}$$

$$= \sqrt{(x_1 + a)^2}$$

$$SP = (x_1 + a)$$

$$\therefore \quad SP^3 = (x_1 + a)^3$$

Now, differentiating equation (1) w.r.t. x, we have

$$2y\frac{dy}{dx} = 4a$$

$$\therefore \quad \frac{dy}{dx} = \frac{2a}{y}$$

Again differentiating $\frac{d^2y}{dx^2} = \frac{-2a}{y^2} \cdot \frac{dy}{dx}$

$$= \frac{-4a^2}{y^3}$$

$$\therefore \qquad (\rho)_P = \left[\frac{1+\left(\dfrac{dy}{dx\rho}\right)^2}{\left(\dfrac{d^2y}{dx^2}\right)_P}\right]^{3/2}$$

$$(\rho)_P = \frac{\left[1+\dfrac{4a^2}{y_1^2}\right]^{3/2}}{\dfrac{-4a^2}{y_1^3}}$$

$$= \frac{\left[y_1^2+4a^2\right]^{3/2}}{-4a^2}$$

$$= \frac{\left[4ax_1+4a^2\right]^{3/2}}{-4a^2}$$

$$= \frac{2}{\sqrt{a}} \cdot (x_1+a)^{3/2}$$

$$\rho^2 = \frac{4}{a}(x_1+a)^3$$

or $$\rho^2 \alpha (SP)^3.$$

Radius of curvature [Parametric curves]

Let $x = f_1(t), y = f_2(t)$ be the parametric equation of a curve.

Then $$\frac{dy}{dx} = \frac{\dfrac{dy}{dt}}{\dfrac{dx}{dt}} = \frac{y'}{x'} \quad \text{[dashes rep. diff. w.r.t. } t\text{]}$$

$$\frac{d^2y}{dx^2} = \frac{y''x' - y'x''}{x'^2} \cdot \frac{dt}{dx}$$

$$= \frac{x'y'' - y'x''}{x'^2} \cdot \frac{1}{x'}$$

$$= \frac{x'y'' - y'x''}{x'^3}$$

Now $$\rho = \frac{\left[1 + \left(\frac{dy}{dx}\right)^2\right]^{3/2}}{\frac{d^2y}{dx^2}}$$

$$= \frac{\left[1 + \frac{y'^2}{x'^2}\right]^{3/2}}{\frac{x'y'' - y'x''}{x'^3}}$$

$$\rho = \frac{\left[x'^2 + y'^2\right]^{3/2}}{x'y'' - y'x''}$$

or $$\boxed{\rho = \frac{\left[x'^2 + y'^2\right]^{3/2}}{x'y'' - y'x''}}$$

SOLVED EXAMPLES

Example 1. Show that curvature of a circle is constant at every point.

Solution: Let $x = a \cos\theta$, $y = a \sin\theta$ be the equation of a circle

$\therefore$ $$\frac{dx}{d\theta} = -a \sin\theta$$

$$\frac{dy}{d\theta} = a \cos\theta$$

or $$x' = -a \sin\theta$$

$$x'' = -a \cos\theta$$

$$y' = +a \cos\theta$$

$$y'' = -a\sin\theta$$

$$\therefore \qquad \rho = \frac{\left[x'^2 + y'^2\right]^{3/2}}{x'y'' - y'x''} = \frac{\left[a^2\sin^2\theta + a^2\cos^2\theta\right]^{3/2}}{-\left(a^2\sin^2\theta + a^2\cos^2\theta\right)}$$

or
$$\rho = \frac{\left(a^2\right)^{3/2}}{a^2} = a$$

$$\therefore \qquad \text{Curvature} = \frac{1}{\rho} = \frac{1}{a}$$

(Constant, $\because$ a is constant for a given circle)

Example 2. Show that the radius of curvature at a point on the curve $x = ae^{\theta}(\sin\theta - \cos\theta)$, $y = ae^{\theta}(\sin\theta + \cos\theta)$ is two times the distance of the tangent at that point from the origin.

Solution: For the given curve

$$x = ae^{\theta}(\sin\theta - \cos\theta)$$

$$y = ae^{\theta}(\sin\theta + \cos\theta)$$

$$\therefore \qquad x' = ae^{\theta}(\sin\theta - \cos\theta) + ae^{\theta}(\cos\theta + \sin\theta)$$

$$x' = 2\,ae^{\theta}\sin\theta$$

$$y' = ae^{\theta}(\sin\theta + \cos\theta) + ae^{\theta}(\cos\theta - \sin\theta)$$

$$= 2\,ae^{\theta}\cos\theta$$

$$\therefore \qquad \frac{dy}{dx} = \cot\theta \qquad \text{...(1)}$$

$$\therefore \qquad \frac{d^2y}{dx^2} = -\operatorname{cosec}^2\theta \cdot \frac{d\theta}{dx}$$

$$= -\operatorname{cosec}^2\theta \cdot \frac{1}{2ae^{\theta}.\sin\theta}$$

$$= \frac{-1}{2ae^{\theta}.\sin^3\theta} \qquad \text{...(2)}$$

$$\therefore \qquad \rho = \frac{\left[1 + \left(\frac{dy}{dx}\right)^2\right]^{3/2}}{\frac{d^2y}{dx^2}}$$

$$= \frac{\left(1+\cot^2\theta\right)^{3/2}}{\dfrac{-1}{2ae^{\theta}.\sin^3\theta}}$$

$$|\rho| = \text{cosec}^3\theta \ . \ 2ae^{\theta} \ . \ \sin^3\theta$$

$$\rho = 2ae^{\theta} \qquad ...(3)$$

Now, the equation of tangent at the above point is

$$y - ae^{\theta}(\sin\theta + \cos\theta) = \cot\theta \, [x - ae^{\theta}(\sin\theta - \cos\theta)]$$

or $\quad x\cos\theta - y\sin\theta + ae^{\theta} = 0 \qquad ...(4)$

$\therefore \quad p$, the length of perpendicular on this tangent from the origin

$$p = \frac{ae^{\theta}}{\sqrt{\cos^2\theta + \sin^2\theta}} = ae^{\theta} \qquad ...(5)$$

From equation (4) and (5),

$$\rho = 2P.$$

Example 3. The tangents at two points P and Q on the cycloid $x = a(\theta - \sin\theta)$, $y = a(1 - \cos\theta)$ are at right angles, show that $\rho_1^2 + \rho_2^2 = 16a^2$, where ρ_1 and ρ_2 are the radii of curvature at these points.

Solution: For the given curve

$$x = a(\theta - \sin\theta) \qquad ...(1)$$

$$y = a(1 - \cos\theta) \qquad ...(2)$$

$$\therefore \qquad x' = a(1 - \cos\theta)$$

$$y' = a\sin\theta)$$

$$\therefore \qquad \frac{dy}{dx} = \frac{a\sin\theta}{a(1-\cos\theta)}$$

$$= \frac{2a\sin\frac{\theta}{2}\cos\frac{\theta}{2}}{2a\sin^2\frac{\theta}{2}}$$

$$\frac{dy}{dx} = \cot\frac{\theta}{2} \quad ...(3)$$

$$\frac{d^2y}{dx} = -\text{cosec}^2\frac{\theta}{2} \cdot \frac{1}{2}\frac{d\theta}{dx}$$

$$= -\frac{1}{2\sin^2\frac{\theta}{2}} \cdot \frac{1}{a(1-\cos\theta)}$$

$$= \frac{-1}{4a}\text{cosec}^4\frac{\theta}{2}$$

$$\therefore \quad \rho = \frac{\left[1+\cot^2\frac{\theta}{2}\right]^{3/2}}{-\frac{1}{4a}.\text{cosec}^4\frac{\theta}{2}}$$

$$\therefore \quad = \frac{\text{cosec}^3\frac{\theta}{2}}{-\frac{1}{4a}\text{cosec}^4\frac{\theta}{2}}$$

$$\therefore \quad \rho = -4a\sin\frac{\theta}{2} \quad ...(4)$$

Now let the values of θ at P and Q be θ_1 and θ_2

$$\therefore \quad \rho_1 = -4a\sin\frac{\theta_1}{2}$$

$$\rho_2 = -4a\sin\frac{\theta_2}{2}$$

$\because$ The tangents at P and Q are at right angles

$$\therefore \quad \cot\frac{\theta_1}{2} \cdot \cot\frac{\theta_2}{2} = -1$$

$$\cot\frac{\theta_1}{2} = -\tan\frac{\theta_2}{2}$$

$$\cot\frac{\theta_1}{2} = \cot\left(\frac{\pi}{2}+\frac{\theta_2}{2}\right)$$

$$\Rightarrow \qquad \frac{\theta_1}{2} = \frac{\pi}{2} + \frac{\theta_2}{2}$$

$$\rho_1^2 + \rho_2^2 = \left(4a\sin\frac{\theta_2}{2}\right)^2 + \left[4a\sin\left(\frac{\pi}{2} + \frac{\theta_2}{2}\right)\right]^2$$

$$= 16a^2 \sin^2\left(\frac{\theta_2}{2}\right) + 16a^2 \cos^2\left(\frac{\theta_2}{2}\right)$$

$$\therefore \qquad \rho_1^2 + \rho_2^2 = 16a^2.$$

RADIUS OF CURVATURE OF POLAR CURVES

Let $\qquad r = f(\theta) \qquad \ldots(1)$

be the polar equation of a curve.

$$\because \qquad x = r\cos\theta$$

$$y = r\sin\theta$$

$$\therefore \qquad x = f(\theta)\,.\,\cos\theta$$

and $\qquad y = f(\theta)\,.\,\sin\theta$

$$\therefore \qquad x' = f'(\theta)\,.\,\cos\theta - f(\theta)\,.\,\sin\theta$$

$$x'' = f''(\theta)\,.\,\cos\theta - f'(\theta)\,.\,\sin\theta - f'(\theta)\,.\,\sin\theta$$

$$-f(\theta)\,.\,\cos\theta$$

$$= f''(\theta)\,.\,\cos\theta - 2f'(\theta)\sin\theta - f(\theta)\cos\theta$$

$$y' = f(\theta)\,.\,\sin\theta + f(\theta)\cos\theta$$

$$y'' = f''(\theta)\,.\,\sin\theta + 2f'(\theta)\cos\theta - f(\theta)\,.\,\sin\theta$$

$$\because \qquad \rho = \frac{\left[x'^2 + y'^2\right]^{3/2}}{x'y'' - y'x''}$$

$$= \frac{\left[\left[f(\theta)\right]^2 + \left[f'(\theta)\right]^2\right]^{3/2}}{\left[f(\theta)\right]^2 + 2\left[f'(\theta)^2\right] - f(\theta).f''(\theta)}$$

$$\therefore \qquad \rho = \frac{\left[r^2 + \left(\frac{dr}{d\theta}\right)^2\right]^{3/2}}{r^2 + 2\left(\frac{dr}{d\theta}\right)^2 - r\frac{d^2r}{d\theta^2}}.$$

SOLVED EXAMPLES

Example 1. Find the radius of curvature of the following curves:

(i) $r = a\,(1 - \cos\theta)$

(ii) $r^n = a^n \sin n\theta$.

Solution: Here $\quad r = a\,(1 - \cos\theta)$

$$\frac{dr}{d\theta} = a\sin\theta$$

$$\therefore \qquad \frac{d^2r}{d\theta^2} = a\cos\theta$$

$$\therefore \qquad \rho = \left[\frac{r^2 + \left(\frac{dr}{d\theta}\right)^2}{r^2 + 2\left(\frac{dr}{d\theta}\right)^2 - r\frac{d^2r}{d\theta^2}}\right]^{3/2}$$

$$= \frac{\left[a^2\left(1 + \cos^2\theta - 2\cos\theta\right) + a^2\sin^2\theta\right]^{3/2}}{a^2\left(1 + \cos^2\theta - 2\cos\theta\right) + 2.a^2\sin^2\theta - a^2\cos\theta + a^2\cos^2\theta}$$

$$= \frac{a^3.\left[2(1 - \cos\theta)\right]^{3/2}}{3a^2 - 3a^2\cos\theta}$$

$$= \frac{2\sqrt{2}\,a^3\,(1 - \cos\theta)^{1/2}}{3a^2}$$

$$= \frac{2}{3}\sqrt{2ar}$$

$$\therefore \qquad \rho = \frac{2}{3}\sqrt{2ar}$$

(ii) Here $\qquad r^n = a^n . \sin n\theta \qquad$ ...(1)

$$\therefore \qquad n \log r = n \log a + \log \sin n\theta$$

$\therefore$ Differentiating w.r.t.θ, we have

$$n\frac{1}{r}.\frac{dr}{d\theta} = 0 + \frac{1}{\sin n\theta} . n \cos n\theta.$$

$$\therefore \qquad \frac{dr}{d\theta} = r \cot n\theta \qquad ...(2)$$

Again differentiating w.r.t. θ, we have

$$\frac{d^2r}{d\theta^2} = \frac{dr}{d\theta} . \cot n\theta - nr \operatorname{cosec}^2 n\theta$$

$$= r \cot^2 n\theta - nr \operatorname{cosec}^2 n\theta$$

$$\therefore \qquad \rho = \frac{\left[r^2 + \left(\frac{dr}{d\theta}\right)^2\right]^{3/2}}{r^2 + 2\left(\frac{dr}{d\theta}\right)^2 - r\frac{d^2r}{d\theta^2}} s$$

$$= \frac{\left[r^2 + r^2 \cot^2 n\theta\right]^{3/2}}{r^2 + 2r^2 \cot^2 n\theta - r^2 \cot^2 n\theta + nr^2 \operatorname{cosec}^2 n\theta}$$

$$= \frac{\left[r^3 \operatorname{cosec}^3 n\theta\right]}{r^2\left[1 + 2\cot^2 n\theta - \cot^2 n\theta + n \operatorname{cosec}^2 \theta\right]}$$

$$= \frac{r \operatorname{cosec}^3 n\theta}{(n+1)\left(\operatorname{cosec}^2 n\theta\right)}$$

$$= \frac{r \operatorname{cosec} n\theta}{(n+1)}$$

$$= \frac{r}{(n+1)} \cdot \frac{a^n}{r^n}$$

$$\therefore \qquad \rho = \frac{a^n}{(n+1)\, r^{n-1}}$$

Example 2. If $r^2 = a^2 \cos 2\theta$, show that $\rho = \dfrac{a^2}{3r}$.

Solution: Here $r^2 = a^2 \cos 2\theta$.

$$\therefore \qquad 2 \log r = 2 \log a + \log \cos 2\theta.$$

$$\therefore \qquad 2 . \frac{1}{r} . \frac{dr}{d\theta} = 0 + \frac{1}{\cos 2\theta} (-2 \sin 2\theta)$$

$$\frac{dr}{d\theta} = - r \tan 2\theta.$$

Again diff. w.r.t. θ, we have

$$\frac{d^2 r}{d\theta^2} = -\frac{dr}{d\theta} . \tan 2\theta - r . 2 . \sec^2 2\theta$$

$$= r \tan^2 2\theta - 2r \sec^2 2\theta$$

$$\rho = \frac{\left[r^2 + r^2 \tan^2 2\theta\right]^{3/2}}{r^2 + 2r^2 \tan^2 2\theta - r^2 \tan^2 2\theta + 2r^2 \sec^2 2\theta}$$

$$= \frac{\left[r^3 \sec^3 2\theta\right]}{r^2\left[1 + 2\tan^2 2\theta - \tan^2 2\theta + 2\sec^2 2\theta\right]}$$

$$= \frac{r \sec^3 2\theta}{3 \sec^2 2\theta}$$

$$= \frac{r}{3} \sec 2\theta$$

$$= \frac{r}{3} \cdot \frac{a^2}{r^2}$$

$$\therefore \qquad \rho = \frac{a^2}{3r}.$$

Example 2. If ρ_1 and ρ_2 are the radii of curvature at the extremities of any chord of the cardioid $r = a\,(1 + \cos\theta)$, which passes through the pole, then show that $\rho_1^2 + \rho_2^2 = \dfrac{16a^2}{9}$

Solution: Here $\qquad r = a\,(1 + \cos\theta) \qquad$ ...(1)

$$\therefore \qquad \frac{dr}{d\theta} = -a \sin\theta$$

$$\text{and,} \qquad \frac{d^2r}{d\theta^2} = -a \cos\theta$$

$$\therefore \rho = \frac{\left[a^2\left(1+\cos^2\theta+2\cos\theta\right)+a^2\sin^2\theta\right]^{3/2}}{a^2\left(1+\cos^2\theta+2\cos\theta\right)+2a^2\sin^2\theta+a^2\cos\theta+a^2\cos^2\theta}$$

$$= \frac{a^3\left[2(1+\cos\theta)\right]^{3/2}}{a^2\left[3+3\cos\theta\right]}$$

$$= \frac{a2\sqrt{2}\,(1+\cos\theta)^{1/2}}{3}$$

$$= \frac{4a}{3}\cos\left(\frac{\theta}{2}\right) \qquad \text{...(2)}$$

Now, if the value of the vectorial angle is θ_1 at p, then at the other end of the chord passing through the pole, it will be $\pi + \theta_1$.

$$\therefore \qquad \rho_1 = \frac{4a}{3}\cos\frac{\theta_1}{2} \qquad ...(3)$$

$$\therefore \qquad \rho_2 = \frac{4a}{3}\cos\left(\frac{\pi}{2}+\frac{\theta_1}{2}\right)$$

$$= \frac{-4a}{3}\sin\frac{\theta_1}{2} \qquad ...(4)$$

$$\therefore \qquad \rho_1^2 + \rho_2^2 = \frac{16a^2}{9}$$

Example 3. If ρ_1 and ρ_2 be the radii of curvature at the extremities of two conjugate diameters of ellipse $\frac{x^2}{a^2}+\frac{y^2}{b^2} = 1.$

Prove that $\left(\rho_1^{2/3}+\rho_2^{2/3}\right)$ $(ab)^{2/3} = a^2 + b^2$.

Solution: Let $\qquad x = a \cos t$

$\qquad y = b \sin t,$

be the parametric equation of the given ellipse.

$$\therefore \qquad x' = -a \sin t$$

$$x'' = -a \cos t$$

$$y' = +b \cos t$$

$$y'' = -b \sin t$$

$$\therefore \qquad \rho = \frac{\left[x'^2 + y'^2\right]^{3/2}}{x'y'' - y'x''}$$

$$= \frac{\left[a^2\sin^2 t + b^2\cos^2 t\right]^{3/2}}{ab\sin^2 t + ab\cos^2 t} \qquad ...(1)$$

Let P and Q be the extremities of the conjugate diameters, then, if P is $P(t_1)$ then Q is $Q\ (t_1 + \pi/2)$.

$$\rho_1 = \frac{\left[a^2\sin^2 t_1 + b^2\cos^2 t_1\right]^{3/2}}{ab}$$

$$\therefore \qquad \rho_1^{2/3} \cdot (ab)^{2/3} = a^2 \sin^2 t_1 + b^2 \cos^2 t_1 \qquad ...(2)$$

and $\rho_2^{2/3} \cdot (ab)^{2/3} = a^2 \sin^2\left(t_1 + \frac{\pi}{2}\right) + b^2 \cos^2\left(t_1 + \frac{\pi}{2}\right)$

$$= a^2 \cos^2 t_1 + b^2 \sin^2 t_1 \quad ...(3)$$

Adding (2) and (3), we have

$$\therefore \left(\rho_1^{2/3} + \rho_2^{2/3}\right) \cdot (ab)^{2/3} = a^2 + b^2.$$

Example 4. Show that for the curve $s = ae^{x/c}$

$$\rho = \frac{s}{c}\sqrt{s^2 - c^2}, \text{ where } s \text{ is the arc length.}$$

Solution: The given curve is

$$s = ae^{x/c} \quad (1)$$

Differentiating w.r.t. x, we have

$$\frac{ds}{dx} = a \cdot e^{x/c} \cdot \frac{1}{c}$$

$$\frac{ds}{dx} = \frac{s}{c}$$

or $$\sqrt{1 + \left(\frac{dy}{dx}\right)^2} = \frac{s}{c} \qquad \left[\because \frac{ds}{dx} = \sqrt{1 + \left(\frac{dy}{dx}\right)^2}\right]$$

$$\therefore \quad 1 + \left(\frac{dy}{dx}\right)^2 = \frac{s^2}{c^2}$$

$$\therefore \quad \frac{dy}{dx} = \frac{1}{c} \cdot \sqrt{s^2 - c^2}$$

$$\frac{d^2y}{dx^2} = \frac{1}{c} \cdot \frac{1}{2} \cdot \frac{2s}{\sqrt{s^2 - c^2}} \cdot \frac{ds}{dx}$$

$$= \frac{s}{c} \frac{1}{\sqrt{s^2 - c^2}} \cdot \frac{s}{c} = \frac{s^2}{c^2} \frac{1}{\sqrt{s^2 - c^2}}$$

$$\therefore \qquad \rho = \frac{\left[1+\left(\frac{dy}{dx}\right)^2\right]^{3/2}}{\frac{d^2y}{dx^2}}$$

$$= \frac{\frac{s^3}{c^3}}{\frac{s^2}{c^2\sqrt{s^2-c^2}}}$$

$$= \frac{s^3}{c^3}.\frac{c^2}{s^2}.\sqrt{s^2-c^2}$$

$$= \frac{s}{c}\sqrt{s^2-c^2}$$

$$\therefore \qquad \rho = \frac{s}{c}\sqrt{s^2-c^2}$$

EXERCISE

1. Find the radius of curvature of $y^2 = 4x$ at (1, 2).
2. Find the radius of curvature of $y = \log x$ at (1, 0).
3. Find the point on the curve $y = e^x$ at which curvature is maximum.
4. Find the point on the curve $y^2 = 8x$ at which curvature is $7\frac{13}{16}$.
5. Find the radius of curvature at any point t on the following curves:
   (i) $x = a \cos^3 t,\ y = b \sin^3 t$
   (ii) $x = a\ (\cos t + \log \tan t/2),\ y = a \sin t.$
   (iii) $x = e^t \cos t,\ y = e^t \sin t.$
6. If ρ_1 and ρ_2 be radii of curvature at the extremities of a focal chord of a parabola whose latus rectum is $2l$, prove that $\rho_1^{-2/3} + \rho_2^{-2/3} = l^{-2/3}$.
7. Show that the radius of curvature at any point on the curve $x = a \cos^3\theta$, $y = a \sin^3\theta$ is equal to three times the length of perpendicular from the origin to the tangent at that point.

8. Prove that for the ellipse $\frac{x^2}{a^2}+\frac{y^2}{b^2}=1$, at any point $\rho=\frac{a^2b^2}{p^3}$, where ρ is the length of perpendicular from the centre of the ellipse, upon the tangent at that point.

9. If CP and CD be a pair of conjugate semi-diameters of an ellipse $\frac{x^2}{a^2}+\frac{y^2}{b^2}=1$ with centre C, prove that the radius of curvature at p is $\frac{(\text{CD})^3}{ab}$.

10. For the curve $y=\frac{ax}{a+x}$ if ρ is the radius of curvature at any point P (x, y), show that $\left(\frac{2\rho}{a}\right)^{2/3}=\left(\frac{y}{x}\right)^2+\left(\frac{x}{y}\right)^2$.

11. Show that for the curve $y=\frac{a}{2}[e^{x/a}+e^{-x/a}]$ $\rho=\frac{y^2}{2a}$.

12. Show that for the curve $r=a(1+\cos\theta)$, $\frac{\rho^2}{r}$ is constant.

13. For the curve $r^m=a^m\cos m\theta$, show that $\rho=\frac{a^m}{(m+1)r^{m-1}}$

14. Show that at each point on the curve $r^2=a^2\cos^2\theta$, the curvature is proportional to the radius vector of that point.

15. Show that for the catenary

$$x=c\log[s+\sqrt{s^2+c^2}]$$

$$y=\sqrt{s^2+c^2}\text{, have}$$

$$\rho=\frac{s^2+c^2}{c}.$$

Answers:

1. $4\sqrt{2}$
2. 3/2
3. $\left(-\frac{1}{2}\log 2, \frac{\sqrt{2}}{2}\right)$
4. $\left(\frac{9}{8}, \pm 3\right)$
5. (i) $\dfrac{3\sin t\cos t\left[a^2\cos^2 t + b^2\sin^2 t\right]^{3/2}}{ab}$

   (ii) $a\cos t$

   (iii) $\sqrt{2}\,e^t$.

7

Curve Tracing

INTRODUCTION

In many engineering applications we need the length of a curve or something distributed along the length of a curve. Area of some region or something distributed over the region bounded by a closed curve, volume of solids formed by the revolution of the area bounded by a curve about a line something distributed in that volume, surface formed by the revolution of the arc of a curve about a line.

In all these cases we need an approximate shape of that curve.

TRACING OF CARTESIAN CURVES

Few of the important points which help us to have an approximate shape of a curve are:

1. Symmetry:

- If a curve below and above x-axis has the same shape then we say that it is symmetric about x-axis.
- If to the left and right of y-axis, the curve has the same shape, it is said to be symmetric about y-axis.
- If below and above $y = x$ line, shape of a curve is same, we say it is symmetric about $y = x$ line.
- If below and above $y = -x$ line, shape of a curve is same, then it is symmetrical about $y = -x$ line.
- If in the Ist and IIIrd quadrants or in II and IV quadrants, shape of a curve is same, then it is said to be symmetric in opposite quadrants.

- How to check symmetry if there is any:

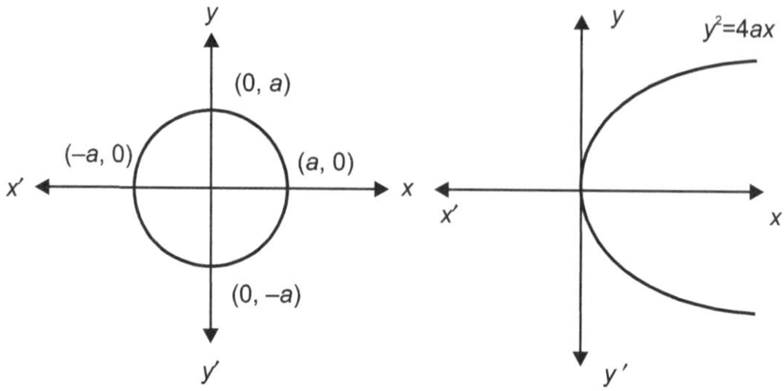

If a curve has the same shape above and below x-axis, *i.e.*, symmetry about x-axis, then corresponding to each point P (x, y) on the curve there exists a point Q $(x, -y)$ on the curve. Thus, for one value of x there are two values of y, both numerically equal but of opposite sign, which can be only if the equation of a curve is of the form $y^2 = f(x)$, $y^4 = f(x)$ ... etc.

- That is if the equation of a curve contains even and only even powers of y, then the curve is symmetrical about x-axis.
- If the equation of a curve contains even and only even powers of x, then it is symmetrical about y-axis.
- If even and only even powers of both x and y, then the curve is symmetrical about both the axes.
- If the equation of a curve does not change when x and y are interchanged, then the curve is symmetrical about $y = x$ line.
- If x is changed to $-y$, y is changed to $-x$ and equation of the curve does not change, then the curve is symmetrical about $y = -x$ line.
- If x is changed to $-x$, y is changed to $-y$ and the equation of the curve does not change, then the curve is symmetric in opposite quadrants *i.e.*, in the first and third quadrants or in second and fourth quadrants, shapes of the curves are same.

2. Origin: Find, whether the curve passes through the origin or not (If the coordinates of origin satisfy the equation of the curve).

- If passes through the origin then equation of tangent(s) at the origin is (are) obtained by equating to zero the lowest degree term.
- If more than one tangents are at the origin, then the origin is a multiple point. If the tangents are real and distinct then it is a node. If tangents are real and coincident the origin is a cusp and if the tangents are imaginary then it is an isolated point.

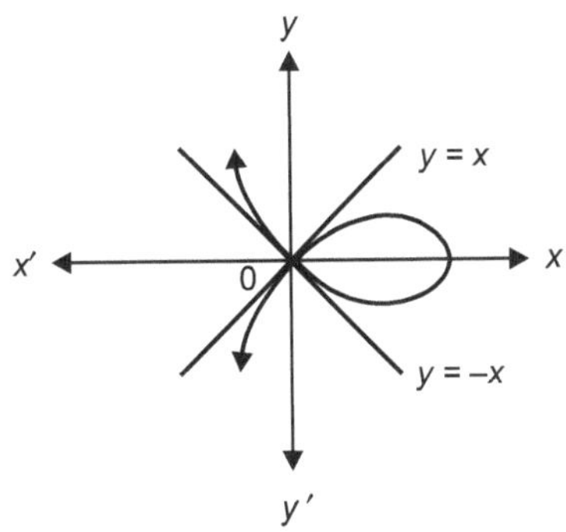

Node

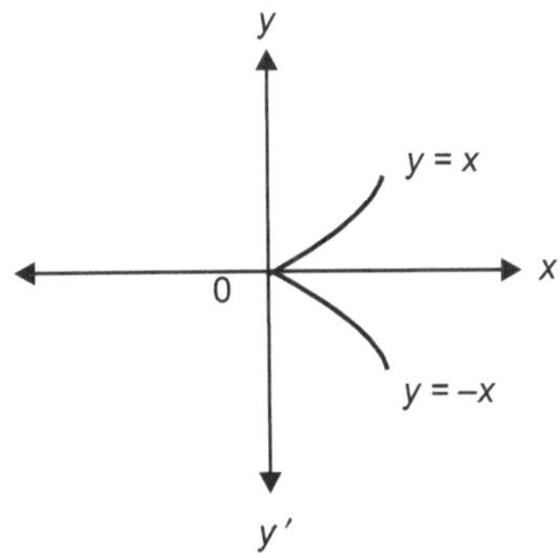

Cups

3. Intersection with coordinate axes: Find the points of intersection on x-axis by solving the equation of the curve for $y = 0$ and vice-versa.

- Tangents at these points (if any) are obtained by shifting the origin at that point and then equating to zero the lowest degree term.
- Find the points of intersection of the curve with the lines $y = x$ and or $y = -x$, if the curve is symmetric about these lines and then the equation(s) of tangents, thereat.

4. Asymptotes: Generally asymptotes || to the coordinate axes are needed, which can be obtained as:

- || to x-axis : by equating to zero to coefficient of highest power of x (if not a constant).
- || to y-axis : by equating to zero the coefficient of highest power of y (if not a constant). If the coefficient of highest powers are (is) constant then no asymptote || to coordinate axes exist(s). Hardly we require oblique asymptotes. If needed they can be obtained by the methods discussed earlier.

5. Region: Find the region in which the curve exists or does not exist.

If y becomes imaginary for values of x in some interval, then the curve does not exist for those values of x and vice-versa.

6. Special Points:

- Those points where

$$\frac{dy}{dx} = 0 \text{ or } \infty.$$

We note down these points at which the curve changes its nature.

- Points, where there may be maxima or minima.

SOLVED EXAMPLES

Example 1. Trace the curve $a^2y^2 = x^3(2a - x)$

Solution:

1. Symmetry: The equation of the curve contains even and only even powers of y. Therefore, the curve is symmetric about x-axis.

2. Origin : The curve passes through the origin and equation of tangents at the origin is

$$a^2y^2 = 0$$

i.e. $$y^2 = 0$$

Here the two tangents given by $y^2 = 0$ *i.e.*, x-axis, are identical, therefore origin is a cusp, *i.e.*, two branches of the curve pass through the origin touching x-axis, one below and one above x-axis.

3. Intersection with coordinate axes:

- on x-axis.

putting $y = 0$ in the equation of the curve, we obtain

$$x^3(2a - x) = 0$$

$\therefore$ $$x = 0$$

and $$= 2a.$$

$\therefore$ The curve intersects x-axis at (0, 0) and $(2a, 0)$.

Tangents at (0, 0) are x-axis and the tangent at $(2a, 0)$ are obtained by shifting origin at $(2a, 0)$ *i.e.*

Substituting

$$x = X + 2a$$

$$y = Y + 0$$

we have

$$a^2Y^2 = (X + 2a)^3(2a - X - 2a)$$

$$a^2Y^2 = -X[X^3 + 8a^3 + 6aX^2 + 12a^2X]$$

or $$a^2Y^2 + X^4 + 8a^3X + 6aX^3 + 12a^2X^2 = 0$$

$\therefore$ Tangent at the new origin $(2a, 0)$ is

$$8a^3X = 0$$

$$i.e.\ X = 0$$

$$i.e.\ x - 2a = 0$$

$$x = 2a$$

- on y-axis, is given by

$$a^2y^2 = 0$$

$$i.e.\ y = 0$$

$\therefore$ at (0, 0) only

4. Asymptotes: Since the coefficient of highest powers of x and y are constant, therefore there is no asymptote || to coordinate axes.

5. Region:

$$a^2y^2 = x^3 (2a - x)$$

y^2 is –ve when $x < 0$ or $x > 2a$

For $x < 0$ and $x > 2a$, the curve does not exist.

$\therefore$ The curve exists for $0 \le x \le 2a$ and y attains maxima for $x = \frac{3a}{2}$

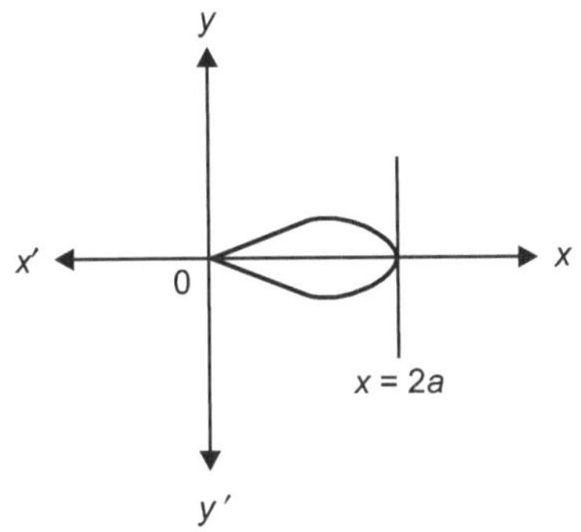

Example 2. Trace the curve $y^2 (2a - x) = x^3$.

Solution:

1. Symmetry: The equation of the curve contains even and only even powers of y, therefore the curve is symmetrical about x-axis.

2. Origin : The curve passes through the origin and equation of tangents at the origin is

$$2ay^2 = 0$$

$$i.e.\ y^2 = 0$$

i.e. x-axis is a double tangent. Thus, origin is a cusp.

3. Intersection with coordinate axes:

- on x-axis.

Putting $y = 0$ in the equation of the curve

we have $x = 0$

$\therefore$ Intersection with x-axis only at the origin.

- on y-axis

For $x = 0$,

we have $y = 0$

$\therefore$ The curve intersects y-axis at the origin only.

4. Asymptotes:

- No asymptote || to x-axis as the coefficient of highest power of x is a constant.
- Asymptote || to y-axis is $x = 2a$.

5. Region: y^2 is –ve for $x < 0$ or $x > 2a$.

$\therefore$ The curve does not exist for $x < 0$ and for $x > 2a$.

The curve lies in $0 \leq x < 2a$.

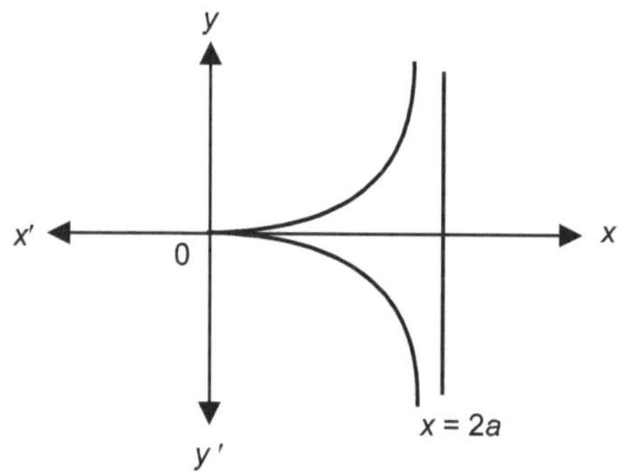

Example 3. Trace the curve $a^2y^2 = a^2x^2 - x^4$.

Solution: Equation of the curve is

$$a^2y^2 = x^2 (a^2 - x^2) \quad \text{...(1)}$$

1. Symmetry: Equation of the curve contains even and only even powers of x and y. Therefore, the curve is symmetrical about both the axes.

2. Origin : The curve passes through the origin and tangents at the origin are given by!

$$a^2y^2 = a^2x^2$$

$$i.e. \ y = \pm x$$

3. Intersection with coordinate axes: (i) on x-axis at

$$x^2 (a^2 - x^2) = 0$$

$$\therefore \quad x = 0, \pm a$$

i.e. $(0, 0)$ $(\pm a, 0)$

$\therefore$ Tangent at $(a, 0)$ is obtained by shifting the origin at $(a, 0)$

Substituting

$$x = X + a$$

$$y = Y + 0$$

In the equation of the curve,

We have

$$a^2Y^2 = (X + a)^2 [a^2 - (X + a)^2]$$
$$= (X^2 + a^2 + 2aX) (2a + X) (-X)$$

$\therefore$ Tangent at the new origin is given by

$$2a^3X = 0$$

i.e. $X = 0$

i.e. $x = a$

Similarly at $(-a, 0)$ is $x = -a$

(ii) Intersection with y-axis only at the origin.

4. Asymptotes: Since the coefficient of highest powers of x and y both, are constants, so there is no asymptote || to coordinate axes.

5. Region:

$$a^2y^2 = x^2 (a^2 - x^2)$$

Here, $y^2 < 0$ for $x > a$ and $x < -a$.

$\therefore$ The curve lies in $-a \le x \le a$.

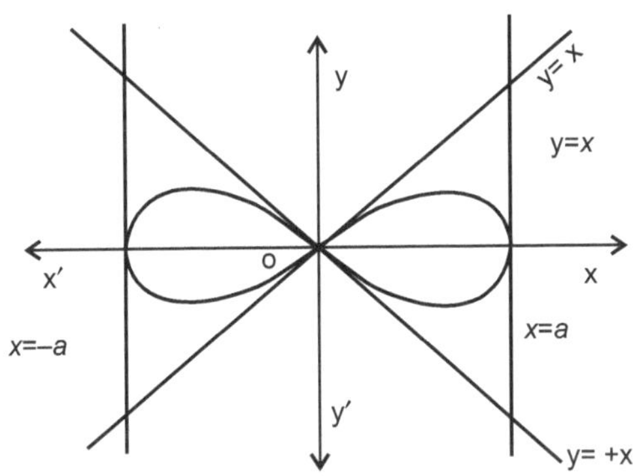

Example 4. Trace the curve $y^2 (a + x) = x^2 (3a - x)$.

Solution:

1. Symmetry: The equation of the curve contains even and only even powers of y, so the curve is symmetrical about x-axis.

2. Origin: The curve passes through the origin and the equation of tangents at the origin is

$$ay^2 = 3ax^2$$

$$\therefore \quad y = \pm \sqrt{3}\, x$$

3. Intersection with coordinate axes:

- on x-axis : Putting $y = 0$, we have

$$x^2 (3a - x) = 0$$

$\therefore$ $x = 0$

$x = 3a$

$\therefore$ Intersection at (0, 0) and $(3a, 0)$.

Now the tangent at $(3a, 0)$ is obtained by shifting origin at (3a, 0), By putting,

$$x = X + 3a$$
$$y = Y$$

In the equation of the curve, we have

$$a^2Y^2 (4a + X) = (X^2 + 9a^2 + 6aX) (3a - X - 3a)$$
$$= -X (X^2 + 9a^2 + 6aX).$$

$\therefore$ The tangent at the new origin is given by

$-9a^2X = 0$, we have

i.e. $X = 0$

i.e. $x = 3a$

$\therefore$ The tangent at $(3a, 0)$ is *i.e.* $= 3a$.

- On y-axis:

Putting $x = 0$

We have $y^2 = 0$

$\therefore$ or $y = 0$

(0, 0) is the point of intersection with y-axis.

4. Asymptotes: (i) || to y-axis : is $a + x = 0$ *i.e.* $x = -a$ and no asymptote || to x-axis.

5. Region:

$y^2 < 0$ for $x < -a$ and $x > 3a$.

$\therefore$ The curve lies in $-a < x \leq 3a$.

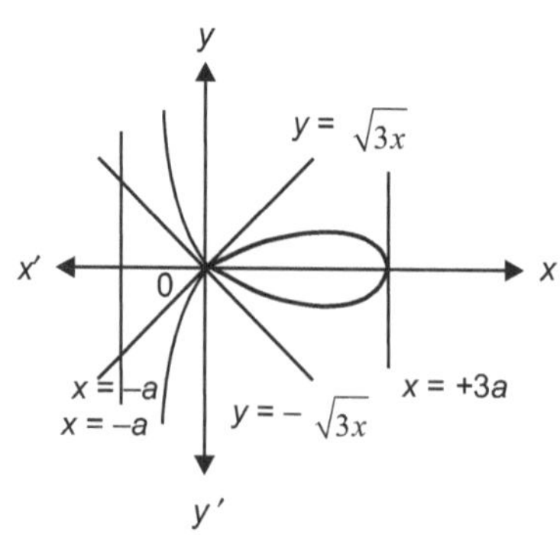

Example 5. Trace the curve $xy^2 = a^2(a - x)$.

Solution:

1. Symmetry: The equation of the curve contains even and only even powers of y, so the curve is symmetric about x-axis.

2. Origin: The curve does not pass through the origin.

3. Intersection with coordinate axes:

- Putting $y = 0$, we have $x = a$

  Intersection on X-axis at $(a, 0)$.

- No intersection with y-axis, since

$$\text{as } x \to 0, y \to \infty$$

Tangent at $(a, 0)$ is obtained by shifting the origin at (a, 0)

i.e. Substituting

$$x = X + a$$

$$y = Y + 0$$

In the equation of the curve, we have

$$(X + a)\,Y^2 = a^2(a - X - a)$$

$$(X + a)\,Y^2 = -a^2X.$$

$\therefore$ Tangent at the new origin is

$$a^2X = 0$$

i.e. $$X = 0$$

i.e. $$x = a$$

$\therefore$ *i.e.* $= a$ is the equation of tangent at $(a, 0)$

4. Asymptotes:

- $\|$ to X-axis is

$$y^2 + a^2 = 0$$

$$y = \pm\, i\, a$$

$\therefore$ Asymptote is imaginary. So no asymptote $\|$ to x-axis.

- $\|$ to y-axis is $x = 0$, *i.e.* y-axis itself.

5. Region:

$y^2 < 0$ for $x < 0$ and $x > a$.

$\therefore$ The curve lies in $0 < x \le a$.

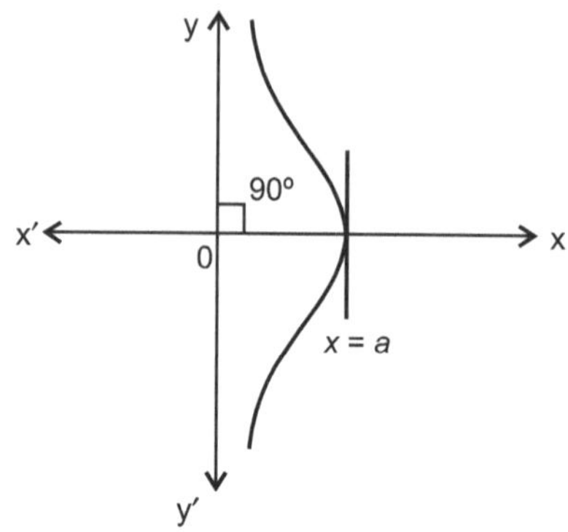

Example 6. Trace the curve $x^3 + y^3 = 3axy.$

Solution:

1. Symmetry: The given curve is symmetric about $y = x$ line as the equation of the curve does not change when x is changed into y and y into x.

2. Origin: The curve passes through the origin and the equation of tangents at the origin is given by

$$3axy = 0$$
$$x = 0$$
$$y = 0$$

i.e. x-axis and y-axis are tangents at the origin.

3. Intersection with coordinate axes: The curve intersects the axes at the origin only.

And the curve intersects $y = x$ line at $(3a/2, 3a/2)$

where $\left(\dfrac{dy}{dx}\right)_{3a/2,\ 3a/2} = -1$

i.e. the tangent is $\perp$ to the line $y = x$.

4. Asymptotes: No asymptote $\|$ to the coordinate axes.

Now the oblique asymptote

$$\phi_3(m) = 1 + m^3$$
$$\phi_2(m) = -\,3\,am.$$

Slopes of asymptotes are given by $\phi_3(m) = 0$

$$1 + m^3 = 0, \text{ gives}$$
$$m = -\,1, \text{ only real value}$$

and $$c = \frac{-\phi_2(m)}{\phi_3^1(m)}$$

$$= +\frac{3am}{3m^2}$$

$$= +\frac{3a}{3m}$$

$$(C)_{m=-1} = -1$$

$\therefore$ The asymptote is

$$y = -x - a$$

or $$= x + y + a = 0.$$

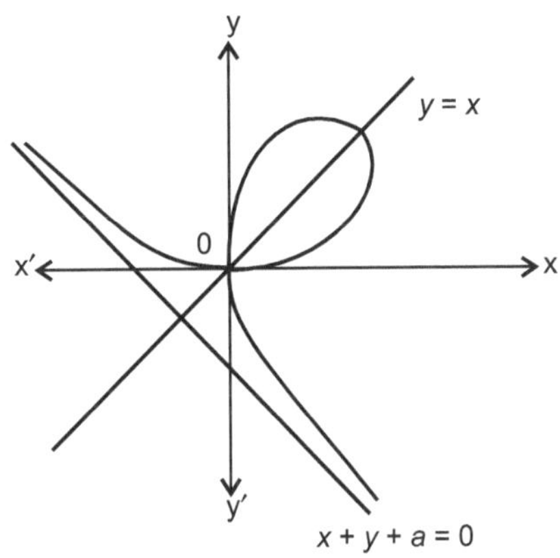

EXERCISE

Trace the following curves:

1. $3ay^2 = x(x - a)^2$
2. $y^2(a^2 + x^2) = x^2(a^2 - x^2)$
3. $y(x^2 - 1) = x^2 + 1$
4. $x^2y^2 = a^2(x^2 + y^2)$
5. $y^2(1 - x^2) = x^2(1 + x^2)$
6. $(x^2 - a^2)(x^2 - b^2) = a^2b^2$

Answers:

1.

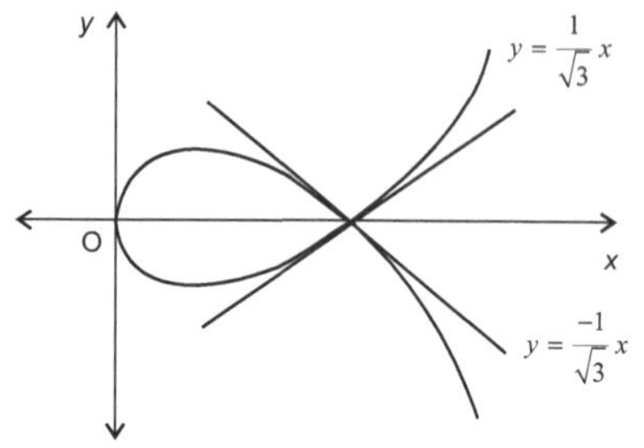

2.

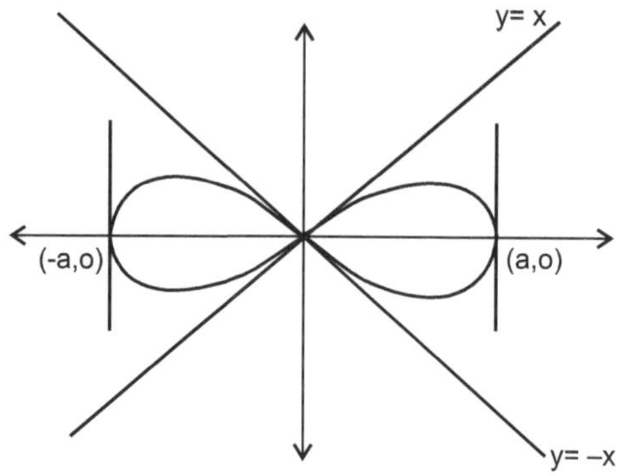

3.

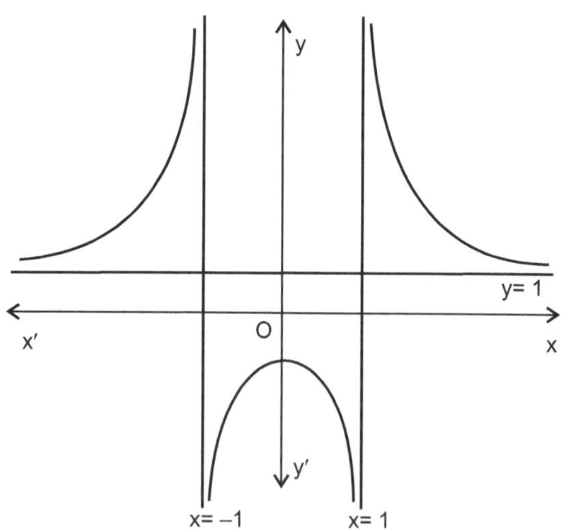

4.

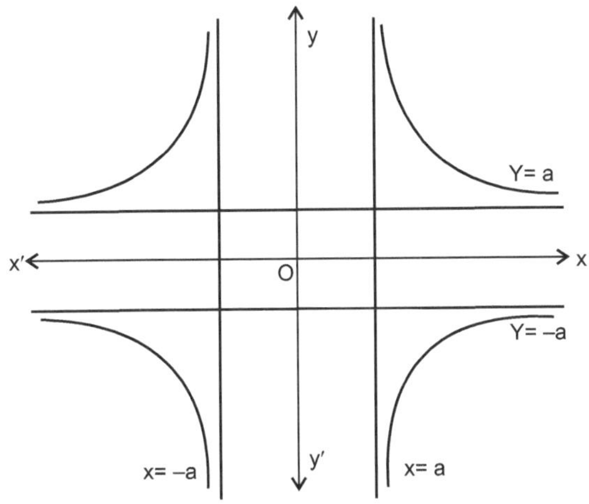

5.

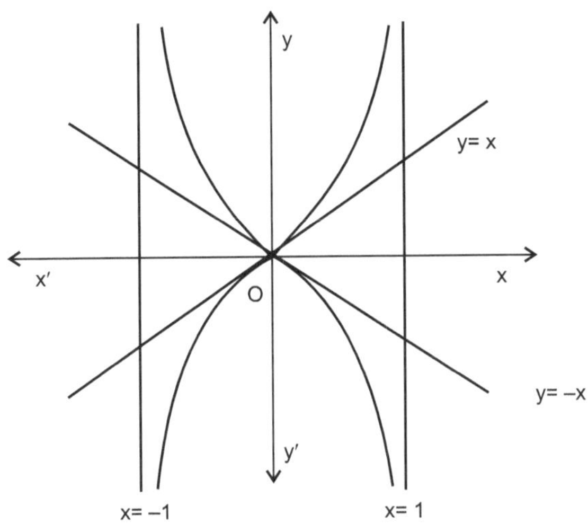

6.

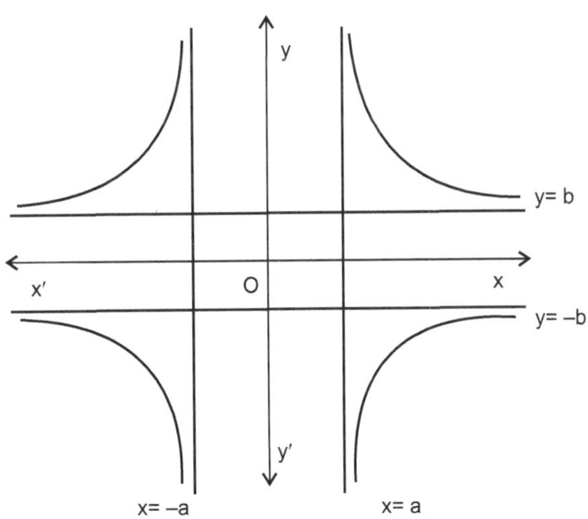

TRACING OF PARAMETRIC CURVES

Let the equation of a curve in parametric form be given by

$$x = f(t) \quad \text{... (1)}$$

$$y = \psi(t) \quad \text{...(2)}$$

The steps which are helpful in tracing of parametric curves are :

1. Symmetry:

- If x is an even function of t and y is an odd function of t, then the curve is symmetric about x-axis.
- If x is an odd function of t and y is an even function of t, then the curve is symmetric about y-axis.
- The curve is symmetric about both the axes if x and y are such functions of t that for each value of x there exist two equal and of opposite sign, values of y and for each value of y there exist two equal and of opposite sign, values of x.

2. Origin: If $x = 0$, $y = 0$ for some real value of t, then the curve passes through the orign. We note that (those) values of t.

3. Intersection with coordinate axes:

- We find (if any) the value or values of t for which $x = 0$, $y \neq 0$, which gives the point of intersection with y-axis.
- We find (if any) the value(s) of t for which $x \neq 0$, $y = 0$, which gives the point of intersection with y-axis.

Values of $\frac{dy}{dx}$ at these points play an important role.

4. Maximum / Minimum of x and (or) y, we note those values of t and values of $\frac{dy}{dx}$, which give important imformation about the curve and its behaviour at these points.

5. Region: The region in which the curve lies or does not lie.

6. If either x or y is perodic, then the curve is traced for one period only and then it is repeated.

SOLVED EXAMPLES

Example 1. Trace the curve

$$x = a \cos t,\ y = b \sin t\ (a > b).$$

Solution: Here

$$x = a \cos t \tag{1}$$

$$y = b \sin t \tag{2}$$

1. Symmetry:

- As x is even function of t and y is odd function of t, therefore, the curve is symmetric about x-axis.
- As it is obvious that for t and $(\pi - t)$ values of y are same but the value of x are equal numerically but of opposite sign.

Therefore, the curve is symmetrical about y-axis also.

Thus, the curve is symmetrical about both the axes.

2. Origin: The curve does not pass through the origin.

3. Intersection with coordinate axes:

- $x = \pm a$ for $y = 0$ at $t = 0$ or π.
- $y = \pm b$ for $x = 0$ at $t = \dfrac{\pi}{2}, \dfrac{3\pi}{2}$.

$\therefore$ The curve intersects x-axis at $(\pm a, 0)$ and y-axis at $(0, \pm b)$

for $\quad t = 0$ or π and $\pi/2$ or $3\pi/2$ respectively.

$$\frac{dy}{dx} = \frac{\frac{dy}{dt}}{\frac{dx}{dt}} = \frac{b\cos t}{-a\sin t}$$

$$= \frac{-b}{a}\cot t.$$

for $\quad t = 0$, A $(a, 0)$, $\dfrac{dy}{dx} = \infty$

for $\quad t = \pi$, A′ $(-a, 0)$, $\dfrac{dy}{dx} = \infty$

for $\quad t = \pi/2$, B $(0, b)$, $\dfrac{dy}{dx} = 0$

for $\quad t = 3\pi/2$, B′ $(0, -b)$, $\dfrac{dy}{dx} = 0$

4. Max/Min of x and (or) y:

$$\text{Max } |x| = a \text{ for } t = 0, \pi$$

$$\text{Min } |y| = b \text{ for } t = \pi/2, 3\pi/2.$$

5. **Region:** the curve lies in $-a \le x \le a, -b \le y \le b$.

6. Since, max/min of x and y are finite, therefore no asymptote of the curve exists.

7. Since both x and y are periodic. We can have the curve traced, if we trace it in the first quadrant only.

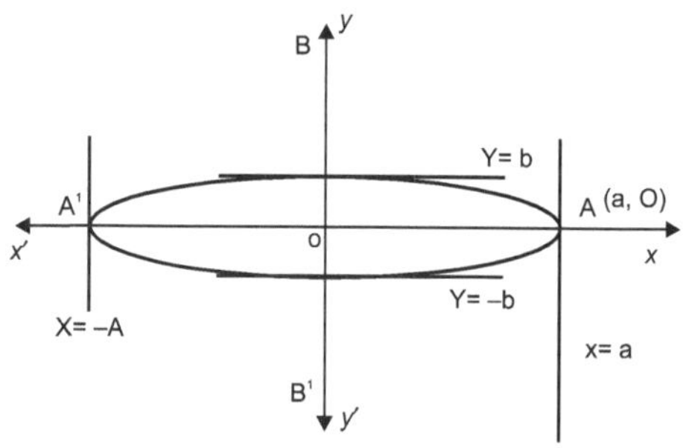

Example 2. Trace the curve

$$x = a\,(t - \sin t)$$

$$y = a\,(1 - \cos t).$$

Solution: Here

$$x = a\,(t - \sin t)$$

$$y = a\,(1 - \cos t)$$

1. **Symmetry:** (i) x is an odd function of t and y is an even function of t.

$\therefore$ The curve is symmetrical about y-axis.

2. **Origin:** For $t = 0, x = 0, y = 0$

$\therefore$ The curve passes through the origin

$$\frac{dy}{dx} = \frac{a\sin t}{a(1-\cos t)}$$

$$= \frac{2\sin t/2\cos t/2}{2\sin^2 t/2} = \cot t/2$$

$$\therefore \qquad \frac{dy}{dx} = \cot\,(t/2)$$

$$\therefore \qquad \left(\frac{dy}{dx}\right)_{t=0} = \infty$$

$\therefore$ At origin tangent is $\|$ to y-axis.

3. Intersection with coordinate axes:

$$x = a\,(t - \sin t)$$

$$y = a\,(1 - \cos t)$$

(i) $\therefore\ x = 0$ for $t = 0$ for which $y = 0$

$\therefore$ Intersection on y-axis only at the origin.

(ii) $y = 0$ for $t = 0, 2\pi, 4\pi \ldots = 2n\pi$.

For which $x = 0, 2a\pi, 4a\pi, \ldots 2an\pi$.

$\therefore$ We will trace the curve between $t = 0$ and 2π, since y is periodic of period 2π.

$$\therefore \qquad \left(\frac{dy}{dx}\right)_{t=0} = \infty,$$

$$\left(\frac{dy}{dx}\right)_{t=2\pi} = \infty$$

4. (i) Maxima of x : x is not bounded above.

Minima of x : x is not bounded below.

(ii) Max. of y : Max $y = 2a$ for $t = \pi, 3\pi \ldots (2n + 1)\pi$

Min $y = 0$ for $t = 0, 2\pi \ldots 2n\pi$.

$$\left(\frac{dy}{dx}\right)_{t=\pi} = 0$$

5. Region: Along y-axis the curve lies in $0 \le y \le 2a$.

Along x-axis it extends form $-\infty$ to ∞.

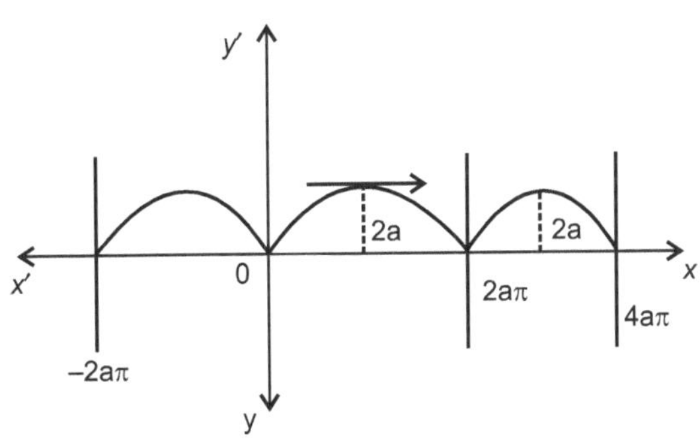

EXERCISE

Trace the following curves :

1. $x = a\,(t - \sin t),\ y = a\,(1 + \cos t)$
2. $x = a\,(t + \sin t),\ y = a\,(1 - \cos t)$
3. $x = a\,(t + \sin t),\ y = a\,(1 + \cos t)$
4. $x = a \cos^3 t,\ y = b \sin^3 t.\ (a > b)$

Answers:

1.

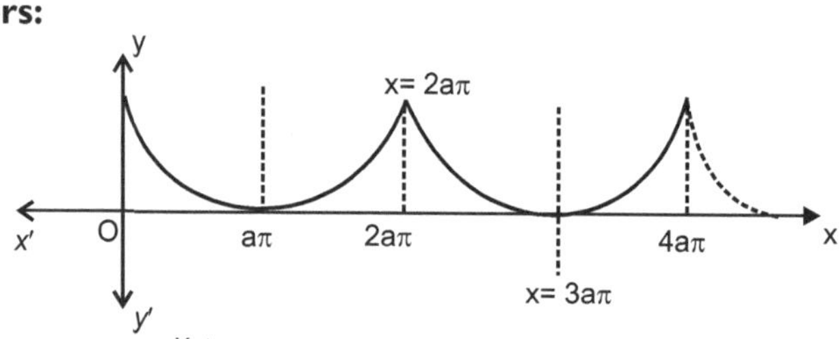

2.

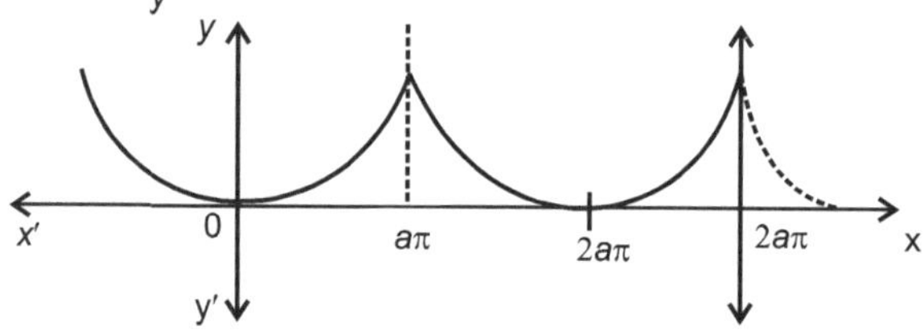

3.

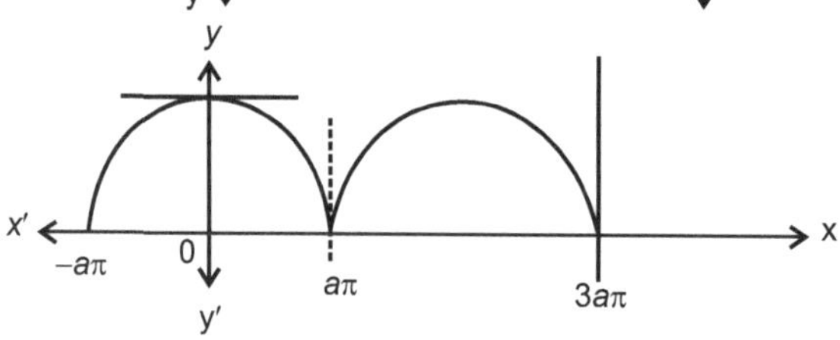

4.

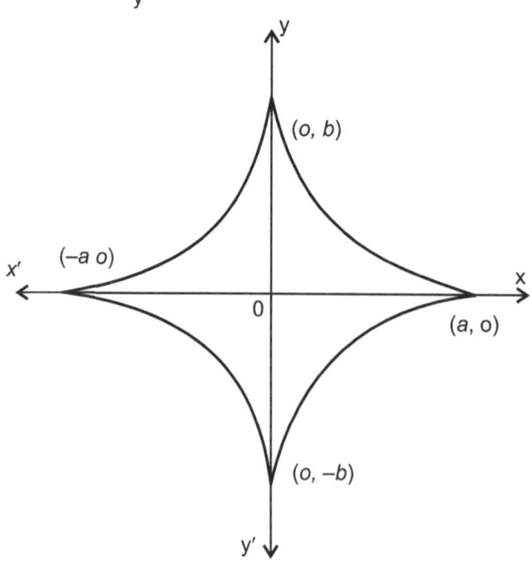

TRACING OF POLAR CURVES

Location of a point when its coordinates are given in Polar form. Location of a point $P(r, \theta)$ is, on a line which makes an angle θ with initial line (*i.e.* +ve direction of x-axis), at a distance r from the pole (origin) and $Q(-r, \theta)$ in on a line which makes an angle θ with initial line and at a distance r is opposite direction from the pole.

(i) $P(r, \theta)$

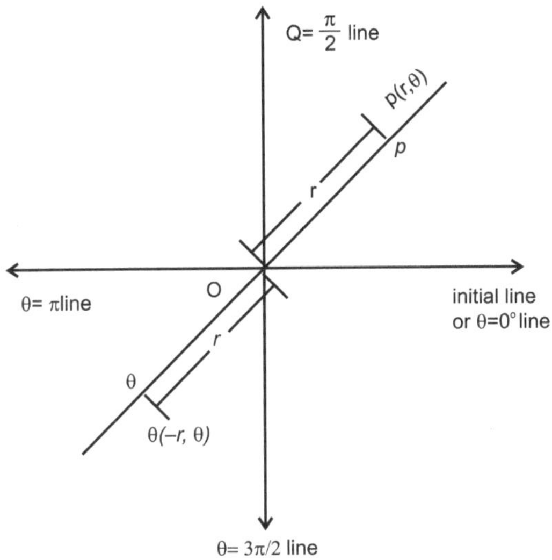

1. Symmetry: The two points $P(r, \theta)$ and $Q(r, -\theta)$ are images of each other in initial line, means value of r is same for θ and $-\theta$. A curve is a collection of points satisfying a given condition. If value of r is same for θ and $-\theta$, for all values of θ, then we an say that the curve is symmetrical about $\theta = 0$ line or initial line. We can say that equation of the curve does not change when θ is changed to $-\theta$.

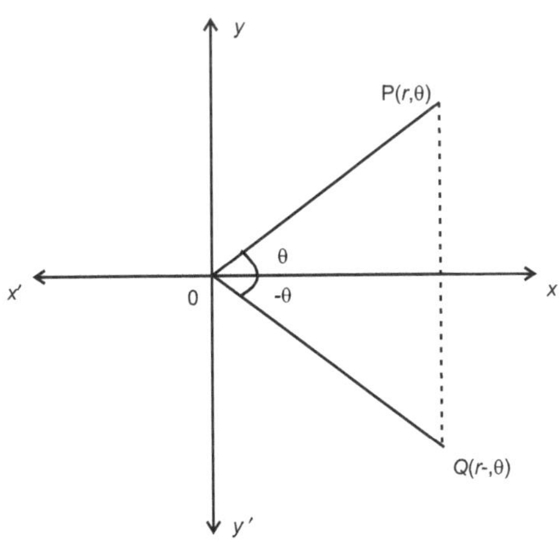

In this situation the curve is symmetrical about initial line ($\theta = 0$ line)

(i) Thus a curve is symmetrical about initial line if the equation of the curve does not change when θ is changed by $-\theta$.

(ii) If the equation of the curve does not change when θ is changed by π-θ, then the curve is symmetrical about $\theta = \frac{\pi}{2}$ line.

(iii) If the equation of the curve does not change when θ is changed by $\frac{\pi}{2} - \theta$, then the curve is symmetrical about $\theta = \frac{\pi}{4}$ line.

(iv) If the equation of the curve does not change when θ is changed to $\frac{\pi}{3} - \theta$, then the curve is symmetrical about $\theta = \frac{\pi}{6}$ line.

(v) If the equation of the curve does not change when θ is changed by $\frac{3\pi}{2} - \theta$, then the curve is symmetrical about $\theta = \frac{3\pi}{4}$ line.

(vi) if the equation of a curve does not change when r is changed to $-r$, then the curve is symmetrical about the pole.

2. Pole: If $r = 0$ for some $\theta = \alpha$ (real), then the curve passes through the pole and $\theta = \alpha$ line is tangent to the curve at the pole, *i.e.*, the curve leaves or approaches the origin along with this line.

3. Max./min. of *r* (if any): Values of θ for which r is minimum or maximum.

4. ϕ, the angle between radius vector and tangent at a point on the curve, which is given by

$$\tan \phi = r \frac{d\theta}{dr}$$

specially at the points of max/min. of r, ϕ is needed.

5. Region: Find $\alpha < \theta < \beta$ for which r is real, then the curve will lie in this interval. If for some $\alpha < \theta < \beta$, r is imaginary, then the curve will not lie in this interval.

6. Asymptote: If $r \to \infty$ for some $\theta = \alpha$, then the asymptotes exist.

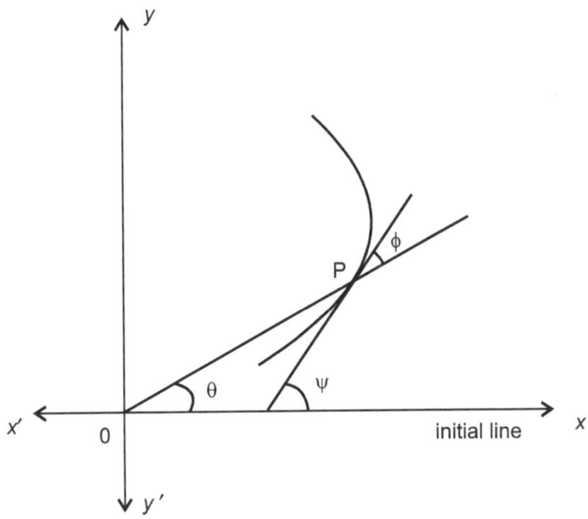

7. Some points on the curve: Give θ some values and find the corresponding values of r.

SOLVED EXAMPLES

Example 1. Trace the curve $r = a\cos\theta$.

Solution:

1. Symmetry: The given curve is symmetric about initial line, *i.e.*, since the equation of the curve does not change when θ is replaced by –θ.

2. Pole: The curve passes through the pole

since

$$r = 0$$

for

$$\theta = \pm\frac{\pi}{2}$$

$$\therefore \quad \theta = \pm\frac{\pi}{2} \text{ lines are tangents at the pole.}$$

3. Max. $r = a$ for $\theta = 0$

Min. $r = -a$ for $\theta = \pi$.

4.

$$\tan\phi = \frac{r}{\frac{dr}{d\theta}}$$

$$= \frac{a\cos\theta}{-a\sin\theta}$$

$$\tan\phi = -\cot\theta$$

$$\tan\phi = \tan\left(\frac{\pi}{2}+\theta\right)$$

$\therefore$ $$\phi = \frac{\pi}{2} + \theta$$

5. Asymptotes: No Asymptote.

When

$$\theta = 0, r = a$$

$$\theta = \pi, r = -a$$

Both these points are the same, at the point of maxima *i.e.* for $\theta = 0°$.

At the point of Max; $\phi = \frac{\pi}{2} + 0$

$\therefore$ $$\phi = \frac{\pi}{2}$$

Thus, at $r = a$, tangent is perpendicular to the radius vector $\theta = 0°$.

No part of the curve will be in second and third quadrants.

Since for $\frac{\pi}{2} < \theta < \frac{3\pi}{2}$, r is –ve and will go in opposite quadrants.

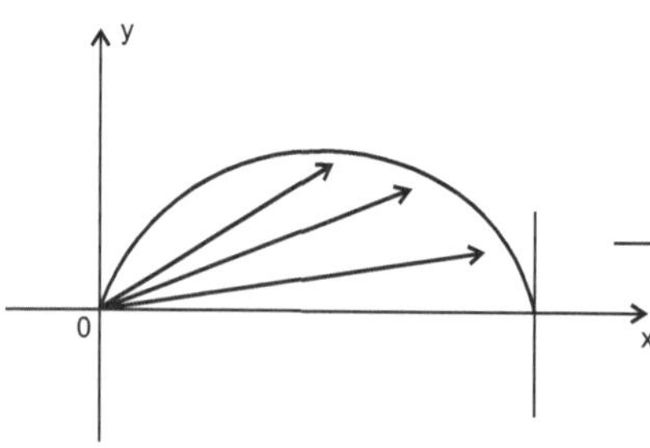

(*i*)

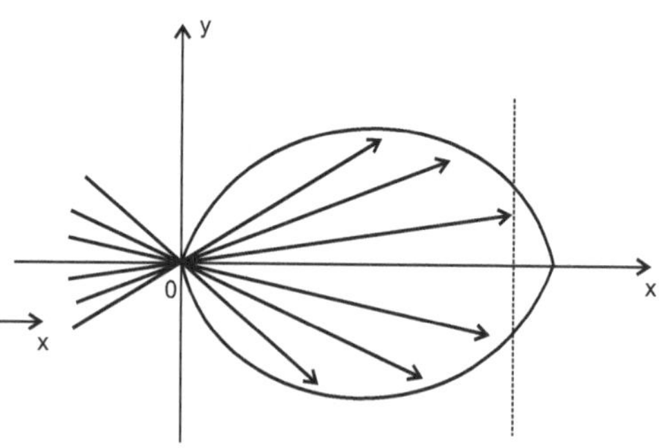

(*ii*)

$\theta =$	0	$\frac{\pi}{6}$	$\frac{\pi}{4}$	$\frac{\pi}{3}$	$\frac{\pi}{2}$	$\frac{2\pi}{3}$	$\frac{3\pi}{4}$	π
$r =$	a	$\frac{\sqrt{3}a}{2}$	$\frac{a}{\sqrt{2}}$	$\frac{a}{2}$	0	$\frac{-a}{2}$	$\frac{-a}{\sqrt{2}}$	$-a$

Since the function cosθ is periodic and the curve is symmetric about initial line, so we consider the portion of the curve from $\theta = 0$ to $\theta = \pi$ and rest will be traced by symmery.

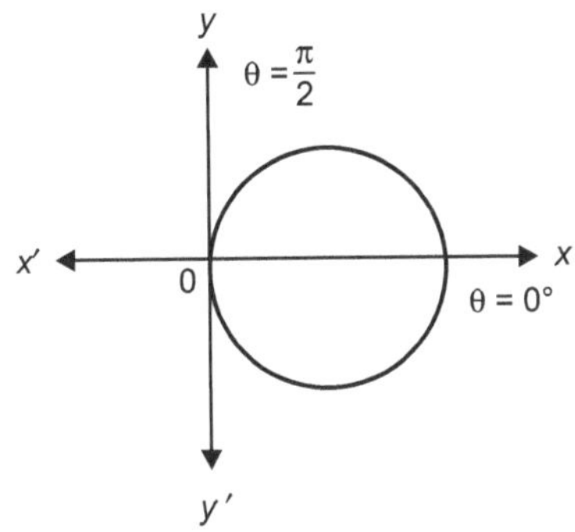

Example 2. Trace the curve $r = a\,(1 - \cos\theta)$.

Solution:

1. Symmetry: The given curve is symmetrical about initial line. Since equation of the curve does not change when θ is changed to –θ.

As the curve is symmetric about initial line, so we trace the curve in $0 \le \theta \le \pi$ only.

2. Pole: The curve passes through the pole.

Since $r = 0$

for $\theta = 0°$ $\quad \therefore\ \theta = 0°$ line is tangent at the pole.

3. Max. $r = 2a$ for $\theta = \pi$

Min. $r = 0$ for $\theta = 0$.

4.
$$\tan\phi = \frac{a(1-\cos\theta)}{a\sin\theta}$$

$$= \frac{2\sin^2\theta/2}{2\sin\theta/2\,\cos\theta/2}$$

$$\Rightarrow \quad \tan\phi = \tan\,(\theta/2)$$

$$\therefore \quad \phi = (\theta/2)$$

5. Asymptote: No asymptote.

When

$\theta =$	$0°$	$\frac{\pi}{6}$	$\frac{\pi}{3}$	$\frac{\pi}{2}$	$\frac{2\pi}{3}$	$\frac{3\pi}{4}$	$\frac{5\pi}{6}$	π
$r =$	0	$a\left(1-\frac{\sqrt{3}}{2}\right)$	$\frac{a}{2}$	a	$\frac{3a}{2}$	$a\left(1+\frac{1}{\sqrt{2}}\right)$	$a\left(1+\frac{\sqrt{3}}{2}\right)$	$2a$

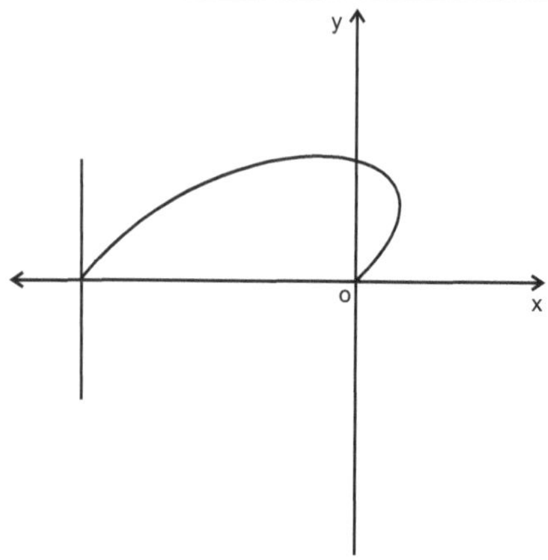

(*i*)

By symmetry about initial line, we have the shape of the corve as:

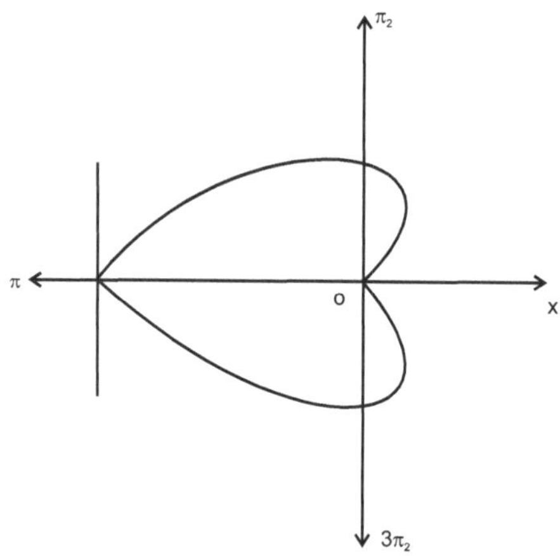

(*ii*)

Example 3. Trace the curve $r = a \sin 2\theta$. $(a > 0)$

Solution:

1. **Symmetry:** The given curve is symmetric about $\theta = \frac{\pi}{4}$ line and

$\theta = \frac{3\pi}{4}$ line.

As the equation of the curve does not change when θ is changed to $\frac{\pi}{2}-\theta$ and $\frac{3\pi}{2}-\theta$.

2. Pole: The curve passes through the pole as

$$r = 0$$

for $$\theta = 0, \pm\frac{\pi}{2}, \theta = \pi$$

and $\theta = 0°, \pm\frac{\pi}{2}$ $\theta = \pi$ lines are tangents at the pole.

3. Max $r = a$ for $\theta = \frac{\pi}{4}, \frac{5\pi}{4}$.

Min $r = -a$ for $\theta = \frac{3\pi}{4}, \frac{7\pi}{4}$.

4. $$\tan\phi = \frac{r}{\frac{dr}{d\theta}}$$

$$= \frac{a\sin 2\theta}{2a\cos 2\theta}$$

$$= \frac{1}{2}.\ \tan 2\theta.$$

$\therefore \quad (\tan\phi)_{\theta=\pi/4} = \infty \quad \therefore \quad \phi = \frac{\pi}{2}$

$\therefore \quad (\tan\phi)_{\theta=3\pi/4} = -\infty \quad \therefore \quad \phi = \frac{\pi}{2}$

$\therefore \quad (\tan\phi)_{\theta=5\pi/4} = \infty \quad \therefore \quad \phi = \frac{\pi}{2}$

$\therefore \quad (\tan\phi)_{\theta=7\pi/4} = \infty \quad \therefore \quad \phi = \frac{\pi}{2}$

$\therefore$ At all the points for $\theta = \frac{\pi}{4}, \frac{3\pi}{4}, \frac{5\pi}{4}, \frac{7\pi}{4}$ tangents are perpendicular to the radius vector.

5. Asymptote: No asymptote exists.

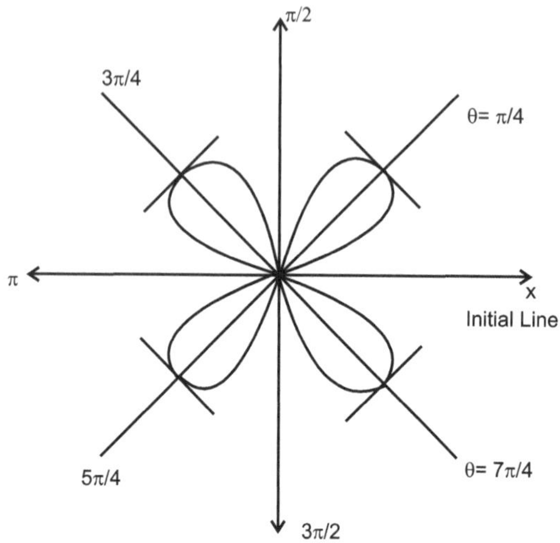

Example 4. Trace the curve $r = 1 + 2\cos\theta$.

Solution: Here, $r = 1 + 2\cos\theta$.

1. Symmetry: The given curve is symmetric about initial line.

2. Pole: The curve passes through the pole,

since $r = 0$ for $\theta = \frac{2\pi}{3}$ and $\frac{4\pi}{3}$

therefore, $\theta = \frac{2\pi}{3}$ and $\theta = \frac{4\pi}{3}$ lines are tangents at the pole.

3. Max. $r = 3$ for $\theta = 0°$

Min. $r = -1$ for $\theta = \pi$.

4.
$$\tan\phi = \frac{r}{\frac{dr}{d\theta}}$$

$$= \frac{1 + 2\cos\theta}{-2\sin\theta}$$

$$= -\frac{1}{2}\left[\frac{(1 + 2\cos\theta)}{\sin\theta}\right]$$

$\therefore \qquad (\tan\phi)_{\theta=0} = \infty \quad \therefore \ \phi = 90^o$

$\therefore \qquad (\tan\phi)_{\theta=\pi} = \infty \quad \therefore \ \phi = 90^o$

$\therefore$ Tangent at both the points P (3, 0) and Q (–1, π) are perpendicular to the radius vector.

5. **Asymptote:** No asymptote exists.

$\theta =$	0	$\frac{\pi}{6}$	$\frac{\pi}{4}$	$\frac{\pi}{3}$	$\frac{\pi}{2}$	$\frac{2\pi}{3}$	$\frac{5\pi}{6}$	π
$r =$	3	$1+\sqrt{3}$	$1+\sqrt{2}$	2	1	0	$1-\sqrt{3}$	-1

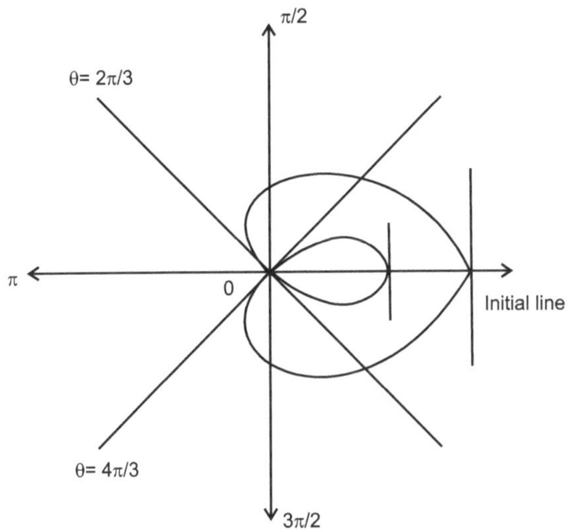

EXERICSE

Trace the following curves:

1. $r = a \sin\theta$
2. $r = a \cos 2\theta$
3. $r = a \cos 3\theta$
4. $r^2 = a^2 \cos 2\theta$
5. $r = a\,(1 + \sin\theta)$
6. $r = a\,(1 - \sin\theta)$
7. $r = 2 + 3 \cos\theta.$
8. $r = a\,(\sec\theta + \cos\theta).$

Answers:

1.

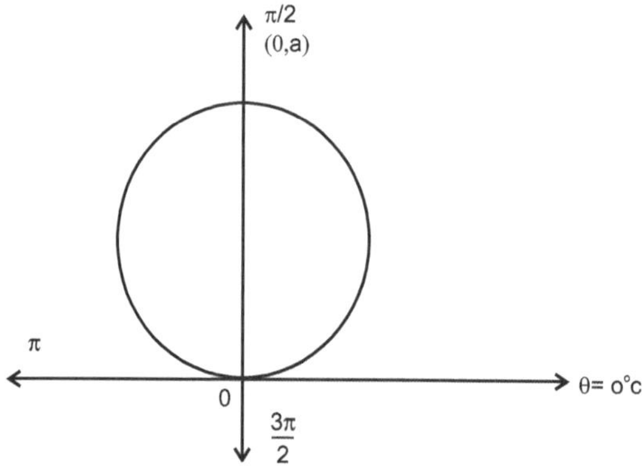
π/2
(0,a)
π
θ= o°c
0
3π/2

2.

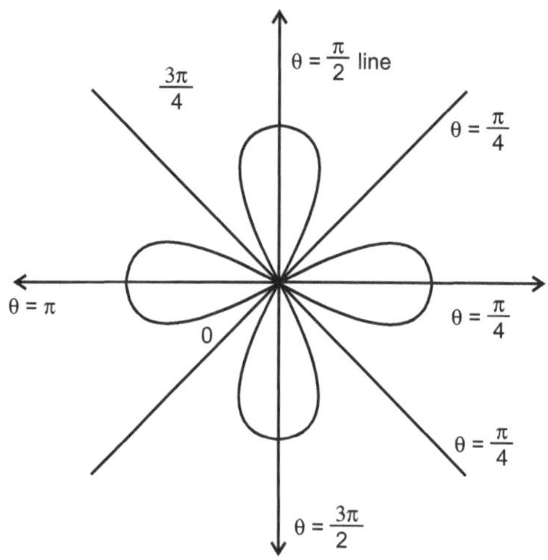
θ = π/2 line
3π/4
θ = π/4
θ = π
θ = π/4
0
θ = π/4
θ = 3π/2

3.

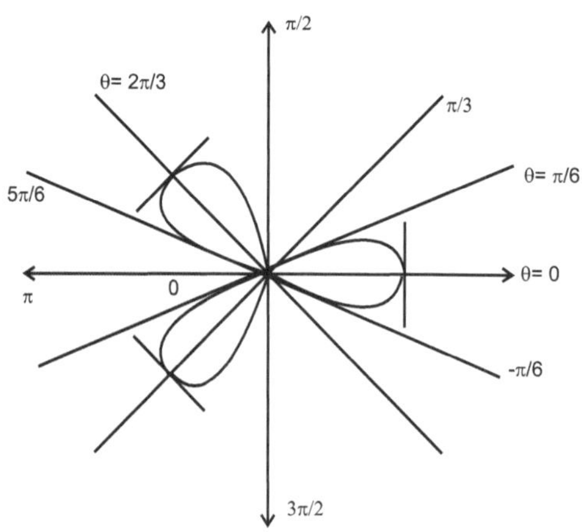
π/2
θ= 2π/3
π/3
θ= π/6
5π/6
θ= 0
π
0
-π/6
3π/2

4. 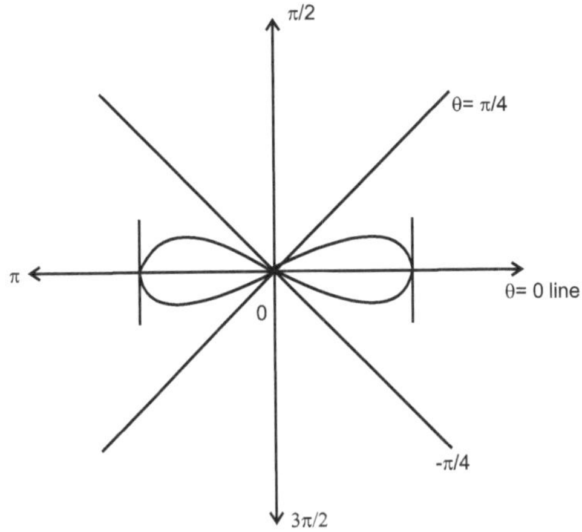
π/2
θ= π/4
π
θ= 0 line
0
-π/4
3π/2

5. 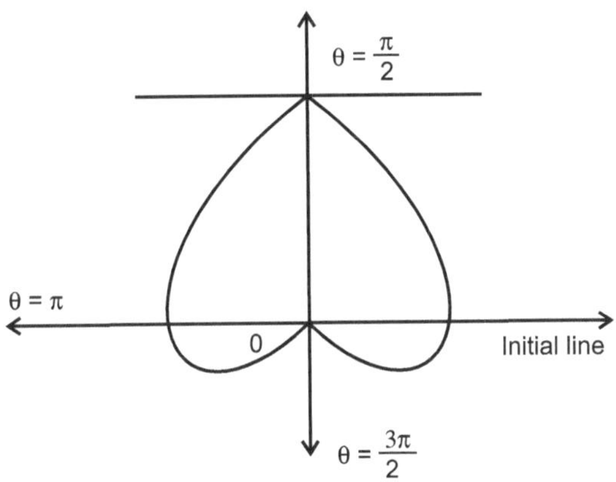
θ = π/2
θ = π
0
Initial line
θ = 3π/2

6. 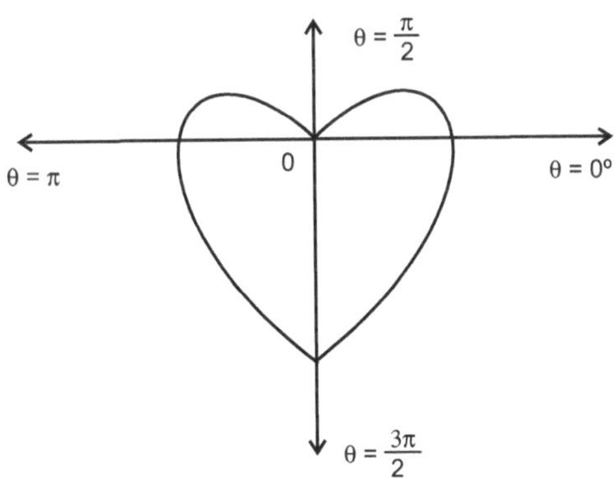
θ = π/2
θ = π
0
θ = 0°
θ = 3π/2

7. 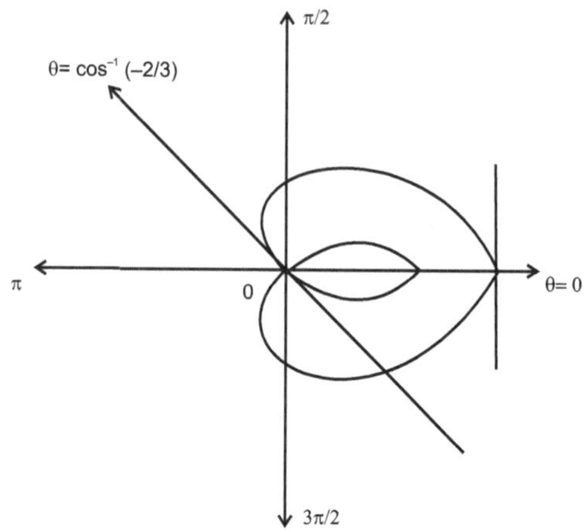

8. 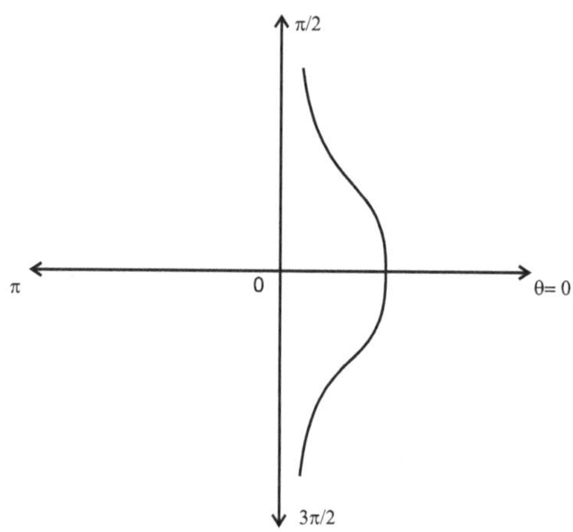

8

Integration

INTRODUCTION

Integration is the reverse process of differentiation.

If $\frac{d}{dx}[\phi(x)] = f(x)$, then

$\phi(x)$ is said to be the integral of $f(x)$ and is denoted by

$\int f(x)\,dx = \phi(x) + C$, where C is a constant known as constent of integration.

Students are very well known about the methods of integration by:

1. Substitution.
2. Integration by parts.
3. Using partial fractions.

Here, we are providing some of the standard results:

1. $\frac{d}{dx}(\sec x) = \sec x \,.\, \tan x \quad \therefore \int \sec x.\tan x\,dx = \sec x + C$

2. $\frac{d}{dx}(\text{cosec } x) = -\text{cosec } x.\cot x \quad \therefore \int \text{cosec}\,x.\cot x\,dx = -\text{cosec } x + C$

3. $\frac{d}{dx}\left[\tan^{-1}\left(\frac{x}{a}\right)\right] = \frac{a}{x^2+a^2} \quad \therefore \int \frac{1}{x^2+a^2}dx = \frac{1}{a}\tan^{-1}\left(\frac{x}{a}\right) + C$

4. $\frac{d}{dx}\left[\sin^{-1}\left(\frac{x}{a}\right)\right] = \frac{1}{\sqrt{a^2-x^2}} \quad \therefore \int \frac{1}{\sqrt{a^2-x^2}}dx = \sin^{-1}\left(\frac{x}{a}\right) + C$

5. $\frac{d}{dx}\left[\sec^{1}\left(\frac{x}{a}\right)\right] = \frac{a}{x\sqrt{x^2 - a^2}}$ $\therefore \int \frac{1}{x\sqrt{x^2 - a^2}} dx = \frac{1}{a}\sec^{-1}\left(\frac{x}{a}\right) + C$

6. $\frac{d}{dx}[\sin hx] = \cos hx$ $\therefore \int \cosh x \, dx = \sin hx + C$

7. $\frac{d}{dx}[\cos hx] = \sin hx$ $\therefore \int \sinh x \, dx = \cos hx + C$

8. $\frac{d}{dx}[\tan hx] = \sec h^2 x$ $\therefore \int \sec h^2 x \, dx = \tan hx + C$

9. $\frac{d}{dx}[\cot hx] = -\text{cosech}^2\, x$ $\therefore \int \text{cosec}\, h^2 x \, dx = -\cot hx + C$

10. $\frac{d}{dx}[\sec hx] = -\sec hx.\tan hx$ $\therefore \int \text{sech}\, x \,.\, \tan hx \, dx = -\sec hx + C$

11. $\frac{d}{dx}[\text{cosec}\, hx] = -\text{cosec}\, hx.\cot hx$

$\therefore \int \text{cosec}\, hx.\cot hx \, dx = -\, \text{cosec}\, hx + C$

12. (i) $\int e^{ax}\cos(bx + c)\, dx = \frac{e^{ax}}{a^2 + b^2}[a \cos (bx + c) + b \sin (bx + c)]$

(ii) $\int e^{ax}\sin(bx + c)\, dx = \frac{e^{ax}}{a^2 + b^2}[a \sin (bx + c] - b \cos (bx + c)]$

13. $\int \frac{1}{x^2 - a^2}\, dx = \frac{1}{2a}\log\left|\frac{x - a}{x + a}\right| + C$

14. $\int \frac{1}{a^2 - x^2}\, dx = \frac{1}{2a}.\log\left|\frac{a + x}{a - x}\right| + C$

15. $\int \frac{1}{\sqrt{a^2 - x^2}}\, dx = \sin^{-1}\left(\frac{x}{a}\right) + C$

16. $\int \frac{1}{\sqrt{a^2 + x^2}}\, dx = \log\left[x + \sqrt{x^2 + a^2}\right] + C$

17. $\int \frac{1}{\sqrt{x^2 - a^2}}\, dx = \log\left[x + \sqrt{x^2 - a^2}\right] + C$

18. $\int \sqrt{a^2 - x^2}\, dx = \frac{x}{2}\sqrt{a^2 - x^2} + \frac{a^2}{2} . \sin^{-1}\left(\frac{x}{a}\right) + C$

19. $\int \sqrt{x^2 - a^2}\, dx = \frac{x}{2}\sqrt{a^2 - x^2} - \frac{a^2}{2} \log\left[x + \sqrt{x^2 - a^2}\right] + C$

20. $\int \sqrt{x^2 + a^2}\, dx = \frac{x}{2}\sqrt{x^2 + a^2} + \frac{a^2}{2} \log\left[x + \sqrt{x^2 + a^2}\right] + C$

INTEGRATION OF IRRATIONAL FUNCTIONS

Type I. When we have an integral of the form

$\int \phi(x)\sqrt{ax+b}\, dx$ or $\int \frac{\phi(x)}{\sqrt{ax+b}}\, dx$, where $\phi(x)$ is a rational function of x.

We substitute

$$ax + b = t^2$$

$$\therefore \quad a\, dx = 2t\, dt$$

$$\therefore \quad dx = \frac{2}{a} t\, dt.$$

Which makes the function integrable by either of the methods known earlier.

Type II. When we have an integral of the form

$$\int \frac{dx}{(ax+b)^n \sqrt{px^2 + qx + r}} \quad \text{or} \quad \int \frac{\phi(x)\, dx}{(ax+b)\sqrt{px^2 + qx + r}}.$$

In this we substitute

$$ax + b = \frac{1}{t}$$

$$\therefore \quad dx = -\frac{1}{at^2}\, dt.$$

and now the integral can be evaluated by any one of the methods discussed earlier.

Type III. When we have an integral of the form

$$I = \int \frac{dx}{(ax^2 + b)\sqrt{cx^2 + d}}$$

then we make substitution

$$x = \frac{1}{t}$$

or $$\frac{cx^2 + d}{ax^2 + b} = t^2$$

and the integral is converted into simpler form.

Type IV. When we have an integral of the form

$$I = \int \frac{dx}{(ax^2 + bx + c)\sqrt{dx^2 + ex + f}}$$

we substitute

$$\frac{dx^2 + ex + f}{ax^2 + bx + c} = t^2$$

and then it is evaluated easily.

SOLVED EXAMPLES

Example 1. Evaluate $\int \frac{dx}{(x+2)\sqrt{x^2 + 3x + 4}}$.

Solution: Let $x + 2 = \frac{1}{t}$

$$\therefore \quad dx = -\frac{1}{t^2}\, dt$$

$$\therefore \quad x = \frac{1-2t}{t}$$

$$\therefore \quad I = \int \frac{-1/t^2 dt}{\frac{1}{t}\sqrt{\left(\frac{1-2t}{t}\right)^2 + 3\left(\frac{1-2t}{t}\right) + 4}}$$

$$= -\int \frac{dt}{\sqrt{2t^2 - t + 1}}$$

$$= \frac{-1}{\sqrt{2}} \int \frac{dt}{\sqrt{\left(t - \frac{1}{4}\right)^2 + \left(\frac{\sqrt{7}}{4}\right)^2}}$$

$$= \frac{-1}{\sqrt{2}} \sin h^{-1} \left(\frac{t - \frac{1}{4}}{\frac{\sqrt{7}}{4}} \right)$$

$$= \frac{-1}{\sqrt{2}} .\sin h^{-1} \left(\frac{4t - 1}{\sqrt{7}} \right)$$

$$= \frac{-1}{\sqrt{2}} .\sin h^{-1} \left[\frac{2 - x}{\sqrt{7}(2 + x)} \right].$$

Example 2. Evaluate: $I = \int x\sqrt{1 + x - x^2}\ dx.$

Solution: We have $x = \frac{-1}{2} . (1 - 2x) + \frac{1}{2}$

$\therefore$ $$I = \frac{-1}{2} \int (1 - 2x) \sqrt{1 + x - x^2}\ dx + \frac{1}{2} \int \sqrt{1 + x - x^2}\ dx$$

$$I_1 = \int (1 - 2x) . \sqrt{1 + x - x^2}\ dx$$

Let $1 + x - x^2 = t$

$\therefore$ $(1 - 2x)\ dx = dt$

$\therefore$ $$I_1 = \int \sqrt{t}\ .\ dt$$

$$= \frac{2}{3} t^{3/2} = \frac{2}{3} (1 + x - x^2)^{3/2}$$

$$I_2 = \frac{1}{2} \int \sqrt{1 + x - x^2}\ dx$$

$$= \frac{1}{2}\int\sqrt{-\left(x^2 - x - 1\right)}\ dx$$

$$= \frac{1}{2}\int\sqrt{-\left[\left(x-\frac{1}{2}\right)^2 - 1 - \frac{1}{4}\right]}\ dx$$

$$= \frac{1}{2}\int\sqrt{\frac{5}{4} - \left(x-\frac{1}{2}\right)^2}\ dx$$

$$= \frac{1}{2}\int\sqrt{\left(\frac{\sqrt{5}}{2}\right)^2 - \left(x-\frac{1}{2}\right)^2}\ dx$$

$$= \frac{1}{2}\left[\frac{1}{2}\left(x-\frac{1}{2}\right)\sqrt{\left(\frac{\sqrt{5}}{2}\right)^2 - \left(x-\frac{1}{2}\right)^2}\right.$$

$$\left. + \frac{5}{8}\sin^{-1}\left(\frac{2x-1}{\sqrt{5}}\right)\right]$$

$$= \frac{(2x-1)}{8}\sqrt{1+x-x^2} + \frac{5}{16}\sin^{-1}\left(\frac{2x-1}{\sqrt{5}}\right)$$

$\therefore$ $$I = I_1 + I_2$$

$$= \frac{-1}{3}(1 + x - x^2)^{3/2} + \frac{1}{8}\ (2x-1)\ \sqrt{1+x-x^2}$$

$$+ \frac{5}{16}\sin^{-1}\left(\frac{2x-1}{\sqrt{5}}\right) + C$$

Example 3. Evaluate $$I = \int\frac{dx}{\left(2x^2+3\right)\sqrt{3x^2-4}}.$$

Solution: Let $\dfrac{3x^2-4}{2x^2+3} = y^2$

$\therefore$ $$x^2 = \frac{3y^2+4}{3-2y^2}$$

$$2x^2 + 3 = \frac{17}{3-2y^2}$$

so, $$x\,dx = \frac{17y\,dy}{\left(3-2y^2\right)^2}$$

and $$3x^2 - 4 = \frac{17y^2}{3-2y^2}$$

or $$dx = 17y \cdot \frac{\left(3-2y^2\right)^{1/2}}{\left(3y^2+4\right)^{1/2}} \cdot \frac{1}{\left(3-2y^2\right)^2}dy$$

so $$I = \int \frac{17y\left(3-2y^2\right)^{1/2}}{\left(3y^2+4\right)^{1/2}.\left(3-2y^2\right)^2} \frac{\left(3-2y^2\right)}{17} \frac{\left(3-2y^2\right)^{1/2}}{17y} dy$$

$$= \frac{1}{\sqrt{17}} \int \frac{1}{\sqrt{3y^2+4}}\, dy$$

$$= \frac{1}{\sqrt{51}} \int \frac{1}{\sqrt{y^2 + \left(\frac{2}{\sqrt{3}}\right)^2}} dy$$

$$= \frac{1}{\sqrt{51}} \,.\log \left[y + \sqrt{y^2 + \left(\frac{2}{\sqrt{3}}\right)^2} \right]$$

$$= \frac{1}{\sqrt{51}} \,.\log \left[\sqrt{3}y + \sqrt{3y^2+4} \right]$$

$$= \frac{1}{\sqrt{51}} \,.\log \left[\sqrt{3}.\sqrt{\frac{3x^2-4}{2x^2+3}} + \sqrt{\frac{x^2-4}{2x^2+3}} \right] + C.$$

EXERCISE

Evaluate the following integrals:

1. $\int \frac{1}{(1+x)\sqrt{1+x+x^2}}\,dx.$

2. $\int \frac{1}{(2x+1)\sqrt{1+3x-2x^2}}\,dx.$

3. $\int \frac{1}{\left(1+x^2\right)\sqrt{1-x^2}}\,dx.$

4. $\int \frac{1}{x^2\sqrt{a^2-x^2}}\,dx.$

5. $\int \frac{x^2+1}{(3x+2)\sqrt{x-1}}\,dx.$

6. Show that

$$\int_0^{1/2} \frac{dx}{\left(1-2x^2\right)\sqrt{1-x^2}} = \frac{1}{2}\log\left[2+\sqrt{3}\right].$$

Answers:

1. $-\sin h^{-1}\left[\frac{1-x}{\sqrt{3}(1+x)}\right] + C$

2. $\frac{1}{2}\sin^{-1}\left[\frac{10x+1}{\sqrt{17}(2x+1)}\right] + C$

3. $-\frac{1}{2}\sin^{-1}\sqrt{\frac{1-x^2}{1+x^2}} + C$

4. $\frac{-\sqrt{a^2-x^2}}{a^2x} + \text{C}$

5. $\frac{1}{2}\log(2x+3)+\log(x-1)+C$

REDUCTION FORMULAE

This is the process in which an integral is expressed in terms of the integral of the same type but of lower orders and by the repeated applications, the integral is evaluated.

Reduction formulae of some standard integrals:

1. Reduction formula for $\int sin^n x\, dx$.

Let
$$I_n = \int \sin^n x\, dx$$
$$= \int \sin^{n-1} x \,.\sin x\, dx$$

Integrating by parts, we have

$$I_n = -\sin^{n-1} x \,.\, \cos x + \int (n-1)\ \sin^{n-2} x \,.\, \cos x \,.\, \cos x\, dx$$

$$= -\sin^{n-1} x \,.\, \cos x + (n-1) \int \sin^{n-2} x\,(1-\sin^2 x)\, dx$$

$$I_n = -\sin^{n-1} x \,.\, \cos x + (n-1) \int \sin^{n-2} x\ dx - (n-1)\, I_n$$

$$\therefore I_n\,[1+n-1] = -\sin^{n-1} x \,.\, \cos x + (n-1)\, I_{n-2}$$

$$\therefore \quad \boxed{I_n = -\frac{\sin^{n-1} x \cos x}{n} + \frac{n-1}{n} I_{n-2}}$$

In case of definite integral $\int_0^{\pi/2} sin^n x dx$

or
$$I_n = \left[\frac{-\sin^{n-1} x \cos x}{n}\right]_0^{\pi/2} + \frac{n-1}{n} I_{n-2}$$

or
$$I_n = \frac{n-1}{n} I_{n-2} \qquad (n \neq 1)$$

$$I_{n-2} = \frac{n-3}{n-2}\, I_{n-4}$$

$$I_{n-4} = \frac{n-5}{n-4} I_{n-6}$$

....

$$I_n = \frac{n-1}{n}.\frac{n-3}{n-2}.\frac{n-5}{n-4}...$$

(a) if *n* is even

$$I_n = \frac{n-1}{n}.\frac{n-3}{n-2}.\frac{n-5}{n-4}...\frac{1}{2}.I_0$$

where

$$I_0 = \int_0^{\pi/2} (\sin x)^\circ \, dx$$

$$\int_0^{\pi/2} 1.dx = \frac{\pi}{2}$$

$\therefore$ $$\boxed{\boldsymbol{I_n = \frac{n-1}{n}.\frac{n-3}{n-2}.\frac{n-5}{n-4}...\frac{1}{2}.\frac{\pi}{2}}}$$

(b) if *n* is odd

$$I_n = \frac{n-1}{n}.\frac{n-3}{n-2}.\frac{n-5}{n-4}...\frac{2}{3} I_1$$

$$= \frac{n-1}{n}.\frac{n-3}{n-2}.\frac{n-5}{n-4}...\frac{2}{3} 1 \quad \left[\because \quad I_1 = \int_0^{\pi/2} \sin dx = 1\right]$$

$\therefore$ $$\boxed{\boldsymbol{I_n = \frac{n-1}{n}.\frac{n-3}{n-2}.\frac{n-5}{n-4}...\frac{2}{3}}}$$

2. If $$I_n = \int \cos^n x \, dx$$

$\therefore$ $$I_n = \frac{n-1}{n} I_{n-2} + \frac{\sin x.\cos^{n-1} x}{n}$$

If $$I_n = \int_0^{\pi/2} \cos^n dx .$$

$$\therefore \int_0^{\pi/2} \cos^n dx = \int_0^{\pi/2} \sin^n dx$$

$\therefore$ We get the same reduction formula for $\int_0^{\pi/2} \cos^n x \, dx$.

$$\int_0^{\pi/2} \cos^n x dx = \begin{cases} \dfrac{n-1}{n}.\dfrac{n-3}{n-2}.\dfrac{n-5}{n-4}...\dfrac{1}{2}.\dfrac{\pi}{2}, \text{ if } n \text{ is even} \\ \dfrac{n-1}{n}.\dfrac{n-3}{n-2}.\dfrac{n-5}{n-4}...\dfrac{2}{3}.1, \text{ if } n \text{ is odd} \end{cases}$$

Example I. Evaluate $\int_0^{\infty} \frac{1}{\left(1+x^2\right)^{\frac{7}{12}}} dx.$

Solution: $I = \int_0^{\infty} \frac{1}{\left(1+x^2\right)^{\frac{7}{12}}} dx.$

Let $x = \tan\theta$

$\therefore$ $dx = \sec^2\theta \; d\theta$

when $x = 0, \theta = 0$

when $x = \infty, \theta = \frac{\pi}{2}$

$$\therefore \quad I = \int_0^{\pi/2} \frac{\sec^2\theta}{\left(1+\tan^2\theta\right)^{7/2}} d\theta$$

$$= \int_0^{\pi/2} \cos^5\theta \; d\theta$$

$$= \frac{4}{5}.\frac{2}{3}.1 = \frac{8}{15}.$$

Example 2. Evaluate $I = \int_0^{\pi/2} \sin^8\theta \; d\theta$.

Solution: $I = \frac{7}{8}.\frac{5}{6}.\frac{3}{4}.\frac{1}{2}.\frac{\pi}{2}$

$$= \frac{35\pi}{256}.$$

Reduction formula for $\int sin^m x.cos^n x \; dx$.

Let $I_{m,\,n} = \int \sin^m x.\cos^n x \; dx.$

$$= -\int \sin^{m-1} x \,.\, \{\cos^n x\,(-\sin x)\}\, dx$$

$$= -\sin^{m-1} x \,.\, \frac{\cos^{n+1} x}{n+1} + \int (m-1)\sin^{m-2} \,.$$

$$\cos x \;\frac{\cos^{n+1} x}{n+1} dx$$

$$= \frac{-\sin^{m-1} x \cos^{n+1} x}{n+1} + \frac{m-1}{n+1}\int \sin^{m-2} x \cos^n x \cos^2 x\, dx$$

$$I_{m,\,n} = \frac{-\sin^{m-1} x \cos^{n+1} x}{n+1} + \frac{m-1}{n+1}\int \sin^{m-2} x \cos^n x\, dx$$

$$- \frac{m-1}{n+1} I_{m,\,n}$$

$$\therefore\; I_{m,\,n}\left[1+\frac{m-1}{n+1}\right] = -\frac{\sin^{m-1} x.\cos^{n+1} x}{n+1} + \frac{m-1}{n+1} I_{m-2,\,n}$$

$$\therefore\qquad \boxed{I_{m,n} = -\frac{\sin^{m-1} x.\cos^{n+1} x}{m+n} + \frac{m-1}{m+n} I_{m-2,n}.} \qquad \ldots (1)$$

Above is the reduction formula for $\int \sin^m x.\cos^n x dx$

If $\qquad I_{m,\,n.} = \int_0^{\pi/2} \sin^m x \cos^n x\, dx$

Then $\qquad I_{m,\,n} = -\left[\frac{\sin^{m-1} x.\cos^{n+1} x}{m+n}\right]_0^{\pi/2} + \frac{m-1}{m+n} I_{m-2,\,n.}$

$$= 0 + \frac{m-1}{m+n} I_{m-2,\,n.} \qquad (n \neq 1)$$

$$\therefore\qquad I_{m,\,n.} = \frac{m-1}{m+n} I_{m-2,\,n.} \qquad \ldots (2)$$

$$\therefore\qquad I_{m-2,\,n} = \frac{m-3}{(m-2+n)} I_{m-4,\,n}$$

$$I_{m-4,\,n} = \frac{m-5}{m-4+n} I_{m-6,\,n}$$

... .

Now, if m is even

then $$I_{m,\,n} = \frac{m-1}{m+n}\cdot\frac{m-3}{m-2+n}\cdot\frac{m-5}{m-4+n}\cdots\frac{1}{2+n}\,I_{o,\,n}$$

where $$I_{o,\,n} = \int_0^{\pi/2}\cos^n dx = \frac{n-1}{n}\cdot\frac{n-3}{n-2}\cdot\frac{n-5}{n-4}\cdots\frac{1}{2}\cdot\frac{\pi}{2} \text{ if } n \text{ is even.}$$

$$= \frac{n-1}{n}\cdot\frac{n-3}{n-2}\cdots\frac{2}{3}.1 \text{ if } n \text{ is odd.}$$

(a) If m is even, then

$$\mathbf{I}_{m,\,n} = \frac{m-1}{m+n}\cdot\frac{m-3}{m-2+n}\cdot\frac{m-5}{m-4+n}\cdots\frac{1}{2+n}\cdot\frac{n-1}{n}\cdot\frac{n-3}{n-2}\cdots\frac{1}{2}\cdot\frac{\pi}{2},$$

if n is even

$$= \frac{m-1}{m+n}\cdot\frac{m-3}{m-2+n}\cdot\frac{m-5}{m-4+n}\cdots\frac{1}{2+n}\cdot\frac{n-1}{n}\cdot\frac{n-3}{n-2}\cdots\frac{2}{3}.1$$

if n is odd.

(b) If m is odd then

$$\mathbf{I}_{m,\,n} = \frac{m-1}{m+n}\cdot\frac{m-3}{m-2+n}\cdot\frac{m-5}{m-4+n}\cdots\frac{2}{3+n}\,\mathbf{I}_{1},\,n$$

Now $$I_1,\, n = \int_0^{\pi/2}\sin x.\cos^n x\, dx$$

$$= -\left|\frac{\cos^{n+1} x}{n+1}\right|_0^{\pi/2}$$

$$= \frac{1}{n+1}$$

$\therefore$ $$I_{m,\,n} = \frac{m-1}{m+n}\cdot\frac{m-3}{m-2+n}\cdot\frac{m-5}{m-4+n}\cdots\frac{2}{3+n}\cdot\frac{1}{n+1},$$

if m is odd.

Example 1. Evaluate $I = \int_0^{\pi/2}\sin^7\theta\cos^4\theta\, d\theta$.

Solution: Using the reduction formula for $\int_0^{\pi/2}\sin^m x\cos^n x\, dx$

we have

$$I = \frac{6}{11}.\frac{4}{9}.\frac{2}{7}.\frac{1}{5} = \frac{16}{1155}.$$

Example 2. Evaluate $I = \int_0^{2a} x^2\sqrt{2ax - x^2}\,dx$

Solution: Let $x = 2a\sin^2\theta$

$dx = 4a\sin\theta\cos\theta\,d\theta.$

$$\therefore \quad I = \int_0^{\pi/2} 4a^2.\sin^4\theta\sqrt{2a.2a\sin^2\theta - 4a^2\sin^4\theta}\;.\;4a\sin\theta\cos\theta\,d\theta.$$

$$= 32a^4\int_0^{\pi/2}\sin^6\theta\cos^2\theta\,d\theta$$

$$= 32a^4\;.\;\frac{5}{8}.\frac{3}{6}.\frac{1}{4}.\frac{1}{2}.\frac{\pi}{2} = \frac{5\pi a^4}{8}.$$

Example 3. Evaluate $I = \int_0^{\infty}\frac{x^3}{(1+x^2)^{9/2}}dx.$

Solution: Let $x = \tan\theta$

$\therefore \quad dx = \sec^2\theta\,d\theta$

$$\therefore \quad I = \int_0^{\pi/2}\frac{\tan^3\theta}{(1+\tan^2\theta)^{9/2}}\;.\;\sec^2\theta\,d\theta$$

$$= \int_0^{\pi/2}\frac{\tan^3\theta}{\sec^9\theta}\sec^2\theta\,d\theta$$

$$= \int_0^{\pi/2}\frac{\sin^3\theta}{\cos^3\theta}\cos^7\theta\,d\theta$$

$$= \int_0^{\pi/2}\sin^3\theta\,.\,\cos^4\theta\,d\theta$$

$$= \frac{2}{7}.\frac{1}{5} = \frac{2}{35}.$$

Example 4. Show that $\int_0^a \frac{x^n}{\sqrt{ax - x^2}}dx = \frac{1.3.5...(2n-1)}{2.4.6...(2n)}\;.\;\pi a^n$

Solution: let $I_n = \int_0^a \frac{x^n}{\sqrt{ax - x^2}} dx$

$x = a \sin^2\theta$

$\therefore \quad dx = 2\, a \sin\theta \cos\theta\, d\theta$

$$\therefore \quad = \int_0^{\pi/2} \frac{a^n . \sin^{2n}\theta}{a \sin\theta \cos\theta} 2a \sin\theta \cos\theta\, d\theta$$

$$= 2a^n \int_0^{\pi/2} \sin^{2n}\theta\, d\theta$$

$$= 2a^n . \frac{(2n-1)}{2n} . \frac{(2n-3)}{(2n-2)} ... \frac{1}{2} . \frac{\pi}{2}$$

$$= a^n . \frac{1.3.5...(2n-1)}{2.4.6...(2n)} \pi.$$

Reduction formula for $\int \tan^n x\, dx.$

$$I_n = \int \tan^n x\, dx$$

$$= \int \tan^{n-2} x . \tan^2 x dx$$

$$= \int \tan^{n-2} x . \sec^2 x dx - \int \tan^{n-2} x dx$$

$$I_n = \frac{\tan^{n-1} x}{n-1} - I_{n-2}$$

$$\therefore \quad \boxed{I_n = \frac{\tan^{n-1} x}{n-1} - I_{n-2}}$$

Reduction formula for $\int \sec^n x\, dx.$

let $I_n = \int \sec^n x\, dx$

$$= \int \sec^{n-2} x . \sec^2 x\, dx$$

$$= \sec^{n-2} x \,.\, \tan x - \int (n-2) \sec^{n-3} x . \sec x . \tan x . \tan x\, dx$$

$$= \sec^{n-2} x \,.\, \tan x - (n-2) \int \sec^{n-2} x . \tan^2 x\, dx$$

$$= \sec^{n-2} x \,.\, \tan x - (n-2) \int \sec^{n-2} x \left(\sec^2 x - 1\right) dx$$

$$= \sec^{n-2} x \tan x - (n-2) I_n + (n-2) I_{n-2}$$

$$\therefore \quad I_n [n-1] = \sec^{n-2} x \,.\, \tan x + (n-2) I_{n-2}$$

$$\therefore \quad \boxed{I_n = \frac{\sec^{n-2} x . \tan x}{n-1} + \frac{n-2}{n-1} . I_{n-2} .}$$

is the reduction formula for $\int \sec^n x\, dx.$

Reduction formula for (i) $\int x^n \sin mx\, dx$ and (ii) $\int x^n \cos mx\, dx$

(i) let $\quad I_{n,\, m} = \int x^n \sin mx\, dx \qquad \ldots (1)$

Integrating by parts taking sin mx as second function.

$$I_{n,\, m} = -x^n \frac{\cos mx}{m} + \int nx^{n-1} . \frac{\cos mx}{m} dx$$

$$= -\frac{x^n \cos mx}{m} + \frac{n}{m} \int x^{n-1} . \cos mx\, dx$$

$$= -\frac{x^n \cos mx}{m} + \frac{n}{m} \left\{ x^{n-1} \frac{\sin mx}{m} - \int (n-1) x^{n-2} . \frac{\sin mx}{m} dx \right\}$$

$$= -\frac{x^n \cos mx}{m} + \frac{n}{m^2} x^{n-1} . \sin mx - \frac{n(n-1)}{m^2} I_{n-2,m}$$

$$\therefore \quad \boxed{I_{n,m} = -\frac{x^n \cos mx}{m} + \frac{n}{m^2} x^{n-1} . \sin mx - \frac{n(n-1)}{m^2} I_{n-2,m}}$$

is the reduction formula for $\int x^n \sin mx\, dx$.

(ii) $I_{n,\,m} = \int x^n \cos mx\, dx$

Integrating by parts we obtain the reduction formula for the above as

$$\therefore \quad \boxed{I_{n,m} = \frac{x^n \sin mx}{m} + \frac{n}{m^2} x^{n-1} . \cos mx - \frac{n(n-1)}{m^2} I_{n-2,m}}$$

Reduction formula for (i) $\int e^{ax} \sin^n x\, dx$ and (ii) $\int e^{ax} \cos^n x\, dx$

(i) $$I_n = \int e^{ax} . \sin^n x\, dx$$

$$= \sin^n x \frac{e^{ax}}{a} - \int n \sin^{n-1} x \cos x \frac{e^{ax}}{a} dx$$

$$= \frac{e^{ax} . \sin^n x}{a} - \frac{n}{a} \int \sin^{n-1} x \cos x\ e^{ax}\, dx$$

$$= \frac{e^{ax} . \sin^n x}{a} - \frac{n}{a} \left\{ \frac{e^{ax}}{a} . \left(\sin^{n-1} x \cos x \right) \right.$$

$$\left. - \int \frac{d}{dx} \left(\sin^{n-1} x \cos x \right) \frac{e^{ax}}{a} dx \right\}$$

$$= \frac{e^{ax} . \sin^n x}{a} - \frac{n}{a^2} \left\{ e^{ax} \sin^{n-1} x \cos x \right.$$

$$\left. - \int (n-1) \sin^{n-2} x . \cos^2 x + \sin^{n-1} x (-\sin x) e^{ax} dx \right\}$$

$$= \frac{e^{ax} . \sin^n x}{a} - \frac{n}{a^2} e^{ax} . \sin^{n-1} x \cos x$$

$$+ \frac{n(n-1)}{a^2} \int e^{ax} . \sin^{n-2} x \cos^2 x\, dx - \frac{n}{a^2} \int \sin^n x\, e^{ax} dx$$

$$= \frac{e^{ax} . \sin^n x}{a} - \frac{n}{a^2} e^{ax} . \sin^{n-1} x \cos x + \frac{n(n-1)}{a^2}$$

$$\int e^{ax}.\sin^{n-2} xdx - \frac{n(n-1)}{a^2}\int e^{ax}.\sin^n xdx$$

$$-\frac{n}{a^2}\int \sin^n e^{ax}dx$$

$$= \frac{e^{ax}.\sin^n x}{a} - \frac{n\, e^{ax}}{a^2}\sin^{n-1} x\cos x + \frac{n(n-1)}{a^2} I_{n-2}$$

$$-\frac{n}{a^2}\int\{(n-1)+1\}e^{ax}.\sin^n x\,dx$$

$$I_n\left[1+\frac{n^2}{a^2}\right] = \frac{e^{ax}.\sin^n x}{a} - \frac{n}{a^2}e^{ax}\sin^{n-1} x.\cos x + \frac{n(n-1)}{a^2} I_{n-2}$$

$$I_n = \frac{e^{ax}.\sin^{n-1} x(a\sin x - n\cos x)}{n^2+a^2} + \frac{n(n-1)}{a^2} I_{n-2}$$

$$\boxed{I_n = \frac{e^{ax}.\sin^{n-1} x(a\sin x - n\cos x)}{n^2+a^2} + \frac{n(n-1)}{a^2} I_{n-2}}$$

(ii) Similarly

If $\quad I_n = \int e^{ax}\cos^n x\,dx$

then $\quad I_n = \dfrac{e^{ax}.\cos^{n-1} x(a\cos x + n\sin x)}{n^2+a^2} + \dfrac{n(n-1)}{(n^2+a^2)} I_{n-2}.$

Reduction formula for $\int x^n e^{ax}dx.$

Let $\quad I_n = \int x^n e^{ax}dx$

$$= x^n.\frac{e^{ax}}{a} - \int nx^{n-1}.\frac{e^{ax}}{a}dx$$

$$I_n = \frac{e^{ax}.x^n}{a} - \frac{n}{a}\int x^{n-1}.e^{ax}dx$$

$$\therefore \qquad \boxed{\boldsymbol{I_n = \frac{x^n e^{ax}}{a} - \frac{n}{a} I_{n-1}}}$$

is the reduction formula for $\int x^n e^{ax} dx$.

Reduction formula for $\int x^m (\log x)^n \, dx$

Let $\qquad I_{m,n} = \int x^m (\log x)^n \, dx$

$$= (\log x)^n \cdot \frac{x^{m+1}}{m+1} - \int n.(\log x)^{n-1} \cdot \frac{1}{x} \frac{x^{m+1}}{m+1} dx$$

$$= \frac{x^{m+1}}{m+1} \cdot (\log x)^n - \frac{n}{m+1} \int x^m (\log x)^{n-1} . dx$$

$$= \frac{x^{m+1}}{m+1} \cdot (\log x)^n - \frac{n}{m+1} I_{m,\,n-1}$$

$$= \boxed{\boldsymbol{I_{m,n} = \frac{x^{m+1}}{m+1} (\log x)^n - \frac{n}{(m+1)} I_{m,n-1}}}$$

Reduction formula for $\int x^m \left(a + bx^n\right)^p dx$

Let $\qquad I_{m,\,p} = \int x^m \left(a + bx^n\right)^p dx$

$$= \frac{x^{m+1}}{m+1} . \left(a + bx^n\right)^p - \int p\left(a + bx^n\right)^{p-1} . nbx^{n-1} . \frac{x^{m+1}}{m+1} dx$$

$$= \frac{x^{m+1}}{m+1} . \left(a + bx^n\right)^p - \frac{bnp}{m+1} \int x^m . x^n . \left(a + bx^n\right)^{p-1} . dx$$

$$= \frac{x^{m+1}}{m+1} . \left(a + bx^n\right)^p - \frac{bnp}{m+1}$$

$$\left[\int x^m . \left(\frac{a + bx^n - a}{b}\right) . \left(a + bx^n\right)^{p-1} dx\right]$$

$$= \frac{x^{m+1}}{m+1}.\left(a+bx^n\right)^p - \frac{np}{m+1}$$

$$\left[\int\left\{x^m.\left(a+bx^n\right)^p - ax^m\left(a+bx^n\right)^{p-1}\right\}dx\right]$$

$$= \frac{x^{m+1}}{m+1}.\left(a+bx^n\right)^p - \frac{np}{m+1}\int x^m.\left(a+bx^n\right)^p dx$$

$$+\frac{anp}{m+1}\int x^m\left(a+bx^n\right)^{p-1}dx$$

$$\therefore \quad = \frac{x^{m+1}}{m+1}.\left(a+bx^n\right)^p - \frac{np}{m+1}.I_{m,p} + \frac{anp}{m+1}I_{m,\,p-1}$$

$$\therefore \quad I_{m,\,p}\left[1+\frac{np}{m+1}\right] = \frac{x^m\left(a+bx^n\right)^p}{m+1} + \frac{anp}{m+1}.I_{m,p-1}.$$

$$\boxed{\boldsymbol{I_{m,p} = \frac{x^m\left(a+bx^n\right)^p}{(np+m+1)} + \frac{anp}{(np+m+1)}.I_{m,p\text{-}1}}}$$

Gamma function It is a mathematical tool to evaluate complicated integrals. It is defined as

$$\overline{|n} = \int_0^\infty e^{-x}.x^{n-1}dx. \qquad (n > 0)$$

PROPERTIES OF GAMMA FUNCTION:

(i) $\overline{|n+1} = n\overline{|n}$

$$\overline{|n+1} = \int_0^\infty e^{-x}.x^n dx$$

$$= x^n.\left.\frac{e^{-x}}{(-1)}\right|_0^\infty + \int_0^\infty nx^{n-1}.e^{-x}dx$$

$$= 0 + n\int_0^\infty e^{-x}.x^{n-1}dx$$

$$= n\Gamma(n).$$

(ii) $\Gamma(1) = 1$

(iii) $\Gamma\left(\frac{1}{2}\right) = \sqrt{\pi}$

(iv) $\Gamma(n+1) = n!$ (if n is a +ve integer)

(v) $$\int_0^{\pi/2} \sin^m x \cos^n x = \frac{\Gamma\left(\frac{m+1}{2}\right) \cdot \Gamma\left(\frac{n+1}{2}\right)}{2\Gamma\left(\frac{m+n+2}{2}\right)}$$

This result, students may use while evaluating the integral of the form $\int_0^{\pi/2} \sin^p \theta \cos^q \theta \, d\theta$, without remembering the reduction formula, occuring in the evaluation of area bounded; length of a curve, surface and volume of the solids of revolution.

9

Area of Plane Curves (Quadrature)

INTRODUCTION

The process of finding the area bounded by a curve is known as quadrature.

AREA OF THE CURVES, GIVEN BY CARTESIAN EQUATIONS

I. The area bounded by the curve $y = f(x)$, x-axis and the ordinates $x = a$ and $x = b$.

Let AB be the arc of the curve $y = f(x)$, where the function $f(x)$ is continuous in the interval $a \leq x \leq b$.

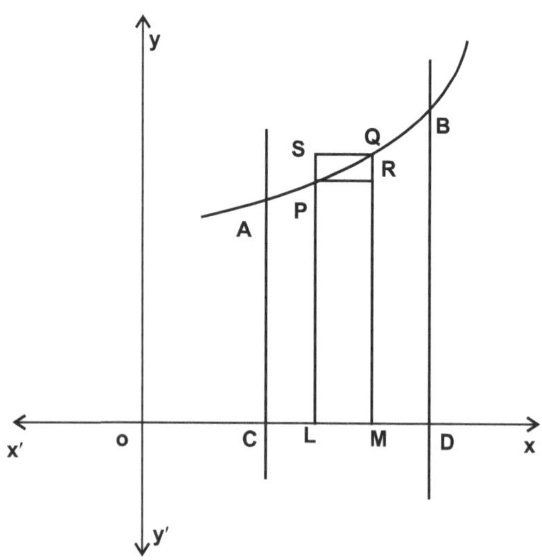

and AC and BD be the ordinates $x = a$ and $x = b$.

Let $P(x, y)$ and $Q(x + \delta x, y + \delta y)$ be two neighbouring points on the curve with their ordinates PL and QM.

Let A, be the area ACLP

and $A + \delta A$ = Area ACMQ

$\therefore$ δA = Area PLMQ

From the fig., it is clear that the

Area PLMR < δA < Area SLMQ

or $y\,\delta x < \delta A < (y + \delta y)\,\delta x$.

$$\therefore \quad y < \frac{\delta A}{\delta x} < (y + \delta y)$$

Taking, limit as $\delta x \to 0$.

Then, $\lim\limits_{\delta x \to 0} \dfrac{\delta A}{\delta x} = \dfrac{dA}{dx}$ and the inequalities convert into equality, giving

$$\therefore \quad \frac{dA}{dx} = y$$

$$\therefore \quad \int_{x=a}^{b} \frac{dA}{dx}.dx = \int_{x=a}^{b} y\,dx$$

The area bounded by the curve $y = f(x)$, x-axis and the ordinates $x = a$ and $x = b$ is

$$\boxed{A = \int_a^b y\,dx}$$

II. Similarly, the area bounded by the curve $x = \phi(y)$, y-axis and the lines $y = c$ and $y = d$ is

$$\boxed{A = \int_{y=c}^{b} x\,dy}$$

- The area bounded by the curve $y = f(x)$, $y = c$ line and the ordinates $x = a$ and $x = b$ is

$$A = \int_a^b (y - c)\,dx$$

- The area bounded by the curved $x = \phi(y)$, the line $x = a$ and the lines $y = c$, $y = d$ is

$$\boxed{A = \int_c^d (x - a)\,dy}$$

SOLVED EXAMPLES

Example 1. Find the area bounded by the parabola $y^2 = 4ax$ and its latus rectum.

Solution: As it is obvious that the curve is symmetrical about x-axis.

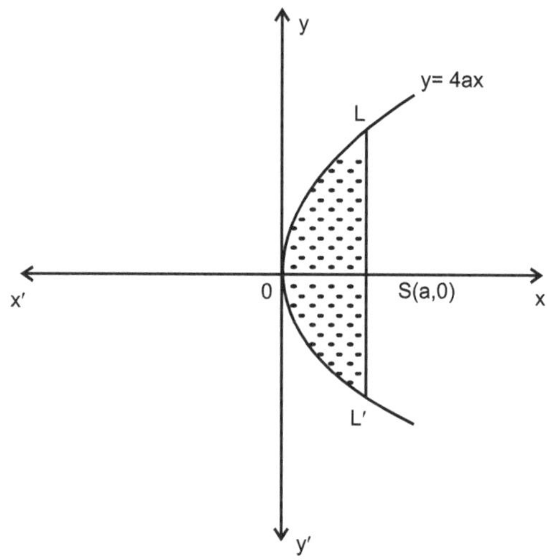

The required area

Area (OL′LO) = 2. area (OSLO)

= 2. Area bounded by the curve $y^2 = 4ax$, X-axis

and the lines $x = 0, x = a$

$$= 2 \cdot \int_0^a y dx$$

$$= 2 \int_0^a 2\sqrt{a}.\sqrt{x} dx$$

$$= 2.2\sqrt{a} \left| \frac{x^{3/2}}{3/2} \right|_0^a$$

$$= 4.\sqrt{a}.\frac{2}{3} \cdot a^{3/2}$$

$$= \frac{8}{3} a^2.$$

Example 2. Find the area of the loop of the curve. $a^2y^2 = a^2x^2 - x^4$

Solution: The loop of the curve is symmetric about x-axis and lies between $x = 0$ and $x = a$.

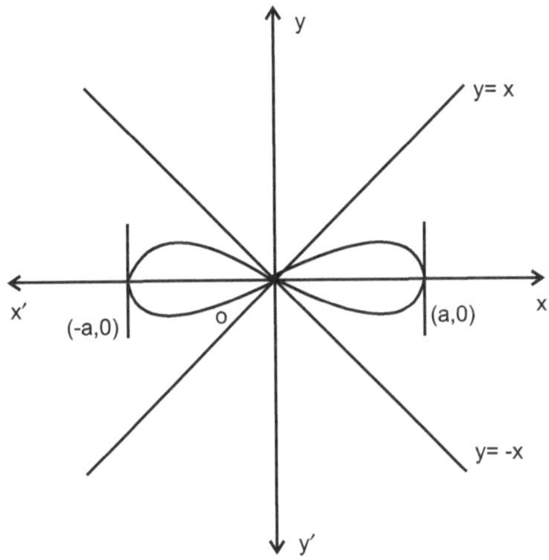

$\therefore$ Area of one loop of the curve

$$= 2. \text{ Area of the loop of the curve above } x\text{-axis}$$

$$= 2. \int_0^a y\,dx$$

$$= 2 . \int_0^a \frac{x}{a}\sqrt{a^2 - x^2}\,dx$$

Let $x = a \sin\theta$

$\therefore$ $dx = a \cos\theta \, d\theta$

$\therefore$ $$A = 2 . \int_0^{\pi/2} \sin\theta . a\cos\theta . a\cos\theta \, d\theta$$

$$= 2a^2 \int_0^{\pi/2} \cos^2\theta . \sin\theta \, d\theta$$

$$= 2a^2 \left[\frac{-\cos^3\theta}{3}\right]_0^{\pi/2}$$

$$= \frac{-2a^2}{3}[0 - 1] = \frac{2a^2}{3}.$$

And, the area of the whole curve is

$$= 2 \,.\, A = \frac{4a^2}{3}$$

Example 3. Find the area between the curve $y^2\,(a + x) = x^2\,(3a - x)$ and its asymptote.

Solution: Asymptote of the curve is $a + x = 0$, *i.e.*, $x = -a$ and dotted area is the required area.

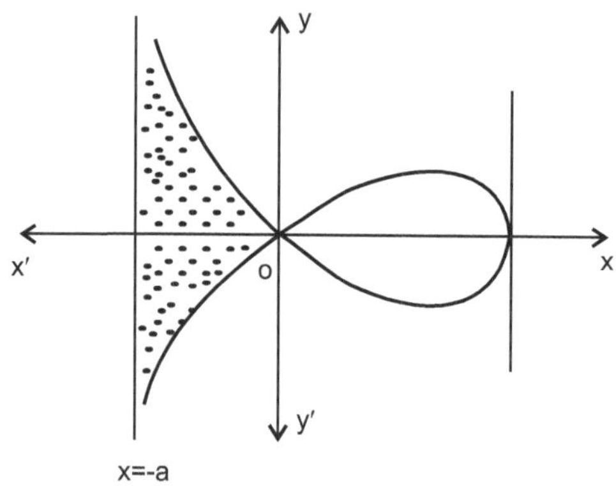

As the curve is symmetrical about x-axis.

$\therefore$ Required area = 2. Area lying above x-axis.

$$A = 2 \,.\, \int_{-a}^{0} x\sqrt{\frac{3a - x}{a + x}}dx$$

$$A = 2 \,.\, \int_{-a}^{0} x\sqrt{\frac{2a + (a - x)}{2a - (a - x)}}\, dx$$

Let $\quad a - x = 2a\,\cos\theta$

$\therefore \quad dx = 2a\,\sin\theta\, d\theta$

$$A = 2 \,.\, \int_{0}^{\pi/3} (a - 2a\cos\theta)\,\sqrt{\frac{2a + 2a\cos\theta}{2a - 2a\cos\theta}}\;(2a\,\sin\theta)\,d\theta$$

$$= 4a^2 \int_{0}^{\pi/3} (1 - 2\cos\theta)\,\sqrt{\frac{1 + \cos\theta}{1 - \cos\theta}}\;\sin\theta\, d\theta$$

$$= 4a^2 \int_{0}^{\pi/3} (1 - 2\cos\theta)\,(1 + \cos\theta)\,d\theta$$

$$= 4a^2 \int_0^{\pi/2} \left(1 - 2\cos\theta + \cos\theta - 2\cos^2\theta\right) d\theta$$

$$= -4a^2 \int_0^{\pi/3} (\cos\theta + \cos 2\theta)\, d\theta$$

$$= -4a^2 \left[\sin\theta + \frac{\sin 2\theta}{2}\right]_0^{\pi/3}$$

$$= -4a^2 \left[\sin\frac{\pi}{3} + \frac{1}{2}\sin\frac{2\pi}{3}\right]$$

$$= -4a^2 \left[\frac{\sqrt{3}}{2} + \frac{1}{2}\cdot\frac{\sqrt{3}}{2}\right]$$

$$= -3\sqrt{3}\, a^2.$$

Since the area is always positive

$\therefore$ $A = 3\sqrt{3}\, a^2$

• **The area bounded by the curves $y = f_1(x)$, $y = f_2(x)$. [$(f_2(x) > f_1(x))$] and the ordinates $x = a$, $x = b$ is given by:**

$$A = \int_a^b \left[f_2(x) - f_1(x)\right] dx$$

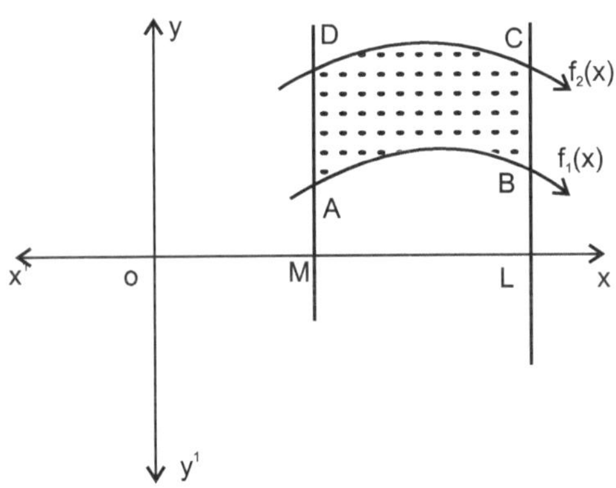

Area ABCD = Area DMLC – Area AMLB

$$= \int_a^b f_2(x)\, dx - \int_a^b f_1(x)\, dx$$

$$= \int_a^b \left[f_2(x) - f_1(x)\right] dx.$$

Example 4. Find the area enclosed by the curves $y^2 = 4ax$ and $x^2 = 4ay$.

Solution: The curves are

$$y^2 = 4ax \qquad (1)$$

$$y^2 = 4ay \qquad (2)$$

Both the curves intersect each other at (0, 0) and $(4a, 4a)$

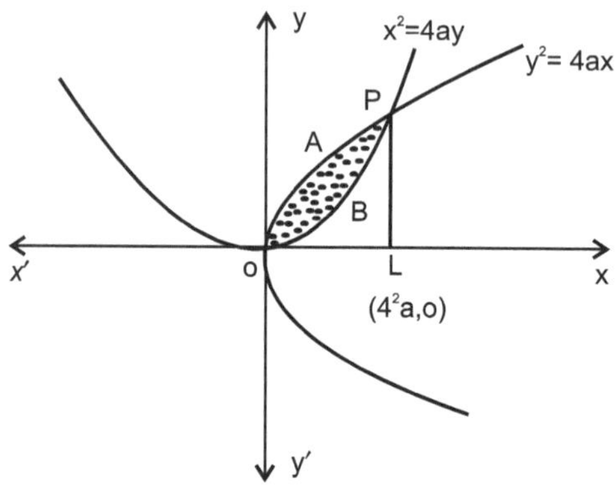

Required area is the area OBPAO

$$= \text{Area OLPAO} - \text{Area OLPBO}$$

$$= \int_0^{4a}\left(2\sqrt{ax} - \frac{x^2}{4a}\right) dx$$

$$= \left[2\sqrt{a}\,.\,\frac{x^{3/2}}{3/2} - \frac{x^3}{12a}\right]_0^{4a}$$

$$= 2\sqrt{a}\,.\,\frac{2}{3}\,.\,(4a)^{3/2} - \frac{64a^3}{12a}$$

$$= \frac{32}{3}a^2 - \frac{16a^2}{3} = \frac{16a^2}{3}.$$

Example 5. Find the area bounded by the curve $\sqrt{x} + \sqrt{y} = \sqrt{a}$ and the coordinate axis.

Solution: The given curve is $x^{1/2} + y^{1/2} = a^{1/2}$. It is symmetrical about $y = x$ line and exists in the first quadrant only. The curve intersects the line $y = x$ at $\left(\frac{a}{4}, \frac{a}{4}\right)$.

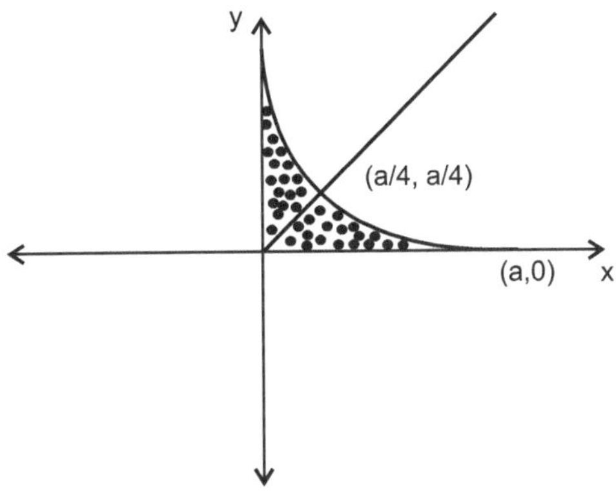

$\therefore$ Area above the line $y = x$ is same as below the line.

$$\therefore \text{Required area} = \int_0^a \left(\sqrt{a} - \sqrt{x}\right)^2 dx$$

$$= \int_0^a \left(a + x - 2\sqrt{ax}\right) dx$$

$$= \frac{a^2}{6}.$$

Area bounded by parametric curves:

The area bounded by the curve $x = \phi(t)$, $y = f(t)$, x-axis and ordinates where $t = t_1$ and $t = t_2$ is

$$\boxed{A = \int_{t_1}^{t_2} y \frac{dx}{dt} dt}$$

and that bounded by the curve $x = \phi(t)$, $y = f(t)$ and the abscissae at the points where $t = t_1$ and $t = t_2$ and y-axis is.

$$\boxed{A = \int_{t_1}^{t_2} x \frac{dy}{dt} dt}$$

Example 6. Find the area enclosed by the curve

$$x = a\cos^3 t,$$
$$y = b\sin^3 t, \quad (a > b).$$

Solution: The given curve is symmetrical about both the axis.

Required area = 4 . Area lying in first quadrant.

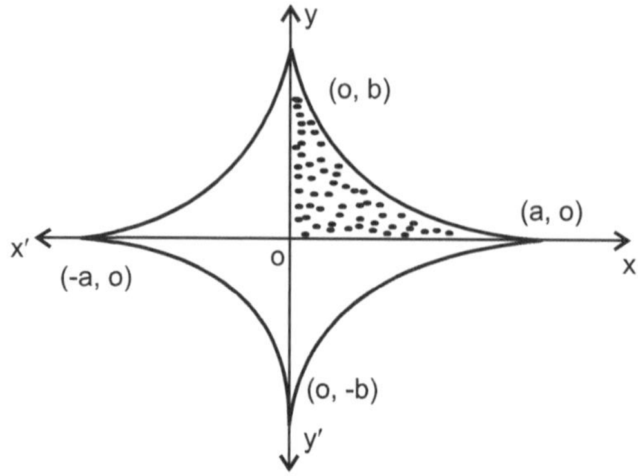

$\because$ $x = a\cos^3 t$

$y = b\sin^3 t$

$\therefore$ $$A = 4\ .\int_0^{\pi/2} y\frac{dx}{dt}\ .\ dt$$

$$= 4\ .\int_0^{\pi/2} b\sin^3 t.3a\cos^2 t(-\sin t).dt$$

$$= 4\int_0^{\pi/2}(-3ab)\sin^4 t\cos^2 t\ dt$$

$$= -12ab\left[\frac{\Gamma(5/2).\Gamma(3/2)}{2\Gamma\left(\frac{5+3}{2}\right)}\right]$$

$$= -12ab\ \frac{\frac{3}{2}.\frac{1}{2}.\sqrt{\pi}.\frac{1}{2}.\sqrt{\pi}}{2.3.2.1}$$

$$= -\frac{3\pi ab}{8}$$

$\therefore$ $$A = \frac{3\pi ab}{8}.$$

Example 7. Find the area between the curve $x = a\ (\theta + \sin\theta)$, $y = a\ (1 + \cos\theta)$ and its base from one cusp to another cusp.

Solution: Area between curve and its base (*i.e.*, between the curve and the x-axis) is symmetrical about y-axis.

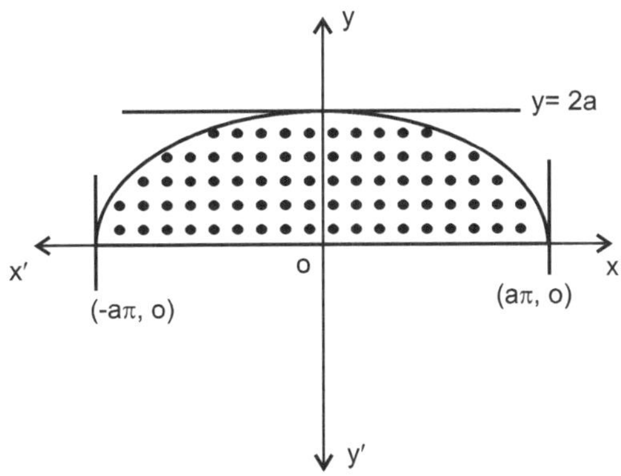

$\therefore$ Required area = 2 . Area in the first quadrant

$$= 2 \,.\, \int_0^{\pi} y\frac{dx}{d\theta}.d\theta$$

$$= 2 \,.\, \int_0^{\pi} a(\theta + \sin\theta)(-a\sin\theta)\,d\theta$$

$$= -2a^2 \int_0^{\pi} \left(\theta\sin\theta + \sin^2\theta\right)d\theta$$

$$= 3\pi a^2.$$

Example 8. Find the area of the loop of the curve $x = t^2$, $y = t - \dfrac{t^3}{3}$.

Solution: Eliminating the parameter t, we have

$$9y^2 = x\,(x - 3)^2$$

or

$$9y^2 = x\,(3 - x)^2$$

$\therefore$ The loop of the curve lies between $x = 0$ and $x = 3$ and as the curve is symmetrical about x-axis, so area of the loop above and below x-axis is same.

$\therefore$ Required area = 2. $\displaystyle\int_0^3 y\,dx$

$$= 2 \,.\, \int_0^3 \frac{(3 - x)\sqrt{x}}{3}\,dx$$

$$= \frac{2}{3} \int_0^3 \left(3\sqrt{x} - x\sqrt{x}\right)dx$$

$$= \frac{2}{3}\left[3x^{3/2}.\frac{2}{3} - x^{5/2}.\frac{2}{5}\right]_0^3$$

$$= \frac{8}{5}\sqrt{3}.$$

The area bounded by the curve $r = f(\theta)$, the radii vectors $\theta = \alpha$ and $\theta = \beta$ is

$$\boxed{A = \frac{1}{2}\int_{\alpha}^{\beta} r^2 d\theta}$$

Proof: Let AB, be the arc of the curve $r = f(\theta)$ and P (r, θ), Q$(r + \delta r, \theta + \delta\theta)$ be two adjacent points on the curve such that the function $r = f(\theta)$ is an increasing function of θ from P to Q.

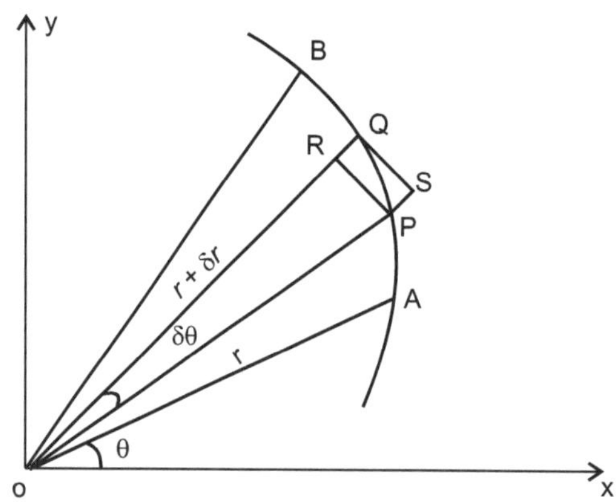

Now, we draw two arcs PR and QS with centre at O and OP, OQ as radii. Let

$$A = \text{area AOP}$$

$$A + \delta A = \text{area AOQ}$$

$\therefore$ $$\delta A = \text{area POQ}$$

As $$PR = r\delta\theta$$

$$QS = (r + \delta r)\,\delta\theta.$$

The area OPQ is more than the area OPR and less than the area OSQ. If $\delta\theta$ is small, then

$$\frac{1}{2} . \text{OP} . \text{PR} < \delta A < \frac{1}{2} . \text{OS} . \text{SQ}$$

or $$\frac{1}{2} r . r\delta\theta . < \delta A < \frac{1}{2} (r + \delta r) . (r + \delta r)\,\delta\theta$$

or $$\frac{1}{2} r^2\,\delta\theta < \delta A < \frac{1}{2} (r + \delta r)^2\,\delta\theta$$

or $$\frac{1}{2}r^2 < \frac{\delta A}{\delta\theta} < \frac{1}{2}(r+\delta r)^2$$

Taking limits as $\delta\theta \to 0$, then

$\lim_{\delta\theta\to 0} \frac{\delta A}{\delta\theta} = \frac{dA}{d\theta}$ and the inequality becomes equality.

$$\therefore \quad \frac{1}{2}r^2 = \frac{dA}{d\theta}$$

$$\therefore \quad \int_{\theta=\alpha}^{\beta} \frac{dA}{d\theta}.d\theta = \int \frac{1}{2}r^2\, d\theta$$

$$\therefore \quad \boxed{A = \frac{1}{2}\int r^2 d\theta}$$

Example 9. Find the area enclosed by the curve $r = a\sin\theta$.

Solution: The curve $r = a\sin\theta$ is symmetrical about the line $\theta = \frac{\pi}{2}$

and the curve lies in the first and second quadrants.

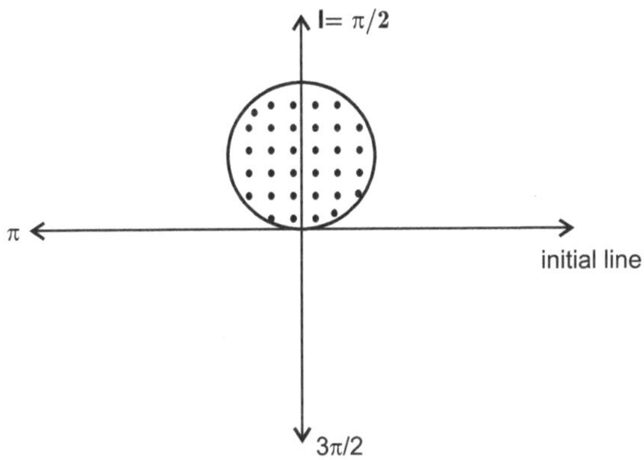

$$\text{Required area} = 2.\frac{1}{2}\int_0^{\pi/2}(a\sin\theta)^2\, d\theta$$

$$= 2a^2\ \frac{1}{2}\int_0^{\pi/2}\sin^2\theta\, d\theta$$

$$= 2a^2\ \frac{1}{2}\cdot\frac{1}{2}\int_0^{\pi/2}(1-\cos 2\theta)\, d\theta$$

$$= \frac{\pi a^2}{4}$$

Example 10. Find the area enclosed by the curve $r = a\,(1 + \cos\theta)$.

Solution: As the curve is symmetric about initial line.

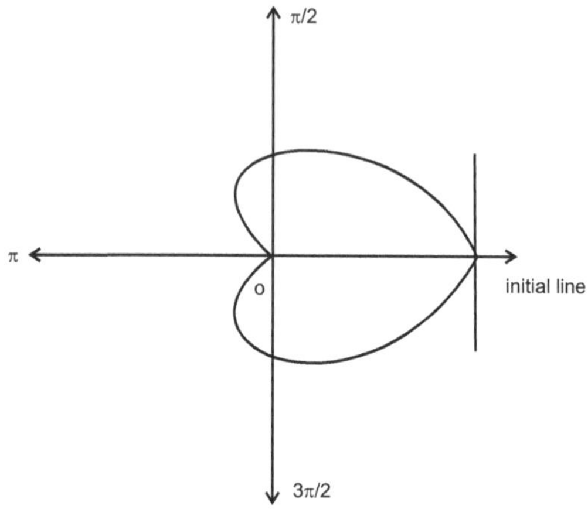

$\therefore$ Required area = 2 . Area above initial line

$$= 2 \cdot \frac{1}{2} \cdot \int_{\theta=0}^{\pi} r^2 \, d\theta$$

$$= \int_{\theta=0}^{\pi} a^2 (1+\cos\theta)^2 \, d\theta$$

$$= 4a^2 \int_0^{\pi} \cos^4 \frac{\theta}{2} d\theta$$

$$= 8a^2 \int_0^{\pi/2} \cos^4 \phi \, d\phi.$$

$$= 8a^2 \left\{ \frac{\overline{|5/2} \,.\, \overline{|1/2}}{2\overline{|6/2}} \right\}$$

$$= 4a^2 \left\{ \frac{\frac{3}{2} \cdot \frac{1}{2} \cdot \sqrt{\pi} \cdot \sqrt{\pi}}{2.1} \right\}$$

$$= \frac{3a^2\pi}{2}.$$

Example 11. Find the area of one loop of the curve $r = a \cos 2\theta$ and hence the whole area of the curve.

Solution:

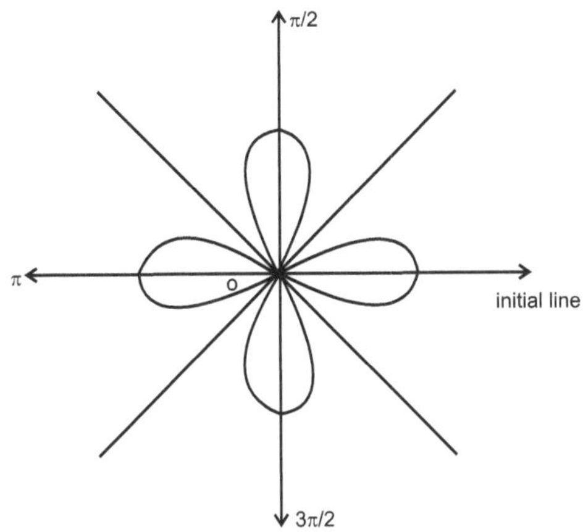

Note: The curves $r = a \cos n\theta$ or $r = a \sin n\theta$ consist of n identical loops if n is odd and $2n$ loops if n is even.

The given curve consists of four loops and one loop lies between

$\theta = \frac{-\pi}{4}$ to $\frac{\pi}{4}$.

$$A = \text{Area of one loop}$$

$$= \frac{1}{2}\int_{-\pi/4}^{\pi/4} r^2\, d\theta$$

$$A = \frac{1}{2}\int_{-\pi/4}^{\pi/4} a^2 \cos^2 2\theta\, d\theta$$

$$= 2\,.\,\frac{1}{2}\,.a^2 \int_0^{\pi/4} \cos^2 2\theta\, d\theta$$

$$= \frac{2a^2}{2}\int_0^{\pi/4}\left(\frac{1+\cos 4\theta}{2}\right) d\theta$$

$$= \frac{a^2}{2}\left[\theta + \frac{\sin 4\theta}{4}\right]_0^{\pi/4}$$

$$= \frac{a^2\pi}{2.4} = \frac{a^2\pi}{8}$$

∴ Area of the whole curve = 4A

$$= \frac{a^2\pi}{2}.$$

Example 12. Find the area of one loop of the curve $r^2 = a^2 \sin 2\theta$.

Solution: The given curve is symmetric about $\theta = \frac{\pi}{4}$ line.

There are two loops in the curve, one of them lies from $\theta = 0$ to $\theta = \frac{\pi}{2}$ and the other from $\theta = \pi$ to $\frac{3\pi}{2}$.

Now, the loop of the curve lying in first quadrant is equally divided by the line $\theta = \frac{\pi}{4}$.

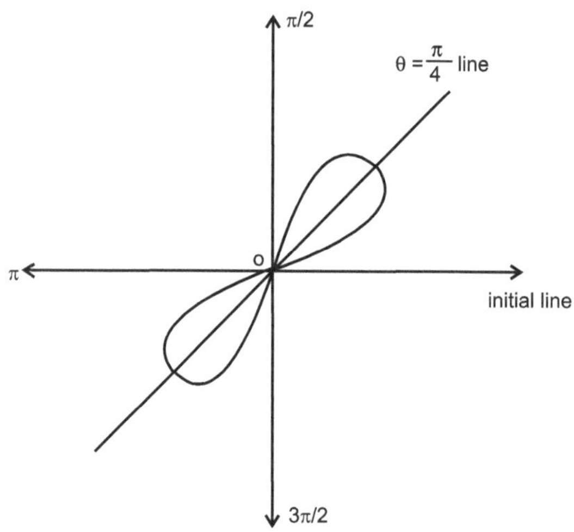

Area of the loop of the curve = 2 . Area of the loop below the line

$$\theta = \frac{\pi}{4}$$

$$= 2 \cdot \frac{1}{2} \int_{\theta=0}^{\pi/4} a^2 \sin 2\theta \, d\theta$$

$$= a^2 \int_0^{\pi/4} \sin 2\theta \, d\theta$$

$$= -a^2\left[\frac{\cos 2\theta}{2}\right]_0^{\pi/4}$$

$$= -\frac{a^2}{2}\left[\cos\frac{\pi}{2} - \cos 0\right]$$

$$= \frac{a^2}{2}.$$

Example 13. Find the area of a loop of the curve

$$x^4 + y^4 = 4a^2xy.$$

Solution: Changing into polar form, we have

$$r^2 = \frac{4a^2 \sin\theta\cos\theta}{\cos^4\theta + \sin^4\theta}$$

$\therefore$ $r = 0$ for $\theta = 0$ and $\theta = \dfrac{\pi}{2}$

$\therefore$ One loop of the curve lies between $\theta = 0$ and $\theta = \dfrac{\pi}{2}$

Area of one loop of the curve

$$A = \frac{1}{2}.\int_{\theta=0}^{\pi/2} r^2 d\theta$$

$$= \frac{1}{2}.\int_0^{\pi/2} \frac{4a^2 \sin\theta\cos\theta}{\cos^4\theta + \sin^4\theta} d\theta$$

$$= 2a^2 \int_0^{\pi/2} \frac{\sin\theta\cos\theta}{\cos^4\theta + \sin^4\theta} d\theta$$

$$= 2a^2 \int_0^{\pi/2} \frac{\tan\theta.\sec^2\theta}{1 + \tan^4\theta} d\theta$$

Let $\tan^2\theta = t$

$\therefore$ $2\tan\theta \,.\, \sec^2\theta \, d\theta = dt$

$\therefore$ $$\text{A} = a^2 \int_0^{\infty} \frac{dt}{1+t^2}$$

$$= a^2\left[\tan^{-1} t\right]_0^\infty$$

$$= \frac{\pi a^2}{2}.$$

Example 14. Show that the area of a loop of the curve $r = a \cos n\theta$ is $\frac{\pi a^2}{4n}$, n being integral. Also prove that the whole area is $\frac{\pi a^2}{4}$ or $\frac{\pi a^2}{2}$ accordingly as n is odd or even.

Solution: The given curve $r = a \cos n\theta$, is symmetrical about initial line.

$$r = 0 \text{ for } n\theta = \pm\frac{\pi}{2} \text{ or } \theta = \pm\frac{\pi}{2n}.$$

$\therefore$ One loop of the curve lies between $-\frac{\pi}{2n}$ and $\frac{\pi}{2n}$.

$$A = 2.\frac{1}{2}.\int_{\theta=0}^{\pi/2n} a^2.\cos^2 n\theta \, d\theta$$

$$= \frac{a^2}{n}.\int_0^{\pi/2} \cos^2 t \, dt$$

$$= \frac{\pi a^2}{4n}$$

$$A = \frac{\pi a^2}{4n}$$

Now, if n is even then there are $2n$ loops in the curve and if n is odd there are, n loops in the curve.

$\therefore$ If n is odd, total area

$$= nA = n\,\frac{\pi a^2}{4n}$$

$$= \frac{\pi a^2}{4}.$$

If n is even, total area

$$= 2n \,.\, A$$

$$= 2n \,.\, \frac{\pi a^2}{4n}$$

$$= \frac{\pi a^2}{2}.$$

EXERCISE

1. Find the area of the ellipse $\frac{x^2}{a^2} + \frac{y^2}{b^2} = 1$.

2. Show that the area of the loop of the curve $ay^2 = x^2 (a - x)$ is $\frac{8a^2}{15}$.

3. Find the whole area of the curve $a^2x^2 = y^3 (2a - y)$

4. Show that the area of the loop of the curve $a^2y^2 = x^2 (x - a) (2a - x)$ is $\frac{3a^2\pi}{8}$.

5. Find the area between the curve $y^2 (a + x) = (a - x)^3$ and its asymptote.

6. Find the area of the loop of the curve $y^2 (a - x) = x^2 (a + x)$.

7. Show that the area cut off from a parabola by any double ordinate is two thirds of the corresponding rectangle contained by the double ordinate and its distance from the vertex.

8. Show that the area bounded by the curve $|x| + |y| = 2a$ is $8a^2$ $(a > 0)$.

9. Find the area enclosed by the ellipses $a^2x^2 + b^2y^2 = 1$ and $b^2x^2 + a^2y^2 = 1$.

10. Find the area enclosed by the curves $x^2 + y^2 = 1$ and $(x - 1)^2 + y^2 = 1$.

11. Find the area enclosed by the curves $x^2 = 4ay$ and $y (x^2 + 4a^2) = 8a^3$.

12. Find the area between the curves $y^2 = ax$ and $x^2 + y^2 = 4ax$.

13. Find the area enclosed by the curve $x^{2/3} + y^{2/3} = a^{2/3}$.

14. Find the area bounded by the curve $x = a (\theta - \sin\theta)$, $y = a (1 - \cos \theta)$ and its base.

15. Find the area of the loop of the curve

    $x = (1 - t^2)$, $y = t (1 - t^2)$, $-1 \le t \le 1$.

16. Find the area between the curves $x = a\sin^2 t$, $y = \dfrac{a\sin^3 t}{\cos t}$ and its asymptote.
17. Find the area of one loop of the curve $r = a\sin 3\theta$.
18. Show that the area common to the curves $r = a\sqrt{2}$ and $r = 2a\cos\theta$ is $a^2(\pi - 1)$.
19. Find the area common to the curves $r = a(1 + \sin\theta)$ and $r = a(1 - \sin\theta)$.
20. Find the area common to the circles r $= a\cos\theta$ and $r = a\sin\theta$.
21. Find the area lying between the cardioid $r = a(1 - \cos\theta)$ and its double tangent.
22. Prove that the sum of the areas of the two loops of the curve loops of the curve $r = a + b\cos\theta$ $(a < b)$ is $\pi\left(a^2 + \dfrac{b^2}{2}\right)$.
23. Find the area of the loops of the following curves:

(i) $x^5 + y^5 = 5a\,x^2 y^2$

(ii) $x^3 + y^3 = 3axy$

(iii) $x^6 + y^6 = a^2x^2y^2$.

Answers:

1. πab
3. πa^2
5. $3a^2\pi$
6. $\dfrac{a^2}{2}(4 - \pi)$
9. $\dfrac{4}{ab}\tan^{-1}\left(\dfrac{a}{b}\right)$
10. $\left(\dfrac{2\pi}{3} - \dfrac{\sqrt{3}}{2}\right)$
11. $\dfrac{2a^2}{3}(3\pi - 2)$

12. $a^2\left(3\sqrt{3}+\frac{4\pi}{3}\right)$

13. $\frac{3a^2\pi}{8}$

14. $3a^2\pi$

15. $\frac{8}{15}$

16. $\frac{3a^2\pi}{8}$

17. $\frac{\pi a^2}{12}$

19. $\frac{a^2}{2}(3\pi-8)$

20. $\frac{a^2}{8}(\pi-2)$

21. $\frac{a^2}{16}\left(15\sqrt{3}-8\pi\right)$

23. (i) $\frac{5a^2}{2}$

(ii) $\frac{3a^2}{2}$

(iii) $\frac{\pi a^2}{12}$

NUMERICAL INTEGRATION

APPROXIMATE VALUE OF A DEFINITE INTEGRAL

Introduction

It is the process of evaluating a definite integral $I = \int_a^b f(x)\ dx$, when the

Integrand $f(x)$ is not integrable or when the Integrand is not given but the values of integrand are given for some equally spaced values of x in $[a, b]$. If it is applied to the integration of function of a single variable, the process is known as quadrature.

In this process the integrand is first aproximated by a polynomial and then integrating this expression between the desired limits, the value of the integral is approximated.

I. Trapezoidal Rule

In this method the function $f(x)$ is approximated by a line between the points A, B, C, D.

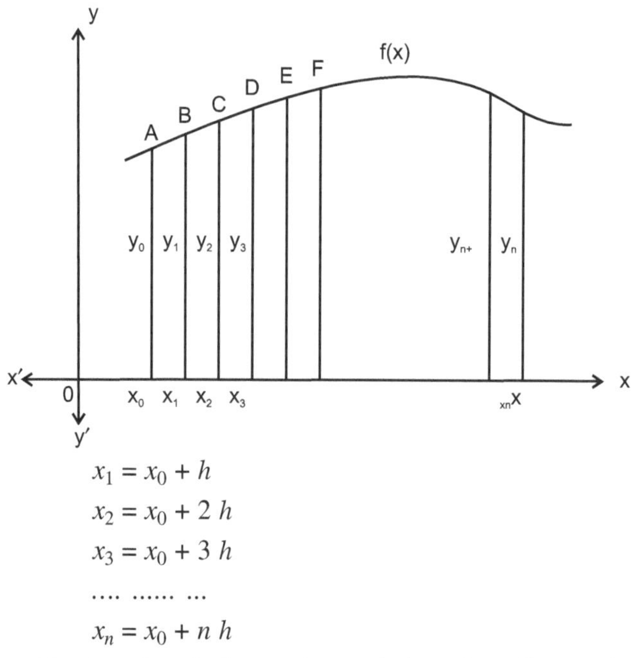

Let $$x_1 = x_0 + h$$
$$x_2 = x_0 + 2\,h$$
$$x_3 = x_0 + 3\,h$$
....
$$x_n = x_0 + n\,h$$

We consider that the whole area is consisting of small trapeziums.

Then, whole area = Sum of the areas of all the trapeziums.

Now, area of the first trapezium

$$A_1 = \frac{1}{2}\,[y_0 + y_1]\,.\,h$$

$$= \frac{h}{2}\,[y_0 + y_1]$$

Area of the second trapezium

$$A_2 = \frac{h}{2}[y_1 + y_2]$$

....

Area of the *n*th trapezium

$$= \frac{h}{2}[y_{n-1} + y_n]$$

∴ The total area

$$A = A_1 + A_2 + A_3 + ... + A_n.$$

$$= \frac{h}{2}[(y_0 + y_1) + (y_1 + y_2) + (y_{n-1} + y_n)]$$

$$= \frac{h}{2}[(y_0 + y_n) + 2\,(y_1 + y_2 + y_3 + y_{n-1})]$$

Let $x_0 = a$, $x_0 + (n)h = b$

$$\therefore \int_{x=0}^{x_0+nh} f(x)\,dx = \frac{h}{2}[(y_0 + y_n) + 2\,(y_1 + y_2 + y_3 + y_{n-1})]$$

$$\therefore \quad \int_a^b f(x)\,dx = \int_{x_0}^{x_0+nh} f(x)dx = \frac{h}{2}[(y_0 + y_n) + 2\,(y_1 + y_2 + y_3 + y_{n-1})]$$

And this is known as trapezoidal rule.

II. Simpson's one third rule

This is the process in which the curve $f(x)$ through (x_0, y_0), (x_1, y_1), (x_2, y_2), is approximated as a polynomial of second degree *i.e.*, as a parabola and the formula obtained is:

$$\int_{x_0}^{x_0+nh} f(x)dx = \frac{h}{3}[(y_0 + y_n) + 4\,(y_1 + y_3 + y_5 + ... + y_{n-1})$$

$$+ 2\,(y_2 + y_4 + y_6 + ... + y_{n-2})]$$

This is known as Simpson's one-third rule or simply Simpson's rule.

Note : While applying the Simpson's one-third rule, the given interval must be divided into even number of equal sub intervals, this is because in one step, we find the area of two strips at a time instead of one, as in trapezoidal rule.

Simpson's three-eight rule: This is the process in which we approximate a curve $f(x)$ as a polynomial of third degree. The formula obtained is known as Simpson's three eight rule.

$$\int_{x_0}^{x_0+nh} f(x)\,dx = \frac{3h}{8}\,[(y_0 + y_n) + 3\,(y_1 + y_2 + y_4 + y_5 + \ldots + y_{n-1}) +$$

$$2\,(y_3 + y_6 + y_9 + \ldots\, y_{n-3}] \text{ or}$$

$$\int_{x_0}^{x_0+nh} f(x)\,dx = \frac{3h}{8}\,[(y_0 + y_n) + 3\,(y_1 + y_2 + y_3 + \ldots + y_{n-1}) +$$

$$2\,(y_3 + y_6 + y_9 + \ldots\, y_{n-3})]$$

Note: While applying Simpson's three eight rule, the number of subintervals should be multiple of 3, Since at a time we take three strips.

SOLVED EXAMPLES

Example 1. A curve passes through the points given by the following table :

x :	1.0	1.5	2	2.5	3	3.5	4
y :	2.0	2.4	2.7	2.8	3	2.6	2.1

Find the approximate area bounded by the curve, x-axis and the lines $x = 1$ and $x = 4$.

Solution:

Here $\quad x_0 = 1,\ x_6 = 4$

$$\therefore \quad n = \frac{x_6 - x_0}{6}$$

$$= \frac{3}{6} = 0.5$$

$\therefore$ By Trapezoidal rule

$$A = \frac{0.5}{2}\,[(2 + 2.1) + 2\,(2.4 + 2.7 + 2.8 + 3 + 2.6)]$$

$$= \frac{0.5}{2}\,[4.1 + 2\ (13.5)]$$

$$= \frac{0.5}{2}\,[31.1]$$

$$A = 7.775 \text{ sq. units.}$$

By Simpson's one-third rule

$$A = \frac{0.5}{3}\ [(2.0 + 2.1) + 4\ (2.4 + 2.8 + 2.6) + 2\ (2.7 + 3)]$$

$$= \frac{0.5}{3}\ [4.1 + 31.2 + 11.4]$$

$$= 7.783 \text{ sq. units}$$

By Simpson's three-eight rule

$$A = \frac{3h}{8}\ [y_0 + y_n) + 3\ (y_1 + y_2 + y_4 + y_5 + \ldots$$

$$+ 2\ (y_3 + y_6 + \ldots)]$$

$$= \frac{3(.5)}{8}[(2 + 2.1) + 3\ [2.4 + 2.7 + 3 + 2.6] + (2.8)]$$

$$= \frac{3}{16}[4.1 + 32.1 + 5.6]$$

$$= 7.837 \text{ sq. units.}$$

Example 2 . Calculate by Simpson's rule and by Trapezoidal rule, the approximate value of $\int_{-3}^{3} x^4 dx$ by subdividing the interval into six equal subintervals. Compare it with the exact value.

Solution: Here, the interval (–3, 3) is sub divided into six equal, sub intervals.

$$\therefore \qquad h = \frac{3-(-3)}{6} = 1$$

$$\therefore \qquad x_0 = -3,\ x_1 = -2,\ x_2 = -1,\ x_3 = 0 \ \ldots\ x_6 = 1$$

x:	–3	–2	–1	0	1	2	3
y:	81	16	1	0	1	16	81

I. By Simpson's one third rule, we have

$$\int_{-3}^{3} x^4 dx = \frac{1}{3}\ [(y_0 + y_6) + 4\ (y_1 + y_3 + y_5) + 2\ (y_2 + y_4)]$$

$$= \frac{1}{3}\ [162 + 4\ (16 + 0 + 16) + 2\ (1 + 1)]$$

$$= \frac{1}{3}[162 + 128 + 4]$$

$$= \frac{1}{3}\ [294]$$

$$= 98$$

II. By Trapezoidal rule, we have

$$\int_{-3}^{3} x^4 dx = \frac{1}{2}\ [162 + 2(34)]$$

$$= \frac{1}{2}[162 + 68]$$

$$= \frac{230}{2}$$

$$= 115$$

III. The actual value is

$$\int_{-3}^{3} x^4 dx = \left[\frac{x^5}{5}\right]_{-3}^{3}$$

$$= \frac{1}{5}[243 + 243]$$

$$= \frac{486}{5} = 97.2$$

It is obvious that Simpson's rule gives better approximation than Trapezoidal rule.

Example 3. The velocity v in km per minute of a vehicle which starts from rest is given below at equally spaced time (min) intervals.

t:	0	2	4	6	8	10	12	14	16	18	20
v:	0	10	18	25	29	32	20	11	5	2	0

Find approximate distance covered in 20 minutes.

Solution: We know that $\text{v} = \dfrac{ds}{dt}$ $\quad \therefore \quad ds = vdt$

$$\therefore \qquad s = \int \text{v} dt$$

$$\therefore \qquad |s| = \int_{0}^{20} \text{v} dt$$

II. By Simpson's rule

$$s = \frac{h}{3}\ [(0 + 0) + 4\ (10 + 25 + 32 + 11 + 2)$$

$$+ 2\ (18 + 29 + 20 + 5]$$

$$= \frac{2}{3}\ [0 + 4\ (80) + 2\ (72)]$$

$$= \frac{2}{3}\ [320 + 144]$$

$$= \frac{2}{3}\ [464]$$

$$= 309.33 \text{ km.}$$

Example 4. Evaluate $\int_0^1 \frac{dx}{1+x^2}$ by Simpson's $\frac{'1'}{3}$ and $\frac{'3'}{8}$ rules and hence, find the approximate value of π.

Solution: Dividing the interval $1 - 0 = 1$, in six equal parts, we have $h = \frac{1}{6}$.

Here $$y = \frac{1}{1+x^2}$$

$x:$	0	$\frac{1}{6}$	$\frac{2}{6}$	$\frac{3}{6}$	$\frac{4}{6}$	$\frac{5}{6}$	1
$y:$	1	0.97297	0.9	0.8	0.69231	0.59016	1/2

∴ By Simpson's Rule

$$\int_0^1 ydx = \frac{h}{3}\ [(y_0 + y_6) + 4\ (y_1 + y_3 + y_5) + 2\ (y_2 + y_4)]$$

$$= \frac{1}{18}\ [(1.5) + 4\ (.97297 + .\ 80000 + .59016)$$

$$+ 2\ (.90000 + .69231]$$

$$= 0.785395$$

By Simpson's three-eight rule

$$\int_0^1 ydx = \frac{3h}{8}\ [(y_0 + y_6) + 3\ (y_1 + y_2 + y_4 + y_5) + 2\ (y_3 + 0]$$

$$= \frac{1}{16}\ [(1.5) + 3\ (.97297 + .900 + .69231 + .59016)$$
$$+ 2\ (.80000)]$$
$$= \frac{1}{16}\ [1.5 + 9.46632 + 1.6]$$
$$= 0.785395$$

Now

$$\int_0^1 \frac{1}{1+x^2}\,dx = \left[\tan^1 x\right]_0^1$$
$$= \tan^{-1}(1) - \tan^{-1}(0)$$
$$= \frac{\pi}{4}$$

By equating the two values obtained, we have

$$\frac{\pi}{4} = 0.785395$$

$\therefore$ $\pi = 3.14158.$

EXERCISE

1. Using Simpson's $\frac{'1'}{3}$ rule, find $\int_0^6 \frac{dx}{(1+x)^2}$.
2. Using Simpson's one-third rule find the approximate area of cross section of a river 80m wide, the depth y (in m) at a distance x from its bank is given below :

x:	0	10	20	30	40	50	60	70	80
y:	0	4	7	9	12	15	14	8	3

3. The velocity v of a particle at time t is given below :

Time (sec):	0	2	4	6	8	10	12
v (m/sec):	4	6	16	34	60	94	136

Find the distance covered by the particle in 12 seconds.

4. Calculate $\int_2^{10} \frac{1}{1+x}\,dx$, by dividing the range into eight equal parts.
5. Show that $\int_0^1 \frac{1}{1+x}\,dx = \log 2 = 0.69315.$

Answers:

1. 0.8946
2. 710 sq. m
3. 552 m.
4. 1.2996

10

Rectification

RECTIFICATION

Process of finding the length of the arc of a curve is called rectification.

The length s, of arc of the curve $y = f(x)$ from the point, where $x = a$ to the point where $x = b$ is given by

$$s = \int_a^b \sqrt{1+\left(\frac{dy}{dx}\right)^2}\, dx$$

where the functions y and $\frac{dy}{dx}$ are continuous and single valued in $a \le x \le b$.

Let AB be an arc of the curve $y = f(x)$.

Let A be a fixed point on the curve such that arc length AP

$$\overset{\frown}{AP} = s.$$

$$\overset{\frown}{AQ} = s + \delta s.$$

Where P (x, y) and Q $(x + \delta x, \delta y)$ are two neighbouring points on the curve, then along the curve as x changes by δx, s changes by δs.

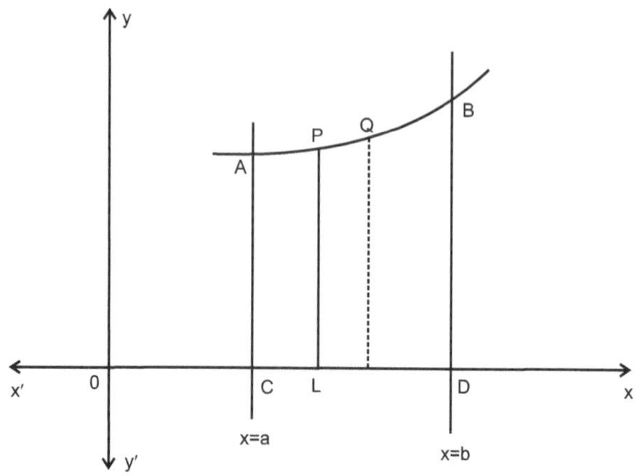

We know that

$$\frac{ds}{dx} = \sqrt{1+\left(\frac{dy}{dx}\right)^2}$$

$$\frac{ds}{dy} = \sqrt{1+\left(\frac{dx}{dy}\right)^2}$$

$$\frac{ds}{dt} = \sqrt{\left(\frac{dx}{dt}\right)^2+\left(\frac{dy}{dt}\right)^2}$$

$$\frac{ds}{d\theta} = \sqrt{r^2+\left(\frac{dr}{d\theta}\right)^2}$$

$$\frac{ds}{dr} = \sqrt{1+r^2\left(\frac{d\theta}{dr}\right)^2}$$

Then the expressions for the length of arc of the curve in cartesian, parametric and polar coordinates are as:

1. Length of the curve $y = f(x)$, between the points where $x = a$ and $x = b$, is

$$s = \int_a^b \sqrt{1+\left(\frac{dy}{dx}\right)^2}\; dx$$

2. Length of the curve $x = \phi(y)$, between the points where $y = c$ and $y = d$, is

$$s = \int_c^d \sqrt{1+\left(\frac{dx}{dy}\right)^2}\, dy$$

3. Length of the curve $x = f(t)$, $y = \phi(t)$, between the points where $t = t_1$ and $t = t_2$ is

$$s = \int_{t_1}^{t_2} \sqrt{\left(\frac{dx}{dt}\right)^2 + \left(\frac{dy}{dt}\right)^2}\, dt$$

4. Length of the curve $r = f(\theta)$, between the points where $\theta = \alpha$ and $\theta = \beta$, is

$$s = \int_\alpha^\beta \sqrt{r^2 + \left(\frac{dr}{d\theta}\right)^2}\, d\theta$$

5. Length of the curve $r = f(\theta)$ between the points where $r = r_1$ and $r = r_2$, is

$$s = \int_{r_1}^{r_2} \sqrt{1 + r^2\left(\frac{d\theta}{dr}\right)^2}\, dr$$

SOLVED EXAMPLES

Example 1. Find the length of the arc of the parabola $y^2 = 4ax$, intercepted between the vertex and an extremity of the latus rectum.

Solution: The equation of the curve is $y^2 = 4ax$

$$\therefore \quad 2y\frac{dy}{dx} = 4a$$

$$\therefore \quad \frac{dy}{dx} = \frac{2a}{y}$$

$$\therefore \quad \frac{dx}{dy} = \frac{y}{2a}$$

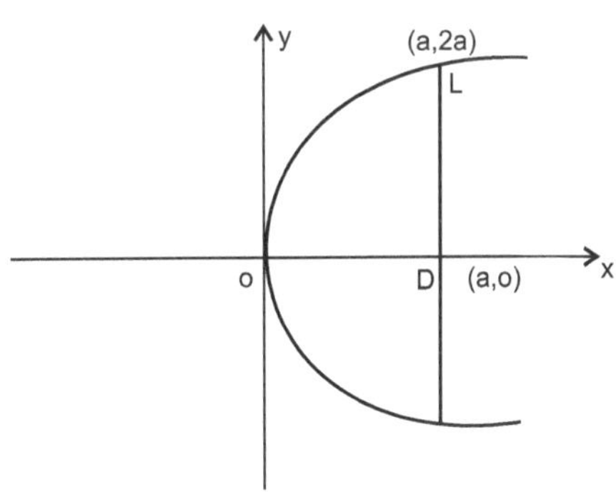

$\therefore$ The required length

$$= \int_0^{2a} \sqrt{1+\frac{y^2}{4a^2}}\, dy$$

$$= \frac{1}{2a} \int_0^{2a} \sqrt{(2a)^2 + y^2}\, dy$$

$$= \frac{1}{2a}\left[\frac{y}{2}\sqrt{y^2+4a^2} + \frac{4a^2}{2}.\log\left(y+\sqrt{y^2+4a^2}\right)\right]_0^{2a}$$

$$= \frac{1}{4a}\left[2a\sqrt{8a^2} + 4a^2\log\left(2a+\sqrt{8a^2}\right) - 4a^2\log 2a\right]$$

$$= a\left[\sqrt{2} + \log\left(1+\sqrt{2}\right)\right]$$

$$\therefore \qquad s = a\left[\sqrt{2} + \log\left(1+\sqrt{2}\right)\right].$$

Example 2. Find the length of the curve $x^2 (a^2 - x^2) = 8a^2y^2$.

Solution: The given curve is symmetric about both the axis and consists of two loops one lying from $x = -a$ to $x = 0$ and other from $x = 0$ and $x = a$.

Since each loop is symmetrical about x-axis.

∴ The required length

= 4 . Length of the loop in first quadrant

$$= 4 \cdot \int_0^a \sqrt{1+\left(\frac{dy}{dx}\right)^2}\, dx$$

From the equation of the curve

$$8a^2y^2 = x^2 (a^2 - x^2)$$

$$\therefore \qquad 16a^2y\frac{dy}{dx} = 2x (a^2 - x^2) - 2x^3$$

$$= 2x (a^2 - 2x^2)$$

$$\frac{dy}{dx} = \frac{x\left(a^2-2x^2\right)}{8a^2y}$$

$$1+\left(\frac{dy}{dx}\right)^2 = 1 + \frac{x^2\left(a^2-2x^2\right)^2}{64a^4y^2}$$

$$= 1 + \frac{x^2\left(a^2-2x^2\right)^2}{8a^2.x^2\left(a^2-x^2\right)}$$

$$= 1 + \frac{\left(a^2 - 2x^2\right)^2}{8a^2\left(a^2 - x^2\right)}$$

$$= \frac{8a^2\left(a^2 - x^2\right) + \left(a^2 - 2x^2\right)^2}{8a^2\left(a^2 - x^2\right)}$$

$$= \frac{\left(3a^2 - 2x^2\right)^2}{8a^2\left(a^2 - x^2\right)}$$

$$\therefore \qquad = \sqrt{1 + \left(\frac{dy}{dx}\right)^2} = \frac{\left(3a^2 - 2x^2\right)}{2\sqrt{2}a.\sqrt{a^2 - x^2}}$$

$$\therefore \qquad s = 4\int_0^a \frac{\left(3a^2 - 2x^2\right)}{2\sqrt{2}.a.\sqrt{a^2 - x^2}}\, dx$$

$$= \frac{4}{2\sqrt{2}a} \cdot \int_0^a \frac{a^2 + 2\left(a^2 - x^2\right)}{\sqrt{a^2 - x^2}}\, dx$$

$$= \frac{4}{2\sqrt{2}a}\left[a^2 \int_0^a \frac{1}{\sqrt{a^2 - x^2}}\, dx + 2\int_0^a \sqrt{a^2 - x^2}\, dx\right]$$

$$= \left\{\frac{4}{2\sqrt{2}a}\left[a^2.\sin^{-1}\left(\frac{x}{a}\right)\right]_0^a\right.$$

$$\left. + 2\left[\frac{x}{2}\sqrt{a^2 - x^2} + \frac{a^2}{2}.\sin^{-1}\left(\frac{x}{a}\right)\right]_0^a\right\}$$

$$= \frac{4}{2\sqrt{2}a}\left[a^2.\frac{\pi}{2} + 0 + 2.\frac{a^2}{2}.\frac{\pi}{2}\right]$$

$$= \frac{4}{2\sqrt{2}} a [\pi] = \pi a\sqrt{2}$$

$\therefore$ Length of the curve is $\pi a\sqrt{2}$.

Example 3. Find the length of the loop of the curve $6ay^2 = x (x - 2a)^2$.

Solution: Here the loop of the curve lies along x-axis between $x = 0$ and $x = 2a$. As the curve is symmetrical about x-axis. So the length of the loop of the curve above and below x-axis will be the same.

$\therefore$ Whole length of the loop = 2 . Length of the loop above x-axis

$$= 2\int_0^{2a} \sqrt{1+\left(\frac{dy}{dx}\right)^2}\, dx$$

For the curve $6ay^2 = x (x - 2a)^2$

$$12ay\frac{dy}{dx} = (x - 2a)^2 + 2(x - 2a) . x$$

$$= (x - 2a) [x - 2a + 2x]$$

$$= (x - 2a) (3x - 2a)$$

$$\therefore \quad \left(\frac{dy}{dx}\right)^2 144 a^2y^2 = (x - 2a)^2 (3x - 2a)^2$$

$$\left(\frac{dy}{dx}\right)^2 24a\, x (x - 2a)^2 = (3x - 2a)^2 (x - 2a)^2$$

$$\therefore \quad \left(\frac{dy}{dx}\right)^2 = \frac{(3x-2a)^2}{24ax}$$

$$\text{so} \quad 1+\left(\frac{dy}{dx}\right)^2 = \frac{24ax+9x^2+4a^2-12ax}{24ax}$$

$$= \frac{9x^2+4a^2+12ax}{24ax}$$

$$1+\left(\frac{dy}{dx}\right)^2 = \frac{(3x+2a)^2}{24ax}$$

$$\therefore \quad \sqrt{1+\left(\frac{dy}{dx}\right)^2} = \frac{3x+2a}{\sqrt{24a}.\sqrt{x}}$$

Let $$s = \int_0^{2a} \frac{(3x+2a)}{\sqrt{24a}.\sqrt{x}}\, dx$$

$$= \frac{1}{\sqrt{24a}} \int_0^{2a} \left(\frac{3x}{\sqrt{x}} + \frac{2a}{\sqrt{x}}\right) dx$$

$$= \frac{1}{\sqrt{24a}} \left[3.\frac{x^{3/2}}{3/2} + 2a\frac{x^{1/2}}{1/2}\right]_0^{2a}$$

$$= \frac{1}{\sqrt{24a}} \left[2x^{3/2} + 4a\sqrt{x}\right]_0^{2a}$$

$$= \frac{1}{\sqrt{24a}} \left[2(2a)^{3/2} + 4a\sqrt{2a}\right]$$

$$= \frac{1}{\sqrt{24a}} \left[4a\sqrt{2a} + 4a\sqrt{2a}\right]$$

$$= \frac{8a.\sqrt{2a}}{\sqrt{24a}} = \frac{8a}{2\sqrt{3}}$$

$$= \frac{4a}{\sqrt{3}}$$

$\therefore$ whole length = $2s$

$$= \frac{8a}{\sqrt{3}}$$

Example 4. Find the length of one arc of the cycloid

$$x = a\,(\theta + \sin\theta)$$

$$y = a\,(1 - \cos\theta).$$

Solution: The given curve is symmetrical about y-axis and has a complete arc between $\theta = -\pi$ and $\theta = \pi$, which is symmetrical about y-axis.

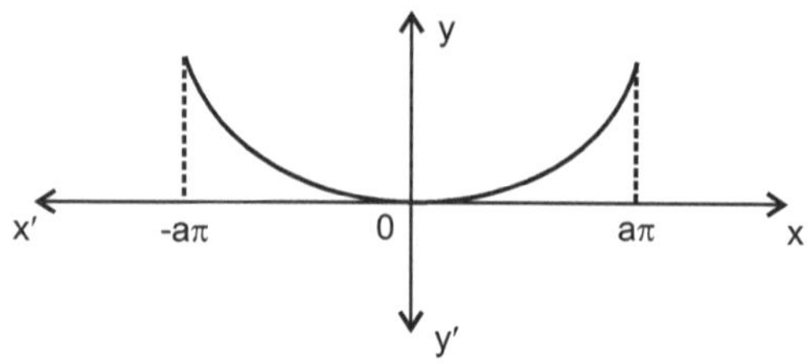

∴ The required length

$$s = 2\int_0^{\pi}\sqrt{\left(\frac{dx}{d\theta}\right)^2 + \left(\frac{dy}{d\theta}\right)^2}\, d\theta$$

$$\therefore \quad x = a\,(\theta + \sin\theta)$$

$$\therefore \quad y = a\,(1 - \cos\theta)$$

$$\therefore \quad \frac{dx}{d\theta} = a\,(1 + \cos\theta)$$

$$\frac{dy}{d\theta} = a\sin\theta$$

$$\therefore \quad \left(\frac{dx}{d\theta}\right)^2 + \left(\frac{dy}{d\theta}\right)^2 = a^2\,[1 + \cos^2\theta + 2\cos\theta + \sin^2\theta]$$

$$= 2a^2\,[1 + \cos\theta]$$

$$= 4a^2 \,.\, \cos^2\frac{\theta}{2}\cdot$$

$$\therefore \quad s = 2\,.\,2a\int_0^{\pi}\left(\cos\frac{\theta}{2}\right) d\theta$$

$$= 4a\left[2\sin\frac{\theta}{2}\right]_0^{\pi}$$

$$= 8a.$$

Example 5. Find the length of the loop of the curve

$$x = t^2$$

$$y = t - \frac{t^3}{3}.$$

Solution: Here eliminating t, we have equation of the curve.

$$9y^2 = x\,(x - 3)^2$$

$\therefore$ The curve is symmetrical about x-axis and the loop of the curve lies between $x = 0$ and $x = 3$.

i.e. $t = 0$ and $t = \sqrt{3}$.

$\therefore$ The required length of the loop

$$s = 2\int_0^{\sqrt{3}} \sqrt{\left(\frac{dx}{dt}\right)^2 + \left(\frac{dy}{dt}\right)^2}\, dt$$

$$= 2\int_0^{\sqrt{3}} \sqrt{(2t)^2 + \left(1-t^2\right)^2}\, dt$$

$$= 2\int_0^{\sqrt{3}} \sqrt{4t^2 + 1 + t^4 - 2t^2}\, dt$$

$$= 2\int_0^{\sqrt{3}} \sqrt{1 + t^4 + 2t^2}\, dt$$

$$= 2\int_0^{\sqrt{3}} \left(1 + t^2\right) dt$$

$$= 2\left[t + \frac{t^3}{3}\right]_0^{\sqrt{3}}$$

$$= 2\left[\sqrt{3} + \sqrt{3}\right]$$

$$= 4\sqrt{3}.$$

Example 6. Find the length of the curve

$$x = a\cos^3\theta$$
$$y = a\sin^3\theta.$$

Solution: As the curve is symmetrical about both the axes.

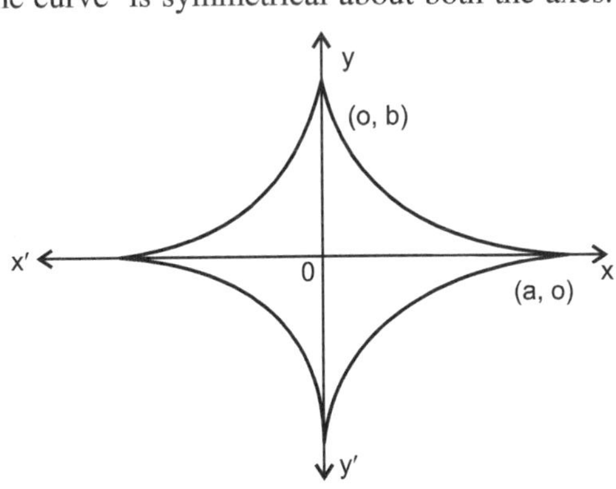

∴ Required length

$$= 4 \,.\, \text{Length in the first quadrant}$$

$$= 4 \,.\, \int_0^{\pi/2} \sqrt{\left(\frac{dx}{d\theta}\right)^2 + \left(\frac{dy}{d\theta}\right)^2}\; d\theta$$

$$= 4 \int_0^{\pi/2} \sqrt{\left(-3a\cos^2\theta\sin\theta\right)^2 + \left(3a\sin^2\theta\cos\theta\right)^2}\; d\theta$$

$$= 4 \int_0^{\pi/2} 3a\sin\theta\cos\theta\sqrt{\cos^2\theta + \sin^2\theta}\; d\theta$$

$$= 4.\, 3a \int_0^{\pi/2} \sin\theta\cos\theta\, d\theta$$

$$= 4.\, \frac{3a}{2} \,.\, \int_0^{\pi/2} \sin 2\theta\, d\theta$$

$$= 2.3a \,.\, \left[\frac{\cos 2\theta}{2}\right]_0^{\pi/2}$$

$$= 6a\left[\frac{-1-1}{2}\right]$$

$$\therefore \qquad = -6a$$

$$s = 6a.$$

Example 7. Find the perimeter of the curve $r = a\,(1 - \cos\theta)$.

Solution: The curve is symmetrical about initial line

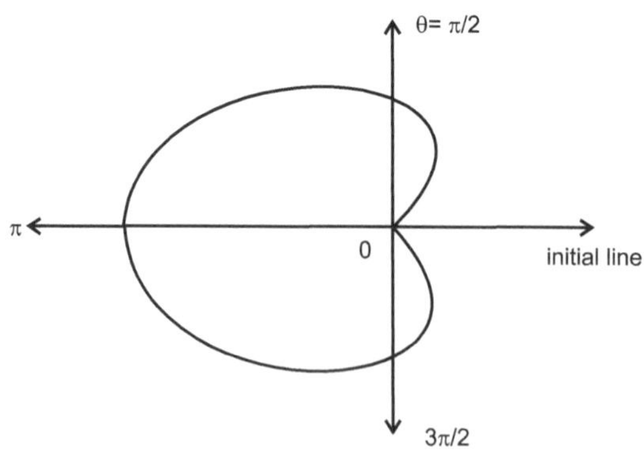

$\therefore$ Whole length of the curve

$$= 2. \text{ Length above initial line}$$

$$= 2 \cdot \int_{\theta=0}^{\pi} \sqrt{r^2 + \left(\frac{dr}{d\theta}\right)^2}\, d\theta$$

$$= 2 \int_0^{\pi} \sqrt{a^2\left(1+\cos^2\theta - 2\cos\theta\right) + a^2\sin^2\theta}\, d\theta$$

$$= 2\int_0^{\pi} a\sqrt{2(1-\cos\theta)}\, d\theta$$

$$= 2a \int_0^{\pi} 2\sin\frac{\theta}{2}\, d\theta$$

$$= 4a \cdot \left[2\left(-\cos\frac{\theta}{2}\right)\right]_0^{\pi}$$

$$= 8a\,[-0+1]$$

$$= 8a.$$

Example 8. Show that upper half of the cycloid $r = a\,(1 + \cos\theta)$ is bisected by $\theta = \dfrac{\pi}{3}$.

Solution: As the curve is symmetrical about initial line.

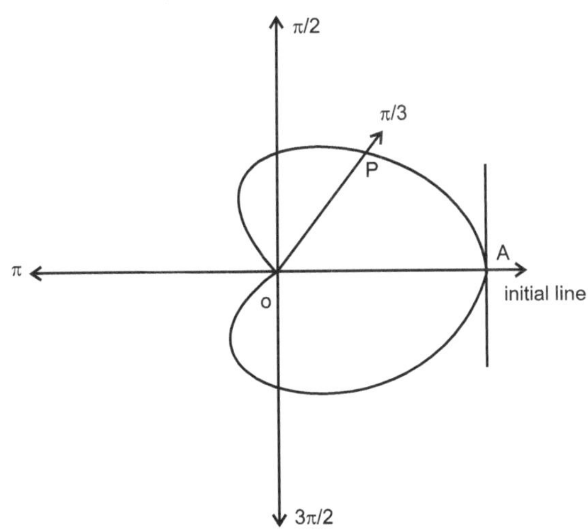

∴ Length of the curve above initial line and below initial line, are same.

Here $r = a\,(1 + \cos\theta)$

∴ $\dfrac{dr}{d\theta} = -a\sin\theta$

∴ Total length of the curve above initial

$$s = \int_0^{\pi} \sqrt{r^2 + \left(\frac{dr}{d\theta}\right)^2}\, d\theta$$

$$= \int_0^{\pi} \sqrt{a^2\left(1+\cos^2\theta + 2\cos\theta + \sin^2\theta\right)}\, d\theta$$

$$= a \int_0^{\pi} \sqrt{2+2\cos\theta}\, d\theta$$

$$= a\,.\int_0^{\pi} 2\cos\left(\frac{\theta}{2}\right) d\theta.$$

$$= 4a\,.\left[\sin\frac{\theta}{2}\right]_0^{\pi}$$

$$s = 4a$$

Now, Length of the curve from the point A to the point P

$$s_1 = \int_0^{\pi/3} \sqrt{r^2 + \left(\frac{dr}{d\theta}\right)^2}\, d\theta$$

$$= 4a\left[\sin\frac{\theta}{2}\right]_0^{\pi/3}$$

$$= 4a\left[\sin\frac{\pi}{6} - \sin 0\right]$$

$$= 2a$$

∴ $s_1 = \dfrac{s}{2}$

∴ The length $s = 4a$ is bisected by the line $\theta = \dfrac{\pi}{3}$.

Example 9. Find the length of the arc of the parabola $\frac{l}{r} = 1 + \cos\theta$ cut off by the latus rectum.

Solution: Equation of the parabola is $\frac{l}{r} = 1 + \cos\theta$, whose latus rectum is $\theta = \frac{\pi}{2}$ line.

$\therefore$ The required length

$$s = 2 \cdot \int_0^{\pi/2} \sqrt{r^2 + \left(\frac{dr}{d\theta}\right)^2}\, d\theta$$

$$r = \frac{l}{1+\cos\theta}$$

$$= \frac{l}{2}\sec^2\frac{\theta}{2}$$

$$\therefore \quad \frac{dr}{d\theta} = \frac{l}{2}.2\sec^2\frac{\theta}{2}.\tan\frac{\theta}{2}.\frac{1}{2}$$

$$= \frac{l}{2}.\sec^2\frac{\theta}{2}.\tan\frac{\theta}{2}$$

$$s = 2. \int_0^{\pi/2} \sqrt{\frac{l^2}{4}.\sec^4\frac{\theta}{2} + \frac{l^2}{4}.\sec^4\frac{\theta}{2}.\tan^2\frac{\theta}{2}}$$

$$= l \int_0^{\pi/2} \sec^3\frac{\theta}{2}\, d\theta$$

$$= l \int_0^{\pi/2} \sqrt{1+\tan^2\frac{\theta}{2}}.\sec^2\frac{\theta}{2}\, d\theta.$$

Let $\tan\frac{\theta}{2} = t$

$$\therefore \frac{1}{2}\sec^2\frac{\theta}{2}\, d\theta = dt$$

$$\therefore \quad s = 2l \int_0^1 \sqrt{1+t^2}\, dt$$

$$= 2l\left[\frac{t}{2}\sqrt{1+t^2} + \frac{1}{2}.\log\left(t+\sqrt{1+t^2}\right)\right]_0^1$$

$$= 2l\left[\frac{\sqrt{2}}{2} + \frac{1}{2}.\log\left(1+\sqrt{2}\right)\right]$$

$$= l\left[\sqrt{2} + \log\left(1+\sqrt{2}\right)\right].$$

EXERCISE

1. Show that the whole length of the curve $3ay^2 = x(x-a)^2$ is $\frac{4}{\sqrt{3}}a$.
2. Find the length of the arc of the semi cubical parabola $ay^2 = x^3$, from the origin to the point (a, a).
3. Find the length of the loop of the curve

$$9ay^2 = (x-2a)(x-5a)^2$$

4. Find the circumference of the circle $x^2 + y^2 = a^2$.
5. Find the length of the curve $y = \log\left|\frac{e^x-1}{e^x+1}\right|$ from $x = 1$ to $x = 2$.
6. Find the length of the curve $y = \log\sec x$ from $x = 0$ to $x = \pi/3$.
7. Show that the length of an arc of the cycloid $x = a(\theta + \sin\theta)$

   $y = a(1 + \cos\theta)$ is $8a$.
8. Show that whole length of the hypocycloid $x = a\cos^3 t$, $y = b\sin^3 t$ is

   $4\left(\frac{a^2+b^2+ab}{a+b}\right)$.
9. Show that for the curve $x = a(\theta + \sin\theta)$, $y = a(1 - \cos\theta)$, the length of the arc from the vertex to the point (x, y) is $\sqrt{8ay}$.
10. If s be the length of the arc of the curve $x = a(\theta + \sin\theta\cos\theta)$,

    $y = a(1 + \sin\theta)^2$, measured from the point where $\theta = -\pi/2$ to a point θ, then show that $s \propto y^3$.
11. Find the perimeter of the curve $r = a\cos\theta$.

12. Prove that the perimeter of the limacon $r = a + b\cos\theta$ if b/a is small, is approximately given by $2\pi a\left(1+\frac{b^2}{4a^2}\right)$.

Answers:

2. $\frac{a}{27}\left(13\sqrt{13}-8\right)$

3. $4\sqrt{3}a$

4. $2\pi a$.

5. $\log\left(e+\frac{1}{e}\right)$

6. $\log\left(2+\sqrt{3}\right)$

11. πa.

11

Volume and Surface of Solids of Revolutions

VOLUME OF SOLIDS OF REVOLUTIONS

The Volume V, of the solid generated by the revolution of the area bounded by the curve $y = f(x)$, x-axis and the ordinates $x = a$, $x = b$, about the axis of X is

$$\boxed{V = \pi \int_a^b y^2 dx}$$

where the curve $y = f(x)$ is continuous, single valued in $a \le x \le b$ and does not cross the x-axis (the axis of revolution).

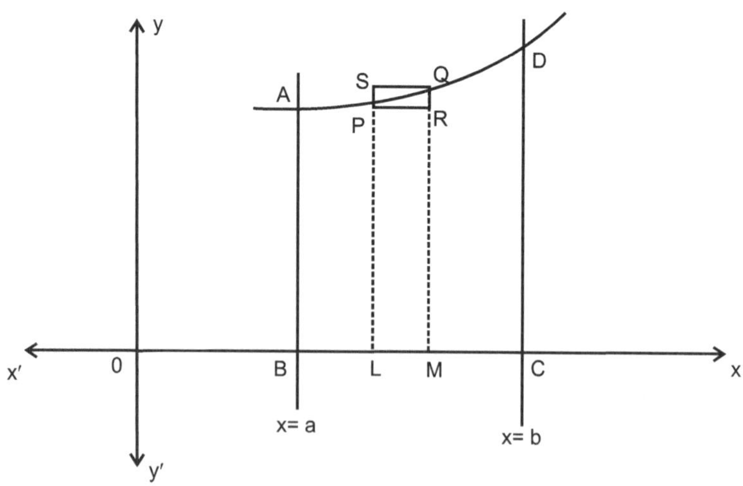

Let AD be the arc of the curve $y = f(x)$, and let P (x, y) and Q $(x + \delta x, y + \delta y)$ be two neighbouring points on the curve.

Let BA, CD be two ordinaters given by $x = a$ and $x = b$, and $y = f(x)$ be increasing in $a \le x \le b$.

Let V = Volume of the solid generated when area ABLP revolves about x-axis.

$V + \delta V$ = Volume of the solid generated when the area ABMQ revolves about x-axis.

$\therefore$ δV = Volume of the solid generated when the area PLMQ revolves about x-axis.

Along the curve as x changes by δx, volume of the solid generated changes by δV.

δV is less then the volume of the solid generated when area of the rectangle SLMQ revolves about X-axis and greater than the volume of the solid generated where area of the rectangle PLMR revolves about X-axis.

$$\therefore \quad \pi y^2 \delta x < \delta V < \pi (y + \delta y)^2 \delta x$$

$$\text{or} \quad \pi y^2 < \frac{\delta V}{\delta x} < \pi (y + \delta y)^2$$

Taking Limit as $\delta x \to 0$, we have

$$\lim_{\delta x \to 0} \frac{\delta V}{\delta x} = \frac{dV}{dx}$$

and the inequality becomes equality.

$$\therefore \quad \pi y^2 = \frac{dV}{dx}$$

$$\text{or} \quad \frac{dV}{dx} = \pi y^2$$

$$\therefore \quad \int_{x=a}^{b} \frac{dV}{dx} dx = \int_a^b \pi y^2 dx$$

The required volume

$$\boxed{V = \pi \int_a^b y^2 dx}$$

- **If the revolution is about the line $y = c$, then**

$$\boxed{\mathbf{V} = \pi \int_a^b (y - c)^2 \, dx.}$$

• **The volume of the solid generated, when area bounded by the curve $x = \phi(y)$, y-axis and the lines $y = c$, $y = d$, revolves about y-axis is**

$$V = \pi \int_{y=c}^{d} x^2 dy$$

• If revolution is about $x = a$ line, then

$$V = \pi \int_{c}^{d} (x - a)^2 dy$$

• Volume of the solid, when the area bounded by the curve $x = f(t)$, $y = \phi$ (t) , x-axis and the ordinates where $t = t_1$ and t_2, revolves about x-axis is

$$V = \pi \int_{t_1}^{t_2} y^2 \frac{dx}{dt} dt$$

• Volume of the solid generated when the area bounded by $x = f(t)$, $y = \phi(t)$, y-axis and abscissae where $t_1 = t_1$ and t_2, revolve about y-axis is

$$V = \pi \int_{t_1}^{t_2} x^2 \frac{dy}{dt} .dt$$

• Volume of the solid generated when the area bounded by the curves $y = f_1(x)$ and $y = f_2(x)$ $[f_2(x) > f_1(x)]$ and the lines $x = a$, $x = b$ revolves about X-axis is given by

$$V = \pi \int_{a}^{b} \left[f_2^2(x) - f_1^2(x) \right] dx$$

• Volume of the solid generated when the area bounded by the polar curve $r = f(\theta)$ and the lines $\theta = \alpha$, $\theta = \beta$

(i) Revolves about initial line, then

$$V = \frac{2\pi}{3} \int_{\alpha}^{\beta} r^3 sin\theta\, d\theta$$

(i) If revolution is about $\theta = \frac{\pi}{2}$ line, then

$$V = \frac{2}{3}\pi \int_{\alpha}^{\beta} r^3 cos\theta\, d\theta$$

SOLVED EXAMPLES

Example 1. Find the volume of the solid generated when area bounded by the curve $xy^2 = 4\,(2 - x)$ and its asymptote, revolves about the asymptote.

Solution: The given curve is

$$xy^2 = 8 - 4x$$

or $\quad (y^2 + 4)\,x = 8.$

asymptote is $x = 0$ *i.e,.* y-axis.

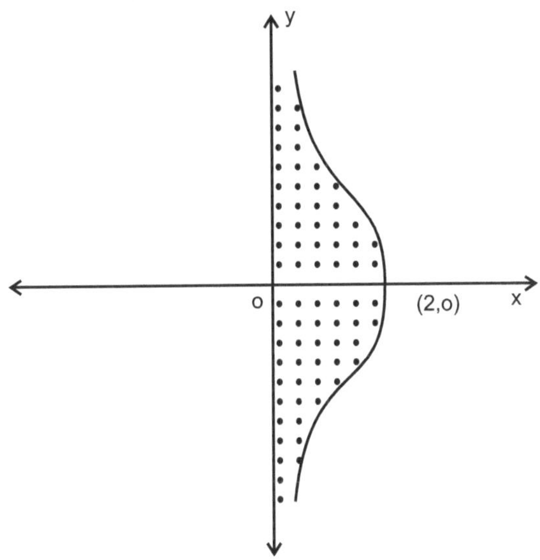

As the curve is symmetrical about x-axis and revolution is about y-axis.

∴ The required volume

$$V = 2\pi \int_0^\infty x^2 dy$$

$$= 2\,.\,\pi \int_0^\infty \frac{64}{\left(y^2+4\right)^2} dy$$

$$= 128\pi \int_0^\infty \frac{1}{\left(y^2+4\right)^2} dy$$

Let $\qquad y = 2\tan\theta$

∴ $\qquad dy = 2\sec^2\theta\; d\theta$

∴ $\qquad V = 256\pi \int_0^{\pi/2} \frac{\sec^2\theta}{16\sec^4\theta} d\theta$

$$= 16\pi \int_0^{\pi/2} \cos^2 \theta d\theta$$

$$= 16\pi \cdot \frac{1}{2} \cdot \frac{\pi}{2}$$

$$= 4\pi^2 \text{ units.}$$

Example 2. Find the volume of the solid generated when area bounded by the loop of the curve $y^2 (a + x) = x^2 (a - x)$, revolves about X-axis.

Solution: The given curve is

$$y^2 = \frac{x^2 (a - x)}{(a + x)},$$

which is symmetrical about X-axis and the revolution is also about X-axis. So the areas above and below X-axis will generate the same solid.

$\because$ The loop of the curve lies between $x = 0$ and $x = a$.

$$\therefore \quad V = \pi \int_0^a y^2 dx$$

$$= \pi \int_0^a \frac{x^2 (a - x)}{(a + x)} dx.$$

$$= \pi \int_0^a \left\{ -x^2 + 2ax - 2a^2 + \frac{2a^3}{a + x} \right\} dx.$$

$$= \pi \left[-\frac{x^3}{3} + ax^2 - 2a^2 x + 2a^3 \log(a + x)) \right]_0^a$$

$$= \pi \left[-\frac{a^3}{3} + a^3 - 2a^3 + 2a^3 \log\left(\frac{2a}{a}\right) \right]$$

$$= \pi \left[-\frac{1}{3} + 1 - 2 + 2\log 2 \right] a^3$$

$$= a^3\pi \left[-\frac{4}{3} + 2\log 2 \right]$$

$$= \frac{a^3\pi}{3}\ [6 \log 2 - 4]$$

$$= \frac{2\pi a^3}{3}\ [3 \log 2 - 2].$$

$$V = \frac{2\pi a^3}{3}[2 - 3\log 2] \qquad [\because \text{V is positive}]$$

Example 3. Find the volume of the solid generated when the area of the ellipse $\frac{x^2}{a^2} + \frac{y^2}{b^2} = 1 (a > b)$, is revolved about major axis.

Solution: As $(a > b)$

∴ X-axis is the major axis.

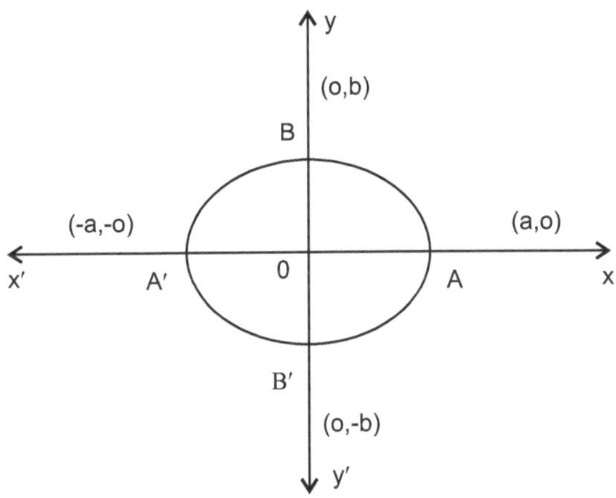

The curve is symmetrical about both the axis and the revolution is about X-axis.

∴ Areas on the left and right of Y-axis will only generate different portions (but equal) of the solid.

∴ The required volume

$$V = 2\pi \int_0^a y^2 dx$$

$$= 2\pi \int_0^a \frac{b^2}{a^2}\ (a^2 - x^2)\ dx$$

$$= \pi \frac{2b^2}{a^2}\left[a^2 x - \frac{x^3}{3}\right]_0^a$$

$$= \pi \frac{2b^2}{a^2} \cdot \left[a^3 - \frac{a^3}{3} \right]$$

$$= \pi \frac{2b^2}{a^2} \cdot \frac{2a^3}{3}$$

$$= \frac{4\pi ab^2}{3}.$$

Example 4. Find the volume of the solid generated when the area bounded by the curve $(a - x)\, y^2 = a^2x$ and its asymptote, revolves about its asymptote.

Solution: The given curve is

$(a - x)y^2 = a^2x$ which is symmetrical about x-axis and has an asymptote || to Y-axis, given by

$$a - x = 0$$

$$\Rightarrow \qquad x = a$$

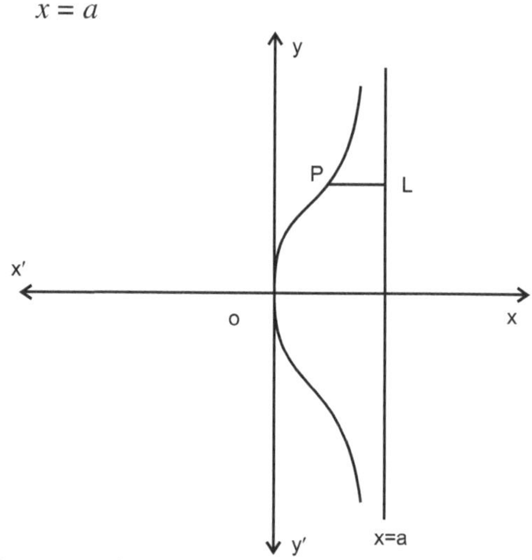

Let P(x, y) be any point on the curve.

$\therefore \qquad \text{PL} = a - x$

$\therefore$ Volume of the solid generated when the area between the curve and its asymptote revolve about $x = a$ line is

$$V = 2 \,.\, \pi \int_0^{\infty} (x - a)^2 \, dy$$

Now $\qquad x = \dfrac{ay^2}{a^2 + y^2}$

$$\therefore \qquad x - a = \frac{a^3}{\left(a^2 + y^2\right)}$$

$$\therefore \qquad V = \pi\, 2 \int_0^{\infty} \frac{a^6}{\left(a^2 + y^2\right)^2} dy$$

Let $\qquad y = a \tan\theta$

$\therefore \qquad dy = a \sec^2\theta\, d\theta$

$$\therefore \qquad V = 2a^6\pi \int_0^{\pi/2} \frac{a \sec^2\theta\, d\theta}{a^4.\left(\tan^2 + 1\right)^2}$$

$$= 2a^3\pi \int_0^{\pi/2} \cos^2\theta\; d\theta$$

$$= 2\pi a^3 \cdot \frac{1}{2} \cdot \frac{\pi}{2}$$

$$= \frac{\pi^2 a^3}{2}$$

$$\therefore \qquad V = \frac{\pi^2 a^3}{2}.$$

Example 5. Show that the volume of the solid generated when the area between the curves $y^2 = x^3$ and $x^2 = y^3$ revolves about X-axis is $\dfrac{5\pi}{28}$.

Solution: Both the curves $y^2 = x^3$ and $x^2 = y^3$ intersect at (0, 0) and (1, 1).

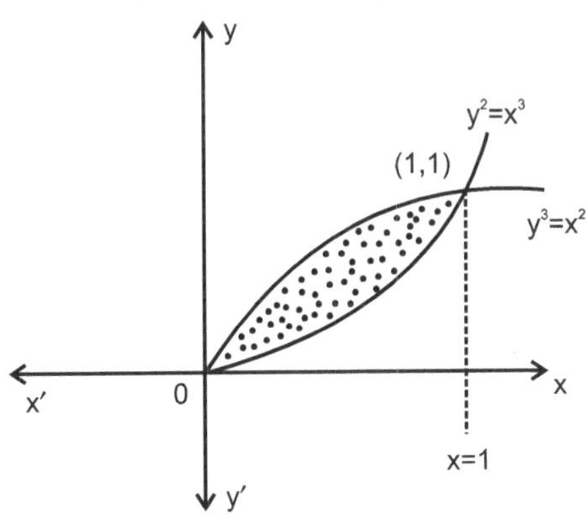

$\therefore$ The required volume

$$V = \pi \int_0^1 \left(x^{2/3}\right)^2 dx - \pi \int_0^1 x^3 dx$$

$$= \pi \int_0^1 \left(x^{4/3} - x^3\right) dx$$

$$= \pi \left[\frac{3}{7}x^{7/3} - \frac{x^4}{4}\right]_0^1$$

$$= \pi \left[\frac{3}{7} - \frac{1}{4}\right]$$

$$= \frac{5\pi}{28}.$$

Example 6. Find the volume of the solid formed when the area between the curves $y^2 = 4ax$ and $27ay^2 = 4(x - 2a)^3$, revolves about X-axis.

Solution: As both the curves are symmetrical about X-axis.

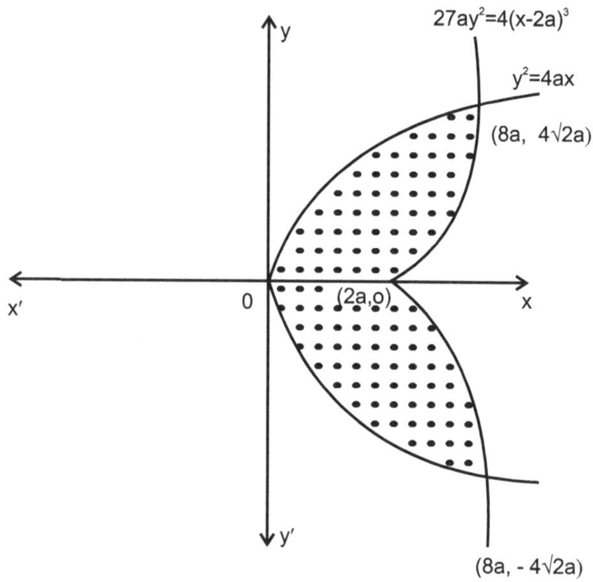

The area between the curves is symmetrical about x-axis.

The curves intersect at $(8a,\ 4\sqrt{2}\,a)$ and $(8a,\ -4\sqrt{2}\,a)$.

$$\therefore \text{ Required volume} = \pi \int_0^{8a} 4ax\,dx - \pi \int_{2a}^{8a} \frac{4(x-2a)^3}{27a}\,dx$$

$$= 4\pi a \left[\frac{x^2}{2}\right]_0^{8a} - \frac{4\pi}{27a}\left[\frac{(x-2a)^4}{4}\right]_0^{8a}$$

$$= 4\pi a \cdot \frac{64a^2}{2} - \frac{4\pi}{27a}[1296a^4]$$

$$= 128\pi a^3 - 48\,\pi a^3$$

$$= 80\,\pi a^3.$$

Example 7. A basin is formed by the revolution of the curve $x^3 = 64y\ (y > 0)$ about the axis of Y. If the depth of the basin is 8 inch, how many cubic inches of water will it hold.

Solution: The volume of water in the basin = volume of the solid generated by the revolution of the area bounded by the curve $x^3 = 64y$, y-axis and the lines $y = 0$, $y = 8$, about y-axis.

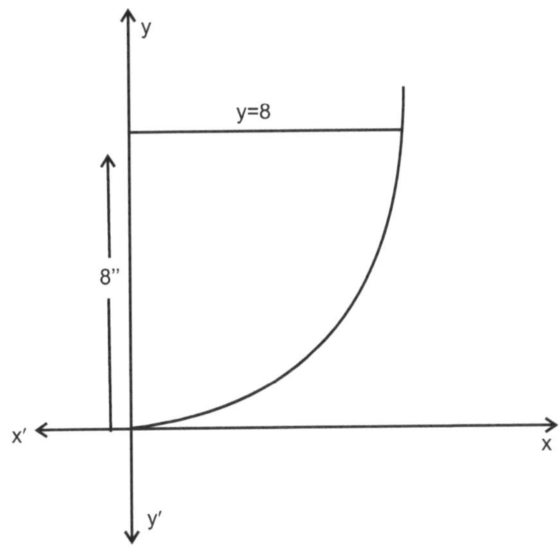

$$= \pi \int_0^8 x^2 dy$$

$$= \pi \int_0^8 (64y)^{2/3} dy$$

$$= 16\pi \int_0^8 y^{2/3} dy$$

$$= 16\pi \left[\frac{y^{5/3}}{5/3}\right]_0^8$$

$$= \frac{48\pi}{5}\left[(8)^{5/3}\right]$$

$$= \frac{48\pi}{5} \cdot 32$$

$$= \frac{1536\pi}{5} \text{ cubic inches.}$$

Example 8. Find the volume of the solid generated when the area bounded by the curve $x = a\,(\theta + \sin\theta)$ $y = a\,(1 - \cos\theta)$ and X-axis, revolves about X-axis.

Solution: As the curve is symmetrical about y-axis.

∴ The areas of the curve on the right and left of Y-axis will generate equal and different solids.

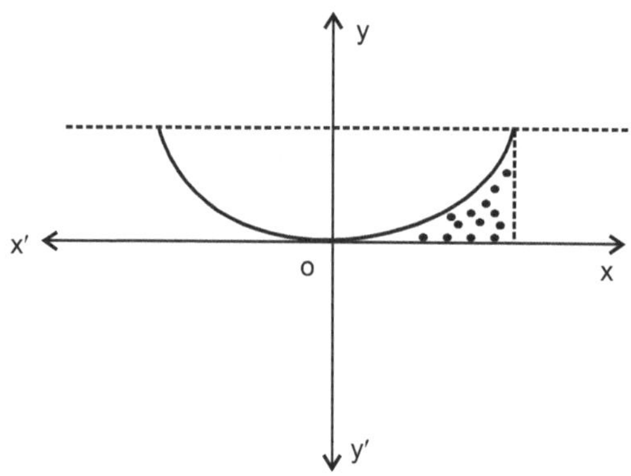

∴The required volume

$$V = 2 \int_{\theta=0}^{\pi} \pi y^2 \frac{dx}{d\theta} d\theta$$

$$= 2\pi \int_0^{\pi} a^2 (1 - \cos\theta)^2 \,.\, a\,(1 + \cos\theta)\, d\theta$$

$$= 16\pi a^3 \int_0^{\pi} \sin^4 \frac{\theta}{2} \cos^2 \frac{\theta}{2} d\theta$$

Let $\quad \dfrac{\theta}{2} = t$

∴ $\quad d\theta = 2\, dt$

$$V = 16\pi a^3 \,.\, 2 \int_0^{\pi/2} \sin^4 t . \cos^2 t\, dt$$

$$= 32\pi a^3 \,.\, \frac{3.1}{6.4.2} . \frac{\pi}{2}$$

$$= \pi^2 a^3.$$

Example 9. Find the volume of the solid generated when the area of the cardioid $r = a\,(1 - \cos\theta)$, revolves about initial line.

Solution: As the curve is symmetrical about initial line and the revolution is also about the same line.

$\therefore$ Upper and lower areas of the curve will generate the same solid. *i.e.*, either upper part revolves or lower part revolves or both revolve, solid will be same.

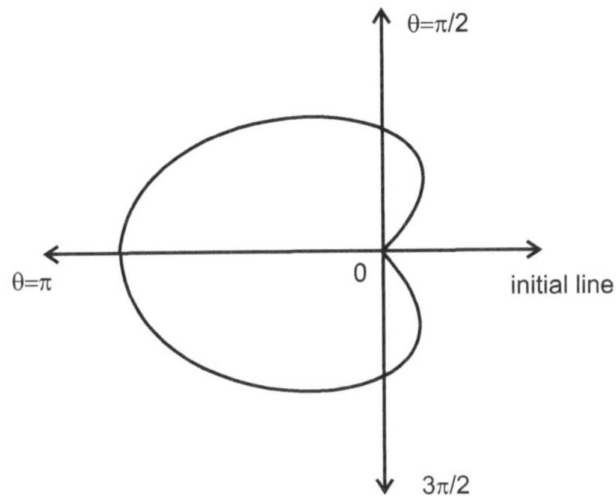

$\therefore$ The required volume

$$V = \frac{2\pi}{3}\int_0^{\pi} r^3 \sin\theta\, d\theta$$

$$= \frac{2\pi}{3}a^3 \int_0^{\pi}(1-\cos\theta)^3 \sin\theta\, d\theta$$

$$= \frac{2\pi}{3}a^3 \int_0^{\pi} 2^3.\sin^6\frac{\theta}{2}.2\sin\frac{\theta}{2}\cos\frac{\theta}{2}\,d\theta$$

$$= \frac{32\pi a^3}{3}\int_0^{\pi}\sin^7\left(\frac{\theta}{2}\right)\cos\frac{\theta}{2}\,d\theta$$

Let $\quad \sin\frac{\theta}{2} = t$

$\therefore \quad \frac{1}{2}\cos\frac{\theta}{2}.d\theta = dt$

$\therefore \quad V = \frac{64\pi a^3}{3}\int_0^{1} t^7\, dt$

$$= \frac{64\pi a^3}{3} \cdot \left[\frac{t^8}{8}\right]_0^1$$

$$= \frac{8\pi a^3}{3}.$$

Example 10. Find the volume of the solid generated when the area of one loop of the curve $r^2 = a^2 \cos 2\theta$, revolves about

(i) the initial line (ii) about $\theta = \frac{\pi}{2}$ line.

Solution: The given curve is symmetrical about initial line and the revolution also, is about initial line. So, the upper part and lower part of the loop will generate the same solid. Upper half of the loop of the curve lies between $\theta = 0$ and $\theta = \frac{\pi}{4}$.

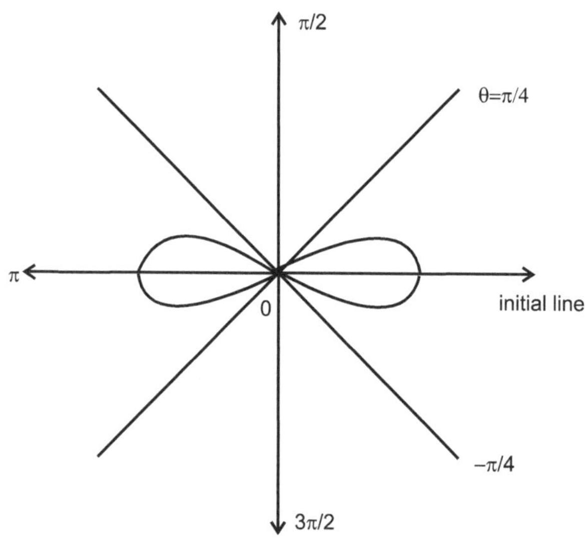

(i) ∴ The required volume $= \frac{2\pi}{3} \int_0^{\pi/4} r^3 \sin\theta \, d\theta$

$$= \frac{2\pi}{3} \int_0^{\pi/4} \left(a\sqrt{\cos 2\theta}\right)^3 \sin\theta \, d\theta$$

$$= \frac{2\pi}{3} \int_0^{\pi/4} a^3 (\cos 2\theta)^{3/2} \sin\theta \, d\theta$$

$$V = \frac{2\pi}{3} a^3 \int_0^{\pi/4} \left(2\cos^2\theta - 1\right)^{3/2} \sin\theta \, d\theta$$

Putting $\sqrt{2}\cos\theta = \sec\phi$

$$V = \frac{\sqrt{2}\pi a^3}{3} \int_{\pi/4}^{0} \left(\sec^2\phi - 1\right)^{3/2} (-\sec\phi \ \tan\phi) \ d\phi$$

$$= \frac{\sqrt{2}.\pi a^3}{3} \int_0^{\pi/4} \tan^4\phi \,.\sec\phi \, d\phi$$

$$= \frac{\sqrt{2}\pi a^3}{3} \int_0^{\pi/4} . \left(\sec^2\phi - 1\right)^2 \sec\phi \ d\phi$$

$$= \frac{\sqrt{2}\pi a^3}{3} \int_0^{\pi/4} . \left(\sec^4\phi + 1 - 2\sec^2\phi\right) \sec\phi \, d\phi$$

$$= \frac{\sqrt{2}\pi a^3}{3} \int_0^{\pi/4} . \left(\sec^5\phi - 2\sec^3\phi + \sec\phi\right) d\phi$$

Using the reduction formula

$$\int \sec^n\phi \, d\phi = \frac{\sec^{n-2}\phi \tan\phi}{n-1} + \frac{n-2}{n-1} \int \sec^{n-2}\phi \, d\phi$$

$$V = \frac{\pi a^3 \sqrt{2}}{24} \ . \left[3\log\left(\sqrt{2}+1\right) - \sqrt{2}\right]$$

$$\therefore \qquad V = \frac{\pi a^3 \sqrt{2}}{24} \left[3\log\left(\sqrt{2}+1\right) - \sqrt{2}\right]$$

(ii) When the revolution is about $\theta = \dfrac{\pi}{2}$ line. Then the areas above and below the initial line will generate equal and different parts of the solids.

$\therefore$ The required volume

$$V = 2 \,.\, \frac{2\pi}{3} \,.\, \int_0^{\pi/2} r^3 \cos\theta \, d\theta$$

$$= \frac{4\pi}{3} a^3 \int_0^{\pi/4} (\cos 2\theta)^{3/2} \ . \cos\theta \ d\theta$$

$$= \frac{4\pi a^3}{3} \int_0^{\pi/4} \left(1 - 2\sin^2\theta\right)^{3/2} . \cos\theta \, d\theta$$

Let $\sqrt{2}\sin\theta = \sin\phi$

$$\therefore \qquad V = \frac{2\sqrt{2}\pi a^3}{3} \int_0^{\pi/2} \left(1 - \sin^2\phi\right)^{3/2} . \cos\phi \, d\phi$$

$$= \frac{2\sqrt{2}\pi a^3}{3} \int_0^{\pi/2} \cos^4\phi \, d\phi$$

$$= \frac{2\sqrt{2}.\pi a^3}{3} \left[\int_0^{\pi/2} \cos^4\phi \sin\phi \, d\phi \right]$$

$$= \frac{2\sqrt{2}.\pi a^3}{3} \left[\frac{\overline{|5/2}.\overline{|1/2}}{2\overline{|3}} \right]$$

$$= \frac{2\sqrt{2}.\pi a^3}{3} \left[\frac{\frac{3}{2}.\frac{1}{2}.\sqrt{\pi}.\sqrt{\pi}}{2.2.1} \right]$$

$$= \frac{2\sqrt{2}.\pi a^3}{3} . \frac{3\pi}{16}$$

$$= \frac{\pi^2 a^3 \sqrt{2}}{8}.$$

Example 11. Find that the volume of the solid formed by the revolution of the area between the curve $y^2 (2a - x) = x^3$ and its asymptote, about its asymptote.

Solution: As the given curve is symetrical about X-axis.

$\therefore$ Area between the curve and its asymptote is symmetrical about X-axis. So, the upper and lower parts of the area will generate the equal and distinct solids when revolution is about the asymptote $x = 2a$.

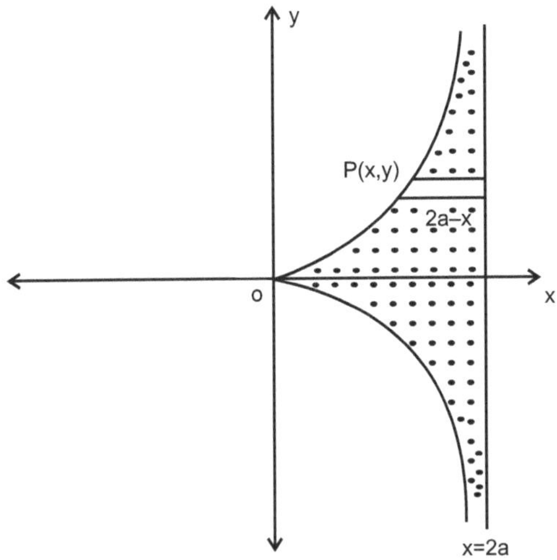

$\therefore$ The required volume = 2. Volume generated by upper part

$$V = 2\pi \int_0^{\infty} (2a - x)^2 \, dy$$

$$= 2\pi \int_0^{2a} (2a - x)^2 . \frac{dy}{dx} . dx$$

$$= 2\pi \int_0^{2a} (2a - x)^2 . \frac{(3a - x)\sqrt{x}}{(2a - x)^{3/2}} \, dx$$

$$= 2\pi \int_0^{2a} (3a - x)\sqrt{2ax - x^2} \, dx$$

$$= 2\pi \int_0^{2a} (a - x)\sqrt{2ax - x^2} \, dx + 2\pi \int_0^{2a} 2a . \sqrt{2ax - x^2} \, dx$$

$$= \frac{2\pi}{2} . \int_0^{2a} (2a - 2x)\sqrt{2ax - x^2} \, dx$$

$$+ 2\pi \int_0^{2a} 2a . \sqrt{2ax - x^2} \, dx$$

$$= \pi . \frac{2}{3}\left[\left(2ax - x^2\right)^{3/2}\right]_0^{2a} + 4\pi a . \int_0^{2a} \sqrt{2ax - x^2} \, dx$$

$$= 0 + 4\pi a . \int_0^{2a} \sqrt{2ax - x^2} \, dx$$

Let $\quad x = 2a \sin^2\theta$

$\therefore \quad dx = 4a \sin\theta \cos\theta \, d\theta$

$$\therefore \quad V = 4\pi a \, . \, 4a \int_0^{\pi/2} 2a \sin\theta\cos\theta \, . \, \sin\theta\cos\theta \, d\theta$$

$$= 32 \, \pi a^3 \, . \int_0^{\pi/2} \sin^2\theta\cos^2\theta \, d\theta$$

$$= 32 \, \pi a^3 \, . \left[\frac{\Gamma\left(\frac{3}{2}\right) . \Gamma\left(\frac{3}{2}\right)}{2\Gamma(3)}\right]$$

$$= 32 \, \pi a^3 \, . \frac{\frac{1}{2}\sqrt{\pi} \, . \, \frac{1}{2} . \sqrt{\pi}}{2.2.1}$$

$$= 2 \, \pi^2 a^3.$$

Example 12. The area bounded by the curves $y = \cos x$, $y = \sin x$ and X-axis between $x = 0$ and $x = \pi/2$, revolves about X-axis. Find the volume of the solid generated.

Solution: The given curves $y = \cos x$ and $y = \sin x$

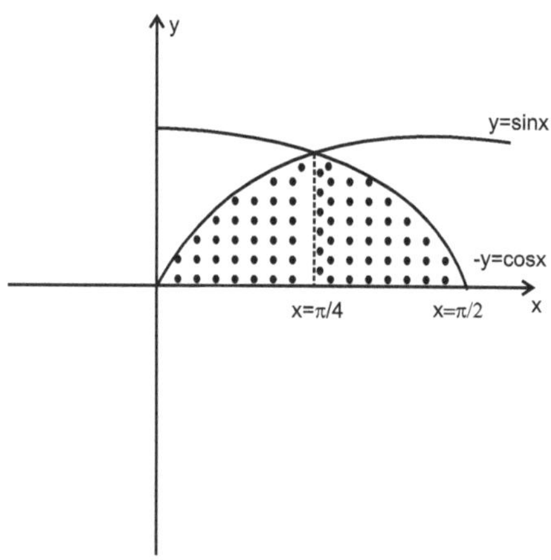

Intersect at $x = \dfrac{\pi}{4}$ and the area between the curves is as shown by the dotted region.

The area between the curves is same on both sides of the line $x = \frac{\pi}{4}$.

$\therefore$ The required volume

$$V = 2\pi \int_0^{\pi/4} \sin^2 x\,dx$$

$$= 2\pi \int_0^{\pi/4} \sin^2 x\,dx$$

$$= \pi \int_0^{\pi/4} (1 - \cos 2x)\,dx$$

$$= \pi \left[x - \frac{\sin 2x}{2} \right]_0^{\pi/4}$$

$$= \pi \left[\frac{\pi}{4} - \frac{1}{2} \right]$$

$$= \frac{\pi}{4}[\pi - 2].$$

Aliter

$$V = \pi \int_0^{\pi/4} \sin^2 x\,dx + \pi \int_{\pi/4}^{\pi/2} \cos^2 x\,dx$$

$$= \frac{\pi}{2}\left[\int_0^{\pi/4} (1 - \cos 2x)\,dx + \int_{\pi/4}^{\pi/2} (1 + \cos 2x)\,dx \right]$$

$$= \frac{\pi}{2}\left\{ \left[x - \frac{\sin 2x}{2} \right]_o^{\pi/4} + \left[x + \frac{\sin 2x}{2} \right]_{\pi/4}^{\pi/2} \right\}$$

$$= \frac{\pi}{2}\left\{ \left[\frac{\pi}{4} - \frac{1}{2} \right] + \left[\left(\frac{\pi}{2} + 0 \right) - \left(\frac{\pi}{4} + \frac{1}{2} \right) \right] \right\}$$

$$= \frac{\pi}{2}\left[\frac{\pi}{4} - \frac{1}{2} + \frac{\pi}{4} - \frac{1}{2} \right]$$

$$= \frac{\pi}{2}\left[\frac{\pi}{2} - 1 \right]$$

$$= \frac{\pi}{4}\,[\pi - 2].$$

EXERCISE

1. The part of the parabola $y^2 = 4ax$ cut off by the latus rectum, revolves about the tangent at the vertex. Find the volume of the solid generated.
2. Area of the curve $a^2x^2 = y^3 (2a - y)$ revolves about Y-axis, find the volume of the solid generated.
3. Calculate by integration the capacity of a half ellipsoid which is formed by revolving an ellipse about its minor axis, the length of axes being $\frac{6}{\pi}$ and $\frac{3}{\pi}$ cm.
4. Find by integration the volume of a sphere of radius a.
5. Find the volume of the solid generated by revolution of the area of one arc of the cycloid $x = a(\theta + \sin\theta)$, $y = a(1 + \cos\theta)$ about X-axis.
6. Find the volume of the solid generated by revolution of the area of the loop of the curve

   $$x = t^2,\ y = t - \frac{t^3}{3},\ \text{about X-axis.}$$

7. Find the volume of the solid generated by revolution about initial of the area of the limacon $r = a + b\cos\theta$ $(a > b)$.
8. Find the volume of a right circular cone of height h and radius a.
9. Find the volume of the solid generated by revolution of the area of the astroid $x = a\cos^3\theta$, $y = a\sin^3\theta$, about X-axis.
10. Find the volume of the torus formed by the rotation of the area of $x^2 + (y - b)^2 = a^2$ $(b > a)$, about X-axis.
11. The area of the loop of curve lying between $\theta = -\frac{\pi}{6}$ and $\theta = \frac{\pi}{6}$, revolves about initial line. Find the volume of the solid generated.

Answers:

1. $\frac{4}{5}\pi a^3$
2. $\frac{8}{5}\pi a^3$

3. $\dfrac{9}{\pi^2}$ cc

4. $\dfrac{4}{3}\pi a^3$

5. $5\pi^2 a^3$

6. $\dfrac{3\pi}{4}$

7. $\dfrac{4\pi a}{3}(a^2 + b^2)$

8. $\dfrac{1}{3}\pi a^2 h$

9. $\dfrac{32\pi a^3}{105}$

10. $2\pi^2 a^2 b$

11. $\dfrac{19\pi a^3}{960}$

SURFACE OF SOLIDS OF REVOLUTION

If the plane area bounded by the curve $y = f(x)$, X-axis and the lines $x = a$, $x = b$, revolves about X-axis, then the surface of the solid thus generated is given by $\boxed{S = \int_{n=a}^{b} 2\pi y \, ds}$

Proof: Let AB be the arc of the curve $y = f(x)$. Let P (x, y), Q $(x + \delta s, y + \delta y)$ be two neighbouring points on the curve, such that y is increasing (or decreasing) function of x in $a \leq x \leq b$.

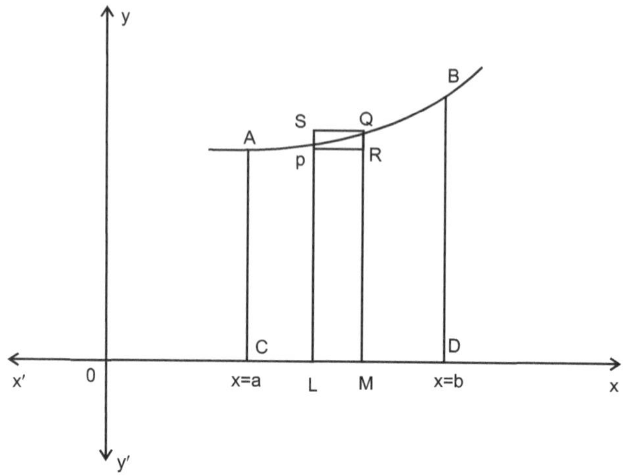

Also let $\widehat{AP} = s$ (arc length AP)

$\widehat{AQ} = s + \delta s$

$\therefore$ $\widehat{PQ} = \delta s$

and Let S = Surface of the solid generated when area ACLP revolves about X-axis.

$S + \Delta S$ = Surface of the solid generated when area ACMQ revolves about X-axis.

$\therefore$ ΔS = Surface of the solid generated when area PLMQ revolves about X-axis.

As long the curve, changes by δs, S changes by δS.

Now, δS is more than the curved surface of the cylinder of radius PL(=y) and thickness δs and less than the curved surface of the cylinder of radius MQ = ($y + \delta y$) and thickness δs.

$\therefore$ $2\pi y\delta s < \delta S < 2\pi\,(y + \delta y)\,\delta s.$

or $$2\pi y < \frac{\delta S}{\delta s} < 2\pi\,(y + \delta y)$$

Taking limit as $\delta s \to 0$, we have

$$\frac{dS}{ds} = 2\pi y$$

Integrating w.r.t. 's' we have

$$\int \frac{dS}{ds}\,ds = \int 2\pi\; y\; ds$$

$$[S]_{x=a}^{x=b} = \int_{x=a}^{b} 2\pi y \frac{ds}{dx} dx$$

$$[S]_{\text{when } x=a} - [S]_{x=b} = 2\pi \int_a^b y \frac{ds}{dx} dx$$

$$S = 2\pi \int_{x=a}^{b} y \sqrt{1+\left(\frac{dy}{dx}\right)^2} dx \tag{i}$$

• When the area bounded by the curve $x = \phi\,(y)$, y-axis and the lines $y = c$, $y = d$ revolves about y-axis, then curved surface of the solid generated is given by

$$S = 2\pi \int_{y=c}^{b} x \sqrt{1+\left(\frac{dx}{dy}\right)^2} dy$$

• Curved surface of the solid generated when the area bounded by the curve $x = f\,(t)$, $y = \phi\,(t)$, x-axis and the ordinates where $t = t_1$ and $t = t_2$, revolves about x-axis is

$$S = 2\pi \int_{t_1}^{t_2} y \sqrt{\left(\frac{dy}{dx}\right)^2 + \left(\frac{dy}{dt}\right)^2} \,.\, dt$$

Similarly, when the revolution is about y-axis, then

$$S = 2\pi \int_{t_1}^{t_2} x \sqrt{\left(\frac{dx}{dt}\right)^2 + \left(\frac{dy}{dt}\right)^2} \,.\, dt$$

• Area of the curved surface generated when area bounded by the curve $r = f\,(\theta)$ and the lines $\theta = \alpha$, $\theta = \beta$ $(\alpha < \beta)$ revolves about the initial line is

$$S = 2\pi \int_\alpha^\beta y \frac{ds}{d\theta} d\theta$$

$$= 2\pi \int_\alpha^\beta (r \sin\theta) \sqrt{r^2 + \left(\frac{dr}{d\theta}\right)^2} \; d\theta$$

• Similarly when revolution is about $\theta = \frac{\pi}{2}$ line, then the area of the curved surface is given by

$$S = 2\pi \int_{\alpha}^{\beta} (r\cos\theta)\sqrt{r^2 + \left(\frac{dr}{d\theta}\right)^2}\, d\theta$$

SOLVED EXAMPLES

Example 1. Find the surface of the solid generated by revolving the arc of the parabola $y^2 = 4ax$ bounded by its latus rectum, about X-axis.

Solution: The required surface area is

$$= 2\pi \int_{x=0}^{a} y\sqrt{1 + \left(\frac{dy}{dx}\right)^2}\, dx$$

$$= 2\pi \int_0^a 2\sqrt{ax}\sqrt{1 + \frac{a}{x}}\, dx$$

$$= 2 \,.\, 2\pi \int_0^a \sqrt{a}\,.\sqrt{a + x}\, dx$$

$$= 4\pi\sqrt{a}\,.\left[\frac{(a+x)^{3/2}}{3/2}\right]_0^a$$

$$= \frac{8\pi}{3}\sqrt{a}\left[2a\sqrt{2a} - a^{3/2}\right]$$

$$= \frac{8\pi\sqrt{a}}{3}\left[2\sqrt{2} - 1\right].a\sqrt{a}$$

$$= \frac{8\pi a^2}{3}\left[2\sqrt{2} - 1\right].$$

Example 2. Find the surface area of the solid formed by revolving the arc of the cycloid

$$x = a\,(\theta + \sin\theta)$$

$$y = a\,(1 + \cos\theta),$$

about x-axis.

Solution: The given curve is symmetric about Y-axis and one arc of the cycloid extends from $\theta = -\pi$ to $\theta = \pi$, which is symmetrical about Y-axis.

$\therefore$ Revolution is about X-axis, then the areas on the right and left of Y-axis will generate equal and distinct parts of the solids.

$\therefore$ The required surface area

$$S = 2\int_{\theta=0}^{\pi} 2\pi y\sqrt{\left(\frac{dx}{d\theta}\right)^2 + \left(\frac{dy}{d\theta}\right)^2}\, d\theta$$

$$= 4\pi \int_0^{\pi} a(1+\cos\theta) \,.\, \sqrt{a^2(1+\cos^2\theta + 2\cos\theta + a^2\sin^2\theta)}\, d\theta$$

$$= 4\pi a \int_0^{\pi}\left(2\cos^2\frac{\theta}{2}\right) .\; a\sqrt{2(1+\cos\theta)}\, d\theta$$

$$= 16\pi a^2 \int_0^{\pi} \cos^3\left(\frac{\theta}{2}\right) d\theta$$

Let $\qquad \dfrac{\theta}{2} = t$

$\therefore \qquad d\theta = 2dt$

$\therefore \qquad S = 32\pi a^2 \displaystyle\int_0^{\pi/2} \cos^3 t\, dt$

$$= 32\pi a^2 \,.\, \frac{2}{3}$$

$$= \frac{64\pi a^2}{3}$$

Example 3. Find the surface of the solid obtained by revolving the cardioid $r = a\,(1 - \cos\theta)$ about the initial line.

Solution: The given curve is symmetrical about initial line. And the revolution also, is about the initial line, so the solid formed will be the same whether to revolve upper half portion or lower half portion or both.

$\therefore$ The required surface

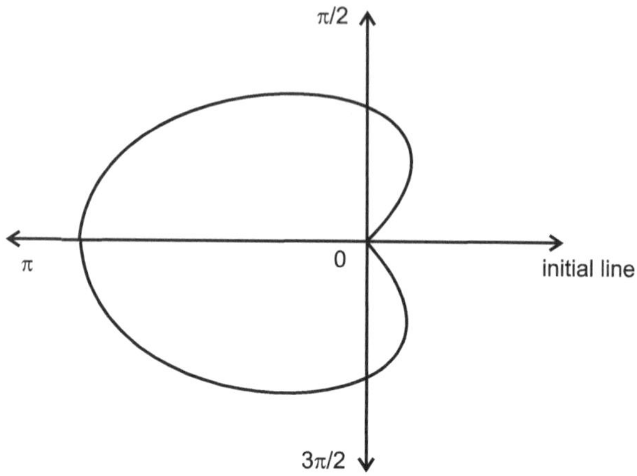

$$S = 2\pi \int_0^{\pi} r\sin\theta.\sqrt{r^2+\left(\frac{dr}{d\theta}\right)^2}\,.\,d\theta$$

$$= 2\pi \int_0^{\pi} a(1-\cos\theta).\sin\theta \;\sqrt{a^2(1-\cos\theta)^2+a^2\sin^2\theta}\,.\,d\theta$$

$$= 2\pi a^2 \int_0^{\pi} 2\sin^2\left(\frac{\theta}{2}\right).\left(2\sin\frac{\theta}{2}\cos\frac{\theta}{2}\right)\; 2.\sin\left(\frac{\theta}{2}\right) d\theta$$

$$= 16\pi a^2 \int_0^{\pi} \sin^4\left(\frac{\theta}{2}\right).\cos\left(\frac{\theta}{2}\right) d\theta$$

Let $\sin\left(\frac{\theta}{2}\right) = t$

$\therefore \quad \cos\frac{\theta}{2}d\theta = 2dt$

$\therefore \quad S = 32\pi a^2 \int_0^1 t^4 dt$

$$= 32\pi a^2 \left[\frac{t^5}{5}\right]_0^1$$

$$S = \frac{32\pi a^2}{5}.$$

Example 4. Find the surface of the solid generated by revolving the lemniscate $r^2 = a^2 \cos2\theta$ about the initial line.

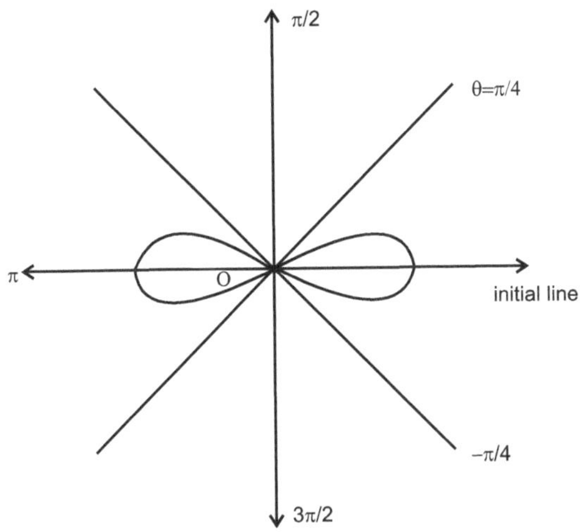

Solution: The given curve is symmetrical about initial line as well as about $\theta = \dfrac{\pi}{2}$ line. When the revolution is about initial line then the required surface area is

$$S = 2.2\pi \int_{\theta=0}^{\pi/4} r\sin\theta\sqrt{r^2 + \left(\frac{dr}{d\theta}\right)^2}\, d\theta.$$

$$= 4\pi \int_{\theta=0}^{\pi/4} \sin\theta\sqrt{r^4 + \left(r\frac{dr}{d\theta}\right)^2}\, d\theta.$$

$$= 4\pi \int_{\theta=0}^{\pi/4} \sin\theta\sqrt{a^4\cos^2 2\theta + a^4 . \sin^2 2\theta}\; d\theta$$

$$= 4\pi a^2 \int_0^{\pi/4} \sin\theta\; d\theta$$

$$= 4\pi\left[-\cos\theta\right]_0^{\pi/4}$$

$$= 4\pi\left[1 - \frac{1}{\sqrt{2}}\right] . a^2$$

$$S = 2\sqrt{2}\pi a^2\left[\sqrt{2} - 1\right].$$

Example 5. Find the surface of the solid generated by revolution of the astroid $x = a\cos^3 t$, $y = a\sin^3 t$, about X-axis.

Solution: The equation of the given curve is

$$x = a\ \cos^3 t$$
$$y = a\ \sin^3 t,$$

which is symmetrial about both the axes.

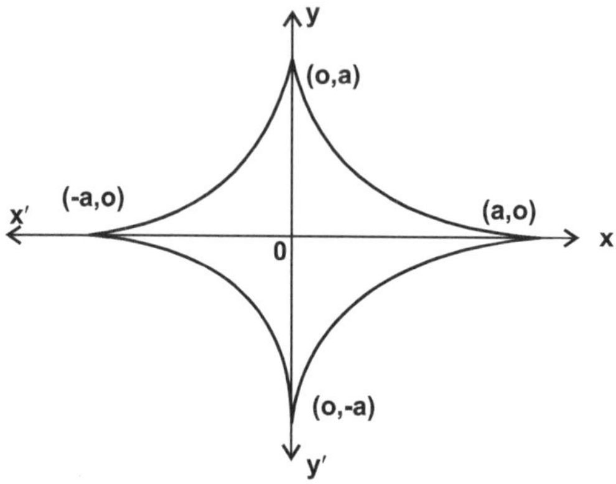

$$\frac{dx}{dt} = -3a\ \cos^2 t\ \sin t$$

$$\frac{dy}{dt} = 3a\ \sin^2 t\ \cos t$$

\ $$\frac{ds}{dt} = \sqrt{\left(\frac{dx}{dt}\right)^2 + \left(\frac{dy}{dt}\right)^2}$$

\ $$\frac{ds}{dt} = \sqrt{9a^2 \cos^4 t \sin^2 t + 9a^2 \sin^4 t \cos^2 t}$$

$$= 3a\ \sin t\ \cos t$$

\The required surface

$$S = 2\ .\ \int_0^{\pi/2} 2\pi y \frac{ds}{dt}\, dt$$

$$= 4pa \int_0^{\pi/2} \sin^3 t\ .\ 3a \sin t\ \cos t\ dt$$

$$= 12pa^2 \int_0^{\pi/2} \sin^4 t \cos t\, dt$$

$$= 12pa^2\ .\ \left[\frac{z^5}{5}\right]_0^1 \qquad \text{Where } z = \sin t$$

$$= \frac{12\pi a^2}{5}.$$

Example 6. Find the surface of the solid when the curve $r = 2a\cos\theta$ revolves about initial line.

Solution: The given equation $r = 2a\cos\theta$ is the equation of a circle passing through the pole and diameter on initial line, it is symmetrical about initial line.

$$r = 2a\cos\theta$$

$$\therefore \quad \frac{dr}{d\theta} = -2a\sin\theta$$

$$\therefore \quad \frac{ds}{d\theta} = \sqrt{r^2 + \left(\frac{dr}{d\theta}\right)^2}$$

$$= \sqrt{4a^2\cos^2\theta + 4a^2\sin^2\theta}$$

$$= 2a$$

$\therefore$ The required surface

$$= \int 2\pi\, y\, ds$$

$$= \int_0^{\pi/2} 2\pi.r\sin\theta \frac{ds}{d\theta} d\theta$$

$$= 2\pi \int_0^{\pi/2} 2a\cos\theta.\sin\theta\; 2a\; d\theta$$

$$= 8\pi a^2 \int_0^{\pi/2} \sin\theta\cos\theta\, d\theta$$

$$= 4\pi a^2.$$

Example 7. One loop of the curve $8a^2y^2 = x^2(a^2 - 2x^2)$ revolves about X-axis. Find the surface of the solid generated.

Solution: The given curve is symmetrical about both the axes and one loop of the curve lies between $x = \dfrac{-a}{\sqrt{2}}$ and $x = 0$ and other between $x = 0$ and $x = \dfrac{a}{\sqrt{2}}$.

$\therefore$ The surface of the solid when one loop lying between $x = 0$ and $x = \dfrac{a}{\sqrt{2}}$ revolves about X-axis is

$$S = \int_0^{a/\sqrt{2}} 2\pi\, y \frac{ds}{dx} .dx$$

Now, $$y^2 = \frac{x^2\left(a^2 - 2x^2\right)}{8a^2}$$

$$\therefore \quad 2y\frac{dy}{dx} = \frac{2x\left(a^2 - 2x^2\right) - 4x^3}{8a^2}$$

$$\therefore \quad \frac{dy}{dx} = \frac{x\left(a^2 - 4x^2\right)}{8a^2 y}$$

$$\therefore \quad \left(\frac{ds}{dx}\right)^2 = 1 + \left(\frac{dy}{dx}\right)^2$$

$$= 1 + \frac{x^2\left(a^2 - 4x^2\right)^2}{64a^4 y^2}$$

$$= \frac{1 + \left(a^2 - 4x^2\right)^2}{8a^2\left(a^2 - 2x^2\right)}$$

$$= \frac{\left(3a^2 - 4x^2\right)^2}{8a^2\left(a^2 - 2x^2\right)}$$

$$\therefore \quad \frac{ds}{dx} = \frac{\left(3a^2 - 4x^2\right)}{2\sqrt{2}a.\left(a^2 - 2x^2\right)^{1/2}}$$

$$\therefore \quad S = 2\pi \int_0^{a/\sqrt{2}} \frac{x\sqrt{\left(a^2 - 2x^2\right)}}{2\sqrt{2}a} \cdot \frac{\left(3a^2 - 4x^2\right)}{2\sqrt{2}a.\sqrt{a^2 - 2x^2}}\, dx$$

$$= \frac{\pi}{4a^2} \int_0^{a/\sqrt{2}} \left(3a^2 - 4x^2\right) x\, dx.$$

$$= \frac{\pi}{4a^2} \int_0^{a/\sqrt{2}} \left(3a^2x - 4x^3\right) dx.$$

$$= \frac{\pi}{4a^2} \left[\frac{3a^2x^2}{2} - x^4\right]_0^{a/\sqrt{2}}$$

$$= \frac{\pi}{4a^2} \left[\frac{3}{2}a^2 \frac{a^2}{2} - \frac{a^4}{4}\right]$$

$$= \frac{\pi a^2}{4} \left[\frac{3}{4} - \frac{1}{4}\right]$$

$$S = \frac{\pi a^2}{8}$$

Example 8. A circular arc revolves about its chord. Prove that the area of the surface generated is $4\pi a^2 (\sin\alpha - \alpha \cos \alpha)$, where a is the radius and 2α, the angle subtended by the arc at the centre.

Solution: Let $x^2 + y^2 = a^2$ ... (i)

be the circle and AB be its chord. Such that the arc AB subtends angle 2α at the centre.

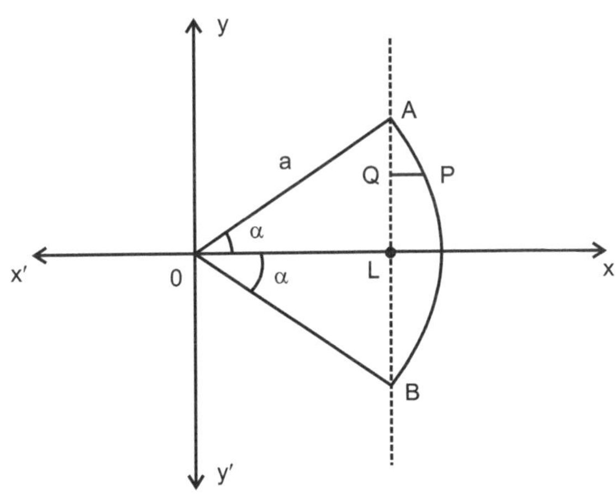

Let $P(x, y)$ be any point on the circular arc AB, draw a perpendicular PQ on the chord AB.

$\therefore$ $PQ = x - a \cos\alpha$ ...(2)

Now from (1)

$$2x + 2y\frac{dy}{dx} = 0$$

$$\therefore \qquad \frac{dy}{dx} = \frac{-x}{y}$$

Since the revolution is about AB, *i.e.*, a line || to y-axis.

$$\therefore \qquad \frac{dx}{dy} = \frac{-y}{x}$$

$$\therefore \qquad 1 + \left(\frac{dx}{dy}\right)^2 = \frac{x^2 + y^2}{x^2} = \frac{a^2}{x^2}$$

so
$$\frac{ds}{dy} = \sqrt{1 + \left(\frac{dx}{dy}\right)^2}$$

$$\frac{a}{x} = \frac{a}{\sqrt{a^2 - y^2}}$$

$\therefore$ The required surface

$$S = 2.2\pi \int_{y=0}^{a\sin\alpha} (x - a\cos\alpha)\frac{ds}{dy}.dy$$

$$= 2.2\pi \int_{y=0}^{a\sin\alpha} (x - a\cos\alpha).\frac{a}{\sqrt{a^2 - y^2}}dy$$

$$= 2.2\pi \int_{y=0}^{a\sin\alpha} \left(\sqrt{a^2 - y^2} - a\cos\alpha\right).\frac{a}{\sqrt{a^2 - y^2}}dy$$

$$= 2.2\pi a \int_{y=0}^{a\sin\alpha} \left(1 - \frac{a\cos\alpha}{\sqrt{a^2 - y^2}}\right)dy$$

$$= 4\pi a \left[y - a\cos\alpha.\sin^{-1}\left(\frac{y}{a}\right)\right]_0^{a\sin\alpha}$$

$$= 4\pi a\ [a\ \sin\alpha - a\ \cos\alpha\ .\ \sin^{-1}\ (\sin\alpha)]$$

$$= 4\pi a^2\ [\sin\alpha - \alpha\ \cos\alpha].$$

EXERCISE

1. Find the surface area of a sphere of radius a.
2. Find the surface of a cone generated by revolution of the line $y = 2x$ from $x = 0$ to $x = 2$ about (i) X-axis (ii) Y-axis.
3. Find the area of the surface formed by the revolution of $x^2 + 4y^2 = 16$ about X-axis.
4. The loop of the curve $x = t^2$, $y = t - \dfrac{t^3}{3}$ revolves about X-axis. Find area of the surface generated.
5. The arc of the cardioid $r = a\,(1+\cos\theta)$ lying between $\theta = -\dfrac{\pi}{2}$ and $\theta = \dfrac{\pi}{2}$ revolves about $\theta = \dfrac{\pi}{2}$ line. Find the area of the surface generated.
6. Find the area of surface of the solid generated by the revolution of the cycloid $x = a\,(\theta + \sin\theta)$, $y = a\,(1 - \cos\theta)$ about X-axis.
7. Find the area of surface of the solid formed by the revolution of the curve $r = a\,(1 + \cos\theta)$ about initial line.
8. A quadrant of a circle of radius r revolves about its chord. Show that area of the surface generated is $2\sqrt{2}\,\pi r^2\,(1 - \dfrac{\pi}{4})$.
9. Find the surface area of the solid generated by revolving the cycloid $x = a\,(\theta - \sin\theta)$, $y = a\,(1 - \cos\theta)$ about

(i) X-axis

(ii) Y-axis

10. Find the surface area of the solid generated by the revolution of the loop of the curve

$$9ay^2 = x\,(3a - x)^2, \text{ about X-axis.}$$

Answers:

1. $4\pi a^2$
2. (i) $8\pi\sqrt{5}$

   (ii) $4\pi\sqrt{5}$

3. $\dfrac{8\pi}{3\sqrt{3}}\,[4\pi + 3\sqrt{3}\,]$

4. 3π

5. $\dfrac{48\sqrt{2}}{5}\,\pi a^2$

6. $\dfrac{32\pi a^2}{3}$

7. $\dfrac{32\pi a^2}{5}$

9. (i) $\dfrac{64\pi a^2}{3}$

   (ii) $\dfrac{64\pi a^2}{3} + 16\pi^2 a^2$

10. $\dfrac{22\pi a\sqrt{3}}{45}$

12

Matrices

ELEMENTARY TRANSFORMATIONS ON A MATRIX

Three operations on a matrix defined below, are called the elementary transformations.

1. Interchange of any two rows (or columns).

   If the ith and j^{th} rows are interchanged then it is denoted by R_{ij} and if i^{th} and j^{th} columns are interchaned then, it is denoted by C_{ij}.

2. Multiplication of any row (or column) by a non-zero number k.

   If i^{th} row is multiplied by k than it is denoted by $k\,R_i$ and if i^{th} columns is multiplied by k it is denoted by kc_i.

3. The addition of k times of jth row to i^{th} row or k times of jth column, to ith column, these are deonted by $R_i + k\,R_j$ or $C_i + k\,C_j$.

   The transformation is called elementary row transformation, if applied between rows and columns transformation if between columns.

- **Equivalent matrices:** Two matrices A and B are said to be equivalent if one is obtained from the other by a series of elementary transformations. It is denoted by A ~ B.
- **Elementary matrices:** A matrix, obtained by a single elementary transformation on an identity matrix, is called an elementary matrix.

Few Important Results

(i) Elementary matrices are same when obtained by R_{ij} or C_{ij}

Let $$I = \begin{bmatrix} 1 & 0 & 0 \\ 0 & 1 & 0 \\ 0 & 0 & 1 \end{bmatrix}$$

$$\therefore \qquad R_{23} = \begin{bmatrix} 1 & 0 & 0 \\ 0 & 0 & 1 \\ 0 & 1 & 0 \end{bmatrix}$$

$$C_{23} = \begin{bmatrix} 1 & 0 & 0 \\ 0 & 0 & 1 \\ 0 & 1 & 0 \end{bmatrix}$$

(*ii*) The elementary matrices obtained by $k\,R_i$ or $k\,C_i$ are the same.

$$\text{let} \qquad I = \begin{bmatrix} 1 & 0 & 0 \\ 0 & 1 & 0 \\ 0 & 0 & 1 \end{bmatrix}$$

$$\therefore \qquad 5\,R_2 = \begin{bmatrix} 1 & 0 & 0 \\ 0 & 5 & 0 \\ 0 & 0 & 1 \end{bmatrix}$$

$$\text{and} \qquad 5\,C_2 = \begin{bmatrix} 1 & 0 & 0 \\ 0 & 5 & 0 \\ 0 & 0 & 1 \end{bmatrix}$$

(*iii*) The elementary matrix obtained by $R_i + k\,R_j$ is the transpose of the matrix obtained by $C_i + k\,C_j$.

$$\text{let} \qquad I = \begin{bmatrix} 1 & 0 & 0 \\ 0 & 1 & 0 \\ 0 & 0 & 1 \end{bmatrix}$$

$$\therefore \qquad E_{23}\,(k) = R_2 + k\,R_3 = \begin{bmatrix} 1 & 0 & 0 \\ 0 & 1 & k \\ 0 & 0 & 1 \end{bmatrix}$$

$$E'_{23}(k) = C_2 + k\,C_3 = \begin{bmatrix} 1 & 0 & 0 \\ 0 & 1 & 0 \\ 0 & k & 1 \end{bmatrix}$$

Clearly $E_{23}(k)$ is the transpose of $E'_{23}(k)$.

(*iv*) An elementary row operation on a matrix A is equivalent to pre-multiplication of A by the corresponding elementary matrix.

let $$I = \begin{bmatrix} 1 & 0 & 0 \\ 0 & 1 & 0 \\ 0 & 0 & 1 \end{bmatrix}$$

$$A = \begin{bmatrix} a & b & c \\ d & e & f \\ g & h & i \end{bmatrix}$$

let B = matrix obtained from A, by inter changing 2nd and 3rd Rows

$$\therefore \quad B = \begin{bmatrix} a & b & c \\ g & h & i \\ d & e & f \end{bmatrix}$$

Corresponding elementary matrix is

$$E_{23} = \begin{bmatrix} 1 & 0 & 0 \\ 0 & 0 & 1 \\ 0 & 1 & 0 \end{bmatrix}$$

$$\therefore \quad E_{23}\, A = \begin{bmatrix} 1 & 0 & 0 \\ 0 & 0 & 1 \\ 0 & 1 & 0 \end{bmatrix} \begin{bmatrix} a & b & c \\ d & e & f \\ g & h & i \end{bmatrix}$$

$$\therefore \quad = \begin{bmatrix} a & b & c \\ g & h & i \\ d & e & f \end{bmatrix}$$

$$\therefore \quad = B$$

$$\therefore \quad B = E_{23}\, A.$$

(*v*) An elementary column operation on a matrix A, is equivalent to post multiplication of *A* by the corresponding elementary matrix.

Let D = A matrix obtained from A by interchanging 2nd and 3rd columns.

$$D = \begin{bmatrix} a & c & b \\ d & f & e \\ g & i & h \end{bmatrix}$$

$$E_{23} = \begin{bmatrix} 1 & 0 & 0 \\ 0 & 0 & 1 \\ 0 & 1 & 0 \end{bmatrix}$$

$\therefore$
$$A.\ E'_{23} = \begin{bmatrix} a & b & c \\ d & e & f \\ g & h & i \end{bmatrix}\begin{bmatrix} 1 & 0 & 0 \\ 0 & 0 & 1 \\ 0 & 1 & 0 \end{bmatrix}$$

$$= \begin{bmatrix} a & c & b \\ d & f & e \\ g & i & h \end{bmatrix} = D$$

$\therefore$ $$D = A.\ E'_{23}\ .$$

(*vi*) An elementary row operation on the product of two matrices is equivalent to the same elementary row operation on the pre-factor.

i.e. $R\ (A\ .\ B) = R(A).\ B$

$$E(AB) = E(A)\ .\ B$$

(*vii*) An elementary column operation on the product of two matrices is equivalent to the same elementary column operation on the post factor.

i.e. $C\ (AB) = A.\ C(B)$

$$E'(AB) = A\ .\ E'\ (B)$$

(*viii*) If a square matrix A is reduced to identity matrix by a series of elementary row transformations, then the same series of operations converts identity matrix into A^{-1}.

Let

$$E_n\ ...\ E_3E_2E_1A = I$$

$\therefore$ $$E_n\ ...\ E_3\ .\ E_2\ .\ E_1\ A\ .\ A^{-1} = I.\ A^{-1}$$

or $$E_n\ ...\ E_3\ .\ E_2\ .\ E_1\ I = A^{-1}.$$

SOLVED EXAMPLES

Example 1. Find the inverse of $A = \begin{bmatrix} 0 & 1 & 2 \\ 1 & 2 & 3 \\ 3 & 1 & 1 \end{bmatrix}$

We have

$$\begin{bmatrix} 0 & 1 & 2 \\ 1 & 2 & 3 \\ 3 & 1 & 1 \end{bmatrix} = \begin{bmatrix} 1 & 0 & 0 \\ 0 & 1 & 0 \\ 0 & 0 & 1 \end{bmatrix} A$$

R_{12}

$$\begin{bmatrix} 1 & 2 & 3 \\ 0 & 1 & 2 \\ 3 & 1 & 1 \end{bmatrix} = \begin{bmatrix} 0 & 1 & 0 \\ 1 & 0 & 0 \\ 0 & 0 & 1 \end{bmatrix} A$$

$R_3 \to R_3 - 3\,R_2$

$$\begin{bmatrix} 1 & 2 & 3 \\ 0 & 1 & 2 \\ 0 & -5 & -8 \end{bmatrix} = \begin{bmatrix} 0 & 1 & 0 \\ 1 & 0 & 0 \\ 0 & -3 & 1 \end{bmatrix} A$$

$R_2 \to R_3 + 5\,R_1$

$$\begin{bmatrix} 1 & 2 & 3 \\ 0 & 1 & 2 \\ 0 & 0 & 2 \end{bmatrix} = \begin{bmatrix} 0 & 1 & 0 \\ 1 & 0 & 0 \\ 5 & -3 & 1 \end{bmatrix} A$$

$R_2 \to R_2 - R_3$

$$\begin{bmatrix} 1 & 2 & 3 \\ 0 & 1 & 0 \\ 0 & 0 & 2 \end{bmatrix} = \begin{bmatrix} 0 & 1 & 0 \\ -4 & 3 & -1 \\ 5 & -3 & 1 \end{bmatrix} A$$

$R_3 \to \frac{1}{2} R_3$

$$\begin{bmatrix} 1 & 2 & 3 \\ 0 & 1 & 0 \\ 0 & 0 & 1 \end{bmatrix} = \begin{bmatrix} 0 & 1 & 0 \\ -4 & 3 & -1 \\ \frac{5}{2} & \frac{-3}{2} & \frac{1}{2} \end{bmatrix} A$$

$R_1 \to R_1 - 2\,R_2 - 3\,R_3$

$$\begin{bmatrix} 1 & 0 & 0 \\ 0 & 1 & 0 \\ 0 & 0 & 1 \end{bmatrix} = \begin{bmatrix} \frac{1}{2} & \frac{-1}{2} & \frac{1}{2} \\ -4 & 3 & -1 \\ \frac{5}{2} & \frac{-3}{2} & \frac{1}{2} \end{bmatrix} A$$

$$\therefore \qquad A^{-1} = \begin{bmatrix} \frac{1}{2} & \frac{-1}{2} & \frac{1}{2} \\ -4 & 3 & -1 \\ \frac{5}{2} & \frac{-3}{2} & \frac{1}{2} \end{bmatrix}$$

$$A^{-1} = \frac{1}{2}\begin{bmatrix} 1 & -1 & 1 \\ -8 & 6 & -2 \\ 5 & -3 & 1 \end{bmatrix}$$

Example 2. Find the inverse of the matrix A using elementary row operation, where.

$$A = \begin{bmatrix} 1 & -1 & 1 \\ 4 & 1 & 0 \\ 8 & 1 & 1 \end{bmatrix}$$

Solution: We have

$$\begin{bmatrix} 1 & -1 & 1 \\ 4 & 1 & 0 \\ 8 & 1 & 1 \end{bmatrix} = \begin{bmatrix} 1 & 0 & 0 \\ 0 & 1 & 0 \\ 0 & 0 & 1 \end{bmatrix} A$$

$$\begin{matrix} R_2 \to R_2 - 4\,R_1 \\ R_3 \to R_3 - 8\,R_1 \end{matrix} \begin{bmatrix} 1 & -1 & 1 \\ 0 & 5 & -4 \\ 0 & 9 & -7 \end{bmatrix} = \begin{bmatrix} 1 & 0 & 0 \\ -4 & 1 & 0 \\ -8 & 0 & 1 \end{bmatrix} A$$

$$\text{By} \quad R_3 \to R_3 - 2\,R_2 \qquad \begin{bmatrix} 1 & -1 & 1 \\ 0 & 5 & -4 \\ 0 & -1 & 1 \end{bmatrix} = \begin{bmatrix} 1 & 0 & 0 \\ -4 & 1 & 0 \\ 0 & -2 & 1 \end{bmatrix} A$$

$$\text{By} \quad R_2 \to R_2 + 4\,R_3 \qquad \begin{bmatrix} 1 & -1 & 1 \\ 0 & 1 & 0 \\ 0 & -1 & 1 \end{bmatrix} = \begin{bmatrix} 1 & 0 & 0 \\ -4 & -7 & 4 \\ 0 & -2 & 1 \end{bmatrix} A$$

By $R_3 \to R_3 + R_2$ $\begin{bmatrix} 1 & -1 & 1 \\ 0 & 1 & 0 \\ 0 & 0 & 1 \end{bmatrix} = \begin{bmatrix} 1 & 0 & 0 \\ -4 & -7 & 4 \\ -4 & -9 & 5 \end{bmatrix} A$

By $R_1 \to R_1 + R_2 - R_3$ $\begin{bmatrix} 1 & 0 & 0 \\ 0 & 1 & 0 \\ 0 & 0 & 1 \end{bmatrix} = \begin{bmatrix} 1 & 2 & -1 \\ -4 & -7 & 4 \\ -4 & -9 & 5 \end{bmatrix} A$

$\therefore$ $A^{-1} = \begin{bmatrix} 1 & 2 & -1 \\ -4 & -7 & 4 \\ -4 & -9 & 5 \end{bmatrix}.$

Minors of a matrix: Minor of a matrix A, is a determinant by taking few rows and equal number of columns of the matrix.

Thus minor of order one is a determinant obtained by taking any one row and any one column of a matrx.

Minor of order two is a determinant obtained by taking any two rows and any two columns of the matrix A.

Thus if A is a matrix of order $m \times n$

then the number of minors of order one

=No. of ways of selecting one row from m rows × No. of ways of selecting one column from n columns.

$= (mc_1)\ (n_{c1})$

No. of minors of order two $= (m_{c2})\ (n_{c2})$

....

No. of minors of order, $r = (m_{cr})\ (n_{cr})$

Rank of a matrix: If $(A)_{m \times n}$ is a matrix, then the rank of A is said to be r; if

(i) there is at least are minor of A of order r which is not zero, and

(ii) all minors of orders higher than r, are zero. It is denoted by $\rho(A)$.

Rank of a matrix does not change by elementary transformations.

1. If any two rows (or columns) of a matrix are interchanged, then the value of the determinant of the matrix does not change numerically, only its sign is changed.

2. If any row (or column) of a matrix is multiplied by a non-zero constant k than the value of the determinant of the matrix becomes k times.
3. Value of the determinant does not change when k times of any row (or column) is added to another row (or column).

Thus, we can say that the rank of a matrix does not change by elementary transformations.

Example 3. Find the rank of the matrix A given by:

$$A = \begin{bmatrix} 1 & 2 & 3 \\ 2 & 3 & 4 \\ 3 & 4 & 5 \end{bmatrix}$$

Solution:

$$A = \begin{bmatrix} 1 & 2 & 3 \\ 2 & 3 & 4 \\ 3 & 4 & 5 \end{bmatrix}$$

$$\begin{matrix} R_2 \to R_2 - 2R_1 \\ R_3 \to R_3 - 3R_1 \end{matrix} \quad \begin{bmatrix} 1 & 2 & 3 \\ 0 & -1 & -2 \\ 0 & -2 & -4 \end{bmatrix}$$

$$R_3 \to R_3 - 2R_2 \quad \begin{bmatrix} 1 & 2 & 3 \\ 0 & -1 & -2 \\ 0 & 0 & 0 \end{bmatrix}$$

we have $$M_{11} = \begin{bmatrix} -1 & -2 \\ 0 & 0 \end{bmatrix} = 0$$

$$M_{31} = \begin{bmatrix} 2 & 3 \\ -1 & -2 \end{bmatrix} = -4 + 3 = -1 \neq 0$$

$\therefore$ the rank of $A = 2$

or $\rho(A) = 2$.

Example 4. Find the rank of the matrix.

$$A = \begin{bmatrix} 5 & 3 & 14 & 4 \\ 0 & 1 & 2 & 1 \\ 1 & -1 & 2 & 0 \end{bmatrix}$$

Solution:

$$A = \begin{bmatrix} 5 & 3 & 14 & 4 \\ 0 & 1 & 2 & 1 \\ 1 & -1 & 2 & 0 \end{bmatrix}$$

By R_{13}

$$A = \begin{bmatrix} 1 & -1 & 2 & 0 \\ 0 & 1 & 2 & 1 \\ 5 & 3 & 14 & 4 \end{bmatrix}$$

$$= \begin{bmatrix} 1 & -1 & 2 & 0 \\ 0 & 1 & 2 & 1 \\ 0 & 8 & 4 & 4 \end{bmatrix} \text{by } R_3 \to R_3 - 5R_1$$

$$= \begin{bmatrix} 1 & -1 & 2 & 0 \\ 0 & 1 & 2 & 1 \\ 0 & 0 & -12 & -4 \end{bmatrix} \text{by } R_3 \to R_3 - 8R_2$$

Thus, matrix is in triangular form and we can not make more zeroes in the third row without disturbing the zeroes, made already, so there exist minors of order three, whose values are non-zero.

$\therefore$ rank is 3

or $\rho\ (A) = 3.$

Example 5. Find the rank of the matrix A given by:

$$A = \begin{bmatrix} 1 & 1 & 1 & 1 \\ 1 & 3 & -2 & 1 \\ 2 & 0 & -3 & 2 \\ 3 & 3 & 0 & 3 \end{bmatrix}$$

Solution: Here

$$A = \begin{bmatrix} 1 & 1 & 1 & 1 \\ 1 & 3 & -2 & 1 \\ 2 & 0 & -3 & 2 \\ 3 & 3 & 0 & 3 \end{bmatrix}$$

$$= \begin{bmatrix} 1 & 1 & 1 & 1 \\ 0 & 2 & -3 & 0 \\ 0 & -2 & -5 & 0 \\ 0 & 0 & -3 & 0 \end{bmatrix} \text{ by } \begin{array}{l} R_2 \to R_2 - R_1 \\ R_3 \to R_3 - 2R_1 \\ R_4 \to R_4 - 3R_1 \end{array}$$

$$= \begin{bmatrix} 1 & 1 & 1 & 1 \\ 0 & 2 & -3 & 0 \\ 0 & 0 & -8 & 0 \\ 0 & 0 & -3 & 0 \end{bmatrix} \text{ by } R_3 \to R_3 + R_2$$

$$= \begin{bmatrix} 1 & 1 & 1 & 1 \\ 0 & 2 & -3 & 0 \\ 0 & 0 & -8 & 0 \\ 0 & 0 & 0 & 0 \end{bmatrix} \text{ by } R_4 \to R_4 - \frac{3}{8} R_3$$

From the above matrix, we can have non-zero minors of third order only.

$\therefore \qquad \rho(A) = 3.$

Example 6. Find the rank of the matrix

$$A = \begin{bmatrix} 1 & 1 & 1 \\ a & b & c \\ a^3 & b^3 & c^3 \end{bmatrix}$$

where $a, b, c \in R$.

Solution:

Here $\qquad |A| = \begin{vmatrix} 1 & 1 & 1 \\ a & b & c \\ a^3 & b^3 & c^3 \end{vmatrix}$

$$= (a-b)(b-c)(c-a)(a+b+c).$$

Now, the rank will depend upon the values of a, b and c.

Case I. When a, b, c all are different and $a+b+c \neq 0$.

$|A| \neq 0$, then the rank is 3.

$\therefore \qquad \rho(A) = 3.$

Case II. When a, b, c all are different but $a+b+c = 0$.

$\therefore \rho(A) \neq 3$, then there is a minor

$$\begin{vmatrix} 1 & 1 \\ a & b \end{vmatrix} \neq 0 \cdot$$

$\therefore$ $\rho\ (A) = 2$

Case III: When two of the numbers a,b,c are equal and different from the third. $|A| = 0$

Let $a = b \neq c$, then

$$\begin{vmatrix} 1 & 1 \\ a & c \end{vmatrix} \neq 0 \cdot$$

then $\rho\ (A) = 2$

Case IV. It $a = b = c$, Then all the miniors of order three and two are zero.

Therefore $\rho\ (A) = 1$.

Normal form of a matrix: By a series of elementary transformations any non-zero matrix A can be reduced to

$$[I_r], [I_r;0], \begin{bmatrix} I_r \\ 0 \end{bmatrix}, or \begin{bmatrix} I_r & 0 \\ 0 & 0 \end{bmatrix} \text{ from}$$

Where I_r is identity matrix of order r and 0 denotes the null matrix of any order. These forms of a matrix A are called the normal form or canonical form of the matrix A.

Example 7. Reduce the matrix $\begin{bmatrix} 5 & 3 & 14 & 4 \\ 0 & 1 & 2 & 1 \\ 1 & -1 & 2 & 0 \end{bmatrix}$

to normal form by E–transformations and hence determine its rank.

Solution:

$$A = \begin{bmatrix} 5 & 3 & 14 & 4 \\ 0 & 1 & 2 & 1 \\ 1 & -1 & 2 & 0 \end{bmatrix}$$

$$= \begin{bmatrix} 1 & -1 & 2 & 0 \\ 0 & 1 & 2 & 1 \\ 5 & 3 & 14 & 4 \end{bmatrix} \text{ by } R_{13}$$

$$= \begin{bmatrix} 1 & -1 & 2 & 0 \\ 0 & 1 & 2 & 1 \\ 0 & 8 & 4 & 4 \end{bmatrix} \text{ by } R_3 \to R_3 - 5R_1$$

$$= \begin{bmatrix} 1 & -1 & 2 & 0 \\ 0 & 1 & 2 & 1 \\ 0 & 0 & -12 & -4 \end{bmatrix} \text{ by } R_3 \to R_3 - 8R_2$$

$$= \begin{bmatrix} 1 & 0 & 0 & 0 \\ 0 & 1 & 2 & 1 \\ 0 & 0 & -12 & -4 \end{bmatrix} \text{ by } C_2 \to C_2 + C_1 \cdot C_3 \to C_3 - 2C_1$$

$$= \begin{bmatrix} 1 & 0 & 0 & 0 \\ 0 & 1 & 0 & 0 \\ 0 & 0 & -12 & -4 \end{bmatrix} \text{ by } C_3 \to C_3 - 2C_2, C_4 \to C_4 - C_2$$

$$= \begin{bmatrix} 1 & 0 & 0 & 0 \\ 0 & 1 & 0 & 0 \\ 0 & 0 & 1 & -4 \end{bmatrix} \text{ by } C_3 \to \frac{-1}{12} C_3$$

$$= \begin{bmatrix} 1 & 0 & 0 & 0 \\ 0 & 1 & 0 & 0 \\ 0 & 0 & 1 & 0 \end{bmatrix} \qquad \text{by } C_4 \to C_4 + 4C_3$$

This is the normal or canonical from of the matrix A, and hence its rank is 3

$\therefore \qquad \rho(A) = 3.$

Example 8. For the matrix $A = \begin{bmatrix} 1 & 1 & 2 \\ 1 & 2 & 3 \\ 0 & -1 & -1 \end{bmatrix}$

Find non singular matrices P and Q such that PAQ is in normal form.

Solution:

We have $\qquad A = I\,A\,I.$

or $$\begin{bmatrix} 1 & 1 & 2 \\ 1 & 2 & 3 \\ 0 & -1 & -1 \end{bmatrix} = \begin{bmatrix} 1 & 0 & 0 \\ 0 & 1 & 0 \\ 0 & 0 & 1 \end{bmatrix} A \begin{bmatrix} 1 & 0 & 0 \\ 0 & 1 & 0 \\ 0 & 0 & 1 \end{bmatrix}$$

operating $$C_2 \to C_2 - C_1$$ $$C_3 \to C_3 - 2C_1$$

we have

$$\begin{bmatrix} 1 & 0 & 0 \\ 1 & 1 & 1 \\ 0 & -1 & -1 \end{bmatrix} = \begin{bmatrix} 1 & 0 & 0 \\ 0 & 1 & 0 \\ 0 & 0 & 1 \end{bmatrix} A \begin{bmatrix} 1 & -1 & -2 \\ 0 & 1 & 0 \\ 0 & 0 & 1 \end{bmatrix}$$

operating $R_2 \to R_2 - R_1$,

we have

$$\begin{bmatrix} 1 & 0 & 0 \\ 0 & 1 & 1 \\ 0 & -1 & -1 \end{bmatrix} = \begin{bmatrix} 1 & 0 & 0 \\ -1 & 1 & 0 \\ 0 & 0 & 1 \end{bmatrix} A \begin{bmatrix} 1 & -1 & -2 \\ 0 & 1 & 0 \\ 0 & 0 & 1 \end{bmatrix}$$

oberating $C_3 \to C_3 - C_2$,

we have

$$\begin{bmatrix} 1 & 0 & 0 \\ 0 & 1 & 0 \\ 0 & -1 & 0 \end{bmatrix} = \begin{bmatrix} 1 & 0 & 0 \\ -1 & 1 & 0 \\ 0 & 0 & 1 \end{bmatrix} A \begin{bmatrix} 1 & -1 & -1 \\ 0 & 1 & -1 \\ 0 & 0 & 1 \end{bmatrix}$$

operating $R_3 \to R_3 + R_2$,

we have

$$\begin{bmatrix} 1 & 0 & 0 \\ 0 & 1 & 0 \\ 0 & 0 & 0 \end{bmatrix} = \begin{bmatrix} 1 & 0 & 0 \\ -1 & 1 & 0 \\ -1 & 1 & 1 \end{bmatrix} A \begin{bmatrix} 1 & -1 & -1 \\ 0 & 1 & -1 \\ 0 & 0 & 1 \end{bmatrix}$$

is the required normal form of the given matrix A.

where $$P = \begin{bmatrix} 1 & 0 & 0 \\ -1 & 1 & 0 \\ -1 & 1 & 1 \end{bmatrix}$$ and

$$Q = \begin{bmatrix} 1 & -1 & -1 \\ 0 & 1 & -1 \\ 0 & 0 & 1 \end{bmatrix}$$

Example 9. Find two non singular matrices P and Q such that PAQ is in normal form, where $A = \begin{bmatrix} 1 & 2 & 3 & -2 \\ 2 & -2 & 1 & 3 \\ 3 & 0 & 4 & 1 \end{bmatrix}$.

Solution: Here, the matrix A is of 3×4 order. So we take pre multiplier of A an identity matrix of order 3 and post multiplier as of order 4.

$$\therefore \quad \begin{bmatrix} 1 & 2 & 3 & -2 \\ 2 & -2 & 1 & 3 \\ 3 & 0 & 4 & 1 \end{bmatrix} = \begin{bmatrix} 1 & 0 & 0 \\ 0 & 1 & 0 \\ 0 & 0 & 1 \end{bmatrix} A \begin{bmatrix} 1 & 0 & 0 & 0 \\ 0 & 1 & 0 & 0 \\ 0 & 0 & 1 & 0 \\ 0 & 0 & 0 & 1 \end{bmatrix}$$

By $R_2 \to R_2 - 2R_1$, $R_3 \to R_3 - 3R_1$

$$\begin{bmatrix} 1 & 2 & 3 & -2 \\ 0 & -6 & -5 & 7 \\ 0 & -6 & -5 & 7 \end{bmatrix} = \begin{bmatrix} 1 & 0 & 0 \\ -2 & 1 & 0 \\ -3 & 0 & 1 \end{bmatrix} A \begin{bmatrix} 1 & 0 & 0 & 0 \\ 0 & 1 & 0 & 0 \\ 0 & 0 & 1 & 0 \\ 0 & 0 & 0 & 1 \end{bmatrix}$$

By $R_3 \to R_3 - R_2$

$$\begin{bmatrix} 1 & 2 & 3 & -2 \\ 0 & -6 & -5 & 7 \\ 0 & 0 & 0 & 0 \end{bmatrix} = \begin{bmatrix} 1 & 0 & 0 \\ -2 & 1 & 0 \\ -1 & -1 & 1 \end{bmatrix} A \begin{bmatrix} 1 & 0 & 0 & 0 \\ 0 & 1 & 0 & 0 \\ 0 & 0 & 1 & 0 \\ 0 & 0 & 0 & 1 \end{bmatrix}$$

By $C_2 \to C_2 - C_3$

$$\begin{bmatrix} 1 & -1 & 3 & -2 \\ 0 & -1 & -5 & 7 \\ 0 & 0 & 0 & 0 \end{bmatrix} = \begin{bmatrix} 1 & 0 & 0 \\ -2 & 1 & 0 \\ -1 & -1 & 1 \end{bmatrix} A \begin{bmatrix} 1 & 0 & 0 & 0 \\ 0 & 1 & 0 & 0 \\ 0 & -1 & 1 & 0 \\ 0 & 0 & 0 & 1 \end{bmatrix}$$

By $C_3 \to C_3 - 5C_2$, $C_4 \to C_4 + 7C_2$

$$\begin{bmatrix} 1 & -1 & 8 & -9 \\ 0 & -1 & 0 & 0 \\ 0 & 0 & 0 & 0 \end{bmatrix} = \begin{bmatrix} 1 & 0 & 0 \\ -2 & 1 & 0 \\ -1 & -1 & 1 \end{bmatrix} A \begin{bmatrix} 1 & 0 & 0 & 0 \\ 0 & 1 & -5 & 7 \\ 0 & -1 & 6 & -7 \\ 0 & 0 & 0 & 1 \end{bmatrix}$$

By $C_2 \to C_2 + C_1$, $C_3 \to C_3 - 8C_1$, $C_4 \to C_4 + 9C_1$

$$\begin{bmatrix} 1 & 0 & 0 & 0 \\ 0 & -1 & 0 & 0 \\ 0 & 0 & 0 & 0 \end{bmatrix} = \begin{bmatrix} 1 & 0 & 0 \\ -2 & 1 & 0 \\ -1 & -1 & 1 \end{bmatrix} A \begin{bmatrix} 1 & 1 & -8 & 9 \\ 0 & 1 & -5 & 7 \\ 0 & -1 & 6 & -7 \\ 0 & 0 & 0 & 1 \end{bmatrix}$$

By $R_2 \to (-1)R_2$

$$\begin{bmatrix} 1 & 0 & 0 & 0 \\ 0 & 1 & 0 & 0 \\ 0 & 0 & 0 & 0 \end{bmatrix} = \begin{bmatrix} 1 & 0 & 0 \\ 2 & -1 & 0 \\ -1 & -1 & 0 \end{bmatrix} A \begin{bmatrix} 1 & 1 & -8 & 9 \\ 0 & 1 & -5 & 7 \\ 0 & -1 & 6 & -7 \\ 0 & 0 & 0 & 1 \end{bmatrix}$$

The matrix on L.H.S. is in normal form,

$$\therefore \qquad P = \begin{bmatrix} 1 & 0 & 0 \\ 2 & -1 & 0 \\ -1 & -1 & 0 \end{bmatrix}$$

$$\text{and} \qquad Q = \begin{bmatrix} 1 & 1 & -8 & 9 \\ 0 & 1 & -5 & 7 \\ 0 & -1 & 6 & -7 \\ 0 & 0 & 0 & 1 \end{bmatrix}$$

are the required matrices

EXERCISE

Find the inverse of the following matrices by E–row operations for the question from 1–6.

1. $A = \begin{bmatrix} 1 & 3 & 3 \\ 1 & 4 & 3 \\ 1 & 3 & 4 \end{bmatrix}$ **Ans.** $\begin{bmatrix} 7 & -3 & -3 \\ -1 & 1 & 0 \\ -1 & 0 & 1 \end{bmatrix}$

2. $A = \begin{bmatrix} 1 & 1 & 1 & 1 \\ 1 & 2 & 3 & 4 \\ 1 & 3 & 6 & 10 \\ 1 & 4 & 10 & 20 \end{bmatrix}$ **Ans.** $\begin{bmatrix} 4 & -6 & 4 & -1 \\ -6 & 14 & -11 & 3 \\ 4 & -11 & 10 & -3 \\ -1 & 3 & -3 & 1 \end{bmatrix}$

3. $A = \begin{bmatrix} 8 & 4 & -3 \\ 2 & 1 & 1 \\ 1 & 2 & 1 \end{bmatrix}$ **Ans.** $\frac{1}{21}\begin{bmatrix} 1 & 10 & -7 \\ 1 & -11 & 14 \\ -3 & 12 & 0 \end{bmatrix}$

4. $A = \begin{bmatrix} 7 & 6 & -2 \\ -1 & 2 & 4 \\ 3 & 6 & 8 \end{bmatrix}$ **Ans.** $\frac{1}{20}\begin{bmatrix} -4 & -18 & 10 \\ 10 & 25 & -15 \\ -6 & -12 & 10 \end{bmatrix}$

5. $A = \begin{bmatrix} 4 & 3 & 3 \\ -1 & 0 & -1 \\ -4 & -4 & -3 \end{bmatrix}$ **Ans.** $\begin{bmatrix} 4 & 3 & 3 \\ -1 & 0 & -1 \\ -4 & -4 & -3 \end{bmatrix}$

6. $\text{A} = \begin{bmatrix} 2 & 2 & -1 \\ -2 & 3 & 1 \\ 4 & 2 & -1 \end{bmatrix}$ **Ans.** $\frac{1}{10}\begin{bmatrix} -5 & 0 & 5 \\ 2 & 2 & 0 \\ -16 & 4 & 10 \end{bmatrix}$

Find of rank of the matrices in the questions from 7-9.

7. $\text{A} = \begin{bmatrix} 1 & 2 & 3 \\ 2 & 1 & 0 \\ 0 & 1 & 2 \end{bmatrix}$

Ans. $\rho\,(A) = 2.$

8. $\text{A} = \begin{bmatrix} 1 & 2 & 3 & 0 \\ 2 & 4 & 3 & 2 \\ 3 & 2 & 1 & 3 \\ 6 & 8 & 7 & 5 \end{bmatrix}$

Ans. $\rho\,(A) = 3.$

9. $A = \begin{bmatrix} 0 & 1 & -3 & -1 \\ 1 & 0 & 1 & 1 \\ 3 & 1 & 0 & 2 \\ 1 & 1 & -2 & 0 \end{bmatrix}$

Ans. $\rho\,(A) = 2.$

10. Reduce the matrix A to normal form and then find its rank.

$$A = \begin{bmatrix} 1 & 1 & 2 & 3 \\ 1 & 3 & 0 & 3 \\ 1 & -2 & -3 & -3 \\ 1 & 1 & 2 & 3 \end{bmatrix}$$

Ans. $\rho\,(A) = 3.$

11. For the matrix matrices A and B, find two matrices P& Q such that Cs PBQ is in normal form.

$$A = \begin{bmatrix} 3 & -3 & 4 \\ 2 & -3 & 4 \\ 0 & -1 & 1 \end{bmatrix} \qquad B = \begin{bmatrix} 2 & 1 & -3 & -6 \\ 3 & -3 & 1 & 2 \\ 1 & 1 & 1 & 2 \end{bmatrix}$$

$$P = \begin{bmatrix} 1 & -1 & 0 \\ 0 & 1 & -4 \\ 0 & 0 & 1 \end{bmatrix} \qquad P = \begin{bmatrix} 0 & 0 & 1 \\ -1 & 0 & 2 \\ \frac{-3}{14} & \frac{1}{28} & \frac{9}{28} \end{bmatrix}$$

$$Q = \begin{bmatrix} 1 & 0 & 0 \\ -2 & 1 & 0 \\ -2 & 1 & 1 \end{bmatrix} \qquad Q = \begin{bmatrix} 1 & -1 & 4 & 0 \\ 0 & 1 & -5 & 0 \\ 0 & 0 & 1 & -2 \\ 0 & 0 & 0 & 1 \end{bmatrix}$$

Solution of the system of linear non-homogeneous equations.

Let us consider the system of m linear equations in n unknowns x_1, x_2, x_3 ... x_n given by

$$a_{11}\,x_1 + a_{12}\,x_2 + \ldots + a_{1n}\,x_n = b_1$$

$$a_{21}\,x_1 + a_{22}\,x_2 + \ldots + a_{2n}\,x_n = b_2$$

....

....

$a_{m1} x_1 + a_{m2} x_2 + \ldots\ldots\ldots\ldots + a_{mn} x_n = b_m$

or
$$\begin{bmatrix} a_{11} & a_{12} & . & a_{1n} \\ a_{21} & a_{22} & . & a_{2n} \\ . & . & . & . \\ . & . & . & . \\ a_{m1} & a_{m2} & . & a_{mn} \end{bmatrix} \begin{bmatrix} x_1 \\ x_2 \\ x_3 \\ . \\ . \\ x_n \end{bmatrix} = \begin{bmatrix} b_1 \\ b_2 \\ b_3 \\ . \\ . \\ b_m \end{bmatrix}$$

or $$AX = B$$

where
$$A = \begin{bmatrix} a_{11} & a_{12} & . & a_{1n} \\ a_{21} & a_{22} & . & a_{2n} \\ . & . & . & . \\ . & . & . & . \\ a_{m1} & a_{m2} & . & a_{mn} \end{bmatrix}$$

$$X = \begin{bmatrix} x_1 \\ x_2 \\ x_3 \\ . \\ . \\ x_n \end{bmatrix}, B = \begin{bmatrix} b_1 \\ b_2 \\ b_3 \\ . \\ . \\ b_m \end{bmatrix}$$

The matrix $[A]_{m \times n}$ is augmented with $[B]_{m\times 1}$, we denote it by D

$\therefore$ $$D = [A : B]$$

Then the, order of the matrix D is $m \times (n + 1)$.

Consistency of the system of equations

(i) The system of equations $AX = B$, is consistent, *i.e.*, has solution if

$$\rho (A) = P (D).$$

(ii) The system of equations $AX = \text{B}$ is inconsistent if $\rho (A) \neq \rho (D)$.

Solution when the system of equations is consistent

(*a*) It $\rho(A) = \rho(D) =$ No. of unknowns, then the system has a unique solution.

(*b*) It $\rho(A) = \rho(D) <$ No. of unknowns, then the system of equations has an infinite number of solutions.

SOLVED EXAMPLES

Example 1. Test the following system of equations for consistency and solve, if found consistent.

$$5x + 3y + 7z = 4$$
$$3x + 26y + 2z = 9$$
$$7x + 2y + 10z = 5$$

Solution: The given system of equations can be written as $AX = B$

Where

$$A = \begin{bmatrix} 5 & 3 & 7 \\ 3 & 26 & 2 \\ 7 & 2 & 10 \end{bmatrix}$$

$$X = \begin{bmatrix} x \\ y \\ z \end{bmatrix}, B = \begin{bmatrix} 4 \\ 9 \\ 5 \end{bmatrix}$$

For the above system, the augmented matrix is

$$D = [A : B] = \begin{bmatrix} 5 & 3 & 7 & : & 4 \\ 3 & 26 & 2 & : & 9 \\ 7 & 2 & 10 & : & 5 \end{bmatrix}$$

$$= \begin{bmatrix} 5 & 3 & 7 & : & 4 \\ 3 & 26 & 2 & : & 9 \\ 1 & -50 & 6 & : & -13 \end{bmatrix} \text{ by } R_3 \to R_3 - 2R_2$$

$$= \begin{bmatrix} 1 & -50 & 6 & : & -13 \\ 3 & 26 & 2 & : & 9 \\ 5 & 3 & 7 & : & 4 \end{bmatrix} \text{ by } R_{13}$$

$$= \begin{bmatrix} 1 & -50 & 6 & : & -13 \\ 0 & 176 & -16 & : & 48 \\ 0 & 253 & -23 & : & 69 \end{bmatrix} \text{ by } \begin{array}{l} R_2 \to R_2 - 3R_1 \\ R_3 \to R_3 - 5R_1 \end{array}$$

$$= \begin{bmatrix} 1 & -50 & 6 & : & -13 \\ 0 & 11 & -1 & : & 3 \\ 0 & 11 & -1 & : & 3 \end{bmatrix} \text{ by } \begin{array}{l} R_2 \to \frac{1}{16} R_2 \\ R_3 \to \frac{1}{23} R_3 \end{array}$$

$$= \begin{bmatrix} 1 & -50 & 6 & : & -13 \\ 0 & 11 & -1 & : & 3 \\ 0 & 0 & 0 & : & 0 \end{bmatrix} \text{ by } R_3 \to R_3 - R_2$$

$\therefore \quad \rho(A) = 2, \rho(D) = 2.$

$\therefore \quad \rho(A) = \rho(D) <$ No. of unknowns

Thus, the system of equations is consistent and has infinitely many solutions.

Re-writing the above system of equations, we have

$$\begin{bmatrix} 1 & -50 & 6 \\ 0 & 11 & -1 \\ 0 & 0 & 0 \end{bmatrix} \begin{bmatrix} x \\ y \\ z \end{bmatrix} = \begin{bmatrix} -13 \\ 3 \\ 0 \end{bmatrix}$$

$\therefore \quad x - 50y + 6z = -13$

$11y - z = 3$

Let $\quad z = k.$

$\therefore \quad 11y - k = 3$

$\because \quad 11y = 3 + k$

$\therefore \quad y = \dfrac{3+k}{11}$

$\because \quad x - 50y + 6z = -13$

$\therefore \quad x - 50\left[\dfrac{9+k}{11}\right] + 6k = -13$

$\because \quad 11x - 150 - 50k + 66k = -143$

$\therefore \quad 11x = 7 - 16k$

$\because \quad x = \dfrac{-16}{11}k + \dfrac{7}{11}.$

$\because$ the solution is $$x = \frac{-16}{11}k + \frac{7}{11}$$

$$y = \frac{3+k}{11}$$

$$z = k.$$

Example 2. Test the following system of equations for consistency and solve, if found consistent.

$$3x + 3y + 2z = 1$$
$$x + 2y + 0z = 4$$
$$x + 10y + 3z = -2$$
$$2x - 3y - z = 5$$

Solution: For the above system of equations, we have

$$A = \begin{bmatrix} 3 & 3 & 2 \\ 1 & 2 & 0 \\ 0 & 10 & 3 \\ 2 & -3 & -1 \end{bmatrix}, x = \begin{bmatrix} x \\ y \\ z \end{bmatrix}, B = \begin{bmatrix} 1 \\ 4 \\ -2 \\ 5 \end{bmatrix}$$

$\therefore$ Augmented matrix

$$D = [A : B]$$

$$= \begin{bmatrix} 3 & 3 & 2 & : & 1 \\ 1 & 2 & 0 & : & 4 \\ 0 & 10 & 3 & : & -2 \\ 2 & -3 & -1 & : & 5 \end{bmatrix}$$

$$= \begin{bmatrix} 1 & 2 & 0 & : & 4 \\ 3 & 3 & 2 & : & 1 \\ 0 & 10 & 3 & : & -2 \\ 2 & -3 & -1 & : & 5 \end{bmatrix} \text{ by } R_{12}$$

$$= \begin{bmatrix} 1 & 2 & 0 & : & 4 \\ 0 & -3 & 2 & : & -11 \\ 0 & 10 & 3 & : & -2 \\ 0 & -7 & -1 & : & -3 \end{bmatrix} \text{ by } \begin{array}{l} R_2 \to R_2 - 3R_1 \\ R_4 \to R_4 - 2R_1 \end{array}$$

$$= \begin{bmatrix} 1 & 2 & 0 & : & 4 \\ 0 & -3 & 2 & : & -11 \\ 0 & 1 & 9 & : & -35 \\ 0 & -1 & -5 & : & 19 \end{bmatrix} \text{ by } \begin{array}{l} R_3 \to R_3 + 3R_2 \\ R_4 \to R_4 - 2R_2 \end{array}$$

$$= \begin{bmatrix} 1 & 2 & 0 & : & 4 \\ 0 & 1 & 9 & : & -35 \\ 0 & -3 & 2 & : & -11 \\ 0 & -1 & -5 & : & 19 \end{bmatrix} \text{ by } R_{23}$$

$$= \begin{bmatrix} 1 & 2 & 0 & : & 4 \\ 0 & 1 & 9 & : & -35 \\ 0 & 0 & 29 & : & -116 \\ 0 & 0 & 4 & : & -16 \end{bmatrix} \text{ by } \begin{array}{l} R_3 \to R_3 + 3R_2 \\ R_4 \to R_4 + R_2 \end{array}$$

$$= \begin{bmatrix} 1 & 2 & 0 & : & 4 \\ 0 & 1 & 9 & : & -35 \\ 0 & 0 & 1 & : & -4 \\ 0 & 0 & 1 & : & -4 \end{bmatrix} \text{ by } \begin{array}{l} R_3 \to \frac{1}{29} R_3 \\ R_4 \to \frac{1}{4} R_4 \end{array}$$

$$= \begin{bmatrix} 1 & 2 & 0 & : & 4 \\ 0 & 1 & 9 & : & -35 \\ 0 & 0 & 1 & : & -4 \\ 0 & 0 & 0 & : & 0 \end{bmatrix} \text{ by } R_4 \to R_4 - R_3$$

Thus, the rank of $A = 3$

and $\rho(D) = 3$

$\therefore$ $\rho(A) = \rho(D) =$ No. of unknowns.

Thus, the system of equations is consistent and has a unique solution.

Given by

$$\begin{bmatrix} 1 & 2 & 0 \\ 0 & 1 & 9 \\ 0 & 0 & 1 \end{bmatrix} \begin{bmatrix} x \\ y \\ z \end{bmatrix} = \begin{bmatrix} 4 \\ -35 \\ -4 \end{bmatrix}$$

$\therefore$ $x + 2y + 0z = 4$

$$y + 9z = -35$$

$$z = -4$$

$\therefore$ $y = 1$

and $x = 4 - 2 = 2$

$\therefore$ The solution is

$$x = 2, y = 1, z = -4.$$

Example 3. Test the following system of equations for consistency and solve if found consistent.

$$2x + 19y - 47z = 32$$

$$3x + y - 3z = 13$$

$$2x - 3y + 7z = 5$$

Solution: For the above system of equations, we have

$$A = \begin{bmatrix} 2 & 19 & -47 \\ 3 & 1 & -3 \\ 2 & -3 & 7 \end{bmatrix}, X = \begin{bmatrix} x \\ y \\ z \end{bmatrix}, B = \begin{bmatrix} 32 \\ 13 \\ 5 \end{bmatrix}$$

$$\therefore \quad D = \begin{bmatrix} 2 & 19 & -47 & : & 32 \\ 3 & 1 & -3 & : & 13 \\ 2 & -3 & 7 & : & 5 \end{bmatrix} \text{ by } R_{12}$$

$$= \begin{bmatrix} 3 & 1 & -3 & : & 13 \\ 2 & 19 & -47 & : & 32 \\ 2 & -3 & 7 & : & 5 \end{bmatrix} \text{ by } \begin{array}{l} R_1 \to R_1 - R_3 \\ R_2 \to R_2 - R_3 \end{array}$$

$$= \begin{bmatrix} 1 & 4 & -10 & : & 8 \\ 0 & 22 & -54 & : & 27 \\ 2 & -3 & 7 & : & 5 \end{bmatrix} \text{ by } R_3 \to R_3 - 2R_1$$

$$= \begin{bmatrix} 1 & 4 & -10 & : & 8 \\ 0 & 22 & -54 & : & 27 \\ 0 & -11 & 27 & : & -11 \end{bmatrix} \text{ by } R_{23}$$

$$= \begin{bmatrix} 1 & 4 & -10 & : & 8 \\ 0 & -11 & 27 & : & -11 \\ 0 & 22 & -54 & : & 27 \end{bmatrix} \text{ by } R_3 \to R_3 + 2R_2$$

$$= \begin{bmatrix} 1 & 4 & -10 & & 8 \\ 0 & -11 & 27 & & -11 \\ 0 & 0 & 0 & : & 5 \end{bmatrix} \text{ by } R_3 \to R_3 + 2\,R_2$$

$\therefore \quad P\,(A) = 2.\ P\,(D) = 3$

$\therefore \quad P\,(\text{A}) \neq P\,(D)$

$\therefore$ The system of equation is inconsistent.

Example 4. Find the values of p and q so that the system of equations

$$2x + 3y + 5z = 9$$

$$7x + 3y - 2z = 8$$

$$2x + 3y + pz = q \qquad \text{has}$$

(i) a unique solution

(ii) an infinite number of solutions

(iii) no solution.

Solution: For the above system of equations, we have

$$A = \begin{bmatrix} 2 & 3 & 5 \\ 7 & 3 & -2 \\ 2 & 3 & p \end{bmatrix}, X = \begin{bmatrix} x \\ y \\ z \end{bmatrix}, B = \begin{bmatrix} 9 \\ 8 \\ q \end{bmatrix}$$

$\therefore \quad D = [A : B]$

$$= \begin{bmatrix} 2 & 3 & 5 & : & 9 \\ 7 & 3 & -2 & : & 8 \\ 2 & 3 & p & : & q \end{bmatrix} \text{ by } R_{12}$$

$$= \begin{bmatrix} 7 & 3 & -2 & : & 8 \\ 2 & 3 & 5 & : & 9 \\ 2 & 3 & p & : & q \end{bmatrix} \text{ by } R_1 \to R_1 - 3\,R_2$$

$$= \begin{bmatrix} 1 & -6 & -17 & : & -19 \\ 2 & 3 & 5 & : & 9 \\ 2 & 3 & p & : & q \end{bmatrix} \text{ by } R_3 \to R_3 - R_2$$

$$= \begin{bmatrix} 1 & -6 & -17 & : & -19 \\ 2 & 3 & 5 & : & 9 \\ 0 & 0 & p-5 & : & q-9 \end{bmatrix} \text{ by } R_2 \to R_2 - 2R_1$$

$$= \begin{bmatrix} 1 & -6 & -17 & : & -19 \\ 0 & 15 & 39 & : & 47 \\ 0 & 0 & p-5 & : & q-9 \end{bmatrix}$$

Now for

(i) unique solution.

$$\rho\ (A) = \rho\ (D) = \text{No. of unknowns} = 3$$

$$\Rightarrow P - 5 \neq 0$$

$$\Rightarrow P \neq 5, \text{ whatever be } q.$$

$\therefore$ The system has unique solution.

when $\quad p \neq 5.$

(ii) For infinitely many solutions

$$P\ (A) = P\ (D) < \text{No. of unknown } (=3)$$

For that $\quad \rho(A) = \rho(D) < 3$

for that $\quad p = 5, q = 9.$

(iii) For no. solution P (A) < P(D)

$$\Rightarrow p = 5, q \neq 9.$$

Example 5. For what values of λ, does the following system of equations have a solution and hence find the corresponding solutions.

$$x + y + z = 1$$

$$x + 2y + 4z = \lambda$$

$$x + 4y + 10z = \lambda^2$$

Solution: For the above system of equations

$$D = [A : B] = \begin{bmatrix} 1 & 1 & 1 & 1 \\ 1 & 2 & 4 & \lambda \\ 1 & 4 & 10 & \lambda^2 \end{bmatrix} \text{ by } \begin{array}{l} R_2 \to R_2 - R_1 \\ R_3 \to R_3 - R_1 \end{array}$$

$$= \begin{bmatrix} 1 & 1 & 1 & 1 \\ 0 & 1 & 3 & \lambda - 1 \\ 0 & 3 & 9 & \lambda^2 - 1 \end{bmatrix} \text{ by } R_3 \to R_3 - 3R_2$$

$$= \begin{bmatrix} 1 & 1 & 1 & 1 \\ 0 & 1 & 3 & \lambda - 1 \\ 0 & 0 & 0 & \lambda^2 - 3\lambda + 2 \end{bmatrix}$$

The given system of equations has a solution if $\lambda^2 - 3\lambda + 2 = 0$

or $(\lambda - 1)(\lambda - 2) = 0$

$\therefore$ $\lambda = 1, 2.$

so, when $\lambda = 1$, we have

$$\begin{bmatrix} 1 & 1 & 1 \\ 0 & 1 & 3 \end{bmatrix} \begin{bmatrix} x \\ y \\ z \end{bmatrix} = \begin{bmatrix} 1 \\ 0 \end{bmatrix}$$

$\therefore$ $x + y + z = 1$

and $y + 3z = 0$

Let $z = k$

$\therefore$ $y = -3k$

$\therefore$ $x = 1 + 2k.$

for $\lambda = 1$

$\therefore$ The solution is $x = 1 + 2k$, $y = -3k$, $z = k$.

Similarly for $\lambda = 2$.

The solution is $x = 2k$, $y = 1-3k$, $z = k$.

EXERCISE

Test the following systems of equations for consistency and solve, if consistent, for *Q*. No. 1–5.

1. $x + 2y + 3z = 6$

   $2x + 3y + \ = 11$

   $4x + y - 5z = -3$

Ans. Consistent and the solution is

$$x = \frac{-16}{5},\ y = \frac{29}{5},\ z = \frac{-4}{5}.$$

$4x - 2y + 6z = 8$

2. $x + y - 3z = -1$

   $15x - 3y + 9z = 21$

Ans. Consistent and the solution is
$x = 1$, $y = 3k$-2, $z = k$.

$$\begin{aligned} x - 2y - z &= 5 \\ x + 8y - 3z &= -1 \\ 2x + y - 3z &= 7 \end{aligned}$$
3.

Ans. Consistent and the solution is

$$x = \frac{7k+19}{5},\ y = \frac{k-3}{5},\ z = k.$$

4.
$$\begin{aligned} 2x - 5y + 7z &= 6 \\ x - 3y + 4z &= 3 \\ 3x - 8y + 11z &= 11 \end{aligned}$$

Ans. Inconsistent.

5.
$$\begin{aligned} x_1 + x_2 + x_3 &= 3 \\ 2x_1 + x_2 + 3x_3 &= 1 \\ 4x_1 + x_2 + 5x_3 &= 3 \\ 3x_1 + 2x_2 + x_3 &= 4 \end{aligned}$$

Ans. Inconsistent.

6. For what value of λ the system of equations

$$\begin{aligned} \lambda x + 2y - 2z &= 1 \\ 4x + 2\lambda y - z &= 2 \\ 6x + 6y + \lambda z &= 3 \end{aligned}$$

has a unique solution and then find the solution.

Ans. If $\lambda \neq 2$. $x = (\lambda + 6)/(\lambda^2 + 2\lambda + 15$

$y = (\lambda + \frac{3}{2}) / (\lambda^2 + 2\lambda + 15)$, $z = (3\lambda - 6) / (\lambda^2 + 2\lambda + 15)$.

7. For what value of λ and μ the follwoing system of equations

$$\begin{aligned} x + y + z &= 6 \\ x + 2y + 3z &= 10 \\ x + 2y + \lambda z &= \mu \end{aligned}$$

has (i) a unique solution (ii) no solution (iii) infinitely many solutions..

Ans. (i) Unique solution for $1 \neq 3$, whatever be it.

(ii) No solution for $\lambda = 3$, $\mu \neq 10$.

(iii) infinitely many solutions for $\lambda = 3$, $\mu \neq 10$.

Solution of System of linear homogeneous equations

Consider the system of linear homogeneous equations

$$\left.\begin{array}{r} a_{11}x_1 + a_{12}x_2 + \dots + a_{1n}x_n = 0 \\ a_{21}x_1 + a_{22}x_2 + \dots + a_{2n}x_n = 0 \\ a_{31}x_1 + a_{32}x_2 + \dots + a_{3n}x_n = 0 \\ \dots\dots \quad \dots\dots \quad \dots\dots \\ \dots\dots \quad \dots\dots \quad \dots\dots \\ a_{m1}x_1 + a_{m2}x_2 + \dots\dots + a_{mn}x_n = 0 \end{array}\right\} \quad \dots(1)$$

The system (1) of linear homogeneous equations always have a solution given by

$x_1 = x_2 = x_3 = \dots \; x_n = 0$

which is called trivial solution.

In addition to the trivial solution, non-trivial solutions also exist if $|A| = 0$.

Thus, if $|A| = 0$, then non-trivial solutions also exist.

and if $|A| \neq 0$, then only the trivial soltuion exists.

If $|A| = 0 \Rightarrow p(A) <$ No. of unknowns

$\Rightarrow$ If non trivial solution exists, then there will be infinitely many non-trivial solution.

Thus the system of linear homogeneous equations either have only trivial solution or an infinitely many solutions.

Example 1. Solve the following system of linear homogeneous equations.

$$x + 2y + 3z = 0$$

$$2x + 3y + 4z = 0$$

$$7x + 13y + 19z = 0.$$

Solution:

Here $$A = \begin{bmatrix} 1 & 2 & 3 \\ 2 & 3 & 4 \\ 7 & 13 & 19 \end{bmatrix}$$

by $R_2 \to R_2 - 2R_1$
$R_3 \to R_3 - 7R_1$

$$= \begin{bmatrix} 1 & 2 & 3 \\ 0 & -1 & -2 \\ 0 & -1 & -2 \end{bmatrix}$$

by $R_3 \to R_3 - R_2$

$$= \begin{bmatrix} 1 & 2 & 3 \\ 0 & -1 & -2 \\ 0 & 0 & 0 \end{bmatrix}$$

$\therefore$ $P(A) = 2 <$ No. of unknowns.

$\therefore$ The system has non trivial solutions also

Given by $x + 2y + 3z = 0$

$$y + 2z = 0$$

let $\quad z = k \therefore y = -2k$ and $x = k$.

$\therefore$ The solution is $\quad x = k$

$$y = -2k.$$

$$z = k.$$

Example 2. Solve the following system of equations:

$$x - y + z = 0$$

$$-3x + y - 4z = 0$$

$$7x - 3y - 9y = 0$$

$$4x - 2y + 5z = 0$$

Solution: Here

$$A = \begin{bmatrix} 1 & -1 & 1 \\ -3 & 1 & -4 \\ 7 & -3 & -9 \\ 4 & -2 & 5 \end{bmatrix}$$

by $R_2 \to R_2 + 3R_1$

$R_3 \to R_3 - 7R_1$

$R_4 \to R_4 - 4R_1$

$$= \begin{bmatrix} 1 & -1 & 1 \\ 0 & -2 & -1 \\ 0 & 4 & -16 \\ 0 & 2 & 1 \end{bmatrix}$$

by $R_3 \to R_3 + 2R_2$

$R_4 \to R_2 + R_2$

$$= \begin{bmatrix} 1 & -1 & 1 \\ 0 & -2 & -1 \\ 0 & 0 & -18 \\ 0 & 0 & 0 \end{bmatrix}$$

Here $\rho(A) = 3$ = No. of unknowns.

$\therefore$ The given system of equations has only trivial solution.

$\therefore$ $x = 0, y = 0, z = 0$ is the only solution.

Example 3. Solve the system of equations

$$x - 2y + z - w = 0$$

$$x + y - 2z + 3w = 0$$

$$4x + y - 5z + 8w = 0$$

and $5x - 7y + 2z - w = 0$

Solution:

Here

$$A = \begin{bmatrix} 1 & -2 & 1 & -1 \\ 1 & 1 & -2 & 3 \\ 4 & 1 & -5 & 8 \\ 5 & -7 & 2 & -1 \end{bmatrix}$$

by $R_2 \to R_2 - R_1$

$R_3 \to R_3 - 4R_1$

$R_4 \to R_4 - 5R_1$

$$= \begin{bmatrix} 1 & -2 & 1 & -1 \\ 0 & 3 & -3 & 4 \\ 0 & 9 & -9 & 12 \\ 0 & 3 & -3 & 4 \end{bmatrix}$$

by $R_3 \to R_3 - 3R_2$

$R_4 \to R_4 - R_2$

$$= \begin{bmatrix} 1 & -2 & 1 & -1 \\ 0 & 3 & -3 & 4 \\ 0 & 0 & 0 & 0 \\ 0 & 0 & 0 & 0 \end{bmatrix}$$

$\therefore \rho(A) = 2 <$ No. of unknowns.

Thus the system of equation has non-trivial solutions, also.

The system of equations can be rewritten as

$$x - 2y + z - w = 0$$
$$3y - 3z + 4w = 0$$

Let $\quad w = k_1,\ z = k_2$

$\therefore \quad 3y = 3k_2 - 4k_1$

$$y = k_2 - \frac{4}{3}k_1$$

and $\quad x = k_1 - \dfrac{5}{3}k_2.$

$\therefore$ The solution is

$$x = k_1 - \frac{5}{3}k_2$$
$$y = k_2 - \frac{4}{3}k_1$$
$$z = k_2$$
$$w = k_1.$$

EXERCISE

Solve the system of equations

1. $$\begin{aligned} x + 2y + 3z &= 0 \\ 2x + 3y + 4z &= 0 \\ 7x + 13y + 19z &= 0 \end{aligned}$$

Ans. $x = k,\ y = -2k,\ z = k$

2. $x_1 + 2x_3 - 2x_4 = 0,\ 2x_1 - x_2 - x_4 = 0$
$x_1 + 2x_3 - x_4 = 0,\ 4x_1 - x_2 + 3x_3 - x_4 = 0$

Ans. $x_1 = x_2 = x_3 = x_4 = 0.$

3. $$\begin{aligned} 3x + 4y - z - 6w = 0, &\quad 2x + 3y + 2z - 3w = 0 \\ 2x + y - 14z - 9w = 0 &\quad x + 3y + 13z + 3w = 0 \end{aligned}$$

Ans. $x = 11k_1 + 6k_2$
$y = -8k_1 - 3k_2$
$z = k_1,\ w = k_2$

4. Find the values λ for which the following system of equations

$$2x + z - 3y = \lambda x$$
$$2x - 3y + 2z = \lambda y$$
$$-x + 2y = \lambda z$$

Can possess a non-trivial solution.

Ans. $\lambda = 1, -3$.

Vector

Here our mean of a vector is an n-tuple or an ordered set of n elements *i.e.* $(a, a_2, a_3 \ldots\ldots a_n)$ etc.

Row Vector

A row vector vector is a $1 \times n$ matrix

$$(a_1, a_2, a_3, a_4, \ldots\ldots\ldots a_n)$$

Column vector

Column vector is a $n \times 1$ matrix, as

$$(a_1, a_2, a_3, a_4 \ldots\ldots\ldots\ldots a_n)^T.$$

Let us consider a linear equation

$2x + 3y + 4z + 7w = o$, the co-efficient of x, y, z, w respectively can be expressed as (2, 3, 4, 7).

Thus, the co-efficients of a system of linear equations

$$a_{11} x_1 + a_{12} x_2 + a_{13} x_3 + \ldots + a_{1n} x_n = b_1$$
$$a_{21} x_1 + a_{22} x_2 + a_{23} x_3 + \ldots + a_{2n} x_n = b_2$$
$$\ldots\ldots \quad \ldots\ldots \quad \ldots\ldots$$
$$\ldots\ldots \quad \ldots\ldots \quad \ldots\ldots$$
$$a_{m1} x_1 + am_2 x_2 \ldots\ldots\ldots + a_{mn} x_n = b_n$$

Can be expressed by the matrix A as are

$$A = \begin{bmatrix} a_{11} & a_{12} & a_{13} & \ldots & a_{1n} \\ a_{21} & a_{12} & a_{13} & \ldots & a_{2n} \\ \ldots & \ldots & \ldots & \ldots & \ldots \\ \ldots & \ldots. & \ldots & \ldots & \ldots \\ a_{mn1} & a_{mn2} & \ldots & \ldots & a_{mn} \end{bmatrix}$$

which consists of n column vectors each having m components or m row vectors each having n components.

Equality of two vectors

Two vectors $\alpha = (\alpha_1\ \alpha_2\ \alpha_3\ ...\alpha_n)$ and

$\beta = (\beta_1, \beta_2, \beta_3\ ...\beta_n)$ are equal

if $\alpha_1 = \beta_1, \alpha_2 = \beta_2\ ...\ \alpha_n = \beta_n$

ie $\alpha_i = \beta_i\ \forall\ i$

Addition of two vectors

If $\alpha = (\alpha_1, \alpha_2, \alpha_3\ ...\ \alpha_n)$

$\beta = (\beta_1, \beta_2, \beta_3\ ...\ \beta_n)$

Then $\alpha + \beta = (\alpha_1 + \beta_1), (\alpha_2 + \beta_2)\ ...\ (\alpha_n + \beta_n)$

if $\gamma = \alpha + \beta$

then $\gamma_i = \alpha_i + \beta_i\ \forall\ i$

Multiplication of a vector by a scalar *k*

Let $\alpha = (\alpha, \alpha_2, \alpha_3\ ...\ \alpha_n)$

$\therefore\ k\alpha = (k\alpha_1, k\alpha_3, ...k\alpha_n)$.

Linear combination of vectors

If $\alpha_1, \alpha_2\ \alpha_3\ ...\alpha_n$ are n vectors

and $a_1, a_2, a_3, a_3\ ...\ a_n$ are n scalars then,

$a_1\ \alpha_1 + a_2\ \alpha_2 + a_3\ \alpha_3 +\ ...\ a_n\ \alpha_n$

is called a linear combination of the vectors $\alpha_1, \alpha_2, \alpha_3\ ...\alpha_n$.

Linearly dependent vectors

The set of vectors $[X_1\ X_2\ X_3\ ...X_n)$ is said to be linearly dependent if there exist scalars $a_1, a_2, a_3\ ...\ a_n$, such that

$a_1\ X_1 + a_2\ X_2 + a_3\ X_3 +\ ...\ a_n\ x_n = 0$, (where all a's are not zero),

where zero on R. H. S is a zero vector.

Linearly independent vectors

The set of vectors $(X_1, X_2\ X_3\ ...\ X_n)$ is said to be linearly independent if

$a_1\ X_1 + a_2\ X_2 + a_3\ X_3\alpha\ ... + a_n\ X_n = 0$

only if $a_1, a_2\ ...\ a_n$ all are zero.

Example 1. Check whether the following vectors are linearly dependent. If so, find the relation between them.

$$X_1 = (2, -1, 3, 2),\ x_2 = (1, 3, 4, 2)$$
$$X_3 = (3, -5, 2, 2)$$

Solution: Let $ax_1 + bX_2 + cX_3 = 0.$

$$\therefore \quad a\,(2, -1, 3, 2) + b\,(1, 3, 4, 2) + c\,(3, -5, 2, 2) = 0$$

$$\therefore \quad \left.\begin{aligned} 2a + b + 3c &= 0 \\ -a + 3b - 5c &= 0 \\ 3a + 4b + 2c &= 0 \\ 2a + 2b + 2c &= 0 \end{aligned}\right\} \quad (1)$$

If the above system (1) of homogeneous equations in a, b, c has a non-trivial solution then the vectors X_1, X_2, X_3 are linearly dependent otherwise not.

$$\therefore \quad A = \begin{bmatrix} 2 & 1 & 3 \\ -1 & 3 & -5 \\ 3 & 4 & 2 \\ 2 & 2 & 2 \end{bmatrix}$$

$$\text{By} \quad R_2 \to (-1)\,R_2 \begin{bmatrix} 2 & 1 & 3 \\ 1 & -3 & 5 \\ 3 & 4 & 2 \\ 2 & 2 & 2 \end{bmatrix}$$

$$\text{By} \quad R_1 \leftrightarrow R_2 \begin{bmatrix} 1 & -3 & 5 \\ 2 & 1 & 3 \\ 3 & 4 & 2 \\ 2 & 2 & 2 \end{bmatrix}$$

$$\begin{aligned} By \quad & R_2 \to R_2 - 2R_1 \\ & R_3 \to R_3 - 3R_1 \\ & R_4 \to R_4 - 2R_1 \end{aligned} \begin{bmatrix} 1 & -3 & 5 \\ 0 & 7 & -7 \\ 0 & 13 & -13 \\ 0 & 8 & -8 \end{bmatrix}$$

By $\quad R_2 \to \frac{1}{7} R_2 \begin{bmatrix} 1 & -3 & 5 \\ 0 & 1 & -1 \\ 0 & 13 & -13 \\ 0 & 8 & -8 \end{bmatrix}$

By $\quad \begin{matrix} R_3 \to R_3 - 13R_2 \\ R_4 \to R_4 - 8R_2 \end{matrix} \begin{bmatrix} 1 & -3 & 5 \\ 0 & 1 & -1 \\ 0 & 0 & 0 \\ 0 & 0 & 0 \end{bmatrix}$

$\Rightarrow \quad \rho(A) = 2 <$ No. of unknowns.

So, it has non-trivial solutions also, which are given by

$$a - 3b + 5c = 0$$

$$b - c = 0$$

Let $\quad c = k \quad \therefore \quad b = k \quad$ and $\quad a = -2k$

$\therefore \quad (-2k), k, k$ is the solution.

Hence the vectors are linearly dependent,

and $\quad -2kX_1 + kX_2 + kX_3 = 0$

or $\quad 2X_1 - X_2 - X_3 = 0$

is the relation between the vectors X_1, and X_3.

Example 2. Check whether the following vectors are linearly dependent. If so, find the relation between them.

$$X_1 = (2, -1, 4), \qquad X_2 = (0, 1, 2)$$

$$X_3 = (6, 1, 16), \qquad X_4 = (4, 0, 12)$$

Solution: Let

$$aX_1 + bX_2 + cX_3 + dX_4 = 0 \tag{1}$$

$$\therefore a(2, -1, 4) + b(0, 1, 2) + c(6, 1, 16) + d(4, 0, 12) = 0$$

$$\therefore \quad \begin{aligned} 2a + 0b + 6c + 4d &= 0 \\ -a + b + c + 0d &= 0 \\ 4a + 2b + 16c + 12d &= 0 \end{aligned} \tag{2}$$

If above system 2 of homo geneous equations has a non-trivial solution also, then these vectors are linearly dependent othewise not.

$$A = \begin{bmatrix} 2 & 0 & 6 & 4 \\ -1 & 1 & 1 & 0 \\ 4 & 2 & 16 & 12 \end{bmatrix}$$

By $\quad R_2 \to (-1)\, R_2 \quad \begin{bmatrix} 2 & 0 & 6 & 4 \\ 1 & -1 & -1 & 0 \\ 4 & 2 & 16 & 12 \end{bmatrix}$

By $\quad R_{12} \quad \begin{bmatrix} 1 & -1 & -1 & 0 \\ 2 & 0 & 6 & 4 \\ 4 & 2 & 16 & 12 \end{bmatrix}$

by $\begin{matrix} R_2 \to R_2 - 2R_1 \\ R_3 \to R_3 - 4R_1 \end{matrix} \quad \begin{bmatrix} 1 & -1 & -1 & 0 \\ 0 & 2 & 8 & 4 \\ 0 & 6 & 20 & 12 \end{bmatrix}$

By $\quad R_3 \to R_3 - 3R_2 \quad \begin{bmatrix} 1 & -1 & -1 & 0 \\ 0 & 2 & 8 & 4 \\ 0 & 0 & -4 & 0 \end{bmatrix}$

As $\rho(A) = 3$. $\therefore$ the system of equations possesses only trivial solution given by

$$a = b = c = d = 0$$

$\therefore$ the given vectors are not dependent.

Linear Transformations

A relation of the form $Y = AX$ .... (1)

where

$$A = \begin{bmatrix} a_{11} & a_{12} & \cdots & a_{1n} \\ a_{21} & a_{22} & \cdots & a_{2n} \\ \cdots & \cdots & \cdots & \cdots \\ a_{a1} & a_{n2} & \cdots & a_{nn} \end{bmatrix}$$

$$Y = \begin{bmatrix} y_1 \\ y_2 \\ \cdots \\ y_n \end{bmatrix}, \qquad X = \begin{bmatrix} x_1 \\ x_2 \\ x_3 \\ \cdots \\ x_n \end{bmatrix}.$$

defines a linear transformation from the vector X into the vector Y.

The matrix A is called the linear operator of the transformation.

If $\quad Y_1 = AX_1, \quad$ and $\quad Y_2 = AX_2$

then $\quad aY_1 + bY_2 = A[aX_1 + bX_2]$, is

called the linear property of the transformation.

the vector Y is said to be the image of X under the transformation defined by the matrix A.

Non-Singular transformation

The linear transformation $Y = AX$ is called a non-singular or regular if the images of different vector X_i are distinct vectors Y_i.

In this case

$$|A| \neq 0.$$

If the images of distinct vectors are not distinct, then the transformation is called singular.

In this case $\quad |A| = 0.$

Inverse Transformation

If the linear transformation

$$Y = AX \qquad \text{...(1) is such that } |A| = 0$$

then

$$X = A^{-1} Y, \qquad \text{...(2)}$$

where A^{-1} is the inverse operator, is called inverse transformation of Y = AX.

Orthogonal Transformation

A linear transformation Y = AX is said to be an orthogonal transformation if it transforms $x_1^2 + x_2^2 + x_3^2 + \ldots + x_n^2$ into $y_1^2 + y_2^2 + y_3^2 + \ldots + y_n^2$.

Condition for orthogonal transformation

we have $$X^T X = (x_1, x_2, x_3, \ldots x_n) \begin{bmatrix} x_1 \\ x_2 \\ x_3 \\ \ldots \\ x_n \end{bmatrix}$$

$$\begin{aligned} &= x_1^2 + x_2^2 + x_3^2 + \ldots + x_n^2 \\ &= y_1^2 + y_2^2 + y_3^2 + \ldots + y_n^2 \\ &= Y'Y \\ &= (AX)' (AX) \\ &= X' A' A X \end{aligned}$$

$$X'X = X' (A'A)X$$

$$\Rightarrow \quad A'A = \text{I}.$$

Thus, the transformation is said to be orthogonal

if $$A'A = \text{I}.$$

or $$A' = A^{-1}.$$

Example 1. Show that the transformation

$$\begin{aligned} y_1 &= 2x_1 + x_2 + x_3 \\ y_2 &= x_1 + x_2 + 2x_3 \\ y_3 &= x_1 - 2x_2 - 2x_3 \end{aligned}$$

is regular. Write down its inverse transformation.

Solution: We can write the above transformation as

$$Y = AX \qquad \ldots(1)$$

where $$Y = \begin{bmatrix} y_1 \\ y_2 \\ y_3 \end{bmatrix},$$

$$A = \begin{bmatrix} 2 & 1 & 1 \\ 1 & 1 & 2 \\ 1 & -2 & -2 \end{bmatrix}, \quad X = \begin{bmatrix} x_1 \\ x_2 \\ x_3 \end{bmatrix}$$

$$\therefore \qquad |A| = \begin{vmatrix} 2 & 1 & 1 \\ 1 & 1 & 2 \\ 1 & -2 & -2 \end{vmatrix} = 5$$

$$\Rightarrow \qquad |A| \neq 0.$$

$\therefore$ The above transformation is regular.

The inverse transformation is

$$X = A^{-1} Y$$

where

$$A^{-1} = \frac{1}{5}\begin{bmatrix} 2 & 0 & 1 \\ 4 & -5 & -3 \\ -3 & 5 & 1 \end{bmatrix}$$

$$\therefore \qquad \begin{bmatrix} x_1 \\ x_2 \\ x_3 \end{bmatrix} = \frac{1}{5}\begin{bmatrix} 2 & 0 & 1 \\ 4 & -5 & -3 \\ -3 & 5 & 1 \end{bmatrix}\begin{bmatrix} y_1 \\ y_2 \\ y_3 \end{bmatrix}$$

or

$$5x_1 = 2y_1 + 0y_2 + y_3$$

$$5x_2 = 4y_1 - 5y_2 - 3y_3$$

$$5x_3 = -3y_1 + 5y_2 + y_3.$$

Example 2. Prove that the matrix

$$A = \frac{1}{3}\begin{bmatrix} -2 & 1 & 2 \\ 2 & 2 & 1 \\ 1 & -2 & 2 \end{bmatrix}$$

defines an orthogonal transformation.

Solution: The transformation $Y = AX$ ...(1)

is said to be orthogonal, if

$$AA^T = I$$

Here

$$A = \frac{1}{3}\begin{bmatrix} -2 & 1 & 2 \\ 2 & 2 & 1 \\ 1 & -2 & 2 \end{bmatrix}$$

$$\therefore \qquad A^T = \frac{1}{3}\begin{bmatrix} -2 & 2 & 1 \\ 1 & 2 & -2 \\ 2 & 1 & 2 \end{bmatrix}$$

$$\therefore \qquad AA^T = \frac{1}{9}\begin{bmatrix} -2 & 1 & 2 \\ 2 & 2 & 1 \\ 1 & -2 & 2 \end{bmatrix}\begin{bmatrix} -2 & 2 & 1 \\ 1 & 2 & -2 \\ 2 & 1 & 2 \end{bmatrix}$$

$$= \frac{1}{9}\begin{bmatrix} 9 & 0 & 0 \\ 0 & 9 & 0 \\ 0 & 0 & 9 \end{bmatrix}$$

$$= \begin{bmatrix} 1 & 0 & 0 \\ 0 & 1 & 0 \\ 0 & 0 & 1 \end{bmatrix}$$

$$= I$$

$$\therefore \qquad AA^T = I$$

$\therefore$ A defines an orthogonal transformation.

Orthogonal Vectors

Two vectors Y = $(x_1, x_2, x_3, \ldots x_n)$ and $Y = (y_1, y_2, y_3 \ldots y_n)$ are said to be orthogonal if $XY^T = 0$.

Complex Matrix

A matrix is said to be a complex matrix if its elements are complex numbers.

If $$Z = \begin{bmatrix} a-ib & e+if \\ e+if & g+ih \end{bmatrix} \qquad \ldots(1)$$

then $$\overline{Z} = \begin{bmatrix} a-ib & c-id \\ e-if & g-ih \end{bmatrix}$$

$$\overline{Z'} = \begin{bmatrix} a-ib & e-if \\ c-id & g-ih \end{bmatrix} \qquad \ldots(2)$$

and $$Z' = \begin{bmatrix} a-ib & c-id \\ e-if & g-ih \end{bmatrix}$$

then $$\left(\bar{Z}'\right) = \begin{bmatrix} a-ib & e-if \\ c-id & g-ih \end{bmatrix} \quad \text{... (3)}$$

From (2) and (3), it is obvious that

$$(\bar{Z})' = \left(\bar{Z}'\right)$$

The conjugate of the transpose of Z, *i.e.*, $(\bar{Z})'$ is called conjugate transpose of Z and is denoted by Z^*.

Hermitian Matrix

A complex matrix Z is said to be a Hermitian matrix if

$$Z = Z^*$$

and skew Hermitian if

$$Z^* = -Z.$$

Unitary Matrix

A Square matrix Z is said to be a unitary matrix if

$$Z^* - Z = I.$$

Characteristic Equation

If A is a square matrix, then the equation $|A - \lambda I| = 0$ is called the characterstic equation of the matrix A, where λ is a scalar and I is an identity matrix of the same order as that of A.

If A is a square matrix of order n given by

$$A = \begin{bmatrix} a_{11} & a_{12} & a_{13} & \cdots & a_{1n} \\ a_{21} & a_{22} & a_{23} & \cdots & a_{2n} \\ \cdots & \cdots & \cdots & \cdots & \cdots \\ \cdots & \cdots & \cdots & \cdots & \cdots \\ a_{n1} & a_{n2} & \cdots & \cdots & a_{nn} \end{bmatrix}$$

then

$$A - \lambda I = \begin{bmatrix} a_{11} - \lambda & a_{12} & \dots & a_{1n} \\ a_{21} & a_{22} - \lambda & \dots & a_{2n} \\ a_{31} & a_{32} & \dots & \dots \\ \dots & \dots & \dots & \dots \\ \dots & \dots & \dots & \dots \\ a_{n1} & a_{n2} & \dots & a_{nn} - \lambda \end{bmatrix}$$

$\therefore$ $|A - \lambda I| = 0$, gives

$$\begin{vmatrix} a_{11} - \lambda & a_{12} & a_{13} & \dots & a_{1n} \\ a_{21} & a_{22} - \lambda & a_{23} & \dots & a_{2n} \\ \dots & \dots & \dots & \dots & \dots \\ \dots & \dots & \dots & \dots & \dots \\ a_{n1} & a_{n2} & \dots & \dots & a_{nn} - \lambda \end{vmatrix} = 0$$

The determinant on its expansion gives the characteristic equation as $(-\lambda)^n + k_1(-\lambda)^{n-1} + k_2(-\lambda)^{n-2} + \dots\dots\dots + k_{n-2}(-\lambda)^2 + k(-\lambda) + k_n = 0$, where $k_1, k_2, \dots\, k_n$ are functions of the elements $a_{11}, a_{12}, \dots$ etc.

Eigen Values

The roots of this equation are called characteristic roots or latent roots or eigen values of the matrix A and are denoted by $\lambda_1, \lambda_2, \lambda_3, \dots \lambda_n$.

Characteristic Vectors

If λ is a characteristic root of the matrix A, then $(A - \lambda I)$ is singular.

If $(A - \lambda I)$ is singular then $(A - \lambda I)X = 0$, a system of homogeneous equations possesses a non-zero solution, *i.e.*, there exists a non-zero column vector X such that

$$AX = \lambda X.$$

A non-zero vector X satisfying the given equation $(A - \lambda I)X = 0$, is called a characteristic vector or eigen vector of the matrix A corresponding to the characteristic root λ.

If X_i is a solution of $(A - \lambda I)X = 0$, for $\lambda = \lambda_i$, then

then

μX_i is also a solution of $(A - \lambda I) X = 0$, where μ is a constant.

$\therefore$ eigen vector of a matrix corresponding to $\lambda = \lambda_i$ is not unique. Any scalar multiple of X_i is also an eigen vector.

Example 1. Find the eigen values and eigen vectors for the matrix A given by

$$A = \begin{bmatrix} 2 & 2 & 1 \\ 1 & 3 & 1 \\ 1 & 2 & 2 \end{bmatrix}$$

Solution: The characteristic equation of the matrix A is

$$|A - \lambda I| = 0$$

or

$$\begin{vmatrix} 2-\lambda & 2 & 1 \\ 1 & 3-\lambda & 1 \\ 1 & 2 & 2-\lambda \end{vmatrix} = 0$$

which gives

$$\lambda^3 - 7\lambda^2 + 11\lambda - 5 = 0$$

$$\text{i.e. } (\lambda - 1)^2 (\lambda - 5)$$

$$\therefore \quad \lambda = 1, 1, 5.$$

$\therefore$ The characteristic roots or eigen values are 1, 1, 5.

The characteristic Vectors

(*i*) Corresponding to $\lambda = 1$.

Let

$$X_1 = \begin{bmatrix} x_1 \\ y_1 \\ z_1 \end{bmatrix},$$

be an eigen vector corresponding to $\lambda = 1$.

$$\therefore \quad (A - I)X_1 = 0 \text{ gives}$$

$$\begin{bmatrix} 2-1 & 2 & 1 \\ 1 & 3-1 & 1 \\ 1 & 2 & 2-1 \end{bmatrix} \begin{bmatrix} x_1 \\ y_1 \\ z_1 \end{bmatrix} = 0$$

or

$$\begin{bmatrix} 1 & 2 & 1 \\ 1 & 2 & 1 \\ 1 & 2 & 1 \end{bmatrix} \begin{bmatrix} x_1 \\ y_1 \\ z_1 \end{bmatrix} = 0$$

gives $\qquad x_1 + 2y_1 + z_1 = 0$

Let $\qquad z_1 = 0 \quad \therefore \quad x_1 + 2y_1 = 0$

If $\qquad y_1 = k_1 \quad \text{then} \quad x_1 = -\,2k.$

$\therefore$ one eigen vector is $\begin{bmatrix} -2k_1 \\ k_1 \\ 0 \end{bmatrix}$ or $\begin{bmatrix} -2 \\ 1 \\ 0 \end{bmatrix}$

Again, let $\qquad y_1 = 0 \quad \text{and} \quad z_1 = k_1 \quad \therefore \quad x_1 = -\,k_1$

$\therefore$ the solution is $\qquad x_1 = -k, \quad y_1 = 0, \quad z_1 = k$

$\therefore$ Another eigen vector is $\begin{bmatrix} -k_1 \\ 0 \\ k_1 \end{bmatrix}$ or $\begin{bmatrix} -1 \\ 0 \\ 1 \end{bmatrix}$

(*ii*) for $\lambda = 5$ let $X_2 = \begin{bmatrix} x_2 \\ y_2 \\ z_2 \end{bmatrix}$ be an eigen vector, then

$$\begin{bmatrix} 2-5 & 2 & 1 \\ 1 & 3-5 & 1 \\ 1 & 2 & 2-5 \end{bmatrix} \begin{bmatrix} x_2 \\ y_2 \\ z_2 \end{bmatrix} = 0$$

or

$$\begin{bmatrix} -3 & 2 & 1 \\ 1 & -2 & 1 \\ 1 & 2 & -3 \end{bmatrix} \begin{bmatrix} x_2 \\ y_2 \\ z_2 \end{bmatrix} = 0$$

by R_{12}

or
$$\begin{bmatrix} 1 & -2 & 1 \\ -3 & 2 & 1 \\ 1 & 2 & -3 \end{bmatrix} \begin{bmatrix} x_2 \\ y_2 \\ z_2 \end{bmatrix} = 0$$

by $R_2 \to R_2 + 3R_1$

$R_3 \to R_3 - R_1$

or
$$\begin{bmatrix} 1 & -2 & 1 \\ 0 & -4 & 4 \\ 0 & 4 & -4 \end{bmatrix} \begin{bmatrix} x_2 \\ y_2 \\ z_2 \end{bmatrix} = 0$$

by $R_3 \to R_3 + R_2$

or
$$\begin{bmatrix} 1 & -2 & 1 \\ 0 & -4 & 4 \\ 0 & 0 & 0 \end{bmatrix} \begin{bmatrix} x_2 \\ y_2 \\ z_2 \end{bmatrix} = 0$$

which gives
$$x_2 - 2y_2 + z_2 = 0$$
$$y_2 - z_2 = 0$$

Let $z_2 = k, \quad y_2 = k \quad \text{and} \quad x_2 = k.$

$\therefore$
$$x_2 = \begin{bmatrix} k \\ k \\ k \end{bmatrix}$$

or
$$X_2 = \begin{bmatrix} 1 \\ 1 \\ 1 \end{bmatrix}$$

is the eigen vector corresponding to $\lambda = 5$.

Properties of eigen values

(*i*) A matrix A and its transpose have the same eigen values.

(*ii*) Value of the determinant of a matrix A is equal to the product of its eigen values.

(*iii*) If $\lambda_1\ \lambda_2\ \lambda_3\ \ldots\ \lambda_n$ are the eigen values of A, then

(*a*) $k\lambda_1,\ k\lambda_2,\ k\lambda_3,\ \ldots\ k\lambda_n$ are the eigen values of kA

(*b*) $\frac{1}{\lambda_1}, \frac{1}{\lambda_2}, \frac{1}{\lambda_3} \ldots \frac{1}{\lambda_n}$ are the eigen values of A^{-1}.

(*c*) $\lambda_1^m, \lambda_2^m, \lambda_3^m, \ldots \lambda_n^m$ are the eigen values of A^m.

(d) $\lambda_1^{-m}, \lambda_2^{-m}, \ldots \lambda_n^{-m}$, are the eigen values of A^{-m}.

Example 2. Find the eigen values and eigen vectors of the matrix

$$A = \begin{bmatrix} 1 & 0 & -1 \\ 1 & 2 & 1 \\ 2 & 2 & 3 \end{bmatrix}$$

Determine whether the eigen vectors are orthogonal.

Solution: Characteristic equation of A is

$$\begin{vmatrix} 1-\lambda & 0 & -1 \\ 1 & 2-\lambda & 1 \\ 2 & 2 & 3-\lambda \end{vmatrix} = 0$$

or $$\lambda^3 - 6\lambda^2 + 11\lambda - 6 = 0$$

or $$(\lambda - 1)(\lambda - 2)(\lambda - 3) = 0$$

$\therefore$ $$\lambda = 1, 2, 3.$$

(*a*) eigen vector for $\lambda = 1$.

Let $X_1 = \begin{bmatrix} x_1 \\ y_1 \\ z_1 \end{bmatrix}$ be an eigen vector corresponding to $\lambda = 1$

$\therefore$ $$\begin{bmatrix} 1-1 & 0 & -1 \\ 1 & 2-1 & 1 \\ 2 & 2 & 3-1 \end{bmatrix}\begin{bmatrix} x_1 \\ y_1 \\ z_1 \end{bmatrix} = 0$$

or $$\begin{bmatrix} 0 & 0 & -1 \\ 1 & 1 & 1 \\ 2 & 2 & 2 \end{bmatrix}\begin{bmatrix} x_1 \\ y_1 \\ z_1 \end{bmatrix} = 0$$

gives $$0x_1 + 0y_1 - z_1 = 0$$
$$x_1 + y_1 + z_1 = 0$$

gives $$z_1 = 0 \text{ and } x_1 + y_1 = 0$$

If $$y_1 = k \quad \text{then} \quad x_1 = -k.$$

$$\therefore \qquad X_1 = \begin{bmatrix} -k \\ k \\ 0 \end{bmatrix}$$

or $$X_1 = \begin{bmatrix} -1 \\ 1 \\ 0 \end{bmatrix}$$ is an eigen vector corresponding to $\lambda = 1$.

(*b*) For $\lambda = 2$

Let $$X_2 = \begin{bmatrix} x_2 \\ y_2 \\ z_2 \end{bmatrix}$$

be an eigen vector for $\lambda = 2$

$$\begin{bmatrix} 1-2 & 0 & -1 \\ 1 & 2-2 & 1 \\ 2 & 2 & 3-2 \end{bmatrix} \begin{bmatrix} x_2 \\ y_2 \\ z_2 \end{bmatrix} = 0$$

$$\therefore \qquad \begin{bmatrix} -1 & 0 & -1 \\ 1 & 0 & 1 \\ 2 & 2 & 1 \end{bmatrix} \begin{bmatrix} x_2 \\ y_2 \\ z_2 \end{bmatrix} = 0$$

or $$x_2 + z_2 = 0, \Rightarrow x_2 + 0y_2 + z_2 = 0$$
$$2x_2 + 2y_2 + z_2 = 0 \Rightarrow 2x_2 + 2y_2 + z_2 = 0$$

$$\therefore \qquad \frac{x_2}{-2} = \frac{y_2}{1} = \frac{z_2}{2} = k.$$

$$\therefore \qquad X_2 = \begin{bmatrix} x_2 \\ y_2 \\ z_2 \end{bmatrix} = \begin{bmatrix} 2 \\ -1 \\ -2 \end{bmatrix}$$

is the eigen vector corresponding to $\lambda = 2$.

(*c*) Now

For $\lambda = 3$

let $X_3 = \begin{bmatrix} x_3 \\ y_3 \\ z_3 \end{bmatrix}$ be an eigen vector corresponding to $\lambda = 3$.

$$\therefore \qquad \begin{bmatrix} 1-3 & 0 & -1 \\ 1 & 2-3 & 1 \\ 2 & 2 & 3-3 \end{bmatrix} \begin{bmatrix} x_3 \\ y_3 \\ z_3 \end{bmatrix} = 0$$

or

$$\begin{bmatrix} -2 & 0 & -1 \\ 1 & -1 & 1 \\ 2 & 2 & 0 \end{bmatrix} \begin{bmatrix} x_3 \\ y_3 \\ z_3 \end{bmatrix} = 0$$

$$\begin{bmatrix} -1 & -1 & 0 \\ 1 & -1 & 1 \\ 2 & 2 & 0 \end{bmatrix} \begin{bmatrix} x_3 \\ y_3 \\ z_3 \end{bmatrix} = 0$$

gives

$$x_3 + y_3 + 0z_3 = 0$$
$$x_3 - y_3 + z_3 = 0$$

$$\frac{x_3}{1} = \frac{y_3}{-1} = \frac{z_3}{-2}$$

$$\therefore \qquad X_3 = \begin{bmatrix} 1 \\ -1 \\ -2 \end{bmatrix}$$

is the eigen vector corresponding to $\lambda = 3$.

Now $$X_1^T X_2 = \begin{bmatrix} -1 \\ 1 \\ 0 \end{bmatrix}^T \begin{bmatrix} 2 \\ -1 \\ -2 \end{bmatrix}$$

$$= \begin{bmatrix} -1 & 1 & 0 \end{bmatrix} \begin{bmatrix} 2 \\ -1 \\ -2 \end{bmatrix} = -3 \neq 0.$$

$$X_2^T X_3 = \begin{bmatrix} 2 & -1 & -2 \end{bmatrix} \begin{bmatrix} 1 \\ -1 \\ -2 \end{bmatrix} = 7 \neq 0.$$

$$X_3^T X_1 = \begin{bmatrix} 2 & -1 & -2 \end{bmatrix} \begin{bmatrix} -1 \\ 1 \\ 0 \end{bmatrix}$$

$$= -3 \neq 0.$$

∴ The eigen vectors are not orthogonal.

Cayley – Hamilton Theorem

It states that every square matrix satisfies its own characteristic equation, *i.e.*, if A is a square matrix of order n and

$$\lambda^n + P_1\lambda^{n-1} + P_2\lambda^{n-2} + \ldots.. + P_n = 0 \qquad (1)$$

is its characteristic equation, then

$$A_n + P_1A^{n-1} + P_2A^{n-2} + \ldots.. + P_nI = 0 \qquad (2)$$

Proof: Let A be a square matrix of order n. The elements of the matrix $(A - \lambda I)$ are at the most of degree one in λ.

Then the elements of Adj $(A - \lambda I)$ are polynomial in λ of degree $(n - 1)$ or less.

Therefore, Adj $(A - \lambda I)$ can be expressed as

$$\text{adj } (A - \lambda I) = B_0\lambda^{n-1} + B_1\lambda^{n-2} + \ldots + B_{n-1}$$

where $B_0, B_1, B_2 \ldots.. B_{n-1}$ are matrices of order $n \times n$, whose elements are functions of the elements of A.

[We know that $A(\text{Adj}(A)) = |A|I$.]

then $$(A - \lambda I)\,\text{Adj}(A - \lambda I) = |A - \lambda I|\, I$$

or $(A - \lambda I)\,(B_0\lambda^{n-1} + B_1{}^{n-2} + \ldots.. + B^{n-1}) = (-1)^n\,[\lambda^n + P_1\lambda^{n-1} + P_2\lambda^{n-2} + \ldots..\ P_nI]$

Now comparing the coefficients of like powers of λ on both sides, we get

$$-IB_0 = (-1)^n\ I$$
$$AB_0 - IB_1 = (-1)^n\ P_1I$$
$$AB_1 - IB_2 = (-1)^n\ P_2I$$
$$\ldots\ldots\ \ldots.. = \ldots..\ \ldots..$$
$$\ldots..\ \ldots.. = \ldots..\ \ldots..$$
$$AB_{n-1} = (-1)^n\ P_n\ I$$

Premultiplying these by A^n, A^{n-1}, A^{n-2} ..... I, respectively and adding we get

$$0 = (-1)^n\,[A^n + P_1A^{n-1} + P_2A^{n-2} + \ldots + P_nI]$$

or $A^n + P_1A^{n-1} + P_2A^{n-2} + \ldots + P_nI = 0.$ Hence proved.

Applications of Cayley-Hamilton theorem

(*i*) To find A^{-1}

We know that if A is a square matrix of order n, then it satisfies its own characteristic equation.

If $\lambda^n + P_1\lambda^{n-1} + P_2\lambda^{n-2} + \ldots\ P_n\,I = 0$

then $A^n + P_1A^{n-1} + P_2A^{n-2} + \ldots\ P_n\,I = 0$

multyplying this by A^{-1}, we have

$$A^{n-1} + P_1A^{n-2} + P_2A^{n-3} + \ldots\ P_n\,A^{-1} = 0.$$

$$\therefore\ A^{-1} = \frac{1}{P_n}\,[A^{n-1} + P_1A^{n-2} + P_2A^{n-3} + \ldots + P_{n-1}I]$$

(*ii*) To find the value of a matrix polynomial

SOLVED EXAMPLES

Example 1. Verify Cayley-Hamilton theorem for the matrix

$$A = \begin{bmatrix} 1 & 3 \\ 2 & 4 \end{bmatrix}$$

and hence find its inverse.

Solution: Characteristic equation of the matrix A is

$$|A - \lambda I| = 0 \Rightarrow \begin{vmatrix} 1-\lambda & 3 \\ 2 & 4-\lambda \end{vmatrix} = 0$$

$\Rightarrow (1 - \lambda)\ (4 - \lambda) - 6 = 0$

or $\qquad \lambda^2 - 5\lambda - 2 = 0 \qquad (1)$

Now

$$A^2 = \begin{bmatrix} 1 & 3 \\ 2 & 4 \end{bmatrix}\begin{bmatrix} 1 & 3 \\ 2 & 4 \end{bmatrix} = \begin{bmatrix} 7 & 15 \\ 10 & 22 \end{bmatrix}$$

$\therefore \qquad A^2 - 5A - 2I$

$$= \begin{bmatrix} 7 & 15 \\ 10 & 22 \end{bmatrix} - \begin{bmatrix} 5 & 15 \\ 10 & 20 \end{bmatrix} - \begin{bmatrix} 2 & 0 \\ 0 & 2 \end{bmatrix}$$

$$= \begin{bmatrix} 7 & 15 \\ 10 & 22 \end{bmatrix} - \begin{bmatrix} 7 & 15 \\ 10 & 22 \end{bmatrix}$$

$$= O$$

$\therefore \qquad A^2 - 5A - 2I = O \qquad (2)$

Thus, A satisfies its own characteristic equation.

Now multiplying (2) by A^{-1}, we have

$A^2A^{-1} - 5A\ A^{-1}\ 2A^{-1} = 0$

or $\qquad A - 5I - 2A^{-1} = 0$

$\therefore \qquad 2A^{-1} = A - 5I$

$$= \begin{bmatrix} 1 & 3 \\ 2 & 4 \end{bmatrix} - 5\begin{bmatrix} 1 & 0 \\ 0 & 1 \end{bmatrix}$$

$$= \begin{bmatrix} 1 & 3 \\ 2 & 4 \end{bmatrix} - \begin{bmatrix} 5 & 0 \\ 0 & 5 \end{bmatrix}$$

$$= \begin{bmatrix} -4 & 3 \\ 2 & -1 \end{bmatrix}$$

$$\therefore \qquad A^{-1} = \frac{1}{2}\begin{bmatrix} -4 & 3 \\ 2 & -1 \end{bmatrix}$$

Example 2. If $A = \begin{bmatrix} 2 & 1 & 1 \\ 0 & 1 & 0 \\ 1 & 1 & 2 \end{bmatrix}$

Find the matrix represented by

$A^8 - 5A^7 + 7A^6 - 3A^5 + A^4 - 5A^3 + 8A^2 - 3A + I.$

Solution: To evaluate the given matrix polynomial we make use of Cayley – Hamilton theorem

The characteristic equation of the given matrix is

$$\begin{vmatrix} 2-\lambda & 1 & 1 \\ 0 & 1-\lambda & 0 \\ 1 & 1 & 2-\lambda \end{vmatrix} = 0$$

or $$\lambda^3 - 5\lambda^2 + 7\lambda - 3 = 0 \qquad (1)$$

$\therefore$ By Cayley-Hamilton theorem

$$A^3 - 5A^2 + 7A - 3I = 0. \qquad (2)$$

The given matrix polynomial can be written as

$$A^8 - 5A^7 + 7A^6 - 3A^5 + A^4 - 5A^3 + 8A^2 - 3A + I$$

$$= (A^5 + A)(A^3 - 5A^2 + 7A - 3I) + A^2 + I$$

$$= (A^5 + A)(0) + A^2 + I.$$

$$= A^2 + I$$

$$= \begin{bmatrix} 5 & 4 & 4 \\ 0 & 1 & 0 \\ 4 & 4 & 5 \end{bmatrix} + \begin{bmatrix} 1 & 0 & 0 \\ 0 & 1 & 0 \\ 0 & 0 & 1 \end{bmatrix}$$

$$= \begin{bmatrix} 6 & 4 & 4 \\ 0 & 2 & 0 \\ 4 & 4 & 6 \end{bmatrix}$$

$\therefore A^8 - 5A^7 + 7A^6 + 3A^5 + A^4 - 5A^3 + 8A^2 - 3A + I$

$$= \begin{bmatrix} 6 & 4 & 4 \\ 0 & 2 & 0 \\ 4 & 4 & 6 \end{bmatrix}.$$

Example 3. If $A = \begin{bmatrix} 1 & 2 \\ -1 & 3 \end{bmatrix}$, express

$A^6 - 4A^5 + 8A^4 - 12A^3 + 14A^2$ as a linear polynomial in A.

Solution: The characteristic equation of the matrix

$$A = \begin{bmatrix} 1 & 2 \\ -1 & 3 \end{bmatrix}$$

$$\begin{vmatrix} 1-\lambda & 2 \\ -1 & 3-\lambda \end{vmatrix} = 0$$

or $(1 - \lambda)(3 - \lambda) + 2 = 0$ or $\lambda^2 - 4\lambda + 3 + 2 = 0$

$$\lambda^2 - 4\lambda + 5 = 0 \qquad \text{... (1)}$$

By Cayley-Hamilton theorem.

$$A^2 - 4A + 5I = 0 \qquad (2)$$

By division algorithm

$$A^6 - 4A^5 + 8A^4 - 12A^3 + 14A^2 = (A^4 + 3A^2 - I)(A^2 - 4A + 5I) - 4A + 5I$$

$\because$ $A^2 - 4A + 5I = 0.$

$\therefore$ $A^6 - 4A^5 + 8A^4 - 12A^3 + 14A^2 = -4A + 5I$

which is the required linear polynomial in A.

Example 4. Find the inverse of the matrix A using Cayley-Hamilton, where

$$A = \begin{bmatrix} 1 & 0 & 2 \\ 0 & 2 & 1 \\ 2 & 0 & 3 \end{bmatrix}$$

Solution: The characteristic equation of the matrix A is

$$|A - \lambda I| = 0$$

or $$\begin{vmatrix} 1-\lambda & 0 & 2 \\ 0 & 2-\lambda & 1 \\ 2 & 0 & 3-\lambda \end{vmatrix} = 0$$

or $$\lambda^3 - 6\lambda^2 + 7\lambda + 2 = 0 \qquad (1)$$

$\therefore$ By Cayley-Hamilton theorem

$$A^3 - 6A^2 + 7A + 2I = 0 \qquad (2)$$

Multiplying equation (2) throughout by A^{-1}, we have

$$A^2 - 6A + 7I + 2A^{-1} = 0$$

$$\therefore \quad A^{-1} = -\frac{1}{2}A^2 + 3A - \frac{7}{2}I.$$

$$= -\frac{1}{2}\begin{bmatrix} 5 & 0 & 8 \\ 2 & 4 & 5 \\ 8 & 0 & 13 \end{bmatrix} + 3\begin{bmatrix} 1 & 0 & 2 \\ 0 & 2 & 1 \\ 2 & 0 & 3 \end{bmatrix} - \frac{7}{2}\begin{bmatrix} 1 & 0 & 0 \\ 0 & 1 & 0 \\ 0 & 0 & 1 \end{bmatrix}$$

$$\therefore \quad A^{-1} = \begin{bmatrix} -3 & 0 & 2 \\ -1 & \frac{1}{2} & \frac{1}{2} \\ 2 & 0 & -1 \end{bmatrix}.$$

Example 5. Verify that the matrix $A = \begin{bmatrix} 1 & 2 & 1 \\ -1 & 0 & 3 \\ 2 & -1 & 1 \end{bmatrix}$

satisfies its characteristic equation.

Solution: The characteristic equation $|A - \lambda I| = 0$, of the given matrix A is

$$\begin{vmatrix} 1-\lambda & 2 & 1 \\ -1 & -\lambda & 3 \\ 2 & -1 & 1-\lambda \end{vmatrix} = 0$$

or $$\lambda^3 - 2\lambda^2 + 4\lambda - 18 = 0.$$

Now for the given matrix A

$$A^3 = \begin{bmatrix} 16 & -6 & 12 \\ 14 & 8 & -8 \\ 2 & 10 & 14 \end{bmatrix}, \quad A^2 = \begin{bmatrix} 1 & 1 & 8 \\ 5 & -5 & 2 \\ 5 & 3 & 0 \end{bmatrix}$$

$$\therefore \quad A^3 - 2A^2 + 4A - 18I = \begin{bmatrix} 16 & -6 & 12 \\ 14 & 8 & -8 \\ 2 & 10 & 14 \end{bmatrix} - 2\begin{bmatrix} 1 & 1 & 8 \\ 5 & -5 & 2 \\ 5 & 3 & 0 \end{bmatrix}$$

$$= +4\begin{bmatrix} 1 & 2 & 1 \\ -1 & 0 & 3 \\ 2 & -1 & 1 \end{bmatrix} - 18\begin{bmatrix} 1 & 0 & 0 \\ 0 & 1 & 0 \\ 0 & 0 & 1 \end{bmatrix}$$

$$= \begin{bmatrix} 0 & 0 & 0 \\ 0 & 0 & 0 \\ 0 & 0 & 0 \end{bmatrix}$$

$\because \quad A^3 - 2A^2 + 4A - 18I = 0.$

Thus, A satisfies its characteristic equation.

Reduction of a Matrix to diagonal form

Let $\lambda_1, \lambda_2, \lambda_3 \ldots \lambda_n$ be n distinct eigen values of a non singular matrix A, with

$$X_1 = \begin{bmatrix} x_{11} \\ x_{21} \\ x_{31} \\ \vdots \\ x_{n1} \end{bmatrix} X_2 = \begin{bmatrix} x_{12} \\ x_{22} \\ x_{32} \\ \vdots \\ x_{n2} \end{bmatrix} \ldots X_n = \begin{bmatrix} x_{1n} \\ x_{2n} \\ x_{3n} \\ \vdots \\ x_{nn} \end{bmatrix}$$

eigen vectors respectively.

Then $$E^{-1}AE = \begin{bmatrix} \lambda_1 & 0 & 0 & \cdots & 0 \\ 0 & \lambda_2 & 0 & \cdots & 0 \\ \cdots & \cdots & \cdots & \cdots & \cdots \\ \cdots & \cdots & \cdots & \cdots & \cdots \\ 0 & 0 & 0 & \cdots & \lambda_n \end{bmatrix}$$

where $E = [X_1, X_2, X_3 \ldots X_n]$.

Proof: Since $X_1, X_2, X_3 \ldots X_n$ are the eigen vectors corresponding to the eigen values $\lambda_1, \lambda_2, \lambda_3 .. \lambda_n$ respectively,

then $AX_1 = \lambda_1 X_1, \quad AX_2 = \lambda_2 X_2 \ldots$

$AX_n = \lambda_n X_n.$

Now, Let $E = [X_1, X_2, X_3 \ldots X_n]$

$$AE = A[X_1, X_2, X_3 \dots X_n]$$
$$= [AX_1, AX_2, AX_3 \dots AX_n]$$
$$AE = [\lambda_1 X_1, \lambda_2 X_2, \lambda_3 X_3 \dots \lambda_n X_n]$$

$$= \begin{bmatrix} \lambda_1 X_{11} & \lambda_2 X_{12} & \cdots & \cdots & \lambda_n X_{1n} \\ \lambda_1 X_{21} & \lambda_2 X_{22} & \cdots & \cdots & \lambda_n X_{2n} \\ \lambda_1 X_{31} & \dots & \cdots & \cdots & \lambda_n X_{3n} \\ \dots & \dots & \cdots & \cdots & \dots \\ \lambda_1 X_{n1} & \lambda_2 X_{n2} & \cdots & \cdots & \lambda_n X_{nn} \end{bmatrix}$$

$$= \begin{bmatrix} X_{11} & X_{12} & X_{13} & \cdots & X_{1n} \\ X_{21} & X_{22} & X_{23} & \cdots & X_{2n} \\ \cdots & \cdots & \cdots & \cdots & \cdots \\ \cdots & \cdots & \cdots & \cdots & \cdots \\ X_{n1} & X_{n2} & \cdots & \cdots & X_{nn} \end{bmatrix} \times \begin{bmatrix} \lambda_1 & 0 & 0 & \cdots & 0 \\ 0 & \lambda_2 & 0 & \cdots & 0 \\ 0 & 0 & \lambda_3 & \cdots & 0 \\ \cdots & \cdots & \cdots & \cdots & \cdots \\ 0 & 0 & 0 & 0 & \lambda_n \end{bmatrix}$$

$$AE = ED$$
$$\therefore \quad E^{-1}AE = E^{-1}ED$$
$$= ID$$
$$\therefore \quad E^{-1}AE = D$$

The matrix E, which diagonalises a matrix A is called modal matrix and the matrix D is called spectral matrix of the matrix A.

SOLVED EXAMPLES

Example 1. Find a matrix P which diagonalises the matrix

$$A = \begin{bmatrix} 4 & 1 \\ 2 & 3 \end{bmatrix}$$

verify that $P^{-1}AP = D$, where D is the diagonal matrix. Hence, find A^4.

Solution: Here the characteristic equation $|A - \lambda I| = 0$, of A is

$$\begin{vmatrix} 4-\lambda & 1 \\ 2 & 3-\lambda \end{vmatrix} = 0$$

$$(4 - \lambda)(3 - \lambda) - 2 = 0$$

$$12 - 3\lambda - 4\lambda + \lambda^2 - 2 = 0$$

$$\lambda^2 - 7\lambda + 10 = 0$$

$$(\lambda - 2)(\lambda - 5) = 0$$

$$\therefore \qquad \lambda = 2, 5.$$

I. For $\lambda = 2$, let $\begin{bmatrix} x_1 \\ y_1 \end{bmatrix}$ be an eigen vector

$$\therefore \qquad \begin{bmatrix} 2 & 1 \\ 2 & 1 \end{bmatrix} \begin{bmatrix} x_1 \\ y_1 \end{bmatrix} = 0$$

$$\therefore \qquad 2x_1 + y_1 = 0$$

$$2x_1 + y_1 = 0$$

$$\therefore \qquad y_1 = -2x_1$$

$$\therefore \qquad \begin{bmatrix} 1 \\ -2 \end{bmatrix}$$

is an eigen vector corresponding to $\lambda = 2$.

II. Let $\begin{bmatrix} x_2 \\ y_2 \end{bmatrix}$ be an eigen vector corresponding to $\lambda = 5$.

$$\therefore \qquad \begin{bmatrix} -1 & 1 \\ 2 & -2 \end{bmatrix} \begin{bmatrix} x_2 \\ y_2 \end{bmatrix} = 0.$$

$$x_2 - y_2 = 0.$$

$$x_2 = y_2$$

$\therefore$ $\begin{bmatrix} 1 \\ 1 \end{bmatrix}$ is an eigen corresponding to $\lambda = 5$.

Since (1, –2) and (1, 1) are linearly independent.

$\therefore$ The model matrix E which diagonolises the given matrix A is

$$E = \begin{bmatrix} 1 & 1 \\ -2 & 1 \end{bmatrix}$$

$$\therefore \qquad E^{-1} = \frac{1}{3}\begin{bmatrix} 1 & -1 \\ 2 & 1 \end{bmatrix}$$

$$\therefore \qquad E^{-1}AE = \frac{1}{3}\begin{bmatrix} 1 & -1 \\ 2 & 1 \end{bmatrix}\begin{bmatrix} 4 & 1 \\ 2 & 3 \end{bmatrix}\begin{bmatrix} 1 & 1 \\ -2 & 1 \end{bmatrix}$$

$$= \frac{1}{3}\begin{bmatrix} 2 & -2 \\ 10 & 5 \end{bmatrix}\begin{bmatrix} 1 & 1 \\ -2 & 1 \end{bmatrix}$$

$$= \frac{1}{3}\begin{bmatrix} 6 & 0 \\ 0 & 15 \end{bmatrix} = \begin{bmatrix} 2 & 0 \\ 0 & 5 \end{bmatrix}$$

= Diagonal matrix D, whose diagonal elements are 2, 5, which are the eigen values of A.

$$D = E^{-1}AE$$

$$\therefore \qquad ED\,E^{-1} = A$$

$$A = ED\,E^{-1}$$

$$A^2 = (ED\,E^{-1})\,(ED\,E^{-1})$$

$$= (E\,D)\,(E^{-1}\,E)\,(D\,E^{-1})$$

$$= E\,D^2\,E^{-1}.$$

Similarly $\qquad A^4 = E\,D^4\,E^{-1}$

$$= \begin{bmatrix} 1 & 1 \\ -2 & 1 \end{bmatrix}\begin{bmatrix} 2^4 & 0 \\ 0 & 5^4 \end{bmatrix}\frac{1}{3}\begin{bmatrix} 1 & -1 \\ 2 & 1 \end{bmatrix}$$

$$= \frac{1}{3}\begin{bmatrix} 16 & 625 \\ -32 & 625 \end{bmatrix}\begin{bmatrix} 1 & -1 \\ 2 & 1 \end{bmatrix}$$

$$= \frac{1}{3}\begin{bmatrix} 1266 & 609 \\ 1218 & 657 \end{bmatrix}$$

$$= \begin{bmatrix} 422 & 203 \\ 406 & 219 \end{bmatrix}$$

$$\therefore \qquad A^4 = \begin{bmatrix} 422 & 203 \\ 406 & 219 \end{bmatrix}.$$

Example 2. Check whether the matrix

$$A = \begin{bmatrix} 1 & 2 & 2 \\ 0 & 2 & 1 \\ -1 & 2 & 2 \end{bmatrix} \text{ is diagonalisable, diagonalise, if it}$$

diagonalisable.

Solution: Here the characteristic equation $|A - \lambda I| = 0$. of the given matrix is

$$\begin{vmatrix} 1-\lambda & 2 & 2 \\ 0 & 2-\lambda & 1 \\ -1 & 2 & 2-\lambda \end{vmatrix} = 0.$$

or $$\lambda^3 - 3\lambda^2 + 6\lambda - 4 = 0.$$

$$(\lambda - 1)(\lambda - 2)^2 = 0.$$

$\therefore$ $$\lambda = 1, 2, 2.$$

Let $$X_1 = \begin{bmatrix} x_1 \\ y_1 \\ z_1 \end{bmatrix}$$

be an eigent vector corresponding to the eigen value $\lambda = 1$.

$\therefore$ $$\begin{bmatrix} 1-1 & 2 & 2 \\ 0 & 2-1 & 1 \\ -1 & 2 & 2-1 \end{bmatrix} \begin{bmatrix} x_1 \\ y_1 \\ z_1 \end{bmatrix} = 0$$

$\therefore$ $$\begin{bmatrix} 0 & 2 & 2 \\ 0 & 1 & 1 \\ -1 & 2 & 1 \end{bmatrix} \begin{bmatrix} x_1 \\ y_1 \\ z_1 \end{bmatrix} = 0$$

or $$y_1 + z_1 = 0$$

$$-x_1 + 2y_1 + z_1 = 0$$

Let $z_1 = k \quad \therefore \quad y_1 = -k$

$\therefore$ $$x_1 = -k$$

$\therefore$ $(-1, -1, 1)^T$ is the eigen vector corresponding to $\lambda = 1$.

Let $$X_2 = \begin{bmatrix} x_2 \\ y_2 \\ z_2 \end{bmatrix}$$

be an eigen vector corresponding to $\lambda = 2$.

$$\therefore \quad \begin{bmatrix} -1 & 2 & 2 \\ 0 & 0 & 1 \\ -1 & 2 & 0 \end{bmatrix} \begin{bmatrix} x_2 \\ y_2 \\ z_2 \end{bmatrix} = 0$$

$$\therefore \quad -x_2 + 2y_2 + 2z_2 = 0$$

$$0x_2 + 0y_2 + z_2 = 0$$

$$-x_2 + 2y_2 + 0z_2 = 0$$

$\therefore \quad z_2 = 0$, Let $\therefore \quad y_2 = k, \quad \therefore \quad x_2 = 2k.$

$\therefore \begin{bmatrix} 2 \\ 1 \\ 0 \end{bmatrix}$ is an eigen vector corresponding to $\lambda = 2$

for another $\lambda = 2$, we will have the same eigen vector.

$\therefore$ The three eigen vectors

$$\begin{bmatrix} -1 \\ -1 \\ 1 \end{bmatrix}, \quad \begin{bmatrix} 2 \\ 1 \\ 0 \end{bmatrix}, \quad \begin{bmatrix} 2 \\ 1 \\ 0 \end{bmatrix}$$

are not linearly independent

$\therefore$ the matrix is not diagonolisable.

Example 3. Diagonalise the matrix

$$A = \begin{bmatrix} 8 & -6 & 2 \\ -6 & 7 & -4 \\ 2 & -4 & 3 \end{bmatrix}$$

and find the modal matrix E.

Solution: The given matrix A is

$$A = \begin{bmatrix} 8 & -6 & 2 \\ -6 & 7 & -4 \\ 2 & -4 & 3 \end{bmatrix}$$

Its characteristic equation $|A - \lambda I| = 0$, is

$$\begin{vmatrix} 8-\lambda & -6 & 2 \\ -6 & 7-\lambda & -4 \\ 2 & -4 & 3-\lambda \end{vmatrix} = 0$$

i.e.

$$\lambda^3 - 18\lambda^2 + 45\lambda = 0.$$

$$\lambda[\lambda^2 - 18\lambda + 45] = 0.$$

$$\lambda(\lambda - 3)(\lambda - 15) = 0$$

$$\therefore \qquad \lambda = 0, 3, 15.$$

Now **I.**

Let $X_1 = \begin{bmatrix} x_1 \\ y_1 \\ z_2 \end{bmatrix}$ be an eigen vector corresponding to $\lambda = 0$.

$$\therefore \qquad \begin{bmatrix} 8 & -6 & 2 \\ -6 & 7 & -4 \\ 2 & -4 & 3 \end{bmatrix} \begin{bmatrix} x_1 \\ y_1 \\ z_1 \end{bmatrix} = 0.$$

By R_{13}

$$\begin{bmatrix} 2 & -4 & 3 \\ -6 & 7 & -4 \\ 8 & -6 & 2 \end{bmatrix} \begin{bmatrix} x_1 \\ y_1 \\ z_1 \end{bmatrix} = 0.$$

$$\begin{matrix} R_2 \to R_2 + 3R_1 \\ R_3 \to R_3 - 4R_1 \end{matrix} \begin{bmatrix} 2 & -4 & 3 \\ 0 & -5 & 5 \\ 0 & 10 & -1 \end{bmatrix} \begin{bmatrix} x_1 \\ y_1 \\ z_1 \end{bmatrix} = 0$$

or $$2x_1 - 4y_1 + 3z_1 = 0$$
$$0x_1 - 5y_1 + 5z_1 = 0$$

$\therefore$ $$y_1 = z_1$$

let $z_1 = k, \quad \therefore \quad y_1 = k$

$\therefore$ $$2x_1 = -3z_1 + 4y_1$$
$$= k$$

$\therefore$ $$x_1 = \frac{k}{2}$$

$\therefore$ an eigen vector corresponding to the eigen value $\lambda = 0$, is $\begin{bmatrix} 1 \\ 2 \\ 2 \end{bmatrix}$

Again let $X_2 = \begin{bmatrix} x_2 \\ y_2 \\ z_2 \end{bmatrix}$ be an eigen vector corresponding to $\lambda = 3$

$\therefore$ $$\begin{bmatrix} 5 & -6 & 2 \\ -6 & 4 & -4 \\ 2 & -4 & 0 \end{bmatrix} \begin{bmatrix} x_2 \\ y_2 \\ z_2 \end{bmatrix} = 0$$

$$\text{By } R_1 \to R_1 - 2R_3 \begin{bmatrix} 1 & 2 & 2 \\ -6 & 4 & -4 \\ 2 & -4 & 0 \end{bmatrix} \begin{bmatrix} x_2 \\ y_2 \\ z_2 \end{bmatrix} = 0$$

$$\text{By } \begin{matrix} R_2 \to R_2 + 6R_1 \\ R_3 \to R_3 - 2R_1 \end{matrix} \begin{bmatrix} 1 & 2 & 2 \\ 0 & 16 & 8 \\ 0 & -8 & -4 \end{bmatrix} \begin{bmatrix} x_2 \\ y_2 \\ z_2 \end{bmatrix} = 0.$$

$\therefore$ $$x_2 + 2y_2 + 2z_2 = 0.$$
$$2y_2 + z_2 = 0$$

$\therefore$ Let $y_2 = k \quad \therefore \quad z_2 = -2k$

so $x_2 = 4k - 2k = 2k$

$$\therefore \qquad X_2 = \begin{bmatrix} x_2 \\ y_2 \\ z_2 \end{bmatrix} = \begin{bmatrix} 2k \\ k \\ -2k \end{bmatrix} = \begin{bmatrix} 2 \\ 1 \\ -2 \end{bmatrix}.$$

Let $X_3 = \begin{bmatrix} x_3 \\ y_3 \\ z_3 \end{bmatrix}$ be an eigen vector corresponding to $\lambda = 15$

$$\therefore \qquad \begin{bmatrix} -7 & -6 & 2 \\ -6 & -8 & -4 \\ 2 & -4 & -12 \end{bmatrix} \begin{bmatrix} x_3 \\ y_3 \\ z_3 \end{bmatrix} = 0$$

$$\text{By } R_2 \to R_2 - R_1 \begin{bmatrix} -7 & -6 & 2 \\ 1 & -2 & -6 \\ 2 & -4 & -12 \end{bmatrix} \begin{bmatrix} x_3 \\ y_3 \\ z_3 \end{bmatrix} = 0$$

$$\text{By } R_{12} \begin{bmatrix} 1 & -2 & -6 \\ -7 & -6 & 2 \\ 2 & -4 & -12 \end{bmatrix} \begin{bmatrix} x_3 \\ y_3 \\ z_3 \end{bmatrix} = 0$$

$$\text{By } \begin{array}{l} R_2 \to R_2 + 7R_1 \\ R_3 \to R_3 - 2R_1 \end{array} \begin{bmatrix} 1 & -2 & -6 \\ 0 & -20 & -40 \\ 0 & 0 & 0 \end{bmatrix} \begin{bmatrix} x_3 \\ y_3 \\ z_3 \end{bmatrix} = 0.$$

$$x_3 - 2y_3 - 6z_3 = 0.$$

$$y_3 + 2z_3 = 0.$$

Let $\quad z_3 = k \quad \therefore \quad y_3 = -2k.$

So $\quad x_3 = 6z_3 + 2y_3$

$$= 6k - 4k$$

$$= 2k$$

$$\therefore \qquad X_3 = \begin{bmatrix} 2k \\ -2k \\ k \end{bmatrix} = \begin{bmatrix} 2 \\ -2 \\ 1 \end{bmatrix}$$

$$\therefore \qquad X_1 = \begin{bmatrix} 1 \\ 2 \\ 2 \end{bmatrix}, X_2 = \begin{bmatrix} 2 \\ 1 \\ -2 \end{bmatrix}, x_3 = \begin{bmatrix} 2 \\ -2 \\ 1 \end{bmatrix}$$

are the eigen vectors, which are linearly independent

$$\therefore \qquad E = [X_1, X_2, X_3]$$

$$= \begin{bmatrix} 1 & 2 & 2 \\ 2 & 1 & -2 \\ 2 & -2 & 1 \end{bmatrix}$$

is the required modal matrix which diagonalises A.

Example 4. Diagonalise the matrix $A = \begin{bmatrix} 1 & 6 & 1 \\ 1 & 2 & 0 \\ 0 & 0 & 3 \end{bmatrix}$ and hence find A^8.

Solution: Here the given matrix A is

$$A = \begin{bmatrix} 1 & 6 & 1 \\ 1 & 2 & 0 \\ 0 & 0 & 3 \end{bmatrix}$$

Its characteristic equation $|A - \lambda I| = 0$, is

$$\begin{vmatrix} 1-\lambda & 6 & 1 \\ 1 & 2-\lambda & 0 \\ 0 & 0 & 3-\lambda \end{vmatrix} = 0.$$

i.e. $\quad (1 - \lambda) [(2 - \lambda) (3 - \lambda) - 0] - 6 [3 - \lambda - 0] + 0 = 0$

$$\therefore \qquad (1 - \lambda) (2 - \lambda) (3 - \lambda) - 6 (3 - \lambda) = 0$$

$$\therefore \qquad (3 - \lambda) [(1 - \lambda) (2 - \lambda) - 6] = 0$$

$$(3 - \lambda) [(\lambda - 1) (\lambda - 2) - 6] = 0$$

$$(3 - \lambda) [\lambda^2 - \lambda - 2\lambda + 2 - 6] = 0$$

$$(3 - \lambda) (\lambda^2 - 3\lambda - 4) = 0$$

$$(3 - \lambda)(\lambda + 1)(\lambda - 4) = 0$$

$\therefore$ $$(\lambda + 1)(3 - \lambda)(\lambda - 4) = 0$$

$\therefore$ $\lambda = -1, 3, 4.$

Now for $\lambda = -1$, Let $X_1 = \begin{bmatrix} x_1 \\ y_1 \\ z_1 \end{bmatrix}$ be an eigen vector, Then

$$\begin{bmatrix} 2 & 6 & 1 \\ 1 & 3 & 0 \\ 0 & 0 & 4 \end{bmatrix} \begin{bmatrix} x_1 \\ y_1 \\ z_1 \end{bmatrix} = 0$$

$\therefore$ $$x_1 + 3y_1 = 0, \quad z_1 = 0$$

$\therefore$ $$x_1 = -3k, \quad y_1 = k, \quad z_1 = 0$$

or $$X_1 = \begin{bmatrix} -3 \\ 1 \\ 0 \end{bmatrix}$$

$\therefore$ $\begin{bmatrix} -3 \\ 1 \\ 0 \end{bmatrix}$ is an eigen vector corresponding to $\lambda = -1$.

For $\lambda = 3$, let $X_2 = \begin{bmatrix} x_2 \\ y_2 \\ z_2 \end{bmatrix}$ be an eigen vector

Processing in the same way, we have

$$-2x_2 + 6y_2 + z_2 = 0$$

$$x_2 - y_2 = 0.$$

$$x_2 = y_2 = k, \quad z_2 = -4k$$

$\therefore$ $$X_2 = \begin{bmatrix} 1 \\ 1 \\ -4 \end{bmatrix}$$

Similarly for $\lambda = 4$, let $X_3 = \begin{bmatrix} x_3 \\ y_3 \\ z_3 \end{bmatrix}$ be an eigen vector,

$\therefore$ we have
$$-3x_3 + 6y_3 + z_3 = 0$$
$$x_3 - 2y_3 = 0$$
$$-z_3 = 0$$

$$\therefore \quad z_3 = 0, \quad x_3 = 2k, \quad y_3 = k$$

$$\therefore \quad X_3 = \begin{bmatrix} 2 \\ 1 \\ 0 \end{bmatrix}$$

$\therefore$ The modal matrix E, is

$$E = [X_1, X_2, X_3]$$

$$= \begin{bmatrix} -3 & 1 & 2 \\ 1 & 1 & 1 \\ 0 & -4 & 0 \end{bmatrix}$$

using elemantary row transformations

we have $$E^{-1} = \frac{1}{20}\begin{bmatrix} -4 & 8 & 1 \\ 0 & 0 & -5 \\ 4 & 12 & 4 \end{bmatrix}$$

Now $$E^{-1} AE$$

$$= \frac{1}{20}\begin{bmatrix} -4 & 8 & 1 \\ 0 & 0 & -5 \\ 4 & 12 & 4 \end{bmatrix}\begin{bmatrix} 1 & 6 & 1 \\ 1 & 2 & 0 \\ 0 & 0 & 3 \end{bmatrix}\begin{bmatrix} -3 & 1 & 2 \\ 1 & 1 & 1 \\ 0 & -4 & 0 \end{bmatrix}$$

$$= \frac{1}{20}\begin{bmatrix} 4 & -8 & -1 \\ 0 & 0 & -15 \\ 16 & 48 & 16 \end{bmatrix}\begin{bmatrix} -3 & 1 & 2 \\ 1 & 1 & 1 \\ 0 & -4 & 0 \end{bmatrix}$$

$$= \frac{1}{20}\begin{bmatrix} -20 & 0 & 0 \\ 0 & 60 & 0 \\ 0 & 0 & 80 \end{bmatrix} = \begin{bmatrix} -1 & 0 & 0 \\ 0 & 3 & 0 \\ 0 & 0 & 4 \end{bmatrix}$$

= Diagonal matrix whose elements are the eigen values of the matrix A.

As, we have

$$D = E^{-1} AE$$

$$\therefore \quad A = E\,D\,E^{-1}$$

and therefore

$$A^n = E\,D^n\,E^{-1}$$

$$\therefore \quad A^8 = E\,D^8\,E^{-1}$$

$$= \frac{1}{20}\begin{bmatrix} -3 & 1 & 2 \\ 1 & 1 & 1 \\ 0 & -4 & 0 \end{bmatrix}\begin{bmatrix} (-1)^8 & 0 & 0 \\ 0 & 3^8 & 0 \\ 0 & 0 & 4^8 \end{bmatrix}\begin{bmatrix} -4 & 8 & 1 \\ 0 & 0 & -5 \\ 4 & 12 & 4 \end{bmatrix}$$

$$A^8 = \begin{bmatrix} 26215 & 78642 & 24574 \\ 13107 & 39322 & 11467 \\ 0 & 0 & 6561 \end{bmatrix}.$$

Example 5. Find the matrix A whose eigen values are 1, –1, 2 and corresponding eigen vectors are $\begin{bmatrix} 1 \\ 1 \\ 0 \end{bmatrix}, \begin{bmatrix} 1 \\ 0 \\ 1 \end{bmatrix}$ and $\begin{bmatrix} 3 \\ 1 \\ 1 \end{bmatrix}$ respectively.

Solution: For the required matrix A the modal matrix E and the spectral matrix D are given as

$$E = \begin{bmatrix} 1 & 1 & 3 \\ 1 & 0 & 1 \\ 0 & 1 & 1 \end{bmatrix} \text{ and}$$

$$D = \begin{bmatrix} 1 & 0 & 0 \\ 0 & -1 & 0 \\ 0 & 0 & 2 \end{bmatrix}$$

$$\therefore \qquad E^{-1} = \begin{bmatrix} -1 & 2 & 1 \\ -1 & 1 & 2 \\ 1 & -1 & -1 \end{bmatrix}$$

Since $\qquad D = E^{-1} A E$

$\therefore \qquad A = E D E^{-1}$

$$= \begin{bmatrix} 1 & 1 & 3 \\ 1 & 0 & 1 \\ 0 & 1 & 1 \end{bmatrix} \begin{bmatrix} 1 & 0 & 0 \\ 1 & -1 & 0 \\ 0 & 0 & 2 \end{bmatrix} \begin{bmatrix} -1 & 2 & 1 \\ -1 & 1 & 2 \\ 1 & -1 & -1 \end{bmatrix}$$

$$= \begin{bmatrix} 1 & -1 & 6 \\ 1 & 0 & 2 \\ 0 & -1 & 2 \end{bmatrix} \begin{bmatrix} -1 & 2 & 1 \\ -1 & 1 & 2 \\ 1 & -1 & -1 \end{bmatrix}$$

$$\therefore \qquad A = \begin{bmatrix} 6 & -5 & -7 \\ 1 & 0 & -1 \\ 3 & -3 & -4 \end{bmatrix}.$$

EXERCISE

1. Show that the vectors
   $X_1 = (1, 2, 4)$, $\quad X_2 = (2, -1, 3)$ $X_3 = (0, 1, 2)$ $\quad X_4 = (-3, 7, 2)$
   are linearly dependent and find the relation among these.

   Ans. $9x_1 - 12x_2 + 5x_3 - 5x_4 = 0.$

2. Check whether the following vectors are linearly dependent. Find a relation among these if linearly dependent.

(*a*) $X_1 = (2, 1, 1, 0), X_2 = (0, 2, 0, 1) X_3 = (1, 1, 0, 2), x_4 = (0, 2, 1, 1)$

Ans. Linearly independent.

(*b*) $X_1 = (1, -1, 0)$, $X_2 = (0, 1, -1)$, $X_3 = (0, 0, 1)$

Ans. Linearly independent

3. Show that the transformation $y = Ax$, defined by

$$y_1 = x_1 + 2x_2 + 5x_3$$
$$y_2 = 0x_1 - x_2 + 2x_3$$
$$y_3 = 2x_1 + 4x_2 + 11x_3$$

is regular and hence find the inverse transformation

Ans. $x_1 = 19y_1 + 2y_2 - 9y_3$

$x_2 = -4y_1 - y_2 + 2y_3$

$x_3 = -2y_1 + 0y_2 + y_3.$

4. A transformation from the variables x_1, x_2, x_3 to y_1, y_2, y_3 is difined by $Y = AX$ and the transformation from the variables y_1, y_2, y_3 to z_1, z_2, z_3 is difined by $Z = BY$, where

$$A = \begin{bmatrix} 2 & 1 & 0 \\ 0 & 1 & 2 \\ -1 & 2 & 1 \end{bmatrix}, \quad B = \begin{bmatrix} 1 & 1 & 1 \\ 1 & 2 & -3 \\ 1 & 3 & 5 \end{bmatrix},$$

find the transformation from the variables x_1, x_2, x_3 to z_1, z_2, z_3 and hence find the inverse transform from z_1, z_2, z_3 to x_1, x_2, x_3.

Ans. $Z = (BA)X = \begin{bmatrix} 1 & 4 & 3 \\ 5 & -3 & 1 \\ -3 & 14 & 11 \end{bmatrix} \begin{bmatrix} x_1 \\ x_2 \\ x_3 \end{bmatrix}$

or $\begin{bmatrix} z_1 \\ z_2 \\ z_3 \end{bmatrix} = \begin{bmatrix} 1 & 4 & 3 \\ 5 & -3 & 1 \\ -3 & 14 & 11 \end{bmatrix} \begin{bmatrix} x_1 \\ x_2 \\ x_3 \end{bmatrix}.$

5. Check whether the transformation $Y = AX$

where $A = \frac{1}{2}\begin{bmatrix} -2 & 1 & 2 \\ 2 & 2 & 1 \\ 1 & -2 & 2 \end{bmatrix}$ is orthogonal.

Ans. Yes.

6. Check whether the following matrices are Hermitian or Skew Hermitian.

(*i*) $\begin{bmatrix} 2 & 3-i & 6+2i \\ 3+i & 0 & 4-7i \\ 6-2i & 4+7i & 8 \end{bmatrix}$

Ans. Hermitian.

(ii) $\begin{bmatrix} 0 & 1-i & 2+3i \\ -1-i & 0 & 6i \\ -2+3i & 6i & 0 \end{bmatrix}$

Ans. Skew Hermition.

7. Find the eigen values and eigen vectors of the following matrices.

(i) $\begin{bmatrix} 3 & 1 & 4 \\ 0 & 2 & 0 \\ 0 & 0 & 5 \end{bmatrix}$

Ans. Eigen values 2, 3, 5

Eigen vectors $\begin{bmatrix} 1 \\ -1 \\ 0 \end{bmatrix}, \begin{bmatrix} 1 \\ 0 \\ 0 \end{bmatrix}, \begin{bmatrix} 2 \\ 0 \\ 1 \end{bmatrix}$

(ii) $\begin{bmatrix} 8 & -6 & 2 \\ -6 & 7 & -4 \\ 2 & -4 & 3 \end{bmatrix}$

Ans. Eigen values are 0, 3, 15

Eigen vectors = $\begin{bmatrix} 1 \\ 2 \\ 2 \end{bmatrix}, \begin{bmatrix} 2 \\ 1 \\ -2 \end{bmatrix}, \begin{bmatrix} 2 \\ -2 \\ 1 \end{bmatrix}$

(iii) $\begin{bmatrix} 2 & 1 & 0 \\ 0 & 2 & 1 \\ 0 & 0 & 2 \end{bmatrix}$

Ans. Eigen values are 2, 2, 2

Eigen vectors $\begin{bmatrix} 1 \\ 0 \\ 0 \end{bmatrix}, \begin{bmatrix} 1 \\ 0 \\ 0 \end{bmatrix}, \begin{bmatrix} 1 \\ 0 \\ 0 \end{bmatrix}$

(iv) $\begin{bmatrix} 6 & -2 & 2 \\ -2 & 3 & -1 \\ 2 & -1 & 3 \end{bmatrix}$

Ans. Eigen values are 2, 2, 8

Eigen vectors $\begin{bmatrix} -1 \\ 0 \\ 2 \end{bmatrix}, \begin{bmatrix} 1 \\ 2 \\ 0 \end{bmatrix}, \begin{bmatrix} 2 \\ -1 \\ 1 \end{bmatrix}$

8. Obtain the eigen values and eigen vectors of the matrix

$\begin{bmatrix} 2 & 0 & 1 \\ 0 & 2 & 0 \\ 1 & 0 & 2 \end{bmatrix}$ and verify that the eigen vectors are orthogonal.

Ans. $\begin{bmatrix} 1 \\ 0 \\ 1 \end{bmatrix}, \begin{bmatrix} 1 \\ 0 \\ -1 \end{bmatrix}, \begin{bmatrix} 0 \\ 1 \\ 0 \end{bmatrix}$

9. Find the characteristic equation of the matrices given below and show that they satisfy their characteristic equations and hence find their inverses.

(*i*) $A = \begin{bmatrix} 1 & 3 & 7 \\ 4 & 2 & 3 \\ 1 & 2 & 1 \end{bmatrix}$

Ans. Characteristic equation $\lambda^3 - 4\lambda^2 - 20\lambda - 35 = 0$

and $A^{-1} = \dfrac{1}{35}\begin{bmatrix} -4 & 11 & -5 \\ -1 & -6 & 25 \\ 6 & 1 & -10 \end{bmatrix}$

(*ii*) $A = \begin{bmatrix} 1 & 2 & 1 \\ 0 & 1 & -1 \\ 3 & -1 & 1 \end{bmatrix}$

Ans. Characteristic equation $\lambda^3 - 3\lambda^2 - \lambda + 9 = 0$

$A^{-1} = \dfrac{1}{9}\begin{bmatrix} 0 & 3 & 3 \\ 3 & 2 & -1 \\ 3 & -7 & -1 \end{bmatrix}.$

10. If $A = \begin{bmatrix} 3 & 1 \\ -1 & 2 \end{bmatrix}$, express

$2A^5 - 3A^4 + A^2 - 4I$ as a linear polynomial in A.

Ans. $138A - 403I$.

11. Find the eigen values of the matrix $A = \begin{bmatrix} 6 & -3 & -2 \\ 4 & -1 & -2 \\ 10 & -5 & -3 \end{bmatrix}$ and using Cayley-Hamilton theorem find A^{-1}.

12. If $A = \begin{bmatrix} 1 & 2 & 3 \\ 2 & 4 & 5 \\ 3 & 5 & 6 \end{bmatrix}$

express $A^8 - 11A^7 - 4A^6 + A^5 + A^4 - 11A^3 - 3A^2 + 2A + I$ as a quadratic polynomial in A.

Ans. $A^2 + A + I$.

13. For the matrix $A = \begin{bmatrix} 1 & 1 & 3 \\ 1 & 5 & 1 \\ 3 & 1 & 1 \end{bmatrix}$.

Find the modal matrix P and hence the spectral matrix D and then find A^4.

Ans. $A^4 = \begin{bmatrix} 251 & 485 & 235 \\ 485 & 1051 & 485 \\ 235 & 485 & 251 \end{bmatrix}$, $E = \begin{bmatrix} -1 & 1 & 1 \\ 0 & -1 & 2 \\ 1 & 1 & 1 \end{bmatrix}$, $D = \begin{bmatrix} -2 & 0 & 0 \\ 0 & 3 & 0 \\ 0 & 0 & 6 \end{bmatrix}$.

14. Find the modal matrix for

$$A = \begin{bmatrix} 7 & -2 & 1 \\ -2 & 10 & -2 \\ 1 & -2 & 7 \end{bmatrix}$$

Ans. $E = \begin{bmatrix} \frac{1}{\sqrt{2}} & \frac{1}{\sqrt{3}} & \frac{1}{\sqrt{6}} \\ 0 & \frac{1}{\sqrt{3}} & \frac{-2}{\sqrt{6}} \\ \frac{-1}{\sqrt{2}} & \frac{1}{\sqrt{3}} & \frac{1}{\sqrt{6}} \end{bmatrix}$.

15. Find a matrix A whose eigen values and the corresponding eigen vectors are

(*i*) eigen values: 3, – 4, 0

eigen vectors: $\begin{bmatrix} -1 \\ 3 \\ -1 \end{bmatrix}, \begin{bmatrix} 1 \\ -1 \\ 3 \end{bmatrix}, \begin{bmatrix} 2 \\ 1 \\ 4 \end{bmatrix}$

Ans. $\dfrac{1}{10}\begin{bmatrix} 73 & 2 & -37 \\ -115 & 10 & 55 \\ 117 & 18 & -93 \end{bmatrix}$

(*ii*) eigen values: 1, 2, 3

eigen vectors: $\begin{bmatrix} -1 \\ -1 \\ 1 \end{bmatrix}, \begin{bmatrix} 0 \\ 1 \\ 0 \end{bmatrix}, \begin{bmatrix} 0 \\ -1 \\ 1 \end{bmatrix}$

Ans. $\begin{bmatrix} 1 & 0 & 0 \\ -2 & 2 & -1 \\ 2 & 0 & 3 \end{bmatrix}$.

13

Differential Equations

An equation which contains an independent variable, dependent variable and differential coefficients of dependent variable with respect to independent variable, is called a Differential Equation.

- **Order of a differential equation:** The order of a differential equation is the order of the highest order devivative involved in the differential equation.
- **Degree of a differential equation:** It is the degree of the highest order derivative when differential coefficients are made free from radicals and fractions.
- **Linear differential equation:** A differential equation is said to be a linear differential equation if can be expressed as

$$P_0 \frac{d^n y}{dx^n} + P_1 \frac{d^{n-1} y}{dx^{n-1}} + P_2 \frac{d^{n-2} y}{dx^{n-2}} + \ldots + P_{n-1} \frac{dy}{dx} + P_n y = Q$$

where P_0, P_1, P_2 ... P_n and Q are either constants or functions of x only.

Thus, the above differential equation will not be linear if :

(*i*) Its degree is more than one.

(*ii*) Any of the derivatives has power more than one.

(*iii*) Power of the dependent variable is more than one.

(*iv*) Any term containing the dependent variable and its derivatives is present in the equation.

- **Solution of a differential equation:** It is a relation between dependent variable and independent which satisfies the given differential equation.
- **General solution:** A solution containing as many arbitrary constants as the order of the differential equation is called the general solution of the differential equation.

- **Particular solution:** A solution obtained by giving particular values to the arbitrary constants is called a particular solution.

For example, solution of the differential equation

$$\frac{d^2 y}{dx^2} + 9y = 0,$$

given by $y = A \cos 3x + B \sin 3x$ is the general solution and

given by $y = 3 \sin 3x + 5 \cos 3x$ is the particular solution which is obtained under some particular condition.

Here, we are mainly concerned about the methods of solving differential equations.

Solution of First order first degree differential equations.

It is not possible to solve all the differential equations. Differential equations which are or can be reduced to some standard forms, can only be solved, which are as:

Differential Equations of the Form

$$\frac{dy}{dx} = f(x) \tag{i}$$

where $f(x)$ is either a constant or a function of x only.

then $dy = f(x)\, dx$

Integrating both sides, we have

$$\int dy = \int f(x)\, dx + C$$

$$y = \int f(x)\, dx + C$$

where C is the constant of integration.

Example 1. Solve $\frac{dy}{dx} - \frac{2x}{x^2+1} = 0$.

Solution: We have from the given differential

$$dy = \frac{2x}{x^2+1} dx. \tag{1}$$

Integrating both sides, we have

$$y = \log(x^2 + 1) + C$$

$\therefore$ $y = \log(x^2 + 1) + C$ is the solution of the given differential equation.

Example 2. Solve $(x + 1)\, dy = (x^2 + 3x + 6)\, dx$.

Solution: From the given differential equation, we have

$$\therefore \qquad dy = \frac{x^2 + 3x + 6}{x+1}\, dx$$

$$dy = \left(x + 2 + \frac{4}{x+1}\right) dx$$

Integrating both sides, we have

$$y = \frac{x^2}{2} + 2x + 4 \log (x + 1) + C$$

is the required solution.

Differential equations in variable separable form

If a differential equation can be expressed as

$$f(x)\, dx = \phi(y)\, dy \qquad (1)$$

where $f(x)$ is function of x only and $\phi(y)$ is function of y only.

Then the solution is obtained by

$$\int f(x)\, dx = \int \phi(y)\, dy + C$$

where C is the constant of integration.

Example 1. Solve: $(x + 3)\dfrac{dy}{dx} = 2xy.$

Solution: We have $$\frac{dy}{dx} = \frac{2xy}{(x+3)}$$

$$\therefore \qquad \frac{1}{y} dy = \frac{2x}{x+3} dx$$

or $$\frac{1}{y} dy = \left(2 - \frac{6}{x+3}\right) dx$$

Integrating both sides, we have

$$\log y = 2x - 6 \log (x+3) + C.$$

$\therefore$ The solution of the given differential equation is

$$\log y = 2x - 6 \log (x + 3) + C.$$

Example 2. Slove the differential equation

$$x(1 + y^2)\,dx - y(1 + x^2)\,dy = 0, \text{ when } y = 0 \text{ for } x = 1.$$

Solution: The given differential equation is

$$x(1 + y^2)\,dx = y(1 + x^2)\,dy \qquad (1)$$

$\therefore$
$$\frac{y}{1+y^2}dy = \frac{x}{1+x^2}dx$$

or
$$\frac{2y}{1+y^2dy} = \frac{2x}{1+x^2}dx$$

Integrating both sides, we have

$$\int\frac{2y}{1+y^2}\,dy = \int\frac{2x}{1+x^2}\,dx + \log C$$

or
$$\log(1 + y^2) = \log(1 + x^2) + \log C$$

$\therefore$
$$\log\left(\frac{1+y^2}{1+x^2}\right) = \log C$$

$\Rightarrow$
$$\frac{1+y^2}{1+x^2} = C \qquad (2)$$

given that $y = 0$ for $x = 1$

$\therefore$
$$\frac{1+0}{1+1} = C \quad \therefore \quad C = \frac{1}{2}$$

$\therefore$ The solution is $\quad 1 + x^2 = 2(1 + y^2)$.

Example 3. Solve $(x^2 - yx^2)\,dy + (y^2 + x^2y^2)\,dx = 0$.

Solution: The given differential equation is

$$(x^2 - yx^2)\,dy + (y^2 + x^2y^2)\,dx = 0 \qquad (1)$$

$\therefore$
$$x^2(1 - y)dy + y^2(1 + x^2)\,dx = 0$$

Dividing throughout by x^2y^2, we have

$$\frac{1}{y^2}(1-y)\,dy + \frac{1}{x^2}\left(1+x^2\right)dx = 0$$

or
$$\left(\frac{1}{y^2} - \frac{1}{y}\right)dy + \left(\frac{1}{x^2} + 1\right)dx = 0 \qquad \ldots(2)$$

Integrating both sides, we have

$$\frac{-1}{y} - \log|y| + \frac{-1}{x} + x + c = 0.$$

$$\frac{1}{y} + \log|y| - \frac{1}{x} + x = C, \text{ is the solution.}$$

Equations reducible to variable separable form

Differential equations of the form

$\frac{dy}{dx} = \phi\,(ax + by + c)$ can be reduced to variable separable form by making the substitution

$$ax + by + c = t$$

$$\therefore \quad a + b\frac{dy}{dx} = \frac{dt}{dx}$$

or
$$\frac{dy}{dx} = \frac{1}{b}\left[\frac{dt}{dx} - a\right].$$

Example 1. Solve the differential equation $\frac{dy}{dx} = \cos(x + y)$.

Solution: The given differential equation is

$$\frac{dy}{dx} = \cos(x + y) \qquad \text{...(1)}$$

Let $x + y = t$

$$\therefore \quad 1 + \frac{dy}{dx} = \frac{dt}{dx} \quad \therefore \quad \frac{dy}{dx} = \frac{dt}{dx} - 1$$

Substituting these in equation (1), we have

$$\frac{dt}{dx} - 1 = \cos(t)$$

$$\therefore \quad \frac{dt}{dx} = 1 + \cos t$$

or
$$\frac{dt}{1 + \cos t} = dx$$

or
$$\frac{dt}{2\cos^2\frac{t}{2}} = dx$$

$$\therefore \qquad \sec^2\left(\frac{t}{2}\right)dt = 2dx.$$

Integrating both sides, we get

$$2\tan\left(\frac{t}{2}\right) = 2x + C$$

$$\tan\left(\frac{t}{2}\right) = x + C'$$

or $\tan\left(\dfrac{x+y}{2}\right) = x + C$, is the required solution.

Example 2. Solve the differential equation

$$(x + y + 1)\frac{dy}{dx} = 1.$$

Solution: The given differential equation is

$$(x + y + 1)\frac{dy}{dx} = 1 \qquad (1)$$

Let $x + y + 1 = t$ (2)

$$\therefore \qquad 1+\frac{dy}{dx} = \frac{dt}{dx}$$

$$\therefore \qquad \frac{dy}{dx} = \frac{dt}{dx}-1. \qquad (3)$$

Making these substitutions, we have

$$t\left(\frac{dt}{dx}-1\right) = 1$$

$$\therefore \qquad \frac{dt}{dx}-1 = \frac{1}{t}$$

$$\therefore \qquad \frac{dt}{dx} = 1+\frac{1}{t}$$

$$= \frac{1+t}{t}$$

$$\frac{t}{1+t}\,dt = dx$$

or $$\left(1-\frac{1}{1+t}\right)dt = dx$$

Integrating both sides, we get

$$t - \log(1+t) = x + C$$

or $$x + y + 1 - \log(x+y+2) = x + C$$

$\therefore$ $$\log(x+y+2) = y + 1 + C'$$

or $\log(x+y+2) = y + k$, is the required solution.

Example 3. Solve the differential equation

$$\frac{dy}{dx} = \frac{(x-y)+3}{2(x-y)+5}.$$

Solution: We are given that

$$\frac{dy}{dx} = \frac{(x-y)+3}{2(x-y)+5} \qquad (1)$$

Let $$x - y = t$$

$\therefore$ $$1 - \frac{dy}{dx} = \frac{dt}{dx}$$

$\therefore$ $$\frac{dy}{dx} = 1 - \frac{dt}{dx}$$

Substituting these in the given differential equation (1), we have

$$1 - \frac{dt}{dx} = \frac{t+3}{2t+5}$$

$\therefore$ $$1-\frac{t+3}{2t+5} = \frac{dt}{dx}$$

or $$\frac{2t+5-t-3}{2t+5} = \frac{dt}{dx}$$

$$\frac{t+2}{2t+5} = \frac{dt}{dx}$$

$\therefore$ $$\frac{2t+5}{t+2}\,dt = dx$$

or $$\frac{2(t+2)+1}{t+2}dt = dx$$

$\therefore$ $$\left(2+\frac{1}{t+2}\right)dt = dx \quad (2)$$

Integrating (2), we have

$$2t + \log(t + 2) = x + C$$

$$2.\ (x - y) + \log(x - y + 2) = x + C$$

$$\log(x - y + 2) = 2y - x + C$$

is the solution of the given differential equation.

Homogeneous Functions

A function is said to be homogeneous, if, when expressed in polynomial form, the degree of each term is same.

For example, Homogeneous function of

(*i*) degree one as $x + y$

(*ii*) degree two $x^2 + k_1 xy + k_2 y^2$

(*iii*) degree three $x^3 + k_1x_2y + 2xy^2 + k_3y^3$

(*iv*) $e^{\frac{y}{x}} . \sin\left(\frac{x}{y}\right)$ etc., are homogeneous functions.

Homogeneous Differential Equations

A differential equation

$$\frac{dy}{dx} = \frac{f(x, y)}{g(x, y)}$$

is said to be homogeneous, if $f(x, y)$ and $g(x, y)$ are homogeneous functions of the same degree.

If a differential equation is homogeneous, it can be transformed to variable separable form by the substitution

$y = Vx$, where V is a function of x.

$\therefore$ $$\frac{dy}{dx} = V + x\frac{dV}{dx}.$$

Example 1. Solve the differential equation

$$(x^2 - y^2)\, dx + 2xy\, dy = 0$$

given that $y = 1$ for $x = 1$.

Solution: From the given differential equation, we have

$$\frac{dy}{dx} = \frac{y^2 - x^2}{2xy} \qquad \text{(i)}$$

here N^r and D^r both are homogeneous functions of degree two.

So, let $y = VX$

$$\therefore \quad \frac{dy}{dx} = V + x\frac{dv}{dx}$$

Substituting these in the given differential equation (1), we have

$$V + x\frac{dV}{dx} = \frac{x^2\left(V^2 - 1\right)}{2x^2 .\ V}$$

$$\therefore \quad V + x\frac{dV}{dx} = \frac{V^2 - 1}{2V}$$

$$\therefore \quad x\frac{dV}{dx} = \frac{V^2 - 1}{2V} - V$$

$$= \frac{V^2 - 1 - 2V^2}{2V}$$

$$x\frac{dV}{dx} = \frac{-\left[1 + V^2\right]}{2V}$$

$$\therefore \quad \frac{2V}{1+V^2}dV = -\frac{1}{x}dx.$$

Integrating both sides, we have

$$\log(1 + V^2) = -\log(x) + \log(C)$$

$$\therefore \quad \log(1 + V^2) + \log x = \log(C)$$

$$\therefore \quad (1 + V^2)\, x = C$$

or

$$\left(1 + \frac{y^2}{x^2}\right) x = C$$

or $x^2 + y^2 = Cx$

Given that $y = 1$ for $x = 1$

$\therefore$ $1 + 1 = C$

$\therefore$ $C = 2.$

$\therefore$ $x^2 + y^2 = 2x$

or $x^2 + y^2 - 2x = 0$, is the solution of the given differential equation.

Example 2. Solve $x\,dy - y\,dx = \sqrt{x^2 + y^2}\ dx$.

Solution: From the given differential equation, we have

$$x\,\frac{dy}{dx} - y = \sqrt{x^2 + y^2}$$

$$\therefore \quad x\,\frac{dy}{dx} = \sqrt{x^2 + y^2} + y$$

$$\therefore \quad \frac{dy}{dx} = \frac{\sqrt{x^2 + y^2} + y}{x} \qquad (1)$$

Equation (1) is a homogeneous differential equation.

So, let $y = Vx$ (2)

$$\therefore \quad \frac{dy}{dx} = V + x\,\frac{dV}{dx} \qquad (3)$$

Substituting (2) and (3) in equation (1), we have

$$V + x\frac{dV}{dx} = \frac{x\left[\sqrt{1+V^2} + V\right]}{x}$$

$$= \sqrt{1+V^2} + V$$

$$x\frac{dV}{dx} = \sqrt{1+V^2}$$

$$\therefore \quad \frac{1}{\sqrt{1+V^2}}\,dV = \frac{1}{x}\,dx.$$

Integrating both sides, we have

$$\log\left[V + \sqrt{1+V^2}\right] = \log x + \log C$$

$$\therefore \quad V + \sqrt{1+V^2} = Cx$$

$$\therefore \quad \frac{y}{x} + \frac{1}{x}\sqrt{y^2 + x^2} = Cx$$

$$y + \sqrt{y^2 + x^2} = Cx^2$$

is the solution of the given differential equation.

Example 3. Solve the differential equation

$$x\frac{dy}{dx} = y - x \tan\left(\frac{y}{x}\right).$$

Solution: The given differential equation can be written as

$$\frac{dy}{dx} = \frac{y - x\tan\left(\frac{y}{x}\right)}{x} \qquad (1)$$

Since $\tan\left(\frac{y}{x}\right)$ is homeneous of degree zero.

$$\therefore \quad \frac{y - x\tan\left(\frac{y}{x}\right)}{x} \text{ is homogeneous.}$$

$\therefore$ Equation (1) is homogeneous differential equation.

So, let $\quad y = Vx \qquad (2)$

$$\therefore \quad \frac{dy}{dx} = V + x\frac{dV}{dx} \qquad (3)$$

Substituting (2) and (3) in equation (1), we have

$$V + x\frac{dV}{dx} = V - \tan V$$

$$\therefore \quad x\frac{dV}{dx} = -\tan V$$

$$\therefore \quad \cot V\, dV = \frac{-1}{x}dx$$

Integrating both sides, we have

$$\log(\sin V) = -\log x + \log C$$

$$\therefore \quad \log(\sin V \,.\, x) = \log C$$

$\therefore \qquad x \,.\, \sin V = C$

or $\qquad x \,.\, \sin\left(\frac{y}{x}\right) = C$

is the solution of the given differential equation.

Differential Equations Reducible to Homogeneous form

A differential equation of the form

$$\frac{dy}{dx} = \frac{a_1 x + b_1 y + c_1}{a_2 x + b_2 y + c_2} \qquad (1)$$

can be reduced to homogeneous form.

Case I.

When $\qquad \frac{a_1}{a_2} \neq \frac{b_1}{b_2}$

We make substitution to eliminate c_1 and c_2.

Let $\qquad x = X + h,$

$\qquad y = Y + k$

$$\therefore \qquad \frac{dy}{dx} = \frac{dY}{dX}$$

$\therefore$ The given differential equation becomes

$$\frac{dY}{dX} = \frac{a_1 X + b_1 Y + (a_1 h + b_1 k + c_1)}{a_2 X + b_2 Y + (a_2 h + b_2 k + c_2)} \qquad (2)$$

Now, choose h and k such that

$$a_1 h + b_1 k + c_1 = 0 \qquad (3)$$

$$a_2 h + b_2 k + c_2 = 0 \qquad (4)$$

Solving these, we have the values of h and k.

Now the equation (2) becomes

$$\frac{dY}{dX} = \frac{a_1 X + b_1 Y}{a_2 X + b_2 Y} \qquad (5)$$

which is homogeneous and can be solved by the method discussed earlier.

Finally, we replace X by $x - h$, Y by $y - k$, and get the solution in terms of x and y.

Example 1. Solve the differential equation

$$\frac{dy}{dx} = \frac{2y - x - 5}{2x - y + 4}.$$

Solution: The given differential equation can be written as

$$\frac{dy}{dx} = \frac{-x + 2y - 5}{2x - y + 4} \tag{1}$$

Here $\frac{a_1}{a_2} \neq \frac{b_1}{b_2}$

$\therefore$ Let

$$x = X + h \tag{2}$$

$$y = Y + k \tag{3}$$

$\therefore$ $\frac{dy}{dx} = \frac{dY}{dX}$ substituting there in equation (1), we have

$$\frac{dY}{dX} = \frac{-X + 2Y + (-h + 2k - 5)}{2X - Y + (2h - k + 4)} \tag{4}$$

Let $\left.\begin{aligned} -h + 2k - 5 = 0 \\ 2h - k + 4 = 0 \end{aligned}\right\} \begin{aligned} h = -1 \\ k = 2 \end{aligned}$

Equation (4) becomes

$$\frac{dY}{dX} = \frac{-X + 2Y}{2X - Y}, \quad \text{which is homo.} \tag{5}$$

Let $Y = VX$

$\therefore$ $\frac{dY}{dX} = V + X\frac{dV}{dX}$

Substitution in equation (5), gives

$$V + X\frac{dV}{dX} = \frac{X[2V - 1]}{X(2 - V)}$$

or

$$V + X\frac{dV}{dX} = \frac{2V - 1}{2 - V}$$

$\therefore$

$$X\frac{dV}{dX} = \frac{2V - 1}{2 - V} - \text{V}$$

$$= \frac{2V - 1 - 2V + V^2}{2 - V}$$

or $$X\frac{dV}{dX} = \frac{1-V^2}{V-2}$$

$\therefore$ $$\frac{V-2}{1-V^2}\,dV = \frac{1}{X}\,dX$$

$$\frac{V}{1-V^2}\,dV + \frac{2}{V^2-1}\,dV = \frac{1}{X}\,dX$$

Integrating, we get

$$-\frac{1}{2}\log(1-V^2) + 2\,.\,\frac{1}{2}\log\left|\frac{V-1}{V+1}\right| = \log X + \log C$$

or $$-\frac{1}{2}\log(1-V^2) + \log\left|\frac{V-1}{V+1}\right| = \log(CX)$$

$\therefore$ $$2\log\left(\frac{V-1}{V+1}\right) - \log(1-V^2) = 2\log(CX)$$

or $$\log\left[\frac{(1-V)^2}{(V+1)^2}\cdot\frac{1}{1-V^2}\right] = \log(C^2X^2)$$

or $$\log\left[\frac{1-V}{(1+V)^3}\right] = \log(C^2X^2)$$

$\therefore$ $$(1-V) = (1+V)^3\,.\,C^2X^2$$

$\because$ $$V = \frac{Y}{X}$$

$\therefore$ $$\left(1-\frac{Y}{X}\right) = \left(1+\frac{Y}{X}\right)^3.\,C^2X^2$$

or $$(X-Y) = (X+Y)^3\,.\,C^2$$

$\because$ $$X = X-1,$$

$$y = Y+2 \text{ putting above, we have}$$

$$(x+1-y+2) = (x+1+y-2)^3\,.\,C$$

or $(x+y-1)^3\,C = (x-y+3)$ is the required solution.

Case 2.

When

$$\frac{a_1}{a_2} = \frac{b_1}{b_2} = \frac{1}{p}$$

$$\therefore \quad a_2 = a_1 p$$

$$b_2 = b_1 p$$

$\therefore$ The given equation reduces to

$$\frac{dy}{dx} = \frac{a_1 x + b_1 y + c_1}{p(a_1 x + b_1 y) + c_2}$$

Now, substitute

$$a_1 x + b_1 y = V$$

$$\therefore \quad a_1 + b_1 \frac{dy}{dx} = \frac{dV}{dx}$$

$$\therefore \quad \frac{dy}{dx} = \frac{1}{b_1}\left(\frac{dV}{dx} - a_1\right)$$

Then the given equation

$$\frac{dy}{dx} = \frac{a_1 x + b_1 y + c_1}{a_2 x + b_2 y + c_2}$$

becomes

$$\frac{1}{b_1}\left[\frac{dV}{dx} - a_1\right] = \frac{V + c_1}{pV + c_2}$$

which can be solved by the method of variable separable

Example 1. Solve the differential equation

$$(2x - y + 2)\, dx + (4x - 2y - 1)\, dy = 0.$$

Solution: The given differential equation can be written as

$$\frac{dy}{dx} = -\frac{(2x - y + 2)}{(4x - 2y - 1)} \quad \text{... (1)}$$

or

$$\frac{dy}{dx} = \frac{2x - y + 2}{-4x + 2y + 1}$$

Here $$\frac{a_1}{b_2} = -\frac{1}{2} = \frac{b_1}{b_2}$$

$\therefore$ Let $$2x - y = V \qquad \text{... (2)}$$

$\therefore$ $$2 - \frac{dy}{dx} = \frac{dV}{dx}$$

or $$\frac{dy}{dx} = 2 - \frac{dV}{dx} \qquad \text{... (3)}$$

Substituting (2) and (3) in (1), we have

$$2 - \frac{dV}{dx} = \frac{V+2}{-2V+1}$$

or $$2 - \frac{V+2}{-2V+1} = \frac{dV}{dx}$$

$\therefore$ $$\frac{dV}{dx} = \frac{-4V+2-V-2}{1-2V}$$

$$\frac{dV}{dx} = \frac{-5V}{1-2V}$$

$$= \frac{5V}{2V-1}$$

$\therefore$ $$\frac{2V-1}{5V} dV = dx$$

or $$\left(\frac{2}{5} - \frac{1}{5}.\frac{1}{V}\right) dV = dx$$

Integrating both sides, we get

$$\frac{2V}{5} - \frac{1}{5}\log V = x + C$$

or $$\frac{2(2x-y)}{5} - \frac{1}{5} \log (2x - y) = x + C$$

$$4x - 2y - \log (2x - y) = 5x + C$$

$\therefore$ $$x + 2y + \log (2x - y) = C$$

is the solution of the given differential equation.

EXERCISE

Solve the following differential equations:

1. $\dfrac{dy}{dx} = \dfrac{x(2\log x+1)}{y\cos y+\sin y}$.

Ans. $y \sin y = x^2 \log x + C$

2. $2xy \dfrac{dy}{dx} = 1 + x + y + xy$.

Ans. $y = x + \log [x (1 + y)]+C$

3. $\dfrac{y}{x}\dfrac{dy}{dx} = \sqrt{1+x^2+y^2+x^2y^2}$.

Ans. $\sqrt{1+y^2} = \dfrac{2}{3}(1 + x^2)^{3/2} + C$

4. $\dfrac{dy}{dx} = (4x + y + 1)^2$.

Ans. $4x + y + 1 = 2 \tan (2x + C)$

5. $\dfrac{dy}{dx} = \sin (x + y) + \cos (x + y)$

Ans. $\log \left[1+\tan\left(\dfrac{x+y}{2}\right)\right] = x + C$

6. $\tan y \dfrac{dy}{dx} = \sin (x + y) + \sin (x - y)$

Ans. $2\cos x + \sec y = C$

7. $(x + y)^2 \cdot \dfrac{dy}{dx} = a^2$.

Ans. $x + y = a \cdot \tan \left(\dfrac{y-C}{a}\right)$

8. $(x + y)\, dx + (y - x)\, dy = 0$.

Ans. $\log (x^2 + y^2) = 2\tan^{-1}\left(\dfrac{y}{x}\right) + C$

9. $[x \tan\left(\frac{y}{x}\right) - y \sec^2\left(\frac{y}{x}\right)]\, dx + x \sec^2\left(\frac{y}{x}\right) dy = 0.$

Ans. $x \tan\left(\frac{y}{x}\right) = C$

10. $(1 + e^{x/y})\, dx + e^{x/y}\left[1 - \frac{x}{y}\right] dy = 0.$

Ans. $x + y\, e^{x/y} = C$

11. $x\frac{dy}{dx} = y\,[\log y - \log x].$

Ans. $y = xe^{1+cx}$

12. $(3y - 7x + 7)\, dx + (7y - 3x + 3)\, dy = 0$

Ans. $(x - y - 1)^2\, (x + y - 1)^5 = \text{C}$

13. $\frac{dy}{dx} + \frac{2x+3y+1}{3x+4y-1} = 0.$

Ans. $x^2 + 3xy + 2y^2 + x - y = C$

14. $\frac{dy}{dx} = \frac{6x-4y+3}{3x-2y+1}.$

Ans. $2x - y = \log\,(3x - 2y + 3) + C$

15. $\frac{dy}{dx} = \frac{x+2y-3}{2x+y-3}.$

Ans. $(x - y)^3 = C\,[x + y - 2]$

16. $(x + y)\,(dx - dy) = dx + dy$

Ans. $x - y = \log\,(x + y) + \text{C}.$

Linear Differential Equation of First Order

The general form of a linear differential equation of first order is

$$\frac{dy}{dx} + Py = Q \quad (1)$$

where P and Q are constants or functions of x only. Also known as Leibnitz's form of linear equation.

The equation (1) can be solved by making its L.H.S., an exact differential of some function, which is done my multiplying the equation (1) by some suitable function $V(x)$, known as an integrating factor (I.F.).

As V (x) is the integrating factor for the differential equation (1).

$$\therefore \qquad V.\frac{dy}{dx} + PVy = QV \qquad (2)$$

$$\text{or} \qquad \frac{d}{dx}(Vy) = QV \qquad (3)$$

Comparing equations (2) and (3), we have

$$PVy = \frac{dV}{dx}.y$$

$$\text{or} \qquad \frac{dV}{dx} = PV$$

$$\therefore \qquad \frac{1}{V}dV = P\,dx \qquad (4)$$

Integrating, we get

$$\log V = \int P\,dx.$$

$$\text{or} \qquad V = e^{\int P\,dx}$$

Substituting V in equation (3), we have

$$\frac{d}{dx}\left[ye^{\int P\,dx}\right] = Qe^{\int P\,dx}$$

Integrating both sides w.r.t. x, we have

$$ye^{\int P\,dx} = \int Q.e^{\int P\,dx}\,dx + C$$

or the solution is given by

$$ye^{\int P\,dx} = \int\left\{Q.e^{\int P\,dx}\right\}dx + C.$$

SOLVED EXAMPLES

Example 1. Solve the differential equation

$$\frac{dy}{dx} + \frac{y}{x} = x^3.$$

Solution: The given differential equation is

$$\frac{dy}{dx} + \frac{1}{x} \cdot y = x^3.$$

which is linear differential equation of Ist order.

Comparing it with the standard form

$$\frac{dy}{dx} + Py = Q,$$

We have

$$P = \frac{1}{x}$$

$$Q = x^3$$

$$\therefore \qquad \text{I.F.} = e^{\int p\,dx}$$

$$= e^{\int \frac{1}{x} dx}$$

$$= e^{\log x}$$

$$= x$$

$\therefore$ The solution is given by

$$y \cdot x = \int x^3 . x\,dx + C$$

$$= \frac{x^5}{5} + C$$

or $$xy = \frac{x^5}{5} + C.$$

Example 2. Solve the differential equation

$$(1 + x^2)\frac{dy}{dx} + y = \tan^{-1}x.$$

Solution: The given differential equation can be wirtten as

$$\frac{dy}{dx} + \frac{1}{1+x^2} \cdot y = \frac{1}{1+x^2} \cdot \tan^{-1}(x) \qquad ...(1)$$

which is linear differential equation of first order.

Here $$P = \frac{1}{1+x^2}$$

$$Q = \frac{1}{1+x^2} \cdot \tan^{-1}(x)$$

$\therefore$ $$\text{I.F.} = e^{\int \frac{1}{1+x^2} dx}$$
$$= e^{\tan^{-1}(x)}$$

$\therefore$ The solution is

$$y \cdot e^{\tan^{-1}(x)} = \int \frac{1}{1+x^2} \cdot \tan^{-1}(x) \cdot e^{\tan^{-1}(x)}\, dx + C$$

or $$y \cdot e^{\tan^{-1}(x)} = \int \frac{\tan^{-1}(x)}{1+x^2} \cdot e^{\tan^{-1}(x)}\, dx + C$$

Now $$\text{I} = \int \frac{e^{\tan^{-1}x} . \tan^{-1}(x)}{1+x^2}\, dx$$

Let $\tan^{-1}x = t$

$\therefore$ $$\frac{1}{1+x^2} dx = dt$$

$\therefore$ $$\text{I} = \int e^t . t\, dt$$

$$= t \cdot e^t - \int 1 \cdot e^t\, dt$$
$$= e^t \cdot t - e^t$$
$$= e^t\, [t - 1]$$
$$= e^{\tan^{-1}}x \cdot (\tan^{-1}x - 1)$$

$\therefore$ The solution is

$$y \cdot e^{\tan^{-1}}x = e^{\tan^{-1}(x)} \cdot [\tan^{-1}(x) - 1] + \text{C}$$

or $y = \tan^{-1}(x) - 1 + C \cdot \text{e}^{-\tan^{-1}x}$, is the solution.

Example 3. Solve the differential equation

$$\frac{dy}{dx} + 2y \tan x = \sin x.$$

Solution: The given differential equations is

$$\frac{dy}{dx} + 2 \tan x \,.\, y = \sin x$$

which is linear differential equation of first order.

Here $\qquad P = 2 \tan x$

$\qquad Q = \sin x$

$\therefore \qquad \text{I.F.} = e^{\int 2 \tan x \, dx}$

$\qquad = e^{2 \log \sec x}$

$\qquad = e^{\log (\sec^2 x)}$

$\qquad \text{I.F.} = \sec^2 x$

$\therefore$ The solution is

$$y \,.\, \sec^2 x = \int \sec^2 x . \sin x dx + C$$

$$= \int \sec x . \tan x \, dx + C$$

$$= \sec x + C$$

$\therefore \qquad y . \sec^2 x = \sec x + C.$

Example 4. Solve the differential equation

$$(x \log x) \frac{dy}{dx} + y = 2 \log x.$$

Solution: The given differential equaion is

$$\frac{dy}{dx} + \frac{1}{x \log x} . y = \frac{2}{x}$$

which is linear differential equation of first order.

Here $\qquad \text{P} = \dfrac{1}{x \log x}$

$\qquad \text{Q} = \dfrac{2}{x}$

$\therefore \qquad \text{I.F.} = e^{\int p \, dx}$

$\qquad = e^{\int \frac{1}{x \log x} dx.}$

$$= e^{\log(\log x)}$$

$$= \log x$$

$\therefore$ The solution is

$$y \,.\, \log x = \int \frac{2}{x} \,.\, \log(x)\, dx + C$$

$$= (\log x)^2 + C$$

$\therefore$ $$y \,.\, \log x = (\log x)^2 + \text{C}.$$

Example 5. Solve the differential equation

$$(1 + x^3)\, \frac{dy}{dx} + 6x^2y = 1 + x^2.$$

Solution: The given differential equation can be written as

$$\frac{dy}{dx} + \frac{6x^2}{1+x^3}\, y = \frac{1+x^2}{1+x^3} \qquad (1)$$

which is linear differential equation of first order

Here $$P = \frac{6x^2}{1+x^3}$$

$$Q = \frac{1+x^2}{1+x^3}$$

$\therefore$ $$\text{I.F.} = e^{\int p\, dx}$$

$$= e^{\int \frac{6x^2}{1+x^3} dx}$$

$$= e^{2\log(1 + x^3)}$$

$$= e^{\log(1 + x^3)^2}$$

$$\text{I.F.} = (1 + x^3)^2$$

$\therefore$ The solution is

$$y \,.\, (1 + x^3)^2 = \int \frac{\left(1+x^2\right)}{\left(1+x^3\right)} \,.\, (1 + x^3)^2\, dx + \text{C}$$

or $$(1 + x^3)^2\, y = \int \left(1+x^2\right)\left(1+x^3\right) dx + C$$

$$= \int\left(1+x^2+x^3+x^5\right)\, dx + C$$

$$(1 + x^3)^2\, y = x+\frac{x^3}{3}+\frac{x^4}{4}+\frac{x^6}{6}+C\,.$$

Example 6. Solve the differential equation

$$\frac{dy}{dx} = \frac{1}{x\cos y+\sin 2y}\,.$$

Solution: The given differential equation can be written as

$$\frac{dx}{dy} = x \cos y + \sin 2y$$

or $$\frac{dx}{dy} - \cos y\,.\,x = \sin 2y \qquad (1)$$

which is a linear differential equation of first order.

Here $$P = -\cos y$$

$$Q = \sin 2y$$

$\therefore$ $$\text{I.F.} = e^{\int -\cos y\, dy}$$

$$= e^{-\sin y}$$

$\therefore$ The solution is

$$x\,.\,e^{-\sin y} = \int e^{-\sin y}.\sin 2y\, dy + C$$

$$= 2\int e^{-\sin y}.\sin y\ \cos y\, dy + C$$

Let $$\text{I} = 2\int e^{-\sin y}.\sin y\ \cos y\, dy$$

Let $$\sin y = t$$

$\therefore$ $$\cos y\, dy = dt$$

$$\text{I} = 2\int e^{-t}\,.\,t\, dt$$

$$= 2\left[t.\frac{e^{-t}}{(-1)}+\int e^{-t}.dt\right]$$

$$= 2[-t\,.\,e^{-t} - e^{-t}]$$

$$= -2e^{-t}\,[t + 1]$$
$$= -2e^{-\sin y}\,[\sin y + 1]$$

∴ The solution is

$$x \,.\, e^{-\sin y} = -2\, e^{-\sin y}\,[\sin y + 1] + C$$

or $$x = -2\,[\sin y + 1] + C \,.\, e^{\sin y}$$

or $$x = c \,.\, e^{\sin y} - 2\,(\sin y + 1).$$

Example 7. Solve the differential equation

$$y\,dx + (x - y^3)\,dy = 0.$$

Solution: The given differential equation is

$$y\,dx + (x - y^3)\,dy = 0 \qquad (1)$$

$$\therefore \qquad y\frac{dx}{dy} + x - y^3 = 0$$

$$y\frac{dx}{dy} + x = y^3$$

or $$\frac{dx}{dy} + \frac{x}{y} = y^2 \qquad (2)$$

Equation (2) is a linear differental equation with integrating factor

$$e^{\int \frac{1}{y} dy} = e^{\log y}$$
$$= y$$

∴ The solution is

$$x \,.\, y = \int y^2 . y\, dy + C$$

$$xy = \frac{y^4}{4} + C.$$

Example 8. Solve the differential equation

$$\frac{dy}{dx} + \frac{y}{x} = \cos x + \frac{\sin x}{x}.$$

Solution: The given differential equation is

$$\frac{dy}{dx} + \frac{1}{x} . y = \cos x + \frac{\sin x}{x} \qquad (1)$$

which is a linear differential equation of first order and first degree, whose I.F. is

$$\text{I.F.} = e^{\int \frac{1}{x} dx}$$
$$= e^{\log x}$$
$$= x$$

∴ The solution is

$$y \,.\, x = \int \left(\cos x + \frac{\sin x}{x} \right) x \, dx + C$$

$$= \int (x \cos x + \sin x) \, dx$$

$$xy = x \sin x + C.$$

EXERCISE

Solve the following differential equations:

1. $\frac{dy}{dx} + \frac{y}{x} = x^3 - 3$

Ans. $10\, x\, y = 2x^5 - 15x^2 + C.$

2. $(x^2 + 1) \frac{dy}{dx} + 2xy = x^2$

Ans. $y\,(x^2 + 1) = \frac{x^3}{3} + C.$

3. $\frac{dy}{dx} + y \,.\, \frac{1}{\sqrt{1+x^2}} = \sqrt{1+x^2}$

Ans. $y\,(x + \sqrt{1+x^2}\,) = \frac{(x^2+1)^{3/2}}{3} + \frac{x^3}{3} + C.$

4. $x \frac{dy}{dx} + y = e^x - xy$

Ans. $xy = \frac{e^x}{2} + C.\, e^{-x}.$

5. $(x + 2y^3)\frac{dy}{dx} = y$

Ans. $x = y^3 + Cy$

6. $(x^2 + 1)\ \frac{dy}{dx} + 2xy = \sqrt{x^2+4}$

Ans. $y\ (x^2 + 1) = \frac{1}{2}\ x\ \sqrt{x^2+4}\ + 2\ \log\left[x+\sqrt{x^2+4}\right] + C$

7. $\frac{dy}{dx} - 2y = \cos 3x$

Ans. $y = \frac{1}{13}\ [3\sin 3x - 2\cos 3x] + C.\ e^{2x}$

8. $\frac{dy}{dx} + y\ = (\cos x - \sin x)$

Ans. $y = \ \cos x + Ce^{-x}$

Differential Equations Reducible to Linear Form

The differential equation

$$\frac{dy}{dx} + Py = Q\ .\ y^n \qquad (1)$$

where P and Q are constants or functions of x only.

The above differential equation is known as Bernoulli's equation.

This equation can be reduced to Leibnitz's form.

Dividing both sides by y^n, we have

$$y^{-n}\ \frac{dy}{dx} + P\ .\ y^{1-n} = Q \qquad (2)$$

Substituting $y^{1-n} = t$

$$\therefore \qquad (1 - n)\ y^{-n}\ \frac{dy}{dx} = \frac{dt}{dx}$$

Substituting in the differential equation (1), we have

$$\frac{1}{(1-n)}\frac{dt}{dx} + P.\,t = Q$$

or $\dfrac{dt}{dx} + (1-n)\ P.\,t = (1-n)Q$

which is linear in t and can be solved by the method discussed earlier.

SOLVED EXAMPLES

Example 1. Solve the differential equation

$$\frac{dy}{dx} + \frac{y}{x} = x^2y^6.$$

Solution: The given differential equation can be written as

$$y^{-6}\frac{dy}{dx} + \frac{1}{x}\,y^{-5} = x^2 \qquad (1)$$

Let $\qquad y^{-5} = t$

$$-5y^{-6}\frac{dy}{dx} = \frac{dt}{dx}$$

$\therefore \qquad y^{-6}\dfrac{dy}{dx} = -\dfrac{1}{5}\dfrac{dt}{dx}$

Substituting these, equation (1) becomes

$$-\frac{1}{5}\frac{dt}{dx} + \frac{1}{x}\,.\,t = x^2$$

$$\frac{dt}{dx} - \frac{5}{x}t = -5\,x^2 \qquad (2)$$

which is a linear differential equation of first order with

$$\text{I.F.} = e^{\int -\frac{5}{x}dx}$$

$$= e^{-5\log x}$$

$$= e^{\log\,(x^{-5})}$$

$$= \frac{1}{x^5}$$

∴ The solution is

$$t \,.\, x^{-5} = \int -5x^2 . \frac{1}{x^5} dx + C$$

or
$$t \,.\, x^{-5} = -5 \int x^{-3} dx + C$$

$$t \,.\, x^{-5} = \frac{-5.x^{-2}}{(-2)} + C$$

$$= \frac{5}{2}\, x^{-2} + C$$

or
$$t = \frac{5}{2} x^3 + C \,.\, x^5$$

Putting $t = \dfrac{1}{y^5}$, we get

$$\frac{1}{y^5} = \frac{5}{2} x^3 + C\;\; x^5.$$

Example 2. Solve the differential equation

$$\frac{dy}{dx} + x \sin 2y = x \cos^2 y.$$

Solution: The given differential equation can be written as

$$\sec^2 y \, \frac{dy}{dx} + 2 \tan y \, x = x \qquad (1)$$

Let $\tan y = t$

$$\therefore \qquad \sec^2 y \frac{dy}{dx} = \frac{dt}{dx}$$

Substituting these, equation (1) can be written as

$$\frac{dt}{dx} + 2x \,.\, t = x \qquad (2)$$

Equation (2) is a linear differential equation with

$$\text{I.F.} = e^{\int 2x\, dx}$$

$$= e^{x^2}$$

and the solution of (2) is given by

$$t \,.\, e^{x^2} = \int x.e^{x^2}\,dx + C$$

$$= \frac{e^{x^2}}{2} + C$$

or $$t = \frac{1}{2} + C\,e^{-x^2}$$

or $$\tan y = C\,e^{-x^2} + \frac{1}{2}.$$

Example 3. Solve the differential equation

$$\frac{dy}{dx} - \frac{\tan y}{1+x} = (1 + x)\,e^x \sec y.$$

Solution: The given differential equation can be written as

$$\cos y\,\frac{dy}{dx} - \frac{1}{1+x}.\left(\frac{\tan y}{\sec y}\right) = (1 + x)e^x$$

or $$\cos y\frac{dy}{dx} - \frac{1}{1+x}\sin y = (1 + x)e^x \tag{1}$$

Let $$\sin y = t$$

$\therefore$ $$\cos y\,\frac{dy}{dx} = \frac{dt}{dx}$$

Substitution equ. (1) gives $$\frac{dt}{dx} - \frac{1}{1+x}\,.\,t = (1 + x)e^x \tag{2}$$

Equation (2) is a linear differential equation of first order.

$$\text{I.F.} = e^{\int \frac{-1}{1+x}dx}$$

$$= e^{-\log(1 + x)}$$

$$\text{I.F.} = \frac{1}{1+x}.$$

$\therefore$ The solution is

$$t\,.\,\frac{1}{1+x} = \int (1+x)e^x \cdot \frac{1}{1+x}dx + C$$

$$\frac{t}{(1+x)} = e^x + C$$

$$t = e^x (1 + x) + C \cdot (1 + x)$$

or $$\sin y = e^x (1 + x) + C (1 + x)$$

$\therefore$ $$\sin y = (e^x + C) (x + 1).$$

Example 4. Solve the differential equation

$$\frac{dy}{dx} + \frac{x}{1-x^2} y = x\sqrt{y}.$$

Solution: Dividing the given differential equation by $\sqrt{y}$, we have

$$\frac{1}{\sqrt{y}}\frac{dy}{dx} + \frac{x}{1-x^2}\sqrt{y} = x \qquad (1)$$

Let $$\sqrt{y} = t$$

$\therefore$ $$\frac{1}{2}\frac{1}{\sqrt{y}}\frac{dy}{dx} = \cdot \frac{dt}{dx}$$

$\therefore$ $$\frac{1}{\sqrt{y}}\frac{dy}{dx} = 2 \cdot \frac{dt}{dx}$$

Substituting in eq. (1),

we have, $$2\frac{dt}{dx} + \frac{x^t}{1-x^2} = x$$

or $$\frac{dt}{dx} + \frac{x}{2(1-x^2)}t = \frac{x}{2} \qquad (2)$$

Equation (2) is linear differential equation, with I.F. as

$$\text{I.F.} = e^{\int \frac{x}{2(1-x^2)} dx}$$

$$= e^{\frac{1}{4}\log(1-x^2)}$$

$$= e^{\log (1 - x^2)^{-1/4}}$$

$$= (1 - x^2)^{-1/4}$$

$\therefore$ The solution is

$$t\,.\,(1-x^2)^{-1/4} = \frac{1}{2}\int x.\left(1-x^2\right)^{-1/4} dx$$

$$= \frac{-1}{4}.\frac{\left(1-x^2\right)^{3/4}}{3/4} + C$$

$$= \frac{-1}{3}\left(1-x^2\right)^{3/4} + C$$

$\therefore$ $$t = \frac{-1}{3}(1-x^2) + C\,.\,(1-x^2)^{1/4}$$

or $$\sqrt{y} = \frac{-1}{3}(1-x^2) + C\,.\,(1-X^2)^{1/4}$$

EXERCISE

Solve the following differential equations:

1. $(x+1)\dfrac{dy}{dx} - y = e^x\,.\,(x+1)^2$

   Ans. $y = (x+1)\,(e^x + C)$

2. $\dfrac{dy}{dx} = \dfrac{y}{2y\log y + y - x}$

   Ans. $xy = y^2\log y + C$

3. $\dfrac{dy}{dx} = 4x\,\text{cosec}\,x - y\cot x.$

   Given $y = 0$ for $x = \dfrac{\pi}{2}$.

   Ans. $y\sin y = 2x^2 - \dfrac{\pi^2}{2}$

4. $x\,dy + dx = e^{-y}\sec^2 y\,dx$

   Ans. $xe^y = \tan y + C$

5. $x^2\dfrac{dy}{dx} = 3x^2 - 2xy + 1$

   Ans. $y = x + \dfrac{1}{x} + \dfrac{C}{x^2}$

6. $x(1-x^2)\dfrac{dy}{dx} + (2x^2-1)\,y = x^3.$

Ans. $y - x = Cx\sqrt{1-x^2}$

7. $\dfrac{dy}{dx} + \dfrac{y\log y}{x} = \dfrac{y.(\log y)^2}{x^2}$

Ans. $3y^2 = x^2\,(2e^{1/x^3} + C)$

8. $y\,(2xy + e^x)\,dx = e^x\,dy$

Ans. $e^x = y(C - x^2)$

Exact Differential Equation

A first order differential equation $M\,dx + N\,dy = 0$, where M and N are functions of x and y or constants, is said to be exact if its left hand side is the exact differential of some function $u(x, y)$. *i.e* If $du = M\,dx + N\,dy$ and its solution is given by $u(x, y) = c$.

Necessary and sufficient conditions for a first order differential equation

$M\,dx + N\,dy = 0$, to be exact.

The differential equation $M\,dx + N\,dy = 0$ is exact if it can be obtained by differentiating a function $u(x, y)$.

Let $$du = M\,dx + N\,dy \qquad (1)$$

But if u is function of x and y, then

$$du = \frac{\partial u}{\partial x}\,dx + \frac{\partial u}{\partial y}\,dy \qquad (2)$$

Equating (1) and (2), we have

$$M\,dx + N\,dy = \frac{\partial u}{\partial x}\,dx + \frac{\partial u}{\partial y}\,dy$$

Therefore, $$M = \frac{\partial u}{\partial x}$$

$$N = \frac{\partial u}{\partial y}$$

$\therefore$ $$\frac{\partial M}{\partial y} = \frac{\partial^2 u}{\partial y\partial x}$$

and $$\frac{\partial N}{\partial x} = \frac{\partial^2 y}{\partial x \partial y}$$

$\because$ $$\frac{\partial^2 y}{\partial x \partial y} = \frac{\partial^2 u}{\partial y \partial x}$$

$\therefore$ $$\frac{\partial M}{\partial y} = \frac{\partial N}{\partial x}$$

is the necessary condition for the given differential equation to be exact.

Condition is sufficient

Let the condition is satisfied

i.e. $$\frac{\delta M}{\delta y} = \frac{\delta V}{\delta x}$$

Let $$\text{P} = \int M \, dx$$

$\therefore$ $$\frac{\partial P}{\partial x} = M$$

and $$\frac{\partial^2 P}{\partial y \partial x} = \frac{\partial M}{dy}$$

But $\dfrac{\partial M}{\partial y} = \dfrac{\partial N}{\partial x}$ as the condition is satisfied.

$\therefore$ $$\frac{\partial N}{\partial x} = \frac{\partial^2 P}{\partial y \partial x}$$

$$= \frac{\partial^2 P}{\partial x \partial y}$$

$$\frac{\partial N}{\partial x} = \frac{\partial}{\partial x}\left[\frac{\partial P}{\partial y}\right]$$

Integrating both sides w.r.t. x, we have

$$N = \frac{\partial P}{\partial y} + \phi(y)$$

$\therefore \quad M\,dx + N\,dy = \dfrac{\partial P}{\partial x}dx + \dfrac{\partial P}{\partial y}\,dy + \phi(y)\,dy$

or $\quad M\,dx + N\,dy = dP + \phi(y)\,dy$

Let $\quad d[h(y)] = \phi(y)\,dy$

$\therefore \quad M\,dx + N\,dy = dP + d\,h(y)$

$\therefore \quad M\,dx + N\,dy = d[P + h(y)]$

which shows that $M\,dx + N\,dy$ is an exact differential equation.

Hence the condition is sufficient.

Procedure to find the solution of an exact differential equation

(i) Integrate M w.r.t. x, taking y as a constant.

(ii) Integrate w.r.t. y, those terms of N which do not contain x.

(iii) Equate the sum of (i) and (ii) to an arbitrary constant.

By the above rule, if $M\,dx + N\,dy = 0$ is exact, then its solution is given by

$$\int_{y \text{ as constant}} M\,dx + \int (\text{terms of } N \text{ which do not contain } x)\,dy = C.$$

SOLVED EXAMPLES

Example 1. Check whether the differential equation

$(x^2 - 4xy - 2y^2)dx + (y^2 - 4xy - 2x^2)\,dy = 0$, is exact. If exact, find its solution.

Solution: Here the given differential equation is

$$(x^2 - 4xy - 2y^2)dx + (y^2 - 4xy - 2x^2)\,dy = 0$$

$\therefore \quad M = x^2 - 4xy - 2y^2$

$\quad N = y^2 - 4xy - 2x^2$

$\therefore \quad \dfrac{\partial M}{\partial y} = -4x - 4y$

$\quad \dfrac{\partial N}{\partial y} = -4x - 4y$

As $\quad \dfrac{\partial M}{\partial y} = \dfrac{\partial N}{\partial y}$

$\therefore$ The given differential equation is exact and its solution is

$$\int_{(y\,\text{constant})} \left(x^2 - 4xy - 2y^2\right)dx + \int y^2 dy = C$$

or
$$\frac{x^3}{3} - 2x^2y - 2y^2x + \frac{y^3}{3} = C$$

or
$$x^3 - 6x^2y - 6xy^2 + y^3 = C.$$

Example 2. Solve the differential equation

$(2xy + y - \tan y)\,dx + (x^2 - x\tan^2 y + \sec^2 y)\,dy = 0$

Solution: Here

$$M = 2xy + y - \tan y$$
$$N = x^2 - x\tan^2 y + \sec^2 y$$

$\therefore$
$$\frac{\partial M}{\partial y} = 2x + 1 - \sec^2 y$$

$$\frac{\partial N}{\partial x} = 2x - \tan^2 y$$
$$= 2x - [\sec^2 y - 1]$$
$$= 2x + 1 - \sec^2 y$$

$\therefore$
$$\frac{\partial M}{\partial y} = \frac{\partial N}{\partial x}$$

So, the given differential equation is exact and hence its solution is

$$\int_{(y\,\text{constant})} (2xy + y - \tan y)\,dx + \int \sec^2 y\,dy = C$$

or
$$x^2y + xy - x\tan y + \tan y = C$$

Example 3. Solve the differential equation.

$$\left(1 + e^{x/y}\right)dx + e^{x/y}\left[1 - \frac{x}{y}\right]dy = 0.$$

Solution: The given differential equation is

$$\left(1 + e^{x/y}\right)dx + e^{x/y}\left[1 - \frac{x}{y}\right]dy = 0$$

Here $$M = 1 + e^{x/y}$$

$$N = e^{x/y}\left[1 - \frac{x}{y}\right]$$

$$\therefore \quad \frac{\partial M}{\partial y} = e^{x/y} \cdot \left(\frac{-x}{y^2}\right)$$

$$= \frac{-x}{y^2} e^{x/y}$$

$$\therefore \quad \frac{\partial N}{\partial x} = e^{x/y} \cdot \frac{1}{y}\left[1 - \frac{x}{y}\right] + e^{x/y}\left[0 - \frac{1}{y}\right]$$

$$= \frac{1}{y} e^{x/y} - \frac{x}{y^2} e^{x/y} - \frac{1}{y} e^{x/y}$$

$$= \frac{-x}{y^2} e^{x/y}$$

$$\therefore \quad \frac{\partial M}{\partial y} = \frac{\partial N}{dx}$$

So, the given differential equation is exact and its solution is given by

$$\int_{(y\,\text{constant})} \left(1 + e^{x/y}\right) dx + \int 0 . dy = C$$

or $$x + y\, e^{x/y} = C.$$

Example 4. Solve the differential equation.

$$[\cos x \tan y + \cos (x + y)]dx + [\sin x \sec^2 y + \cos (x + y)]\, dy = 0.$$

Solution: Here the given differential equation

$$[\cos x \tan y + \cos (x + y)]dx + [\sin x \sec^2 y + \cos (x + y)]\, dy = 0 \tag{1}$$

is of the form $M\, dx + N\, dy = 0$,

where $$M = \cos x \tan y + \cos (x + y)$$

and $$N = \sin x \sec^2 y + \cos (x + y)$$

$$\therefore \quad \frac{\partial M}{\partial y} = \cos x \,.\, \sec^2 y - \sin (x + y)$$

$$\frac{\partial N}{\partial x} = \cos x \,.\, \sec^2 y - \sin(x + y)$$

$$\therefore \qquad \frac{\partial M}{\partial y} = \frac{\partial N}{\partial x}$$

So, the given differential equation is exact and the solution is

$$\int_{(y\,\text{constant})} \cos x.\tan y + \cos(x+y)\,dx + \int 0\,dy = C$$

or $$\sin x \tan y + \sin(x + y) = C.$$

EXERCISE

Check whether the following differential equations are exact and solve, if found exact.

1. $(x^2 + y^2 - a^2)\, x\, dx + (x^2 - y^2 - b^2)\, y\, dy = 0$

Ans. $x^4 + 2x^2y^2 - 2a^2x^2 - y^4 - 2b^2y^2 = C$

2. $(5x^4 + 3x^2y^2 - 2xy^3)\, dx + (2x^3y - 3x^2y^2 - 5y^4)\, dy = 0$

Ans. $x^5 + x^3y^2 - x^2y^3 - y^5 = C.$

4. (sec x tan x tax $y - e^x$) dx + sec x $\sec^2 y\, dy = 0$

Ans. $\sec x \tan y - e^x = C$

6. $ye^{xy}\, dx + (xe^{xy} + 2y)\, dy = 0$

$e^{xy} + y^2 = C.$

8. $\frac{dy}{dx} + \frac{y\cos x + \sin y + y}{\sin x + x\cos y + x} = 0$

Ans. $y \sin x + (\sin y + y)\, x = C.$

Differential Equations Reducible to Exact Form

If a differential equation is not exact, in some of the cases it can be reduced to exact form, by multiplying it by a suitable function, known as Integrating Factor. In some of the cases integrating factor may be found by inspection after rearranging the terms. The following are some differentials which help us in selecting the integrating factor by inspection:

1. $$d[xy] = y\,dx + x\,dy$$

2. $$d\left[\frac{y}{x}\right] = \frac{xdy - ydx}{x^2}$$

3. $$d\left[\frac{x}{y}\right] = \frac{ydx - x\,dy}{y^2}$$

4. $$d\left[\log\left(\frac{y}{x}\right)\right] = \frac{xdy - ydx}{xy}$$

5. $$d\left[\tan^{-1}\left(\frac{y}{x}\right)\right] = \frac{xdy - ydx}{x^2 + y^2}$$

6. $$d[\log(x^2 + y^2)] = \frac{2[xdx + ydy]}{x^2 + y^2}$$

7. $$d\left[\log\left(\frac{x+y}{x-y}\right)\right] = \frac{2[xdy - ydx]}{x^2 - y^2}$$

Example 1. Solve the differential equation

$$x\,dy - y\,dx = xy^2\,dx.$$

Solution: The given differential equation is

$$x\,dy - y\,dx = xy^2\,dx \qquad (1)$$

Dividing through out by $-y^2$, we have

$$\frac{ydx - xdy}{y^2} = -x\,dx$$

$$d\left[\frac{x}{y}\right] = -x\,dx$$

Integrating, we have

$$\frac{x}{y} = \frac{-x^2}{2} + C$$

or $$\frac{x}{y} + \frac{x^2}{2} = C$$

or $x^2y + 2x = 2\,Cy$, is the solution.

Example 2. Solve the differential equation.

$$(x^4e^x - 2m\,xy^2)\,dx + 2mx^2y\,dy = 0$$

Solution: The given differential equation is

$$x^4e^x\,dx - 2m\,xy^2\,dx + 2mx^2y\,dy = 0$$

or $$x^4e^x\,dx - 2m\,[xy^2\,dx - x^2y\,dy]$$

or $$e^x\,dx - m\,\frac{\left[x^2 2y\,dy - y^2 2x\,dx\right]}{x^4} = 0$$

or $$e^x\,dx - m\,.\,d\left[\frac{y^2}{x^2}\right] = 0$$

Integrating, we get

$$e^x - m\,.\,\frac{y^2}{x^2} = C$$

$\therefore$ $x^2e^x - my^2 = Cx^2$, is the solution.

Example 3. Solve the differential equation.

$$y\sin 2x\,dx = (1 + y^2 + \cos^2 x)\,dy.$$

Solution: The given differential equation is

$$(1 + y^2 + \cos^2 x)\,dy - y\sin 2x\,dx = 0$$

$$dy + y^2dy + \cos^2 x\,dy - y\sin 2x\,dx = 0$$

$$dy + y^2\,dy + d\,[y\cos^2 x] = 0$$

Integrating, we get

$$y + \frac{y^3}{3} + y\cos^2 x = C$$

is the required solution.

EXERCISE

Solve the following differential equations:

1. $(4x^3y^3 - 2xy)\,dx + (3x^4y^2 - x^2)\,dy = 0$

   Ans. $x^4y^3 - x^2y = C$

2. $ydx - xdy + 3x^2y^2e^{x^3}dx = 0$

   Ans. $\frac{x}{y} + e^{x^3} = C$

3. $3x^2y\,dx + (y^4 - x^3)\,dy = 0$

   Ans. $3x^3 + y^4 = Cy$

4. $x\,dy - y\,dx = (x^2 + y^2)\,dx$

Ans. $y = x \tan(x + C)$

5. $xdy - ydx = x\sqrt{x^2 - y^2}\,dx$

Ans. $y = x \sin(x + C)$

6. $(x^3 + xy^2 + y)\,dx + (y^3 + x^2y + x)\,dy = 0$

Ans. $x^2 + y^2 + 4xy = C$

I. If the differential equation $M\,dx + N\,dy = 0$, is not exact but $\dfrac{\dfrac{\partial M}{\partial y} - \dfrac{\partial N}{\partial x}}{N}$ is a function of x only, say $f(x)$ then $e^{\int f(x)dx}$ is the integrating factor.

Example I. Solve the differential equation.

$$(xy^2 - e^{1/x^3})\,dx - x^2y\,dy = 0. \tag{1}$$

Solution: Here

$$M = xy^2 - e^{1/x^3}$$

$$N = -x^2y$$

$$\therefore \quad \frac{\partial M}{\partial y} = 2xy$$

$$\frac{\partial N}{\partial x} = -2xy$$

$$\because \quad \frac{\partial M}{\partial y} \neq \frac{\partial N}{\partial x}$$

$\therefore$ The equation is not exact

But
$$\frac{\dfrac{\partial M}{\partial y} - \dfrac{\partial N}{\partial x}}{N} = \frac{4xy}{-x^2y}$$

$$\frac{-4}{x} = f(x)$$

is function of x only.

$\therefore$ The integrating factor is

$$\text{I.F.} = e^{\int \frac{-4}{x} dx}$$

$$= e^{-4 \log x}$$

$$= e^{\log(x^{-4})}$$

$\therefore$ $$\text{I.F.} = x^{-4}$$

$$= \frac{1}{x^4}$$

Multiplying the given equation by $\frac{1}{x^4}$, we have

$$\left(\frac{y^2}{x^3} - \frac{e^{x^{1/3}}}{x^4}\right) dx - \frac{y}{x^2} dy = 0 \tag{2}$$

Now $$M' = \frac{y^2}{x^3} - \frac{e^{x^{1/3}}}{x^4}$$

$$N' = \frac{-y}{x^2}$$

$\therefore$ $$\frac{\partial M'}{\partial y} = \frac{2y}{x^3}$$

and $$\frac{\partial N'}{\partial x} = \frac{2y}{x^3}$$

As $$\frac{\partial M'}{\partial y} = \frac{\partial N'}{\partial x}$$

$\therefore$ The equation (2) is exact differential equation, whose solution is

$$\int_{(y \text{ constant})} \left(\frac{y^2}{x^3} - \frac{e^{1/x^3}}{x^4}\right) dx + \int 0 \, dx = C$$

or $$\frac{-y^2}{2x^2} + \frac{e^{1/x^3}}{3} = C$$

or $$\frac{1}{3} e^{1/x^3} - \frac{y^2}{2x^2} = C$$

or $$2e^{1/x^3} - \frac{3y^2}{x^2} = C, \text{ is the solution.}$$

Example 2. Solve the differential equation

$(x^2 + y^2 - a^2)x\,dx + (x^2 - y^2 - b^2)\,y\,dy = 0.$

Solution: The given differential equaton is

$$(x^2 + y^2 - a^2)x\,dx + (x^2 - y^2 - b^2)\,y\,dy = 0 \qquad (1)$$

Here $$M = x^3 + y^2x - a^2x$$

$$N = x^2y - y^3 - b^2y$$

$$\frac{\partial M}{\partial y} = 2xy$$

$$\frac{\partial N}{\partial x} = 2xy$$

$\because$ $$\frac{\partial M}{\partial y} = \frac{\partial N}{\partial x}$$

$\therefore$ The given differential equation is exact and its solution is

$$\int_{(y\text{ constant})} \left(x^3 + y^2x - a^2x\right)dx + \int\left(-y^2 - b^2y\right)dy = C$$

or $$\frac{x^4}{4} + \frac{x^2y^2}{2} - \frac{a^2x^2}{2} - \frac{y^4}{4} - \frac{b^2y^2}{2} = C$$

or $$x^4 + 2x^2y^2 - 2a^2x^2 - y^4 - 2b^2y^2 = C, \text{ is the solution.}$$

Example 3. Solve the differential equation

$y\,(2x^2 - xy + 1)\,dx + (x - y)\,dy = 0$

Solution: The given differential equation is

$$y\,(2x^2 - xy + 1)\,dx + (x - y)\,dy = 0$$

Here $$M = 2x^2y - xy^2 + y$$

$$N = x - y$$

$\therefore$ $$\frac{\partial M}{\partial y} = 2x^2 - 2xy + 1$$

$$\frac{\partial N}{\partial x} = 1$$

$$\therefore \qquad \frac{\partial M}{\partial y} \neq \frac{\partial N}{\partial x}$$

$\therefore$ The equation is not exact.

As $$\frac{\partial M}{\partial y} - \frac{\partial N}{\partial x} = 2x^2 - 2xy$$

$$= 2x(x - y)$$

$$\frac{\dfrac{\partial M}{\partial y} - \dfrac{\partial N}{\partial x}}{N} = 2x = \text{function of } x \text{ only.}$$

$\therefore$ the integrating factor is as

$$\text{I.F.} = e^{\int 2x\,dx}$$
$$= e^{x^2}$$

Multiplying the equation (1) by e^{x^2}, we have

$$ye^{x^2}(2x^2 - xy + 1)\,dx + e^{x^2}.(x - y).\,dy = 0 \qquad (2)$$

Here $$M' = ye^{x^2}.(2x^2 - xy + 1)$$
$$= e^{x^2}(2x^2y - xy^2 + y)$$
$$N' = e^{x^2}.x - e^{x^2}.y$$

$$\therefore \qquad \frac{\partial M'}{\partial y} = e^{x^2}(2x^2 - 2xy + 1)$$

$$\frac{\partial N'}{\partial x} = e^{x^2}(2x^2 - 2xy + 1)$$

$$\because \qquad \frac{\partial M'}{\partial y} = \frac{\partial N'}{\partial x}$$

$\because$ The equation (2) is exact and the solution is

$$\int_{(y \text{ as constant})} e^{x^2}.\left(2x^2y - xy^2 + y\right)dx + \int 0\,dy = C$$

or $$e^{x^2}(2xy - y^2) = C, \text{ is the solution.}$$

2. If the differential equation $M\,dx + N\,dy = 0$, is not exact but $\dfrac{\dfrac{\partial N}{\partial x} - \dfrac{\partial M}{\partial y}}{M}$ is a function of y only, say $f(y)$, then $e^{\int f(y)dy}$ is the integrating factor.

Example 1. Solve the differential equation.

$$(3x^2y^4 + 2xy)\,dx + (2x^3y^3 - x^2)\,dy = 0.$$

Solution: The given differential equation is

$$(3x^2y^4 + 2xy)\,dx + (2x^3y^3 - x^2)\,dy = 0 \quad (1)$$

Here

$$M = 3x^2y^4 + 2xy$$

$$N = 2x^3y^3 - x^2$$

$$\therefore \quad \frac{\partial M}{\partial y} = 12x^2y^3 + 2x$$

$$\frac{\partial N}{\partial x} = 6x^2y^3 - 2x$$

$$\frac{\partial N}{\partial x} - \frac{\partial M}{\partial y} = -6x^2y^3 - 4x$$

$$\therefore \quad \frac{\dfrac{\partial N}{\partial x} - \dfrac{\partial M}{\partial y}}{M} = \frac{-6x^2y^3 - 4x}{y\left[3x^2y^3 + 2x\right]}$$

$$= \frac{-2}{y} = f(y), \text{ is a function of } y \text{ only}$$

therefore

$$\text{I.F.} = e^{\int -\frac{2}{y}dy}$$

$$= e^{-2\log y}$$

$$= \frac{1}{y^2}$$

Now, multiplying equation (1) by $\frac{1}{y^2}$, we have

$$\left(3x^2y^2 + \frac{2x}{y}\right)dx + \left(2x^3y - \frac{x^2}{y^2}\right)dy = 0 \qquad (2)$$

Here $$M' = 3x^2y^2 + \frac{2x}{y}$$

and $$N' = 2x^3y - \frac{x^2}{y^2}$$

$\therefore$ $$\frac{\partial M'}{\partial y} = 6x^2y - \frac{2x}{y^2}$$

$$\frac{\partial N'}{\partial x} = 6x^2y - \frac{2x}{y^2}$$

As $$\frac{\partial M'}{\partial y} = \frac{\partial N'}{\partial x}$$

$\therefore$ The given differential equation (2) is exact and its solution is

$$\int_{(y\,\text{constant})} \left(3x^2y^2 + \frac{2x}{y}\right)dx + \int 0\,dy = C$$

or $$x^3y^2 + \frac{x^2}{y} = C$$

or $x^3y^3 + x^2 = Cy$, is the solution.

Example 2. Solve the differential equation.

$(xy^3 + y)\,dx + 2(x^2y^2 + x + y^4)\,dy = 0$

Solution: The given differential equation is

$$(xy^3 + y)\,dx + 2(x^2y^2 + x + y^4)\,dy = 0 \qquad (1)$$

Here $$M = xy^3 + y$$

$\therefore$ $$\frac{\partial M}{\partial y} = 3xy^2 + 1$$

$$N = 2(x^2y^2 + x + y^4)$$

$$\frac{\partial N}{\partial x} = 4xy^2 + 2$$

$\because$ $$\frac{\partial M}{\partial y} \neq \frac{\partial N}{\partial x}$$

$\therefore$ The differential equation (1) is not exact.

But $$\frac{\frac{\partial N}{\partial x} - \frac{\partial M}{\partial y}}{M} = \frac{4xy^2 + 2 - 3xy^2 - 1}{y\left(xy^2+1\right)}$$

$$\frac{xy^2+1}{y\left(xy^2+1\right)} = \frac{1}{y}, \text{ is function of } y \text{ only.}$$

$\therefore$ $$\text{I.F.} = e^{\int \frac{1}{y} dy}$$
$$= e^{\log y}$$
$$= y$$

Multiplying the equation (1) by y, we have

$$(xy^4 + y^2)\, dx + 2(x^2y^3 + xy + y^5)\, dy = 0 \qquad (2)$$

Here $$M' = xy^4 + y^2$$

$\therefore$ $$\frac{\partial M'}{\partial y} = 4xy^3 + 2y$$

$$N' = 2(x^2y^3 + xy + y^5)$$

$$\frac{\partial N'}{\partial x} = 2(2xy^3 + y)$$
$$= 4xy^3 + 2y$$

$\because$ $$\frac{\partial M'}{\partial y} = \frac{\partial N'}{\partial x}$$

$\therefore$ Equation (2) is exact and the solution is

$$\int_{(y \text{ as constant})} \left(xy^4 + y^2\right) dx + 2\int y^5 dy = C$$

$$\frac{x^2y^4}{2} + xy^2 + \frac{1}{3}y^6 = C$$

or $$x^2y^4 + 2xy^2 + \frac{2}{3}y^6 = C$$

or $$3x^2y^4 + 6xy^2 + 2y^6 = C, \text{ is the solution.}$$

3. If $M\,dx + N\,dy = 0$, is not exact but is a homogeneous differential equation, then $\frac{1}{Mx + Ny}$ $(Mx + Ny \neq (0)$ is the integration factor.

Example 1. Solve the differential equation.

$$(3xy^2 - y^3)\,dx - (2x^2y - xy^2)\,dy = 0.$$

Solution: The given differential equation is

$$(3xy^2 - y^3)\,dx + (xy^2 - 2x^2y)\,dy = 0 \tag{1}$$

Here
$$M = 3xy^2 - y^3$$
$$N = xy^2 - 2x^2y$$
$$\frac{\partial M}{\partial y} = 6xy - 3y^2$$
$$\frac{\partial N}{\partial x} = y^2 - 4xy$$

As
$$\frac{\partial M}{\partial y} \neq \frac{\partial N}{\partial x}$$

∴ The differential equation (1) is not exact, but

the equation is homogeneous

and
$$Mx + Ny = 3x^2y^2 - y^3x + xy^3 - 2x^2y^2$$
$$= x^2y^2\ (\neq 0)$$

∴
$$\text{I.F.} = \frac{1}{Mx + Ny}$$
$$= \frac{1}{x^2y^2}$$

∴ Multiplying the equation (1) by $\frac{1}{x^2y^2}$, we have

$$\left(\frac{3}{x} - \frac{y}{x^2}\right)dx + \left(\frac{1}{x} - \frac{2}{y}\right)dy = 0 \tag{2}$$

Now, $$M' = \frac{3}{x} - \frac{y}{x^2}$$

$$N' = \frac{1}{x} - \frac{2}{y}$$

$\therefore$ $$\frac{\partial M'}{\partial y} = \frac{-1}{x^2}$$

$$\frac{\partial N'}{\partial x} = \frac{-1}{x^2}$$

As $$\frac{\partial M'}{\partial y} = \frac{\partial N'}{\partial x}$$

$\therefore$ The differential equation (2) is exact and its solution is

$$\int_{(y \text{ constant})} \left(\frac{3}{x} - \frac{y}{x^2}\right) dx + \int \left(\frac{-2}{y}\right) dy = C$$

$$3 \log x + \frac{y}{x} - 2 \log y = C$$

$\therefore$ $$3 \log x + \frac{y}{x} - 2 \log y = C, \text{ is the solution.}$$

Example 2. Solve the differential equation

$$(x^2y - 2xy^2)\, dx - (x^3 - 3x^2y)\, dy = 0.$$

Solution: The given differential equation is

$$(x^2y - 2xy^2)\, dx - (x^3 - 3x^2y)\, dy = 0 \qquad (1)$$

Here $$M = x^2y - 2xy^2$$

$$N = 3x^2y - x^3$$

$\therefore$ $$\frac{\partial M}{\partial y} = x^2 - 4xy$$

$$\frac{\partial N}{\partial x} = 6xy - 3x^2$$

As $$\frac{\partial M}{\partial y} \neq \frac{\partial N}{\partial x}$$

∴ The equation (1) is not exact. The differential equation (1) is a homogeneous differential equation.

$$Mx + Ny = x^3y - 2x^2y^2 + 3x^2y^2 - x^3y$$
$$= x^2y^2 \ (\neq 0)$$

∴ $$\frac{1}{Mx+Ny} = \frac{1}{x^2y^2} \text{ is the I.F.}$$

So, multiplying equation (1) by $\frac{1}{x^2y^2}$, we have

$$\left(\frac{1}{y}-\frac{2}{x}\right)dx+\left(\frac{3}{y}-\frac{x}{y^2}\right)dy = 0 \qquad (2)$$

Here $$M' = \left(\frac{1}{y}-\frac{2}{x}\right)$$

$$N' = \left(\frac{3}{y}-\frac{x}{y^2}\right)$$

$$\frac{\partial M'}{\partial y} = -\frac{1}{y^2}$$

$$\frac{\partial N'}{\partial x} = -\frac{1}{y^2}$$

As $$\frac{\partial M'}{\partial y} = \frac{\partial N'}{\partial x}$$

∴ The equation (2) is exact. And the solution is

$$\int_{(y \text{ as constant})} \left(\frac{1}{y}-\frac{2}{x}\right)dx + \int \frac{3}{y}dy = C$$

or $$\frac{x}{y} - 2\log x + 3\log y = C, \text{ is the solution.}$$

4. When the differential equation $M\,dx + N\,dy = 0$ is not exact and is of the form $\phi_1(x, y)\, y\, dx + \phi_2(x, y)\, x\, dy = 0$, such that $Mx - Ny \neq 0$, then $\frac{1}{Mx - Ny}$ is the I.F.

Example 3. Solve the differential equation.

$(xy^2 + 2x^2y^3)\, y\, dx + (x^2y - x^3y^2)\, x\, dy = 0.$

Solution: The given differential equation is of the form

$$\phi_1(x, y)\, y\, dx + \phi_2(x, y)\, x\, dy = 0$$

where
$$M = xy^2 + 2x^2y^3$$
$$N = x^2y - x^3y^2$$

$$\therefore \quad Mx - Ny = x^2y^2 + 2x^3y^3 - x^2y^2 + x^3y^3$$
$$= 3x^3y^3 \ (\neq 0)$$

$$\therefore \quad \text{I.F.} = \frac{1}{3x^3y^3}$$

Multiplying equation (1) by $\frac{1}{3x^3y^3}$, we have

$$\left(\frac{1}{3x^2y} + \frac{2}{3x}\right) dx + \left(\frac{1}{3xy^2} - \frac{1}{3y}\right) dy = 0 \qquad (2)$$

Here
$$M' = \frac{1}{3x^2y} + \frac{2}{3x}$$

$$N' = \frac{1}{3xy^2} - \frac{1}{3y}$$

$$\therefore \quad \frac{\partial M'}{\partial y} = \frac{-1}{3x^2y^2}$$

$$\frac{\partial N'}{\partial x} = \frac{-1}{3x^2y^2}$$

As
$$\frac{\partial M'}{\partial y} = \frac{\partial N'}{\partial x}$$

∴ The equation is exact and the solution is given by (2)

$$\int_{(y\ \text{constant})} \left(\frac{1}{3x^2y} + \frac{2}{3x}\right) dx + \int \left(-\frac{1}{3y}\right) dy = C$$

or $$\frac{-1}{3xy}+\frac{2}{3}\log x-\frac{1}{3}\log y = C$$

or $$\frac{-1}{xy} + 2\log x - \log y = C, \text{ is the solution.}$$

5. When the differential equation is of the form $x^a y^b$ $(my\,dx + nx dy) + x^c y^d\,(pydx + qxdy) = 0$, where a, b, m, n, c, d, p, q are all constants and $mp - nq \neq 0$.

Then it has an integrating factor of the form $x^h y^k$ where h and k are given by

$$\frac{a+h+1}{m} = \frac{b+k+1}{n}$$

and $$\frac{c+h+1}{p} = \frac{d+k+1}{q}$$

Example 1. Solve the differential equation.

$(2y^2 + 4x^2y)\,dx + (4xy + 3x^3)\,dy = 0.$

Solution: The given differential equation is

$$(2y^2 + 4x^2y)\,dx + (4xy + 3x^3)\,dy = 0 \qquad ...(1)$$

$$M = 2y^2 + 4x^2y$$

$$N = 4xy + 3x^3$$

$\therefore$ $$\frac{\partial M}{\partial y} = 4y + 4x^2$$

$$\frac{\partial N}{\partial x} = 4y + 9x^2$$

As $$\frac{\partial M}{\partial y} \neq \frac{\partial N}{\partial x}$$,so, the equation is not exact.

The above equation may be written as

$$x^2\,(4y\,dx + 3x\,dy) + y\,(2y\,dx + 4x\,dy) = 0 \qquad ...(2)$$

Comparing this equation by

$x^a y^b\,(my\,dx + nx\,dy) + x^c y^d\,(py\,dx + q\,x\,dy = 0$

we have $a = 2, b = 0, c = 0, d = 1, m = 4, n = 3, P = 2, q = 4$

and $$mp - nq = 8 - 12 \neq 0.$$

Now if $x^h y^k$ is the I.F. then h and k are given by

$$\frac{a+h+1}{m} = \frac{b+k+1}{n}$$

and $$\frac{c+h+1}{p} = \frac{d+k+1}{q}$$

then $$\frac{2+h+1}{4} = \frac{0+k+1}{3}$$

$\therefore$ $$9 + 3h = 4k + 4$$

$\therefore$ $$4k - 3h = 5 \quad ...(3)$$

and $$\frac{0+h+1}{2} = \frac{1+k+1}{4}$$

$\therefore$ $$4\,h + 4 = 2k + 4$$

$\therefore$ $$4h - 2k = 0 \quad ...(4)$$

From (3) and (4), we have

$$h = 1$$

$$k = 2$$

$\therefore$ xy^2 is the I.F.

Now multiplying the given equation by xy^2, we have

$$xy^2\,(2y^2 + 4x^2y)\,dx + xy^2\,(4xy + 3x^3)\,dy = 0$$

or $$(2xy^4 + 4x^3y^3)\,dx + (4x^2y^3 + 3x^4y^2)\,dy = 0 \quad ...(5)$$

Hence $$M' = 2xy^4 + 4x^3y^3$$

$$N' = 4x^2y^3 + 3x^4y^2$$

$\therefore$ $$\frac{\partial M'}{\partial y} = 8xy^3 + 12x^3y^2$$

and $$\frac{\partial N'}{\partial x} = 8xy^3 + 12x^3y^2$$

$\therefore$ equation exact and the solution is given by

$$(2xy^4 + 4n^3y^3)\,dx + ody = C\ (y \text{ cost})$$

or $$x^2y^4 + n^4y^3 = C$$

As $$\frac{\partial M'}{\partial y} = \frac{\partial N'}{\partial x}$$

Then by rearranging, we have

$$2xy^4\,dx + 4x^3y^3\,dx + 4x^2y^3\,dy + 3x^4y^2\,dy = 0$$

$$d[x^2y^4] + d\,[x^4y^3] = 0$$

Integrating $\quad x^2y^4 + x^4y^3 = C$, is the solution.

EXERCISE

Solve the following differential equations:

1. $y\,(x + y)\,dx + (x + 2y - 1)\,dy = 0$

   Ans. $y\,(x + y - 1) = C\,.\,e^{-x}$

2. $(xy^3 + y)\,dx + 2\,(x^2y^2 + x + y^4)\,dy = 0$

   Ans. $3x^2y^4 + 6xy^2 + 2y^6 = C.$

3. $2xy\,dy - (x^2 + y^2 + 1)\,dx = 0$

   Ans. $y^2 - x^2 + 1 = Cx$

4. $(x^2y - 2xy^2)\,dx + (3x^2y - x^3)\,dy = 0$

   Ans. $x - 2y \log x + 3y \log y = Cy$

5. $(1 + xy)\,ydx + (1 - xy)\,xdy = 0$

   Ans. $\dfrac{-1}{xy} + \log\left(\dfrac{x}{y}\right) = C$

6. $(3xy - 2ay^2)\,dx + (x^2 - 2axy)\,dy = 0$

   Ans. $x^2\,(ay^2 - xy) = C$

7. $(y^4 + 2y)\,dx + (xy^4 + 2y^4 - 4x)\,dy = 0$

   Ans. $y^3 + {}^2\,x + y^4 = Cy^2$

8. $y^2\,dx + (x^2 - xy - y^2)\,dy = 0$

   Ans. $(x - y)\,y^2 = C\,(x + y)$

9. $(xy + 2x^2y^2)\,dx + (xy - x^2y^2)\,xdy = 0$

   Ans. $2 \log x - \log y = C$

10. $x^2y\,dx - (x^3 + y^3)\,dy = 0$

    Ans. $\log y - \dfrac{x^3}{3y^3} = C$

11. $y\,dx - x\,dy + \log x\,dx = 0$

    Ans. $Cx + y + \log x + 1 = 0$

12. $(x^3 + xy^4)\, dx + 2y^3\, dy = 0$

Ans. $e^{x^2} (x^2 + y^4 - 1) = C$

13. $(y - xy^2)\, dx - (x + x^2y)\, dy = 0$

Ans. $\log \left(\dfrac{x}{y}\right) - xy = C$

14. $(xy^2 - x^2)\, dx + (3x^2y^2 + x^2y - 2x^3 + y^2)\, dx = 0$

Ans. $x^3y^2 + \dfrac{x^2}{y} = C$

15. $(y^3 - 2x^2y)\, dx + (2xy^2 - x^3)\, dy = 0$

Ans. $x^2y^2\,(y^2 - x^2) = C$

16. $2xy\, dx + (y^2 - x^2)\, dy = 0,\ y(2) = 1$

Ans. $x^2 + y^2 = 5y$

17. $[xy \sin (xy) + \cos (xy)]\, y\, dx + [xy \sin (xy) - \cos (xy)]x\, dy = 0$

Ans. $x \sec (xy) = Cy$

18. $x^3y^3\,(2y\, dx + x\, dy) - [5y\, dx + 7x\, dy] = 0.$

Ans. $x^3y^3 + 2 = C \,.\, x^{5/3} \,.\, y^{7/3}$

Linear differetial equations with constant coefficients.

A differential equation of the form

$$\frac{d^n y}{dx^n} + p_1 \frac{d^{n-1} y}{dx^{n-1}} + p_2 \frac{d^{n-2} y}{dx^{n-2}} + \ldots\ p_n\, y = X$$

where $p_1, p_2, p_3 \ldots p_n$ are constants and X is either a constant or a function of x only, is said to be a linear differential equation with contant coefficients.

The operator D

For convenience we write the operators

$$\frac{d}{dx} = D,\ \frac{d^2}{dx^2} = D^2,\ \frac{d^3}{dx^3} = D^3 \ldots \text{etc.}$$

By this

$$\frac{dy}{dx} = Dy,\ \frac{d^2 y}{dx^2} = D^2y,\ \frac{d^n y}{dx^n} = D^n y \ldots \text{etc.}$$

With this, a differential equaiton

$$\frac{d^n y}{dx^n} + p_1 \frac{d^{n-1} y}{dx^{n-1}} + p_2 \frac{d^{n-2} y}{dx^{n-2}} + \ldots\ p_n\, y = X, \text{ is written as}$$

$$D^n y + p_1\, D^{n-1} y + p_2\, D^{n-2} y + \ldots + p_n y = X$$

or $$(D^n + p_1\, D^{n-1} y + p_2\, D^{n-2} + \ldots + p_n) y = X$$

or $$f\,(\mathrm{D}) y = X$$

where $F(D)$ is the polynomial given by

$$F(D) = D^n + \mathrm{P}_1 \mathrm{D}^{n-1} + \mathrm{P}_2\, \mathrm{D}^{n-2} + \ldots + P_n.$$

The operator D can be treated as an algebraic quantity as

$$D\,(\lambda y) = \lambda D\,(y)$$

$$D^n\,(D^m\, y) = D^m\,(D^n y)$$

$$= D^{m+n}\, y$$

The polynomical $F\,(D)$ can be factorised by ordinary rules of algebra and does not depend on the order of the factors.

Solution of a linear differential equation with constant coefficients.

$y = y_1$, is said to be a solution of the differential equation

$$D^n y + p_1\, D^{n-1} y + p_2\, D^{n-2} y + \ldots\ p_n y = X \tag{1}$$

if $D^n y_1 + p_1\, D^{n-1} y_1 + p_2\, D^{n-2} y_1 + \ldots\ p_n y_1 = X.$

Theorem: If $y = y_1, y = y_2 \ldots y = y_n$ are n linearly independent solution of the differential equation.

$$D^n y + p_1 D^{n-1}\, y + p_2\, D^{n-2} y + \ldots + p_n y = X$$

then$y = c_1 y_1 + c_2 y_2 + c_3 y_3 + \ldots + c_n y_n$ is also a solution,

where $c_1,\ c_2, c_3 \ldots c_n$ are arbitrary constants.

Proof:

Since $y = y_1, y = y_2 \ldots y = y_n$ are solutions of the equation.

$$(D^n + p_1\, D^{n-1} + p_2\, D_{n-2} + \ldots\ p_n)\ y = 0 \tag{1}$$

$$\left.\begin{aligned}
&\left(D^n + p_1 D^{n-1} + p_2 D^{n-2} + \ldots + p_n\right) y_1 = 0 \\
&\left(D^n + p_1 D^{n-1} + p_2 D^{n-2} + \ldots + p_n\right) y_2 = 0 \\
&\left(D^n + p_1 D^{n-1} + p_2 D^{n-2} + \ldots + p_n\right) y_3 = 0 \\
&\ldots \qquad \ldots \qquad \ldots \\
&\ldots \qquad \ldots \qquad \ldots \\
\therefore \quad &\left(D^n + p_n D^{n-1} + p_2 D^{n-2} + \ldots + p_n\right) y_n = 0
\end{aligned}\right\} \quad (2)$$

Multiplying the members of equation (2) by $c_1,\ c_2, c_3\ \ldots\ c_n$ respectively and adding, we have

$$\begin{aligned}
D^n\, [c_1y_1 + c_2y_2 + \ldots + c_ny_n] &+ \\
p_1\, D^{n-1}\, [c_1y_1 + c_2y_2 + \ldots + c_ny_n] &+ \\
p_2\, D^{n-1}\, [c_1y_1 + c_2y_2 + \ldots + c_ny_n\ ] &+ \\
\ldots \qquad \ldots \qquad \ldots & \\
\ldots \qquad \ldots \qquad \ldots & + \\
p_n\, [c_1y_1 + c_2y_2 + \ldots + c_ny_n\ ] &= 0
\end{aligned}$$

Thus, $(D^n + p_1\, D^{n-1} + p_2D^{n-2} + \ldots\ p_n)\ v = 0$

where $v = c_1y_1 + c_2y_2 + \ldots + c_ny_n$

Thus, $c_1y_1 + c_2y_2 + c_3y_3 + \ldots + c_ny_n$ is also a solution.

Solution of the differential equation of the form

$$F(D)y = 0,$$

where $F(D) = (D^n + p_1\, D^{n-1} + p_2\, D^{n-2} + \ldots\ p_n)\ y = 0$ (1)

Let $y = e^{mx}$ be a solution, then

$$\begin{aligned}
Dy &= me^{mx} \\
D^2y &= m^2e^{mx} \\
D^3y &= m^3e^{mx} \\
\ldots & \quad \ldots \\
\ldots & \quad \ldots \\
D^ny &= m^n\ e^{mx}
\end{aligned}$$

Substituting y, Dy, D^2y, $D^3y\ \ldots\ D^ny$ in the equation (1), we have

$(m^n + p_1\ m^{n-1} + p_2\ m^{n-2} + \ldots + p_n)\ e^{mx} = 0$

or $\quad m^n + p_1m^{n-1} + p^2\ m^{n-2} + \ldots\ p^n = 0$ (2)

We see that $y = e^{mx}$ is a solution, if m satisfies the equation (2).

The equation (2) is called the **auxiliary equation** for the differential equation (1), which is obtained by replacing D by m in $F(D) = 0$. Solving equation (2) we find the values of m, *i.e.*, the roots of the auxiliary equation.

Let $m = m_1, m_2, m_3 \ldots m_n$ be the roots of the auxiliary equation **(*A.E.*)**. The solution of the differential equation (1) depends upon the nature of the roots of *A.E.*

Case I.

When all the roots of A.E. are real and distinct then the solutions are

$$y_1 = e^{m_1 x},\ y_2 = e^{m_2 x} \ldots y_n = e^{m_n x}$$

and
$$y = c_1 y_1 + c_2 y_2 + c_3 y_3 + \ldots c_n y_n$$
$$y = c_1 e^{m_1 x} + c_2 e^{m_2 x} + c_3 e^{m_3 x} + \ldots c_n\, e^{m_n x}$$

is the complete or general solution.

Case 2.

When two roots of A.E. are euqal and rest are real and distinct.

Let
$$m_1 = m_2 = m$$
then
$$y = (c_1 + c_2)\, e^{m_1 x} + c_3\, e^{m_3 x} + \ldots c_n\, e^{m_n x}$$
$$= a_1\, e^{m_1 x} + c_3\, e^{m_3 x} + \ldots cn\, e^{m_n x}$$

This solution contains $(n - 1)$ arbitrary constants and hence cannot be the general solution, because the general solution must contiain n arbitrary constants.

Now corresponding to $m = m_1$, we have

$$(D - m_1)(D - m_1)y = 0$$

Let
$$(D - m_1)y = V$$
$\therefore$
$$(D - m_1)V = 0 \text{ or } DV = m_1 V$$
$\therefore$
$$\frac{DV}{V} = m_1$$

Integrating we have

$$\log V = m_1 x + \log c_1$$

$$\log\left(\frac{V}{c_1}\right) = m_1 x$$

$\therefore$
$$V = c_1\, e^{m_1 x}$$
$\therefore$
$$(\mathrm{D} - m_1)\, y = c_1\, e^{m_1 x}$$

or $\frac{dy}{dx} - m_1 y = C_1 \quad e^{m_1 x}$, is differential equation with I.F. $e^{-m_1 x}$ and the solution is

$$y \,.\, e^{-m_1 x} = \int c_1 e^{m_1 x} \,.\, e^{-m_1 x} dx + c_2$$

$$= c_1 \,.\, x + c_2$$

$$\therefore \qquad y = (c_1 x + c_2)\, e^{m_1 x}$$

and the complete solution is given by

$$y = (c_1 x + c_2)\, e^{m_1 x} + c_3\, e^{m_3 x} + c_4\, e^{m_4 x} + \ldots\, c_n\, e^{m_n x}.$$

If three roots are real and equal and rest of the roots are real and distinct then the solution is given by

$$y = (c_1 x^2 + c_2 x + c_3)\, e^{m_1 x} + c_4\, e^{m_4 x} + \ldots + c_n\, e^{m_n x}.$$

Similarly if r roots are equal and real and rest of the roots are distinct than the complete soution is

$$y = (c_1 x^{r-1} + C_2\, x^{r-2} + \ldots + c_r)\, x^{m_r x} + C_{r+1}\, e^{m_{r+1} x} + \ldots$$

Case III.

When roots are complex numbers

Let $m_1 = \alpha + i\beta$, $m_2 = \alpha - i\beta$ and rest of the roots are real and distinct.

Then

$$y = A\, e^{(\alpha + i\beta)x} + B\, e^{(\alpha - i\beta)x} + c_3\, e^{m_3 x} + c_4\, e^{m_4 x} + \ldots + c_n\, e^{m_n x}$$

$$= e^{\alpha x}[A\, e^{i\beta x} + B\, e^{-i\beta x} +] + c_3\, e^{m_3 x} + \ldots + c_n\, e^{m_n x}.$$

$$= e^{\alpha x}[(A + B) \cos \beta x + i\,(A - B) \sin \beta x] + c_3\, e^{m_3 x} + \ldots + c_n\, e^{m_n x}$$

$$\therefore \quad y = e^{\alpha x}[c_1 \cos \beta x + c_2 \sin \beta x] + c_3\, e^{m_3 x} + c_4\, e^{m_4 x} + \ldots + c_n\, e^{m_n x}$$

Case-IV.

When the complex roots are repeated, let $m_1 = m_2 = \alpha + i\beta$, $m_3 = m_4 = \alpha - i\beta$ and rest of the roots are real and distinct. Then the solution is

$$y = e^{\alpha x}[(c_1 x + c_2) \cos \beta x + (c_3 x + c_4) \sin \beta x]$$
$$+ c_5\, e^{m_5 x} + c_6\, e^{m_6 x} + \ldots + c_n\, e^{m_n x}$$

Example 1. Solve $\frac{d^2 y}{dx^2} - \frac{5dy}{dx} + 6y = 0.$

Solution: The given differential equaton is

$$(D^2 - 5D + 6)\, y = 0$$

$\therefore$ A.E. $$m^2 - 5m + 6 = 0$$

or $$(m-2)(m-3) = 0$$

$\therefore$ $$m = 2, 3$$

$\therefore$ the complete solution is

$$y = c_1 e^{2x} + c_2 e^{3x}.$$

Example 2. Solve $\dfrac{d^4y}{dx^4} + 13\dfrac{d^2y}{dx^2} + 36y = 0.$

Solution: The given differential equation is

$$(D^4 + 13D^2 + 36)\,y = 0 \qquad (1)$$

$\therefore$ A.E. $$m^4 + 13m^2 + 36 = 0 \qquad (2)$$

$$(m^2 + 4)(m^2 + 9) = 0$$

if $$m^2 + 4 = 0$$

$\therefore$ $$m = \pm 2i$$

if $$m^2 + 9 = 0$$

$$m = \pm 3i$$

$\therefore$ The complete solution is

$$y = c_1 \cos 2x + c_2 \sin 2x$$
$$+ c_3 \cos 3x + c_4 \sin 3x.$$

Example 3. Solve $\dfrac{d^4y}{dx^4} + 8\dfrac{d^2y}{dx^2} + 16y = 0.$

Solution: The given differential equation is

$$(D^4 + 8D^2 + 16)\,y = 0 \qquad (1)$$

$\therefore$ A.E. $$m^4 + 8m^2 + 16 = 0$$

$$(m^2 + 4)^2 = 0$$

$\therefore$ $m^2 + 4 = 0$, is two times repeated.

or $m = \pm\, 2i$, are two times repeated

$\therefore$ The complete solution is given by

$$y = (c_1x + c_2)\cos 2x + (c_3x + c_4)\sin 2x$$

Example 4. Solve $\dfrac{d^3y}{dx^3} + 3\dfrac{d^2y}{dx^2} + 3\dfrac{dy}{dx} - y = 0.$

Solution: The given differential equation is

$$(D^3 - 3D^2 + 3D - 1)\, y = 0 \tag{1}$$

A.E. $m^3 - 3m^2 + 3m - 1 = 0$

or $(m-1)^3 = 0$

$\therefore$ $m = 1, 1, 1.$ three times repeated

$\therefore$ The complete solution is

$$y = (c_1x^2 + c_2x + c_3)\, e^x.$$

Example 5. Solve the differential equation.

$$(D^2 - 1)^3 \,.\, (D^2 + D + 1)^2 y = 0.$$

Solution: The given differential equation is

$$(D^2 - 1)^3 \,.\, (D^2 + D + 1)^2\, y = 0 \tag{1}$$

$\therefore$ A.E. $(m^2 - 1)^3\, (m^2 + m + 1)^2 = 0$

$(m-1)^3\, (m+1)^3\, (m^2 + m + 1)^2 = 0$

$\therefore$ Roots of A.E. are $m = 1, 1, 1\ -1, -1, -1$ and

$$(m^2 + m + 1)^2 = 0$$

$$m = -\frac{1}{2} \pm i\frac{\sqrt{3}}{2}, \text{ repeated twice.}$$

$\therefore$ The complete solution is

$$(c_1x^2 + c_2x + c_3)\, e^x + (c_4x^2 + c_5\, x + c_6)\, e^{-x}$$

$$+ e^{\frac{-x}{2}}\left[(c_7x + c_8) \cos\frac{\sqrt{3}}{2}x + (c_9x + c_{10}) \sin\frac{\sqrt{3}}{2}x\right].$$

The inverse operator : $\frac{1}{F(D)}$

Definition: $\frac{1}{F(D)}$ X is that function of x, independent of arbitrary constants which when operated upon by $F(D)$ gives X.

Thus $F(D)\left[\frac{1}{F(D)}X\right] = X$

$\therefore$ $F(D)$ and $\frac{1}{F(D)}$ are called inverse operators.

Solution of F(D) y = X, where X is either constant or function of x only.

The solution of $F(D)\, y = X$ will consist of two parts:

(1) Solution of $F(D)\, y = 0$, called the complementary function (C.F.)

(2) The solution $\frac{1}{F(D)} X$, called the particular integral (P.I.).

Theorem:

$$\frac{1}{D} X = \int x\, dx$$

Proof:

Let $$u = \frac{1}{D} X$$

$\therefore$ $$Du = X$$

or $$\frac{du}{dx} = X$$

$\therefore$ $$\int \frac{du}{dx} dx = \int X\, dx$$

or $$u = \int X\, dx$$

$\therefore$ $$\frac{1}{D} x = \int X\, dx$$

Theorem:

$$\frac{1}{(D-m)} X = e^{mx} \int e^{-mx} X\, dx$$

Proof:

Let

$$u = \frac{1}{(D-m)} X$$

$\therefore$ $$(D - m)\, u = X$$

or $$Du - mu = X$$

or $\quad \dfrac{du}{dx} - mu = X$, is a linear differential equation with

$$\text{I.F.} = e^{\int -m dx}$$

$$= e^{-mx}$$

$\therefore$ The solution is

$$u \,.\, e^{-mx} = \int e^{-mx} X \, dx$$

or
$$u = e^{mx} \int e^{-mx} X \, dx$$

or
$$\frac{1}{D-m} X = e^{mx} \int e^{-mx} X \, dx \, .$$

Rules for finding particular Integral in some special cases

The particular integral $= \dfrac{1}{F(D)} X$ when.

Case I. $\quad X = e^{ax}$

$$\therefore \quad D\, e^{ax} = a e^{ax}$$

$$D^2 e^{ax} = a^2 e^{ax}$$

$$\dots \quad \dots$$

$$D^{n-1} e^{ax} = a^{n-1} \,.\, e^{ax}$$

$$D^n e^{ax} = a^n \,.\, e^{ax}$$

$$\therefore \ (D^n + p_1 D^{n-1} + p_2 D^{n-2} + \dots + p_n)\, e^{ax}$$
$$= (a^n + p_1 a^{n-1} + p_2 a^{n-2} + \dots p_n)\, e^{ax}$$

or
$$F(D)\, e^{ax} = (F(a)\, e^{ax}$$

Operating both sides by $\dfrac{1}{F(D)}$, we have

$$\frac{1}{F(D)} \{F(D) X\} = \frac{1}{F(D)} [F(a)\, e^{ax}]$$

or
$$e^{ax} = F(a) \,.\, \frac{1}{F(D)} \,.\, (e^{ax})$$

$$\therefore \quad \boxed{\frac{1}{F(D)} \cdot \left(e^{ax}\right) = \frac{e^{ax}}{F(a)}, F(a) \neq 0}$$

$$\therefore \qquad \frac{1}{F(D)}(e^{ax}) = \frac{e^{ax}}{F(a)},\ F(a) \neq 0$$

Case of failure, *i.e.* **if $F(a) = 0$**

Since $F(a) = 0$ then $(D - a)$ is a factor of $F(D)$

Let $\qquad F(D) = (D - a)\,\phi(D),\ \phi(a) \neq 0$

$$\therefore \qquad \frac{1}{F(D)}(e^{ax}) = \frac{1}{(D-a)\phi(D)}e^{ax}$$

$$\therefore \qquad = \frac{1}{(D-a)}\left[\frac{e^{ax}}{\phi(a)}\right]$$

$$= \frac{1}{\phi(a)}\cdot\frac{1}{(D-a)}e^{ax}$$

$$= \frac{1}{\phi(a)}\cdot e^{ax}\int e^{-ax}e^{ax}dx$$

$$= \frac{xe^{ax}}{\phi(a)},\quad \phi(a) \neq 0.$$

Now $\qquad F(D) = (D - a)\,\phi(D)$

$\therefore \qquad F'(D) = \phi(D) + (D - a)\,\phi'(D)$

$\therefore \qquad F'(a) = \phi(a)$

$$\therefore \qquad \frac{1}{F(D)}e^{ax} = \frac{xe^{ax}}{F'(a)},\ F'(a) \neq 0.$$

if $\quad F'(a) = 0$ then

$$\frac{1}{F(D)}e^{ax} = \frac{x^2e^{ax}}{F''(a)},\ F(a) = 0,\ F'(a) = 0,\ F''(a) \neq 0.$$

If $(D - a)$, is r times repeated factor of F(D), then

$$\frac{1}{F(D)}e^{ax} = \frac{x^r e^{ax}}{F^r(a)}.$$

SOLVED EXAMPLES

Example 1. Solve the differential equation.

$$\frac{d^3y}{dx^3} + y = 3 + 5\,e^x.$$

Solution: The given differential equation is

$$(D^3 + 1)\,y = 3 + 5\,e^x$$

$\therefore$ A.E. $\quad m^3 + 1 = 0$

$$(m + 1)\,(m^2 - m + 1) = 0$$

$$m = -1 \text{ and}$$

$$m = \frac{1 \pm \sqrt{1-4}}{2}$$

$$m = -1$$

$$m = \frac{1}{2} \pm \frac{i\sqrt{3}}{2}$$

$\therefore$

$$\text{C.F.} = c_1\,e^{-x} + e^{x/2}\left[c_1 \cos\frac{\sqrt{3}}{2}x + c_3 \sin\frac{\sqrt{3}}{2}x\right]$$

$$\text{P.I.} = \frac{1}{D^3+1}\,(3 + 5\,e^x)$$

$$= 3\,\frac{1}{D^3+1}\,.\,e^{ox} + 5\,.\,\frac{1}{D^3+1}\,.\,e^x$$

$$= 3\,.1 + 5\,.\,\frac{1}{2}\,.\,e^x$$

$$= 3 + \frac{5}{2}\,.\,e^x$$

$\therefore$ The complete solution is

$$y = c_1e^{-x} + e^{x/2}\left[c_2 \cos\frac{\sqrt{3}}{2}x + c_3 \sin\frac{\sqrt{3}}{2}x\right] + 3 + \frac{5}{2}e^{x}.$$

Example 2. Solve the differential equation

$$\frac{d^2y}{dx^2} + \frac{dy}{dx} + y = (1 + e^x)^2.$$

Solution: The given differential equaton is.

$$(D^2 + D + 1)\, y = 1 + e^{2x} + 2e^x$$

$\therefore$ A.E. $\quad m^2 + m + 1 = 0$

$$\therefore \qquad m = \frac{-1}{2} \pm i\frac{\sqrt{3}}{2}$$

$$\therefore \qquad \text{C.F.} = e^{-x/2}\left[c_1 \cos\frac{\sqrt{3}}{2}x + c_2 \sin\frac{\sqrt{3}x}{2}\right]$$

and P.I.

$$= \frac{1}{D^2 + D + 1}\,(1 + e^{2x} + 2\, e^x)$$

$$= \frac{1}{D^2 + D + 1}\, e^{0x} + \frac{1}{D^2 + D + 1}\, e^{2x} + 2\,.\, \frac{1}{D^2 + D + 1}\, e^x$$

$$= 1 + \frac{e^{2x}}{7} + \frac{2}{3}e^x$$

$\therefore$ The complete solution is

$$y = e^{-x/2}\left[c_1 \cos\frac{\sqrt{3}}{2}x + c_2 \sin\frac{\sqrt{3}}{2}x\right] + \frac{1}{7}e^{2x} + \frac{2}{3}e^x + 1.$$

Case II. When $X = \sin(ax + b)$ or $\cos(ax + b)$, then

$$D \sin(ax + b) = a \cos(ax + b)$$
$$D^2 \sin(ax + b) = (-a^2) \sin(ax + b)$$
$$D^3 \sin(ax + b) = -a^3 \cos(ax + b)$$
$$D^4 \sin(ax + b) = (-a^2)^2 \sin(ax + b)$$

....

....

$$(D^2)^n \sin(ax + b) = (-a^2)^n \sin(ax + b)$$
$$\therefore F(D^2) \sin(ax + b) = F(-a^2) \sin(ax + b)$$

Operating both sides by $\frac{1}{F(D^2)}$, we have

$$\frac{1}{F(D^2)}\{F(D^2)\sin(ax+b)\} = \frac{1}{F(D^2)}[F(-a^2)\sin(ax+b)]$$

or $$\sin(ax+b) = F(-a^2)\,.\,\frac{1}{F(D^2)}\sin(ax+b)$$

or $$\frac{1}{F(D^2)}\sin(ax+b) = \frac{1}{F(-a^2)}\sin(ax+b)$$

provided $F(-a^2) \neq 0$.

Similarly,

$$\frac{1}{F(D^2)}\cos(ax+b) = \frac{1}{F(-a^2)}\cos(ax+b)$$

$$F(-a^2) \neq 0.$$

If $F(-a^2) = 0$, then the method fails.

Now

$\therefore$ $$\cos ax + i\sin ax = e^{iax}]$$

$\therefore$ $$\cos(ax+b) + i\sin(ax+b) = e^{i(ax+b)}.$$

$$\therefore \frac{1}{F(D^2)}[\cos(ax+b) + i\sin(ax+b)] = \frac{1}{F(D^2)}e^{i(ax+b)}$$

$$= \frac{e^{i(ax+b)}}{F(-a^2)}$$

But $$F(-a^2) = 0$$

then $$\frac{1}{F(D^2)}e^{i(ax+b)} = \frac{x\,e^{i(ax+b)}}{F'(-a^2)}$$

$\therefore$ If $$F(-a^2) = 0$$

and $$F'(-a^2) \neq 0$$

then

$$\frac{1}{F(D^2)} \cos(ax + b) + i \sin(ax + b) = \frac{x[\cos(ax+b) + i\sin(ax+b)]}{F'(-a^2)}$$

Equating real and imaginary parts, we have

$$\frac{1}{F(D^2)} \cos(ax + b) = \frac{x\cos(ax+b)}{F'(-a^2)},$$

and
$$\frac{1}{F(D^2)} \sin(ax + b) = \frac{x\sin(ax+b)}{F'(-a^2)},$$

If $$\boldsymbol{F'(-a^2) = 0}$$
$$\boldsymbol{F''(-a^2) \neq 0}$$

then, similarly

$$\frac{1}{F(D^2)} \cos(ax + b) = \frac{x^2\cos(ax+b)}{F''(-a^2)}$$

and
$$\frac{1}{F(D^2)} \sin(ax + b) = \frac{x^2\sin(ax+b)}{F''(-a^2)}$$

and so on.

Example 3. Find the P.I. of $(D^3 + 1)\,y = \sin(2x + 3)$.

Solution: The given differential equation is

$$(D^3 + 1)\,y = \sin(2x + 3)$$

$$\therefore \qquad \text{P.I.} = \frac{1}{D^3+1} \sin(2x + 3)$$

$$= \frac{1}{D(D^2)+1} \cdot \sin(2x + 3) \qquad [\because (-a^2) = -4]$$

$$= \frac{1}{D(-4)+1} \sin(2x + 3)$$

$$= \frac{1}{1-4D} \sin(2x + 3)$$

$$= \frac{1+4D}{1-16D^2} \sin(2x+3)$$

$$= \frac{1+4D}{1+16.4} \sin(2x+3)$$

$$= \frac{1}{65} [\sin(2x+3) + 4D \sin(2x+3)]$$

$$\therefore \text{ P.I.} = \frac{1}{65} [\sin(2x+3) + 8\cos(2x+3)].$$

Example 4. Find the P.I. of $\frac{d^4y}{dx^4} - 16y = \cos 2x$.

Solution: The given differential equation is

$$(D^4 - 16)\, y = \cos 2x \quad (1)$$

$$\therefore \quad \text{P.I.} = \frac{1}{D^4 - 16} \cos 2x$$

$$= \frac{1}{(D^2-4)(D^2+4)} \cos 2x$$

$$= \frac{1}{(D^2-4)} \frac{1}{(D^2+4)} \cos 2x$$

$$= \frac{1}{(D^2+4)} \cdot \frac{1}{(-4-4)} \cos 2x$$

$$= \frac{-1}{8} \frac{1}{D^2+4} \cos 2x$$

$$= \frac{-x}{8} \cdot \frac{1}{2D} \cos 2x$$

$$= \frac{-x}{16} \int \cos 2x\, dx$$

$$\therefore \text{ P.I.} = \frac{-x}{32} \sin 2x.$$

Case III. when $X = x^m$, m is a +ve integer

Then $$\text{P.I.} = \frac{1}{F(D)} x^m$$

Take out the lowest degree term from $F(D)$ to make one term unity so that binomial theorem may be applied and then expand by bionomial theorem (for any index), upto the term containing D^m. Then operate on x^m term by term.

Example 5. Find the P.I. of $\frac{d^2y}{dx^2} - 4y = x^2$.

Solution: The given differential equation is

$$(D^2 - 4)\, y = x^2$$

$$\therefore \quad \text{P.I.} = \frac{1}{D^2 - 4} x^2$$

$$= -\frac{1}{4} \frac{1}{\left(1 - \frac{D^2}{4}\right)} x^2$$

$$= -\frac{1}{4}\left[1 - \frac{D^2}{4}\right]^{-1} x^2$$

$$= -\frac{1}{4}\left[1 + \frac{D^2}{4}\right] x^2$$

$$= -\frac{1}{4}\left[x^2 + \frac{1}{4} D^2 \left(x^2\right)\right]$$

$$\therefore \text{P.I.} = -\frac{1}{4}\left[x^2 + \frac{1}{2}\right]$$

$$= -\frac{x^2}{4} - \frac{1}{8}.$$

Example 6. Find the P.I. of $\frac{d^2y}{dx^2} + 2y = x^3 + x^2$.

Solution: The given differential equation is

$$(D^2 + 2)\, y = x^3 + x^2$$

$$\therefore \qquad \text{P.I.} = \frac{1}{(D^2+2)}\, x^3 + x^2$$

$$= \frac{1}{2\left[1+\frac{D^2}{2}\right]}\, x^3 + x^2$$

$$= \frac{1}{2} \cdot \left[1+\frac{D^2}{2}\right]^{-1} x^3 + x^2$$

$$= \frac{1}{2}\left[1-\frac{D^2}{2}+\frac{(-1)(-2)}{2}\frac{D^4}{4}\ldots\right](x^3 + x^2)$$

$$= \frac{1}{2}\left[1-\frac{D^2}{2}\right](x^3 + x^2) \qquad [\because D^4\,(x^3 + x^2) = 0]$$

$$= \frac{1}{2}\,[x^3 + x^2 - \frac{1}{2}\, D^2\,(x^3 + x^2)]$$

$$= \frac{1}{2}\,[x^3 + x^2 - \frac{1}{2}\,(6x + 2)]$$

$$= \frac{1}{2}\,[x^3 + x^2 - 3x - 1)]$$

$$\therefore \qquad \text{P.I.} = \frac{1}{2}\,[x^3 + x^2 - 3x - 1)].$$

Case IV.

when $X = e^{ax} \,.\, V$

where V is a function of x. Then

$$D\,(e^{ax} \,.\, V) = e^{ax} \,.\, DV + a\, e^{ax} \,.\, V$$

$$= e^{ax} \,.\, (D + a)\, V$$

$$D^2(e^{ax}) = ae^{ax} \cdot (D + a) V + e^{ax} \cdot (D^2 + aD) V$$

$$= e^{ax} [D^2 + 2a D + a^2] V$$

$$= e^{ax} \cdot (D + a)^2 V$$

$$D^3(e^{ax} \cdot V) = e^{ax} \cdot (D + a)^3 V$$

$$\therefore \quad F(D)(e^{ax} \cdot V) = e^{ax} \cdot f(D + a) V$$

Operating both sides by $\frac{1}{F(D)}$, we have

$$\frac{1}{F(D)} \cdot [F(D) \cdot (e^{ax} \cdot V)] = \frac{1}{F(D)} [e^{ax} \cdot F(D + a) V]$$

or $$e^{ax} \cdot V = \frac{1}{F(D)} [e^{ax} \cdot F(D + a) V]$$

Let $F(D + a) V = u$

$$\therefore \quad V = \frac{1}{F(D+a)} \cdot u$$

$$\therefore \quad e^{ax} \cdot \frac{1}{F(D+a)} u = \frac{1}{F(D)} (e^{ax} \cdot u)$$

$$\therefore \quad \frac{1}{F(D)} (e^{ax} \cdot u) = e^{ax} \cdot \frac{1}{F(D+a)} u$$

$$\therefore \quad \frac{1}{F(D)} (e^{ax} \cdot V) = e^{ax} \cdot \frac{1}{F(D+a)} V.$$

Example 7. Find the P.I. of $\frac{d^2y}{dx^2} - \frac{2dy}{dx} = e^x \sin x$.

Solution: The given differential equation is

$$(D^2 - 2D) y = e^x \sin x$$

$$\therefore \quad \text{P.I.} = \frac{1}{D^2 - 2D} (e^x \sin x)$$

$$= e^x \cdot \frac{1}{(D+1)^2 - 2(D+1)} \sin x$$

$$= e^x \cdot \frac{1}{D^2+1+2D-2D-2} \sin x$$

$$= e^x \cdot \frac{1}{D^2-1} \sin x$$

$$= e^x \frac{1}{-1-1} \sin x$$

$$= e^x \cdot -\frac{1}{2} \sin x$$

$$\therefore \qquad \text{P.I.} = -\frac{e^x \sin x}{2}.$$

Example 8. Find the P.I. of $(D^2 - 4D + 3)\, y = e^x \cos 2x$.

Solution: The given differential equation is

$$(D^2 - 4\text{D} + 3)\, y = e^x \cos 2x$$

$$\therefore \qquad \text{P.I.} = \frac{1}{D^2-4D+3} e^x \cos 2x$$

$$= e^x \cdot \frac{1}{(D+1)^2-4(D+1)+3} \cos 2x$$

$$= e^x \cdot \frac{1}{D^2+1+2D-4D-1} \cos 2x$$

$$= e^x \cdot \frac{1}{D^2-2D} \cos 2x$$

$$= e^x \cdot \frac{1}{-4-2D} \cos 2x$$

$$= -\frac{e^x}{2(D+2)} \cos 2x$$

$$= -\frac{e^x}{2} \cdot \frac{(D-2)}{(D^2-4)} \cos 2x$$

$$= \frac{e^x}{16} [D - 2] \cos 2x$$

$$= \frac{e^x}{16} [-2 \sin 2x - 2\cos 2x]$$

$$\text{P.I.} = -\frac{e^x}{8} [\sin 2x + \cos 2x].$$

Case V.

When $X = xV$, where V is function of x.

Then $$\frac{1}{F(D)} [xV] = x \frac{1}{F(D)} V - \frac{F'(D)}{[F(D)]^2} V.$$

Example 9. Find the P.I. of $(D^2 - 2D + 1) y = xe^x \sin x$.

Solution: The given differential equation is

$$\text{P.I.} = \frac{1}{D^2 - 2D + 1} e^x . x . \sin x$$

$$= \frac{1}{(D-1)^2} e^x . x . \sin x$$

$$= e^x \frac{1}{(D+1-1)^2} x \sin x$$

$$= e^x . \frac{1}{D^2} x \sin x$$

$$= e^x . \left[x . \frac{1}{D^2} \sin x - \frac{2D}{D^4} \sin x \right]$$

$$= e^x . \left[x . (-\sin x) - \frac{2}{D^3} \sin x \right]$$

$$= e^x . [- x \sin x - 2 \cos x]$$

$$\text{P.I.} = - e^x [x \sin x + 2 \cos x].$$

General Method:

When x is any function.

Let F(D) be resolved into linear factors as

$$F(D) = (D - m_1)(D - m_2) \dots (D-m_n)$$

$$\therefore \quad \frac{1}{F(D)}(X) = \frac{1}{(D-m_1)(D-m_2)(D-m_3)\dots(D-m_n)}(X)$$

$$= \left[\frac{A_1}{(D-m_1)} + \frac{A_2}{(D-m_2)} + \dots + \frac{A_n}{(D-m_n)}\right] X$$

$$= A_1 \frac{1}{D-m_1}(X) + A_2 \frac{1}{D-m_2}(X) + \dots + A_n \frac{1}{D-m_n}$$

(X)

$$= A_1 e^{m_1 x} \int e^{-m_1 x} X dx + A_2 e^{m_2 x} \int e^{-m_2 x} X dx + \dots$$

$$+ A_n e^{m_n x} \int e^{-m_n x} X dx.$$

Example 10. Solve the differential equation.

$$(D^2 - 4D + 3)\, y = 2xe^x + 3e^x \cos 2x.$$

Solution: The given differential equation is

$$(D^2 - 4D + 3)\, y = 2xe^x + 3e^x \cos 2x.$$

$$\therefore \quad \text{A.E.} = m^2 - 4m + 3.$$

$$\text{or} \quad (m-1)(m-3) = 0$$

$$\therefore \quad m = 1, 3$$

$$\text{C.F.} = c_1 e^x + c_2 e^{3x}$$

$$\text{P.I.} = \frac{1}{D^2 - 4D + 3} 2x\, e^x + 3e^x \cos 2x$$

$$= e^x . \frac{1}{(D+1)^2 - 4(D+1) + 3}(2x + 3 \cos 2x)$$

$$= e^x . \frac{1}{D^2 - 2D}(2x + 3 \cos 2x)$$

$$= 2e^x . \frac{1}{D^2 - 2D} x + 3e^x \frac{1}{D^2 - 2D} \cos 2x$$

$$= 2e^x . \left\{ -\frac{1}{2D}\left(1 - \frac{D}{2}\right)^{-1} x \right\} + 3e^x \left[\frac{1}{-4 - 2D} \cos 2x \right]$$

$$= 2e^x . \left\{ \frac{-1}{2D}\left[1 + \frac{D}{2} + \frac{D^2}{4}\right] x \right\} + 3e^x . \left[\left(\frac{-1}{2}\right) \frac{1}{D+2} \cos 2x \right]$$

$$= 2e^x . \left\{ \frac{-1}{2}\left[\frac{1}{D} + \frac{1}{2} + \frac{D}{4}\right] x \right\} - \frac{3e^x}{2} \left[\frac{D-2}{D^2 - 4} \cos 2x \right]$$

$$= 2e^x . \left\{ \frac{-1}{2}\left[\frac{x^2}{2} + \frac{x}{2} + \frac{1}{4}\right] \right\} - \frac{3e^x}{2} \left[\frac{(D-2)}{-8} \cos 2x \right]$$

$$= -e^x \left[\frac{x^2}{2} + \frac{x}{2} + \frac{1}{4} \right] + \frac{3e^x}{16} [D(\cos 2x) - 2\cos 2x]$$

$$= -e^x \left[\frac{x^2}{2} + \frac{x}{2} + \frac{1}{4} \right] - \frac{3e^x}{8} [\sin 2x + \cos 2x]$$

$\therefore$ The complete solution is

$$y = c_1 e^x + c_2 e^{3x} - e^x \left[\frac{x^2}{2} + \frac{x}{2} + \frac{1}{4} \right] - \frac{3e^x}{8} [\sin 2x + \cos 2x].$$

Example 11. Solve the differential equation.

$$(D^2 - 1)\, y = x \sin x + e^x (1 + x^2).$$

Solution: The given differential equation is

$$(D^2 - 1)\, y = x \sin x + e^x (1 + x^2) \qquad ...(1)$$

A.E. $= m^2 - 1 = 0$

$\therefore m = \pm 1$

C.F. $= c_1 e^x + c_2 e^{-x}$

$$\text{P.I.} = \frac{1}{D^2 - 1} x \sin x + \frac{1}{D^2 - 1} e^x (1 + x^2)$$

$$= x \cdot \frac{1}{(D^2-1)} \sin x - \frac{2D}{(D^2-1)^2} \sin x + e^x \frac{1}{D^2+2D} (1+x^2)$$

$$= x \cdot \frac{\sin x}{(-1-1)} - \frac{2D}{(-1-1)^2} \sin x + e^x \frac{1}{D^2+2D} (1+x^2)$$

$$= \frac{-x \sin x}{2} - \frac{1}{2} \text{D} (\sin x) + e^x \cdot \frac{1}{2D\left[1+\frac{D}{2}\right]} (1+x^2)$$

$$= \frac{-x \sin x}{2} - \frac{\cos x}{2} + e^x \cdot \frac{1}{2D}\left[1+\frac{D}{2}\right]^{-1} (1+x^2)$$

$$= -\frac{1}{2} [x \sin x + \cos x] + \frac{e^x}{2} \cdot \frac{1}{D}\left[1-\frac{D}{2}+\frac{D^2}{4}-\frac{D^3}{8}\right] (1+x^2)$$

$$= -\frac{1}{2} [x \sin x + \cos x] + \frac{e^x}{2} \cdot \left[\frac{1}{D}-\frac{1}{2}+\frac{D}{4}-\frac{D^2}{8}\right] (1+x^2)$$

$$= -\frac{1}{2} [x \sin x + \cos x] + \frac{e^x}{2} \left[x+\frac{x^3}{3}-\frac{1}{2}(1+x^2)+\frac{1}{4}(2x)-\frac{1}{8}.2\right]$$

$$= -\frac{1}{2} [x \sin x + \cos x] + \frac{e^x}{2} \left[x+\frac{x^3}{3}-\frac{1}{2}-\frac{x^2}{2}+\frac{x}{2}-\frac{1}{4}\right]$$

$$= -\frac{1}{2} [x \sin x + \cos x] + \frac{e^x}{2} \left[\frac{x^3}{3}-\frac{x^2}{2}+\frac{3x}{2}-\frac{3}{4}\right]$$

∴ The complete solution is

$$= c_1 e^x + c_2 e^{-x} - \frac{1}{2} [x \sin x + \cos x] + \frac{e^x}{2} \left[\frac{x^3}{3}-\frac{x^2}{2}+\frac{3x}{2}-\frac{3}{4}\right].$$

Example 12. Solve the differential equation.

$(D^2 + 1)\ y = \text{cosec}\ x.$

Solution: The given differential equation is $(D^2 + 1)\ y = \text{cosec}\ x$ (1)

$$\text{A.E.} = m^2 + 1 = 0$$

$$m = \pm\, i$$

$$\therefore \quad \text{C.F.} = c_1 \cos x + c_2 \sin x \quad (2)$$

$$\text{P.I.} = \frac{1}{D^2+1}\ \text{cosec}\ x$$

$$= \frac{1}{2i}\left[\frac{1}{D-i} - \frac{1}{D+i}\right]\ \text{cosec}\ x$$

$$= \frac{1}{2i}\left[\frac{1}{D-i}\text{cosec}\ x - \frac{1}{D+i}\text{cosec}\ x\right]$$

Now $\dfrac{1}{D-i}\ \text{cosec}\ x = e^{ix} \int e^{-ix}.\text{cosec}\ x dx$

$$= e^{ix} \int (\cos x - i \sin x)\ \text{cosec}\ x$$

$$= e^{ix} \int (\cot x - i)\, dx$$

$$= e^{ix}\ (\log \sin x - ix)$$

Similarly $\dfrac{1}{D+i}\ \text{cosec}\ x\ = e^{-ix}\ [\log \sin x + ix]$

$$\therefore \quad \text{P.I.} = \frac{1}{2i}\ [e^{ix}\ (\log \sin x - ix) - e^{-ix}\ (\log \sin x + ix)]$$

$$= \log \sin x \left[\frac{e^{ix} - e^{-ix}}{2i}\right] - x\left[\frac{e^{ix} + e^{-ix}}{2}\right]$$

$$= \sin x\ .\ \log \sin x - x \cos x$$

$\therefore$ The combplete solution is

$$y = c_1 \cos x + c_2 \sin x + \sin x \log \sin x - x \cos x.$$

Example 13. Solve the differential equation.

$(D - 2)^2\ y = 8\ e^{2x} + \sin 2x + x^3$

Solution:

$$\text{A.E.} = (m-2)^2 = 0$$

$$\therefore \quad m = 2, 2$$

$$\therefore \quad \text{C.F.} = (c_1 x + c_2)\, e^{2x}$$

$$\text{P.I.} = \frac{1}{(D-2)^2}\; 8e^{2x} + \sin 2x + x^3$$

$$= \frac{8}{(D-2)^2}\, e^{2x} + \frac{1}{(D^2-4D+4)} \sin 2x + \frac{1}{(D-2)^2} \,.\, x^3$$

$$= 8x \,.\, \frac{1}{2(D-2)}\, e^{2x} + \frac{1}{-4-4D+4} \sin 2x + \frac{1}{4\left[1-\frac{D}{2}\right]^2}\, x^3$$

$$= \frac{8.x^2.e^{2x}}{2} + \left(\frac{1}{-4D}\right) \sin 2x + \frac{1}{4}\left[1-\frac{D}{2}\right]^{-2} \,.\, x^3$$

$$= 4x^2e^{2x} + \frac{\cos 2x}{8} + \frac{1}{4}\left[1 + 2\left(\frac{D}{2}\right) + \frac{2.3}{2}.\frac{D^2}{4} + \frac{2.3.4}{3!}\frac{D^3}{8}\right] . \, x^3$$

$$= 4x^2e^{2x} + \frac{1}{8}\cos 2x + \frac{1}{4}\left[1 + D + \frac{3}{4}D^2 + \frac{1}{2}D^3\right] x^3$$

$$= 4x^2e^{2x} + \frac{1}{8}\cos 2x + \frac{1}{4}\left[x^3 + 3x^2 + \frac{9}{2}x + 3\right]$$

$\therefore$ The complete solution is

$$y = 4x^2e^{2x} + \frac{1}{8}\cos 2x + \frac{1}{4}\left[x^3 + 3x^2 + \frac{9}{2}x + 3\right] + (c_1x + c_2)e^{2x}$$

Example 14. Solve the differential equation.

$$\frac{d^4y}{dx^4} - y = \cos x \,.\, \cos hx.$$

Solution: The given equation is $(D^4 - 1)\, y = \cos x \,.\, \cos hx$ (1)

$\therefore$ $\text{A.E.} = m^4 - 1 = 0$

$\therefore$ $(m^2 - 1)(m^2 + 1) = 0$

$m = \pm 1, \pm i$

$\therefore$ $\text{C.F.} = c_1 e^x + c_2 e^{-x} + c_3 \cos x + c_4 \sin x$

$$\text{P.I.} = \frac{1}{D^4 - 1} \cos x \,.\, \cos hx$$

$$= \frac{1}{D^4 - 1} \cos x \left(\frac{e^x + e^{-x}}{2}\right)$$

$$= \frac{1}{2}.\left[\frac{1}{D^4 - 1} e^x.\cos x + \frac{1}{D^4 - 1} e^{-x}.\cos x\right]$$

$$= \frac{1}{2}\left[e^x.\frac{1}{(D+1)^4 - 1}\cos x + e^{-x}.\frac{1}{(D-1)^4 - 1}\cos x\right]$$

$$= \frac{1}{2}\left[e^x.\frac{1}{D^4 + 4D^3 + 6D^2 + 4D}.\cos x\right.$$

$$\left. + e^{-x}.\frac{1}{D^4 - 4D^3 + 6D^2 - 4D}\cos x\right]$$

$$= \frac{1}{2}\left[e^x.\frac{1}{1 - 4D - 6 + 4D}\cos x + e^{-x}\frac{1}{1 + 4D - 6 - 4D}\cos x\right]$$

$$= \frac{1}{2}\left[e^x.\frac{1}{-5}\cos x + e^{-x}.\frac{1}{-5}\cos x\right]$$

$$= -\frac{1}{5}\cos x\left[\frac{e^x + e^{-x}}{2}\right]$$

$$= \frac{-1}{5} \cos x \cos hx.$$

$\therefore$ The complete solution is

$$y = c_1 e^x + c_2 e^{-x} + c_3 \cos x + c_4 \sin x - \frac{1}{5} \cos x \;\; \cos hx.$$

Example 15. Solve.

$$(D^2 + a^2)\, y = \tan(ax)$$

Solution: The given differential equation is $(D^2 + a^2)\, y = \tan(ax)$ (1)

A.E. $m^2 + a^2 = 0$

$$\therefore \quad m = \pm\, ia$$

$$\therefore \quad \text{C.F.} = c_1 \cos ax + c_2 \sin ax \tag{2}$$

$$\text{P.I.} = \frac{1}{D^2 + a^2} \,.\, \tan(ax)$$

$$= \frac{1}{2ia}\left[\frac{1}{D - ia} - \frac{1}{(D + ia)}\right] \tan(ax)$$

$$= \frac{1}{2ia}\frac{1}{(D - ia)} \tan ax - \frac{1}{2ia}\frac{1}{(D + ia)} \,.\, \tan(ax)$$

Now,
$$= \frac{1}{D - ia} \tan ax$$

$$= e^{iax} \int e^{-iax} \tan ax\, dx$$

$$= e^{iax} \int (\cos ax - i \sin ax) \tan ax\, dx$$

$$= e^{iax} \int \left(\sin ax - i \frac{\sin^2 ax}{\cos ax} \right) dx$$

$$= e^{iax} \int \sin ax - i(\sec ax - \cos ax)\, dx$$

$$= e^{iax} \left[\frac{-\cos ax}{a} - \frac{i}{a}\left[\log(\sec ax + \tan ax)\right] + i \frac{\sin ax}{a} \right]$$

$$= \frac{-e^{iax}}{a} [(\cos ax - i \sin ax) + i \log(\sec ax + \tan ax)]$$

$$= -\frac{1}{a} [e^{iax} \,.\, e^{-iax} + i\, e^{iax} \,.\, \log(\sec ax + \tan ax)]$$

$$= -\frac{1}{a} [1 + i\, e^{ax} \,.\, \log(\sec ax + \tan ax)]$$

Similarly changing i by $-i$, we have

$$\frac{1}{D + ia} \tan ax = -\frac{1}{a} [1 - i\, e^{-iax} \log(\sec ax + \tan ax)]$$

$$\text{P.I.} = \frac{1}{2ia}\left\{\frac{-1}{a}(1 + ie^{iax}\log(\sec ax + \tan ax)]\right.$$

$$\left. + \frac{1}{a}[1 - i\,e^{iax}\log(\sec ax + \tan ax]\right\}$$

$$= \frac{-1}{2ia^2}[i\log(\sec ax + \tan ax][e^{iax} + e^{-iax}]$$

$$= -\frac{1}{a^2}(\log\sec ax + \tan ax)\left[\frac{e^{iax} + e^{-iax}}{2}\right]$$

$$= -\frac{1}{a^2}(\log\sec ax + \tan ax)\cos ax$$

∴ The complete solution is

$$y = c_1\cos ax + c_2\sin ax - \frac{1}{a^2}\log(\sec ax + \tan ax)\cos ax.$$

Example 16. Solve $(D^2 + a^2)\,y = \sec ax.$

Solution: The given differential equation is $(D^2 + a^2)\,y = \sec ax$ (1)

A.E. $m^2 + a^2 = 0$

∴ $m = \pm\, ia$

∴ C.F. $= c_1\cos ax + c_2\sin ax$ (2)

$$\text{P.I.} = \frac{1}{D^2 + a^2}\,.\,\sec ax$$

$$= \frac{1}{2ia}\left[\frac{1}{D - ia} - \frac{1}{(D + ia)}\right]\sec(ax)$$

$$= \frac{1}{2ia}\left[\frac{-1}{(D + ia)}\sec ax + \frac{1}{D - ia}\sec ax\right]$$

$$= \frac{1}{2ia}[-I_1 + I_2]$$

where $I_1 = \dfrac{1}{D + ia}\sec ax$

$$= e^{-iax} \int e^{iax}.\sec ax\, dx$$

$$= e^{-iax} \int (\cos ax + i \sin ax) \frac{1}{\cos ax} dx$$

$$= e^{-iax} \int (1 + i \tan ax)\, dx$$

$$= e^{-iax} \left[x + \frac{i}{a} \log \sec ax \right]$$

$\therefore$ Replacing i by $-i$, we have

$$I_2 = \frac{I}{D - ia} \sec ax$$

$$= e^{iax} \left[x - \frac{i}{a} \log \sec ax \right]$$

$$\therefore \qquad \text{P.I.} = \frac{1}{2ia} \left[e^{iax} \left(x - \frac{i}{a} \log \sec ax \right) - e^{-iax} \left(x + \frac{i}{a} \sec ax \right) \right]$$

$$= \frac{1}{2ia} \left[x\left(e^{iax} - e^{-iax}\right) \frac{-i}{a} \log \sec ax \left(e^{iax} + e^{-iax}\right) \right]$$

$$= \frac{x}{a}.\left(\frac{e^{iax} - e^{-iax}}{2i} \right) - \frac{1}{a^2}.\log(\sec ax).\left(\frac{e^{iax} + e^{-iax}}{2} \right)$$

$$= \frac{x}{a} \sin ax + \frac{1}{a^2} \log(\cos ax).\cos ax$$

$\therefore$ The complete solution is

$$y = c_1 \cos ax + c_2 \sin ax + \frac{x}{a} \sin ax + \frac{1}{a^2} \log(\cos ax).\cos ax$$

$$= c_1 \cos ax + c_2 \sin ax + \frac{x}{a} \sin ax + \frac{\cos ax}{a^2} \log(\cos ax).$$

EXERCISE

Solve the following differential equations:

1. $(D^2 + 5D + 6)\, y = 0$

Ans. $y = c_1\, e^{-2x} + c_2\, e^{-3x}$

2. $(D^3 - 4D^2 + 4D)\, y = 0$

Ans. $y = c_1 + (c_2 x + c_3)\, e^{2x}$

3. $(2D^2 + D - 6)\, y = 0$

Ans. $y = c_1 e^{3x/2} + c_2\, e^{-2x}$

4. $(D^2 - 4D + 1)\, y = 0$

Ans. $y = c_1 e^{\left(2+\sqrt{3}\right)x} + c_2 e^{\left(2-\sqrt{3}\right)x}$

5. $(D^3 + a^3)\, y = 0$

Ans. $y = c_1\, e^{-ax} + e^{-ax/2} \left[c_2 \cos\left(\dfrac{\sqrt{3}}{2} ax\right) + c_3 \sin \dfrac{\sqrt{3}}{2} ax \right]$

6. $(D^2 + 4) = e^{3x} + 5$

Ans. $y = c_1 \cos 2x + c_2 \sin 2x + \dfrac{e^{3x}}{13} + \dfrac{5}{4}$

7. $(D^3 - 5D^2 + 8D - 4)\, y = e^{2x} + 2e^x + 3e^{-x}$

Ans. $y = c_1 e^x + c_2\, e^{2x} + c_3 x \,.\, e^{2x} + \dfrac{1}{2}\, x^2\, e^{2x} + 2x\, e^x + \dfrac{e^{-x}}{6}$

8. $(D^3 - 12D + 16)\, y = (e^x + e^{-2x})^2$

Ans. $y = (c_1 x + c_2)\, e^{2x} + c_3\, e^{-4x} + \dfrac{x^2 e^{2x}}{12} + \dfrac{2e^{-x}}{27} + \dfrac{xe^{-4x}}{36}$

9. $(D^2 - D + 1)\, y = \sin hx$

Ans. $y = e^{x/2} \left[c_1 \cos \dfrac{\sqrt{3}}{2} x + c_2 \sin \dfrac{\sqrt{3}}{2} x \right] + \dfrac{1}{6}\left(3e^x - e^{-x}\right)$

10. $(D^2 - 4D - 5)\, y = e^{2x} + 3 \cos (4x + 3)$

Ans. $y = c_1 e^{-x} + c_2 e^{5x} - \dfrac{1}{9} e^{2x} - \dfrac{1}{697}\, [48 \sin (4x + 3) + 63 \cos (4x + 3)]$

11. $(D^3 - 2D^2 + 4D)\, y = e^{2x} + \sin 2x$

$$\textbf{Ans. } y = c_1 + e^x [c_2 \cos \sqrt{3}\,x + c_3 \sin \sqrt{3}\,x] + \frac{1}{8}(e^{2x} + \sin 2x)$$

12. $(D^2 + 5D - 6)\, y = \sin 4x \,.\, \sin x$

$$\textbf{Ans. } y = c_1 e^x + c_2\, e^{-6x} + \frac{1}{2}\left[\frac{\sin 3x - \cos 3x}{30}\right] + \left[\frac{31\cos 5x - 25\sin 5x}{1586}\right]$$

13. $(D^2 + 2D + 1)\, y = e^{2x} - \cos^2 x$

$$\textbf{Ans. } y = (c_1 x + c_2)\, e^{-x} + \frac{1}{5}\,[2\sin 2x + \cos 2x] + \frac{1}{2}$$

14. $(D^2 + D)\, y = x^2 + 2x + 4$

$$\textbf{Ans. } y = c_1 + c_2\, e^{-x} + \frac{x^3}{3} + 4x$$

15. $(D^6 - D^4)\, y = x^2$

$$\textbf{Ans. } y = (c_1 x^3 + c_2 x^2 + c_3 x + c_4) + c_5\, e^x + c_6 e^{-x} - \left[\frac{x^6}{360} + \frac{x^4}{12}\right]$$

16. $(D^2 + 2)\, y = x^3 + x^2 + e^{-2x} + \cos 3x$

$$\textbf{Ans. } y = (c_1 \cos \sqrt{2}\,x + c_2 \sin \sqrt{2}\,x) + \frac{1}{2}(x^3 + x^2 - 3x - 1)$$

$$+ \frac{e^{-2x}}{6} - \frac{1}{7} \cos 3x.$$

17. $(D^3 - D^2 - 6D)\, y = 1 + x^2$

$$\textbf{Ans. } y = c_1 + c_2 e^{-2x} + c_3\, e^{3x} - \frac{1}{18}\left[x^3 - \frac{x^2}{2} + \frac{25}{6}x\right]$$

18. $(D^2 + 2)\, y = x^2 e^{3x} + e^x \cos 2x$

$$\textbf{Ans. } y = c_1 \cos \sqrt{2}\,x + c_2 \sin \sqrt{2}\,x + \frac{e^{3x}}{11}\left(x^2 - \frac{12}{11}x + \frac{50}{121}\right)$$

$$+ \frac{e^x}{17}\,(4\sin 2x - \cos 2x)$$

19. $(D^4 - 1)\, y = \cos x \cos hx$

$$\textbf{Ans. } y = c_1 e^x + c_2 e^{-x} + c_3 \cos x + c_4 \sin x - \frac{1}{5} \cos x \cos hx$$

20. $(D^3 - 2D + 4)\, y = e^x \sin x$

$$\textbf{Ans. } y = c_1 e^{-2x} + e^x [c_2 \cos x + c_3 \sin x] + \frac{xe^x}{20} (3\sin x + \cos x)$$

21. $(D^2 + 4D + 8)\, y = 12e^{-2x} . \sin 3x . \sin x$

$$\textbf{Ans. } y = e^{x/2}\left[c_1 \cos \frac{\sqrt{31}}{2} x + c_2 \sin \sqrt{\frac{31}{2}} x\right] + \frac{1}{2} e^{-2x} (3x \sin 2x + \cos 4x)$$

22. $(D^2 - 1)\, y = xe^x \sin x$

$$\textbf{Ans. } y = c_1 e^x + c_2 e^{-x} + \frac{e^x}{25} [14 \sin x - 2\cos x - 5x (2\cos x + \sin x)]$$

23. $(D^2 + 4)\, y = \sec 2x$

$$\textbf{Ans. } y = c_1 \cos 2x + c_2 \sin 2x + \frac{x}{2} \sin 2x + \frac{1}{4} \cos 2x \log (\cos 2x)$$

24. $(D^2 + 9)\, y = \tan 3x$

$$\textbf{Ans. } y = c_1 \cos 3x + c_2 \sin 3x - \frac{1}{9} \cos 3x . \log (\sec 3x + \tan 3x).$$

Homogeneous linear differential equations

A linear differential equation of the form

$$x^n \frac{d^n y}{dx^n} + p_1 x^{n-1} \frac{d^{n-1} y}{dx^{n-1}} + p_2 x^{n-2} \frac{d^{n-2} y}{dx^{n-2}} \dots + p_n y = X$$

where $p_1, p_2, p_3 \dots p_n$ are all constants and X is function of x (or a constant), is called a Homogeneous linear differential equation. Also known as Cauchy's linear equation.

Solution of Cauchy's linear equation

This equation is reduced to linear differential equation with constant coefficients, by the substitution

$x = e^z$ or $z = \log x$

$$\therefore \qquad \frac{dy}{dx} = \frac{dy}{dz}.\frac{dz}{dx}$$

$$= \frac{1}{x}\frac{dy}{dz}$$

or

$$x\frac{dy}{dx} = \frac{dy}{dz}$$

$$\therefore \qquad x\frac{dy}{dx} \equiv \frac{dy}{dz} = Dy \text{ Where } D = \frac{d}{dz}$$

and

$$\frac{d^2y}{dx^2} = \frac{d}{dx}\left[\frac{dy}{dx}\right]$$

$$= \frac{d}{dx}\left[\frac{1}{x}\frac{dy}{dz}\right]$$

$$= \frac{d}{dx}\left[\frac{1}{x}.\frac{dy}{dz}\right]$$

$$= \frac{d}{dz}\left[\frac{1}{x}\frac{dy}{dz}\right].\frac{dz}{dx}$$

$$= -\frac{1}{x^2}\frac{dy}{dz} + \frac{1}{x^2}\frac{d^2y}{dz^2}$$

$$\therefore \qquad x^2\frac{d^2y}{dx^2} = \frac{-dy}{dz} + \frac{d^2y}{dz^2}$$

$$= \frac{d}{dz}\left[\frac{d}{dz} - 1\right]y$$

$$\therefore \qquad x^2\frac{d^2}{dx^2} = \frac{d}{dz}\left[\frac{d}{dz} - 1\right]$$

$$= D\,(D - 1)\,y$$

Similarly

$$x^3\frac{d^3y}{dx^3} = D\,(D-1)\,(D-2)\,y \text{ etc.}$$

Substitution of these, reduces the given differential to a linear differential equation with constant coefficients, which may be solved by the methods discussed earlier.

Example 1. Solve.

$$x^2 \frac{d^2 y}{dx^2} - x\frac{dy}{dx} - 3y = x^2 \log x$$

Solution: The given equation is Cauchy's linear equation.

$$x^2 \frac{d^2 y}{dx^2} - x\frac{dy}{dx} - 3y = x^2 \log x \qquad (1)$$

Let $$x = e^z \text{ or } z = \log x$$

$$\frac{xdy}{dx} = Dy.$$

and $$x^2 \frac{d^2 y}{dx^2} = D(D-1)\,y$$

Then the equation (1) is reduced to

$$(D(D-1) - D - 3)\,y = x^2 \log x$$

$$= e^{2z} \cdot z$$

or $$(D^2 - 2D - 3)\,y = ze^{2z} \qquad (2)$$

Equation (2) is a linear differential equation with constant coefficients

A.E. $$m^2 - 2m - 3 = 0$$

$\therefore$ $$m = 3, -1$$

$$\text{C.F.} = c_1 e^{3z} + c_2 e^{-z}$$

$$= c_1 x^3 + \frac{c_2}{x}$$

$$\text{P.I} = \frac{1}{D^2 - 2D - 3} e^{2z} \cdot z$$

$$= e^{2z} \frac{1}{(D+2)^2 - 2(D+2) - 3} z$$

$$= e^{2z} \frac{1}{D^2 + 2D - 3} z$$

$$= -\frac{1}{3}e^{2z}\left[z+\frac{2}{3}\right]$$

$$= -\frac{1}{3}x^2\left[\log x+\frac{2}{3}\right]$$

∴ The complete solution is

$$y = c_1x^3 + \frac{c_2}{x} - \frac{1}{3}x^2\left(\log x+\frac{2}{3}\right).$$

Example 2. Solve

$$x^2\frac{d^2y}{dx^2} - 3x\frac{dy}{dx} + 5y = x^2 \sin(\log x)$$

Solution: The given differential equation is Cauchy's linear differential equation.

$$x^2\frac{d^2y}{dx^2} - 3x\frac{dy}{dx} + 5y = x^2 \sin(\log x) \qquad (1)$$

By the substitution $z = \log x$ (2)

$$x\frac{dy}{dx} = Dy$$

$$x^2\frac{d^2y}{dx^2} = D(D-1)y$$

Where $D = \dfrac{d}{dz}$

then from (1), we have

$$(D(D-1) - 3D + 5)y = e^{2z} . \sin z$$

or $(D^2 - 4D + 5)y = e^{2z} . \sin z$ (3)

Equation (3) is linear differential equation with constant coefficients.

∴ A.E. $m^2 - 4m + 5 = 0$

∴ $m = 2 \pm i$

$$\text{C.F.} = e^{2z}[c_1\cos z + c_2 \sin z]$$

$$= x^2 [c_1 \cos(\log x) + c_2 \sin(\log x)]$$

Now, $$\text{P.I.} = \frac{1}{D^2 - 4D + 5} \cdot e^{2z} \cdot \sin z$$

$$= e^{2z} \cdot \frac{1}{(D+2)^2 - 4(D+2) + 5} \sin z$$

$$= e^{2z} \cdot \frac{1}{D^2 + 1} \sin z$$

$$= e^{2z} . z \frac{1}{2D} \sin z$$

$$= e^{2z} . z \left(-\frac{\cos z}{2} \right)$$

$$= -\frac{1}{2} \cdot e^{2z} \cdot z \cdot \cos z$$

$$= -\frac{1}{2} \cdot x^2 (\log x) \cdot \cos (\log x)$$

$\therefore$ The complete solution is

$$y = x^2 (c_1 \cos (\log x) + c_2 \sin (\log x)$$

$$- \frac{x^2}{2} (\log x) \cdot \cos (\log x).$$

Equations Reducible to Homogeneous Form

The general equation of the form

$$(a + bx)^n \frac{d^n y}{dx^n} + p_1 (a + bx)^{n-1} \frac{d^{n-1} y}{dx^{n-1}} + \ldots$$

$$p_{n-1} (a + bx) \frac{dy}{dx} + p_n y = \text{X} \qquad \ldots (1)$$

where $p_1, p_2 \ldots p_n$ are constants and X is function of x or constant, can be reduced to homogeneous form. This equation is known as Legendre's differential equation.

Substituting $\qquad a + bx = t$

$$\therefore \qquad \frac{dt}{dx} = b$$

$$\therefore \qquad \frac{dy}{dx} = \frac{dy}{dt}.\frac{dt}{dx}$$

$$= b \,.\, \frac{dy}{dt}$$

$$\frac{d^2 y}{dx^2} = \frac{d}{dx}\left[b.\frac{dy}{dt}\right]$$

$$= \frac{d}{dt}\left[b.\frac{dy}{dt}\right].\frac{dt}{dx}$$

$$= b \,.\, \frac{d^2 y}{dt^2} \,.\, b$$

$$= b^2 \frac{d^2 y}{dt^2}$$

$$= \frac{d^n y}{dx^n}$$

$$= b^n \,.\, \frac{d^n y}{dt^n}$$

Substituting these, we get

$$t^n b^n \frac{d^n y}{dt^n} + p_1 b^{n-1} t^{n-1} \frac{d^{n-1} y}{dt^{n-1}} + p_2 b^{n-2} t^{n-2} \frac{d^{n-2} y}{dt^{n-2}} + ... + p_n y = F(t)$$

$$\text{or } t^n \frac{d^n y}{dt^n} + \frac{p_1}{b} t^{n-1} \frac{d^{n-1} y}{dt^{n-1}} + ... \frac{p_n}{b^n} y = \frac{1}{b^n} F(t) \qquad (2)$$

Equation (2) is a homogeneous differential equation which can be solved by the method discussed earlier.

Example 1. Solve $(2x + 5)^2 y'' - 6(2x + 5)y' + 8y = 6x$.

Solution: $(2x + 5)^2 y'' - 6(2x + 5) y' + 8y = 6x$ (1)

Let $\qquad 2x + 5 = t$

$\therefore \qquad a = 5, b = 2$

Then making this substitution, we have

$$4t^2 \frac{d^2 y}{dt^2} - 6t_2 \frac{dy}{dt} + 8y = 6\left[\frac{t-5}{2}\right]$$

or $$t^2\frac{d^2y}{dt^2} - 3t\frac{dy}{dt} + 2y = \frac{3}{4}(t-5) \qquad (2)$$

Now let $t = e^z$ or $z = \log t$

$$\therefore \quad t\frac{dy}{dt} = Dy,\ t^2\frac{d^2y}{dt^2} = D(D-1)y$$

where $$D \equiv \frac{d}{dz}$$

$$\therefore D(D-1)y - 3Dy + 2y = \frac{3}{4}(e^z - 5)$$

$$(D^2 - 4D + 2)y = \frac{1}{4}[3e^z - 15] \qquad (3)$$

Equation (3) is linear differential equation with constant coeffcients.

$\therefore$ A.E. $m^2 - 4m + 2 = 0$

$$m = 2 \pm \sqrt{2}$$

$$\therefore \quad \text{C.F.} = e^{2z}\left[c_1e^{\sqrt{2}z} + c_2e^{-\sqrt{2}z}\right]$$

$$\text{P.I.} = \frac{1}{D^2 - 4D + 2}\frac{1}{4}[3e^z - 15]$$

$$= \frac{1}{4}\left[3\frac{1}{D^2 - 4D + 2}e^z - 15\frac{1}{D^2 - 4D + 2}e^{0z}\right]$$

$$= \frac{1}{4}\left[3.\frac{e^z}{-1} - 15.\frac{1}{2}\right]$$

$$= -\frac{1}{4}\left[3e^z + \frac{15}{2}\right]$$

$$= \frac{-3}{4}e^z - \frac{15}{8}$$

$\therefore$ The complete solutions is

$$y = e^{2z}\left[c_1e^{\sqrt{2}z} + c_2e^{-\sqrt{2}z}\right] - \frac{3}{4}e^z - \frac{15}{8}$$

$$= (2x + 5)^2 \left[c_1 (2x+5)^{\sqrt{2}} + c_2 (2x+5)^{-\sqrt{2}} \right]$$

$$-\frac{3}{4} (2x + 5) - \frac{15}{8}.$$

EXERCISE

Solve the following differential equations:

1. $x^3 \dfrac{d^3y}{dx^3} + 2x^2 \dfrac{d^2y}{dx^2} + 2y = 10 \left(x + \dfrac{1}{x} \right)$

Ans. $y = \dfrac{c_1}{x} + x\,[c_2 \cos(\log x) + c_3 \sin(\log x)] + 5x + \dfrac{2}{x} \log x]$

2. $x^3 \dfrac{d^3y}{dx^3} + 3x^2 \dfrac{d^2y}{dx^2} + x\dfrac{dy}{dx} = 24x^2$

Ans. $y = c_1 + c_2 (\log x) + c_3 ((\log x)^2 + 3x^2$

3. $x^4 \dfrac{d^3y}{dx^3} + 2x^3 \dfrac{d^2y}{dx^2} - x^2 \dfrac{dy}{dx} + xy = 1$

Ans. $y = [c_1 + c_2 (\log x)]\, x + \dfrac{c_3}{x} + \dfrac{\log x}{4x}$

4. $x^3 \dfrac{d^3y}{dx^3} - 8x^2 \dfrac{d^2y}{dx^2} + 28x \dfrac{dy}{dx} - 40y = \dfrac{-9}{x}$

Ans. $y = c_1 x^2 + c_2 x^4 + c_3 x^5 + \dfrac{1}{10x}$

5. $x^2 \dfrac{d^2y}{dx^2} - 2x \dfrac{dy}{dx} - 4y = x^2 + 2 \log x$

Ans. $y = \dfrac{c_1}{x} + c_2 x^4 - \dfrac{x^2}{6} - \dfrac{1}{2} \log x + \dfrac{3}{8}$

6. $x^2 \dfrac{d^2y}{dx^2} + 2x \dfrac{dy}{dx} - 12y = x^3 \log x$

Ans. $y = c_1x^3 + c_2 x^{-4} + \dfrac{x^3}{98} (\log x) [7 \log x - 2]$

7. $(2x + 3)^2 \dfrac{d^2y}{dx^2} - 2 (2x + 3) \dfrac{dy}{dx} - 12 y = 6x$

Ans. $y = c_1 (2x + 3)^{-1} + c_2 (2x + 3)^3 - \dfrac{3}{4} (2x + 3) + 3$

8. $(3x + 2)^2 \dfrac{d^2y}{dx^2} + 3 (3x + 2) \dfrac{dy}{dx} - 36y = 3x^2 + 4x + 1$

Ans. $y = c_1 (3x + 2)^2 + c_2 . (3x + 2)^{-2} + \dfrac{1}{108} [(3x + 2)^2 \log (3x + 2) + 1]$

Method of Variation of Parameters

This is the method of finding complete solution of a linear differential equation of second order whose complementary function is known.

Let the differential equation of second order be

$$\frac{d^2y}{dx^2} + P \frac{dy}{dx} + Qy = R \quad (1)$$

where P, Q and R, are functions of x.

Let $y = c_1 \phi (x) + c_2 \psi (x)$ (2)

be the complementary function of (1), where c_1, c_2 are constants.

$\therefore$ $y = c_1 \phi (x) + c_2 \psi (x)$ will satisfy the equation

$$\frac{d^2y}{dx^2} + p\frac{dy}{dx} + Qy = 0$$

$$[c_1\phi'' (x) + c_2 \psi'' (x)] + P [c_1\phi' (x) + c_2 \psi' (x)] + Q [c_1\phi (x) + c_2 \psi (x)] = 0$$

$$\text{or} [c_1\phi'' (x) + P \phi' (x) + Q\phi(x)] + c_2 [\psi'' (x) + P \psi' (x) + Q\psi(x)] = 0$$

$$\therefore \qquad \phi''(x) + P\phi'(x) + Q\phi(x) = 0 \qquad (3)$$

$$\psi''(x) + P\psi'(x) + Q\psi(x) = 0 \qquad (4)$$

Now let us assume that

$$y = A\phi(x) + B\psi(x) \qquad (5)$$

be the complete solution of equation (1), where A, B are functions of x, so choosen that (1) is satistified.

$$\therefore \qquad \frac{dy}{dx} = A\phi'(x) + \mathrm{B}\psi'(x) + \frac{dA}{dx}\phi(x) + \frac{dB}{dx}\psi(x)$$

Now, A and B are choosen is such a way that

$$\frac{dA}{dx}\phi(x) + \frac{dB}{dx}\psi(x) = 0 \qquad (6)$$

$$\therefore \qquad \frac{dy}{dx} = A\phi'(x) + \mathrm{B}\psi'(x)$$

and $$\frac{d^2y}{dx^2} = A\phi''(x) + \mathrm{B}\psi''(x) + \frac{dA}{dx}\phi'(x) + \frac{dB}{dx}\psi'(x)$$

Substituting $y, \frac{dy}{dx}, \frac{d^2y}{dx^2}$ in (1), we have

$$\left[A\phi''(x) + \mathrm{B}\psi''(x) + \frac{dA}{dx}\phi'(x) + \frac{dB}{dx}\psi'(x)\right]$$

$$+ P[A\phi'(x) + \mathrm{B}\psi'(x)] + \mathrm{Q}[A\phi(x) + \mathrm{B}\psi(x)] = \mathrm{R}$$

or $$A[\phi''(x) + p\phi'(x) + \mathrm{Q}\phi(x)] + \mathrm{B}[\psi''(x)$$

$$+ p\psi'(x) + \mathrm{Q}\psi(x)] + \frac{dA}{dx}\phi'(x) + \frac{dB}{dx}\psi'(x) = \mathrm{R}$$

Since $$\phi''(x) + p\phi'(x) + \mathrm{Q}\phi(x) = 0$$

and $$\psi''(x) + p\psi'(x) + \mathrm{Q}\phi(x) = 0$$

$$\therefore \qquad \frac{dA}{dx}\phi'(x) + \frac{dB}{dx}\psi'(x) = \mathrm{R} \qquad (7)$$

Now equations (6) and (7) are simultaneous equations in $\frac{dA}{dx}$ and $\frac{dB}{dx}$, solving these we find the values of A and B and finally substituting in equation (5), we get the required solution.

SOLVED EXAMPLES

Example 1. Solve by the method of variation of parameters.

$$\frac{d^2y}{dx^2} + y = \text{cosec } x$$

Solution: The given equation is

$$\frac{d^2y}{dx^2} + y = \text{cosec } x \qquad (1)$$

$\therefore$ A.E. $\quad m^2 + 1 = 0$

or $\quad m = \pm i$

$\therefore$ C.F. is $\quad y = c_1 \cos x + c_2 \sin x \qquad (2)$

Now, let $\quad y = A \cos x + B \sin x \qquad (3)$

be the complete solution of (1), where A and B are functions of x.

$$\therefore \quad \frac{dy}{dx} = -\text{A} \sin x + \text{B} \cos x + \frac{dA}{dx} \cos x + \frac{dB}{dx} \sin x$$

Let $\frac{dA}{dx} \cos x + \frac{dB}{dx} \sin x = 0 \qquad (4)$

$$\therefore \quad \frac{dy}{dx} = -\text{A} \sin x + \text{B} \cos x$$

$$\text{so,} \quad \frac{d^2y}{dx^2} = -\text{A} \cos x - \text{B} \sin - \frac{dA}{dx} \sin x + \frac{dB}{dx} \cos x$$

Substituting $y, \frac{dy}{dx}, \frac{d^2y}{dx^2}$ in equation (1), we have

$$-A \cos x - B \sin x - \frac{dA}{dx} \sin x + \frac{dB}{dx} \cos x$$

$$+ A \cos x + B \sin x = \text{cosec } x$$

$$\therefore \quad -\frac{dA}{dx} \sin x + \frac{dB}{dx} \cos x = \text{cosec } x \qquad (5)$$

∴ From (4) and (5)

$$\frac{dA}{dx}\cos x + \frac{dB}{dx}\sin x = 0$$

$$-\frac{dA}{dx}\sin x + \frac{dB}{dx}\cos x = \text{cosec } x$$

Eliminating $\frac{dA}{dx}$, we have

$$\frac{dB}{dx}[\cos^2 x + \sin^2 x] = \cot x$$

$$\therefore \qquad \frac{dB}{dx} = \cot x$$

$$B = \int \cot x \, dx$$

$$B = \log(\sin x) + c_2 \qquad (6)$$

Now eliminating $\frac{dB}{dx}$, we have

$$\frac{dA}{dx}[\cos^2 x + \sin^2 x] = -\text{cosec } x \sin x$$

$$\frac{dA}{dx} = -1$$

$$A = -x + c_1$$

Substituting A and B in (3), we have

$$y = (-x + c_1)\cos x + [\log(\sin x) + c_2]\sin x$$

or $$y = c_1 \cos x + c_2 \sin x - x\cos x + \sin x \log(\sin x)$$

is the complete solution.

Example 2. Solve by the method of variation of parameters equation.

$$\frac{d^2 y}{dx^2} + n^2 y = \sec nx$$

Solution: The given differential equation is

$$\frac{d^2 y}{dx^2} + n^2 y = \sec nx \qquad (1)$$

$\therefore$ A.E. $\quad m^2 + n^2 = 0$

$$m = \pm\, in$$

$\therefore$ C.F. is $\quad y = c_1 \cos nx + c_2 \sin nx \qquad (2)$

Let $\quad y = A \cos nx + B \sin nx \qquad (3)$

be the complete solution, where A, B are functions of x.

$$\frac{dy}{dx} = -An \sin nx + Bn \cos nx + \frac{dA}{dx} \cos nx + \frac{dB}{dx} \sin nx$$

Let $\quad \dfrac{dA}{dx} \cos nx + \dfrac{dB}{dx} \sin nx = 0 \qquad (4)$

$$\therefore \quad \frac{dy}{dx} = -An \sin nx + Bn \cos nx$$

$$\therefore \quad \frac{d^2y}{dx^2} = -An^2 \cos nx - Bn^2 \sin nx - n\frac{dA}{dx} \sin nx + n\frac{dB}{dx} \cos nx$$

Substituting $y, \dfrac{dy}{dx}, \dfrac{d^2y}{dx^2}$ in (1), we have

$$-n^2 A \cos nx - n^2 B \sin nx - n\frac{dA}{dx} \sin nx + n\frac{dB}{dx} \cos nx + n^2 A \cos nx + n^2 B \sin nx = \sec nx$$

$$\therefore \quad -n\frac{dA}{dx} \sin nx + n\frac{dB}{dx} \cos nx = \sec nx \qquad (5)$$

$\therefore$ from (4) and (5), we have

$$\frac{dA}{dx} \cos nx + \frac{dB}{dx} \sin nx = 0$$

and $$-\frac{dA}{dx}\sin nx + \frac{dB}{dx}\cos nx = \frac{1}{n}\sec nx$$

Eliminating $\frac{dA}{dx}$, we have

$$\frac{dB}{dx}[\cos^2 nx + \sin^2 nx] = \frac{1}{n}\sec nx \,.\, \cos nx$$

$$\therefore \quad \frac{dB}{dx} = \frac{1}{n}$$

$$\therefore \quad B = \frac{x}{n} + c_2. \qquad (6)$$

Eliminating $\frac{dA}{dx}$, we have

$$\frac{dA}{dx}[\cos^2 nx + \sin^2 nx] = -\frac{1}{n}\tan nx$$

$$\frac{dA}{dx} = -\frac{1}{n}\tan nx$$

$$\therefore \quad A = \frac{1}{n^2}\log(\cos nx) + c_1$$

Substituting A and B in (3), we have the complete solution as

$$y = c_1\cos nx + c_2\sin nx + \frac{1}{n^2}\cos nx\log(\cos nx) + \frac{x}{n}\sin nx.$$

Example 3. Solve by the method of variation of parameters.

$$\frac{d^2y}{dx^2} + 4y = 4\tan 2x$$

Solution: The given differential equation is

$$(D^2 + 4)y = 4\tan 2x \qquad (1)$$

$\therefore$ A.E. $\quad m^2 + 4 = 0$

$$m = \pm 2i$$

$\therefore$ C.F. is $\quad y = c_1\cos 2x + c_2\sin 2x \qquad (2)$

Let $\quad y = A\cos 2x + B\sin 2x \qquad (3)$

be the complete solution, where A and B are functions of x.

$$\frac{dy}{dx} = -2A \sin 2x + 2B \cos 2x + \frac{dA}{dx} \cos 2x + \frac{dB}{dx} \sin 2x$$

Let $\frac{dA}{dx} \cos 2x + \frac{dB}{dx} \sin 2x = 0$ (4)

$$\therefore \quad \frac{dy}{dx} = -2A \sin 2x + 2B \cos 2x$$

$$\text{so,} \quad \frac{d^2y}{dx^2} = -4A \cos 2x - 4B \sin 2x - 2\frac{dA}{dx} \sin 2x + 2\frac{dB}{dx} \cos 2x.$$

Substituting $y, \frac{dy}{dx}$ and $\frac{d^2y}{dx^2}$ in (1), we have

$$-4A \cos 2x - 4B \sin 2x - 2\frac{dA}{dx} \sin 2x$$

$$+ 2\frac{dB}{dx} \cos 2x + 4\text{A} \cos 2x + 4\text{ B} \sin 2x = 4 \tan 2x$$

or $$-2\frac{dA}{dx} \sin 2x + 2\frac{dB}{dx} \cos 2x = 4 \tan 2x \qquad (5)$$

Now from equation (4) and (5), we have

$$-2 \frac{dA}{dx} \sin 2x + 2\frac{dB}{dx} \cos 2x = 4 \tan 2x \qquad (6)$$

$$\frac{dA}{dx} \cos 2\text{x} + \frac{dB}{dx} \sin 2x = 0 \qquad (7)$$

Eliminating $\frac{dB}{dx}$ in (6), we have

$$\frac{dA}{dx} = -2 \tan 2x \,.\, \sin 2x$$

$$= -2\frac{\sin^2 2x}{\cos 2x}$$

$$\frac{dA}{dx} = -2 \frac{\left(1 - \cos^2 2x\right)}{\cos 2x}$$

$$= -2 \sec 2x + 2 \cos 2x$$

$\therefore$ $$A = -\log(\sec 2x + \tan 2x) + \sin 2x + c_1$$

and $$B = -\cos 2x + c_2.$$

$\therefore$ Substituting A and B in (3), we have the complete solution

$$y = c_1 \cos 2x + c_2 \sin 2x - \log(\sec 2x + \tan 2x) \cos 2x.$$

Example 4. Solve the following differential equation by the method of variation of parameters.

$$x^2 \frac{d^2 y}{dx^2} + x\frac{dy}{dx} - y = x^3 e^x$$

Solution: The given differential equation is

$$x^2 \frac{d^2 y}{dx^2} + x\frac{dy}{dx} - y = x^3 e^x \quad (1)$$

which is a homogeneous differential equation.

Let $$x = e^z$$

then the above equation reduces to

$$[D(D-1) + D - 1]\, y = e^{3z} \,.\, e^{e^z}. \quad (2)$$

(2) is L.D.E. with constant coefficient

A.E. $$m^2 - 1 = 0$$

$$m = \pm 1$$

$\therefore$ C.F. $$y = c_1 e^z + c_2 e^{-z}$$

$$y = c_1 x + c_2 \,.\, \frac{1}{x}$$

Let $$y = Ax + B\frac{1}{x} \quad (3)$$

where A, B are functions of x, be the complete solution.

$\therefore$ $$\frac{dy}{dx} = A - \frac{B}{x^2} + \frac{dA}{dx}.x + \frac{dB}{dx}.\frac{1}{x}$$

Let $$\frac{dA}{dx}.x + \frac{dB}{dx}.\frac{1}{x} = 0 \quad (4)$$

$\therefore$ $$\frac{dy}{dx} = A - \frac{B}{x^2}$$

so, $$\frac{d^2y}{dx^2} = \frac{dA}{dx} - \frac{dB}{dx}.\frac{1}{x^2} + \frac{2B}{x^3}$$

Substituting y, $\frac{dy}{dx}$ and $\frac{d^2y}{dx^2}$ in equation (1), we have

$$x^2\frac{dA}{dx} - \frac{dB}{dx} + \frac{2B}{x} + Ax - \frac{B}{x} - Ax - \frac{B}{x} = x^3e^x$$

$$x^2\frac{dA}{dx} - \frac{dB}{dx} = x^3e^x \tag{5}$$

∴ From equation (4) and (5), we have

$$\frac{dA}{dx}.x + \frac{dB}{dx}.\frac{1}{x} = 0$$

$$x^2\frac{dA}{dx} - \frac{dB}{dx} = x^3e^x$$

Eliminating $\frac{dB}{dx}$, we have

$$\frac{2dA}{dx}x = x^2e^x$$

∴ $$\frac{dA}{dx} = \frac{1}{2}x\,e^x$$

∴ $$A = \frac{1}{2}(x-1)\,e^x + c_1.$$

Putting $\frac{dA}{dx}$ in equation $\frac{dA}{dx}.x + \frac{dB}{dx}.\frac{1}{x} = 0$, we have

$$\frac{dB}{dx} = -\frac{1}{2}x^3\,e^x$$

∴ $$B = -\frac{1}{2}[x^3 - 3x^2 + 6x - 6]\,e^x + c_2$$

Substituting A and B in equation (3), we have the complete solution as

$$y = c_1 x + c_2 \cdot \frac{1}{x} + \frac{e^x}{2}\left[2x - 6 + \frac{6}{x}\right]$$

$$= c_1 x + c_2 \cdot \frac{1}{x} + e^x\left[x - 3 + \frac{3}{x}\right].$$

EXERCISE

Solve the following differential equations by the method of variation of parameters.

1. $\frac{d^2y}{dx^2} + y = x \sin x$

Ans. $y = c_1 \cos x + c_2 \sin x + \frac{x}{2} \sin x - \frac{x^2}{4} \cos x$

2. $\frac{d^2y}{dx^2} - \frac{2dy}{dx} + 2y = e^x \tan x$

Ans. $y = e^x (c_1 \cos x + c_2 \sin x) - e^x \cos x \cdot \log (\sec x + \tan x)$

3. $\frac{d^2y}{dx^2} - y = \frac{2}{1+e^x}$

Ans. $y = c_1 e^x + c_2 e^{-x} + e^x \cdot \log\left(\frac{1+e^x}{e^x}\right) - e^{-x} \log (1 + e^x) - 1$

4. $\frac{d^2y}{dx^2} + 9y = \sec 3x$

Ans. $y = c_1 \cos 3x + c_2 \sin 3x + \frac{1}{9} \cdot \cos 3x \log (\cos 3x) + \frac{x}{3} \sin 3x$

5. $x^2 \frac{d^2y}{dx^2} + \frac{xdy}{dx} - y = x^2 e^x$

Ans. $y = c_1 x + \frac{c_2}{x} + e^x - \frac{1}{x} e^x$

6. $\frac{d^2y}{dx^2} + a^2y = \text{cosec } ax$

Ans. $y = c_1 \cos ax + c_2 \sin ax - \frac{x}{a} \cos ax + \frac{1}{a^2} \sin ax \log(\sin ax)$

7. $(D^2 + a^2)\, y = \tan ax$

Ans. $y = c_1 \cos ax + c_2 \sin ax - \frac{1}{a^2} \cos ax \log(\sec ax + \tan ax)$.

Simultaneous linear differential equations with constant coefficients.

These are the differential equations in which there is only one independent variable and two or more dependent variables.

Here we apply the method of elimination:

Let x and y be two dependent variables and t the independent variable.

Let us consider the simultaneous equations.

$$F_1(D)\, x + F_2(D)\, y = T_1 \tag{1}$$

and

$$\psi_1(D)\, x + \psi_2(D)\, y = T_2 \tag{2}$$

where $D = \frac{d}{dt}$ and T_1, T_2 are functions of t.

To eliminate y between (1) and (2), we make the operators of y equal.

So multiplying equation (1) by $\psi_2(D)$ and (2) by $F_2(D)$, we have

$$[F_1(D)\psi_2(D)]\, x + [F_2(D)\, \psi_2(D)]\, y = \psi_2(D)\, T_1 \tag{3}$$

$$[\psi_1(D)F_2(D)]\, x + [\psi_2(D)\, F_2(D)]\, y = F_2(D)\, T_2 \tag{4}$$

Subtracting (4) from (3), we have

$$[F_1(D)\psi_2(D) - \psi_1(D)\, F_2(D)]\, x = \psi_2(D)\, T_1 - F_2(D)\, T_2 \tag{5}$$

Now equation (5) is linear in x and t and can be solved by the methods discussed earlier. Substituting the value of x in (1) or (2), we get the value of y and the system gets a solution.

Note: By making the operator of x, equal we may eliminate x and find the value of y in terms of t and then finally the value of x.

SOLVED EXAMPLES

Example 1. Solve the simultaneous equations.

$$\frac{d^2x}{dt^2} - 3x - 4y = 0, \; \frac{d^2y}{dt^2} + x + y = 0$$

Solution: The given equations can be written as

$$(D^2 - 3)\,x - 4y = 0 \tag{1}$$

$$x + (D^2 + 1)\,y = 0 \tag{2}$$

Eliminating y, we have

$$[D^2 + 1)\,(D^2 - 3) + 4]x = 0$$

or $$[D^4 + D^2 - 3D^2 - 3 + 4]\,x = 0$$

$$(D^4 - 2D^2 + 1)\,x = 0$$

$$(D^2 - 1)^2\,x = 0 \tag{3}$$

Equation (3) is L.D.E. with constant coefficients.

So, A.E. ... is $(m^2 - 1)^2 = 0$

$$m = \pm 1, \pm 1$$

$\therefore$ $$x = (c_1 + c_2t)\,e^t + (c_3 + c_4t)\,e^{-t}$$

$\therefore$ $$\frac{dx}{dt} = (c_1 + c_2t)\,e^t + c_2\,e^t - (c_3 + c_4t)\,e^{-t} + c_4e^{-t}$$

$$\frac{d^2x}{dt^2} = (c_1 + c_2t)\,e^t + 2c_2\,e^t + (c_3 + c_4t)\,e^{-t} - 2c_4e^{-t}$$

$\therefore$ $$4y = \frac{d^2x}{dt^2} - 3x$$

$$= (c_1 + c_2t)\,e^t + 2c_2\,e^t + (c_3 + c_4t)e^{-t} + 2c_4e^{-t}$$
$$-3\,(c_1 + c_2t)\,e^t - 3\,(c_3 + c_4t)\,e^{-t}$$

$$4y = -\,2\,(c_1 + c_2t)e^t + 2c_2e^t - 2\,(c_3 + c_4t)e^{-t}$$

or $$y = -\frac{1}{2}\,[c_1 + c_2t - c_2]e^t - \frac{1}{2}\,[c_3 + c_4t + c_4]e^{-t}.$$

and $x = (c_1 + c_2t)\,e^t + (c_3 + c_4t)\,e^{-t}$ is the solution.

Example 2. Solve the simultaneous equations.

$$\frac{dx}{dt} - 7x + y = 0, \; \frac{dy}{dt} - 2x - 5y = 0$$

Solution: The given differential equations are

$$(D - 7)\, x + y = 0 \qquad (1)$$

$$-2x + (D - 5)\, y = 0 \qquad (2)$$

Eliminating y, we have

$$[(D - 5)(D - 7) + 2]\, x = 0$$

$$\therefore \quad (D^2 - 12D + 37)\, x = 0 \qquad (3)$$

Equation (3) is E.D.E. with constant coefficient

$\therefore$ A.E. $\quad m^2 - 12m + 37 = 0$

$$\therefore \quad m = \frac{12 \pm \sqrt{144 - 148}}{2}$$

$$\therefore \quad = 6 \pm i$$

$$\therefore \quad x = e^{6t}\,[c_1 \cos t + c_2 \sin t] \qquad (4)$$

$$\therefore \quad \frac{dx}{dt} = 6e^{6t}\,[c_1 \cos t + c_2 \sin t] + e^{6t}\,[-c_1 \sin t + c_2 \cos t]$$

Substituting these in equation (1), we have

$$y = 7x - \frac{dx}{dt}$$

$$= 7\, e^{6t}\,[c_1 \cos t + c_2 \sin t] - 6e^{t}\,[c_1 \cos t + c_2 \sin t] - e^{6t}\,[-c_1 \sin t + c_2 \cos t]$$

$$y = e^{6t}\,[(c_1 - c_2) \cos t + (c_1 + c_2) \sin t]$$

$\therefore$ The solution is

$$x = e^{6t}\,[c_1 \cos t + c_2 \sin t]$$

and

$$y = e^{6t}\,[(c_1 - c_2) \cos t + (c_1 + c_2) \sin t].$$

Example 3. Solve the simultaneous equations

$$\frac{dx}{dt} + 4x + 3y = t \text{ and } \frac{dy}{dt} + 2x + 5y = e^t$$

Solution: The given differential equations are

$$(D + 4)\,x + 3y = t \qquad (1)$$

and $$2x + (D + 5)\,y = e^t \qquad (2)$$

Eliminating y, we get

$$[(D + 5)\,(D + 4) - 6]\,x = (D + 5)\,t - 3e^t$$

or $$(D^2 + 9D + 14)\,x = 1 + 5\,t - 3e^t \qquad (3)$$

Equation (3) is a L.D.E. with constant coefficients

$\therefore$ A.E. $\quad m^2 + 9m + 14 = 0$

$\therefore \quad m = -2, -7$

$\therefore$C.F. is $\quad = c_1\,e^{-2t} + c_2 e^{-7t} \qquad (4)$

$$\text{P.I.} = \frac{1}{D^2+9D+14}\,(1 + 5t - 3e^t)$$

$$= \frac{1}{D^2+9D+14}\,.\,e^{0t} + 5\frac{1}{D^2+9D+14}\,.\,t - \frac{3}{D^2+9D+14}\,.\,e^t$$

$$= \frac{1}{14}+\frac{5}{14}\left[1+\frac{D^2+9D}{14}\right]^{-1} .t - \frac{3}{24}e^t$$

$$= \frac{1}{14}+\frac{5}{14}\left[1-\left(\frac{D^2+9D}{14}\right)\right]t - \frac{1}{8}e^t$$

$$= \frac{1}{14}+\frac{5}{14}\left[t-\frac{9}{14}\right]-\frac{1}{8}e^t$$

$$= \frac{5}{14}t-\frac{31}{196}-\frac{1}{8}e^t$$

$$\therefore \quad x = c_1e^{-2t} + c_2e^{-7t} + \frac{5}{14}t-\frac{31}{196}-\frac{1}{8}e^t$$

$$\therefore \quad \frac{dx}{dt} = -2\,c_1e^{-2t} - 7c_2e^{-7t} + \frac{5}{14}-\frac{e^t}{8}$$

Substituting these in equation (1), we have

$$3y = t - \frac{dx}{dt} - 4x$$

$$= t + 2c_1e^{-2t} + 7c_2e^{-7t} - \frac{5}{14} + \frac{e^t}{8}$$

$$-4c_1e^{-2t} - 4c_2e^{-7t} - \frac{10}{7}t + \frac{31}{49} + \frac{e^t}{2}$$

$\therefore$ $$y = \frac{1}{3}\left[-2c_1e^{-2t} + 3c_2e^{-7t} - \frac{3}{7}t + \frac{27}{98} + \frac{5}{8}e^t\right]$$

and $$x = c_1e^{-2t} + c_2e^{-7t} + \frac{5}{14}t - \frac{31}{196} - \frac{e^t}{8}$$

is the solution.

Example 4. Solve $\frac{dx}{dt} + wy = 0$ and $\frac{dy}{dt} - wx = 0$.

Solution: The given simultaneous differential equations are

$$Dx + wy = 0 \qquad (1)$$

and $$-wx + Dy = 0 \qquad (2)$$

Eliminating y, we have

$$(D^2 + w^2)\, x = 0 \qquad (3)$$

Equation (3) is a L.D.E. with constant coefficients

$\therefore$ A.E. $m^2 + w^2 = 0$

$\therefore m = \pm\, iw$

$\therefore$ The solution is $x = c_1 \cos wt + c_2 \sin wt$ (4)

$\therefore$ $$\frac{dx}{dt} = -wc_1 \sin wt + c_2 w \cos wt$$

And from equation (1) $$y = \frac{-1}{w}\frac{dx}{dt}$$

$\therefore$ $y = c_1 \sin wt - c_2 \cos wt$

Hence $x = c_1 \cos wt + c_2 \sin wt$

and $y = c_1 \sin wt - c_2 \cos wt$

in the solution.

Example 5. Solve.

$$x\frac{dy}{dx} + z = 0$$

and $$x\frac{dz}{dx} + y = 0$$

Solution: The given simultaneous differential equations are

$$x\frac{dy}{dx} + z = 0 \qquad (1)$$

and $$x\frac{dz}{dx} + y = 0 \qquad (2)$$

Differentiating equation (1) w.r.t. x, we have

$$x\frac{d^2y}{dx^2} + \frac{dy}{dx} + \frac{dz}{dx} = 0$$

$$\therefore \quad x^2\frac{d^2y}{dx^2} + x\frac{dy}{dx} + x\frac{dz}{dx} = 0$$

Substituting $x\dfrac{dz}{dx} = -y$ form (2), we have

$$x^2\frac{d^2y}{dx^2} + x\frac{dy}{dx} - y = 0 \qquad (3)$$

Equation (3) is homogeneous equation

Let $x = e^z$, them

Equation (3) becomes

$$[D(D - 1) + D - 1]\, y = 0$$

Where $D = \dfrac{d}{dz}$

$$(D^2 - 1)\, y = 0 \qquad (4)$$

Equation (4) is a L.D.E. with constant coefficients

$\therefore$ A.E. $m^2 - 1 = 0$

$$m = \pm 1$$

∴ The solution is

$$y = c_1 e^t + c_2 e^{-t}$$

or $$y = c_1 x + c_2 \frac{1}{x} \tag{5}$$

∴ $$\frac{dy}{dx} = c_1 - \frac{c_2}{x^2}$$

as $$z = -x \frac{dy}{dx}$$

∴ $$= -c_1 x + \frac{c_2}{x^2} . x$$

$$z = -c_1 x + c_2 . \frac{1}{x}$$

Hence $$y = c_1 x + c_2 . \frac{1}{x}$$

and $$z = -c_1 x + \frac{c_2}{x},$$

is the solution of the given equation.

Example 6. Solve

$$\frac{dx}{dt} + \frac{dy}{dt} - 2y = 2 \cos t - 7 \sin t$$

$$\frac{dx}{dt} - \frac{dy}{dt} + 2x = 4 \cos t - 3 \sin t$$

Solution: The given differential equations are

$$Dx + (D - 2) y = 2 \cos t - 7 \sin t \tag{1}$$

$$(D + 2) x - Dy = 4 \cos t - 3 \sin t \tag{2}$$

Eliminating y, we have

$$[D^2 + (D^2 - 4)] x = - 2 \sin t - 7 \cos t - 4 \sin t - 8 \cos t$$

$$-3 \text{ cost } t + 6 \sin t$$

$$2 (D^2 - 2) x = -18 \cos t$$

∴ $$(D^2 - 2) x = -9 \cos t \tag{3}$$

Equation (3) is a L.D.E. with constant coefficients

$\therefore$ A.E. $\quad m^2 - 2 = 0$

$$m = \pm\sqrt{2}$$

so $$\text{C.F.} = c_1 e^{\sqrt{2}t} + c_2 e^{-\sqrt{2}t}$$

$$\text{P.I.} = -9 \,.\, \frac{1}{D^2 - 2} \cos t$$

$$= -9 \,.\, \left(\frac{-1}{3}\right) \cos t$$

$$= 3 \cos t$$

$\therefore$ $$x = c_1 e^{\sqrt{2}t} + c_2 e^{\sqrt{2}t} + 3 \cos t \tag{4}$$

$\therefore$ $$\frac{dx}{dt} = \sqrt{2}c_1 e^{\sqrt{2}t} - \sqrt{2}c_2 . e^{-\sqrt{2}t} - 3\sin t$$

Now adding (1) and (2), we have

$$\frac{2dx}{dt} + 2x - 2y = 6 \cos t - 10 \sin t$$

$\therefore$ $$y = \frac{dx}{dt} + x - 3 \cos t + 5 \sin t$$

$$= \sqrt{2}c_1 e^{+\sqrt{2}t} - \sqrt{2}c_2 e^{-\sqrt{2}t} + c_1 e^{\sqrt{2}t} + c_2 e^{-\sqrt{2}t}$$

$$- 3 \sin t + 3 \cos t - 3 \cos t + 5 \sin t$$

$$= \left(1 + \sqrt{2}\right) c_1 e^{\sqrt{2}t} + \left(1 - \sqrt{2}\right) c_2 e^{-\sqrt{2}t} + 2\sin t$$

$\therefore$ $$x = c_1 e^{\sqrt{2}t} + c_2 e^{-\sqrt{2}t} + 3\cos t$$

and $$y = \left(1 + \sqrt{2}\right) c_1 e^{\sqrt{2}t} + \left(1 - \sqrt{2}\right) c_2 e^{-\sqrt{2}t} + 2\sin t$$

is the solution of the given equation.

EXERCISE

Solve the following simultaneous differential equations:

1. $\frac{dx}{dt} + 5x + y = e^t$

$$\frac{dy}{dt} - x + 3y = e^{2t}$$

Ans. $x = (c_1 + c_2 t)e^{-4t} + \frac{4}{25}e^t - \frac{1}{36}e^{2t}$

$y = -(c_1 + c_2 + c_2 t)\, e^{-4t} + \frac{7}{36}e^{2t} + \frac{1}{25}e^t$

2. $\frac{d^2y}{dt^2} + \frac{dy}{dt} - 2y = \sin t$

$\frac{dx}{dt} + x - 3y = 0$

Ans. $x = \frac{3}{2}c_1 e^t - 3c_2 e^{-2t} + c_3 e^{-t} + \frac{3}{10}e^t\ (\cos t - 2\sin t)$

$y = c_1 e^t + c_2 e^{-2t} - \frac{1}{10}(\cos t + 3\sin t)$

3. $\frac{dx}{dt} - y = 1$

$\frac{dy}{dt} - x = 1$

Ans. $x = c_1 e^t + c_2 e^{-t} - 1$

$y = c_1 e^t - c_2 e^{-t} - 1$

4. $\frac{dx}{dt} - 3x - 6y = t^2$

$\frac{dy}{dt} + \frac{dx}{dt} - 3y = e^t$

Ans. $x = c_1 \cos 3t + c_2 \sin 3t + \frac{3}{5}e^t - \frac{t^2}{3} + \frac{2t}{9} + \frac{2}{27}$

$y = \frac{1}{2}(c_2 - c_1)\cos 3t - \frac{1}{2}(c_1 + c_2)\sin 3t - \frac{e^t}{5} - \frac{2t}{9}$

$$\frac{d^2x}{dt^2} + y = \sin t$$

$$\frac{d^2y}{dt^2} + x = \cos t$$

Ans. $x = c_1e^t + c_2e^{-t} + c_3 \cos t + c_4 \sin t + \frac{t}{4} [\sin t - \cos t]$

$y = -c_1e^t - c_2e^{-t} + c_3 \cos t + c_4 \sin t + \frac{1}{4} (2 + t) [\sin t - \cos t]$

$$\frac{dx}{dt} + \frac{dy}{dt} + 3x = \sin t$$

$$\frac{dx}{dt} + y - x = \cos t$$

Ans. $x = c_1 e^{-t} + c_2e^{3t} + \frac{1}{5} (\cos t - 2 \sin t)$

$y = 2c_1 e^{-t} - 2c_2e^{3t} + \frac{8}{5} \cos t - \frac{1}{5} \sin t)$